The Details of Modern Architecture

Edward R. Ford

The Details of Modern Architecture

The MIT Press

Cambridge, Massachusetts

London, England

Second printing, 1991
© 1990 Massachusetts Institute of Technology

This book was set in Trump Mediaeval and Univers by DEKR Corporation, and was printed and bound by Dai Nippon Printing Company in Japan.

Library of Congress Cataloging-in-Publication Data

Ford, Edward R.
    The details of modern architecture / Edward R. Ford.
        p.   cm.
    Bibliography: p.
    Includes index.
    ISBN 0-262-06121-X
    1. Architecture—Details.   2. Architecture, Modern—19th century.
3. Architecture, Modern—20th century.   I. Title.
NA2840.F67   1989
724'.5—dc20   89-31772
                                                              CIP

Contents

Preface

I did not set out to write a technical history of architecture, or a technical critique of Modernism, or a historical work of any kind. I set out to write a book about detailing, but I found I could not discuss details without discussing styles of building, that I could not discuss styles of building without discussing styles of architecture, and that I could not discuss any of these without discussing history. This is to apologize in advance for the episodic nature of the book. I make no claims to comprehensiveness. Some readers will be puzzled at the inclusion of some obscure buildings; others will be disappointed at the omission of some of their favorites. I share most of these disappointments. The buildings discussed here are limited in part to those for which the construction documents are accessible, but a more important limitation is that far too much of the documentation, not to mention the fabric, of modern architecture has disappeared. A depressing number of the major buildings of the last hundred years survive only in fuzzy photographs; the buildings, the working drawings, and the specifications all have been discarded.

Much of what I have written about these buildings is critical. This is particularly true of my comments on the Modernists of 1920–1940. I did not intend to write a technical critique of Modernism or a technical defense of Postmodernism. I have tried to judge the architects on their own terms, by their own criteria; if some of them failed more than others, it is often because they attempted more. The Gamble house, the Villa Savoie, the Hanna, Eames, and Farnsworth houses, and both Lovell houses were all intended, and all failed, to be prototypes of Modern construction. In explaining the reasons for these failures, I had no intention of criticizing the architects for making the attempt. The history of Modernism would be infinitely poorer without these buildings, and these buildings would be infinitely poorer had they been more conventional. I have tried to avoid the conventional image of the genius architect whose brilliant technical innovations are ignored by society, and that of the irresponsible artist who is oblivious to practical needs; neither image fits the designers of these buildings. I hope to have shown that architectural technology is no more objective or subjective than architectural design, and that an architect's relationship to the building conventions of his time usually mirrors his relationships to the rest of society. I hope I have also shown that, while the technical criticism of architecture is necessary to the criticism of architecture as a whole, it is not sufficient. There is no functional style of building. Modernists have attempted to criticize Postmodernism using technology as an objective basis, just as the Gothic Rationalists attempted to criticize Classicism a hundred years ago. In both cases the technical criticisms were fuzzy, shallow, and often incorrect, and they resulted in a poverty of technical criticism. We cannot use technology as a fixed, objective point from which to measure the rightness or wrongness of architectural forms. It is perhaps for this reason that Postmodern criticism is almost devoid of technical commentary, an exercise that is equally impossible. Architecture and building have resisted all our attempts to neatly separate them.

I have elected to redraw almost all of the working drawings. I realize that many scholars would prefer to study the original drawings, but this was not a reasonable alternative. The majority of these drawings would have been illegible in reduced form, and many are difficult for anyone but the trained professional to understand even at full size. The purpose of working drawings is to show how buildings are constructed, not how they appear. My intent in redrawing these documents in axonometric form was to show construction and appearance simultaneously, while at the same time making the information accessible to a wider audience. The individual drafting style of the architect or the draftsman is lost by this process, but at the same time the buildings may be more effectively compared because of the standardized format. The source material for each drawing is listed in the accompanying legend.

All the drawings in this book are based on construction documents, either published or in archives; as such, they are subject to a certain degree of error, as these documents are sometimes departed from during construction. When it was possible I visited the buildings to verify the drawings; however, many were inaccessible, demolished, or altered, and in those cases I have relied on construction photographs and restoration architects. The sources of this information and the specific points of uncertainty are noted in the legends that accompany the illustrations in question. In the dates given with the figures, I have tried to use dates of construction (when possible) rather than dates of design.

The aspect of this book that I most regret is my inability to name the authors of many of the details. Built architecture is never the work of an individual; in a large office such as that of McKim or that of Lutyens, the chief designer could not have initiated many of the details, and in some cases he could not even have reviewed them. The details in this book include the contributions of hundreds of unnamed individuals. Rather than mention some while omitting many more (some of whom are living), I have opted to mention almost none. Thus, I have assumed that, except in obvious cases, Frank Lloyd Wright was responsible for the details produced by his office, and I have discussed them accordingly while recognizing that Wright did not design and draw every one of them.

This is not a "how to" book of building construction. Few of the details here, if any, are suitable examples for current practice. Many were poor details when executed, and changes in materials, manufacturing, and performance standards have antiquated the rest. However, there is much to be learned from these details, and much of it applies to contemporary situations. Detailing today is far too much a product of a conventional wisdom, and far too many decisions are made on the basis of what is "standard" without much analysis of why a certain practice became standardized. An understanding of how the details in this book are the product of social and economic conditions, of local and national conventions that are independent of style, and of individual architects' versions of the conventional wisdom can lead to the same sort of analysis of our own preconceptions.

I had originally intended for this study to extend from 1877 to the present day. It soon became clear that this would result in an extremely long book if all the relevant material were included. This volume therefore ends in the year 1936; a subsequent volume will deal with work from 1936 onward.

I would like to thank the following institutions and individuals for allowing me to use their archives, to reproduce photographs, and to make new drawings from their archival materials: the Avery Library at Columbia University; the Busch-Reisinger Museum at Harvard University; Country Life, Ltd.; the Frank Lloyd Wright Foundation; the Getty Center for the History of Art and the Humanities; the Greene and Greene Library; the Historic American Buildings Survey of the Library of Congress; the Houghton Library at Harvard University; Hoyle, Doran, and Berry, Architects; Donald Leslie Johnson; the Kings College Library; A. Morancé; Dion Neutra; the New York Historical Society; the Foundation Le Corbusier; the Museum of Modern Art; Gustav Pichelmann; the Princeton University Archives; the Postsparkasse and the Psychiatrisches Krankenhaus Baumgarten in Vienna; the Royal Institute of British Architects Drawing Collection and Library; the Special Collections of the University of California at Los Angeles; the Architectural Drawings Collection of the University Museum at Santa Barbara; the Utrecht Museum; and the Kartographische Sammlung of the Wiener Stadtarchiv.

I would also like to thank these institutions and individuals who allowed me the use of photographs from their collections: Bruce Abbey, the Fiske Kimball and Alderman Libraries of the University of Virginia, *Architectural Record*, the Architectural Association Library, the Burnham and Ryerson Libraries and the Art Institute of Chicago, Herbert Barnett, the Buffalo and Erie County Historical Society, Wayne Cable, the Canadian Center for Architecture, John Eiffler of SOM in Chicago, Volker Döhne, Ezra Stoller of ESTO, Elroy van Groll, Hedrich-Blessing, the Johnson Wax Company, the MacMillan Company of Australia, the Princeton University Press, Marvin Rand, the Regenstein Library at the University of Chicago, Michael Stogner, the Society of the Preservation of New England Antiquities, the Historisches Museum der Stadt Wien, William Wischmeyer, David Woodruff, and the Semper Archive of the Eidgenossischen Technischen Hochschule in Zurich.

I would like to thank Felicity Ashbee for permission to quote from her parents' journals; the numerous institutions and individuals who allowed me to visit, photograph, and survey the buildings they own and occupy (especially the Martin house, the Robie house, the Schindler house, and the Gropius house); Samuel Holloway, Craig Mutter, Matthew Sage, and Carrie Wilson for help with the drawings; Joan Baxter for typing the manuscript; John Hatch and Theo van Groll for help with translation; Anne Wren and Steve Yarnell for help with the initial graphic layout; Robert Maxwell, Robert Gutman, Mike Kihn, and all my colleagues at the University of Virginia for their help and encouragement; and my family for their patience.

The production for this book would have been impossible without the assistance of the Graham Foundation and especially the enthusiasm and patience of Mark Rakatansky and Roger Conover.

Editor's note: The symbol meaning *inches* has generally been omitted from expressions such as "2 × 4," partly as a matter of convention (a 2 × 4 is not actually 2 inches by 4 inches) and partly for the sake of appearance. Whenever dimensions are given without units, the reader may assume that the implicit units are inches— perhaps *approximate* inches, as in the case of the 2 × 4.

1   Introduction

There are styles of design in architecture and there are styles of building in architecture. Styles of building are no more right or wrong and nor more appropriate or inappropriate than styles of architecture. There is a life of forms in architecture and there is a life of ideas in architecture, lives that are not always the same. Ideas may change while forms are constant; forms may change without changes in ideology. The life of a theory of building may not be the same as the life of a theory of form. The nineteenth century saw many styles of design: Classic, Gothic, Queen Anne, Art Nouveau. It also saw several styles of building: monolithic and literal, layered and analogous, and many combinations of these. These styles of building did not correspond to styles in design. The Gothic Revivalists tended toward the monolithic and the literal, but many of them built in the layered style; the Classical Revivalists tended toward the layered and the analogous, but many of them built in the monolithic style.

There is also a difference between ideas of building and realities of building, a difference that is probably much greater than differences in form. Many architects propagated one style of construction while building in another. Many built different buildings in different styles of construction, and some used different styles of construction within the same building. Few were consistent through a large body of work, not because of insincerity but because of necessity and circumstance. To a certain extent this is because the logics of construction often defy generalization; to a greater degree it is because their ideas of building were inappropriate to the conditions to which they were being applied.

There is also in architecture a life of details, which is independent of style. Many details have stylistic and historical associations, and these may or may not correspond to the stylistic and historical associations of the buildings in which they are used. But details serve other functions than historical association. They may articulate the building's mass. They may establish scale or deny it. They may explain or deny the structural behavior of the building. They may express or conceal the way the building has been assembled. Designers whose attitudes toward historical style are identical may differ greatly in their response to these and other questions.

1.1

1.2

Peoples Savings Bank

Louis Sullivan

Cedar Rapids, Iowa, 1911

1.1 exterior
(Art Institute of Chicago.)

1.2 banking room
(Art Institute of Chicago.)

In 1855, after returning from a tour of Northern Italy, George Edmund Street published *Brick and Marble in the Middle Ages: Notes of a Tour of North Italy*. Today the book is forgotten except by historians, but in the nineteenth century it was widely read. Street was no Classicist. He devotes only a short chapter to his visit to Vicenza (where he found the buildings "wretched and ruinous"), while Venice receives four chapters, devoted largely to the Gothic buildings. Street categorizes them in two types: the monolithic style, represented by churches with exposed brick walls, and the incrusted style, represented by the marble-clad walls of St. Marks. Street's preference is for the former:

In my notes upon the buildings as they were passed in my journeys, I have described two modes in which this kind of work was treated: the first was that practised in Venice—the veneering of brick walls with thin layers or coats of marble: the other, that practised at Bergamo, Cremona, and Como—in which the marble formed portion of the substance of the wall.

These two modes led, as would naturally be expected, to two entirely different styles and modes of architecture.

The Venetian mode was rather likely to be destructive of good architecture, because it was sure to end in an entire concealment of the real construction of the work; the other mode, on the contrary, proceeded on true principles, and took pleasure in defining most carefully every line in the construction of the work. It might almost be said that one mode was devised with a view to the concealment, and the other with a view to the explanation, of the real mode of construction.[1]

Street was not the only nineteenth-century writer to make a distinction between clad and monolithic systems of building. Eugène-Emanuel Viollet-le-Duc criticized Roman architecture for the application of veneers and nonstructural columns to brick buildings, contrasting it with Greek architecture, in which decoration and structure were inseparable.

Not all theoreticians of the modern era shared this preference for monolithic, unfinished construction. Many believed, with H. S. Goodhart-Rendel, that

the normal process of design is to aestheticise, to dramatise, the physical character of buildings and to adorn them with sculpture. For sculpture is the proper name given to all the mimic architecture with which real architecture is customarily adorned. The Romanesque wall arcade, . . . [and] the Renaissance rows of pilasters, stand in exactly the same relationship to real arches, roofs, and colonnades as that in which stone saints and statesmen stand to saints and statesmen of flesh and blood. Sculptural too, in their essence are the moldings and flutings by means of which the natural appearances of construction are usually emphasized.[2]

Foremost in this group was Gottfried Semper, who insisted that architecture was structure plus cladding and that the essential element was the cladding itself. In a different stylistic camp but essentially in agreement was John Ruskin, who wrote:

The Architect is not bound to exhibit structure; nor are we to complain of him for concealing it, any more than we should regret that the outer surfaces of the human frame conceal much of its anatomy; nevertheless, that building will generally be the noblest, which to an intelligent eye discovers the great secrets of its structure, as an animal form does, although from a careless observer they may be concealed.[3]

The preference for the monolithic or the layered system transcended stylistic preferences. Although Otto Wagner and Auguste Perret were both essentially Classicists, Wagner used the layered system and Perret the monolithic. Others, including Frank Lloyd Wright, used both systems at different times in their careers. Some theoreticians straddled the fence. Julien Guadet, the chief theoretician of the Beaux-Arts in the late nineteenth century, recognized both systems as acceptable means of building, and many architects—from the Greene brothers to McKim, Mead & White—used both systems simultaneously.

1.3

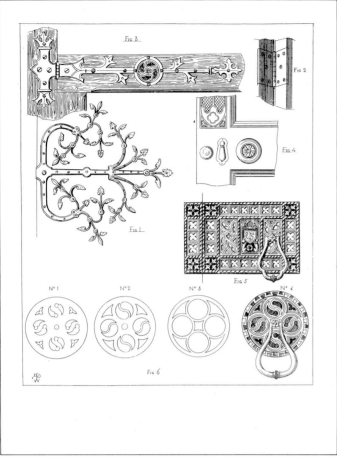

1.4

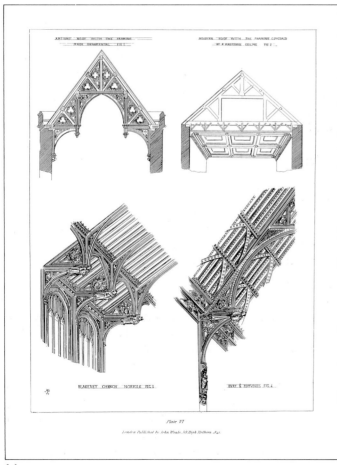

1.5

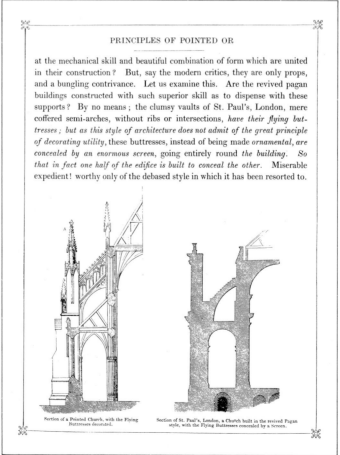

PRINCIPLES OF POINTED OR

at the mechanical skill and beautiful combination of form which are united in their construction? But, say the modern critics, they are only props, and a bungling contrivance. Let us examine this. Are the revived pagan buildings constructed with such superior skill as to dispense with these supports? By no means; the clumsy vaults of St. Paul's, London, mere coffered semi-arches, without ribs or intersections, *have their flying buttresses; but as this style of architecture does not admit of the great principle of decorating utility*, these buttresses, instead of being made *ornamental, are concealed by an enormous screen*, going entirely round *the building. So that in fact one half of the edifice is built to conceal the other. Miserable expedient!* worthy only of the debased style in which it has been resorted to.

Section of a Pointed Church, with the Flying Buttresses decorated.

Section of St. Paul's, London, a Church built in the revived Pagan style, with the Flying Buttresses concealed by a Screen.

The Modernism of the 1920s and the 1930s changed this. That era of revolutionary dogma would not accept two contradictory methods of solving the same problem. The Modernist choice was for the monolithic system, and this preference became stronger in subsequent years. As long as Modernism retained its moral earnestness and its revolutionary rhetoric, it retained its preference for monolithic exposed structural systems. This preference is retained by many today.

The irony in the development of this dogma is that the construction industry—particularly in the United States—was developing along opposite lines, mainly because of the influence of industrialization. Although certain new techniques and materials (e.g. precast concrete) seemed to make the monolithic system desirable, the development of the steel frame encouraged the use of the layered system.

PERCEPTION AND STRUCTURAL RATIONALISM

Many Classical architects of the nineteenth century were no less concerned with rational building than Street, but their priorities were different. Most admired monolithic exposed construction but did not consider it to be a prerequisite of good building. Guadet wrote: "It is a superior beauty, that which results from the construction itself, that is the architecture itself, and does not require further decoration,"[4] but at the same time he recognized that it was often advantageous to clad structures and to exaggerate certain characteristics for the sake of effect.

Guadet's aim was to make solidity "manifest." In many ways this was a more restrictive requirement than any used by the Gothic Revivalists. Certain types of structures, particularly those with flying buttresses, he considered to be visually unstable. Guadet, despite being a Classicist, admired the front of Notre Dame for its solidity:

In art, admiration is a sense of well being, the satisfaction of total repose, while astonishment does not occur without anxiety. Thus apparent solidity, incontestable, captures the spirit more than the tour de force, admiration holds itself back, first one ought to be convinced.

These two impressions are perceptible in the same building, Notre Dame de Paris.

When one views the main facade with its towers so monumental, its portals so well enclosed, the pure lines of its two galleries, one admires the building in its magnificent health; no accident, no inclemency, no passage of time, seems to destroy or compromise this ensemble so well planted, so strong in its proportions.[5]

The rear of Notre Dame, because of the use of buttresses, does not adequately explain how the weight of its masonry finds its way to the ground. It employs what Viollet-le-Duc called the principle of equilibrium, rather than the more desirable system of superimposition. In Guadet's words,

One perceives with pain how fearfully made are the actions and reactions, the thrusts from the interior to the exterior, from the exterior to the interior. The building appears as a ship in drydock, propped up by its buttresses, and the mind wonders what would occur if a shock, a crushed stone, should jeopardize this astonishing equilibrium; astonishing, but one ought to say artificial and precarious in comparison with the marvelous main facade.[6]

Modernists have generally preferred the rear of Notre Dame, and for many this sense of weightlessness was the essence of the modern era. Kazimir Malevich wrote in 1920: "I suppose weight distribution or liberation in weightlessness to have been the reason for God's creation of the world and the Universe. . . . Man too . . . strives for the same thing—to disperse weight and himself become weightless."[7]

Malevich had considerable interest in architecture, and saw the factory as the means of spiritual realization; however, his denial of mass was a manifestation of the spirit, not of construction, as to a lesser degree it was for Gerrit Rietveld. For others, including Wright and Le Corbusier, the lack of mass and the absence of "stability made manifest" were inevitably linked with the steel or concrete frame.

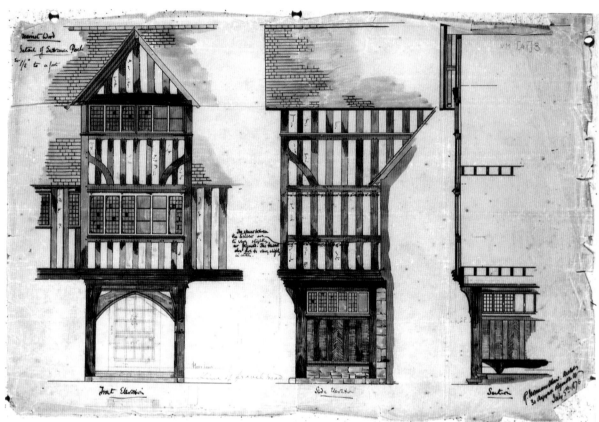

1.6

1.6 Richard Norman Shaw, detail of
entrance porch, Merrist Wood,
1876.
*(RIBA Drawings Collection,
drawing [41] 8.)*

The triumph of Modernism was the triumph of the principle of equilibrium over the principle of superimposition. Few Modernists would criticize the flying buttresses of Notre Dame as Guadet had done. And the perception of tension here is not unlike that one feels at the Villa Savoie, with its floating volume cut by a ribbon window.

Many of the typical Modernist details resulted from this reversal of attitude, and it is one reason why the typical Modernist detail is so often an inversion of a traditional detail, for it seeks to deny what the other seeks to affirm. This, of course, would be contested by most Modernists, who saw such details as the obvious solution to pragmatic problems. If one is to criticize the traditionalists for their nonacceptance of an inevitable characteristic of frame construction, one should compliment them on the recognition that structure and the perception of structure are different things.

We associate the disappearance of ornament with the arrival of modern building systems, but to an extent these events were merely simultaneous rather than interdependent. Many who criticized ornament (among them Adolf Loos) did so for cultural rather than technical reasons, and Modernists more commonly saw the new technology as changing the nature of ornament rather than eliminating it. In fact, so long as buildings were built using layered construction in which the structure was concealed, some form of ornamental cladding was necessary for structural expression. This type of expression exists in all phases of Modernism— a fact that the designers of Modern architecture have been reluctant to acknowledge and Modern historians have been slow to recognize.

CRAFTSMANSHIP

In one sense, detailing was born when craftsmanship died. It is always surprising to see how little the drawings of Renaissance architects resemble the finished buildings, particularly in such details as column capitals. The quality of these elements is due largely to the quality of their execution, and the men who executed them had a fair degree of latitude in their adaption of the design. Drawings were sometimes submitted to the architects for approval, but it is doubtful that Wren, for example, had a great deal to do with the design of the wood paneling in his churches.

That this system is largely dead today there is no question. How and why it died is not so clear. Today there are few stonecarvers in the traditional sense. In 1850 there were plenty, but Ruskin and others lamented that they were little better than slaves, since all they did was mechanically execute forms designed by others. The death of craftsmanship on the level of art and on the level of skill has been ascribed to the Industrial Revolution, but it was not a simple case of machines replacing men. In any case, nineteenth-century architects exercised more and more control over the craft of building, even when preindustrial building methods requiring much handwork were still in use.

Figure 1.6 shows a working drawing for Merrist Wood, a half-timbered building completed in 1876. Note that the architect, Richard Norman Shaw, specified that "the space between the timbers be varied slightly in width," and that the width of the boards be varied also. Shaw was obviously trying to achieve the imprecise look of a vernacular half-timbered house. The irony, of course, is that he had to specify precisely how this imprecision was to be achieved, rather than leaving it to chance. No such note would ever have appeared on a Wren drawing. But however it was achieved, it is noteworthy that the architect desired a lower level of craftsmanship than he would normally receive. This is the legacy of Ruskin's desire for "rudeness" in building.

Ruskin and the Arts and Crafts architects responded to the decline in craftsmanship by attempting to revive the tradition of the craftsman as artist. As a result of this attempt, imperfect craftsmanship came to be valued. As Goodhart-Rendel notes,

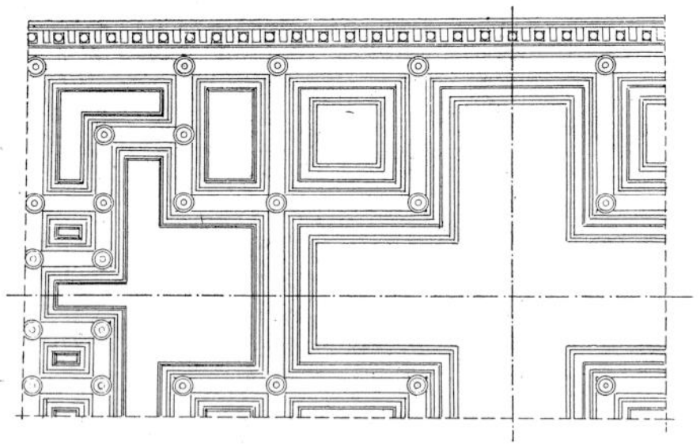

Fig. 417. — Plafond de l'église d'*Ara-Cœli*, à Rome.

Fig. 418. — Plafond de l'église
Sainte-Marie-Majeure, à Rome.

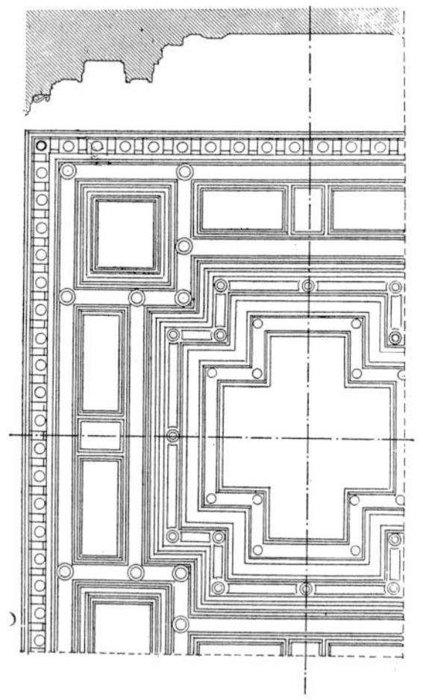

Fig. 419. — Plafond au Palais Farnèse, à Rome.

1.7

Si tous les bois sont laissés apparents, et sont d'ailleurs posés uniquement pour satisfaire aux besoins de la construction, on a le plancher rustique de nos campagnes; si le travail est bien exécuté, les espacements réguliers, les bois bien équarris, on a un plancher d'aspect architectural, qui, avec quelques moulures ou un peu de décoration, deviendra aisément un de ces beaux plafonds à

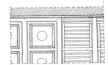

Fig. 414. — Plafond exprimant
la construction d'un plancher.

charpentes apparentes comme vous en voyez à l'École même, à l'hôtel Cluny, à Fontainebleau, et autour de la cour des Invalides.

Ces beaux plafonds ont pour l'architecte un grand charme, leur vérité même. Ils sont non seulement l'expression de la construction, ils sont la construction même. Tel est ce charme

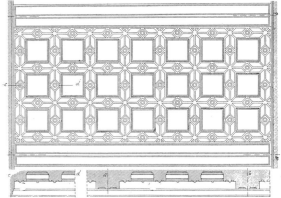

Fig. 415. — Plafond de la Bibliothèque de l'École des Beaux-Arts.

1.8

The tenet . . . that the mark of the worker's tool can add positive value to the finished work, a tenet that is less based upon aesthetics than upon sociological sentimentality . . . was the foundation for the whole movement known as the Arts and Crafts.[8]

But the appeal was not entirely unaesthetic. Ruskin wrote of what he called the principle of rudeness:

I have confined the illustration of [the principle] to architecture, but I must not leave it as if true of architecture only. Hitherto I have used the words imperfect and perfect merely to distinguish between work grossly unskilful, and work executed with average precision and science; and I have been pleading that any degree of unskilfulness should be admitted, so only that the labourer's mind had room for expression. But, accurately speaking, no good work whatever can be perfect, and the demand for perfection is always a sign of a misunderstanding of the ends of art.[9]

As with many other nineteenth-century theories, the idioms and rules of Arts and Crafts design remained long after the core of the belief had been forgotten. Ruskin's and William Morris's respect for the craftsman, their hatred of the mechanical and perfect, and their love of rudeness bequeathed to Modernism an acceptance and even an admiration for less-than-perfect workmanship, and a love of joinery that "explained" itself visually. This acceptance was by no means universal. Mies van der Rohe, generally praised as the finest of modern detailers, went to great lengths to conceal the joints of his buildings so that steel members flowed into one another without visible seams, caps, or fasteners, whereas the Greene brothers are praised as great detailers for their use of exposed fasteners and their articulation of the means of joining wood members.

Construction has always involved various levels of acceptable craftsmanship, from the precise to the crude. In layered forms of construction, the hierarchy of craftsmanship was both logical and obvious: Exposed construction was percise; concealed construction was crude. The Modernist desire for monolithic construction blurred but did not destroy this distinction. Those nineteenth-century writers who advocated uniform craftmanship in construction were well aware that this was an impractical idea, but their concerns were utopian rather than practical. This distinction was not so clear in the minds of the twentieth-century writers who advocated similar ideas of craftsmanship.

Insofar as twentieth-century architects have concerned themselves with the social consequences of their work, they have focused on the way in which buildings affect the behavior of their occupants. Insofar as nineteenth-century architects concerned themselves with the social consequences of their work, they focused on the way in which buildings (and particularly their ornaments) affect those who *build* them. There is perhaps no greater difference between the architects of the nineteenth century and those of the twentieth than that each group was so indifferent to the social concerns of the other.

Ruskin, Morris, and Pugin did not accept the world as it was. They did not like the buildings their society was producing, and they sought to better the buildings by bettering the society. The architects who followed them had to reconcile the realities of their commissions with a set of rules for building that were highly utopian in origin. It is not an accident that William Morris and his architect, Philip Webb, were socialists, despite the fact that their clients included the royal family. Subsequent architects, including Frank Lloyd Wright, were to experience considerably more difficulty in reconciling the differences between their ideas of rational construction and the constraints imposed by the societies in which they lived.

ORNAMENT AND CONSTRUCTION
In his 1912 review of Louis Sullivan's Peoples Savings Bank at Cedar Rapids, Montgomery Schuyler was generally sympathetic and found much to praise. However, he disliked certain aspects of the detailing, particularly in the interior:

Fig. 29. — Notre-Dame de Paris. Façade principale.

1.9

---

la satisfaction est entière, rien ne l'inquiète, et si ce sentiment ne s'analyse pas, il s'impose cependant : vous admirez avec bonheur, en vous livrant tout entier.

Faites le tour, et considérez le chevet de Notre-Dame (fig. 30).

Certes, pour ce que vous voyez maintenant, il a fallu plus de science ou d'expérience, plus de hardiesse heureuse. On conçoit à peine comment peuvent se faire équilibre ces actions et ces réactions, ces poussées du dedans au dehors, du dehors au dedans. Le monument apparaît comme un vaisseau sur son chantier de lancement, maintenu par ses étrésillons, et l'esprit se demande ce qu'il ad-

Fig. 30. — Chevet de Notre-Dame de Paris.

viendrait si un choc, une pierre écrasée, compromettait cet équilibre étonnant. Étonnant, oui — mais il faut le dire, artificiel et précaire en comparaison de cette merveilleuse façade principale, si majestueuse dans l'évidence de son inébranlable solidité.

1.10

The absence of what we called functional modelling is as marked, almost, in the interior as on the exterior. If it be not so noticeable, that proceeds from a circumstance which here explains and tends to justify the omission. The material itself of this interior is of great beauty and great sumptuosity. The marble of the counters, the oak of the partitions have evidently been carefully sought with reference to their decorative effect, and sought successfully. Material of this kind shows to the best advantage when employed in unbroken surfaces as extensive as may be. One willingly foregoes, in such expanses, the moulded framing of the marble, the panelling of the woodwork. But elsewhere and throughout it is evident that a square arris has no terrors whatever for this designer and that he willingly omits what to the designer of another school, to the designer, we may say, of any "school," would be the irreducible minimum of "finish." This is seen in the detail throughout, in the joinery of the counters, in the framing of the mural pictures, in the "trim" of the subordinate rooms. And the willingness to forego traditional transitions and modifications is as evident in the columns, which are hardly columns, of which the capital that mediates and forms a graduated transition between the shaft and the abacus is an essential member, but rather posts, upon which the spread of the abacus is directly superposed, or rather interposed, for the posts which carry the clerestory walls are "produced" into the strips of pier which we have seen terminating in the grotesques of the exterior. Even so, it must be admitted that some form of capital, either the swell of a bell in stonework or spreading braces in wood or metal, supporting and relieving the abacus, is demanded not only by tradition but by the nature of the construction and that the omission of it is a lapse in structural logic.[10]

To Schuyler the purpose of moldings and ornaments was to create transitions. His criticisms of Sullivan betray the source of this idea: Viollet-le-Duc, who said that "the molding serves three purposes: it either supports a projection, or it forms a footing, or it marks a height, or defines an opening. In the first case the molding is a cornice; in the second a base, in the third a stringcourse, a jamb, a frame. Except for these three functions a molding has no rational purpose."[11]

In the view of Schuyler and Viollet-le-Duc, the molding should be coincident with the joint, often covering it. This is the case in most traditional architecture, where moldings often serve such functional purposes as covering difficult joints between dissimilar materials (as in baseboards and window trim). In the traditional system, ornament and moldings are distinct elements, a molding being a continuous, often curved section to which the ornament—a repetitive pattern, such as egg and dart— is applied. Sullivan's ornament is not the result of a lack of structural logic; it simply follows a different set of rules. Joints without moldings are common in his work. Sullivan's ornament is independent of both moldings and joints, and it flows across joints and surfaces independent of constructional constraints. His terra cotta blocks are often designed to create the illusion of continuity. In the Gage Building, whose columns have the Sullivanesque equivalents of fluting and capitals, these elements flow across the surfaces of the terra cotta and its joints rather than forming terminations.

Pugin, in his writings on Gothic, argued that many ornaments and moldings serve practical purposes; for example, drip moldings on windows and buttresses keep water away from critical joints. While this is true in isolated cases, it is not true of the vast majority of moldings in Gothic or in any other style. Ruskin, although a lover of Gothic, dismissed the idea that ornament had a functional or symbolic relationship to structure:

. . . the false theory that ornamentation should be merely decorated structure is so pretty and plausible, that it is likely to take away your attention from the far more important abstract conditions of design. Structure should never be contradicted, and in the best buildings it is pleasantly exhibited and enforced . . . yet so independent is the mechanical structure of the true design, that when I begin my Lectures on Architecture, the first building I shall give you as a standard will be one in which the structure is wholly concealed. It will be the Baptistery of Florence. . . .[12]

A more convincing case for the relationship of ornament and structure was made by Leopold Eidlitz, H. H. Richardson's collaborator, who argued that moldings, ornaments, and textures serve to express the structural forces at work in an architectural element:

The object of decorating the surfaces of building material is . . . to give artificial texture to it, which shall re-enforce its apparent capability to resist pressure. . . . Carved ornament being intended to decorate a structural mass with the view of accentuating its function, the mass itself must not be entirely absorbed or covered up by the ornament, but must be clearly perceptible, and express in its form also the function performed by it. . . . The bell of the capital and of the corbel will serve as an illustration of this. To erect a leaf or an animal form, whether it be conventionalized or not, and use this leaf, animal, or human form as a structural part, or, what is still worse, for the mere purpose of a convenient transition from one part of structure to another, is contrary to the nature of art-work.[13]

The Classical Rationalists had equally strong feelings on the subject of ornament and structure. Like Eidlitz, they acknowledged the role of perception in rational building: that certain characteristics must be articulated or exaggerated in order to make structural forces evident.

CONCLUSION

There was not, in the last quarter of the nineteenth century, much agreement among theoreticians and architects as to what constituted rational building, as to how structure was related to form, or as to how construction affected style. Was architecture ornamented construction, or was it structure plus cladding? Could it be some combination of the two? Was good building solid and monolithic, or could it be veneered? What was the role of ornament: Was it the inevitable result of function? Was it the exterior expression of internal structural forces, or was it simply a language independent of its structural base? What was the role of craftsmanship in architecture: Was it most successful when least noticeable, when it achieved seamless and geometrically perfect joinery, or was this perfection degenerate? And what was craftsmanship's relation to ornament: Was the purpose of ornament to hide poor craftsmanship, or to display good craftsmanship? In an era when craftsmanship seemed to be disappearing, should ornament disappear as well?

These questions predated the industrialization of building that took place between 1875 and 1920, and were based on the analysis of buildings constructed by archaic means. However, the ideas behind them were not abandoned when the processes of building changed. The life of forms in art and the life of ideas in art are often not the same, and many of these conceptions of good building have outlived many changes in style. A brick is still a brick; a piece of wood is still a piece of wood. Good building was and is described as solid, honest, and craftsmanlike. Even the most iconoclastic of the Modernists were seldom able to discuss construction without some knowledge of and some reference to precedent. This accounts in part for the discrepancies that occur in the examples that follow. How could the same architects be so perceptive of one phenomenon in construction and so blind to another? And how could some be so oblivious to the practicalities of realizing their ideas? The answer is sometimes, but not often, ignorance. The technological history of Modernism and of Traditionalism in the modern era is a history that is no less utopian in its technology than in its imagery.

2   H. H. Richardson, Ralph Adams Cram, and the Gothic Revival

She met Henry, who was a cathedral builder. He built cathedrals in places where there were no cathedrals—Twayne, Nebraska, for example. Every American city needed a cathedral, Henry said. The role of the cathedral in the building of the national soul was well known. We should punish ourselves in our purses, Henry said, to shape up the national soul. An arch never sleeps, Henry said, pointing to the never-sleeping arches in his plans. Architecture is memory, Henry said, and the nation that had no cathedrals to speak of had no memory to speak of either. . . . Cathedrals are mostly a matter of thrusts, Henry said. You got to balance your thrusts. The ribs of your vaults intersect collecting the vertical and lateral thrusts at fixed points which are then buttressed or grounded although that's not so important anymore when you use a steel skeleton as we do which may be cheating but I always say that cheating in the Lord's name is O.K. as long as He don't catch you at it.

Donald Barthelme, *Sadness*

There are styles of design in architecture and there are styles of construction in architecture, and the two do not always coincide. Architects who have advocated one style of building in print have built numerous buildings in another. Architects using radically different styles of design have built in the same style of construction, and architects building in the same style of construction have built in radically different styles of design.

These paradoxes have no better illustration than the ideas and buildings of the architects of the Gothic Revival. Some of these architects were interested only in picturesque effects and were indifferent to the methods and materials of building. Others saw Gothic architecture as rational building, although there was little agreement as to what aspects of Gothic architecture constituted rational building. One group saw Gothic buildings as the logical result of the application of principles of construction, while others thought rational building was more than a question of practical and scientific concerns. The latter group of architects and critics believed not only in the superiority of Gothic architecture but also in the superiority of the society that produced it, and felt that the concerns of rational building included not only its physical results but also the means of production. As a result, there are two different strains of Gothic Rationalism, one of which deals largely with empirical concerns and one of which deals with concerns that are largely utopian.

Henry Hobson Richardson and Ralph Adams Cram both loved the Medieval, but they loved different eras for different reasons. Richardson loved the Romanesque for its romantic associations; Cram loved the Gothic for its social and religious associations. Cram and Richardson were separated by time, personality, and taste, but they faced similar problems in construction. Although they attacked these problems differently, they often used similar elements.

The Gothic Revival began in the late eighteenth century. Richardson and Cram, working in the late nineteenth century, faced different technical problems than the theoreticians and architects of the early and middle Gothic Revival. Nevertheless, in order to understand the intellectual climate in which Richardson and Cram worked, one must understand these theoreticians, particularly Augustus Welby Pugin and Eugène-Emanuel Viollet-le-Duc.

2.1

pente, qui n'est susceptible d'aucune déformation ni dislocation. Re-

32

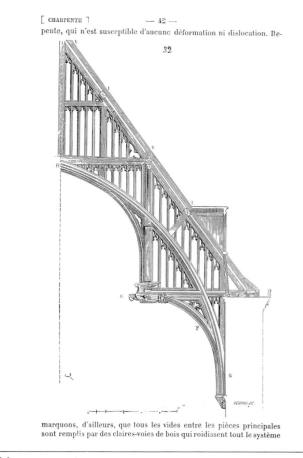

marquons, d'ailleurs, que tous les vides entre les pièces principales
sont remplis par des claires-voies de bois qui roidissent tout le système

2.2

21, 23, 26, 28, car elles ne couvrent généralement que des salles d'une

34

médiocre largeur. Si la Normandie ou la Picardie ont possédé des char-

2.3

construction. Les charpentes qui nous sont restées de ce temps sont

33

simples et ne diffèrent guère de celles données ci-dessus figures 19,

2.4

pentes de combles élevées conformément au système anglo-normand,
ce qui est possible, elles ne sont pas parvenues jusqu'à nos jours.
Nous trouvons cependant, près de Maubeuge, dans la petite église de
Hargnies (Nord), une charpente dont la combinaison se rattache aux
deux systèmes anglo-normands et français. Cette charpente est, ou plu-
tôt était dépourvue d'entraits; car, vers le milieu du XVIᵉ siècle, des
tirants furent posés de deux en deux fermes sous les arbalétriers. Les

34 bis

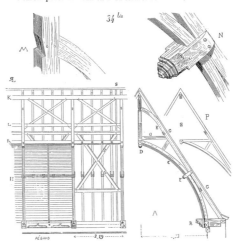

fermes maîtresses, dont nous donnons le profil en A (fig. 34 bis), repo-
sent sur de forts blochets B; elles se composent de deux courbes C
s'assemblant à l'extrémité inférieure du poinçon D, d'arbalétriers E
courbes eux-mêmes à leur point de rencontre avec le poinçon, afin de
trouver des assemblages solides indiqués dans le détail M. La courbe et
l'arbalétrier sont bridés à la tangente, au moyen de deux petites moises
F, dont le détail N explique la forme et les attaches. Sous les arbalétriers sont chevillés et assemblés à mi-bois deux cours d'entretoises ou
pannes G dans lesquelles viennent s'assembler des croix de Saint-André
inclinées suivant la pente du chevronnage, et figurées en I dans la coupe
longitudinale. Ces pannes soulagent le chevronnage profilé en P, mais

AUGUSTUS WELBY PUGIN

Pugin did not wish to define rational building, or to establish a new style. He wished to restore Britain to a Christian society, with a Christian architecture, by returning to medieval society and medieval architecture. The purpose of his writing on construction was to establish the superiority of Gothic methods of building to classical and contemporary methods. His major book on this subject, *Principles of Pointed or Christian Architecture,* was a series of comparisons between Gothic and Classic showing the superiority of the former. For example, he criticized Wren for concealing the flying buttresses of St. Paul's behind a screen. But Pugin did more than condemn "deceits." He also issued commandments: "The two great rules of design are: (1st) There should be no features about a building which are not necessary for convenience, construction, or propriety. (2nd) That all ornament should consist in the essential construction of the building. In pure architecture the smallest detail should have a meaning or a purpose."[1]

Most of the elements that Pugin considered to be constructed ornament would today be called finish materials. By requiring that ornament be limited to essential construction, Pugin set up a model that equated rational building with monolithic construction, in which the structural materials are also the finish materials.

According to Pugin, rational buildings did not conceal their roof trusses; they exposed them (figure 1.4). The logical way to build with timber was to expose the timbers on the inside, so that they could be carved, rather than to conceal the frame behind sheathing or carve a second piece of wood and apply it to the frame. Pugin condemned the dome of St. Paul's—which Classicists considered a model of engineering and rational building—for consisting of *three* domes rather than one, since the second dome is concealed and the inner envelope does not match the outer. Logical construction, he felt, should be monolithic and exposed, with little if any cladding.

The same rules apply in more subtle ways to architectural details. Figure 1.3 shows what Pugin considered a correct design for a door based on medieval models. The hinges are exposed, as are the fasteners, and the door is made with exposed pegs. Pugin wrote: " . . . hinges, locks, bolts and nails, etc., which are always concealed in modern design, were rendered in pointed architecture rich and beautiful decorations. . . . [These hinges] have been most religiously banished from public edifices as unsightly, merely on account of our present race of artists not exercising the same ingenuity as those of ancient times in rendering the useful as a vehicle for the beautiful."[2]

The last point is a crucial one, since Pugin's conception of building was closely connected with a conception of craftsmanship. A system of construction in which everything is exposed requires a much higher level of craftsmanship than one in which major structural elements are concealed.

Pugin's influence on ideas about rational building continued long after the Gothic Revival. He was the principal author of a concept that is very much alive today: that an honest building is one in which the structural frame and the means of its connections are exposed, in which there is no distinction between structural materials and finish materials, and in which these structural elements are for the most part monolithic. This ideal, to which architects as diverse as Wright, Le Corbusier, Mies, and Kahn subscribed, is in many ways ill suited to the systems of modern building as they have evolved in the twentieth century.

EUGÈNE-EMANUEL VIOLLET-LE-DUC

If Pugin illustrates the utopian school of Gothic Revival theory, then Viollet-le-Duc may be said to represent the empirical school of thought. Viollet-le-Duc's opinions about Gothic architecture were as strong as Pugin's, but his writings examined Gothic building at greater length and with more care. Pugin's *Principles of Pointed Architecture* is only 76 pages long; Viollet-le-Duc's *Entretiens* runs to two volumes and 900 pages, and the section on construction in his *Dictionnaire* is longer than Pugin's entire book. Viollet-le-Duc's ideas and prejudices were similar to Pugin's, but he did not reduce them to slogans.

2.5

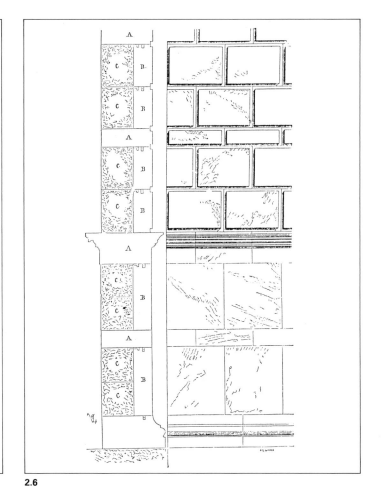

2.6

2.7

2.5 Mode of building of the Romans, from Viollet-le-Duc's *Lectures on Architecture.*

2.6 Example of Roman masonry, from Viollet-le-Duc's *Lectures on Architecture.*

2.7 **Trinity Church,** Boston
H. H. Richardson, 1877.
(Society for the Preservation of New England Antiquities.)

2.8 **Trinity Church,**
competition design, interior.
(Houghton Library, Harvard University.)

2.8

Like Pugin, Viollet-le-Duc preferred monolithic and unclad construction but did not demand it. He was particularly willing to make exceptions in the case of the wall. Figure 2.6 shows his drawing of a Roman wall consisting of concrete, brick, and a cladding of dressed stone, bound together with string courses. This was not dishonest, since the string corners revealed the clad nature of the wall.

Viollet-le-Duc also preferred, but did not demand, exposed timber in wooden roofs. In the *charpente* (framing) section of the *Dictionnaire* he describes two basic types of timber construction: the French and the Anglo-Norman. A typical Anglo-Norman example is Westminster Hall, which has the exposed and ornamented monolithic timber structure that Pugin thought was essential to Gothic. In the French system, much of the framing is often concealed by a semicircular wood vault. Viollet-le-Duc did not consider this a dishonest structure or the imitation of a stone form in wood, since the wood vault strengthened the roof; he was only critical of the type shown in figure 2.4 when no horizontal tie beam was used at the bottom. But the monolithic Anglo-Norman type was, he wrote, clearly superior, in that the structure was exposed and thus expressed.

Although Viollet-le-Duc preferred monolithic exposed roof structures, he was ready to accept structures that were concealed to some degree—provided that the cladding was structural. But he still felt, with Pugin, that architecture was essentially ornamented structure: "... all architecture proceeds from structure, and the first condition at which it should aim is to make the outward form accord with that structure."[3]

There was within Gothic Rational thinking the recognition that good buildings could not always be exposed, monolithic structures, and that it was sometimes necessary to use building systems that used layered systems that concealed structure. George Edmund Street recognized the virtues of the "incrusted" style of Venetian Gothic, but considered the monolithic style to be superior. John Ruskin, by contrast, considered the incrusted style of Venetian Gothic to be superior, despite his dislike of deceits in architecture. But the majority of Gothic Revival architects agreed with Pugin and Viollet-le-Duc that the superior form of architectural construction was that in which the structure and architecture were the same, without cladding or finish materials.

The difficulty with the attitude of Pugin and Viollet-le-Duc was that modern building was slowly evolving away from monolithic systems of construction in which structure and finish were unified. Building systems in the late nineteenth century made increasing use of structural frames, elaborate systems of finish materials, and layered construction, and architects whose ideas of rational building grew out of traditional Gothic Revival theory faced increasing difficulty applying these ideas to the building problems at hand. These architects dealt with these problems in different ways. Like Gothic Revival thoreticians, some of these architects were utopian in their outlook and some were pragmatic. Among the latter was Henry Hobson Richardson.

H. H. RICHARDSON

It is a tempting but frustrating exercise to try to connect Richardson's work with nineteenth-century theory. He was one of the best-educated architects of the time, could read French, and had an extensive library. Major writers were his close friends: Frederick Law Olmsted was his neighbor and collaborator; Henry Adams was his client and classmate at Harvard. Julien Guadet, the chief theoretician of the Beaux-Arts, was his classmate in Paris and remained in touch with him in later life. But Richardson wrote almost nothing of consequence, nor is his work consistent in attitude. Complicating the issue is the fact that, although educated in the Classical manner at the Ecole des Beaux-Arts, Richardson was stylistically a descendant of the Gothic Revivalists and his work shows the influence of the ideals of the structural rationalists of the Gothic Revival.

H. H. Richardson's attitude toward Viollet-le-Duc was largely negative. While a student at the Ecole des Beaux-Arts, he was arrested during a protest against Viollet-le-Duc's appointment to the Ecole. (He later said he had been protesting

2.9

2.10

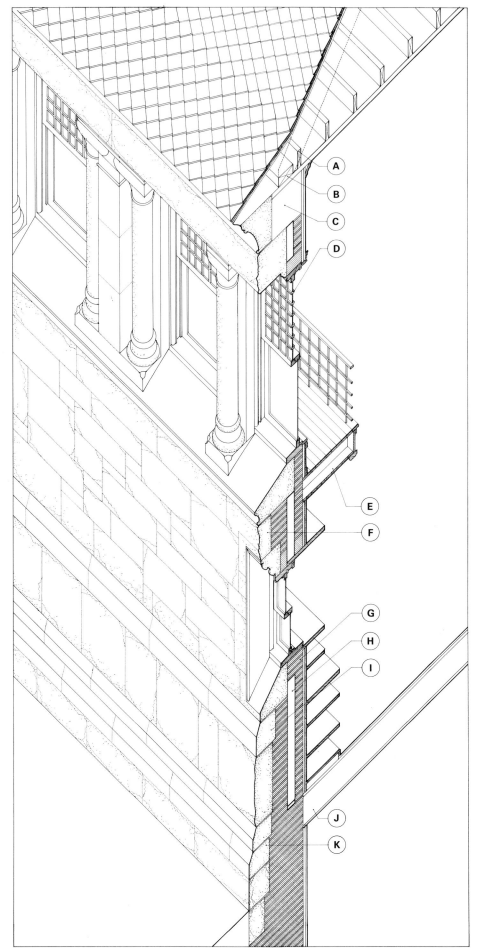

2.11

Winn Memorial Library

H. H. Richardson

Woburn, Massachusetts, 1879

2.9   **exterior facade**

2.10   **wall of stack wing**

2.11   **wall section at stack wing**

A Roof construction: 3 × 9 rafters supporting tiles nailed to sheathing or wood nailers.

B 4 × 10 wood plate. The bottoms of rafters rest on this plate, which provides a nailing surface and distributes the roof load to the wall.

C Longmeadow sandstone lintel with carved Ohio stone string course above.

D Wood double-hung window. The lintel is of ashlar Longmeadow stone cased with a carved molding of Ohio stone. The sill is Ohio stone.

E Balcony construction: Wood joists, 16″ on center, with floor and soffit of tongue-and-groove wood boards.

F Longmeadow stone lintel.

G Interior wood finish and bookcases.

H Air space. This was probably not a waterproofing cavity but a means of preventing humidity from reaching the books, a practice used in libraries since Classical antiquity.

I Base of Ohio stone with Longmeadow stone ashlar above.

J Floor construction: 12″-deep wood joists, 16″ on center, with finish-wood floor.

K Base of Ohio stone with Longmeadow sandstone above and granite below.

(Houghton Library, Harvard University, drawing WLM-C-3.)

against the manner of the appointment, not against Viollet-le-Duc's stylistic or ideological bias.) Peter Wight wrote that Richardson was a "studious reader of . . . Viollet . . . and I think his influence was patent in shaping his teachings."[4] Richardson's library included both the *Entretiens* and the *Dictionnaire*, but in 1885 he wrote to Henry Adams: "The depths to which you must have fallen in quoting [Viollet-le-Duc] as an authority on design is painful."[5]

During his lifetime Richardson was criticized by some of the orthodox Gothic Revivalists for "dishonest" construction, principally because of the interior of Trinity Church. In the competition Richardson had proposed a completely exposed wood roof structure (figure 2.8), but after being awarded the commission he redesigned the project substantially. Henry-Russell Hitchcock and others have described the difficulty of designing a tower for the crossing that could be supported in the poor soil of Boston's Back Bay. In the redesign, the roof was altered to that shown in figure 2.7. Henry Van Brunt wrote in the *Atlantic Monthly:*

The ceilings of the auditorium are of light furring and plaster in the form of a large barrel-vault of trefoil section, abutting against the great arches of the crossing, which are furred down to a similar shape, with wooden tie-beams casing iron rods carried across on a level with the cusps of the arches. The four great granite piers which sustain the weight of the tower are encased with furring and plastering, finished in the shape of grouped shafts with grouped capitals and bases. The whole apparent construction is thus, contrary to the conviction of the modern architectural moralist, a mask of the construction. We do not propose here to enter upon the question as to whether or to what extent the architect was justified in thus frankly denying his responsibility to the ethics of design as practiced and expounded by the greatest masters, ancient and modern. . . . [6]

Richardson was sensitive to this criticism. In his description of the design of the church, he wrote:

In the construction of the great arches and for tying the piers at the summit to the walls of the nave and transept iron was used, but sparingly, and as a matter of precaution rather than necessity, the weights and points of application of the adjoining walls having been calculated to furnish sufficient resistance to the thrust of the arches without the aid of ties. In general, throughout the building, the use of iron was avoided as far as might be, and with the exception of the staircase turret, which is supported by a double set of iron beams over the vestibule below, no masonry in the church is dependent on metal for support. . . . [7]

But Richardson had never intended to leave the walls unplastered; he had said that he desired "a color church." In 1883, six years after the completion of Trinity Church, he proposed a similar treatment for the interior of the Albany Cathedral. (This was a major factor in his loss of the commission for that building.) Richardson felt that "honest building" did not require walls with identical finishes on both sides. The problem of the vault, however, was more complex.

Why did Richardson change the design of the roof of Trinity Church? His reasons may have been stylistic (he may not have wanted a completely exposed structure on the interior), or they may have been pragmatic. The roof structure of the competition design of Trinity uses a number of large, solid wood timbers. The roof structure of Trinity as built uses a smaller number of timbers, many of which are not solid but are built up of smaller pieces of wood. The original design may be more "honest," since it exposes more of the structure; however, it may be more expensive, since it requires more finish-grade wood. Lumber, when cut, is subject to certain defects (such as knots) that weaken it and make it visually unacceptable. The larger a piece of timber is cut, the more likely it is to have defects. Thus, larger timbers become increasingly more expensive, not just because they require more material, but because they are harder to find free of defects. A given piece of timber may have defects that are visually undesirable but structurally acceptable, so wood is usually graded into finish grade and construction grade. There are also certain species of wood (fir, for example) that are good structurally but poor in terms of finish, since they lack hardness and beauty of grain. These woods are

2.12

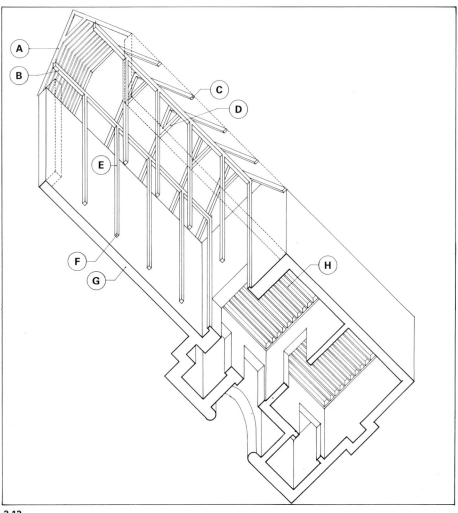

2.13

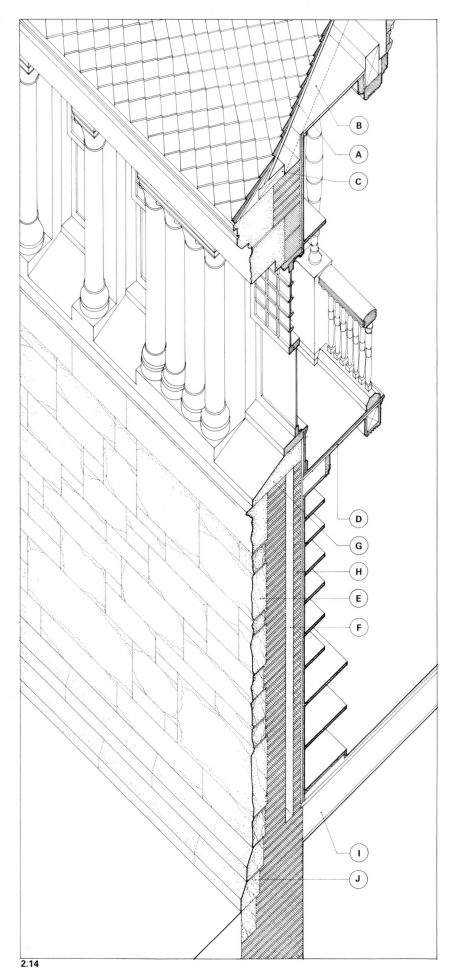

2.14

Ames Free Library

H. H. Richardson

North Easton, Massachusetts, 1879

2.12 exterior facade

2.13 roof framing axonometric

A Roof construction: Flat tiles on nailers or sheathing supported by rafters.

B 6 × 8 wood beam supporting rafters.

C Doubled joist at column. This adds to the bracing by tying the columns together.

D Collar beam. This ties the rafters together, preventing them from spreading as well as forming a truss.

E Upper wood column. Here the finish-wood column is monolithic and is a true structural support.

F Lower wood column. This is a rough wood column encased in the finish woodwork of the book stacks and the ornamental columns.

G Load-bearing wall of brick and granite. Like many late-nineteenth-century buildings, this one has load-bearing exterior walls and internal columns.

H Lobby ceiling. In contrast with the stack area, the smaller beams here are monolithic and exposed.
(Houghton Library, Harvard University, drawing ALNE-A-1-6.)

2.14 wall section at stack wing

A Roof construction: flat tiles nailed to wood boards spanning between rafters.

B 8″ rafters spaced at 1′8″ on center and supported by masonry wall.

C Wood sill. This provides a level nailing surface for the rafters and transfers their load to the masonry wall.

D Ceiling of 1 × 3 tongue-and-groove boards.

E Gray Milford granite and pink granite wall.

F Air space to protect books from moisture

G Longmeadow sandstone trim. The carved and dressed portions of the wall are of sandstone, which is softer and easier to carve than the granite.

H Brick. As much of the wall as possible is made of common brick, laid simultaneously and interlocking with the stone (brick being much less expensive).

I Floor construction: 2 × 12 wood joists 12″ on center supporting wood finish floor.

J Foundation. The wall is thickened at the base and made of the same stone as the wall although it is dressed.
(Houghton Library, Harvard University, drawing ALNE-C-1 and survey.)

generally cheaper than finish woods such as oak, which, being heavy and expensive, is a poor choice for structural timber. This is why the final design of Trinity Church is probably a less expensive construction than the original design. It is perhaps why Richardson chose this method, and it is what is wrong with Pugin's theory of monolithic construction.

As Van Brunt's criticism of Trinity Church indicates, the theories and the realities of architectural construction were beginning to diverge. It is remarkable that this criticism came from a practicing architect whose work hardly meets his own standards in this regard. Although some of Van Brunt's buildings—for example, Hemenway Gymnasium at Harvard University (1881)—use exposed monolithic wood trusses, his Unitarian Church in Waltham, Massachusetts (also 1881) has most of its wood trusses covered with a wood-and-plaster ceiling, so that they are partially exposed in the manner of Trinity Church.

Although Viollet-le-Duc certainly would have agreed with Van Brunt about Richardson's use of iron ties encased in wood, the drawings of medieval French wood trusses contained in his *Dictionnaire raisonné de l'architecture française* (1854–1868) may have provided precedents for Richardson's design. However, Henri Labrouste's roof for the Bibliotheque St. Geneviève—with which Richardson was undoubtedly familiar because of his work in the office of Theodore Labrouste—may be a more important precedent. Like the roof of Trinity Church, this is a barrel-vaulted space with a partially exposed and partially concealed structure.

In any case, the structure of Trinity Church was both demanding and unique. More typical examples of Richardson's attitude toward exposed structure are found in the building type for which he is best known: the small library.

In Massachusetts, between 1879 and 1882, Richardson built three of his best-known works: the Woburn, North Easton, and Quincy libraries. In its design, each of the buildings took as a point of departure the plan of the preceding one. The library in Quincy is one of Richardson's finest buildings. He built two subsequent libraries: one at Malden, Massachusetts (1885) and one at Burlington, Vermont (1886). These fit less neatly into a course of development, and Hitchcock calls the Burlington library a "workshop piece" (i.e., one not designed by Richardson).

All the libraries have load-bearing brick walls faced with stone on the exterior and wood and plaster on the interior. All are roofed with wood trusses which usually, but not always, are concealed from view. Woburn, the largest of the libraries, is composed of a series of separate volumes, each with its own type of framing. Quincy, the smallest, accommodates a similar plan within one structural envelope. The bookstacks of the libraries are the most similar in plan of all the parts; thus, they show in detail the process of development.

It is doubtful that any of these structures is acceptable by the standards of Pugin or Viollet-le-Duc. All are something like a basilica in plan, with a nave with alcoves on either side and with columns at the ends of the alcoves to support the roof. The first and the second, Woburn and North Easton, have barrel vaults executed in wood; Quincy has a flat, beamed ceiling. The two wood-sheathed barrel vaults would be unacceptable to Pugin, being stone forms in wood. However, they approximate one of Viollet-le-Duc's examples of timber roofs. And although they lack tie beams, the sheathing reinforces the wood framing, which the plaster vault of Trinity Church does not do. But there is an order to these systems. They are not deceits so much as they are mixtures of exposed structural members, clad structural members, and analogous structural members—that is, structural ornaments that describe concealed elements.

The nature and the advantages of the principle discussed above can be seen in the framing of the library at North Easton. The major girders and beams of the stack wing are made of construction-grade wood and then concealed or clad with a finish wood. In contrast, the framing of the smaller spaces is of exposed monolithic wood joists. Again we see the real structure in some places, but in others we see an

2.15

2.16

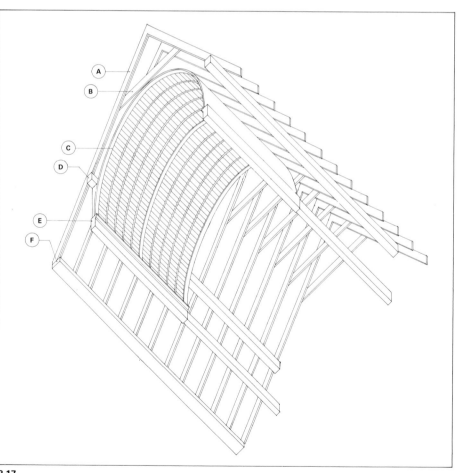

2.17

Ames Free Library

H. H. Richardson

North Easton, Massachusetts, 1879

2.15 **interior of stack wing**

(Society for the Preservation of New England Antiquities.)

2.16 **exterior of stack wing**

2.17 **roof framing axonometric**

A   Rafters supporting roof deck.

B   Collar beam. Structurally it would be better located at the top of the wall, but it is raised to avoid interfering with the vault.

C   Wood vault of tongue-and-groove boards. This vault is not structural but is supported by the wood framing above

D   Beam supported by columns to support rafters.

E   Beam cased with wood trim.

F   Plate to receive rafters resting on masonry wall (not shown).

(Houghton Library, Harvard University, drawings ALNE-A-1-6, ALNE-C-1 and survey.)

analogous cladding of finish wood. To have built these major girders of solid finish-grade wood would have been inordinately expensive; furthermore, they would have had to be larger, and they would have been much more susceptible to cracking than the veneered beams. What good is a theory of construction that requires this? And if the analogous structure of the flat lobby ceiling is acceptable, why not the vault?

There is much to support the above interpretation of Richardson's idea of structural expression, but there is much to contradict it as well. If we look at the stack area at Woburn, another set of questions arise. Parallel to the long sides are a series of thin wood arches. These and the main ribs of the vault are supported by engaged tripartite pilasters, with each column supporting an arch in the manner of a Gothic cathedral. It is hard to know what to make of this. It is hard to believe that the small columns that support the wood arches, which are Classical in their ornamentation, were designed by a former student of the Ecole des Beaux-Arts and the larger columns below have no capitals at all. The arches can in no way be seen as structurally rational; they are clearly stone forms executed in wood. In fact they resemble the masonry arches of the main lobby, but their extreme thinness reveals their purely ornamental status while robbing them of any suggestion of the quality of stone.

Did Richardson consider it acceptable to imitate forms of one material in another, provided the nonstructural nature of the form was made clear? North Easton provides a partial explanation. The wood structure of the stack area is similar to that at Woburn in its use of a major column flanked by two smaller ones, but different in other important ways: There are no false arches and no other blatantly non-functional elements, and the columns themselves, far from being imitations of stone construction, are in what might be called the language of furniture. But the crucial characteristic is that rather than resembling the stone details of the buildings, they match almost precisely the stair balusters (figure 2.15), which in turn match the design of the table legs. In the typical Gothic building, as we will see in the case of Cram, it is common for the language of structure to invade the language of furniture. In Richardson's work, the language of furniture enters the language of structure.

The difference between furniture design and structural design is not so much a difference in style as it is a difference in what functions are being articulated. In traditional styles of architecture, particularly those employing masonry, the building visually explains how its weight finds its way to earth. The plinth, the base, the battered wall, the bracket, and the capital are all visual and sometimes structural devices for "making the stability of the structure apparent," as Guadet would say. In furniture design these forces are sometimes contradicted, while at times other forces are articulated. Elements of furniture such as spiral flutes and curved joints often display the lightness of the loads they carry, whereas traditional architectural columns flare out at the bottom to emphasize the weight of the building reaching earth. The bottoms of most furniture legs, through tapering or other devices, emphasize their discontinuity with the ground plane, and thus their mobility. Some architects (Wright, for example) do not make this distinction—a Wrightian piece of furniture is a miniature Wrightian building. However, for most architects—Gothic, Classic, or otherwise—there is a point of division between architecture and furniture.

The detailing of the North Easton library is somewhat "Queen Anne." The typical door casing, for example, is the square block with bull's-eye shown in Eastlake's *Hints on House Hold Taste,* as opposed to the more common mitered joint. Although based on historical precedent, the Queen Anne style often magnifies traditionaly small elements into full-fledged architectural elements. For example, a typical Queen Anne gable might be composed entirely of volutes and half-circles—details usually seen on a smaller scale and in more limited use. At North Easton, a type of column commonly seen as a porch support in shingle-style houses is applied systematically in the interior. When used as a random porch support,

2.18

2.19

2.20

2.21

the main virtue of such a column is the impression of naiveté—the architect wishes to create the impression of a vernacular building designed by someone who does not know the rules. At North Easton there is no sense of naiveté; rather, there is a systematic contradiction of the visual structural order of traditional design.

The Burlington library brings this series to an interesting end. Hitchcock disliked it, preferring the more compact plan and the lighter-colored granite of Quincy. The exterior of Burlington is not so successful as Quincy; however, some of the interior details are among Richardson's finest.

There is little carving in the Burlington interior, and most of it is near the entry. Figure 2.20 shows the column "capitals." The pilasters themselves are Classical in feeling, but the flutes dissolve into ornamental foliage. Each capital is based on a different plant type. They have the combination of the Classic and the Romantic, and of the serious and the humorous, that characterizes Richardson's finest ornamentation.

What is most difficult to explain about Burlington is that Richardson used a monolithic exposed structure for the first time since the North Congregational Church (Springfield, Mass.). Although the interior walls are plastered in the style of Trinity Church, the roof structures of the lobby and the gallery are of monolithic exposed pine; the sketch that appears in Marianna Griswold Van Rensselaer's book[8] suggests that the stack area was intended to be as well (figure 2.19). The roof of the lobby matches exactly Viollet-le-Duc's illustration of the "French" system of wood roofs. The polygonal roof of the gallery is less easily classified. In section it resembles English Hammerbeam roofs, but again in the tripartite columns and flanking arches there seems to be a mimicking of stone in wood. In the unexecuted design we have a mingling of the languages of structure and furniture, with spiral columns atop piers that resemble the "Classical" ones at Quincy.

There is some evidence that Richardson considered the roof of exposed monolithic timbers as an ideal. If so, it was one he was seldom able to achieve. Many of his projects, such as Trinity Church and the Burlington library, began with this type of structure and were altered in the course of development to totally or partially concealed systems. Most of Richardson's train stations had exposed monolithic timbers, but inferior woods were used for these. Even at Burlington, Richardson was forced to use pine. The major exception other than the train stations is the Emmanuel Episcopal Church in Pittsburgh, which was built with solid exposed brick walls and framed with trusses of solid timber.

As to the variety of Richardson's interior detailing, we may assume that it is what it appears to be and that some of the simple facts of Richardson's life explain it: (1) He preferred to use monolithic exposed roof systems when it was possible, but he was willing to use partially or totally concealed structures when it was not. (2) He was being intentionally manneristic. Richardson's old friends from the Beaux-Arts days envied him the freedom he enjoyed as an American away from the strictures of the academy. There is every reason to think he enjoyed and exploited this freedom by breaking the rules of Classicism. Perhaps the reason for his love of the Romanesque was that it was, in its own way, a violation of the rules of Classicism. (3) Many of his details are examples of architectural wit. He was a jovial man, and there is much evidence of this in his work. It is obvious in the ornamental puns at Quincy, but is also present in the baluster that becomes a column at North Easton and in the fluted columns that burst into leaves at Burlington. (4) The one Gothic Revival theory to which he steadfastly adhered was the idea of a relationship between ornament and material. Although he used wood for arches and vaults—structural forms peculiar to masonry—there is always a stark contrast between his delicate wood interiors, with their motifs from furniture, and his massive stone exteriors.

2.22

2.23

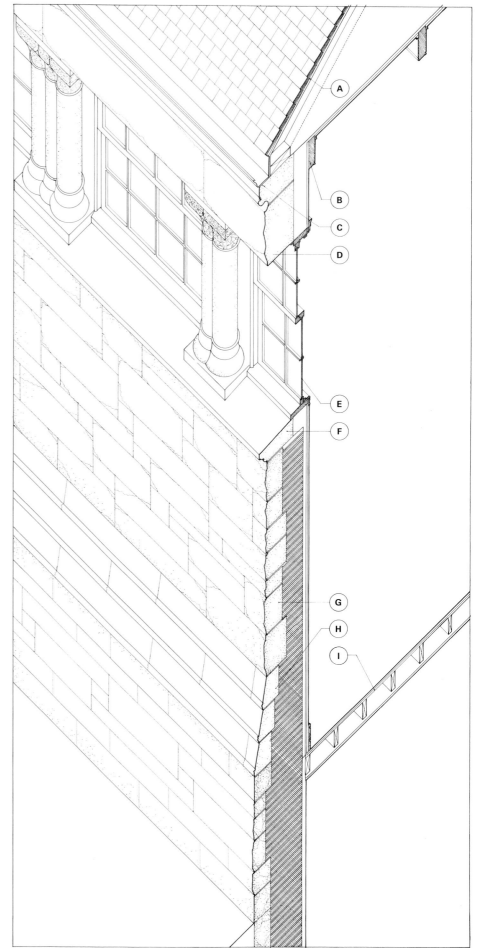

2.24

Austin Hall

H. H. Richardson

Harvard University, 1884

2.22 exterior facade
(Houghton Library, Harvard University.)

2.23 detail

2.24 wall section at small lecture room

A Roof construction: 4 × 12 rafters, 5′ on center.

B Ceiling construction. The exposed beams of this space are structural and form the bottom chord of the roof trusses. Other beamed ceilings in the building are more loosely related to the real structure.

C Metal gutter.

D Rough ashlar Ohio stone lintel.

E Double-hung wood window.

F Dressed Ohio stone sill.

G Wall construction: rough ashlar Longmeadow stone exterior with brick behind. Since this is a classroom and not a library, the air space used at North Easton and Woburn is omitted.

H Base of Ohio stone.

I Floor construction: 2 × 8 wood joists, 16″ on center, supporting wood floor.

(Houghton Library, Harvard University, drawing AH-D-109.)

Richardson's sensitivity to materials is more than a simple recognition of the massive characteristics of stone versus the delicate nature of wood; it also shows a careful exploration of the characteristics of different types of stone. Figures 2.11 and 2.14 show the elevations of the stack wings of the Woburn and North Easton libraries and the types of stone employed in each. The basic elements are the same, but the proportions and the types of stone differ. Only the softer stones, such as puddingstone, are carved; the granites are seldom dressed on their exposed faces. The elements are arranged, as always in Richardson's work, to emphasize mass. The walls are battered, the base projects, and the windows are grouped at the top of the wall—all to emphasize the bottom-heavy quality of the form.

The individual types of stones are arranged so as to increase this effect. The North Easton wall begins with two projecting courses of Milford gray granite, dressed on their sloped edges but rough on their thin vertical faces. Atop this is a string course of pink granite, uniform in height but narrow. Above this is an unbroken expanse of wall, slightly battered and composed of gray and pink granite in what looks like, but is not, a random pattern. The larger stones are gray, the smaller ones pink. The gray stones are flatter than the pink ones and more regular, so that they have less shadow on their faces. Atop this is a string course of Longmeadow sandstone, rough-faced but with a top molding that forms a tiny drip for the windowsill. Projecting drip molds or sills are small if they occur at all in Richardson's work, so as not to detract from the mass. His ornament is incised, not applied. The columns framing the windows are of puddingstone, as are the rough lintels, which are topped with dressed moldings.

In the case of Austin Hall, at Harvard University, we can see more clearly Richardson's intentions in relation to his accomplishments. The construction documents and the building are well preserved, and a plan exists which is overlaid with notes to the contractor and to the office. The instruction to "consider showing beams of conference above" could be taken as an explanation of intent regarding conformance with the ideas of Pugin: Follow them when you can.

The structure is, in principle, similar to those of the libraries. The walls are load-bearing brick, with stone exteriors and with plaster facing on the inside. The roof structures are wood, and vary in type and detail for each component. They can be roughly grouped as follows (see figure 2.28): (1) Standard wood floor framing of joists spaced 16″ on center, plastered over to give a flat ceiling (used in service areas and other less important areas). (2) Exposed oak beams spaced ±4′0″ on center, with oak-clad spruce planks spanning between them (used in major corridors and lobbies). (3) Exposed oak beams and deck supported by built-up steel girders faced with 1″ boards to appear monolithic (used to frame the ceiling of the large lecture room). (4) A trussed roof system, with the concealed truss supporting a flat ceiling of exposed wood beams. The bottom chord of the truss projects through the plane of the ceiling and is marked with a dropped beam. (This is used in the smaller lecture rooms and in the library stacks.) (5) A roof of exposed solid trusses supporting exposed beams but carrying a concealed substructure of rafters to support the roof above (used in the reading room of the law library, the largest space in the building). The importance Richardson attached to exposure and expression of structure in relation to the importance he attached to programmatic spaces is more evident from this system than from his libraries.

There is a clear hierarchy of programmatic spaces in Austin Hall, and there is a clear hierarchy of the structural systems that follow this hierarchy. The most important space, the library reading room, has exposed monolithic trusses and beams. It is not a Puginesque structure (its outer and inner forms do not coincide), but it is certainly an exposed one. Spaces of secondary importance are given exposed beams, most of which are structural. Whether these beams are under a roof or a floor does not matter. It is their relative importance, not their position, that determines the type of structure. Elements of tertiary importance have plaster ceilings with no exposed structure at all. The more important the space, the more exposed the structure. Richardson clearly must have felt that the structure of the reading room was the most desirable one but not the only acceptable one.

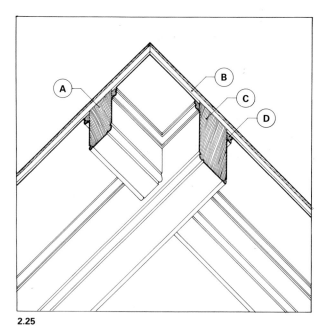

2.25

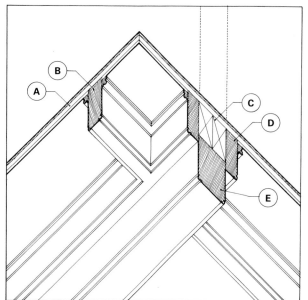

2.26

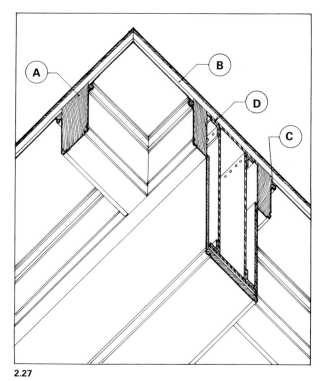

2.27

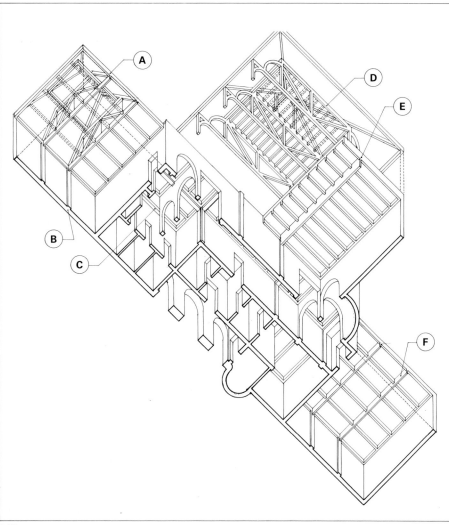

2.28

Austin Hall

H. H. Richardson

Harvard University, 1884

2.25 beam detail at monolithic beam

A 10 × 12 wood beams spaced at about 4' on center.

B Typical floor construction. The thick center portion of the floor is spruce boards. It is finished below with thinner oak boards and above with a wood-finished floor on a layer of building paper.

C 12 × 16 girder.

D Wood trim, covering rough ends of oak ceiling board.

(Houghton Library, Harvard University, drawing AH-A-21-57.)

2.26 beam detail at wood truss

A Typical floor construction, with oak ceiling below.

B 4 × 12 wood beam. This beam is structural, supporting the wood deck above

C Bottom chord of wood truss.

D 2 × 12 wood beam.

E 8 × 12 wood beam. This beam and the beam in D are largely ornamental, as the bottom chord of the truss supports the 4 × 12 beams.

(Houghton Library, Harvard University, drawing AH-A-21-57.)

2.27 beam detail at steel girder

A Solid 10 × 12 wood beam.

B Typical floor construction.

C Molding and 5 × 12 wood beam.

D 3'-deep steel girder built up from ½"-thick plates and angles. This detail was a deceit to Gothic Rationalists, since it was a steel beam clad to look like a solid wood beam.

(Houghton Library, Harvard University, drawing no. AH-A-21-57.)

2.28 framing plan

A Roof structure of small lecture hall. (See figure 2.26.)

B Pier in masonry wall to support truss above.

C Floor structure of corridors and smaller rooms. (See figure 2.25.)

D Truss in library. (This truss is only part of the roof structure; there is a triangular wood truss above.)

E Library floor construction over lecture hall. (See figure 2.27.)

F Ceiling beams in small lecture hall. (See figure 2.26.)

(Houghton Library, Harvard University, drawing AH-A-21-57.)

The exterior of Austin Hall, particularly the side wings, is similar to those of the libraries. Similar techniques were used to emphasize mass: battered walls, graduated colors and textures of stone from bottom to top, and deep-set windows concentrated at the top of the wall. But Richardson introduced an interesting variant here, deemphasizing the mass of the two end blocks to neutralize the central block. This was done in simple but effective fashion by varying the details of the roof parapet. Underneath both eaves runs a band of stone, forming lintels over the window openings. Although the span is about the same in each window, the lintel appears deeper in the central portion. In fact the lintel proper is almost the same size in each case as the gutter that joins the roof with the wall. The difference is in the carved piece between the two. At the side wings the transition is made with a roll molding (¾ of a circle), which overhangs the lintel, casting a shadow. At the central block the transition is made with an ovolo, with a cavetto below. The shape of the ovolo is not as complete a segment and casts no shadow. This, along with its greater depth, gives additional mass to the central portion.

Richardson's moldings show two other subtle devices he used to increase the apparent mass. His moldings are almost always convex. (Those that are concave are usually filled with projecting roll moldings, carved as in figure 2.30.) Typical Gothic moldings are concave, and when used in quantity they decrease the apparent mass of a building.

The most common of Richardson's convex moldings is the roll. Almost every corner of Austin Hall is formed by this molding. It is often given a base and a capital to make a slender engaged column, but it often continues in the arch above at the same diameter. Although most of the walls are rough-faced, they seldom form irregular corners, and they always meet in a straight line. The irregular surface adds to the apparent mass, but when its irregular edge is seen against the sky it softens the form. But Richardson does not always follow this detail. He uses it at Austin Hall and the Burlington library, where the primary wall materials are sandstone. At the North Easton and Quincy libraries, where the walls are of the harder-to-carve granite, the roll molding is omitted and the stone is simply carved to a sharp corner.

If Austin Hall is taken as the primary example, it can be said that Richardson's model of good construction is one that uses both literal (monolithic) and analogous (layered) systems of construction, that the choice of one of these systems for a given space is based on the programmatic importance of that space, and that the proper use of details is to articulate the mass, the qualities of the materials, and, occasionally, the programatic importance of the spaces in which the details occur.

RICHARDSON AND THE NATURE OF CONSTRUCTION IN 1880

One of the few larger Richardson buildings that are still standing and for which extensive drawings exist is City Hall in Albany, New York. It is not one of Richardson's finer works; the interior is rather bare in comparison with some of his others, owing to a limited budget, and the exterior lacks the originality of ornamentation of his best work. But because of its size and its function (it is essentially an office building), this building offers a standard of comparison by which developments in architecture and construction over the past century can be judged.

The construction is strikingly modern in some ways. Most of the essential materials and processes of modern construction are present, although insulation, gypsum drywall, and metal decking and studs are missing. Rolled iron and steel sections are used extensively, but in small pieces. Forced-air heating and ductwork are used, but not in modern configurations. Only the absence of elevators dates this building in its basic systems. The building differs from modern ones not so much in materials (brick, steel, and concrete are used) as in the processes by which they were used and in their tightly integrated relationship. The aspects of the building that have become antiquated since its completion in 1883 are the structure, the walls, and the distribution of services.

2.29

2.30

2.31

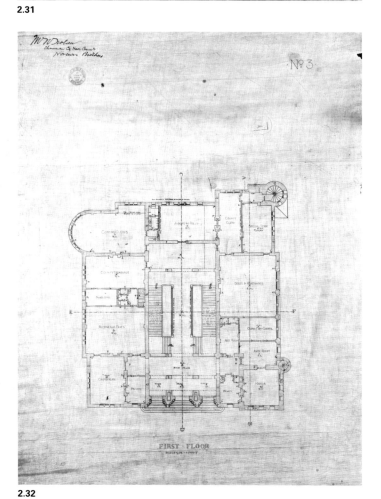

2.32

City Hall

H. H. Richardson

Albany, New York, 1883

2.29 **exterior facade**

2.30 **detail**

2.31 **section**

Note the use of steel girders in the
center section and wood joists at
the perimeter. The exterior walls
are load-bearing masonry, while
internally the floors are supported
by a steel frame.
*(Houghton Library, Harvard University,
drawing ACH-C-3.)*

2.32 **first-floor plan**

Note that there are no ceiling
cavities for utilities but numerous
wall cavities for ducts and shafts.
*(Houghton Library, Harvard University,
drawing ACH-C-6.)*

The structure is what we might today call a hybrid; it is composed of a number
of materials and systems. The vertical supports are load-bearing brick walls, which
form a doughnut-like configuration (figure 2.31). The walls increase noticeably in
thickness at each floor as the load increases. Spanning between these walls are
iron and steel beams, which support wood joists, which support a wood-plank
floor (figure 2.32). A complex series of wood trusses with iron ties supports the
roof. (Compare this with William Le Baron Jenney's Home Insurance Building—
begun in 1884, the year after the completion of the Albany City Hall—which was
the first of a series of Chicago office buildings to rely primarily on a complete
steel frame. Even though conditions in Chicago favored the curtain-wall system,
which the complete frame made possible, Richardson's Marshall Field Wholesale
Store [1885–1887] was a hybrid of load-bearing and frame construction. The historian Carl Condit has seen this hybrid type of building as inferior to the pure
frame. Independent frames eventually became almost mandatory in modern architecture and construction; however, the hybrid system was still an economical
one in 1880, and it continued to be so for some time. Wright used it in the Larkin
Building in 1903, and Otto Wagner used it in the Postsparkasse [Post Office Savings
Bank]. Should these architects be criticized for putting the masonry exteriors of
their buildings to structural use? This seems inconsistent even with modernist
theory.)

Even by the standards of 1880, the Albany City Hall is susceptible to fire. It
certainly met the minimum requirements of the day, but those requirements were
not high. A present-day building code would recognize three types of construction
in this building: "combustible" (the wood floor and roof, which will burn), "non-
combustible but unprotected" (the iron girders, which will not burn but will lose
their strength under intense heat), and "noncombustible protected" (the masonry
walls, which cannot easily be structurally damaged by fire). The code would
prohibit the use of these three types of construction together, or of using wood
and unprotected steel in a building this large. (Wood would be acceptable for a
single-family house; unfireproofed steel would be acceptable for a small one- or
two-story building.)

Although the organization of the work at Albany is not known precisely, it must
have required extensive coordination between carpenters, ironworkers, and masons; this is evident from the intertwining of wood joists, iron beams, and brick
walls. Indeed, there may not have been precise distinctions among the men doing
these three trades. In some ways this is the most antiquated aspect of the building.
Only a few different types of workmen were involved, and close coordination was
required between them. One of the principal developments of modern construction
was the rise of specialized workmen and specialized subcontractors. Norcross
Brothers, who built almost all of Richardson's major buildings, owned their own
stone quarries, did their own engineering, and hired most of their workmen directly
rather than through a subcontractor. Their organization bore little resemblance to
a modern contractor, who is often simply the manager of a series of independent
subcontractors. In all of architectural history there is a correspondence between
systems of building organizations and the methods of their assembly. In 1885
highly integrated buildings were built by a highly integrated method of contracting.
In 1989, buildings of highly independent subsystems are built by a highly independent system of subcontractors.

Integration of form and assembly can also be seen in the distribution of services
within this building. Although the extensive services of a modern office building
are not present, there is plumbing, gas lighting, and a primitive system for distributing heated air. All these services are located in cavities in the load-bearing
walls. Like the building's structure, this required a close coordination between
structure and services.

The wall details of the Albany City Hall are the result of a happy marriage between
Richardson's aesthetics and the requirements of load-bearing masonry construction. The walls increase in thickness as the load increases; at their thickest point

2.33

First Unitarian Church
Ralph Adams Cram
Newton, Massachusetts

2.33 exterior facade
(*Cram Goodhue and Ferguson,* Pencil
Points Press.)

2.34 interior
(*Cram Goodhue and Ferguson, Pencil
Points Press.*)

2.34

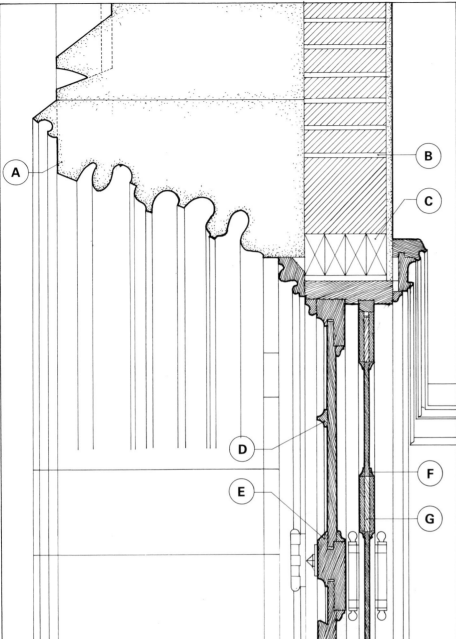

2.35

First Unitarian Church

Ralph Adams Cram

Newton, Massachusetts

2.35 door detail

A Limestone arch. Note that the Gothic moldings have complete curves and deep reveals.

B Brick wall, plastered on interior.

C Wood nailers. These serve as an intermediate fastener between the brick opening and the finish-wood door frame.

D Molding of outer door. Compare these panel moldings with those in figure 3.60.

E Rail of outer door.

F Molding of inner door.

G Rail of inner door. The outer door is solid; the inner door is partially veneered.

(F. M. Snyder, *Building Details*.)

2.36 door detail

2.36

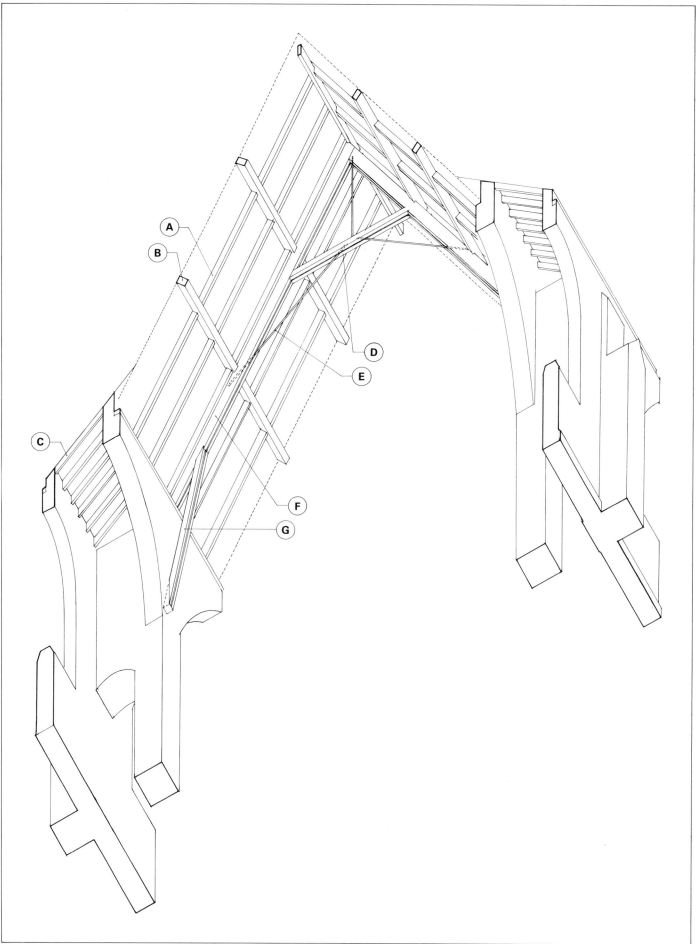

2.37 roof framing

(showing structure only)

A 4 × 6 pine rafters supporting smaller rafters and wood deck (not shown).

B 6 × 10 pine purlin supporting rafters spanning between trusses.

C 2 × 8 wood rafters supporting aisle roof.

D Two 5 × 8 pine collar beams.

E $1\frac{1}{2}''$ round steel rods. In those portions of the truss that are in pure tension, steel rods are substituted for wood.

F Two 5 × 14 pine truss rafters. The double beam construction simplifies the connection of steel rods to wood rafters.

G Two 3 × 6 pine struts. These direct a portion of the lateral thrust developed by the truss to a lower section of the wall, lessening the tendency of the lateral thrust to overturn the wall.

(F. M. Snyder, *Building Details,* Hoyle, Doran, and Berry.)

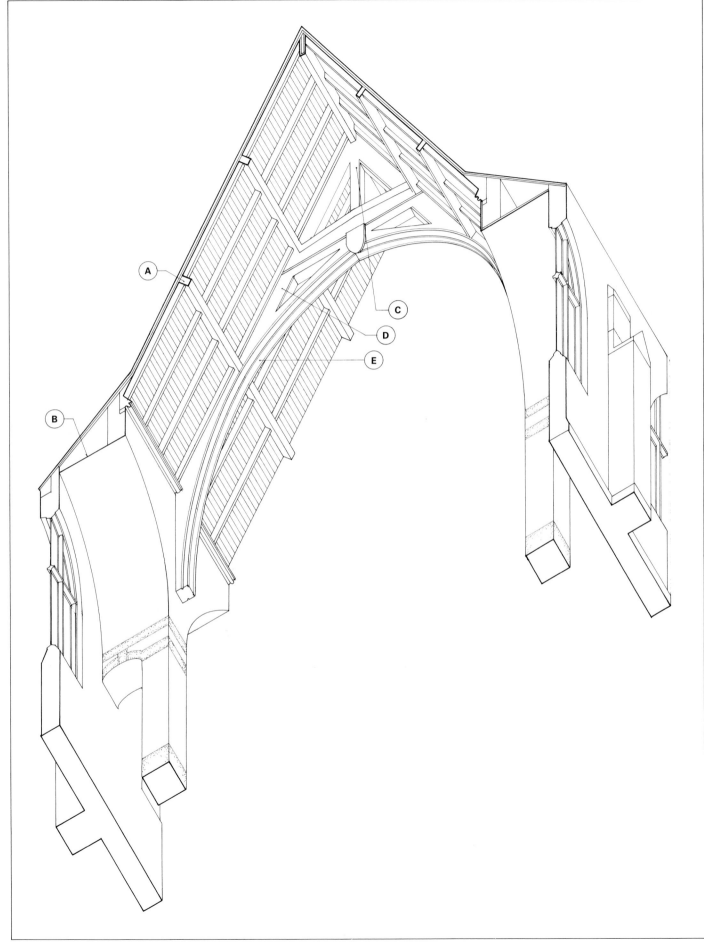

First Unitarian Church
Ralph Adams Cram
Newton, Massachusetts

2.38 **roof framing**
      (showing finish materials)
   A Unlike the larger timbers, the
      smaller rafters, purlins and
      sheathing are monolithic and
      exposed.
   B The rafters supporting the aisle
      roof are concealed under plaster
      vaults, a practice Cram referred to
      as "utterly and forever impossible
      to an honest architect."
   C Steel rods encased in cypress box
      beams.
   D Pine beams cased in cypress and
      carved.
   E The arched beam, unlike the other
      cypress casings, is completely
      ornamental and encloses no
      structural elements.
      (F. M. Snyder, *Building Details,* Hoyle,
      Doran, and Berry.)

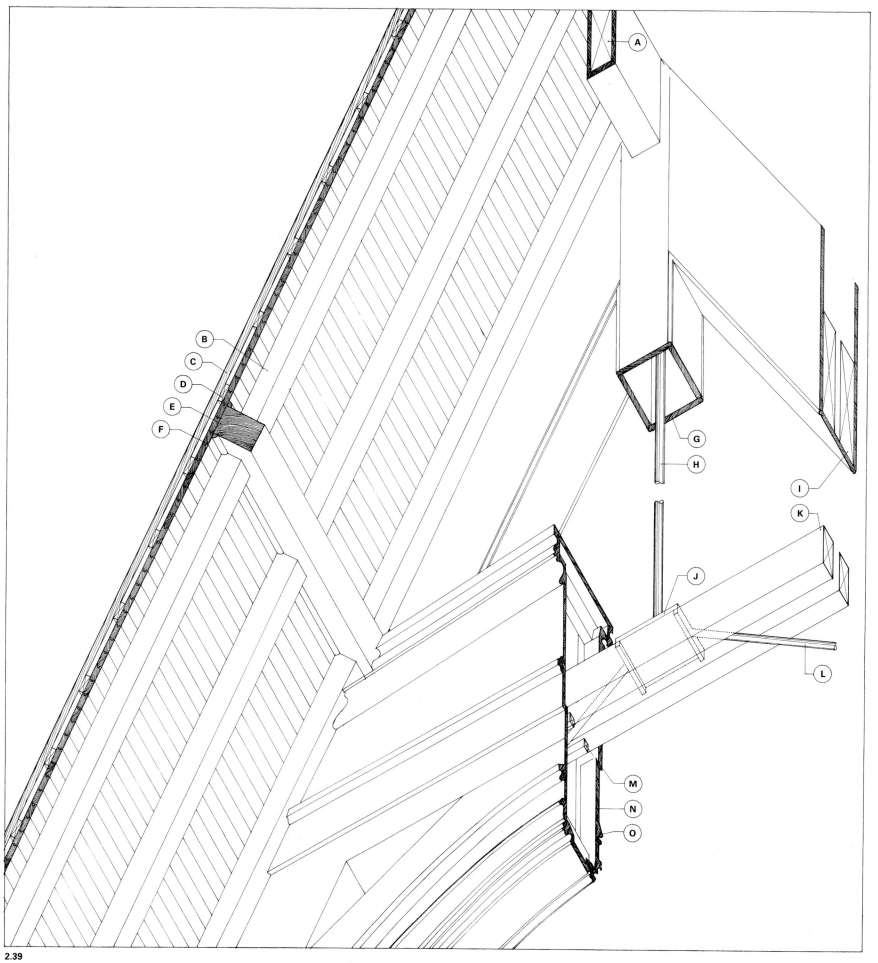

First Unitarian Church

Ralph Adams Cram

Newton, Massachusetts

2.39   roof detail

A   4 × 12 pine ridge beam cased in $\frac{7}{8}$″ cypress boards.

B   4 × 6 pine rafters spaced at 2′ on center.

C   Slate shingles (not shown) on $1\frac{1}{4}$ × 6 tongue-and-groove boards.

D   1 × 3 furring.

E   6 × 10 hard pine purlins.

F $\frac{7}{8}$ × 3 cypress sheathing.

G $\frac{7}{8}$″ cypress casing (partially shown) enclosing steel rods.

H $1\frac{1}{2}$″ round steel rods.

I   Two 5 × 14 pine truss rafters. The double rafter allows for easier joining of truss members and for steel rods to penetrate the beam.

J   Cast-iron shoe, lag-bolted to pine beams. This transfers the tensile stress in the rods to the wood beam distributing it over a larger area of wood.

K   Two 5 × 8 pine beams. These are the actual structural members. The cypress casing is only a finish material.

L $1\frac{1}{2}$″ round steel rod.

M   Blocking. This serves to join and support the hollow cypress sheathing.

N   Cypress casing. The boards are joined so as to make the casing appear monolithic and indistinguishable from the solid beams.

O   Trim. Note the deep-set reveals.
(F. M. Snyder, *Building Details,* Hoyle, Doran, and Berry.)

above ground they are over 3 feet thick. As a result the windows are deep-set, and the building's profile is enlarged at its base, giving the effect of mass and solidity that Richardson desired.

The walls are layered in the sense that they are composed of stone on the outside, common brick in the middle, and plaster on the inside. They are monolithic in the sense of being composed entirely of masonry, without voids or other materials. They are not monolithic in the same sense as the Greek and Roman walls described by Viollet-le-Duc, but they are more nearly monolithic than contemporary stone or brick walls.

More important, the walls of this building are generalized in function. All of the tasks which a wall is called upon to perform—to keep out water, to keep in heat, and to hold up the building—are accomplished by masonry. Brick is a poor material for accomplishing any of these tasks but the last, but it is used here in such quantity as to accomplish its purpose.

Despite the fact that he used numerous modern materials in buildings such as the Albany City Hall, Richardson never had to face the most difficult conflict between traditional architecture and modern construction. His death coincided with the development of the complete steel frame, which made load-bearing walls unnecessary. The rational basis of the Gothic Revival ideal of good building was dependent to a great extent on the limitations imposed by masonry load-bearing walls. Once these limitations disappeared, reconciling the images of Gothic and Romanesque architecture with modern building systems became increasingly difficult.

RALPH ADAMS CRAM

Ralph Adams Cram began practicing in 1889—three years after Richardson's death—and continued until 1942. Cram was only two years older than Frank Lloyd Wright, and he witnessed most of the technical and aesthetic changes that produced modern architecture. Despite the fact that he was one of the last Gothic Revival architects, Cram was as devoted a disciple as Pugin was to have—certainly much more so than Richardson.

In Cram's writings, one architect is constantly singled out for criticism. It is not McKim, nor White, nor one of the Art Nouveau architects or one of the early Modernists, but H. H. Richardson. While Cram always prefaced his comments by stating that Richardson was a genius, he considered Richardson's influence disastrous: "His was an alien style, with no historic nor ethnic propriety. . . . With his death the fatal weakness of Romanesque became apparent. . . . It degenerated into the most shocking barbarism and passed into history as an episode."[9]

Cram was critical of Richardson's work for three reasons: (1) Cram followed the doctrinaire principles of the Ecclesiological Movement in church planning, whereas Richardson had not; thus, for example, he criticised Richardson's Trinity Church for its deep chancel, which he considered inappropriate to a low church without a high altar at the rear of the chancel. (2) He was equally critical of Richardson's rustic and picturesque design and detailing: ". . . sprawling irregular plans, chaotic roofs, silly turrets and meaningless towers, windows of a dozen shapes, united in only one thing—their incorrigible badness. No repose, no simplicity, no self respect; just a delicious attempt at hectic picturesqueness through the use of silly elaboration."[10] (3) He subscribed, in theory if not in practice, to Pugin's ideas about the correctness of exposed, monolithic construction; thus, he wrote that, in the ideal village church, "floor and walls should be of dressed stone. Stone vaulting is practically out of the question. . . . I need hardly say that vaults of lath and plaster, or of steel construction, are utterly and forever impossible to an honest architect or a God-fearing congregation. . . . A fine roof of simple open beams supported on carved stone corbels is infinitely better for such a church. . . ."[11]

2.40

2.41

2.42

Princeton University Chapel

Ralph Adams Cram

1922

2.40 **exterior facade**
(Hoyle, Doran, and Berry.)

2.41 **interior**
(Hoyle, Doran, and Berry.)

2.42 **choir stall**
(Hoyle, Doran, and Berry.)

Cram's sympathy for Pugin's ideas is clear in his condemnation of a stone church that contained a steel frame:

[The church] was given the height and the simplicity of mass that were necessary; but most unfortunately it was built after an evil fashion; falsely and unpardonably, with a frame of steel like an office building, supporting the sheathing of stone that was worked into the forms of honest construction. It is therefore an example of all that should be avoided, when it might quite well have been a marvel of ecclesiastical beauty and holiness, had it but been a piece of self-respecting and honorable construction.[12]

This passage was written when the steel frame was already well established, particularly in the skyscraper. Cram had little use for American commercial architecture (which he referred to as "veneered engineering"[13]), although his firm was later to design several steel-framed office buildings.

Cram preferred monolithic construction even for residences built of wood. He praised the work of the Greene brothers, which he thought was monolithic (it was not), and in his book *Impressions of Japanese Architecture* he described the virtues of Japanese wood construction:

There is no ornament for the sake of ornament, no woodwork or carving not demanded by the exigencies of construction. . . . The spirit of ornamented construction and no other ornament whatever that characterized Greek architecture finds its echo in Asia. . . . No greater contrast to our own fashion could be imagined. With us the prime object appears to be the complete concealment of all construction of whatever nature by an overlay of independent ornament. With wainscot and marble and tiles, plaster, textiles, and paper-hangings, we create a fictitious shell that masks all construction and exists quite independently of it.[14]

Anyone who applied a theory of construction based on the analysis of thirteenth-century churches to the building problems of the early twentieth century was bound to encounter some difficulty. Cram certainly did, but he was pragmatic and willing to compromise on certain issues—particularly that of honesty. He did not share the Modernist ideal of one universal system and ethics of building. Cram did his best work for organizations to which he was ideologically sympathetic, such as the High Episcopal Church. As he believed in hierarchies of society, he believed in hierarchies of building; and as he believed in hierarchies of building, he believed in hierarchies of construction. Thus a clad steel frame might be acceptable for a commercial office building, but not for a church. Cram's work shows little consistency, but it indicates by example what he considered the ideal system to be.

Cram's work at Princeton University, which is among his best, is organized in clear hierarchies of type of form and type of construction. The major program elements (chapel, refectory [dining hall], and cloister [dormitory]), the natural adaptation of Collegiate Gothic, and the generous budgets all allowed him to come as close as he could to his ideals.

Cram was made supervising architect at Princeton in 1907. In 1909 he began work on the Graduate College on a site away from the older campus. This program also provided a clear hierarchy of elements: large dining room, small dining rooms, kitchen, common rooms, dormitory rooms, and a memorial tower. These elements are loosely grouped around two quadrangles. All the buildings are connected, but the more important elements, such as the dining hall, stand out as individual buildings (figure 2.47).

The budget reinforced Cram's tendency to demand "honest" systems of construction for the more important spaces, since a separate large gift was made for the dining hall. But although there was a hierarchy of program, out of which grew a natural hierarchy of construction types, hierarchy of detail was a problem. Cram wrote that this was his most difficult problem—particularly in the design of the exterior of the dining hall, which he wanted to set off from the dormitory rooms without making it look "ecclesiastical."

Princeton University Chapel

Ralph Adams Cram

1922

2.43 **entrance**

(Hoyle, Doran, and Berry.)

2.44 **section at door**

A   Limestone facing.

B   Masonry-core wall. Although the walls are monolithic, the exposed outer layer is of limestone.

C   Keystone.

D   Brick arch with limestone below.

E   Concrete deck, lintels, and bond beams.

F   Door trim.

(Hoyle, Doran, and Berry.)

2.43

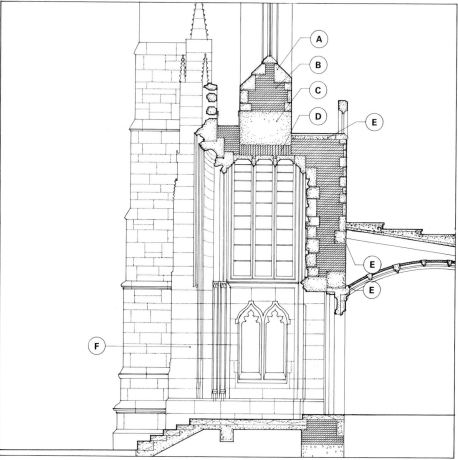

2.44

2.45

Austin Hall

H. H. Richardson

Harvard University, 1884

2.45 **Austin Hall,** detail

2.46 **City Hall, Albany**
section at door
A Gray granite wall.
B Longmeadow sandstone arches.
Note the use of the roll molding.
C Brick arch. The sandstone facing
arch carries part of the load of the
wall around the door opening, but
most of it is borne by this
concealed brick arch.
(Houghton Library, Harvard University.)

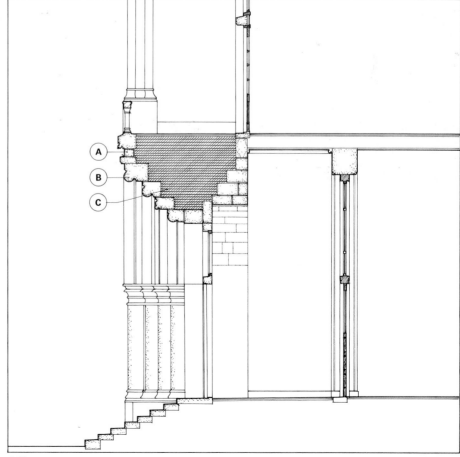

2.46

2.47

2.48

Princeton Graduate School

Ralph Adams Cram

1909

2.47   exterior
(Hoyle, Doran, and Berry.)

2.48   interior of dining hall
(Hoyle, Doran, and Berry.)

The dining hall or refectory is the most important element in the hierarchy. Appropriately, it is almost entirely of monolithic construction. Cram considered it one of his finest achievements, and wrote in his autobiography that "one thing [that] was done in the case of the great refectory that was rather unusual in modern times . . . was to construct the wide-spanned hammer-beam trusses of solid and honest balks of timber without recourse to hidden steel in any place."[15] As figure 2.49 shows, this is not quite true. While the beams are solid oak, they are assisted by steel tie rods concealed by the screens that infill the truss openings. Since hammerbeam roofs do not have horizontal bottom members, they have a tendency to push out the stone walls below. The exterior buttresses could have been enlarged to counter this, but that would have resulted in a more "ecclesiastical" look. The "hidden steel" type of hammerbeam truss which Cram described can be found in Richardson's Trinity Church, and also in Cram's First Unitarian Church in Newton, Massachusetts. Although the trusses of the Newton church appear monolithic, they are actually built of rough timber trusses covered with thin slabs of finish cypress. In the voids thus created run steel rods, which increase the tensile strength of the wood in the manner of reinforced concrete. These beams were much less expensive than the large monolithic beams of the Princeton refectory. There is another difference between the two systems of truss construction that is equally important: the process of construction. The trusses at Princeton are both structure and finish material. They had to be erected early in the construction process, and much of their ornamentation had to be carved in place. The wood also had to be protected from damage during construction. The trusses at Newton have separate sections of wood for structure and finish. The roof trusses were put in place first; the finish wood could be carved on the ground or in the shop and installed much later in the construction process, when it would be less susceptible to damage.

The truss construction of the church at Newton is not one that Ruskin or Viollet-le-Duc would approve; it falls definitely into the category of deceits. Cram considered it an inferior system, but not an unacceptable one; a system that exposed the steel rods would have been unacceptable. Interestingly enough, the medieval roof of Westminster Hall in London, in many ways a model for Princeton's Graduate College, had been dismantled and reinforced with steel rods, and William Butterfield—one of the leaders of the Gothic Revival—had used concealed iron rods in wood roofs (Cram was probably not aware of this). But it should be remembered that Cram had other options. In their dining hall at Princeton, built in 1910, Day and Klauder were forced by economic constraints to use a system of rough trusses with steel rods covered in finished wood; however, they elected to use a paneled ceiling in which the truss was expressed but not exposed. Despite its lack of deceits, Day and Klauder's roof is not the monolithic exposed type preferred by Pugin and Cram. As was to be the case in much of Modern architecture, the desire for monolithic exposed structures had become the end, not the means, even when defying those rules it was to have illustrated.

Cram's dormitories at Princeton are a step down the hierarchy of types from the refectory, and are, accordingly, built by less noble means. The construction systems are less monolithic and more economical, and the details are altered to place them within the hierarchy. The exterior finish (schist, with limestone trim) is the same as that of the refectory, but the interior walls are finished primarily in plaster whereas those of the refectory are finished in sandstone. Although the exterior walls are bearing, the floors are steel encased in concrete (a great improvement in fire safety over wood floors). In the dorm rooms the brick and concrete are plastered. (Cram hoped that some students would pay for wood paneling.) The common rooms, which are located on the ground floor of each dormitory building, had a place in the hierarchy between the refectory and the dorm rooms; thus, Cram gave them wainscoting and wood ceilings.

Pugin would not like Cram's use of steel beams encased in concrete, covered in wood, and given stone corbels. Here again, Cram probably thought he was employing an inferior but not unacceptable system. (In portions of Day and Klauder's

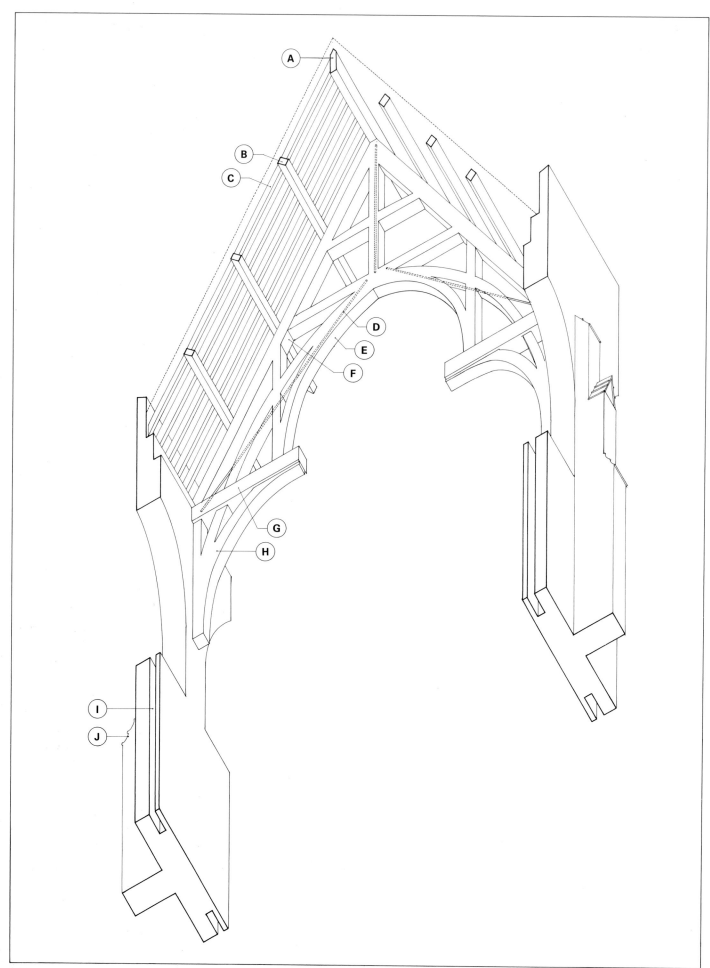

2.49

Princeton Graduate School

Ralph Adams Cram

1909

2.49 roof framing of dining hall
Unlike the West Newton roof, this
one is built of solid monolithic
beams made possible by a
generous budget.

A   8 × 18 ridge beam.

B   10 × 15 purlins.

C   4 × 6 rafters supporting wood deck
     (not shown).

D   2″ round steel rods. Contrary to
     Cram's statement in his
     autobiography, this roof does have
     steel reinforcing. These rods are
     concealed by an ornamental wood
     screen (not shown).

E   12″-thick arched beam. The
     longitudinal braces are not shown.

F   12 × 14 wood. All roof timbers in
     the Graduate School are solid, with
     no wood veneers or hollow beams.

G   14 × 16 wood beam. The ends of
     these were carved after they were
     in place.

H   10″-thick bracket.

I   Shaft for air-supply ductwork.

J   Schist-and-masonry wall.
     (Hoyle, Doran, and Berry.)

nearby dining hall the beams are exposed concrete. This to Cram would have been an impropriety and a confirmation of the inferior nature of modern society.) To Cram the *appearance* of monolithic construction was more important than conformance to the principles of monolithic construction. He attached overriding importance to the articulation of typology, to the relative importance of the parts of his program. On the exterior of the college buildings this is accomplished by means of parapet and eave details. The typical roof throughout is slate nailed to wood boards and supported by timber framing. In the dining room the wood is exposed; in the dormitories it is concealed. The slates are not set in even courses but become progressively thinner and closer together toward the top of the roof. This, like many of the details, emphasizes the building's weight at the bottom and its lightness at the top. At the dining hall there is a parapet, and the water is carried off by a concealed gutter and exterior leaders. In order for the dorms to have a less important profile, the roof overhangs to form an eave. This eave has a slightly flatter angle than the roof itself, as was common at this time, and here the gutter is exposed. In the block between the dining hall and the tower, perhaps feeling that an overhanging eave would present too great a contrast, Cram added another floor of rooms to create a series of gables connected with a parapet wall, still subordinate to but more in keeping with the tower and the dining hall. The common rooms are called out by buttresses and by two-tiered windows on the ground floor. Although these buttresses correspond to the locations of the steel beams inside, they are probably overdesigned structurally.

The articulation of programmatic types is continued in the smaller details such as the windows. There are three primary types, with variations: larger, pointed windows subdivided by stone tracery for the dining hall (figure 2.53); smaller, two-tiered windows, also subdivided with stone, for the common room; and pairs of simple rectangular windows with limestone surrounds for the dorm rooms (figure 2.52). The latter are sometimes given a drip cap (to call out a study or some other room more important than a bedroom) and sometimes used merely for picturesque variety. This is another violation of Puginesque principles, as the purpose of the drip cap is to keep water away from the window head and not to articulate the importance of the room it serves. The mullions are similar in profile but vary slightly with the spaces they serve. In the dining hall the glass is set the deepest and is primarily fixed leaded glass; in the common rooms the glass is set less deep and the frames are primarily steel with lead inserts; in the dorm rooms the windows are steel casements and the glass is closest to the surface. Thus, the most important space—the dining hall—has the most medieval windows.

The limestone trim and mullions reinforce these programmatic distinctions. The mullion of the dining hall has a double concave molding; the common room a single concave, and the dorm rooms a single flat. However, the primary purpose of the molding design is not to articulate the program but to articulate the mass. This is to some extent the same thing, since different programmatic pieces of the building also have their own characteristic massing.

Whereas Richardson used convex moldings almost exclusively (particularly the roll), Cram used concave moldings almost exclusively, at least on the exteriors of the majority of his buildings. Convex moldings have the effect of increasing mass; concave ones have the effect of decreasing it. Most of Cram's moldings use an incised form with a fillet, so that they appear to be cut out of the mass. This does not mean that Cram was less interested in massiveness than Richardson. Rather, he seems to have been interested in greater contrasts in mass between the heaviest portions and the lightest.

Another fundamental difference between Cram's trim and Richardson's is the treatment of materials. Richardson developed completely different systems for exterior stone and interior wood, and seldom used exterior finish materials in an interior. Cram recognized that interior trim should be less pronounced and coarse than exterior, and that wood details should be more delicate than stone; however, he used essentially the same forms, so many of his wood details are small-scale replicas of his stone details. Figures 2.52 and 2.56 show the window and wood

2.50

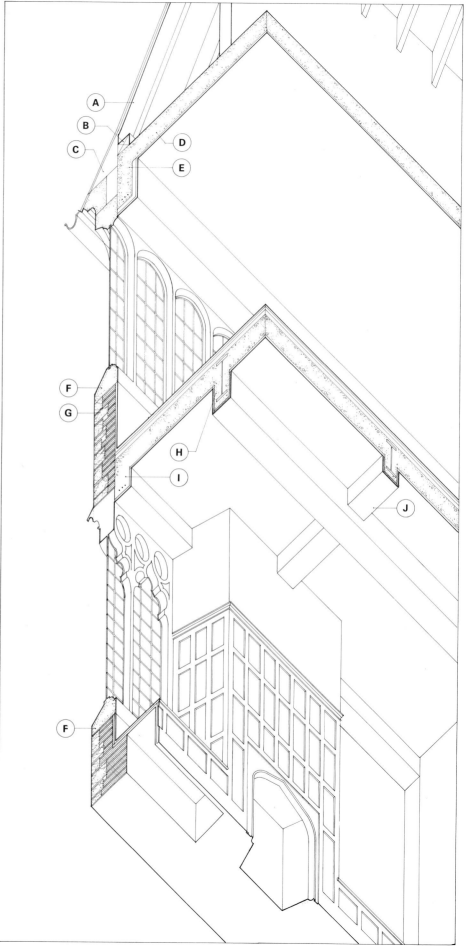

A

B

C

D

E

F

G

H

I

J

F

2.51

Princeton Graduate School
Ralph Adams Cram
1909

2.50 common room in new quad
(Hoyle, Doran, and Berry.)

2.51 wall section

A Roof construction. Slates on wood nailers on deck supported by rafters. The slates vary in size, becoming thicker toward the bottom of the roof.

B Wood plate to receive rafters. This distributes the load of the rafters to the wall and acts as a nailer.

C An additional rafter is added here to change the slope of the roof to a more horizontal angle.

D Concrete slab. Except for the rafters, the structure is built of non-combustible materials.

E Concrete beam over window. The slab supported, at least in part, by the masonry walls.

F Steel and lead windows in limestone trim.

G Wall construction: brick load-bearing wall faced with schist. Although the building contains a great deal of concrete and steel, it is essentially a load-bearing-wall building.

H Steel beam cased in wood trim. Although Cram encases steel beams in wood, he did not construct false beams in this building.

I Concrete slab and edge beam.

J Steel beam cased in wood trim.
(Hoyle, Doran, and Berry, Princeton University Archives.)

paneling details of the Old Common Room; figure 2.57 shows the panel details of the New Quad Common Room. In the Old Common Room, the window jamb is a simple concave curve and the sill a simple but steep slope. This pattern is repeated in the edges of a typical wood panel. Whereas the bottom of the horizontal rail is a single concave, the top is a simple slope in imitation of the window sill. This same repetition is seen in the New Quad Room, this time with a simpler convex curve. Appropriately, this system is repeated in a more complex fashion in the details of the windows and the wood screens of the dining hall, where the jamb pattern becomes a double concave molding (reflecting not only this hall's greater size but its greater importance as well).

The extensive use of exposed fasteners in the interior of the Graduate College is in accordance with Pugin's desire for expression through exposure. The paneling in the East Wing Common Room has exposed dovetails at the corners, while that in the New Quad Common Room has a roll molding at the corner and exposed pegs at the mortise-and-tenon joint of the rail. As is obvious from the differences in detail between these two systems, they expose only selected joints and fasteners. In the truss of the Great Hall there are numerous exposed pegs, but they give no indication of the steel rods and bolts.

The chapel, at the time of its completion in 1922, was called Princeton's $2 million protest against materialism—a quip which time and inflation have deprived of its bite. This project logically completed the hierarchy of types set up in the Graduate College, since to Cram the chapel was the most important building on a college campus. It carries the ideal (if not the reality) of monolithic construction to its logical Gothic conclusion. Because there is only one room, the details have type-articulating meaning only by comparison with the Graduate College. Nonetheless, the chapel continues the parallel systems of stone and wood detailing and the principle of mass at the base and lightness at the top.

As in the Graduate College, the roof structure is the primary means of articulating the importance of the chapel as a building type. In contrast with the wood roof of the Graduate College, the chapel is vaulted—with a vault not like any Gothic one. The plan of the chapel resembles the typical Christian basilica system of nave, side aisles, transcept, and choir, but the aisles are narrowed down to corridors so that there are no seats behind columns. With a traditional vault this might not have been possible, since there would not have been sufficient room for the buttresses. Cram was able to achieve his clever solution by building the vault of Guastavino tiles with an acoustic facing instead of stone, thus greatly reducing its weight and the size of the buttresses needed to support it. (Guastavino tiles are terra-cotta-like squares set in thin layers with portland cement. Vaults of these tiles were thinner, lighter, and stronger than traditional vaults of stone set with lime mortar. Besides being a boon to Gothic Revivalists who loved masonry vaulting, they were used extensively by McKim, Mead & White.)

In technology, if not in form, the Princeton chapel is an extremely modern building. Instead of the traditional Gothic wood roof over the vault, there are steel trusses and a concrete deck. But all this is hidden from view, and the building has the appearance of a monolithic construction. No visual distinction can be made between tile, interior stone, and exterior stone. The building appears to be made of only limestone, lead, and glass. One has no awareness of the tile, the steel, and the concrete and concrete block that make up so much of the building.

Completing the hierarchy of window types set up in the Graduate College, the windows of the chapel (none of which are operable) are fixed stained glass set in lead. They are slightly larger and have more stone subdivisions than the windows of the Graduate College.

A comparison of Cram's door details will illustrate further not only his typology of detail but also his attitude toward mass. Compare first the door jamb of the chapel shown in figure 2.44 with the Richardson door shown in figure 2.34. Each of these has a series of progressively smaller moldings, which were common in both Gothic and Romanesque architecture; however, Cram and Richardson used

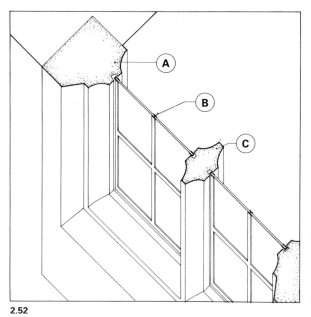

2.52

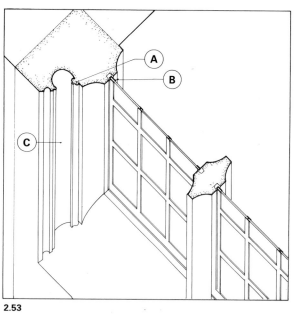

2.53

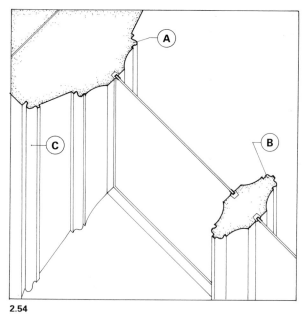

2.54

2.55

2.56

2.57

Princeton Graduate School

Ralph Adams Cram

1909

2.52 **window detail of typical room**

A   Limestone jamb. Being the smallest and least important room, this has the simplest jamb.

B   Fixed glass set with H-shaped lead joints. Unlike Medieval prototypes, these metal sections were preformed.

C   Limestone mullion. The windows of the small rooms have large, simple moldings with minimal shadows (Survey.)

2.53 **window detail of dining hall**

A   Lamb's-tongue molding on limestone jamb. The larger window of the dining hall has a molding applied at the perimeter, but not the central mullion, to denote the greater importance of the room and the increased scale of the window.

B   Fixed glass set with lead.

C   A deep cove is added to the typical window here to create a shadow line around the window, while the center stone mullion has the same profile as in figure 2.52.

(Survey, Hoyle, Doran, and Berry.)

2.54 **Princeton University Chapel**
window detail

A   Limestone jamb. The notches to receive the glass are deeper on two adjacent sides to allow the glass to be set in place, a task made difficult by the absence of any type of glazing bead.

B   Lamb's-tongue molding on limestone mullion. The mullion here is deeper than those in the Graduate School, since it must span a greater distance due to the larger opening.

C   One half lamb's-tongue molding at jamb. Here, in the most important buildings, moldings are applied to both jamb and mullions.

(Survey, Hoyle, Doran, and Berry.)

2.55 **Old Common Room**

2.56 **panel detail of Old Common Room**
Note that the trim moldings match the window in figure 2.53 and the dovetail joint at the corner.

2.57 **panel detail at common room in New Quad**
The joints here are pegged rather than dovetailed, but again are stone details replicated at smaller scale in wood.

these moldings in opposite ways. Richardson's moldings are convex; Cram's are concave. Richardson's appear to be added on; Cram's are incised. Richardson's articulate the independence of the parts; Cram's emphasize the geometric completeness of the whole. The incised and unified nature of Cram's details, in combination with the smooth stonework, gives an impression of an almost Modernist ideal form controlling the design, in contrast with the material-conscious articulated details of Richardson. Where Cram uses a convex molding, it is at a main structural pier supporting the ribs above. For Cram the primary purpose of ornament was not to articulate structure or to bring out the qualities of materials, but to show the importance of the spaces in which the ornament is used.

Much of the quality of the woodwork in the interior of the chapel is due to the individual craftsmen, but the details maintain the principle of wood details following the general outlines of stone details. Perhaps the greatest contrast between the interior detailing of Cram and Richardson is that whereas Richardson used details characteristic of furniture for architectural purposes, Cram used characteristics of architectural detailing in furniture. Figure 2.42 shows an end support of one of the choir stalls. It is tapered toward the top; it sits on a plinth with a base molding; it has incised miniature buttresses at the corners, with their own bases topped with miniature pinnacles. While much too delicate to be made of anything but wood, it is (particularly in its bottom-heaviness) suggestive of stone construction. As with Cram's stone details, primarily concave shapes with fillets are used to give an impression of lightness at the upper portions and mass at the base.

Like the building itself, the woodwork of the Princeton chapel emphasizes its importance by being of monolithic construction. But in contrast with the building, the appearance of the woodwork reflects reality: almost every piece is solid. Cram emphasizes this fact through the carving, particularly the holes cut through the centers of the oak panels. Today the use of this much solid oak would be beyond the reach of all but the most generous budgets.

From the evidence of their work, both Cram and Richardson considered exposed monolithic structural systems to be of the highest order, but not the only acceptable solutions. This can be interpreted in two ways: (1) Both men had large offices and numerous commissions, so some degree of flexibility and compromise was necessary; perhaps they were simply pragmatic. (2) Both men recognized the aesthetic choice played a factor in the choice of technology—something the Modernists failed to do. Richardson and Cram recognized hierarchies of buildings, of use, and of forms. Cram did not require that an office building adhere to the constructional ideology that he applied to a cathedral.

It can be argued that there was a gap between the Gothic Revival theory of rational building and the realities of building in any age, but there was certainly an even wider gap between Gothic Revival theory and the realities of modern building. This was evident to the sensitive observer at the end of Richardson's career in 1886; it was obvious to anyone who wanted to see it at the end of Cram's in 1942. Strangely enough, the ideas of Gothic Rationalism outlived the style itself and became tenets of modernist rationalism—particularly the idea of monolithic and exposed construction as the most desirable system. The result was that the inherent conflict between these ideals and the common practice of building was to continue to the present day. But before we examine this development, it is necessary that we look at another equally strong tradition of rational building: the Classical.

3 McKim, Mead & White and Classical Rationalism

To teach the orders, one teaches images; to teach the wall, first one teaches reality.

Julien Guadet

Frank Lloyd Wright wrote in 1901:

In our so-called skyscrapers good granite or Bedford stone is cut into the fashion of the Italian followers of Phidias and his Greek slaves. Blocks so cut are cunningly arranged about a structure of steel beams and shafts (which structure secretly robs them of any real meaning), in order to make the finished building resemble the architecture depicted by Palladio and Vitruvius—in the schoolbooks. It is quite as feasible to begin putting on this Italian trimming at the cornice, and come on down to the base, as it is to work, as the less fortunate Italians were forced to do, from the base upward. Yes, "from the top down" is often the actual method employed. The keystone of a Roman or Gothic arch may now be "set"—that is to say, "hung"—and the voussoirs stuck alongside or "hung" on downward to the haunches. Finally this mask, completed, takes on the features of the pure "classic," or any variety of "renaissance," or whatever catches the fancy or fixes the "convictions" of the designer. . . . The "classical" aspect of the sham front must be preserved at any cost to sense.[1]

To Wright, it was mandatory that the Modern era produce its own style of building. The use of the steel frame alone would "require" the development of a new architecture. The buildings of McKim, Mead & White were unacceptable by this standard, in that they adapted forms from Roman and Renaissance sources to clad-steel-frame buildings.

From this viewpoint, one of the worst offenders is Charles McKim's Pennsylvania Station, in New York. The main waiting room, which duplicates fairly closely the hall of a Roman bath, is built not in brick and concrete (as was the original) but with plaster ceilings suspended from steel trusses. By the standards of Guadet or those of Ruskin, the vault of the main waiting room—a plaster ceiling suspended from a steel frame pretending to be a monolithic coffered concrete vault of the Roman type—is a "deceit." Unlike the contemporary vaults of Otto Wagner, it makes no attempt to show that it is not a structural form. Pennsylvania Station represented to many, when it was built and for years after, all that was wrong with the architecture of the American Renaissance. Being one of McKim, Mead & White's best-known buildings, it is largely responsible for their reputation of indifference to the real structure of buildings.

3.1

3.2

3.3

3.4

However, the testimony of McKim's biographer, Charles Moore, concerning the construction of the marble walls at the Morgan Library, contradicts the view discussed above:

To Mr. Morgan [McKim] said in substance: "I would like to build after the manner of the Greeks, whose works have lasted through the ages; but to do so will be very expensive, and the results will not be apparent. . . . When I have been in Athens, I have tried to insert the blade of my knife between the stones of the Erechheum, and have been unable to do it. I would like to follow their example but it would cost a small fortune and no one would see where the money went. . . . So the building was planned with the stones filed to make perfect horizontal joints, being doweled by a cement mortice in a shallow groove at the center, with a cup-like provision for moisture; the vertical joints being laid with sheets of lead one sixty-fourth of an inch in thickness; and an air chamber being provided between the inner and outer walls.[2]

This episode and many others suggest that McKim and Stanford White were dedicated to good building as well as to good design. Neither of them ever wrote or spoke on the subject. The evidence of their "rationalism" is in their work. The evidence, however, is far from clear.

Figures 3.1 and 3.3 show two buildings by McKim: Bates Hall of the Boston Public Library (1895) and the Army War College (1908). The interiors of both are geometrically similar to the waiting room of Pennsylvania Station, with a trussed roof on top of a vaulted interior. However, the structural systems are different to the point of being contradictory. At Bates Hall a semicircular plaster vault is suspended from iron trusses on load-bearing walls. The War College, has a real, self-supporting masonry vault. These two buildings are built in different styles of construction (one layered, the other monolithic), and each is built with a different attitude toward the architectural style which is implied by the type of construction.

The construction of the Boston Public Library was complicated by the lack of a clear relationship between the interior and the exterior. For example, the hall is not centered on the truss above. McKim and White were often criticized for working from the outside in, and the Boston Library is often cited as an example. Even to their admirers, planning was the least of their skills. There is a great deal of "shoehorning"—forcing the plan to meet the elevation—throughout the library. The assemblage of rooms of different heights and shapes beneath the trussed roof made the reconciliation of plan, structure, and elevation difficult from the start.

The structural system of the Boston Public Library is a layered one. Load-bearing brick walls support iron trusses at each pier. From these is suspended the great vault of Bates Hall, the reading room. To many this would be the worst form of architectural deceit. A stone form, the vault is imitated in iron and plaster. A structural form has become an ornamental form. Others might argue that this is an analogous structure, since each rib of the plaster vault corresponds to a truss above, and the enlargement of every third pier might also be justified as buttressing the wall. Supporting this theory is the use of extensive real vaults of Guastavino tile in other areas, such as the adjacent special-collections area. But to most rationalists, Classic or Gothic, plaster vaults were examples of falsehood.

The War College, by contrast, is almost a model of nineteenth-century rationalism. The plan is much more coherently organized than that of the Boston Library, and thus more easily reconciled with the structure. The vaults are true masonry vaults (of tile); the brick columns and pilasters carry the load of the vault and the floors. There is no concealed frame, and nothing is plastered over, although some Classical rationalists would have criticized the use of pilasters on the outside wall. (Marc-Antoine Laugier called the use of pilasters "one of the great abuses that have found their way into architecture."[3])

It is difficult not to admire the "rationality" of the War College. It is a monolithic building; structure and finish are one. There are no suspended ceilings. There are no vestigial forms. The vaults are all real structural vaults, and the columns are

3.5

3.6

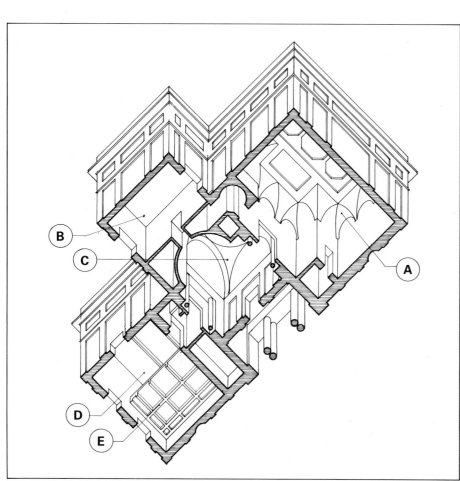

3.7

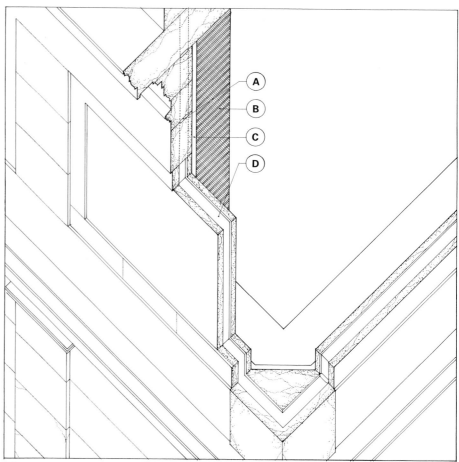

3.8

Morgan Library

McKim, Mead & White

New York, 1900

3.5 **exterior facade**

(New York Historical Society.)

3.6 **interior of East Room**

(New York Historical Society.)

3.7 **framing plan**

A East Room roof vaults of Guastavino tile with steel beams at ridges. Supported by load-bearing walls and plastered over.

B Second-floor structure: Conventional steel beam and tile framing. There is little wood structure in the building except for the antique ceilings (E). All other materials are noncombustible.

C Vestibule: Guastavino tile dome with steel-framed roof above. All the vaults and domes are true masonry vaults, although their ridges are formed by steel sections. All are concealed by the ornamental plaster ceilings.

D West Room roof structure: Steel beams and tile roof.

E Wood ceiling. This is a reassembled Renaissance wood ceiling brought from Italy. Although the roof is the same height as the library, the ceiling is much lower.

(New York Historical Society.)

3.8 **wall detail**

A Horizontal joint in white Vermont marble wall. All joints are built to zero tolerance and filled with thin sheets of lead.

B Brick wall.

C Air space. An air space is provided for waterproofing. The marble is anchored to the brick.

D Slot. All horizontal and vertical joints were given pockets, which were then filled with portland cement. Although the joints appear to have been set dry (without mortar), they were not. The masonry contractor felt that this type of marble was too irregular in consistency for "perfect" joints.

(New York Historical Society.)

all real structural columns. In short, it is, as Pugin would say, construction ornamented rather than ornament constructed. Ironically, it was finished the year after Wagner's Church of St. Leopold, in which vestigial forms, such as metal domes and plaster vaults, carried by steel trusses, abound. This was rational construction in Wagner's terms, but it was not by the standards of Modernism. That Wagner should be seen as progressive and McKim as reactionary is a testament to the naiveté or the ignorance of many who have written about them.

But neither the War College nor Pennsylvania Station coincides with what McKim considered to be good construction, for both are products of circumstance. The perception of the War College as a rational building is due largely to the monolithic nature of its construction, and that is a product of the building's program and client. Because documents were to be stored in the building, the client desired fireproof construction; and although steel and plaster are not combustible, monolithic tile vaults are safer than hollow plaster vaults suspended from exposed steel.

The supervising engineer of the War College, Captain John Sewall (who presumably had a career of building solid fortifications behind him), desired that the building's structure be exposed wherever possible. He felt that plaster (or furring, as he called it) only concealed moisture and cost money. In 1905 he wrote to McKim: "When we first started out on the War College Building, I protested against the use of any inside furring, and my understanding at that time is that it be committed except where absolutely essential to secure architectural lines."[4] Likewise, many of the more rational interior details, such as the brick piers, were not (as McKim would have preferred) executed in limestone or terra cotta, which would have been too costly. However admirable the War College is, it is not McKim's or White's model of rational building; it is a product of circumstance. But it would be incorrect to assume that McKim and White were always pragmatic or empirical, solving the constructional problems of each building in the way the situation demanded. They did have their own model of good building. For evidence of this, we must look to the Morgan Library, in New York. This library contains three major spaces, two of which are vaulted (in the third, a reassembled Renaissance ceiling brought from Italy is covered with a steel-framed roof). The two vaults are covered with ornamental plaster and mural paintings. They have no structural expression about them, yet they are in fact real vaults (or at least the modern equivalent thereof, being built of Guastavino tile). There is considerable steel framing in the building—particularly in the vaults, where steel sections act as the modern equivalents of the ribs in Gothic vaulting. None of the vaulting is exposed, and much of the structure is concealed, but there is no false structure (as in the Boston Library), no suspended vaults of plaster, and no false columns.

Just as the vaults of the Morgan Library are not really traditional vaults, the wall is not really a traditional Greek wall but a modern, rational equivalent. Finely built traditional stone walls of this type were solid and monolithic, used "perfect" joints (with no spaces), and were set dry or with lime mortar. The Morgan Library's wall appears to have perfect joints on its face. The stone is thick, even for an early-twentieth-century building. But in other respects it is modern. It uses portland cement (the basic component of modern concrete) set within a notch to the rear of the joint. It is not monolithic, but a cavity wall, with an air space to prevent water from getting to the books inside (lead sheets were placed in the joints for additional waterproofing), and in this respect it is technically progressive.

McKim preferred solid if not precisely monolithic structures. He did not require the structure to be exposed, but preferred usually for it to be concealed, provided that it was not concealed in a deceitful way. When possible he used real vaults, but invariably he plastered them over. He advocated the use of modern materials provided they did not invalidate the forms they were applied to. A tile vault was, to him, simply a more efficient form of masonry vaulting. Not surprisingly, McKim's ideal conception of building was a Roman one, with structural forms clad in stone and plaster. His love of Roman architecture went deeper than the copying of forms. He wished in principle to copy techniques as well.

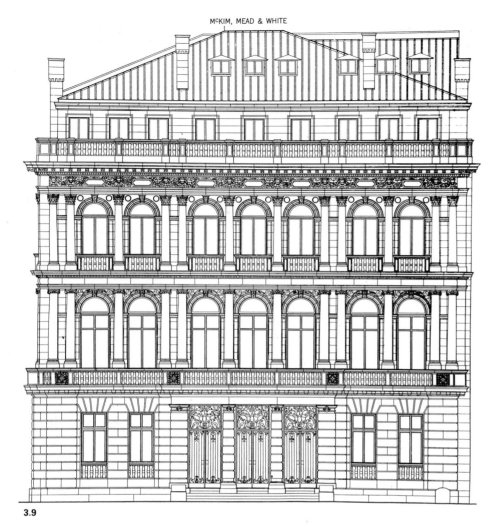

3.9

3.10

3.11

3.9 Pulitzer residence,
McKim, Mead & White, New York,
1903, elevation.
(New York Historical Society.)

3.10 Basilica of Giants, Agrigentum.
(Viollet-le-Duc, *Lectures on Architecture.*)

3.11 J. H. Choate house,
McKim, Mead & White,
Stockbridge, Mass., 1887, gable
detail. Note the combination of
Classical elements (the Serlian
window and eave molding with
dentils) with rustic and vernacular
ones. The Classical details are not
quite correct; for example, the half-
circle is much too small.

To understand McKim's attitude toward Classicism and rational building, one must understand the climate in which it arose: the school of Classical Rationalism in general and the Ecole des Beaux-Arts in particular.

RATIONAL BUILDING AND THE ECOLE DES BEAUX-ARTS
During a visit to Paris in 1939, Frank Lloyd Wright was given a tour of the city by the director of the Ecole des Beaux-Arts. Wright remarked that he did not think much of the American version of that institution. "We don't think much of it either," his host replied.[5] The work of the American Classicists was never popular at the Ecole, and for reasons of substance. The idea of the facade as the articulation of the program, for example, is totally missing from the work of McKim, Mead & White. Thus, it cannot be assumed that McKim's ideas about the relation of architecture and construction were acquired at the Ecole.

Even if one assumes that McKim's ideas were those of a student of the Ecole, it is not easy to establish what those ideas were. The masters of the Ecole were concerned with building, but there was a diversity of ideas, and they were hardly systematic, coherent, or consistent. In a review of an exhibition of student work at the Ecole in 1839, Henri Labrouste wrote:

The construction products are always sufficiently numerous, and one is obliged to congratulate the authors, nevertheless one notices little of imagination in these projects, they appear copied from one to the next. . . . The students seem to take part in these courses with a certain reluctance, and, so to speak, to rid themselves of them, for the sole reason that they are obligatory. The cause of it is perhaps the plan of the building which they are obliged to study. The construction is imposed by the program; the study of construction becomes in that case a study of the details . . . that they copy from the manuals of metalwork or carpentry, and has little of interest when it consists in the combination of all the architectural parts that must converge not only to the convenience and to the beauty of a building, but also to its solidity, and to the provision of the means of executing it.[6]

Interestingly enough, McKim received his early education in architecture from Gothic rationalists. His first job was with Henry Van Brunt, an American disciple of Viollet-le-Duc, and perhaps because of this he hoped to study with the latter in Paris and to translate his lectures into English. But Viollet-le-Duc was not accepting students, and so McKim joined the atelier of P. G. H. Daumet, one of the eclectic (as opposed to the rational) masters of the Ecole. In later life McKim certainly would have found his flirtation with Gothic, rational or otherwise, to be embarrassing.

Stanford White was just as reticent as McKim on matters of theory. He had no formal training in the practical or theoretical aspects of building, but this did not impede his exploration of structural rationalism any more than his lack of formal training in history or aesthetics impeded his design abilities.

But these disclaimers aside, there is a parallel between McKim and White's ideas in practice and the ideas in theory of Julien Guadet, who finally codified many of the traditions of the Ecole in his *Eléments et Théories de l'Architecture.* Guadet was a classmate and friend of Richardson. He and McKim were probably aquaintances when the latter was in Paris, but the similarity of Guadet's ideas and McKim's practice was a result of a common education. Like Ruskin, Pugin, Laugier, and most architectural writers since Vitruvius, Guadet condemned "deceits": "Truth is required in architecture: any architectural lie is vicious."[7]

Guadet's attitude toward the relationship between exposed construction and rational building is evident in his article on floors and ceilings in the *Eléments.* He lists three types of ceilings which are acceptable:

·*a system of coffers made of exposed, solid wood timbers such as that in the Library of the Ecole des Beaux-Arts.* Of the aforementioned, Guadet says: "These

3.12

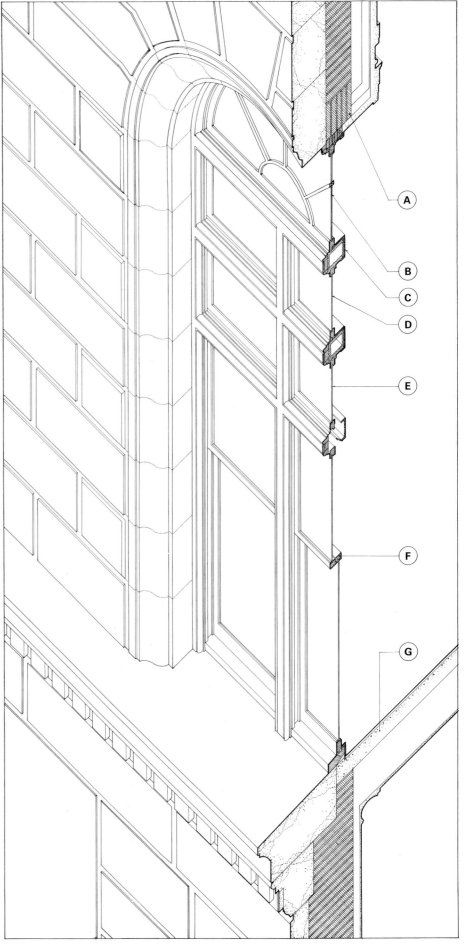

3.13

3.14

3.15

University Club

McKim, Mead & White

New York, 1900

3.12 exterior facade
(New York Historical Society.)

3.13 wall section

A   Wall construction: Pink granite facing with brick backup and hollow tile. This wall is monolithic and contains no cavity.

B   Horizontally pivoting wood sash (in-swinging). The windows are of three different woods: English oak, yellow pine and white pine.

C   Wood frame to support operable sash.

D   Horizontally pivoting wood sash (in-swinging.)

E   Horizontally pivoting wood sash (in-swinging). Note that the frame below has a hinged opening to allow the double-hung window sash to pass.

F   Meeting rail of double-hung window.

G   Floor construction. Concrete-and-hollow-tile vaults with steel framing, supported by load-bearing masonry walls.
(F. M. Snyder, Building Details.)

3.14 cornice

3.15 detail

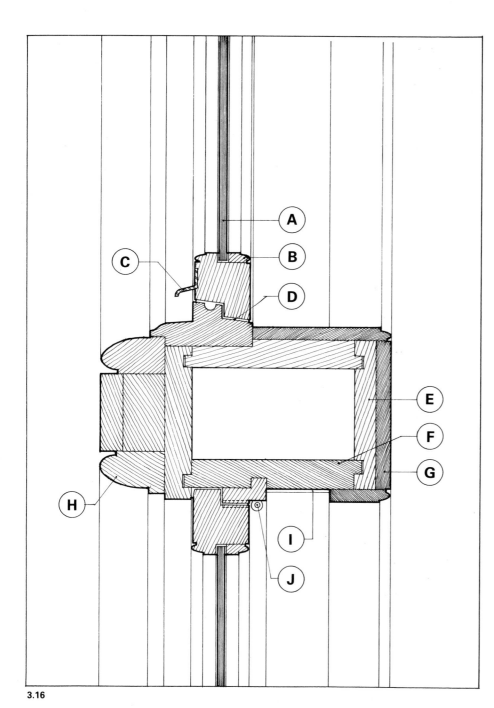

3.16

University Club

McKim, Mead & White

New York, 1900

3.16   window profile

- **A** Glass in horizontal in-swinging wood window.
- **B** Glass stop. Compare this profile with the half-round profile in figure 4.15. One school of thought held that the most attractive moldings were those that were not geometric curves as in Greek antiquity.
- **C** Brass drip. This prevents water from accumulating at the bottom of the sash near the vulnerable sill joint of the in-swinging window.
- **D** The rabbet joint, which is normally sloped outward, is reversed here since the window swings in. The half-round air pocket prevents water from being sucked in through capillary action.
- **E** White pine frame. The portions of the frame that were concealed or to be painted were made of less expensive wood. White pine is soft and has little grain.
- **F** Yellow pine jamb. Since this piece is struck by the sash below when it is opened, it is sturdier than oak veneer on white pine.
- **G** English oak finish on interior. Those interior portions of the frame that were to receive a clear finish were made of oak, although the oak is little more than a veneer on the white pine.
- **H** Exterior white pine trim. This is now, and probably always was, painted.
- **I** Brass strike plate. This pocket receives the double-hung sash below when it is raised.
- **J** Hinge of out-swinging horizontal window.

(F. M. Snyder, *Building Details.*)

3.17   detail

3.17

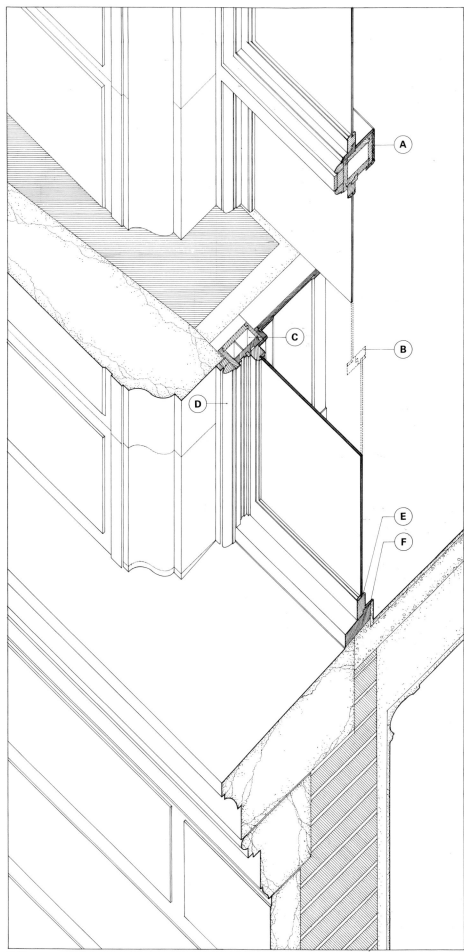

3.18

3.18 window detail

A   Fixed rail at top of double-hung window. The major window pieces are made from white pine, a paint-grade finish wood. The interior portions are clad with English oak, which has a more beautiful grain and is finished with a clear varnish. Those sections of the painted sash that receive the most wear are of yellow pine.

B   Meeting rail of double hung sash. The slanting Z joint ensures that the crack will not open as the wood expands and contracts.

C   Jamb of white pine with yellow pine for the grooved section. The square pockets are for the sash weights. Like all the pine sections, it is faced with English oak on the interior.

D   Trim mold of white pine. This was put in place after the window was set, to cover the irregular gap between masonry opening and window.

E   Bottom sash of white pine.

F   Sill of yellow pine clad with English oak and marble on the interior.

(F. M. Snyder, *Building Details.*)

3.19

Gould Library
McKim, Mead & White
New York University, 1903

3.19 **exterior facade**
(New York Historical Society.)

3.20 **section of original dome structure**
The original design was to have
two structural tile domes, the inner
dome resting on a row of steel
columns encased with plaster Ionic
decorations (see figure 3.23). An
auditorium, also vaulted with tile
on steel ribs, is located below.
(New York Historical Society.)

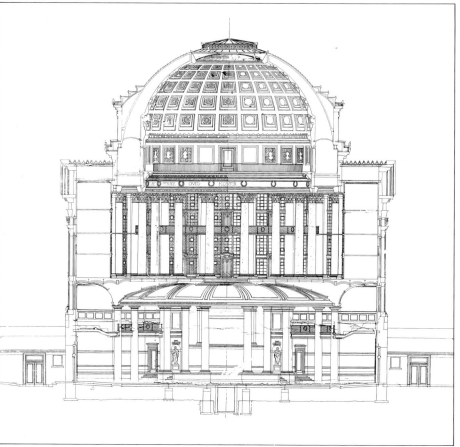

3.20

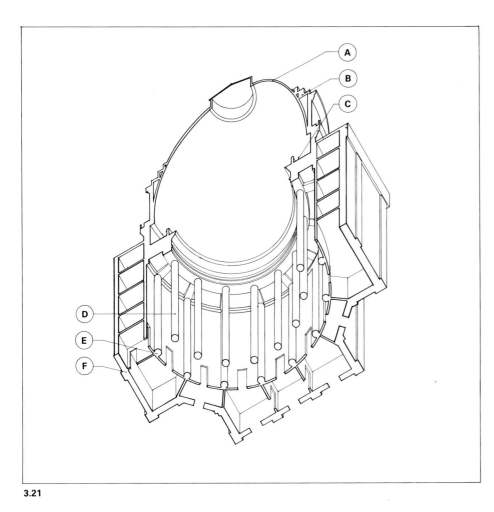

3.21

3.21 framing plan

A Guastavino tile dome. Unlike the final design of Low Library dome, this is a true masonry dome.

B Tile buttressing arches. These brace the dome laterally, transferring the horizontal thrust developed by the dome to the walls.

C Balcony. In the original version this area was to contain seminar rooms.

D Interior columns of solid Connemara marble. These were originally to be constructed as shown in figure 3.23, but were changed to solid stone at the client's request.

E Perimeter columns of steel. The less visible pilasters are steel sections encased in brick and plaster.

F Exterior wall: load-bearing brick
(New York Historical Society.)

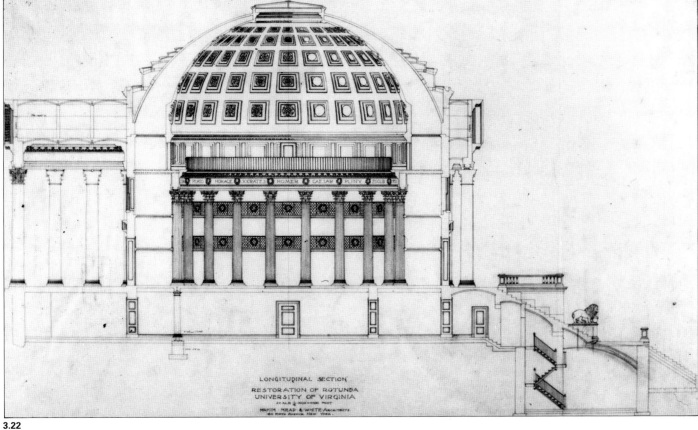

3.22

3.22 reconstruction of rotunda interior, McKim, Mead & White, University of Virginia, Charlottesville, 1899, section. Both inner and outer domes were of Guastavino tile, supported by steel columns covered with brick and plaster.
(Alderman Library, University of Virginia.)

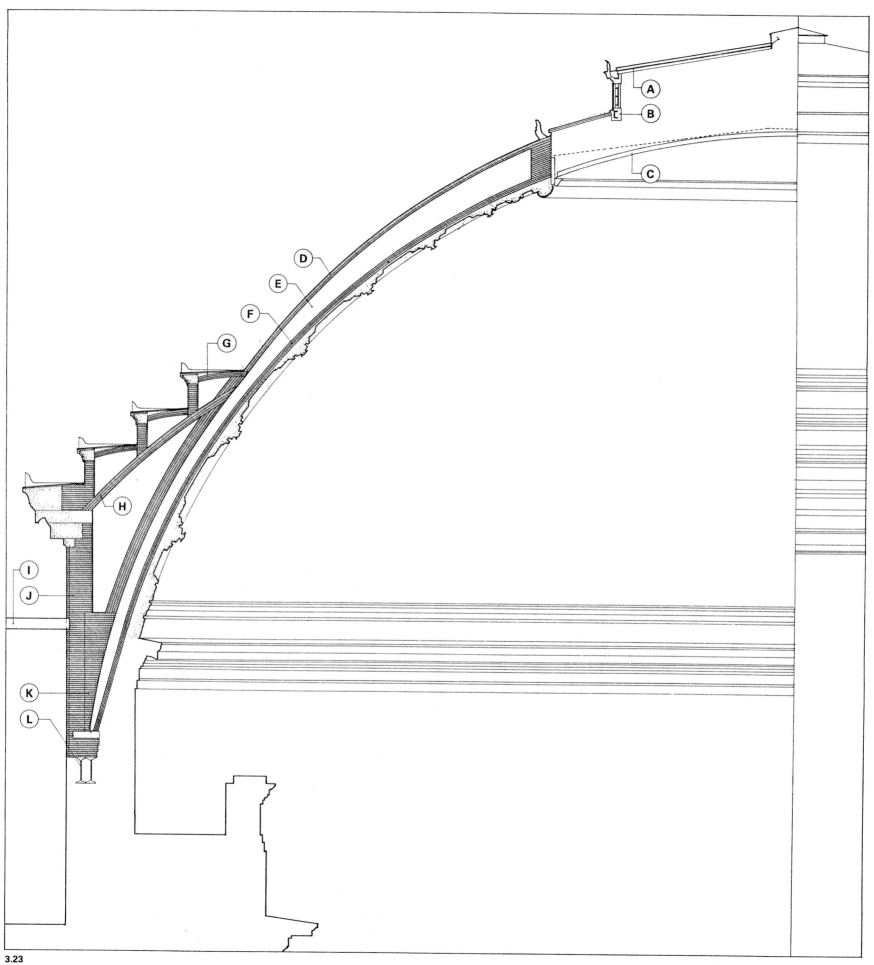

3.23

Gould Library

McKim, Mead & White

New York University, 1903

3.23 **section of dome as built**

A Wood-and-glass skylight.

B Steel structure supporting skylight.

C Inner window of skylight.

D Outer tile dome. The final design (see figure 3.20) retains the two-dome arrangement for structural purposes by building in effect a hollow dome. While it has the stiffness of a solid dome of similar depth, it does not have the same weight.

E Tile ribs. These tie the two domes together structurally.

F Inner tile dome with ornamental plaster coffers. The original square coffers were a reflection of tile ribs in the structure they clad. These diagonal coffers are applied to a flat tile surface.

G Secondary tile buttressing arch.

H Tile buttressing arch.

I Roof structure of steel beams and flat hollow tile arches.

J Load-bearing brick wall.

K Brick impost to receive thrust of dome.

L Steel beams supporting brick wall above.

(New York Historical Society.)

3.24 **details of original column construction**

A Steel column built up from plates and angles.

B Brick.

C Plaster. This detail was omitted and replaced with a solid marble shaft at the request of the client.

(New York Historical Society.)

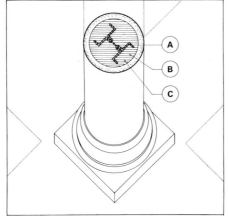

3.24

beautiful ceilings have for the architect a great charm. They are not only the expression of construction but construction itself."[8] And, like the Gothic Rationalists, he felt that producing this type of ceiling by cladding an iron construction with wood was an unacceptable deceit: "One cannot defend the imitation by artificial means, that one sees sometimes under floors of iron, the imitation of wood joists . . . like hypocrisy, it is the homage rendered by vice to virtue."[9] But Guadet did not require the use of monolithic exposed construction; he recognized that this would severely limit the possibilities of architectural expression: "[this type of ceiling] cannot be varied . . . and as floors are the occasion of beautiful artistic combinations and of a grand decorative richness, one seeks to introduce the variety by elements which are not the construction itself of the floor, by combinations purely decorative."[10]

· *a system in which major beams are exposed, and minor ones are covered with wood panels*, "which are the expression of the construction, but a construction informed by the decoration, and thus the floors have exposed beams, but where the space between the beams forms a decorative panel, in sculpted wood."[11] Even this was not mandatory, and in many ceilings no structure was exposed.

· *a wood ceiling completely encased in plaster.* "A great number of admirable ceilings," Guadet wrote, "are purely decorative. . . . [These] are in reality large applied panels."[12] His examples vary greatly in their relationship to the structure of the floors above. Some, such as that in the upper portion of figure 1.7, have no relation to the construction above. Others, such as that in the lower portion of figure 1.7, replicate almost exactly in plaster the structure above. The main criterion, again, is apparent solidity—that is, the beams should be of sufficient depth to appear to support the ceiling.

Beaux-Arts ideas in general, and Guadet's theories in particular, were flexible in this regard. Structural systems might be fully exposed, partially exposed, or completely concealed. Structures might be monolithic or layered, and structural systems might be literal or analogous. Ornament might be constructed, or construction might be ornamented. All were subordinated to two requirements: the absence of deceits and the presence of stability (not simple stability, but stability made manifest). Perhaps the great virtue of late-nineteenth-century Classicism was that it acknowledged the role of perception in rational architecture.

The Beaux-Arts and the French Classical tradition included many points of view and embraced architects who advocated or built in different styles. Louis Duc, although a structural innovator, built in monolithic masonry; Henri Labrouste, the leader of the Beaux-Arts rationalists, built hybrid systems of masonry and iron which were sometimes exposed and sometimes concealed; J. I. Hittorf, an advocate of applied polychromy, argued that Classical construction was layered and clad while using exposed iron in his own work.

The issue of the proper use of iron was particularly important both to the French architects and to McKim. Some opposed its use for anything other than fasteners. Hittorf maintained that concealed metal had been used structurally in ancient Greek work, and that there was no reason modern architects should not use it in the same way. In 1807 the French rationalists condemned the use of iron framing in the dome of François-Joseph Belanger's proposal for the Halle au Blé as "ce genre de construction parasite."[13] As McKim's and White's careers progressed, the structural use of iron and steel in stone buildings became more common and the controversy as to whether or not this was proper became more intense.

MCKIM, WHITE, AND THE ORDERS

In 1934, H. Van Buren Magonigle recalled his apprenticeship with McKim and White:

[McKim] anxiously consulted the books, and had his assistants spend hours and hours looking up data for him, particularly in Letarouilly [Edifices de Rome Moderne] which was a kind of office bible—if you saw it in Letarouilly, it was so! And if he could not find, somewhere, authority for a certain combination of

3.25

Low Library
McKim, Mead & White
Columbia University, 1903

3.25   **exterior facade**

3.26   **proposed concrete and plaster dome**
(Left half of the drawing shows structural elements only.)

A   Concrete dome faced with stone. Although similar to the final design, this dome was self-supporting and required no steel trusses.

B   This series of steps, which contain the buttressing arches in the tile solution as in figure 3.27, was retained here for visual reasons.

C   Brick arch supporting dome.

D   Suspended plaster ceiling. Although deemed superior to figure 3.28 because it used no steel, the vault visible from the interior was not a true one but was suspended by cables from the vault above.

E   Brick arch supporting dome.
(New York Historical Society.)

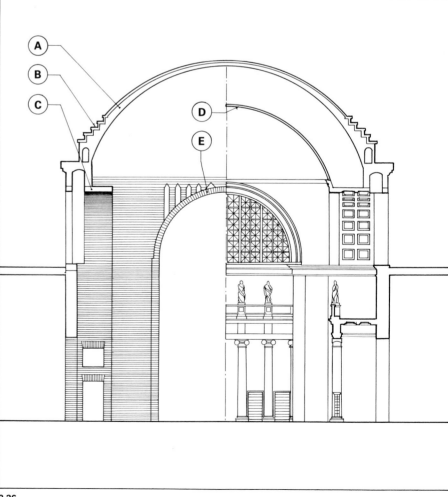

3.26

Low Library

McKim, Mead & White

Columbia University, 1903

3.27 proposed tile dome

(Left half of the drawing shows structural elements only.)

A Guastavino tile dome faced with stone.

B Buttressing arches of Guastavino tile. These transfer the lateral forces developed by the dome to the adjacent wall.

C Brick arch supporting dome.

D Inner dome of Guastavino tile. This was the only version in which both vaults were true structural vaults.

E Brick arch supporting dome.

(New York Historical Society.)

3.28 dome as built

(Left half of the drawing shows structural elements only.)

A Brick dome faced with stone and supported by steel trusses. This roof weighed considerably less than the concrete version and thus placed the least lateral thrust on the corner piers. It was also the most economical, probably because it required less centering or form work.

B As in figure 3.26, the nonfunctional coverings of the buttressing arches are retained for visual effect.

C Brick arch supporting dome.

D Suspended plaster ceiling.

E Brick arch supporting dome.

(New York Historical Society.)

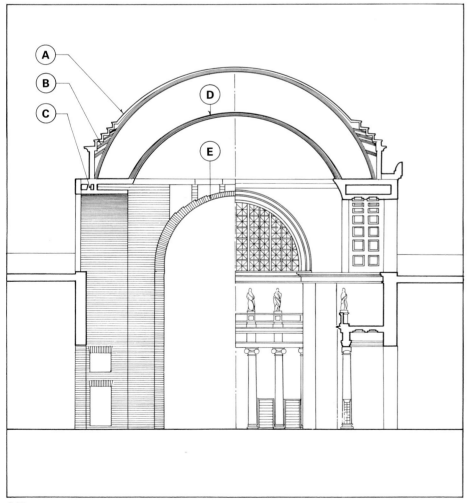

3.27

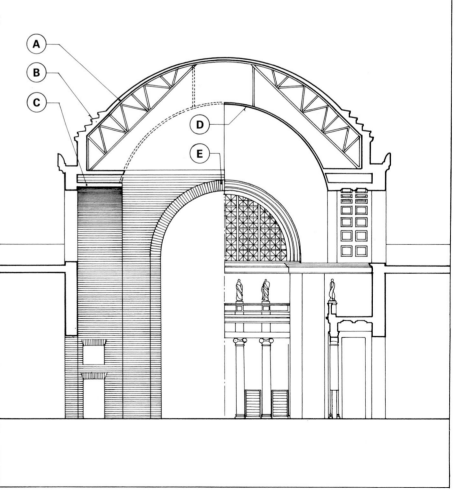

3.28

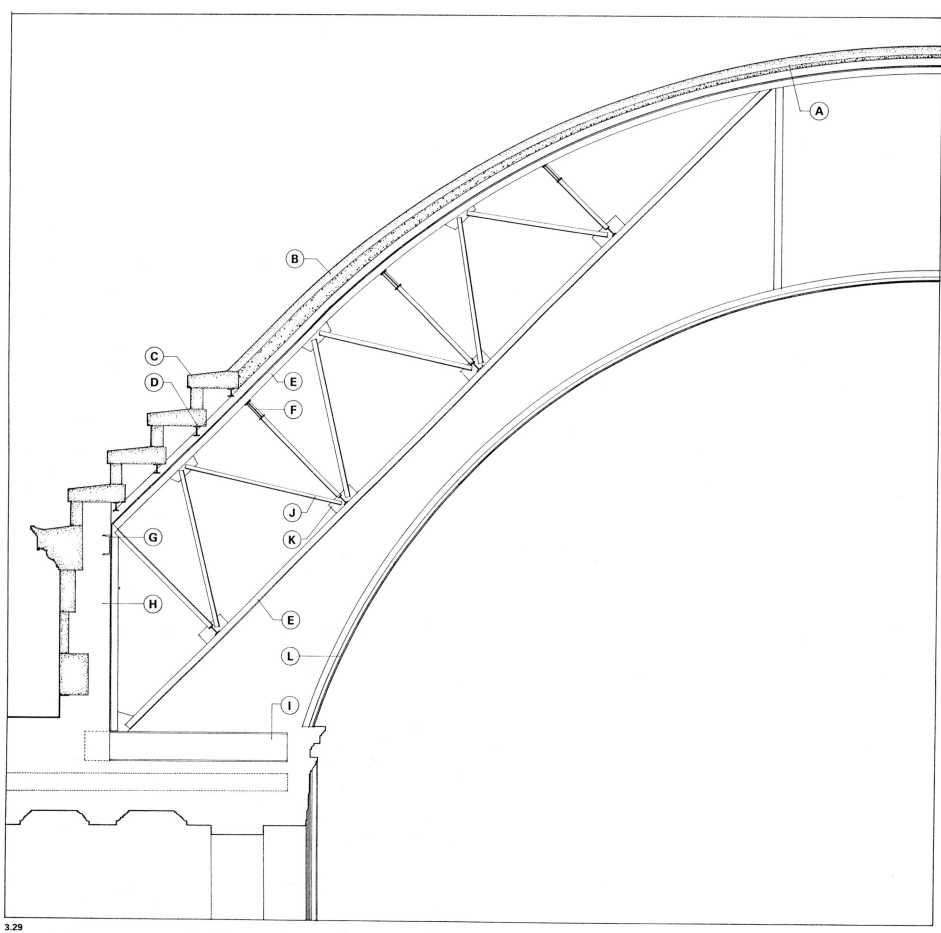

3.29

Low Library

McKim, Mead & White

Columbia University, 1903

3.29 section through dome

(This drawing represents the dome as it was intended to be built when construction began. Changes were made during construction.)

A McKim had wanted a skylight at the top, as at the University of Virginia and as in the Gould Library. The client refused, but McKim directed that the dome be framed so as to allow one to be installed later.

B 5″-thick concrete dome faced with 8″ of stone. This was later changed to brick covered with metal. The concrete was to be laid on closely spaced steel tees.

C Stone trim at base. These steps were to cover the tile buttressing arches made unnecessary by the use of steel trusses.

D Steel beam supporting stone steps.

E Top and bottom chords of truss made up of pairs of $5″ \times 3\frac{1}{2}″$ steel angles. Doubling the structural members enabled the connections at gusset plates to be more easily constructed.

F Horizontal purlins of 4×15 steel I section.

G Steel channel and bracket. This anchors the truss to the load-bearing wall.

H Brick-and-limestone wall.

I Steel brace made up of two 20″-deep I sections to support plaster dome and pendentives.

J Intermediate truss members made from steel angles.

K Gusset plate.

L Plaster ceiling suspended from truss. The support structure for the plaster is a grid of $3\frac{1}{2}″$ and $2\frac{1}{2}″$ steel tees.

(New York Historical Society.)

---

mouldings or other elements he desired to make, he would give it up and use something else for which he could find a precedent. He was the most convinced authoritarian I have ever encountered. . . . To find virtue only in that which has been done before is a form of ancestor worship from which White, thank God, saved me at a very impressionable time of life. . . . [McKim] liked to . . . design out loud . . . the room reverberated with architectural terms that sounded most recondite to a green boy of 20: Cyma Recta, Cyma Reversa, Fillet above, Fillet below, Dentils, Modillions, and so on. When he went away and quiet reigned again I stole from my alcove to see this imposing assemblage of members. . . . All I found was a top and bottom line and a few faint pencil marks that didn't even suggest a cornice to me; I wanted particularly to see a Cyma Recta but couldn't find one.

White's methods of design were as different from McKim's as day from night. He would tear into your alcove [and] in five minutes make a dozen sketches of some arrangement of detail or plan, slam his hand down on one of them—or perhaps two or three of them if they were close together—say 'Do that' and tear off again.[14]

To some, Classicism is an architecture of absolutes. Ratios, proportions, and even plan types are fixed. To depart from them is to diminish them. The Classicism of McKim and White was relative. It was based not on mathematics but on perception. Ratios, proportions, and ideal plans were subject to variations—variations which were sometimes systematic and sometimes not, but which were always seen to improve and not diminish the original.

That McKim was an eclectic (or, more bluntly, a copyist) is not news. What is significant is the sources he was copying from. When he was "fishing," as he called it, one of his principal sources was Letarouilly's book, which describes precisely the Renaissance buildings of Rome. Other sources may have been the L'Envois of Prix de Rome winners (reconstructions of Greek and Roman ruins in ink washes; many of these were by P. G. H. Daumet, the master of McKim's atelier at the Ecole des Beaux-Arts). McKim seldom copied from contemporary French sources, and there is no evidence that he consulted Palladio, Vignola, or Serlio. McKim was not a theoretician and did not look to theories or treatises for his ideas. He looked to built precedents, particularly Roman ones.

Although McKim's use of the orders is usually correct, this is more often due to the correctness of what he was copying than to his adherence to absolute ratios set out by theoreticians. McKim's grasp of Classicism was, in its way, just as intuitive as White's. On occasion, for specific purposes, McKim would depart from any standard system of proportion, as he did with the Bank of Montreal. There are also many elements in his work that do not specifically correspond to any one precedent—the cornice of the University Club, for example, incorporates portions of the Farnese Palace and the Pallazzo Massimo alle Colonne. For the most part, however, precedent was his guide.

THE DOMES

McKim and White's greatest problem in building was, as we have seen, the problem of vaults, particularly domes. A number of their buildings of the 1890s had suspended plaster vaults. Most of these vaults were fairly small, such as the vestibules of the Naugatuck library and the Walker Art Building at Bowdoin College. Around the turn of the century, however, McKim and White began to explore the possibility of building real structural vaults. This began with the development of the winning design in the 1891 competition for the Rhode Island State Capitol. The dome of this project was much larger than any that McKim and White had attempted, and they felt an obligation to build in traditional masonry. The design was of the double-shell type used by Renaissance architects, and the dome was built entirely of masonry. By contrast, the dome of the U.S. Capitol, built 40 years earlier, has cast-iron trusses with plaster shells suspended below. Today the U.S. Capitol is noted for its progressive technology, but McKim would have considered its method of construction inferior. To him, only the solidity of monolithic masonry was proper for a dome or a vault.

3.30

3.31

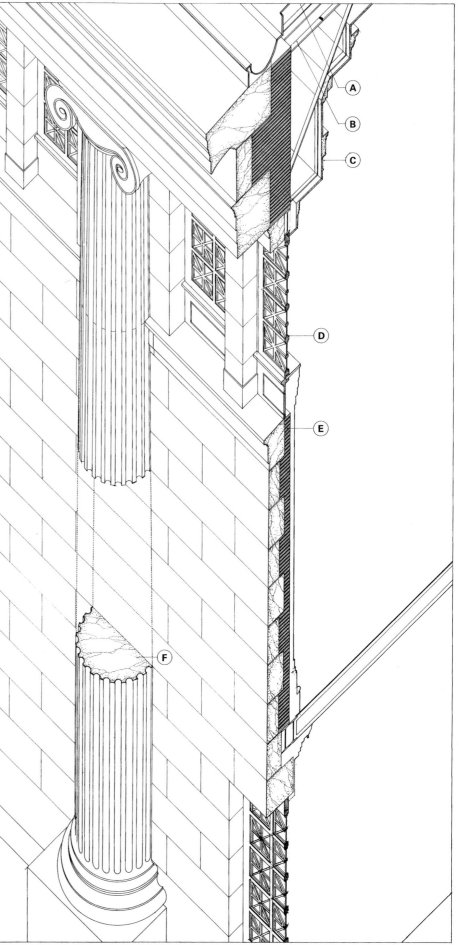

3.32

Cullum Memorial

McKim, Mead & White

U.S. Military Academy

West Point, New York, 1898

3.30 **exterior facade**

(New York Historical Society.)

3.31 **wall detail**

3.32 **wall section**

A Roof construction: steel tees supporting tile roof. The steel members are encased in concrete for fire protection.

B Steel trusses.

C Ornamental plaster ceiling.

D Wood window with wood screen.

E Wall construction: load-bearing brick and Milford granite facing.

F Granite column. This was in four sections, two of which are T shaped in order to bond to the wall. Unlike later buildings by White, the columns here are the actual structure.

(New York Historical Society.)

While the Rhode Island Capitol was under construction, both McKim and White received major commissions with similar structural and programmatic problems. White's Gould Library at New York University (1903) and McKim's Low Library at Columbia University (1898) are both centrally planned buildings with large domes. There are many precedents for this type of library. James Gibbs's Radcliffe Camera at Oxford is one, but the most obvious is Thomas Jefferson's library at the University of Virginia. Ironically, while the Gould and Low libraries were under design, White was asked to redesign the interior of Jefferson's building after it was partially destroyed by fire in 1895. Thus, in the years 1894–1900 the firm of McKim, Mead & White was working on three libraries, all topped with domes.

In all three cases, McKim and White looked to Rome for precedents—specifically, to the Pantheon. This was not the obvious choice of a precedent for a domed building. The interior had an obvious appeal, the space being defined by a perfect sphere. The difficulty stemmed from the exterior: the dome was so low as to not be visible. The typical dome of the nineteenth century more closely resembled that of the Rhode Island Capitol, where there are actually two domes—an interior one and an exterior one—which have little to do with each other. But McKim and White felt the Classical Roman type of dome to be superior. In 1894 McKim wrote to the building committee for the Low Library explaining his design, perhaps defensively:

The proposed new structures being Roman in scale and, generally speaking, in type, the Roman dome has been adapted rather than any later form as the commanding feature of the central building.

The Roman dome is invariably a low dome, and is the classic dome par excellence.

See Pantheon of Agrippa at Rome, also of Minerva Medica at Rome.

See Baths of Agrippa also Baths of Caracalla.

St. Sophia, the last note of the classic dome, is usually regarded as the most perfect dome in the world.

The low dome is a higher order of composition and much more monumental in its character than the later forms.[15]

McKim also argued that there was a programmatic link between his design and the use of the dome in Roman architecture:

The perfect examples of the low dome are to be found in Thermae. Some of the ends that the Thermae served, besides use as actual baths were as

1. Academies where public lectures were delivered

2. Clubs for young men

3. Rooms for philosophers to hold their conversations

4. Theatrical representations, concerts

5. Places of physical culture, gymnasiums, etc.

6. Public libraries—for example the library of Trajan. . . .[16]

With these Roman domes as a precedent, McKim and White developed their own ideal form for all three libraries, using a double-shell dome but generally preserving the Roman proportions. The Pantheon has a double-shell wall and a single-shell dome, which is scarcely visible from the ground. Jefferson's dome also has a double wall, but that wall aligns with the outer shell, creating an inner arcade and making the dome more prominent on the exterior. White combined the two in a double-shell dome, lowering the floor to create the ideal spherical shape.

Jefferson's dome was built of wood—a sham in the eyes of many, since the dome is a form appropriate to stone, not to wood. Both shells of White's reconstruction were Guastavino tile. The outer dome rests on steel columns braced against the existing walls. The inner dome is supported by a row of Corinthian columns made of brick covered with plaster. The Guastavino tile dome was considerably lighter than an equivalent mass of stone, and thus produced less lateral thrust, but it maintained the solidity associated with the concrete and masonry domes of antiquity. For McKim and White, this spherical double-shell tile dome represented the ideal form. They used it, or attempted to use it, on many other buildings.

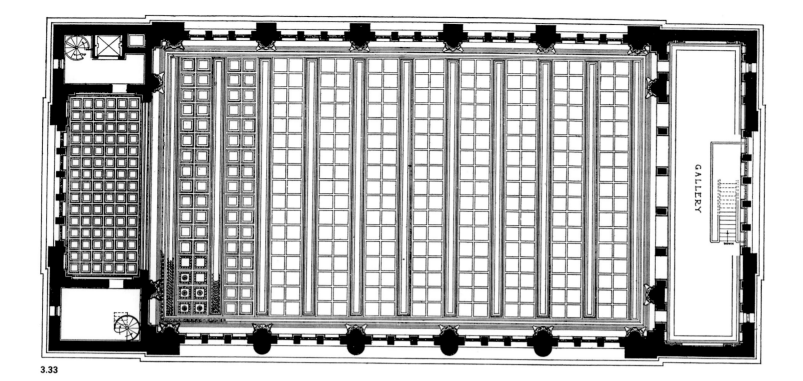

3.33

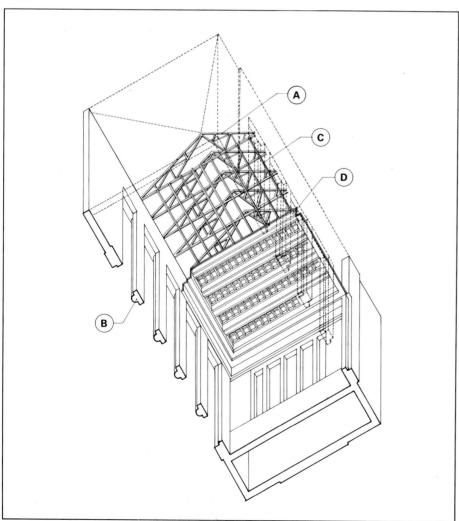

3.34

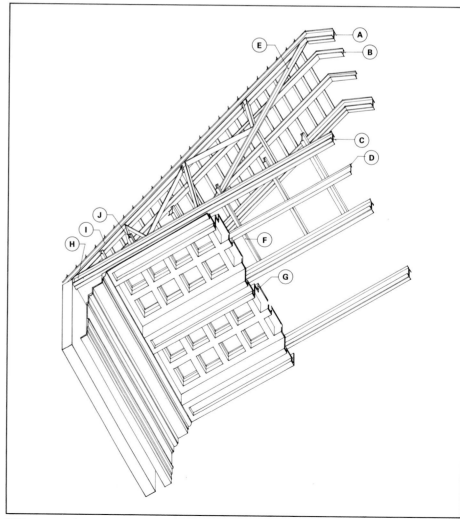

3.35

Cullum Memorial

McKim, Mead & White

U.S. Military Academy

West Point, New York, 1898

3.33 plan showing reflected ceiling

(New York Historical Society.)

3.34 framing plan

A Steel trusses spaced at 12' on center.

B Brick-and-granite piers, located under every second truss.

C Steel purlins.

D Ornamental plaster ceiling. This describes in an analogous fashion the steel structure which it conceals.

(New York Historical Society.)

3.35 framing detail

A Top chord of truss, made up from two 12"-deep steel channels.

B 4"-deep steel I section.

C Bottom chord of truss, made up from two 10"-deep steel channels. The major plaster beams of the ceiling align with the trusses above.

D 6"-deep steel I section.

E Diagonal truss members, made of steel angles.

F Ceiling purlins made from 4"-deep steel I sections.

G Plaster ceiling. The location of the coffers corresponds, in one direction, to the location of the bottom chords of the truss above.

H Wall construction: brick and Milford granite.

I Roof construction.

J Truss connection. These are made with flat steel gusset plates.

(New York Historical Society)

White's plan for the construction of the dome of Gould Library at N.Y.U. followed closely the model represented by the Virginia library. Structurally and ornamentally more complex than the Virginia dome, the Gould dome sits within a cruciform shape and is supported by two circular rows of columns. In the original design there were two almost independent tile vaults. The outer dome was braced by three rings formed of tile vaulting and anchored against the weight of the masonry enclosing them. The inner dome was coffered. Although plastered over, the ribs between vaults were to be made of tile and were to reinforce the dome much as the ribs of a waffle slab reinforce a concrete floor. The columns supporting the dome were to be plaster, but they were not to be false, since each was to contain a built-up steel column. The design remained in this state until the completion of working drawings, but in September 1898 Henry MacCracken, the client, wrote to White voicing his concern over the design of the dome. After noting that the cost of the building was excessive, he wrote: "I am still dissatisfied with the reading room which I fear will prove a barn-like rotunda, dimly lighted, never warm in coolest weather. Then we do not get interior richness with 24 sham marble columns. I should have esthetic pains every time I saw them. Domes, although imposing, are dreary things to live in."[17] At MacCracken's suggestion the inner dome was omitted, primarily to save money but also to make the dome appear larger and to allow for additional windows around the base to let more light into the reading room. The inner circle of columns remained, supporting only an arcade with statues, but they were changed from steel covered with plaster to monolithic marble. The outer row, being less prominent and still structural, remained in the original materials. White also changed the design of the coffers to a smaller, shallower diagonal pattern. (Domes can be divided into those that display their weight, as at the Pantheon, and those that appear to float or be suspended, as at the Hagia Sophia. In altering the coffering, and in retaining the arcade so that the edges of the dome would not be visible, White was moving from the Pantheon type toward the floating, Hagia Sophia type.)

McKim's original intentions for the construction of the Low Library dome are not clear. However, in the contract drawings, issued in 1895, the dome is not a true masonry dome but a shell of concrete supported by steel trusses and clad with limestone. There is an inner shell, but it is nonstructural, consisting of plaster suspended from the trusses. McKim was clearly never happy with this design, and in 1896, while the base was under construction, he tried to convince Columbia to build a more "substantial" dome—one that would be monolithic and truly structural. Rafael Guastavino, McKim's consulting engineer and the inventor of Guastavino tile, developed two alternative schemes (figures 3.26, 3.27). The first of these involved a double-shell vault of Guastavino tile that was structurally identical to White's original design for Gould Library, with three concentric buttressing vaults at the base; the second involved a concrete dome, which would be self-supporting (thus eliminating the steel trusses), although it also used a suspended plaster dome. There was never any question but that the steel-supported dome was the easiest, fastest, and cheapest of the three to build, which was undoubtedly the reason for its choice in the first place. Nevertheless, up until the last minute, McKim's firm (he was away in Europe) tried to convince Columbia to adopt one of the other alternatives.

McKim's partner William Mead asked William Ware, dean of the Columbia School of Architecture and an old friend of McKim's, to write to the building committee and to urge the use of tile or concrete, and perhaps to explain why the architects were so insistent on a choice that was so uneconomical. In his letter, Ware first considers the functional issues:

It does not appear that there is any essential difference in respect of safety, between a dome held up by iron trusses and a self supporting dome of tiles. The objection that the iron and the masonry that rests upon it will expand and contract unequally, has, I understand no scientific support [,but] the mixed construction of iron and masonry is complicated and heterogeneous, and the iron itself a highly artificial product, chemically unstable so to speak, and only to be prevented from rusting . . . by constant vigilence. It is in its nature to decay. This

3.36

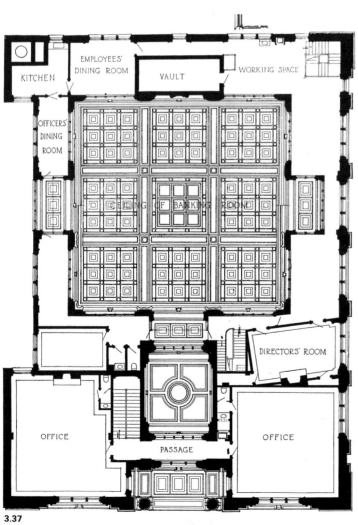

KITCHEN

EMPLOYEES'
DINING ROOM

VAULT

WORKING SPACE

OFFICERS'
DINING
ROOM

CEILING OF BANKING ROOM

DIRECTORS' ROOM

OFFICE

OFFICE

PASSAGE

3.37

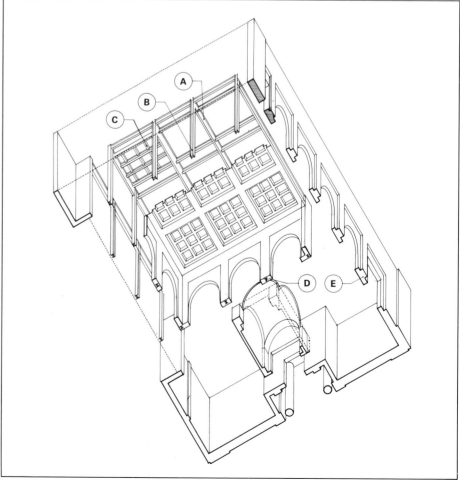

3.38

Detroit State Savings Bank

McKim, Mead & White

1900

3.36   exterior facade

(New York Historical Society.)

3.37   plan

(New York Historical Society.)

3.38   framing plan

A   Steel-plate girders. Although the pattern of plaster coffers reflects the structure above, it does not show the greater structural importance of these girders.

B   Steel column. Although never exposed, they correspond in location to the ornamental columns and pilasters.

C   Intermediate steel beams. Their primary role is to support the ceiling as the roof is supported by trusses above.

D   Marble facing on interior steel columns.

E   Load-bearing exterior wall and piers.

(New York Historical Society.)

does not commend it to my mind as a material for monumental purposes. Domes of tile on the other hand, are simple in design and homogeneous in construction, and the material of which they are composed is the most indestructible that the arts have produced.[18]

An engineer writing today would not disagree with this reasoning. It is not true, as Viollet-le-Duc believed, that concrete and iron are subject to radically different thermal movements and cannot be used closely together. It is true that steel, commonly left exposed in enclosed voids, is subject to rust via condensation and must be maintained. But Ware's objections were not really functional; they were more purely architectural:

. . . the charm of a dome lies not in its shape but in one's conception of it, in the idea that is self supported and hangs in the air. It is even more captivating to the mind than the eye. But the proposed construction is not a real dome, it is only an ingenious contrivance to produce the effect of one. I think this sort of thing . . . is disturbing and distasteful. One does not like the idea, one takes no satisfaction in the result, for there is always something which has to be forgotten or forgiven. Domes of tile, on the other hand, really are what they appear to be.[19]

In the end both the tile and concrete alternatives were rejected, for structural as well as economic reasons. Norcross Brothers, the contractor for the Low Library and the great majority of both Richardson's and McKim's buildings, refused to guarantee the stability of the Guastavino-tile dome. This left only the option of self-supporting concrete with a plaster inner dome, the heaviest and most expensive of the three. When the decision was made, the four piers that would carry the dome were already under construction, and they were too small to carry the concrete dome unless voids reserved for mechanical ductwork could be filled in. When President Low realized that changing to a concrete dome would require an additional $15,000 and a redesign of the mechanical system, he directed McKim to retain the steel-truss dome and the plaster vault. The concrete shell which they were to support was later changed to brick to avoid the need to pour concrete in freezing weather.[20]

The above episode reveals that McKim was neither as idealistic nor as superficial as his admirers and his critics have believed. On the one hand, McKim was clearly concerned with the structural reality as well as the structural appearance of buildings. All three of the proposed domes would have looked the same. The vault would undoubtedly have been plastered over, as it was in most of McKim's tile vaults. McKim did not want to expose the structure; he wanted the structural substrate to conform to the clue given by the surface. At the same time, he was perfectly willing to build a sham vault if that was what the situation and the client demanded. He had done so ten years earlier in the Boston Public Library, and he was to do so fourteen years later in Pennsylvania Station. But whenever he could, he would reconcile structural appearance and structural reality.

Later, both McKim and White built domed buildings of the Roman type, but not on the scale of the university libraries. With his renovation of the Bank of Montreal in 1904, McKim was finally able to achieve his ideal type of a hemispherical dome built of two concentric tile vaults. White's last dome was that of the Madison Square Presbyterian Church in New York. Here, rather than return to the coffered double-shell dome he had developed for the University of Virginia, he (oddly) developed the type of dome he had been forced by the client to adopt at New York University.

The various controversies surrounding the domes of McKim and White show a great deal about the relationship between the realities and the theories of construction at the turn of the century. They show how prevalent was the prejudice against "shams" in architecture—not only among architects (such as McKim and Ware, who felt that a suspended plaster ceiling should not imitate a masonry dome) but also among their clients (such as MacCracken, who "should have [had] esthetic pain" at the sight of White's proposed steel columns encased in plaster Ionic). The prevalence of this prejudice may have been due to the tremendous popularity of John Ruskin, although Guadet has also condemned "architectural lies."

3.39

3.40

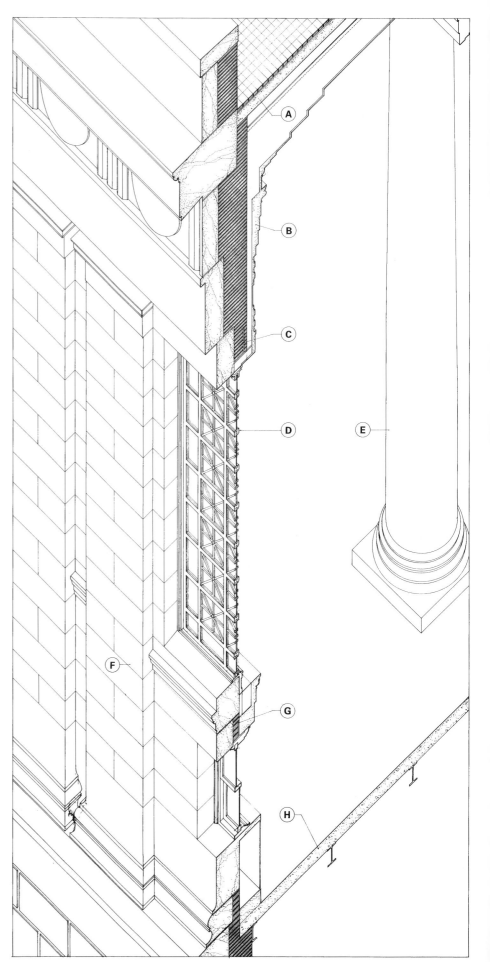

3.41

Bank of Montreal

McKim, Mead & White

1904

3.39 **exterior facade**

(New York Historical Society.)

3.40 **banking hall**

(New York Historical Society.)

3.41 **wall section**

A Roof construction. Steel trusses with ornamental plaster ceiling below.

B Wall construction: Chelmsford granite facing with brick backup. The interior is a mixture of stone and plaster ornaments.

C Steel tee lintel to support brick wall above. The stone lintel is self-supporting.

D Bronze window.

E Green Syenite column with black marble base and cast bronze gilt capitals.

F Pilaster. The location of these corresponds to the steel trusses inside.

G Steel tee lintel supporting brick wall above.

H Floor construction: Steel beams with flat tile arches.

(New York Historical Society.)

None of the structural materials contemplated for Low Library could be said to be traditional. Concrete and Guastavino tile are no less modern than steel. The virtues of the steel-supported dome did not have to do with materials; they had to do with the organization of materials and the process of construction. That the steel-frame dome proved to be the most economical solution is not surprising, but there are considerations unique to the problems of vaulting—for example, steel-frame domes did not require the construction of centering (a labor-intensive operation), as did masonry domes whether they were of traditional stone or modern tile. Among the reasons that the steel dome was so disliked by Ware were its complexity, its configuration, and the multiplicity of materials required. The concrete and tile domes were closer to traditional methods in their monolithic simplicity. But trends in construction—the minimization of on-site labor and the increasing number, complexity, and specialization of building systems—were making this difficult.

Most important, this controversy tells us something about McKim's and White's conception of architectural appreciation. To appreciate a dome, one must know that it is what it appears to be structurally. "Lies" and "shams" were not excusable, whether perceptible or not. At the same time, a building was not required to explain itself. White might switch from the structurally explicit coffer-type dome to the "floating" or celestial dome, which is silent as to its structural nature. One was required only not to lie; one was not required to tell the truth.

THE CULLUM MEMORIAL AND THE BANK BUILDINGS

Writing in the *Architectural Record* in 1904, Montgomery Schuyler praised White's recently completed Knickerbocker Trust Building, calling it "a modern classic":

It is by no means often that a modern architect has a project which will allow itself to be simplified to Greek Construction, and in which a single system of uprights and cross pieces can be made the whole visible structure of the modern building. (When that exceptionally happens, the most convinced Medievalist or Modernist can hardly cavil at the adaption of the "order," in which that construction was once and for all so beautifully developed and expressed that no construction more complicated has attained equal perfection.) A case is clearly made out for classic when the architect can employ the order as the structure, instead or reducing it to the place of a superficial decoration, or of taking it apart and undertaking to reassemble its elements in other connections than that for which they were devised.[21]

Schuyler's ideals of building were essentially those of Viollet-le-Duc. Both condemned the Romans for cladding vaulted construction with the post-and-lintel system of orders, and both praised the Greeks for making the orders and the structure one. The model of correct construction for Viollet-le-Duc, for Schuyler, and perhaps for White was the Basilica of the Giants at Agrigentum, in which the Doric columns are joined with a thin stone screen.

In the article cited above, Schuyler says of White's Cullum Memorial at West Point that "the order is not only the structure but the whole structure," and that "besides the essential structure there is also the screen wall of Agrigentum." This is essentially true, but the building as a whole is somewhat more complex in its relation to its structure. The screen walls, for example, are bonded with the column drums in the manner shown in figure 3.32, so that walls and columns act together as a structural unit. The interior of the major room corresponds only loosely to Schuyler's concept of columns and structure as one. The interior columns are plaster and are not structural, although they mark the locations of the real columns on the exterior. The ceiling of this space is formed of a series of plaster beams connecting the columns; the space between beams is infilled with square coffers. This is not, by Beaux-Arts standards, an irrational system of building, as the plaster ceiling describes fairly precisely the steel structure which it clads. Each plaster beam corresponds to a truss above; each smaller beam and coffer corresponds to a steel purlin. This is rational building for Guadet, but it is not for Viollet-le-Duc or (if he had looked at the building more closely) for Schuyler. It is a mixture of

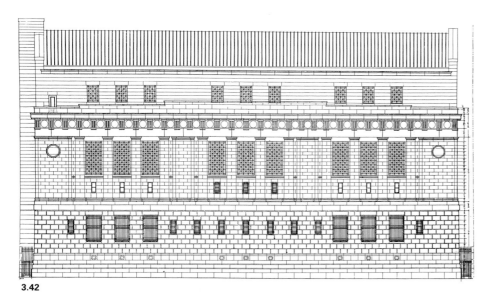

3.42

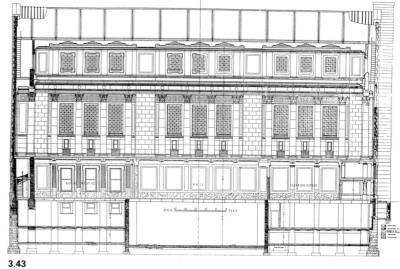

3.43

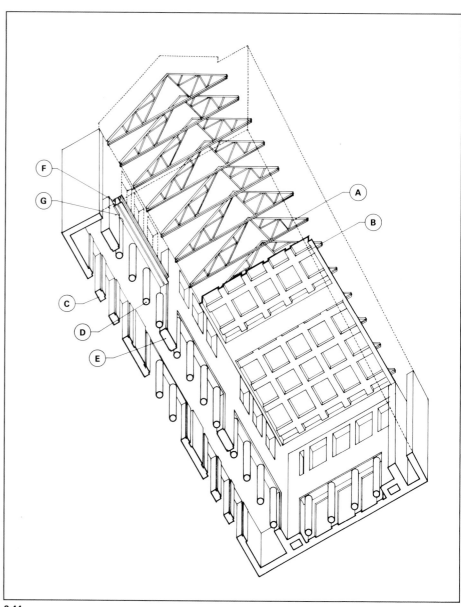

3.44

Bank of Montreal

McKim, Mead & White

1904

3.42   Craig Street elevation

(New York Historical Society.)

3.43   section

Note the location of the steel
trusses in relation to the columns
below and to the pilasters in figure
3.42.

(New York Historical Society.)

3.44   framing plan

A   Steel trusses. The location of the
trusses corresponds to the location
of the columns and pilasters below.

B   Plaster ceiling. While the coffers
correspond in location to the steel
beams above, the size of the
plaster beams does not reflect the
various sizes and strengths of the
steel beams.

C   Load-bearing exterior wall of brick
and Chelmsford granite.

D   Green Syenite interior columns
with black marble bases and cast
bronze gilt capitals.

E   Intermediate piers. Their purpose—
to divide the hall into three square
bays—is more visual than
structural.

F   Steel lintels, made from three steel
I sections. While the stone columns
are load-bearing, their entablatures
are not. The load of walls and
trusses is transferred to piers and
columns through steel beams.

G   Cast-iron shoe. This transfers the
load of the steel lintels to the stone
columns below.

(New York Historical Society.)

the two systems of building identified in chapter 1: the literal and the analogous. For White, as for most of his Classical contemporaries, the literal was better but not mandatory. Despite this mixture of systems, the Cullum Memorial, in its simplicity, is a paradigm of rational construction. The Cullum Memorial and the Knickerbocker Trust Building are among the first and the last of McKim and White's small Classical works. In detail they show a rational bias, but not the one that Schuyler saw.

It seems curious that McKim and White's subsequent works were not as successful as the Cullum Memorial, but the reason is simple: This type of rationalism is dependent on a certain type of program. If one ignores the base, the Cullum Memorial is a single great room with smaller support spaces at the end. It requires a single span from one exterior wall to the other. In this it resembles its prototypes in antiquity. A majority of buildings in antiquity were single-room buildings, and many Renaissance buildings as well. In more complex buildings with numerous smaller rooms, this type of rationality proved more elusive.

White's Metropolitan Club and McKim's University Club, both designed around the same time as the Cullum Memorial, have none of that building's clear structural order or its expression. Here again, the complexity of the framing is due largely to the complexity of the plan and to the shoehorning of rooms into a preconceived envelope. McKim and White were able to duplicate the character of the Cullum Memorial only when they had an equally simple program. The most frequent opportunities for this came in commissions for small banks.

White began the State Savings Bank in Detroit five years after the Cullum Memorial. Faced with a slightly more complex program, he achieved a slightly less orderly structural result. The program required a larger banking hall with a number of smaller support spaces. By using a large hall surrounded by a layer of small support spaces, he was able to approximate the structural order of the Cullum Memorial.

The State Savings Bank is a building within a building. The banking hall, with its nine-square grid of columns, sits within a rectangular one-story building. The structural order matches fairly closely the architectural order. The exterior walls are load-bearing masonry. The inner structure is a steel frame of columns and beams matching precisely the nine-square grid. There are no false columns or even false vaults, the small domed vestibule being built of Guastavino tile. But the structure is neither monolithic or exposed. The interior steel columns are clad in marble Ionic pilasters. The tile dome is plastered over. The ceiling structure of the banking room is divided into nine square plaster coffers, each of which is divided into nine more squares. The beams of the coffers correspond in location but not in size to the steel beams they enclose. These plaster coffers imply a two-way structural system, with the beams on both sides of the square bay contributing equally toward carrying the load (figure 3.38). The actual steel structure is a one-way system, with four 36-inch-deep plate girders running along the transverse axis and four pairs of 12-inch-deep channels running along the short axis. Of course, this structure corresponds only in a very crude way to the roof structure above. It could be argued that the correspondences between the real steel structure and the ornamental plaster structure are circumstantial, and that adherence to the Roman prototype is more important than adherence to the description of the underlying steel structure; however, in comparison with a ceiling by Robert Adam or one by Christopher Wren, which are coffered but in ways that are completely unlike their structural substrates, White's ceiling is rigorous in its adherence to the real structure.

McKim's first bank in the Classical style was the Girard Bank in Philadelphia. It is domed, and is essentially the Low Library parti executed with a Guastavino-tile vault and a marble exterior. It provides evidence, if any is necessary, that McKim's idea of type was independent of program, and that McKim believed that the palazzo and other forms could be adapted to a house, a club, or a bank provided it was of adequate size. It was to the palazzo form that McKim turned in his subsequent banks, beginning with the Bank of Montreal.

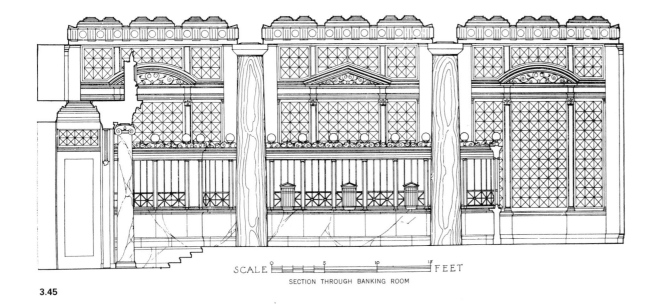

SCALE |0 5 10 15| FEET

SECTION THROUGH BANKING ROOM

3.45

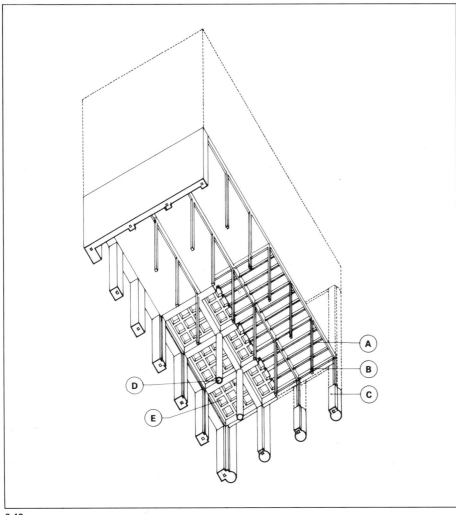

A
B
C
D
E

3.46

3.47

The Bank of Montreal, although unnoticed by Schuyler, comes the closest of any of the firm's banks to the model of rational building, where the columns are the structure. The bank has two sections, linked by a bridge. The smaller portion was an existing square building, into which McKim inserted a small double-shell tile dome like that used in the firm's libraries. The larger section was new, a rectangular block containing on its top floor the main banking hall. Here White's plan of a building within a building was used. The inner building is defined by columns and piers, which support a clerestory. Although these piers and columns stand only 15 feet inside the bearing walls of the building, both the walls and the columns are load-bearing, as is all the masonry in the building.

There is little in the walls and columns of this bank that could be called an analogous or clad system. The inner columns are all solid and all structural, supporting the roof trusses above and the adjacent floor beams. The pilasters of the outer walls all support major beams. In contrast with the State Savings Bank and the Gould Library, there are no steel columns clad in plaster. The entablature is more complex. The architrave is solid stone and self-supporting, but it does not carry the wall above. Concealed within the wall are three steel lintels, connected to the column below with a cast-iron shoe.

The floors, roofs, and ceilings of the Bank of Montreal follow a different concept than the monolithic columns and walls. The structural system here, as at Detroit, is an analogous rather than a literally exposed structure. The main hall is spanned by a series of equally spaced steel trusses, resting on pilasters which in turn rest on the solid columns below (figure 3.43). Supporting the first floor below are a series of steel beams with the same spacing. Although these beams and trusses are not exposed, their centerlines correspond exactly to the centerlines of the Corinthian columns of the banking hall and the Doric pilasters of the exterior. Here McKim, like White, used a simple squared coffer system similar to that of the Cullum Memorial and the Detroit bank.

A comparison of the real and symbolic structural systems of White's bank at Detroit and McKim's at Montreal suggests similar conceptions of building. However, the two men differed considerably on other points, including the expression of wall structure and the treatment of interior detail in relation to exterior detail.

Although the Bank of Montreal has pilasters, it does not have traditional construction of the kind that is associated with them. Those who condemned pilasters as structurally illogical felt that supports should be either column or wall, not both. But here the wall between pilasters is dropped to create a clerestory at the top, making the infill walls into screens not unlike those in the Cullum Memorial. No pilasters occur on the full-height walls, only thin strips at each end to suggest the column that is not there (figure 3.42). Thus, if one discounts the piers between every three columns, which divide the hall into square bays, the building is a sort of flattened out version of the Cullum Memorial and the Basilica at Agrigentum, but one in which there is a unity between column and wall.

The detailing of the exterior of the Bank of Montreal might serve as an illustration of what Guadet meant by "effective strength." The wall is detailed to explain literally how the load from the roof trusses finds its way to the ground. The wall becomes progressively thicker toward the ground, and the stones in the base are noticeably larger, as it logical in the construction of any load-bearing masonry wall since the loads are greatest at the base. The joints of the stones at the base are rusticated to create deeper shadows and the appearance of greater mass. There are more subtle graduations as well. The stone courses in the zone occupied by the columns appear to be of equal height, but in fact each series of five stones is $\frac{1}{2}$ inch smaller than the five below. This has a subtle but noticeable impact on the perception of the wall: It appears to be more massive at its base, and the cornice appears to be higher than it is (since the eye measures the joints as equal). This was a common practice in nineteenth-century Classical buildings; it occurs in the Boston Library, in Low Library, and in many other buildings where every stone is a different size. Perhaps the most surprising detail of the Bank of Montreal is the

3.48

3.49

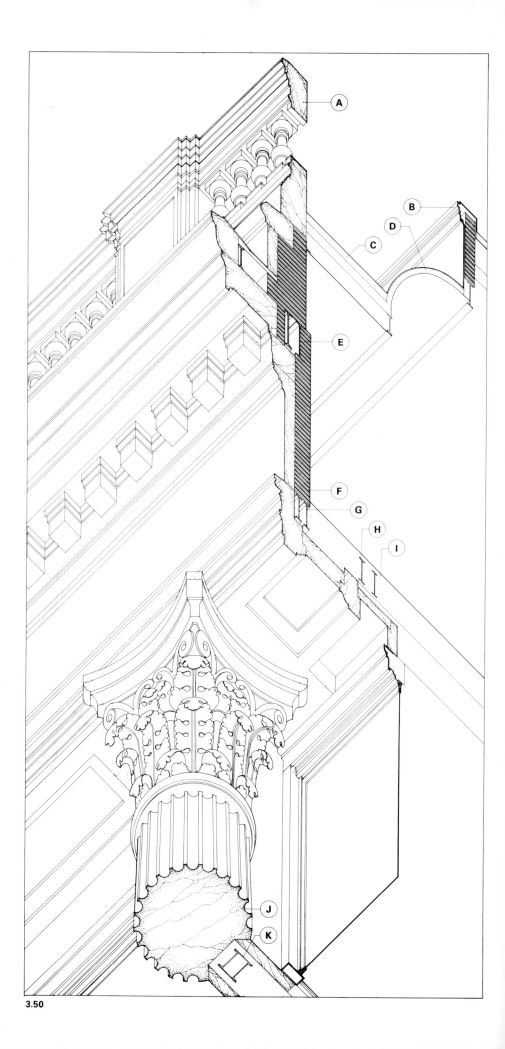

3.50

Knickerbocker Trust Co.

McKim, Mead & White

New York, 1904

3.48 cornice

(New York Historical Society.)

3.49 exterior facade

(New York Historical Society.)

3.50 wall section at cornice

A Baluster. This was a typical device used to establish scale in Classical buildings.

B Brick wall faced with copper.

C Roof construction: steel beams supporting flat hollow tile arches covered with concrete, a layer of waterproofing, and roof tiles.

D Tile blocks covered with copper.

E Steel beams supporting cornice.

F Typical wall construction: white Vermont marble with brick backup. In contrast with the other banks, this is a curtain wall and not a load-bearing wall. The windows are of wood faced with copper to minimize maintenance and to achieve the archaic appearance of a bronze screen.

G Steel beams supporting masonry wall. Since the edges of the floors are recessed behind the massive columns, two layers of steel framing are required on the perimeter—one to support the floor and one to support the entablature.

H Steel beams supporting floor.

I Floor construction: steel beams and flat tile arches.

J Column of solid marble. While horizontal joints were acceptable in columns, vertical ones were not; hence, these are the most massive stone sections in the structure.

K Steel column built up from two channels and two plates. The stone columns here are symbolic rather than structural, as at the Cullum Memorial.

(New York Historical Society.)

alteration of the proportions of the Doric order to unify the facade and increase the perception of mass. The column is the correct height of 7 column diameters, but the entablature is $2\frac{1}{2}$ diameters high rather than the standard 2.

The walls of the Cullum Memorial are notable for the absence of these details. Of course the Ionic columns, with their projecting capitals, their entasis, and their attic bases, are deeply expressive of the loads they are carrying; but the screen walls between them are flat and simple. There is one projection at the base, but there are no rusticated joints. The masonry courses are equal in height, and the Ionic order is of the correct proportions (at least according to Scamozzi). Here again White emphasized the separateness of column and screen as well as the lightness of the screen itself.

The Cullum Memorial is extremely simple in its ornamentation. None of the moldings are carved with enrichments, such as the egg-and-dart or the water leaf of which White was so fond. At first this seems very odd—White is associated with complex ornamentation and produced buildings as rich as Madison Square Garden. However, the materials must be considered. White's mature Classical style had four different modes of ornamentation, based on the four principal groups of materials he used: granite, limestone, brick and terra cotta, and metal. Many thin groups of elements, which were subject to surface irregularities, were purposely ornamented to hide these defects. Likewise, terra cotta was seldom used in a way that exposed large unbroken planes to light. White always heavily molded the surface of terra cotta, and used it in conjunction with rough brick. His limestone and granite, by comparison, were often quite plain, with a minimum of moldings and ornament, because of their solidity. Granite, being the most difficult of these materials to carve, received the simplest treatment. Cullum is unusual in White's work in being entirely of granite, and its simplicity is in part a response to this fact. McKim was much less sensitive than White to the nature of materials; his highly modeled University Club is also entirely of granite.

The greatest difference between the Cullum Memorial and the Bank of Montreal, and perhaps the greatest difference between White and McKim, is in the treatments of the interiors and the relation of these treatments to the exteriors. White's taste ran toward the ornamental, McKim's toward the monumental. In the Cullum Memorial, the interior details are much smaller and finer and the projections are generally shallower than those of the exterior. It was standard Neo-Classical practice to reduce the size, scale, and relief of interior details, which do not receive as much light or show as much shadow as exterior details. Details in a building interior will appear much larger than the same details outside. At Cullum the reduction in column size is in fact necessary because the main room extends only two-thirds the height of the facade, but the practice is followed in many buildings where it is unnecessary—e.g., Low Library, where the interior Ionic columns are only about two-thirds of the height of the exterior ones. With the Bank of Montreal, McKim reversed this practice. Here the Doric pilasters of the facade are a full 2 feet shorter than the interior composite pilasters. This is necessitated by the choice of orders, since the ratios of height to diameter of the two orders are fixed at different quantities, while the column spacing is the same. But other details of this interior are enlarged rather than reduced. The typical interior limestone block, for example, is almost twice the height of the typical exterior granite block. The net result is a deception of scale implying a much larger and imposing room than actually exists, as in the great halls of ancient Rome (and in Pennsylvania Station).

The Knickerbocker Trust Building was one of the last banks that White completed. Although elegant in its simplicity, particularly on the exterior, it was not typical of his bank buildings. The banking hall occupied a much smaller proportion of the building's volume than in the previous banks. In addition, the building was intended as a base for a much larger building of fifteen stories, and thus had a much more elaborate structural system.

3.51

3.52

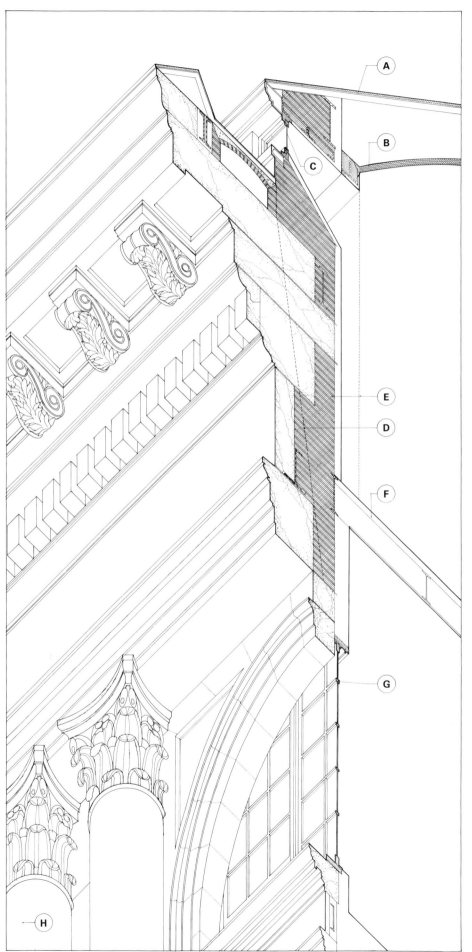

3.53

Tiffany Building

McKim, Mead & White

New York, 1906

3.51 **exterior facade**
(New York Historical Society.)

3.52 **detail**

3.53 **wall section at cornice**

A Roof construction: steel beams supporting tile roof.

B Vault of Guastavino tile. This vault occurs only at the top floor.

C Clerestory window.

D Steel bracket (beyond) to support cornice.

E Wall construction: non-load-bearing brick-and-marble wall with steel column beyond.

F Floor construction: steel beams with flat tile arches.

G Double-hung wood window. There is in effect one window every two floors, giving the building a deceptive scale.

H Marble column. Each stone column corresponds to a steel column behind, although the stone columns are sometimes doubled.
(New York Historical Society.)

What Montgomery Schuyler found so admirable about the Knickerbocker Trust Building—that the order is the structure—was not actually true of that building, although it was true of the Cullum Memorial, the Bank of Montreal, and portions of the State Savings Bank. The Knickerbocker Trust Building had a complete steel frame. There were no stone columns in the building that did not correspond to hidden steel columns, but there were no stone columns that supported anything other than themselves. This resulted in a rather complex arrangement, in which exterior steel columns projected beyond the spandrel edge beams so that the stone columns would appear to be free-standing. White even added an extra steel column at the corner so that there would be an exact correspondence between steel and stone columns.

The interior structure followed a similar but more complex pattern. The banking hall, as in all of White's other banks, was a nine-square grid, but in this case there was a column at each intersection. The columns were taken from the mansion of A. T. Stevens, which had previously stood on the site. How White reconciled these columns with the steel frame is not known, since the drawings and the building have disappeared. The ceiling coffers, and the structure which they clad, followed exactly the pattern used in the State Savings Bank.

Despite Schuyler's comments, it cannot be said that the Knickerbocker Trust Building had the same precise relationship of interior, exterior, and structure as the Cullum Memorial. The banking hall occupied only half of the floor area and two of the building's five stories. As a result, a great many structural elements were suppressed rather than articulated. The top floor was hidden completely behind the cornice, and the spandrels of the intermediate floors were clad in metal so that they would appear to be only a part of the window system. This, in a nutshell, was the problem of applying Classical columns to steel buildings: In order to maintain correct spacing and have the steel and stone columns align, the order had to extend over several floors. But the major difference between the two buildings is in the nature of the columns on the exterior. In the Cullum Memorial the columns are the literal structure. In the Knickerbocker Trust Building the columns are analogous; they represent the real steel columns behind. These two systems of structural expression—one real, the other symbolic—occur throughout White's work, even within the same building. He did not consider one system to be superior to the other, but thought either could be appropriate to a given situation. However, the Knickerbocker Trust Building, with its steel frame, is more typical of the problems of building in the early twentieth century. McKim built few buildings that used a complete steel frame. White, however, in the last years of his life, designed several skyscrapers, all of which were built with complete steel frames and non-load-bearing masonry walls; thus he was faced with the necessity of using systems that were largely analogous, and with the necessity of reconciling a symbolic structural language based on Classical precedent with a real structure based on the pragmatic demands of steel construction.

WHITE AND THE SKYSCRAPER

In 1896 Louis Sullivan wrote:

. . . the tall office building should not, must not, be made a field for the display of architectural knowledge in the encyclopaedic sense; . . . too much learning in this instance is fully as dangerous, as obnoxious, as too little learning; . . . miscellany is abhorrent to their sense; . . . the sixteen-story building must not consist of sixteen separate, distinct and unrelated buildings piled one upon the other until the top of the pile is reached.

To this latter folly I would not refer were it not to the fact that nine out of every ten tall office buildings are designed in precisely this way in effect, not by the ignorant, but by the educated. It would seem, indeed, as though the "trained" architect, when facing this problem, were beset at every story, or at most, every third or fourth story, by the hysterical dread lest he be in "bad form"; lest he be not bedecking his building with sufficiency of quotation from this, that, or the other "correct" building in some other land and some other time; lest he be not

3.54

3.55

3.56

Gorham Building

McKim, Mead & White

New York, 1906

3.54   **exterior facade**

(New York Historical Society.)

3.55   **detail**

3.56   **wall section at cornice**

A   Steel tees supporting terra cotta blocks.

B   Wood planks on nailers supporting copper roof. The voids between nailers are filled with cement.

C   Copper cornice, supported by triangular steel angle brackets. The large cantilever here prohibited the use of stone because of weight.

D   Wall construction of brick and limestone.

E   Roof construction of Guastavino tile vaults and concrete. See figure 3.59.

F   Steel I-section beams.

G   Double-hung wood window.

H   Wall construction: Bedford Indiana limestone with back up of brick or terra cotta tile.

I   Steel column built up from two plates and two channels, behind limestone Corinthian column. There is a steel column behind very other limestone column.

(New York Historical Society; F. M. Snyder, Building Details.)

copious enough in the display of his wares; lest he betray, in short, a lack of resource.[22]

Here Sullivan would seem to be describing a building similar to White's Tiffany Building of 1906. Along with McKim's plaster vaults, this criticism contributed to the Modernist sentiment that the firm of McKim, Mead & White was indifferent to structural expression. It was not until Leland Roth's book of 1983 that White's interest in structural rationalism (particularly in the last years of his life) was revealed.[23] White was not indifferent to the problems of programmatic expression and compositional imbalance created by the tall building. In the period 1900–1906, White approached the ornamentation of tall buildings and smaller ones in fundamentally different ways.

In 1903, after considerable difficulties with the client, White completed the Joseph Pulitzer residence in New York. Like most of his medium-size urban buildings, it is a palazzo type, suggesting but not precisely reproducing several specific Italian models. The orders are superimposed in "correct" order from base to top: a rusticated Tuscan order for the ground floor, Ionic for the second, and Corinthian for the third. Each of the orders is correctly proportioned in the ratio of column diameter to height (at least by Serlio's standards, which are less than those of Palladio or Vitruvius). The Ionic columns at the second floor are 8 column diameters high, the Corinthian columns at the top floor are $8\frac{1}{2}$ diameters high, and the two rusticated columns at the entry are 6 diameters high.

Since the eighteenth century, architects had recognized that the apparent proportion of the orders changed in taller buildings, since the orders at the top of a tall building were further away and thus appeared smaller. There was considerable debate as to whether traditional proportioning systems needed to be modified for taller buildings. Laugier said no, but Claude Perrault and others said yes and suggested that elements high off the ground be enlarged by the method illustrated in figure 3.62, whereby the moldings are enlarged to the size that would make them appear to match those at ground level. This became the standard method of adjustment, and it was recommended by McKim's friend William Ware.

White, out of ignorance or genius, did not use this method but invented his own. In 1906 he completed the Tiffany building. Despite the difference in size and program, it closely resembles the Pulitzer house. Again there are three tiers of orders, but here each corresponds to two stories. The orders are not superimposed, but each tier is a Corinthian order of different size and proportion. The correct height of a Corinthian column is 10 diameters according to Vignola and $9\frac{1}{2}$ according to Palladio and Vitruvius. None of the columns of the Tiffany building match this ratio exactly. Those at the top floor are almost correct, being 10 diameters high, but they sit on a base that is almost a full diameter high. Those at the second tier are 11 diameters high, so they are thinner, and those at the base (actually pilasters) are $10\frac{1}{2}$ diameters, again thinner but not by the same degree. But look again at the upper tier. If we consider that from street level we will not see the oversized base, the column becomes correct, but only if we disregard perspective distinction (i.e., that it will appear smaller than it really is). The base serves the purpose of raising the scotia and the torus of the column above the entablature below, so that they can be seen from street level. If the top order is thus correct, White reversed the method of Perrault and Ware by making the top order, and not the bottom, to traditional proportions, and attenuated the lower orders. The result is that all the order appear somewhat lighter than when used in their traditional proportions.

The apparent structure of the Tiffany Building is not analogous; it is idealized, as Goodhart-Rendel would say. The real structure is a steel-frame building with square bays. Corresponding to each real steel column is a pair of stone columns. Corresponding to each floor beam is a stone lintel. But the stone columns are two stories high, and every other floor has an arch.

The Tiffany Building stretched the Palazzo type to its extreme height, and it is perhaps for this reason that it is so different from the Gorham Office Building,

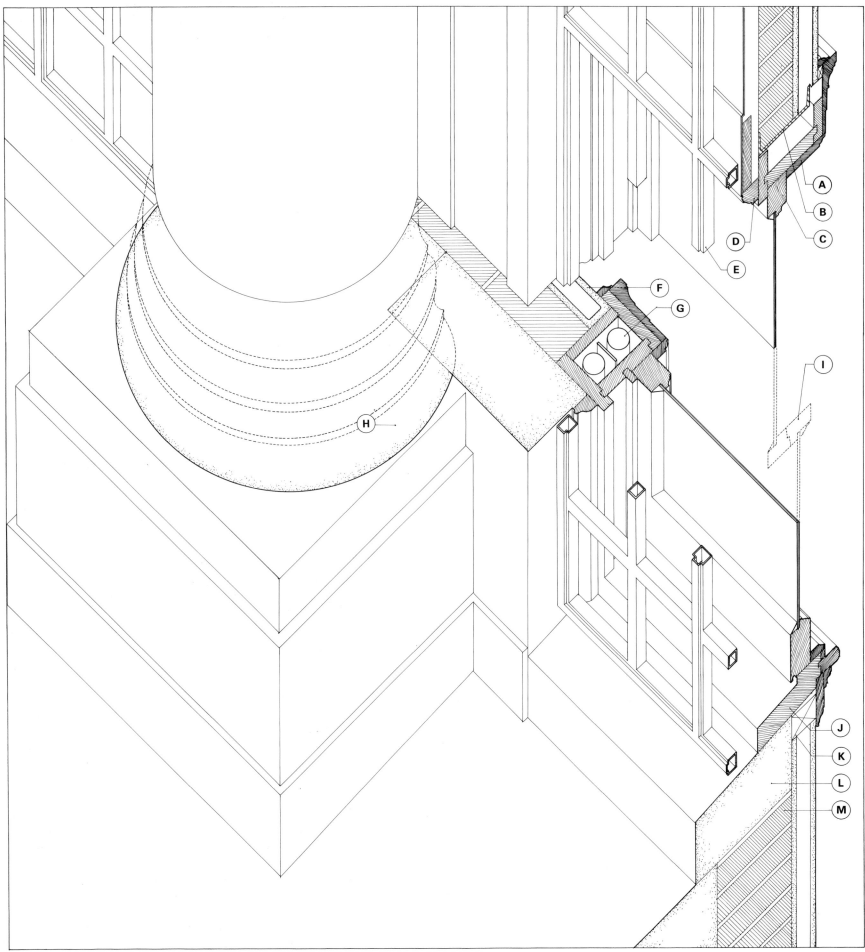

A
B
C
D
E
F
G
H
I
J
K
L
M

3.57

Gorham Building

McKim, Mead & White

New York, 1906

3.57 window details at upper floor

A Finish wood trim. The windows were constructed of two woods: a quality finish wood for the interior (to be stained or varnished) and a poorer-grade wood for the exterior (to be painted.)

B Steel channel supporting brick over window opening.

C Sash of double-hung window.

D Wood panel faced with copper. The copper protects the wood from rot, minimizes maintenance, and gives an antique look to the windows.

E Copper grille. This serves no functional purpose but recalls similar grillwork in antiquity.

F Terra cotta tile.

G Sash weight in jamb pocket. Because the large windows are so heavy, counterweights attached to the sash with ropes and pulleys are provided.

H Limestone column base.

I Meeting rail of double hung window.

J Wood sill. All sills are sloped to shed water.

K Wood nailer. This serves to support the window and the trim.

L Limestone sill.

M Brick backup wall faced with Bedford Indiana limestone.
(New York Historical Society; F. M. Snyder, Building Details.)

designed at the same time. The Gorham Building is eight stories as opposed to Tiffany's seven, but it is a much thinner building, and White here uses a composition of base, shaft, and cornice in a concept not unlike Sullivan's contemporary work. The wall of columns and entablatures creating a frame expression is abandoned in favor of a more unified mass of sheer walls with punched openings. To the problem of accommodating the orders and their proportions to the tall building, White creates here a third solution, differing from Ware's and from his own in the Tiffany Building. But there is evidence that White wished to do more than accommodate the visual order of Classicism to the tall office building; he wished to accommodate the structural order of Classicism as well.

The ornamentation of the Gorham Building is sparse for White. Ionic columns at the base support arches, and Corinthian columns at the top two floors support a huge metal cornice that overhangs the building by 8 feet. As in the Tiffany Building, the uppermost order is correctly proportioned while the lower is not; however, this has a different purpose here. Just as the lower columns of the Tiffany Building are made thinner to emphasize the building's frame qualities, the lower columns of the Gorham Building are made thicker to increase the building's mass. Typical Ionic columns are 9 diameters high, although Serlio thought they should be 8. Those of the Gorham Building are $7\frac{3}{4}$ diameters high and are bulkier as a result. The Corinthian columns of the Gorham Building are $10\frac{1}{2}$ diameters high, and are thinner than the normal 10-diameter columns, and (as at the Tiffany Building) they rest on extremely high plinths. The entablature is 5 diameters high, twice its normal size.

The cornice and the entablature of the Gorham Building are not proportioned to the height of the columns, but to the height of the entire building. (This could have been done by enlarging the typical Corinthian cornice to the desired size, but that would have destroyed the relationship between the Corinthian columns and the cornice, and would have reduced the apparent scale of the building in the manner of one of Robert Venturi's oversized ornaments.) Some of the elements of entablature and cornice are enlarged; but the more important ones are doubled. The frieze (the flat middle portion) is its normal height at one diameter. The architrave (the lowest portion) is enlarged from its normal $\frac{3}{4}$ diameter to a full diameter. However, the cornice proper is not enlarged but is expanded to its full size by the doubling of the modillion. This cornice is in all other respects a typical Corinthian one, and if the second modillion were omitted it would be almost the correct size for the Corinthian columns below. The result is a double reading, whereby the cornice may be seen both as the cap to the entire building and as the entablature of the order immediately below.

The double readings that occur in the Gorham Building make it an obvious object of study for Postmodernists, who are trying with far less success to do the same. But one of the more remarkable aspects of the building—one that history has been ignorant of and the installation of suspended ceilings has obscured—is the structural rationalism of the floor and wall systems. Like White's systems of proportion it follows no precedented pattern, and by the standards of a Viollet-le-Duc it is inconsistent in its methods. In the terms defined in chapter 1, it is sometimes a monolithic system of exposed and ornamented structure and sometimes a layered system of analogous structure, where the real structural system is clad with an ornamental one.

The typical floor construction of the Gorham Building is a monolithic system that even Pugin or Cram would call rational. Each floor is divided into 20-foot-square bays. Each of these is framed with a cross-vault of Guastavino tile, resting on braces of iron angles and ornamented with plaster. The vaults are supported by square bays of steel beams and box columns; the interior columns have round plaster covers. The walls, on the other hand, are layered and are analogous in their rationalism. Unlike those of the Cullum Memorial or the Bank of Montreal, the Ionic columns of the base and the Corinthian columns of the attic are not structural. The building has a complete steel frame, and the masonry, although it adds stiffness to the structure, is not load-bearing.

3.58

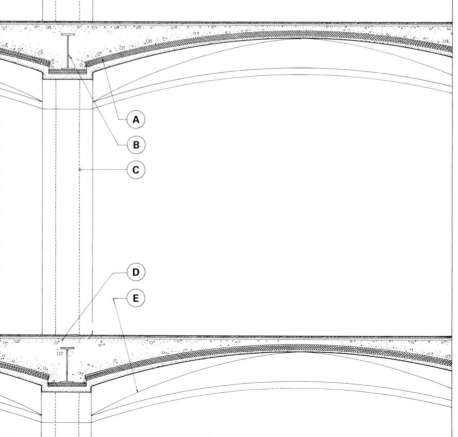

3.59

Gorham Building

McKim, Mead & White

New York, 1906

3.58 **interior of ground floor**

(New York Historical Society.)

3.59 **tile vault**

A Guastavino tile vault. Floors were typically made of tiles at this time, but usually hollow tiles which formed flat arches rather than vaults.

B 15″-deep steel I section.

C Steel column, built up from one channel and two plates.

D Concrete fill. This serves only to provide a flat floor above the vaults.

E $5 \times 9\frac{3}{4}$ curved steel I section. This forms the rib of the finished vault, providing both reinforcement and formwork.

(New York Historical Society.)

Unlike the Tiffany and Knickerbocker Trust buildings, the Gorham Building does not have an exact correspondence between the ornamental Classical columns and the real steel columns which they conceal. The steel columns of the Gorham Building are spaced at twice the distance of the Classical columns, so that only every other stone column marks the location of a real steel column. In contrast with the Tiffany Building, both the scale of the spaces of the plan and the traditional spacing of Classical columns are preserved, but this is done at the expense of an exact correspondence between the real steel structural system and the ornamental stone structural system. In contrast with the floor structure, where the real and ornamental structural systems are the same, the wall system of the Gorham Building can only be described as a highly idealized representation of the real structure.

This was the universal problem of applying the Classical orders to a steel frame. The traditional spacing of Classical columns is quite small, since it is based on the limitations of masonry construction. In steel construction the economical spacing of columns is much wider, but to space traditional columns at this same interval would be visually unacceptable to most Classical architects. In the Tiffany Building, White solved this problem by making the Classical columns two stories tall, thus preserving the traditional spacing, but he did so at the expense of the building's scale. At first glance the Tiffany Building appears to be three stories tall; in fact it is seven.

Thus, neither the Tiffany Building nor the Gorham Building was an ideal solution to the problem of representing a steel frame with Classical orders. (Louis Sullivan faced the same problem with the Wainwright Building, where only every other brick pier of the facade corresponds to a steel column.) The radical differences between the two buildings would suggest that White was struggling with this problem at the time of his death, shortly after the completion of these buildings. McKim, who retired shortly thereafter, may have deliberately avoided designing any large steel-frame office buildings. Thus, neither McKim nor White can be said to have come to terms with the essential contradictions between Classical proportions and the proportions resulting from steel framing.

CONCLUSION

In hindsight, there is little doubt that McKim and White practiced their own version of structural rationalism. Their best buildings were, in their own terms, just as rational as those of Louis Sullivan, Frank Lloyd Wright, H. P. Berlage, or Otto Wagner. Their rationalism has inconsistencies, and it breaks its own rules (though no more so than the rationalism of Mies).

McKim and White faced the same problem as most successful firms of the Modern era: There was no dogma of building that could be successfully applied to the number and variety of commissions they received. Those who remained inflexible, such as Wright, ended up concentrating on large houses; they were unable to compete in the market for large buildings. That their rationalism has been largely ignored is a result of the bias of Wright and the Modernists. It is not the type of rationalism we have wanted to see, for our perception of them is quite different from their own.

Our perception of their mode of building is that it is a reactionary one—that they realized that the steel frame would make obsolete the traditional forms of building, and were making a futile attempt to save those forms by adapting new materials (such as Guastavino tile) to old forms.

McKim and White saw their place in history differently. They were not trying to save the old, but to establish something new. The saw themselves as establishing an American tradition of architecture, building, and craft. They considered American architecture to have been inferior to European architecture in every respect, and they wished to make it equal. Technically and aesthetically, they did not have the Modernists' faith in the beneficial effects of the new methods of building. The U.S. Capitol is to us a technically progressive work in its use of cast iron to support the dome, but to McKim and White it was an example of the inferiority

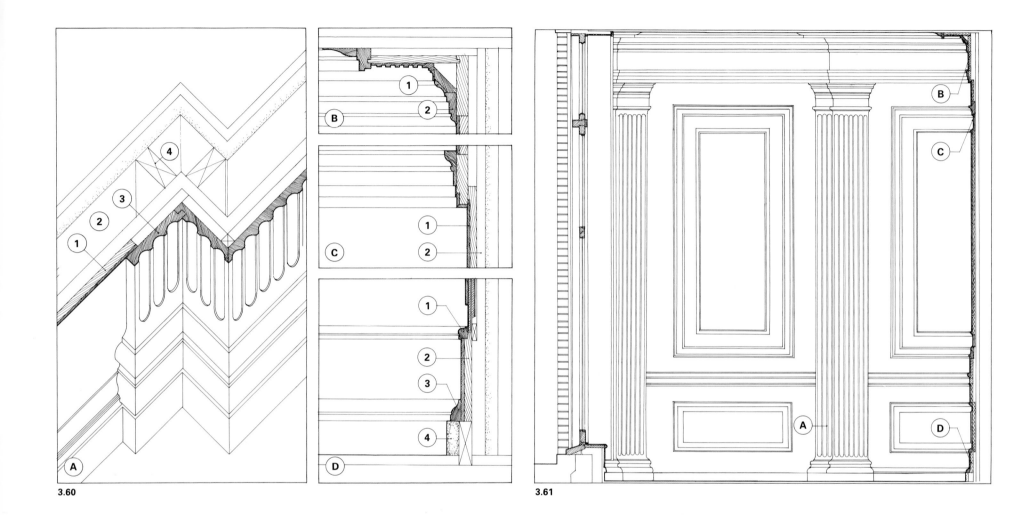

3.60

3.61

C. Gibson house

McKim, Mead & White

New York, 1903

3.60 wood paneling details

A Plan details at column.

1 Cherry veneer on ash board.

2 Air space. This ensures that the wood remains dry on both sides to prevent warping.

3 Solid cherry pilaster. Those sections which are carved or molded are of solid wood.

4 Wood blocking. This provides a rough nailer to which the finish paneling is attached.

B Crown mold.

1 Composition molding. Cast from wood fibers.

2 Solid cherry trim. The molded pieces, since they must be milled and carved, cannot be veneered.

C Picture rail details.

1 Cherry veneer on four-ply ash plywood. The major panels are too large to be fabricated from a single piece of wood.

2 Blocking attached to plaster wall. An air space is usually provided between wood paneling and wall to ensure that the wood remains dry and responds uniformly to changes in humidity.

D Base detail.

1 Solid cherry panel molding. The moldings used here serve to soften the transitions by eliminating horizontal surfaces.

2 Cherry veneer on solid ash board.

3 Solid cherry base molding. Note that the top and bottom base moldings are similar but not identical.

4 Gray Sienna marble base.

(F. M. Snyder, *Building Details.*)

3.61 paneling details

(F. M. Snyder, *Building Details.*)

3.62 Method of adjusting proportions of entablatures. (Plate CXXXII of Batty Langley's *City and Country Builder's and Workman's Treasury of Designs.*)

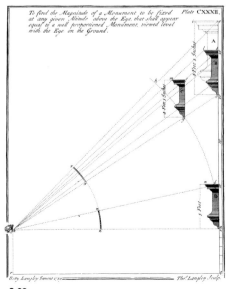

3.62

of American building techniques. Americans had never built a dome of stone on the scale of St. Peter's and St. Paul's. Their aim was to establish a tradition of building that would equal the achievements of Europe, not to explore the possibilities of old forms in new materials. (Now that we see more clearly the long-term effects of steel framing on modern architecture, we should perhaps be less critical of them for not wholeheartedly embracing it.)

McKim's and White's attitude toward architectural construction is best summed up by Guadet's comment that "science has axioms, art has principles. . . . Principles, like axioms, are proved only by the enduring superiority of the works which have most faithfully abided by them. . . . Principles are not restrictions, they are a light."[24]

McKim's building practices are based on principles, but they are also full of compromises brought on by "impinging necessities." He was willing to build "dishonest" domes and vaults suspended from steel trusses when the situation demanded, as in the cases of Low Library and Pennsylvania Station. He would build monolithic exposed brick and tile buildings, such as the War College, where structure and architecture were the same, if that was demanded by "impinging necessity." But his preferred style was that which was, according to his principles, represented by the Bank of Montreal and the Morgan Library. This style was characterized by monolithic stone walls and by columns that were literal and real structural members. Where McKim used domes, the domes are built of steel-supported tile, and they are real structural domes although they are covered with plaster. McKim's ceilings are of steel, and are clad with plaster systems that describe the structures above (and also recall Roman examples). The reason for his preference and the depth of his thinking probably went no deeper than this. Such construction was solid, it was enduring, and it recalled Rome in its configurations. It is not a reactionary system or even a conservative one. It had little to do with contemporary American practice. It used a number of technological innovations—Guastavino tile, portland cement, structural steel, and cavity walls—but in ways that were reminiscent of and continuous with European (particularly Roman) precedent. It was a style that many thought had built-in contradictions, such as the mixture of exposed, clad, and analogous structural systems within the same building.

White's mature style contains few "deceits" on the order of the Low Library dome or the waiting room at Pennsylvania Station, but the use of analogous and clad structural systems is much more prevalent. The Cullum Memorial is very close to McKim's work in its use of load-bearing stone columns with a plaster ceiling describing the trusses above. However, the interiors of most of White's smaller buildings are, like that of the State Savings Bank, plaster claddings on steel structures. Each column in these structures is expressive in the sense of being a plaster casing around a real column and beam. No plaster columns occur where real columns do not, but no real steel columns are exposed. Despite some of his clients' dislike for this system, White was satisfied, and it is perhaps because of this that he was to take on the high office building with more confidence than McKim. In the Knickerbocker Trust, Tiffany, and Gorham buildings this system evolved into one in which the orders were "a mimic architecture with which real architecture is adorned." Each steel column was faced with a real column of stone that bore only its own weight.

It is not difficult to understand why McKim's and White's interest in construction has been largely ignored. Their ideas of rational building were based largely on precedent rather than on impartial analyses of actual conditions, and although they used modern materials and systems, they used them for a conservative reason: to maintain the quality of traditional building. When they died, their work was only beginning to feel the impact of modern materials and systems. To examine the history of Classicism in the twentieth century, it is necessary to examine another career: that of Edwin Lutyens.

4 Edwin Lutyens and the Language of Classicism

In 1928 Hannes Meyer, one of the leaders of the movement known as *Neue Sachlichkeit* [New Objectivity], wrote in the journal *Bauhaus* that "building is not an aesthetic process. . . . Architecture as 'a continuation of the traditions of building' means being carried along by the history of architecture. . . . Pure construction is the basis and the characteristic of the new world of forms."[1] Meyer's position is unusual for a Modernist in the 1930s. In contrast, Gropius, Mies, and Le Corbusier all acknowledged the importance of studying traditional building techniques. Meyer's fear was that traditional methods would lead inevitably to traditional forms. Other Modernists solved this dilemma by confining their study to vernacular building techniques, which were seen as being without style. The history of Modernism is filled with such paradoxes. At the Illinois Institute of Technology in the 1950s, under the leadership of Mies, while courses in architectural history were deemphasized, students were required to build a joint of an archaic timber-frame building to learn construction.

For those who used traditional forms, traditional techniques presented no problems other than being antiquated. In 1931, three years after Meyer's manifesto, Edwin Lutyens wrote:

. . . we cannot get rid of the body of the tradition, murder it how we may, it is always with us. . . . By tradition I do not mean the unthinking repetition of antique forms—the hanging of Roman togas on Victorian towel horses. Tradition to me consists in our inherited sense of structural fitness, the evolution of rhythmic form by a synthesis of needs and materials, the avoidance of arbitrary faults by the exercise of common sense coupled with sensibility.[2]

Lutyens described himself as an architect of traditional forms and traditional techniques. It is difficult to reconcile this attitude with Lutyens's later work, for the technology of his buildings of the 1920s was far from traditional. Of Lutyens's Midland Bank and Britannic House, Roderick Gradidge wrote:

. . . in these big buildings commercial firms of some distinction like Whinney Son & Austen Hall or Lawrence Gotch would produce steel frames and draw out plans of the rows of office floors, and on to them Lutyens would hang his stone facades. There is nothing wrong in facing a steel building in stone. . . . Without a doubt the Classical style is the most suitable style to use for this purpose. But

4.1

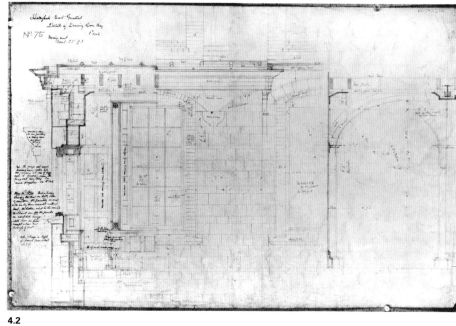

4.2

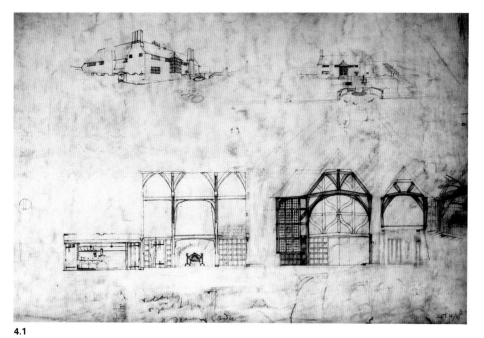

4.3

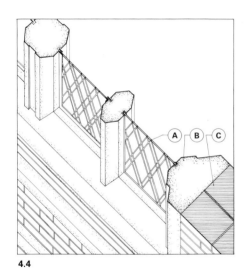

4.4

if the consultant architect's facade bears little relation to the functional requirements of the building to which it is fixed, then it is obvious that the design integrity of that architect must be called into question. Too often on these office blocks the fenestrations bear little or no relation to what is going on behind. Some offices, for instance, are lit with enormous arched windows that run from floor to ceiling while next-door offices of equal importance have but one small opening.[3]

This view was reinforced by Lutyens's biographers. His assistant W. A. S. Lloyd recalled that

. . . the office dealt only in surfaces. Lut was not interested in what held the building up or composed the core, heated, or drained it. He left generous tolerances in these respects, and Thomas or collaborating architects and builders put in the stuffing and bones. All his buildings could have been built of the materials on the face (and he would have regarded them as noble had they been), but he did not really mind, or recognize, the supporting steel, or concern himself greatly with the bonding of the thin bricks he liked using to the common backers.[4]

Gradidge argues that this was true of Lutyens only later in his career, and that his earlier work is more integral in that its forms are reconciled with the technology that produced them. Gradidge points out that, unlike other late-nineteenth-century architects (e.g. Richard Norman Shaw), Lutyens never used false half-timbering, and that "he was educated at home. . . . He was allowed to wander through the woods and fields of still unsuburban Surrey, and to visit the small country builders' yards in the neighbouring villages. In this way he learnt about the craft of building many years before he learnt of the art of architecture."[5]

Which was the real Lutyens: the stylist indifferent to what lay beneath the surface of his buildings, or the rational traditional architect who failed to reconcile his formal language with changes in technology? Or is there some way in which Lutyens's formal language, like McKim's and White's, can be read as an expression of the buildings that it clads? There is no simple answer, but the idea of Lutyens's designs as language is crucial in understanding his work.

Lutyens often spoke of the grammar of architecture. In 1931 he wrote:

. . . I regret the passing, be it temporary or permanent, of humanism and the personal note; the eclipse by impersonal machines of bricklayer, mason, and joiner as the makers of buildings. . . . Traditional ways of handling materials are the basis of style in architecture.

There are innumerable things that an educated humanist "does not do," just as there are things that a writer does not commit: platitudes, jingles, slipshod construction, journalese. It would be very easy to write if one invented one's own language. That is what I feel about the average modern building. It has been easy to design because there is, as yet, no grammar.[6]

The idea of architecture as language is neither original nor unique to Lutyens. But it is particularly appropriate to Lutyens's architecture, primarily because of the operations he performed on that grammar and that language. Although Lutyens probably never heard of Gottfried Semper, he would have agreed that the grammar of architecture takes on a life of its own, and that vestigial forms disassociated from their original purposes have their place in architecture. The question, as always, is how far may the language of architecture depart from the reality of construction.

Lutyens had probably never read the linguist Roman Jakobson, but they would probably have agreed on the nature of language—that it is creative and constantly changing, that it is subject to structure but not necessarily to rules, and that meanings can be changed by transformations of that language, by juxtaposition, displacement, or inversion. Lutyens's Classicism was a modern Classicism, and its language was a modern conception of that language. It was not based on an inviolate set of harmonic proportions, although it used proportional systems; it was not based on a set of orders with predetermined components and ratios,

4.5

4.6

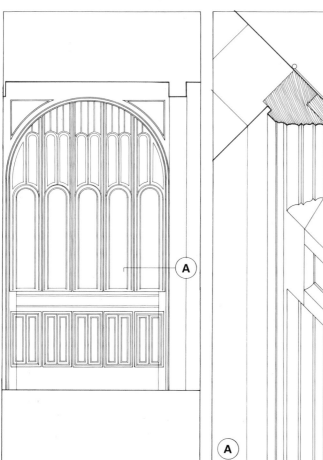

4.7

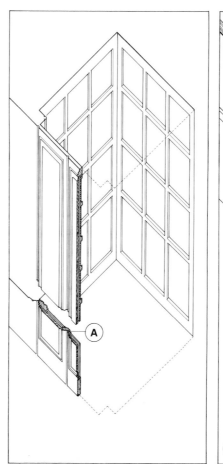

A

1
2

A

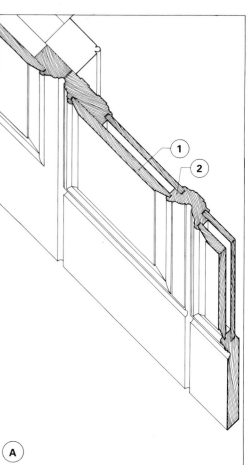

4.8

A

1
2

A

Castle Drogo

Edwin Lutyens

Devon, 1910–1930

4.5 **door from library to hall**

(Country Life.)

4.6 **best dressing room**

(Country Life.)

4.7 **door from library to hall**

A   Rail at hinge. These moldings are more Gothic in character than those below, since they use concave curves to form sharp edges rather than the convex segmented curves used in Classical moldings.

1 Solid wood panel.

2 Molding covering panel joint. Note that this is a butt joint covered with trim.

(Butler, *The Lutyens Memorial,* volume I, plate LX.)

4.8 **door in best dressing room**

A   Rail at hinge. The moldings in this door are more typically Classical in character than those in figure 4.7.

1 Panel. On one side the panel is recessed in accordance with conventional practice.

2 Rail panel joint. Unlike the library door, the panel is rabbeted into the rail.

(*Country Life*; Butler, *The Lutyens Memorial,* volume I, plate LX.)

although it used these elements and had its own ratios. Lutyens wrote of the orders that "you cannot copy: you find if you do you are caught, a mess remains. It means hard labour, hard thinking, over every line in all three dimensions and in every joint; and no stone can be allowed to slide. You alter one feature (which you have to, always), then every other feature has to sympathize and undergo some care and invention. Therefore it is no mean game, nor is it a game you can play lightheartedly."[7]

LUTYENS'S HOUSES AND THOSE OF HIS MENTORS

Sorting out Lutyens's country houses by the use of similar features, if not precisely styles, three groups can be identified. The first are those in the "Surrey vernacular," such as Munstead Wood, which are his most rustic and picturesque. The second are those in what Goodhart-Rendel called the "vigorous" style: Marshcourt, Lindisfarne, and Castle Drogo. This style was based on Medieval and Jacobean stone details; however, the elimination of all nosings, projections, and moldings from windowsills, buttresses, and other elements resulted in a degree of abstract formalism that approached Modernism. The third group of houses are in the classic "Wrenaissance" styles, ranging from the brick-and-limestone Georgian of Ednaston Manor to the more rigorous Classicism of Heathcote. Although the tone of Lutyens's work became more classical in the course of his career, he continued to design in all three styles into the 1930s, and although there are details associated with each of these styles, two or even three of these styles of detailing may be present in one building. Marshcourt, the exterior of which is totally in the Jacobean vigorous style, is filled with rooms that are mostly in a pristine Classical style but sometimes in the solid, pegged-oak manner of the Surrey buildings.

Lutyens's detailing, even his Classical detailing, is a product of his apprenticeship in the "Queen Anne" era. He was particularly influenced by the men he called his two great masters: Richard Norman Shaw and Philip Webb. Lutyens's planning techniques owe little to these two architects, but his elevations, the details he chose to use, and the way he chose to combine them were refinements of their techniques (particularly Webb's). Lutyens said of Webb that "he conceived his buildings more in the spirit of a constructor rather than that of a scenic painter. . . . His right use of material was masterly."[8] Lutyens's early work in Surrey, although it resembles Shaw's half-timbered style, is heavily indebted in its values to the ideals of Webb.

Gradidge has maintained that early in his career Lutyens was deeply interested in rational construction, and that he made a careful study of not only the traditional style but also the traditional building techniques of Surrey. Few construction drawings survive from this period, but an 1889 project for a house in Surrey shows more than a surface interest in the traditional wood construction of the region (figure 4.3). The structure is exposed throughout; it is monolithic and conforms to the Puginesque theory of good building. This project also shows the considerable influence of Arts and Crafts ideals of celebrating the means of connection.

Lutyens's interest in local craft was also due to the influence of Webb, whom Goodhart-Rendel credits with the invention of modern architectural detailing:

This change in practice . . . was probably as much due to Webb as anybody else. That it was great can be realized now when every architect designs or pretends to design everything in a house down to the handrail of the back staircase; and when authorities on seventeenth-century architecture profess to see the hand of Wren himself in every drawing for woodwork submitted by a joiner for his approval. There is no real evidence that Wyatt, Salvin, Burn or any but a very few of their predecessors or contemporaries, ever themselves, drew a bedroom chimney-piece or the back stair banisters in their lives. All matters of process too, of the pointing of brickwork, or the tooling of stone, had customarily been controlled by a clerk of the works interpreting a conventional specification, until Webb, and of course, William Morris, awoke their age to full consciousness of craftsmanship.[9]

4.9

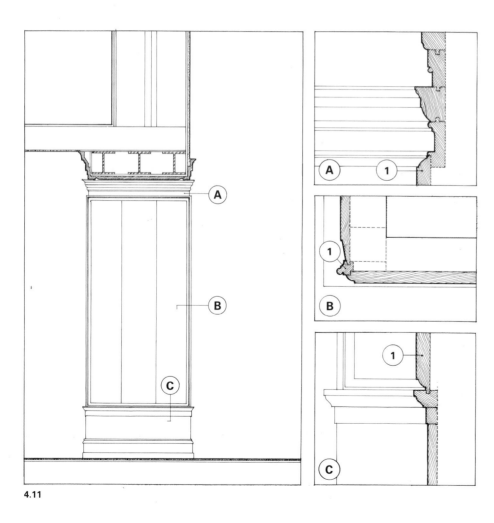

4.11

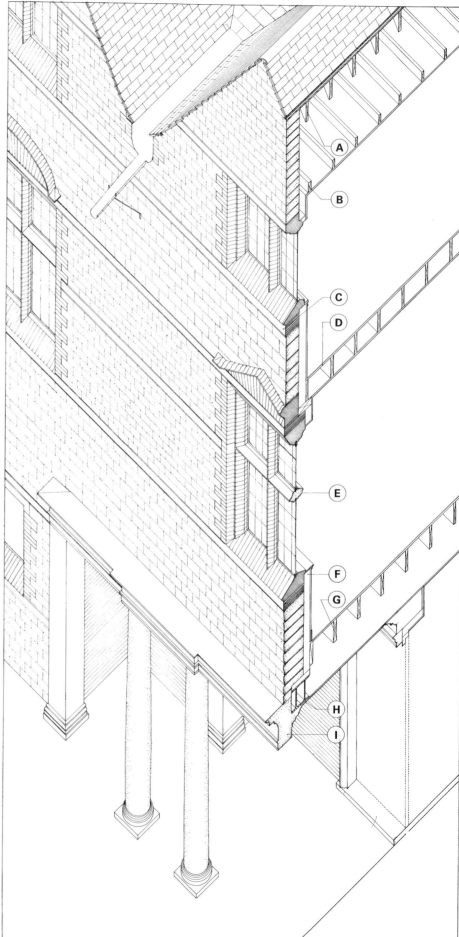

4.10

Tigbourne Court

Edwin Lutyens

Surrey, 1899

4.9 **exterior**

(Country Life.)

4.10 **wall section**

A Roof construction: tiles on wood nailers supported by wood rafters.

B Plaster ceiling supported by wood joists.

C String course made from three courses of tiles.

D Floor construction: 2 × 12 wood joists at 14″ on center.

E Window mullions of pressed brick. This is Lutyens's "frameless" window with a metal rather than a wood frame.

F Wall construction. Brick may have been used as a backup for the facing stone.

G Floor construction: 2 × 12 wood joists at 14″ on center.

H Two 10″-deep steel beams. The stone entablature is not sufficient to carry the large mass of masonry above.

I Stone entablature and columns.

(RIBA Drawings Collection, drawing [303] 3.)

4.11 **Marshcourt,** Hampshire, E. Lutyens, 1901–1924. Trim details of great room.

A Detail at capital below lintel. At (1) The typical panel is inverted from conventional practice (see figure 3.60; rather than receding, it projects to the plane of the capital above.

B Corner detail. At (1) the panel is recessed on the long side of the pier while projecting on the short side.

C Detail at base. At (1) the panel projects to align with the rail below.

(Country Life; Butler, *The Lutyens Memorial,* volume I, plate XIII.)*

Webb certainly documented and supervised his buildings with unprecedented precision, and it is revealing to compare the drawings of the young Lutyens with those of the elder Webb. (See figures 4.1 and 4.2.) Webb's drawings are covered with notes and dimensions explaining precisely how certain things are to be done, and those elements of construction that will be concealed are drawn and detailed with the same precision as those that will be exposed. Lutyens's drawings of Deanery Garden, with its exposed solid timber framing, show a similar aesthetic, and we know that Lutyens spent much time at the site to ensure correct fabrication; however, his drawing shows no information about and no concern with the concealed portions of the wood truss. Lutyens admired Webb's attention to minute details in all that he did, but his own work—even that from early in his career—reveals his indifference to what lay below the surface.

But if Lutyens did not learn this lesson from Webb well, there is another that he learned better: the virtues of juxtaposing of different styles of detailing. Lutyens's work is full of inconsistencies in detail: Tudor casements with Georgian paneling, a rustic eave atop a classic entablature, a precise Palladian window in a crude clapboard wall. These juxtapositions are common in older English houses, built and remodeled over several centuries, but they are also common in the houses of Philip Webb. When Webb built Standen, in 1896, he incorporated an existing farmhouse into the design. Aside from the stylistic difference between Webb's portion of the building, and the old portion, there are many inconsistencies within the new portion.

Despite the Classical character of many of Webb's details, there are no literally Classical elements other than moldings in Standen. There are no columns or pilasters that belong to any recognizable order, no triglyphs, metopes, or capitals, no egg-and-dart, no bead-and-reel. Webb used cyma rectas and ovolos not because they occurred in antiquity but because they occurred in Sussex. Webb used vernacular buildings for his models in part because they were astylistic. Like many Modernists, he thought he saw in vernacular building a functional architecture born out of innocence, designed by men ignorant of stylistic convention. Webb began his career as a Gothic Revivalist, believing that kind of building to be rational. When Gothic became popular, it also seemed to become simply another style in the eclectic climate of the nineteenth century, and Webb abandoned it.

Lutyens's Tigbourne Court shows similar contrasts of precision and rusticity, and of the Classical with the vernacular. The entry is marked by what appears to be a precisely executed and complete Tuscan order, and except for some of the windows there is not another molding to be found on the exterior of the house. The juxtaposition is deliberate; it could not be misread as a later addition to a traditional building. But it is itself a contradictory Classical element: On the one hand, it has none of the naïveté of Webb's Classical pieces. It is modeled on antiquity and done by an educated architect, not a vernacular builder. On the other hand, it is not Classically "correct." The order combines a Doric column (two tori at the base, rather than one as in Doric) with a Tuscan entablature (no metopes or triglyphs on the frieze). The column is $7\frac{1}{2}$ diameters high—acceptable for a Tuscan column, but too tall for a Doric. The entablature is $1\frac{3}{4}$ diameters high, which would be correct for a column 6 or 7 diameters in height but not for one of $7\frac{1}{2}$ diameters (which should have an entablature of at least 2 diameters). Even at this early stage in his use of Classical elements, Lutyens was taking liberties with standard proportions.

Just as Lutyens sometimes simultaneously designed two buildings in different styles, he occasionally used different styles of detailing at the same time. Corresponding to each of the house styles identified as Surrey Vernacular, Vigorous, and Wrenaissance, there is an associated style of detailing. But the use of one of these detailing styles is not limited to the building style with which it is associated; thus, in one building (e.g. Marshcourt), Classical and vernacular details are evident as well as details associated with the style of the house. The exterior is in the Vigorous style; the interiors of the major rooms are Classical; the stair hall has a vernacular, Arts and Crafts character. This results in some strange juxtapositions.

4.12

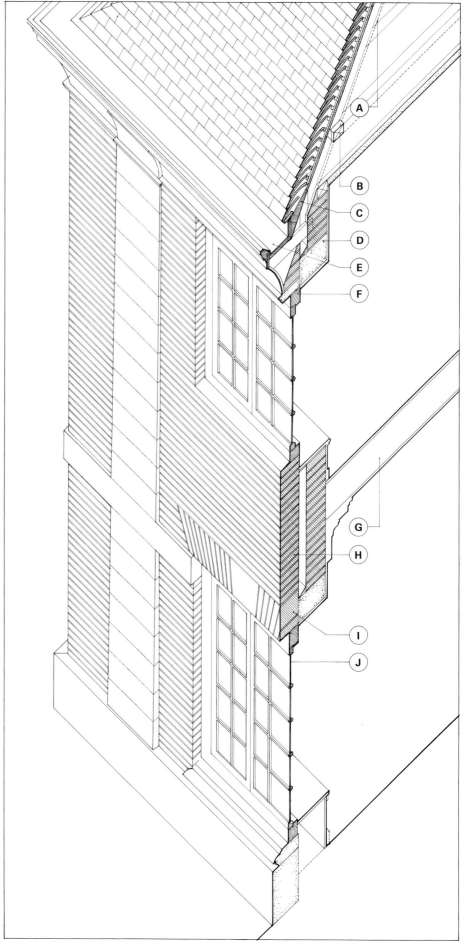

A

B

C

D

E

F

G

H

I

J

4.13

Ednaston Manor
Edwin Lutyens
Derbeyshire, 1913

4.12   exterior
(Country Life.)

4.13   wall section

A   Tile roof on $1\frac{1}{2}'' \times \frac{3}{4}''$ wood nailers, attached to $\frac{7}{8}''$ boarding supported by rafters. A layer of felt is placed on top of the boards to intercept any water that may penetrate the tiles.

B   Roof structure: $2 \times 5\frac{1}{2}$ wood rafters and 3×11 ceiling joists. Both are set on a cork pad and nailed to the continuous $4\frac{1}{2} \times 5$ horizontal wood piece at the top of the brick wall.

C   Lutyens uses a tapered piece of wood here to achieve the typical horizontal "flair" of the roof pitch at the edge. The roof proper is pitched at 54° so that the ridge at the intersection will appear at 45°.

D   Concrete lintel. Backup lintels of concrete rather than steel were common in English building at this time.

E   Gutter concealed in wood entablature, lined with felt and then lead to protect the wood from rot caused by water standing in the gutter. It is given a slight pitch to achieve drainage.

F   Out-swinging wood casement window.

G   Floor construction: 3×12 wood joists with wood finish floor above and plaster below.

H   Wall construction: two wythes of brick (common brick on the interior and special facing bricks on the exterior). Lutyens here uses something resembling the modern cavity wall with a triangle of grout at the bottom to help drain the cavity.

I   Flat brick arch lintel on the exterior wythe; cast-in-place concrete lintel for the interior brick wythe.

J   Out-swinging wood casement window.
(Butler, The Lutyens Memorial, volume I, plate LXIV.)

At Castle Drogo, the exterior doors are in the Vigorous style (as is the building as a whole), but the inner doors are Classical in character—they have the moldings and proportions of a typical style-and-rail door such as that in figure 3.61. But something is wrong: the parts that would ordinarily project are recessed, and vice versa. (The door and its paneling, if designed correctly, might be something like White's paneling in the Gibson house.) The effect of reversing the rail element is to create a deep valley, Gothic in character. It might be said that, while Lutyens used Gothic and Classical elements, he Classicized the Gothic details and Gothicized the Classical ones. Using modern terms, we would say that this door has been transformed by means of inversion.

The consistency of Lutyens's work is found not in the stylistic elements themselves, but in the way in which they are adapted. Just as he seldom used the orders without modifying them in some way, he altered the character of any historical element he used. His transformations may be roughly classified as elimination, inversion, and planar recession.

Compare, for example, the typical windows of Marshcourt with those of Ednaston Manor. Both may well be adaptations of vernacular prototypes. (The medieval stone mullioned window at Westwood may have been a prototype for Marshcourt.) The windows at Ednaston recall Georgian prototypes, although they have little of the surrounding trim that is associated with the Georgian style. The upper-story windows have concealed lintels, and there is nothing save a sloped bed of mortar where there would normally be a stone sill (or at least a rollock course). The jambs have no stone trim, and although in the house called Salutation Lutyens used a different color and texture of brick to define the opening, here he does nothing. The lower window is more elaborate, with a flat arch for a lintel (although the continuation of the stone string course could have accomplished the same thing). The jambs are untreated. There is a stone sill, but it is in the very un-Classical shape of a quarter-circle with its flat side down. This gives it a knife-edge profile with a deep shadow, which makes it effectively disappear. The brick panel below the sill is pulled out to its leading edge so that they are in the same plane. This is a simple example of two of Lutyens's common transformations: elimination in the entablature and window head and jambs and planar recession in the window sills.

There are other characteristic Lutyens details in the Marshcourt wall, such as the inversion of the stone coursing. The wall is of smooth white chalk with small pieces of flint mixed in checkerboard courses. Since the flint does not appear to be as heavy as the chalk, one would expect it to be mostly at the top of the wall. The reverse is true, and the building has a visually soft base as a result. There are few moldings in the wall, but when they occur (as they do under some of the eaves) they are again recessed so that their leading edges are flush with the face of the wall, rather than projecting to visually support the roof.

The paneling of the Great Room at Marshcourt shows similar transformation on a more subtle scale (figure 4.11). Note how the typical relationship of style to rail has been reversed by inverting the quarter-round molding. This is inversion, which was to become one of the popular techniques of Modernist detailing. But the techniques used on the facade are used here as well. The panel is pressed forward and the capital and the base are recessed, so that many of the elements are in one plane. This, as with the exterior molding, is an example of planar recession. The usual character of molding in wood or stone is additive, a piece tacked on to the construction. By recessing these moldings (which usually project), he makes them subtractive, as if carved out of the mass. At the same time, Lutyens projects by inversion moldings that one would expect to see recessed.

Planar recession and elimination are particularly evident in Lutyen's Wrenaissance and Classical buildings, where the source of these elements—the Classical orders—is more easily recognized. On the subject of the elimination (or what Lutyens called telescoping) of an entablature, Lutyens wrote to Herbert Baker in 1910: "I am rather fond of an entablature with the frieze omitted and the top member of

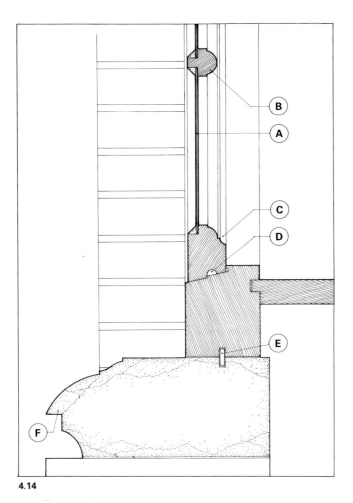

4.14

4.16

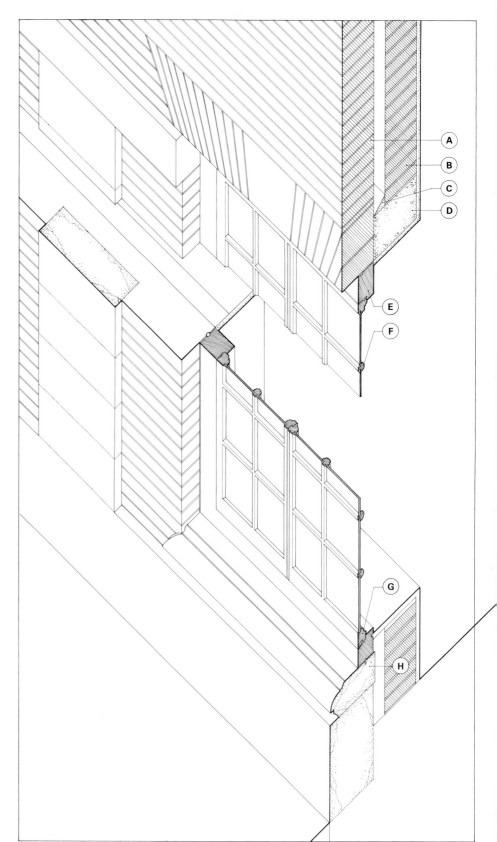

4.15

Ednaston Manor

Edwin Lutyens

Derbeyshire, 1913

4.14   window profile

A   Glass in out-swinging wood casement.

B   Typical wood muntin. The glass is placed from the outside and held in place with putty. The curve acts to soften the corner and avoids the sharp, glaring contrast that would occur if light were to strike a square muntin.

C   At the edge the convex muntin curve is echoed with a concave molding framing the whole window. This is a typical Classical molding, with two contrasting curves of unequal size separated by a rectangular fillet.

D   The joint of the sash and the fixed sill is sloped to drain rainwater, and is provided with two air pockets to prevent water from being pulled through the joint by capillary action.

E   Spline. This prevents water from seeping through the joint.

F   Stone sill. This very unclassical molding, with a knife edge and a sharp shadow, almost disappears in elevation. It is functionally useless, since it is flat and does not project. Like all Lutyens's curves, these are fragments rather than full quarter- and half-circles.

(Butler, *The Lutyens Memorial*, volume I, plate LXV.)

4.15   window details

A   Outer brick wythe. Lutyens used thinner facing bricks to give more horizontal lines on the exterior.

B   Inner brick wythe. Brick walls at this time were usually monolithic. The use of cavity walls for waterproofing did not become commonplace until much later.

C   Cavity with cement wash at bottom. The wash drains water toward the exterior.

D   Concrete lintel faced with jack arch. The less labor-intensive concrete lintel is used in the unexposed location.

E   Head of wood casement.

F   Typical window muntin.

G   Sill of wood casement.

H   Stone sill. This profile, with its deep undercut and sharp edge, almost disappears on the exterior.

(*Country Life*; Butler, *The Lutyens Memorial*, volume I, plate LXV.)

4.16   British Embassy, E. Lutyens, Washington, D.C., 1925.

The entablature is dropped well below the eaves, and the roof tiles meet the brick wall without a molding.

(*Fiske Kimball Library, University of Virginia.*)

the architrave becoming the lower member of the cornice."[10] An example of this is the eave detail at Ednaston (figure 4.33), where the column capitals, rather than support the plaster cove above, are absorbed by it. (At Heathcote, a similar effect is achieved by elimination rather than by telescoping. The Doric columns of the ground floor have a full entablature, while the building as a whole has only a small cornice.)

On one level, Lutyens's telescoping recalls the juxtaposition of Classical and vernacular details common in Lutyens's seventeenth-century Queen Anne prototypes and in the work of Webb. But Lutyens's juxtaposition is more systematic. Perhaps he felt that the "ideal" qualities of Classicism were made manifest by juxtaposition with the rudeness of vernacular details. On another level, this telescoping of a cornice has a profound impact on our perception of the scale and mass of a building. It makes the building appear taller than it actually is, since the entablature, being smaller, seems farther away. It also makes the top of the building appear lighter, so the base and the building as a whole appear more massive. This elimination, minimizing, and displacement of the cornice is common to almost all of Lutyens's mature work, regardless of size and style.

Almost all Lutyens's houses have un-Classical roofs. In his Classical and Georgian houses, Lutyens never used the Classical technique of raising the parapet to hide the roof slope. Occasionally he used a parapet in a more Tudor building, such as Castle Drogo or Crooksbury, but in his truly Classical works (such as Heathcote or Ednaston Manor) there is always a steeply pitched, visible roof. The roof was invariably at an angle of 54.45° (as were the moldings) so that it appeared to be 45° at the corners. An extra rafter at a shallower slope is always placed at the edge (figure 4.13) to visually ease the transition and to allow the rafter to brace on the inner part of the wall.

Heathcote is considered pivotal in Lutyens's work, in part because many of its details appear in his larger Classical buildings and in part because of his letter to Herbert Baker describing its design, in which he says that "in Architecture Palladio is the Game."[11] Just as important in this letter is a reference to Michele Sanmichele, the source of many of Lutyens's details. This letter is often quoted as illustrating Lutyens's belief that the proportions of the orders should be changed to fit circumstances; however, the proportions at Heathcote are nearly correct— the column is 8 diameters high, the entablature 2 diameters.

The crucial transformation at Heathcote is not the alteration of proportions but, again, planar recession. In Sanmichele's prototype (the Porta Palio, at Verona), the columns stood in front of the wall. At Heathcote they are set into recesses with wide end pieces. Again Lutyens's ornament is not additive but subtractive, not tacked on but carved out. Certain elements are in front of the plane of the wall, particularly the "phantom columns." The base and the capital sit at the top and the bottom of the rusticated wall (figure 4.18). It appears as if the column was never finished, or—in Cubist terms—that the column and the wall have interpenetrated to form what Colin Rowe calls a phenomenal transparency: "two figures that are able to interpenetrate without an optical destruction of each other." This type of transparency, which results in a double reading of the wall and/or the column, was to become the basis of Lutyens's Classicism.

Another transformation can be seen in the moldings at Heathcote, which are all made slightly heavier than normal by the use of enlarged curves. Lutyens disliked what he called "spent curves"—i.e., perfect quarter- or half-circles. Each of Lutyens's curves has a larger radius than necessary, so that it never reaches its point of tangency. (Perhaps this is an imitation of Greek moldings, which were seldom pure geometric forms.) Lutyens's assistant Lloyd wrote:

The "spent curve," as he called it, was anathema. All mouldings were built up of arcs of various simple constructions. This also applied to domes, niches, etc., the semicircle never being allowed, except in the arch, to complete itself. He thought continually in three dimensions, if not four, and set no store by a drawing other than as a statement of intention. . . .[12]

4.17

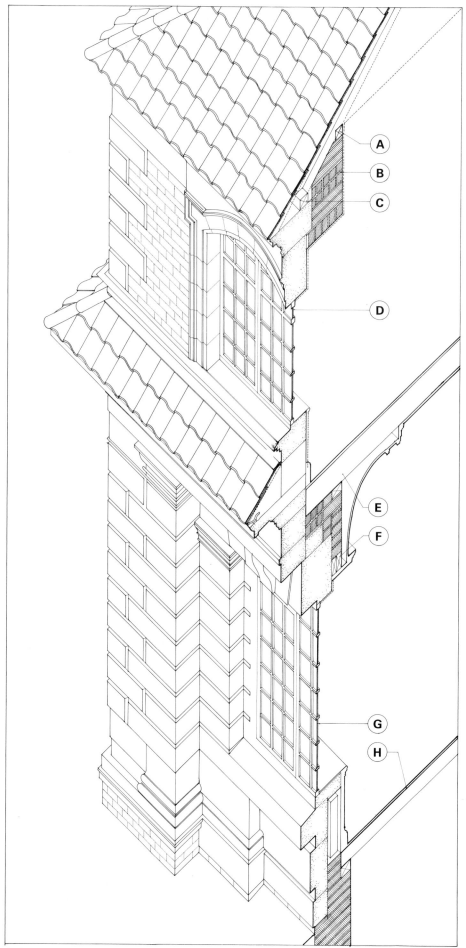

4.18

Heathcote

Edwin Lutyens

Ikley, Yorkshire, 1907

4.17 exterior

4.18 wall section at end of pavilion

A Wood nailer to support rafters. Roof construction: tiles on $1\frac{1}{4}'' \times \frac{3}{4}''$ battens on wood rafters.

B Brick relieving arches. These assist in carrying the loads on the wall around the window openings.

C Wood plate to support rafters.

D Wood casement window.

E Floor construction: 2 × 10 wood joists supporting subfloor and finish floor.

F Wood nailers below relieving arch. These close the opening between the curved arch and the flat soffit of the window.

G Wood window.

H Floor construction: 2 × 6 wood joists.

(RIBA Drawings Collection, drawing LC-[101]6.)

What was the purpose of these distortions and juxtapositions? Why manipulate the mass and the scale of a building in this way? Lutyens probably never read Guadet, but he would have agreed that functional stability is not sufficient in a building, and that stability must be rendered apparent. Lutyens's dislike of thin partitions and ribbon windows, which emphasize the lightness of the wall, and for other modern devices which suggest a frame that is in equilibrium rather than superimposition, recalls Guadet's criticism of the rear of Notre Dame. Most of Lutyens's distortions act to lower the apparent center of gravity of the building, making the base appear massive and precise while making the top seem light and difficult to perceive. When Lutyens began to receive commissions for much taller buildings, he made even more use of these devices.

NEW DELHI

The first designs for the Viceroy's House at New Delhi were done in 1912, but the building did not open officially until 1929. The Indian independence movement may have had some effect on the decisions as to what style to use—Classic, Mogul, or something else. Lord Hardinge (the viceroy) and Herbert Baker (Lutyens's collaborator) favored what would today be called a contextual approach; they felt that the buildings should be Indian in character, if not specifically in form. Lutyens was not unsympathetic, but he strongly opposed the use of such literal quotations as the Ogee arch, which Baker was to use in his buildings at New Delhi. In 1912–13, Lutyens undertook a study of Indian architecture in the hopes of devising a compromise. He learned a great deal about Indian architecture, and in the process he learned a great deal about Western Classical architecture as well.

In 1912, Lutyens wrote to his wife:

Personally I do not believe there is any real Indian architecture of any great tradition. . . . It is essentially the building style of children. . . . I shall try and start an Indian school and Western tradition must be there. As Englishmen we cannot help it and then send the Indians straight to nature and let them invent and conventionalize to fit given spaces . . . and to build in stone for stone and in wood for wood. When they build it is exactly like children's bricks and they put stone beams in tension. [See figure 4.32.]

Take the Fort at Delhi. The stones (marble) are like this. How does A stick up. Nonsense by Gum! Towers this shape. Why should we throw away the lovely subtlety of a Greek column for this uncouth and careless unknowing and unseeing shape?[13]

Another aspect of Indian architecture Lutyens disliked was the use of veneers, particularly marble. In 1917 he wrote of the Taj Mahal:

Having got this mass built in concrete, each face has a carpet of marble and stone veneer stuck onto it, and then to further adorn the building they put on five domes. Four little and one big. And then further embellishments with chattris and little arcades with toy drums in rows like pearls on a necklace.

Compare this method with a building like the Parthenon or any of the great French Cathedrals—where the stones are the bones of the building and make their construction their own decoration and then everything thought out relatively to make the whole design one organism approaching a work of nature.[14]

At this point in his career, Lutyens's ideas of rational building, insofar as he had any, were very much in the tradition of Gothic Rationalism: that materials could be used only in certain ways, that monolithic construction was preferable to veneered, and that the orders, when used, should be used structurally. Lutyens's work at New Delhi shows the influence of these ideas—which served him well in the India of the 1920s, with its largely preindustrial building methods.

The structure of the Viceroy's House reflects Lutyens's newfound interest in Classical Rationalism—or at least in monolithic construction, since he came the closest here to reconciling his architectural forms with the structures supporting them. Load-bearing walls support steel-and-concrete floors and roofs, and brick

4.19

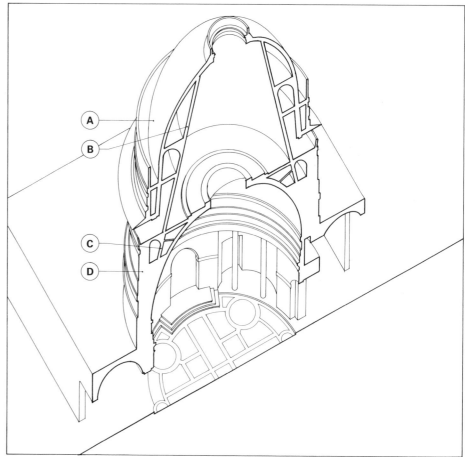

4.21

4.20

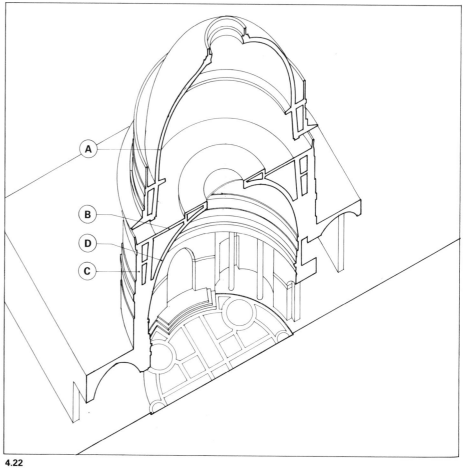

4.22

Viceroy's House

Edwin Lutyens

New Delhi, 1929

---

vaults. The walls are of brick, faced with stone on the exterior and plaster on the interior. A dome of brick and concrete covers Durbar Hall, the main reception area; roofs of steel and concrete, with supplemental brick vaults, cover the main reception areas; steel-and-concrete floors cover the smaller rooms.

Although the two domes have little in common formally, Lutyens's original concept for the dome of the Viceroy's House bears a close structural resemblance to Wren's dome for Saint Paul's. Wren's dome consists of three shells, the innermost made of masonry. The second shell, also of masonry, does the real structural work, carrying the weight of the outer dome to the supporting piers without developing lateral thrusts that would require buttresses. Lutyens's dome is smaller and lower than Wren's and thus has less lateral thrust. Its decoration is predominantly Indian, and it seems to have little in common with Wren's much taller design. Lutyens had used Wren's three-shell system previously in a much smaller dome for the Free Church in Hampstead, with the difference that the inner dome was of concrete. The original design for New Delhi closely followed (technically, if not formally) Wren's model of two hemispheres separated by a cone to carry the load of the outer dome to the piers below. All three shells were to be brick; concrete was unavailable because of the war. The inner dome was to be plastered; the outer dome was to be covered with copper plates (see figure 4.21). The dome as built differs from the original design for two reasons. First, when construction was resumed after the war, concrete was more readily available, and the inner dome was changed to concrete. J. L. Sayle, the supervising engineer, suggested that the second shell (the brick cone) be omitted and replaced by a concrete floor at the top of the inner dome, and that the sides of the outer dome be slanted inward below the roof line. Omitting the second shell would save money and allow work to proceed on the finishing of the interior, since much less centering (formwork) would be required.

Much has been written about the "Delhi Order" of the front colonnade of the Viceroy's House and its mixture of Western and Eastern elements. There are Indian elements (the *chigi* or cornice; the railings); however, the columns may not be Indian at all, but rather Lutyens's abstraction of the standard Corinthian order. They may be superficially "Indian" in appearance, but Lutyens's subsequent use of these columns in entirely different contexts (Campion Hall at Oxford in 1934 and Middleton Park in 1935) contradicts this interpretation. Lutyens was not so exotic as to use an Indian element at Oxford, and he was not so lazy as to reuse the order out of reluctance to design another one.

If Lutyens's interest in transformations is considered, particularly his proportional distortion of the Classical elements, the Delhi order is a unique case. First it should be noted that there are actually at least three orders, each of which corresponds to one of the Classical orders. The order of the entry portico is based on the Corinthian. It is flanked by smaller columns in a fairly straightforward Doric order, although both use the same entablature. In the west garden loggia is a smaller Corinthian order. In the interior, in addition to the Corinthian of Durbar Hall, there is the Ionic order of the state dining room, which is transformed in a manner similar to the Corinthian of the front facade. Lutyens takes some of the usual liberties with the standard proportions. The Doric and Corinthian columns of the front facade share an entablature of 2 column diameters; however, in contrast with almost all of Lutyens's previous uses of the orders, the exterior columns have the correct ratio of height to width. The Corinthian columns are 10 diameters high, as Vignola specifies, whereas the unmodified Doric are $7\frac{1}{2}$ diameters high (rather than the usual 8) and the Corinthian of the west garden loggia are $9\frac{1}{2}$ diameters high (as specified by Vitruvius and Palladio). The reasons for this are obvious: As long as the form of the column remained inviolate, it was acceptable to alter the proportions. When the ornament of the form itself began to be transformed, Lutyens felt obliged to maintain the correct ratios. This practice is continued in the interior of the building, where the Ionic orders of the state dining room are 9 diameters high, with an entablature of $1\frac{3}{4}$ diameters. Again, when Lutyens modified the design of the order he maintained the correct proportion.

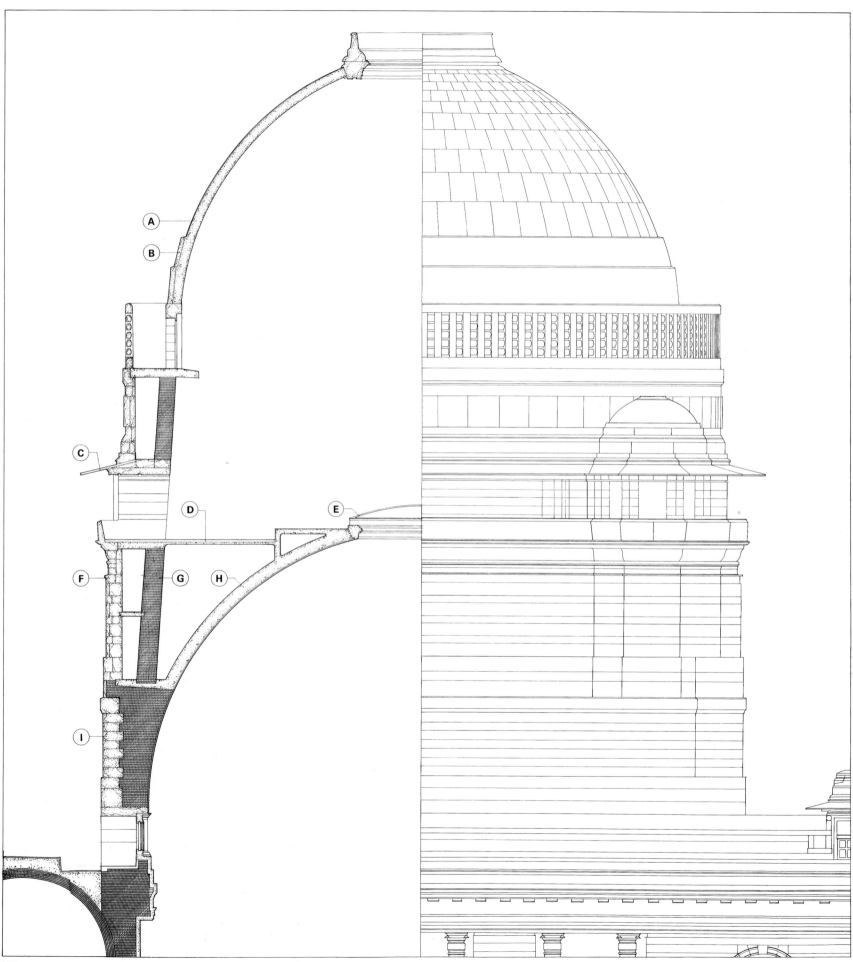

4.23

Viceroy's House

Edwin Lutyens

New Delhi, 1929

4.23   dome section

A   Copper plates on concrete dome.

B   Stone facing of buff Dholpur sandstone on concrete.

C   Stone chujja. (an element taken from traditional Mogul architecture). This is an example of the use of stone in tension, of which Lutyens was so critical in his letters.

D   Concrete diaphragm. (See figure 4.22.)

E   Skylight.

F   Drum wall of brick faced with Red Dholpur sandstone. The sandstone's color changes to buff at the chujja.

G   Brick cone. (See figure 4.22.)

H   Concrete dome faced with plaster. Although Lutyens used false vaults and domes (i.e. suspended plaster) elsewhere, he did not do so here.

I   Solid masonry wall. Since this receives the weight and the lateral thrust of both domes, it is the most massive section.

(Butler, *The Lutyens Memorial,* volume II, plates XLVI and XLVII.)

Lutyens's contact with Indian architecture reinforced his turn toward Classicism, but this reaffirmation or affirmation of the superiority of Western tradition included a reaffirmation of the Western tradition of monolithic building. His ideas on construction were to change rapidly when he returned to London to do buildings of comparable size with steel framing.

THE WAR MEMORIALS

As is true of many artists, particularly British artists, Lutyens's work was not the same after 1914 as it had been before. Lutyens was not touched directly by the war, and the endless succession of war memorials, cemeteries, and monuments he designed in its aftermath do not seem to have made him more cynical, depressed, or idealistic than before—in fact, he was probably more affected by his visits to India, where he had struggled with the client and with himself over the appropriate style for British buildings in India and where he had argued the virtues of Classicism before a hostile audience. But whatever the reason, Lutyens's work became increasingly Classical after the Great War, although it was his own personal Classicism, originating with his work at Heathcote. This was more a trend than a deliberate change. He continued to design picturesque houses (Plumpton Place, 1928; Halnaker Park, 1936), but his prominent style became a highly abstracted Classicism. Herbert Baker spoke of Lutyens's "fascination with the intellectual allurement of geometry and the grand manner."[15] It is important to remember that while Lutyen's Classicism was unacceptable to Modernists, his abstraction was unacceptable to many Classicists.

In 1925 Lutyens completed a monument to the missing of the Battle of the Somme at Thiepval, France. It was, like his London Cenotaph, more an object than a building. It was more complex than the Cenotaph, since it had to provide enough surface area for the 70,000 names. Gradidge and Summerson have shown how this form originates in a triumphal arch expanded along its axis, and how the building ascends in a series of arches which multiply themselves, each parallel row of arches supporting a larger row perpendicular to it. The Thiepval monument incorporates many of the same techniques of abstract Classicism that were used in the Cenotaph, but it also introduces some new ones.

Whereas the Cenotaph was designed by simplifying a Classical form to its most abstract shape, the Thiepval monument is really two objects—one Classical, one abstract—which interpenetrate each other to create what Colin Rowe would call a phenomenal transparency. From a distance the monument appears to be abstract, with few moldings or ornaments. As one comes closer, and particularly as one enters the monument, more and more moldings and trim are visible. The flat limestone band becomes an elaborate cornice upon turning the corner into an interior passage. The arrangement of moldings is not arbitrary. If the base molding, the wall, and the architrave are examined together, they form the typical elements of the Tuscan order; only the columns are missing. The contradiction and the resulting tension between the literal and the abstract portions of the trim continue throughout the other details.

Many of Lutyens's characteristic devices for manipulating perceptions of mass and scale, used at Heathcote and in the Cenotaph, are repeated in the Thiepval monument. The sides of the building taper slightly. The base is ornamented while the cornice is not, and where an entablature is used it is held well below the parapet. The entablature at Thiepval is a string course which, in either abstract or literal form, never becomes a cornice. The general effect again is both to lower the visual center of gravity (and thus increase the perception of stability) and to eliminate the major scale-rendering elements at the top of the building (and thus increase its apparent height).

At Thiepval, Lutyens began to experiment with articulating the nonstructural nature of the Classical elements by flattening the Classical facade by pulling back projections to the face of the wall and thus making the elements appear to be carved out rather than added on. This is most noticeable at the base, where the Portland stone band containing the names is pulled forward to the face of

4.24

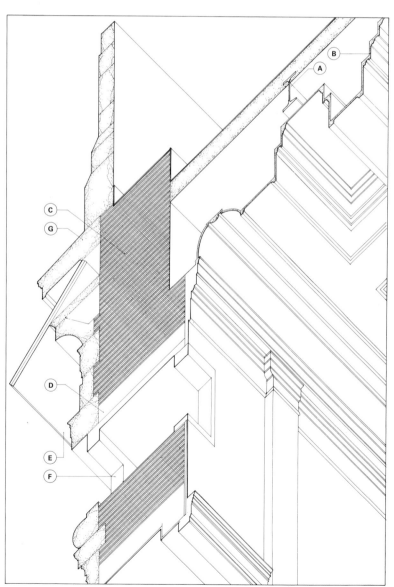

4.25

Viceroy's House

Edwin Lutyens

New Delhi, 1929

4.24 **library**
(Country Life.)

4.25 **wall section at South State Drawing Room**

A Steel beam supporting concrete roof deck.

B Coffered plaster ceiling. Here the coffers, unlike those in the library, have no relation to the steel structure above.

C Brick load-bearing wall.

D Brick or concrete lintel.

E Sandstone chujja.

F Ventilation opening.

G Buff Dholpur sandstone and brick wall.

(Butler, *The Lutyens Memorial*, volume II, plate LV.)

4.26

Viceroy's House

Edwin Lutyens

New Delhi, 1929

4.26 **North State Drawing Room**
(Country Life.)

4.27 **wall section at North State Drawing Room**
- A Steel beam supporting concrete deck and ceiling.
- B Concrete roof deck.
- C Concrete on steel beams supporting concrete roof. The roof is covered with asphalt and stone slabs.
- D Metal flashing.
- E Brick load-bearing wall.
- F Brick or concrete lintel.
  (RIBA Drawings Collection.)

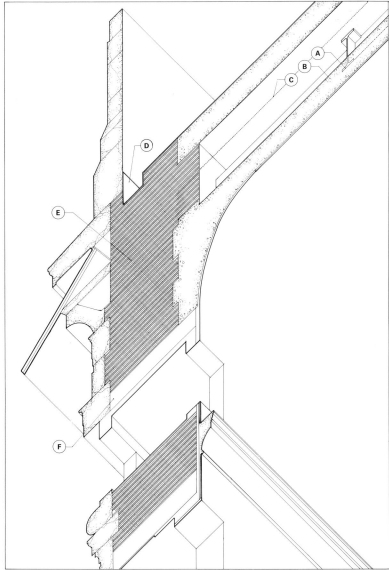

4.27

4.28

4.30

4.29

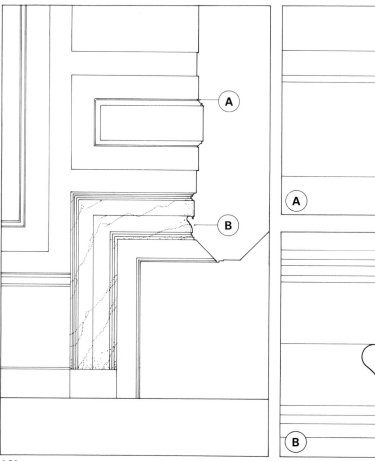

4.31

Viceroy's House
Edwin Lutyens
New Delhi, 1929

4.28 **fireplace in private dining room**
(Country Life.)

4.29 **fireplace in guest's bedroom**
A Head/Mantel.
  1 Curved mirror attached with brass screws.
  2 Gray marble.
  3 White marble.
B Jamb. Lutyens's moldings are inverted from normal practice; they slope away from rather than toward the fireplace opening. This device is not unknown in Georgian buildings, but Lutyens made it particularly his own.
(Butler, The Lutyens Memorial, volume II, plate LXXIII.)

4.30 **Cenotaph**
E. Lutyens, London.

4.31 **Bank of Montreal**
McKim, Mead & White
fireplace detail.
A Head/Mantel of marble with plaster above.
B Jamb. Compare the principal molding around the fireplace with figure 4.29.
(New York Historical Society.)

4.32 **Cantilevered stone in Indian construction**
(After Edwin Lutyens to Emily Lutyens, June 4, 1912.)

4.33 **Telescoping cornice**
(After E. Lutyens to H. Baker, Feb. 1, 1910.)

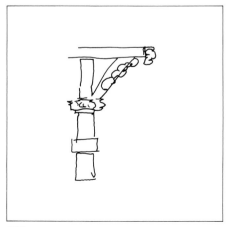

4.32

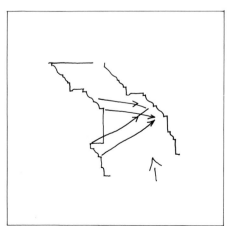

4.33

the torus below, thus negating the base's visual role of bringing the mass of the building to the ground. This effect is accentuated by the use of brick or visually "soft" material for the base, where logic would demand the heavier Portland stone. This strategy of enhancing the symbolic function of ornaments and denying their structural function by reducing them to two dimensions was used before by Otto Wagner and after by Robert Venturi, but Lutyens did not flatten these elements; he only recessed them. He never allowed this operation to destroy the sculptural quality of an element.

The quality of the Thiepval monument is just as much a result of the Classical elements that were retained as it is of those that were eliminated. One of the chief virtues of ornament is to give scale, and the chief means of doing so is to multiply ornaments as their size increases. Just as White multiplied the modillions of the cornice of the Gorham Building, so Lutyens multiplied some of the ornamentation at Thiepval. The smallest of the architrave moldings is the correct one for the Tuscan order. When this is applied to a larger arch, it is not enlarged but multiplied. The concave moldings are expanded by combining them with convex (or at least partially convex) ones; for example, the cavetto of the small arch is combined with a cyma recta. The moldings are always separated by a rectilinear shape or a fillet mold, and they are never the same size, so no one molding is dominant. Since we know the size of the smallest architrave (the one closest to us), we can judge the size of the higher architrave by recognizing the same element, at the same size above, at the largest area where it is farthest away; its extent is called out by a band of bead and reel. As the size of each architrave increases, one would expect its projection to increase, thus increasing its shadow. But Lutyens did not want so large a projection at the top of the building, so—as he did at the base—he recessed the projecting elements to form a single plane. A molding was necessary to make this transition; Lutyens used the familiar projecting knife-edged ovolo. This is a very un-Classical element. It breaks all the rules by its harsh profile and by curving in the wrong direction. Seldom found in Classical building, it is found somewhere in almost every one of Lutyens's buildings.

The scale-rendering quality of the architrave moldings of the Thiepval monument are in direct contrast to the absence or confusion of scale created by the lowered and sometimes eliminated entablature. However, the result is not contradiction but tension, and this is the essence of the monument: tension between the abstract and the literal, between the elements that establish the visual stability of the building and those that undermine it, and between the elements that establish scale and those that deny it.

THE MIDLAND BANK
Lutyens's commission to collaborate in the design of the Midland Bank (in London's Financial District) called for him to design only the exteriors and the major public spaces. Since the technology of building was changing (steel columns and complete steel frames were now commonplace), the language Lutyens had developed in the context of load-bearing wall construction at Heathcote, New Delhi, and Thiepval could not be applied here with any claim to traditional "rationality." In addition, Lutyens was not free to manipulate interior space in relation to the elevations, so there is no correspondence between the size and type of openings and the rooms beyond. Lutyens's solution, for the most part, was to ignore both of these problems.

The wall details of the Midland Bank recall the transformations Lutyens made in his country houses. The "phantom columns" used at Heathcote reappear in the ground floor of the Midland Bank (figure 4.36). The base and capital of a Doric column are interlocked with the rusticated wall of the building so that there is a transparency between wall and colonnade. Butler has described how Lutyens thickened these columns beyond the normal Palladian proportions to make the building appear more massive at the base. While these columns have a full entablature, the building itself has no cornice, recalling the detail used at Ednaston Manor. This tendency to increase the mass of the building at the base while decreasing

4.34

4.35

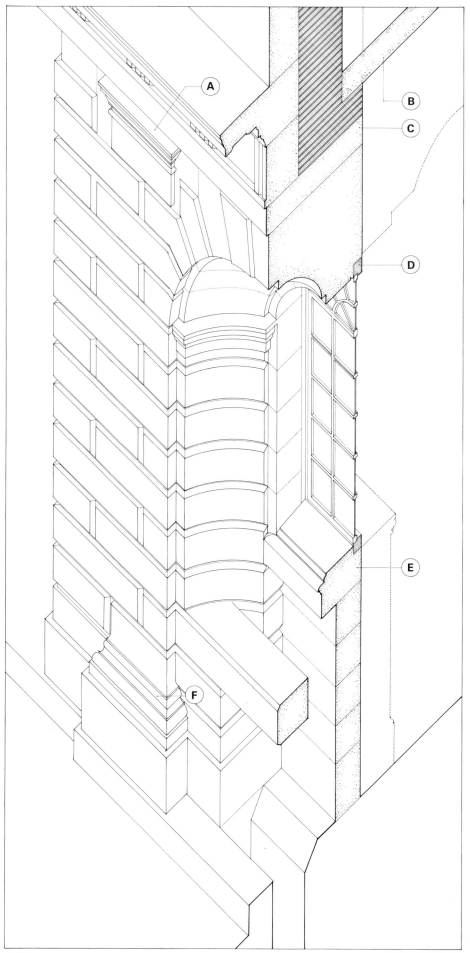

4.36

Midland Bank

Edwin Lutyens

London, 1924–1939

4.34   **exterior facade**

4.35   **detail**

4.36   **wall section at base**

A   Doric capital. Lutyens reduced the height and projection of the capital from what it normally would have been. This is an example of his practice of telescoping or reducing and combining of details at the top of a building.

B   Floor structure. The building has a complete steel frame with floors of composite concrete and steel.

C   Brick wall faced with Portland stone. Each stone course is $\frac{1}{8}''$ smaller than the one below (a device also used by McKim and White).

D   Wood window.

E   Portland stone sill.

F   Doric base. The base and the capital form an implied Doric column that is $7\frac{1}{2}$ rather than 8 column diameters high, making the column appear more massive.
(Butler, *The Lutyens Memorial, volume III*, plates XXXIV and XXXV.)

both mass and detail at the top is reinforced by a number of other transformations. The wall, in addition to its numerous setbacks, is tapered so that it slopes away from the street. The vertical stone courses, which appear to be of uniform height, are reduced by $\frac{1}{8}$ inch at each course (as McKim had done in the Bank of Montreal and elsewhere). The effect of all these moves is to assert the mass and stability of the wall at grade and to deny the scale of the building at the top—precisely the opposite of the effect intended by Stanford White in the Gorham Building.

Opinions of the result vary widely. Butler and Hussey, the authors of the official biography and memorial volumes, thought the Midland Bank to be one of Lutyens's finest works. Modernists considered it to be an example of all that was wrong with traditional architecture: a steel-frame building hidden by what appears to be a load-bearing building. Contemporary admirers of Lutyens's work, such as Gradidge, considered the Midland Bank to be well below the quality of his other buildings.

Although Lutyens would not change his forms to fit the new technology, he would change his ideas to accommodate his forms. In India he had criticized the Taj for its use of veneers and for not making structure and finish one, and in reaction had built the Viceroy's House in the monolithic style of Western Classicism. But by 1932 Lutyens was arguing that traditional Classical construction was not monolithic but veneered: "The prototype of the steel framed building is to be found at Bath and other places as well, where the timber frames of terraced houses—greatly admired—are hung with mechanical slabs of stone to represent ashlar."[16] Lutyens was arguing, with some justification, that if his buildings concealed their true structure, so did most modern buildings: "Many of the so-called modern concrete buildings are of brick and plaster, and in appearance are as much in fancy dress as when clothed in traditional costumes."[17]

MIDDLETON PARK
After 1914, the great days of the English country house were over, and Lutyens had far fewer house commissions. He was preoccupied with larger projects, such as New Delhi and the Liverpool Cathedral, and with a few exceptions the plans and elevations of his late houses lack the cleverness and originality of his earlier houses. However, this is not true of the details, for the simple reason that Lutyens began to apply the techniques he had developed for larger buildings to these houses.

Middleton Park, on which Lutyens's son Robert collaborated, was finished in 1935. The plan and the general outlines are, at best, restatements of old themes. The closer one approaches this building, however, the more one sees. Regardless of the quality of the whole, one can find here, within the height of one section, all of the transformations Lutyens had developed for the Thiepval monument and the Midland Bank.

The most noticeable transformation here is planar recession, particularly in the west front. It is used here, as in the Midland Bank, to achieve interpenetration of the literal Classical element and the abstract geometrical element. The plane of reference is defined by the rubble faces of the outside portion of the wall (figures 4.38, 4.39). The only portions that project in front of this plane are the base and the capitals of the phantom columns (which are similar to those of Heathcote and the Midland Bank) and the entablature above. As in the larger buildings, and in contrast with the earlier houses, the wall is given a 3-inch batter (slope). A center section is recessed 3 inches, its edges forming one side of the phantom columns, so that the bottom of the recess is in the same vertical plane as the top of the projecting wall. The lower part of the recess is filled with a stone surround with alternating molded and unmolded quoins. As he did at Marshcourt, Lutyens recesses the moldings into the form, so that they appear to be cut out of a solid stone. The face of this projecting surround aligns with the reference plane at the bottom. But the surround is vertical and the wall is not; thus, as the wall rises, the projection increases. As at Thiepval, an abstract building seems to have absorbed a Neoclassical one.

4.37

4.38

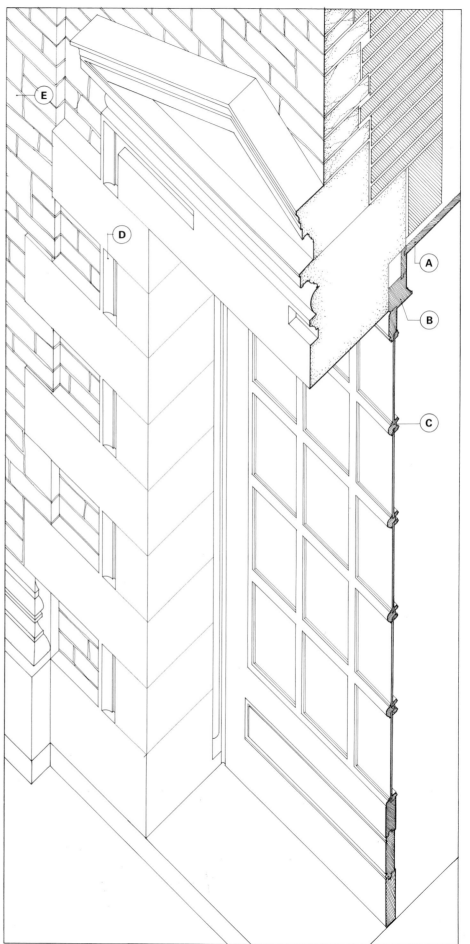

4.39

Middleton Park

Edwin Lutyens
Bicester, Oxford, 1935

4.37 **exterior facade**
(James Cox, Betty Hill.)

4.38 **door detail**
(Country Life.)

4.39 **door detail**

A   Wood paneling on typical wall
construction of stone and brick.

B   Wood door frame.

C   Typical door muntin. The glass
stops are inverted here in a manner
reminiscent of Wright in that they
project rather than recede.

D   Door molding. Although this is
flush with the wall face at the base,
the door frame remains perfectly
vertical while the walls are battered
so that its projection increases as
the wall rises.

E   Column base. Lutyens again uses
the "phantom" column defined
only by a capital base. The rough
stone work is Clipsham stone from
Rutland.
(Butler, *The Lutyens Memorial*, volume I,
plate LXXXIX.)

The door is a product of inversion. Its basic type is that of Ednaston Manor, but here the frame is recessed into niches in the wall. In his brick buildings, Lutyens emphasized the contrast of the white frame and the brick by exposing as much of the sash width as possible; in his stone buildings, he minimized this contrast of color of materials in order to emphasize the contrast of solid and void.

CONCLUSION

Charles McKim and Stanford White were twenty years older than Edwin Lutyens, but their careers and his were parallel in many ways. All began their practices designing picturesque country houses. All, in mid-career, switched to a predominantly Classical style of design. All were faced in the course of their long careers with adapting a style based on load-bearing masonry construction to the realities of steel-frame construction. The principal difference is in the length of their careers. McKim died in 1910 and White in 1906; Lutyens lived through the heyday of the International Style, dying in 1944.

McKim and White responded more positively to the changes in technology than Lutyens, who never completely reconciled himself to it. But then Lutyens had to deal with more than just the new technology; he also had to deal with Modernists' criticism of his failure to "express" that technology. Perhaps if his career had been different—if he had built his first large buildings in London instead of New Delhi, or if he had been forced to design large office buildings with steel frames earlier in his career—he might have responded to the new building as did Wagner or Perret, but this is doubtful. Lutyens was interested in the nature of construction. His early houses are just as "honest" as Webb's, and more so than Shaw's. He certainly was interested in the nature of construction in India, where he saw New Delhi as a demonstration of the quality of European building and craft. And, in his own way, he was interested in construction when he worked on the Midland Bank—but his interest was in the *language* of construction, not the reality.

In his later writings, Lutyens speaks repeatedly of the "grammar" of an architecture style, and of style as synonymous with the craft tradition. Once established, an architectural style became a language, with its own grammar. Whether or not style and grammar in architecture are the results of the traditions of craft and materials (an unusual statement from one who was supposed to be a Classicist), and whether or not Lutyens really believed this, there is no doubt that the concept of language was essential to Lutyens's architecture.

Although Lutyens was willing to use different traditional languages of architecture simultaneously, he was less willing to combine the traditional languages with the modern or to transform the latter into the former. He wrote in 1931 that "the most unhappy productions of [Modern architecture] are to be found where an architect has tried to combine Traditionalism and Modernism."[18] Lutyens, White, and McKim saw rational building as the tradition of Classicism; Pugin and Cram saw it as the tradition of Gothic architecture. But a third group, perhaps the most important of the three, saw rational building as the language of vernacular tradition.

5 The Arts and Crafts Movement: The Greene Brothers and Their English Contemporaries

So she went in and the draught from inside slammed the door behind. Desolation greeted her. Dirty finger prints were on the hall-windows, flue and rubbish on its unwashed boards. . . . Dining-Room and Drawing-Room—right and left—were guessed only by their wall-papers. They were just rooms where one could shelter from the rain. Across the ceiling of each ran a great beam. The Dining-Room and Hall revealed theirs openly, but the drawings-room's was match-boarded—because the facts of life must be concealed from ladies?

E. M. Forster, *Howard's End*

John Ruskin did not like the world he lived in. He did not like the machine; he did not like cities; he did not like Victorian architecture or Victorian architects. He hated the Crystal Palace and the steam engine. In 1878 he admitted to his friends that he was going insane. Obsessed with the quality of the air in Britain, he was convinced that he was being poisoned by factory exhaust. It is prophetic that a man so alienated from his world should have had such an influence on modern building. Ruskin's influence was probably greater than that of Laugier, Choisy, or Guadet, and honesty in building and truth to materials are concepts that are owed to him.

If Ruskin is forgotten, or at least not well remembered, it is because his ideas came to Modernism indirectly through the Arts and Crafts movement. That movement is associated most strongly with William Morris, but its primary architectural works and ideas came from his associates: Philip Webb, William Lethaby, and others. The chief American advocate of Arts and Crafts was the essayist and furniture maker Gustav Stickley, but the greatest architectural achievements of the American movement were the houses built in California by Charles and Henry Greene between 1900 and 1914.

Many have questioned whether the Greene brothers' dedication to the Arts and Crafts ideal was not superficial. But to understand the Greene brothers, one must first understand Ruskin. His published works run to forty volumes, but his enduring architectural ideas are contained in two short works. The first is "The Lamp of Truth," from *The Seven Lamps of Architecture*, in which he wrote:

. . . Architectural Deceits are broadly to be considered under three heads:

1st. The suggestion of a mode of structure or support, other than the true one; as the pendants in late Gothic roofs.

2nd. The painting of surfaces to represent some other material than that of which they actually consist (as in the marbling of wood) or the deceptive representation of sculptured ornament upon them.

3rd. The use of cast or machine-made ornaments of any kind.[1]

5.1

5.2

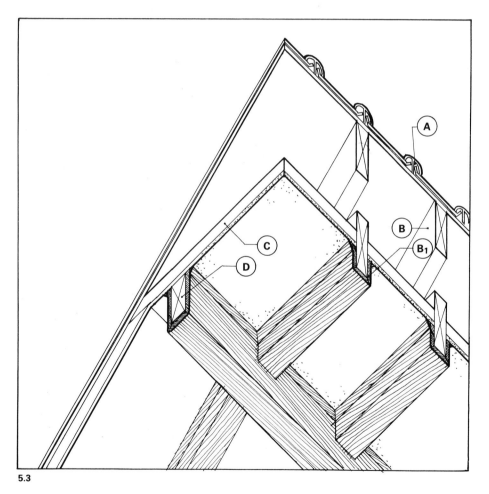

5.3

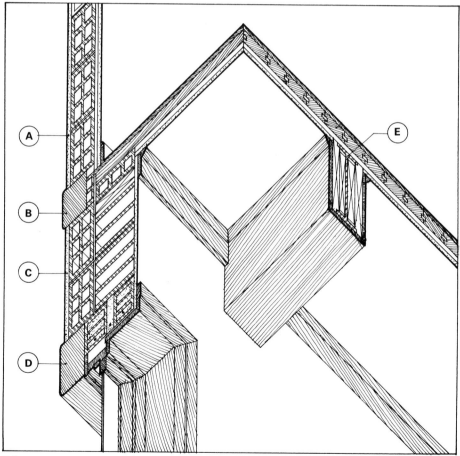

5.4

Stickley house

Gustav Stickley

Morris Plains, New Jersey, 1908

5.1   exterior
(The Craftsman.)

5.2   interior
(The Craftsman.)

5.3   roof detail
(Final construction may have
differed from published drawings.)

A   Roman tiles, 15″ on center, on
roofing felt and sheathing. The felt
intercepts any water that penetrates
the joints of the tiles.

B   3 × 8 wood rafters spaced at 24″
on center.

B1   4 × 8 purlin with finish wood
sheathing.

C   Ceiling construction: 2″ × 12″ × 20″
porous ceiling book tiles covered
with plaster on metal lath. Stickley
felt that the tiles acted as
insulation.
(The Craftsman, October, 1908, p. 78.)

5.4   wall details
A   Pebble dash finish on exterior.
Inner wall is of structural clay tile.

B   6 × 8 chestnut timber squared on
three sides. Stickley said that these
were not ornamental but were part
of the actual construction.

C   Reinforced concrete lintel. Over
openings the voids in the tile are
filled with concrete and reinforcing
bars.

D   6 × 12 chestnut timber squared on
three sides.

E   Main girder: steel I section with
2 × 14 wood blocking and finish-
wood casing.
(The Craftsman, October 1908, p. 78.)

Ruskin is quick to qualify each of these rules. For example, he points out that truth in structure does not necessarily require exposure of structure: "The architect is not *bound* to exhibit structure; nor are we to complain of him for concealing it, any more than we should regret that the outer surfaces of the human frame conceal much of its anatomy. . . ."[2] He also notes that the prohibition of deceit in cladding does not mean that it is unacceptable to cover one material with another. The important thing, he claimed, is not to deceive. Gilding of buildings was acceptable, gilding of jewelry was not. Ruskin's architectural preference was for what he called the "incrusted style" (represented by St. Mark's in Venice, where brick walls are clad in marble).

It is a measure of Ruskin's naiveté or of our cynicism that what was obvious to him is strange to us: that a good building could only be produced by good men in a good society. Gothic architecture and Gothic society were the model. Ruskin loved the variety of Gothic ornament, partly for its own sake and partly because it was the work of craftsmen:

Wherever the workman is utterly enslaved, the parts of the building must of course be absolutely like each other; for the perfection of his execution can only be reached by exercising him in doing one thing, and giving him nothing else to do. . . . Only do not let us suppose that love of order is love of art. It is true that order, in its highest sense, is one of the necessities of art, just as time is a necessity of music; but love of order has no more to do with our right enjoyment of architecture or painting, than love of punctuality with the appreciation of an opera.[3]

The implications of this idea went well beyond ornament. The love of rudeness and the hatred of perfection led to a revolution in ideas regarding joinery and finish. Ruskin wrote:

I shall perhaps press this law farther elsewhere, but our immediate concern is . . . never to demand an exact finish, when it does not lead to a noble end. . . . The rule is simple: Always look for invention first, and after that, for such execution as will help the invention, and as the inventor is capable of without painful effort, and no more. *Above all, demand no refinement of execution where there is no thought, for that is slaves' work, unredeemed. Rather choose rough work than smooth work, so only that the practical purpose be answered, and never imagine there is reason to be proud of anything that may be accomplished by patience and sand-paper.*[4]

William Morris was not an architect, or even an architectural critic. The primary historian and critic of the Arts and Crafts group was William Lethaby, but the clearest expression of the ideas the group held in common is found in his writings on the work of Morris's collaborator Philip Webb. "Modern Architecture, if we ever have any, will be mastership in building craft developed out of contact with needs and materials," wrote Lethaby.[5] This summarized the four principal ideas of the Arts and Crafts architects: the importance of learning and respecting traditional crafts, the correct relationship of design to materials, the relationship of buildings to their sites, and the reverence for vernacular architecture and its building techniques.

"Architecture is building traditionally," wrote Lethaby. "There can be no arts of the old kind until by some means folk traditions are once more regained so that builders and employers accept the natural expression of the moment. . . ."[6] Along with the reverence for traditional methods, particularly vernacular ones, went a reverence for vernacular forms. Lethaby again: "All style imitation is trivial and futile. . . . The spirit and essence of such designs in the styles has nothing whatever in common with the natural work of old buildings."[7] The perception of vernacular building as the pure expression of building became a key legacy of the Arts and Crafts movement to Modernism, and the same idea was expressed again by Walter Gropius, Le Corbusier, Marcel Breuer, and others. Furthermore, wrote Lethaby, local materials must be used in the right way: "We owe it to England and the landscape to build in a reverent way with suitable materials. Materials must be

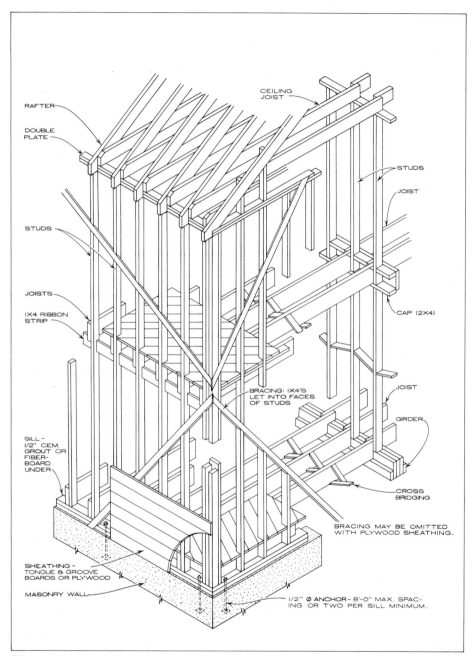

RAFTER

DOUBLE
PLATE

STUDS

JOISTS

IX4 RIBBON
STRIP

CEILING
JOIST

STUDS

JOIST

CAP (2X4)

BRACING: IX4'S
LET INTO FACES
OF STUDS

JOIST

GIRDER

SILL -
1/2" CEM.
GROUT OR
FIBER-
BOARD
UNDER

CROSS
BRIDGING

BRACING MAY BE OMITTED
WITH PLYWOOD SHEATHING.

SHEATHING -
TONGUE & GROOVE
BOARDS OR PLYWOOD

MASONRY WALL

1/2" Ø ANCHOR- 8'-O" MAX. SPAC-
ING OR TWO PER SILL MINIMUM.

5.5

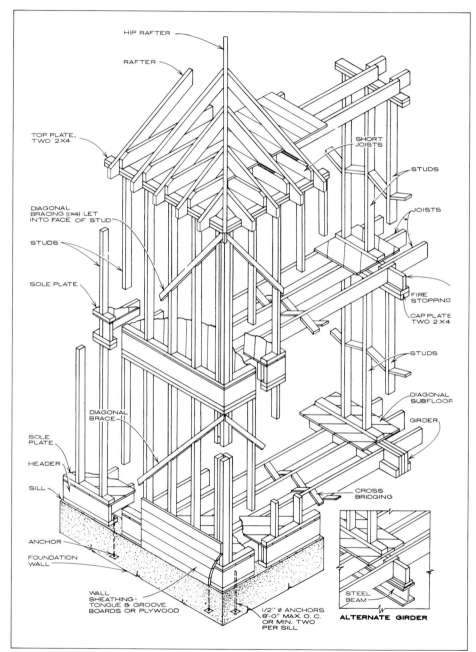

HIP RAFTER

RAFTER

TOP PLATE,
TWO 2X4

SHORT
JOISTS

STUDS

DIAGONAL
BRACING (IX4) LET
INTO FACE OF STUD

STUDS

JOISTS

SOLE PLATE

FIRE
STOPPING

CAP PLATE
TWO 2X4

STUDS

DIAGONAL
SUBFLOOR

DIAGONAL
BRACE

GIRDER

SOLE
PLATE

HEADER

SILL

CROSS
BRIDGING

ANCHOR

FOUNDATION
WALL

WALL
SHEATHING -
TONGUE & GROOVE
BOARDS OR PLYWOOD

1/2" Ø ANCHORS
8'-O" MAX. O. C.
OR MIN. TWO
PER SILL

STEEL
BEAM

ALTERNATE GIRDER

5.6

used so as to express their essential qualities; these essential qualities are what rhythm is to poetry. This applies as well to decoration as to structure."[8] Webb echoed this sentiment: ". . . the gist of all decorative design is the hand and glove fitness for the material reception."[9] But what an architect like Frank Lloyd Wright meant by truth to materials is not the same as what Lethaby and Webb meant. The Arts and Crafts architects were concerned with the appropriateness of ornament to the material to receive it, and with the use of techniques that would emphasize the natural qualities of materials, such as the grain of wood. This idea that form was inherent in the nature of materials is the result of the influence of Japan, and of Wright's reinterpretation of the Arts and Crafts ideas.

The Greene brothers have received as much criticism as adulation. The criticism has been that their understanding of the principles of the Arts and Crafts movement was superficial and that their work is "dishonest," consisting of imagery without substance. R. J. Clark has pointed out that many of their exposed clamps, pegs, and wedges are structurally unnecessary and were added to the buildings after completion, and that many of their exposed ebony pegs either hide screws or are unnecessary. Reyner Banham has used the Greenes as an example of what he believes is the American tendency to strip architectural forms of the ideas that support them: ". . . European art movements lose their moral content and become forms of styling when they arrive on U.S. soil. If the Gamble House is one of the gems of the Craftsman Movement in California, it is also—in part—a paste jewel. Look into the roof spaces and you will find the construction that isn't seen, far from being carefully and lovingly wrought, tends to be the usual old U.S. carpenter's crude work, trued up with odds and ends of lumber and spliced together with cockeyed six inch nails."[10]

The criticism of the Greene brothers has centered around the degree to which their beams are not really beams and their fasteners are not really fasteners, and around other "dishonest" elements in their work. The critics, perhaps without realizing it, have aligned themselves with Pugin in the belief that the rational and the monolithic are synonymous and that, in good building ornament, structure and finish are integral with each other in a single material. Before critically examining this doctrine, one must ask whether it is a doctrine of the Arts and Crafts movement.

Banham's view is that in true Arts and Crafts building the level of craftsmanship is uniformly high. Many, but not all, of the writers and designers of the Arts and Crafts movement would have concurred in principle. Their models of ideal wood buildings were vernacular ones: the Japanese house, the Swiss chalet, or the old English house or barn. All of these had few finish materials, monolithic construction, and a uniform (if not always high) level of craftsmanship.

Christopher Dresser, an associate of William Morris, said of the Japanese house that "every part of the edifice, whether seen or unseen, manifests an amount of honest workmanship which in its finish is simply perfect; and in no part of the building can we find slovenly work, however small or perfectly concealed that part may be. . . . No one can have failed to notice that all good Japanese works . . . are as well finished in the parts that are seen as in the parts are not seen." This practice, he asserts, is a result of the Shinto attitude toward materials: "Here we have the very essence of Shinto, and an embodiment in spirit of that passage in our own scriptures: 'Whatsoever thy hand findeth to do, do it with thy might.'"[11]

The Japanese house, like the traditional English house, had a traditional handmade wood frame, made using the local equivalents of the pit saw, the draw plane, and the mortise-and-tenon joint. Like the traditional English frame, it was not easily adapted to modern conditions in America. It required large timbers and handcrafted joints, and in the modern world it was grossly expensive in comparison with the platform frame. The closest thing to such a frame that can be found in the works of the Arts and Crafts movement exists in the buildings designed by Ernest Gimson at the turn of the century. After being trained and apprenticed as an architect in London, Gimson moved to the Cotswolds to study local craft traditions such as chair caning and wheelwrighting. He is remembered today for his furniture designs,

5.7

5.8

Standen

Phillip Webb

East Grinstead, Sussex, 1896

5.7 **exterior**

5.8 **detail**

Within this small area of the elevation there are four different types of windows and sets of details.

5.9 **beam detail**

A Plaster ceiling.

B Wood joists.

C Wood.

D Steel I section.

E Finish-wood casing around steel beam.

(RIBA Drawings Collection, drawing V21[42].32.)

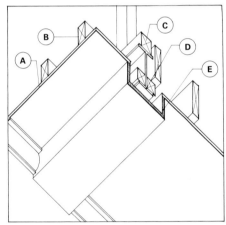

5.9

but he also built several cottages, a church, and a library. The typical American wood-frame house of the late nineteenth century had a balloon or platform frame, built from small pieces of lumber which were milled in a factory and connected with nails at the site. In Britain, where lumber was less plentiful, houses tended to have masonry walls and roofs and floors of milled lumber. This was in sharp contrast with the pre-1850 timber frame, which, like the Japanese frame, was made up of a small number of large hand-cut timbers connected with elaborate pegged joints. The frames of Gimson's buildings were attempts to reestablish the preindustrial wood frame in form and in process of construction.

The best known of Gimson's buildings is Stoneywell Cottage, finished in 1899. It was built of local materials—fieldstone, English oak, and thatch—by local craftsmen using local vernacular forms and techniques. Despite having been completed 70 years after the development of the balloon frame, it is an excellent example of the preindustrial wood frame. The major timbers were first cut from logs by hand—a time-consuming process requiring two men. The saw marks were then cut off with a plane or an adze, also a lengthy process. Connections were made primarily with mortise-and-tenon joints, a process that was not only time-consuming but required a great deal of skill. The principal problem in the traditional wood structure was finding suitable timbers of sufficient size. All lumber contains numerous defects—knots, checks, shakes, etc.—and the larger the piece of wood one desires, the more difficult it is to find one free of defects. Gimson compensated for this somewhat by accepting crooked and bowed timbers and using the gentle curves to create shallow arches and other effects. The structure of the first floor is composed of closely spaced 6 × 6 beams covered with a deck of boards. The beams are supported by solid masonry walls at the perimeter and major beams (some as large as 18 × 18) on the interior. The timber is local English oak, cut by local craftsmen using a hand saw and smoothed with an adze and a plane (the marks of which are visible on the large beams). One might say that the idea of the traditional wood frame is to use the minimum number of pieces and the minimum number of joints, and hence the minimal amount of labor.

Sigfried Giedion and James Marston Fitch have described the impact on modern construction of the invention of the balloon frame in the 1830s. In subsequent years it has been largely replaced by its close relative, the platform frame. The platform frame (figure 5.6) uses a much greater number of structural members and joints, but these joints require much less time and skill to execute. The technical inventions that made this possible were the power-driven circular saw and the wire-cut nail. The circular saw made it possible to cut logs into a number of smaller boards (usually 2 × 4's) much more quickly than was possible with the pit saw. It was also easier to find boards free of defects, since a smaller board is less likely to contain them. More boards meant more joints, but this problem was solved by the wire-cut nail, with which joints could be made quickly, cheaply, and with little skill. Lateral bracing was achieved by diagonal boards "let" into the uprights, and also by the sheathing.

The platform frame also greatly simplified the problem of cladding. We usually associate the traditional frame with exposed construction in which the spaces between the timber are filled with brick or plaster. This system was aesthetically appealing and structurally "honest," but it was never a good system in practice. Both the frame and the infill expanded and contracted with changes in temperature and humidity, resulting in cracks and thus leakage and infiltration. Thus, the frame could sometimes be used in Britain, but never in North America, which has much greater temperature extremes. Even in medieval times these frames were often completely encased, but infilling materials were often still required, since the thin clapboards and plaster could not easily span from timber to timber. The platform frame, with its tightly spaced uprights or studs, gave much more support to interior and exterior finish materials.

To architects such as Gimson, the architectural shortcomings of the platform frame were that it was hidden by sheathing on the outside and that its crude craftsmanship made it unacceptable to expose it on the interior. Those who wished

5.10

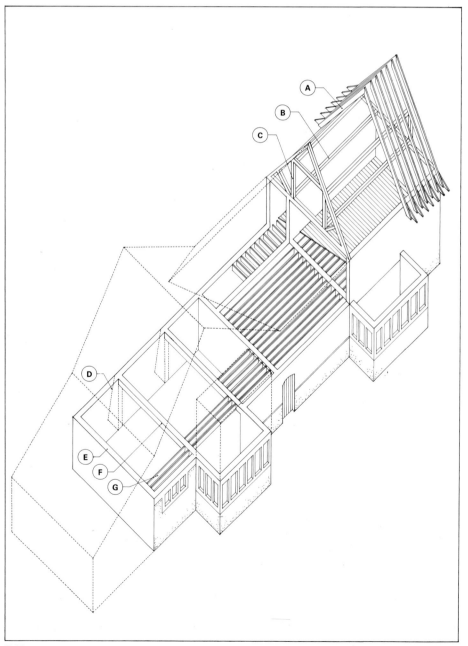

5.11

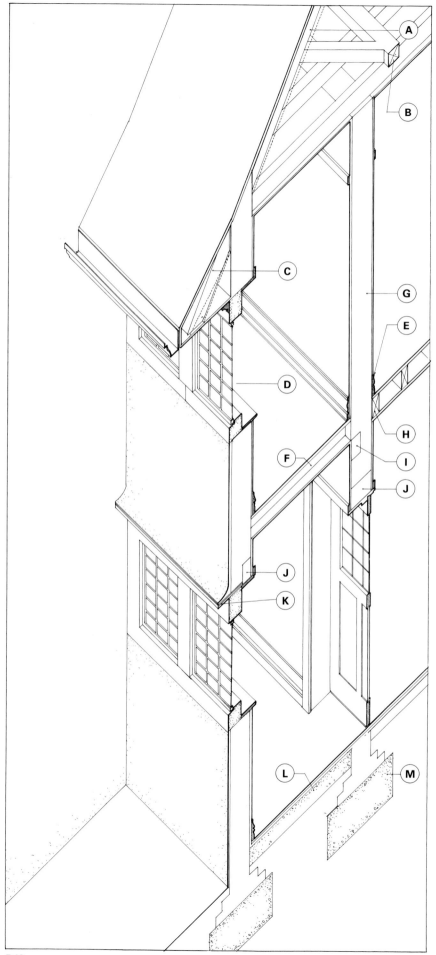

5.12

Greyfriars

Charles Voysey

Surrey, 1897

5.10 rendering

(RIBA Drawings Collection, drawing [117].3.)

5.11 framing plan

A 2 × 7½ wood rafters.

B 4 × 6 wood beams. These support the rafters and tie the trusses together.

C 4 × 4 wood queen post truss columns.

D Buttresses. Although these correspond to the locations of the major beams, they are probably not structurally necessary.

E Load-bearing masonry wall.

F Major beams. These are the only exposed structure in the house.

G Typical floor construction: 3 × 6½ joists, 14″ on center, supporting wood floor.

(RIBA Drawings Collection, drawing [117].5–8.)

5.12 wall section

A Roof construction: Slates on wood nailers on 7½″ rafters.

B 4 × 6 beam and 3 × 4 beam supporting roof rafters and ceiling joists connected by 4 × 4 wood posts.

C Like Lutyens, Voysey adds an additional 3 × 7½ to change the roof slope at the eave, giving it a more gentle pitch.

D Metal window set in stone surrounds, similar to figure 5.17.

E Wood base. See figure 5.13.

F Floor construction: 3 × 6½ beams spaced at 14″ on center.

G Masonry load-bearing wall faced with stucco and plaster.

H Floor construction: 3 × 6½ wood beams spaced at 14″ on center, in this case spanning between parallel interior walls.

I Concrete bond beam. This gives additional strength to the masonry wall at the point where it supports the floor joists.

J Concrete lintels. These support the masonry over the window opening.

K Drip over stone window surround, made from tile and stucco. This keeps water away from the joints between window and wall.

L Floor construction: 6″ concrete slab on grade supporting wood flooring on sleepers or tile on grout bed.

M Foundation: concrete pads supporting brick foundation walls.

(RIBA Drawings Collection, drawing [117] 8.)

to express the platform frame by exposing it were doomed to frustration, and the common solution was to build an ornamental or analogous frame on the exterior. H. H. Richardson overlaid clapboards with uprights and diagonals simulating an exposed timber frame; Richard Norman Shaw clad brick walls with a thin layer of boards and plaster simulating old English timberwork. This was clearly a deceit in Ruskinian terms, but the brick backup was required by fire laws in many parts of Britain. The wood frame of Gimson's Stoneywell Cottage, like those of all his buildings, has all the qualities of the Japanese or the English prototype. The structure is entirely exposed, is monolithic (with no veneers or cladding), and has a uniformly high level of craftsmanship.

Architects who had larger practices than Gimson, greater constraints of time and money, and the need for a level of craft with less "rudeness" had to pursue other alternatives. To realistically evaluate the British Arts and Crafts movement, we must examine the buildings of the more active architects of the movement, such as Charles Voysey and Philip Webb. These men were as sincere as Gimson in their own way, but they built numerous houses for varied clients, and they dealt with a more complex set of demands than Gimson, who realized only five buildings in 25 years of practice. Voysey, while perhaps not an official member of the Arts and Crafts circle, is generally perceived to be one of its adherents; Webb was one of its key architects and designers. If Banham was correct in stating that "moral content" is lost when European ideas are changed into American "styling," then we should expect to find this moral content in the work of Voysey and Webb.

Webb's Standen (1896) and Voysey's Greyfriars (1897) differ in finish and in style, but the basic structural systems are the same: load-bearing masonry walls, wood-joist floors, and some steel framing. If one accepts Ruskin's theories as the basis of the Arts and Crafts movement, if the use of structural iron is prohibited, if the concealment of one element with another with the intention of deceiving is prohibited, and if covering steel with plaster falls into the latter category, then Webb is a much worse offender than the Greenes.

Standen has a considerable amount of structural steel framing, little of which is exposed. The ground floor is framed in a series of rectilinear masonry boxes, one corresponding to each major room. The floors are framed in wood joists, spaced 14 inches apart. The joists do not span the short dimension except in the smaller rooms; more typically they are supported by pairs of steel beams, which reduce their lengths to acceptable dimensions. Webb would probably have made these girders of wood if it had been structurally and economically possible. The second floor uses a similar arrangement, with two long steel beams supporting the main ridge and with shorter beams supporting portions of the five gables of the main facade. In fact, the lineal quantity of steel in Standen equals or exceeds that in Wright's Robie House.

Whereas in Gimson's work the structure is entirely visible, at Standen it is almost entirely concealed. There is no exposed wood framing on the interior, and little on the exterior. The only exposed steel occurs in the conservatory. It is not true that the structure goes unexpressed. The bottom of each of the steel beams is lower than the ceiling, and a plaster cover encloses and marks its location (figure 5.9). On the ground floor, where beams do not extend between rooms, they are given moldings to match the walls; on the upper floors, where the beams are continuous, they are given simple rectilinear cases. The beam cases are no deeper than is necessary to cover the beam and to provide space for wood blocking and plaster, so they appear quite shallow in the rooms below. Guadet would undoubtedly dislike these plaster beam covers, since they appear too small to visually support the floor above. Ruskin would undoubtedly dislike the use of steel, but neither he nor Guadet would fault the concealment—beams are not made of plaster, and Webb's plaster is obviously cladding a true beam. Did Webb see this as a compromise of his principles? Probably not; his use of steel is much too systematic to be the result of economic or procedural necessity. And Webb was as principled as any architect of his era. He simply did not consider the exposure of structure to be mandatory.

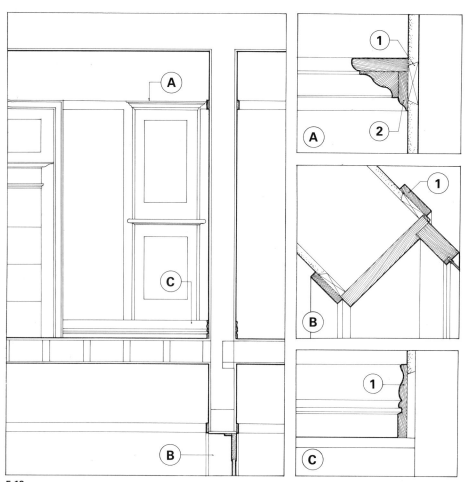

5.13

5.14

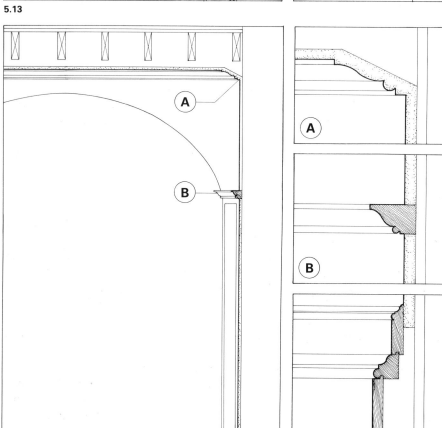

5.15

5.16

Greyfriars

Charles Voysey

Surrey, 1897

5.13 **trim details**

A Picture rail.

  1 Wood ground. This serves to give the plasterer an even surface to finish his work, and as a nailer for the molding.

  2 Wood molding. Compare the deliberately crude and awkward design of this trim with figure 3.60.

B Door jamb.

  1 Casing. Although the joints are covered with trim, no moldings are used.

C Base.

  1 Base molding. The curves of the base seem deliberately awkward. The moldings do not create transitions, and are combined without rectilinear elements to separate them.

  (RIBA Drawings Collection, drawing [117].4.)

5.14 **New Place,** Charles Voysey, Surrey, 1899, interior.

  (W. S. Sparrow, The British Home of Today.)

5.15 **Standen, interior details at drawing room**

A Crown mold. Although Classical shapes (such as the cyma recta) are used, they are combined in a unclassical way, as in Voysey's details.

B Picture rail. This profile replicates the crown mold at a smaller scale.

C Base detail. The profile of the upper molding is repeated at a smaller scale at the base. This is the traditional method of achieving relative scale by "doubling" of a profile.

  (RIBA Drawings Collection, drawing V21[42].32.)

5.16 **Standen, drawing room**

What was mandatory was respect for craftsmanship. The respect is there in Webb's work, but not in the same way as it is in Gimson's. Gimson used a monolithic exposed frame, as did the Japanese, and thus a fairly uniform level of craftsmanship. Since Webb used layered and concealed construction, the craftsmanship in his buildings varies from the very crude to the fairly precise. His crudest work is not as precise as Gimson's, his precision work not as crude. As in any layered building, the precision work occurs in the finish materials and the cruder work is concealed under the succeeding layers of construction. Several different levels of craftsmanship are associated with different styles of detailing in Webb's buildings. Monolithic timber structures like Gimson's do appear in Webb's work, but only in elements such as gates, porches, and bridges.

Voysey's structural system at Greyfriars is simpler than Webb's. Wood joists span between transverse load-bearing walls. There are a few pieces of steel (in the tower, for example), but the predominant materials are wood and masonry. In this respect Ruskin would have found Greyfriars more acceptable than Standen. But like Standen it has little exposed framing, and unlike Standen it has little framing that is expressed. It does have exterior buttresses and wrought-iron brackets at the eaves, but these are, if not ornamental, probably structurally redundant. Many of the lintels are concealed under plaster or wood trim, and most of the ceilings are almost completely flat, with no expression of the joists or the trusses above. While it cannot be said with certainty, it seems highly unlikely that the joists or the timbers of the truss are finished to the precision of Gimson's, or even that they were finished by hand. What would be the point of such an expenditure in a house in which they were entirely concealed? Voysey might have preferred a wood frame like Gimson's had his budget permitted it, but the frame as built is largely concealed.

Thus, within the Arts and Crafts movement there were two models of good building, which were not seen as excluding each other: the monolithic exposed structure of Gimson's Stoneywell Cottage, with its uniform level of craftsmanship, and the layered and concealed system of Webb's Standen and Voysey's Greyfriars, with their variations in craftsmanship.

Gustav Stickley—in some ways the primary American exponent of the Arts and Crafts movement—reached a similar intellectual position to his European contemporaries by a different route. Trained as a mason and carpenter, he was inspired after reading Ruskin and Morris to found the Craftsman Workshops. His primary interests were the design and construction of furniture ("Mission" furniture, as it came to be known) and the publication of a magazine (*The Craftsman*) in which he echoed the English ideas of truth to material, response to site, structural fitness, and absence of conscious style.

Perhaps because the American traditions of building were not as well established as the English ones, Stickley was more willing than many of his English contemporaries to use innovative materials and methods. He shared with Morris a concern for the effect of industrial society on the quality of labor, but he did not let this prejudice him against industrial products. Many of the house designs published in *The Craftsman* specified steel beams and concrete. A typical example of this is a design published in *The Craftsman* in 1908 (figures 5.1, 5.2). (The house was built in Morris Plains, N.J., but Stickley later admitted that much of the information published in *The Craftsman* was deceptive and inaccurate.) At first glance there is nothing particularly remarkable about Stickley's house. It is a simple box, with rough stone walls on the ground floor and half-timbered plaster on the second floor. Attached to the rear is a rustic log pergola. The construction is anything but typical, however. On the second floor Stickley wanted an exposed timber frame, but a true half-timber frame was unacceptable for environmental reasons. But Stickley did not resort to a purely ornamental frame. His solution was to combine timber, concrete, clay tile, and plaster into a complex but structurally integrated whole. The wall is composed of two layers. The inner layer is structural clay tile covered with plaster. The openings in this layer are spanned by reinforced concrete beams inside the clay tiles. The outer layer is also composed of clay tiles covered

5.17

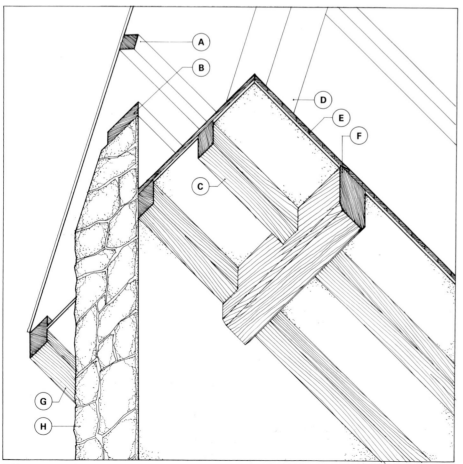

5.18

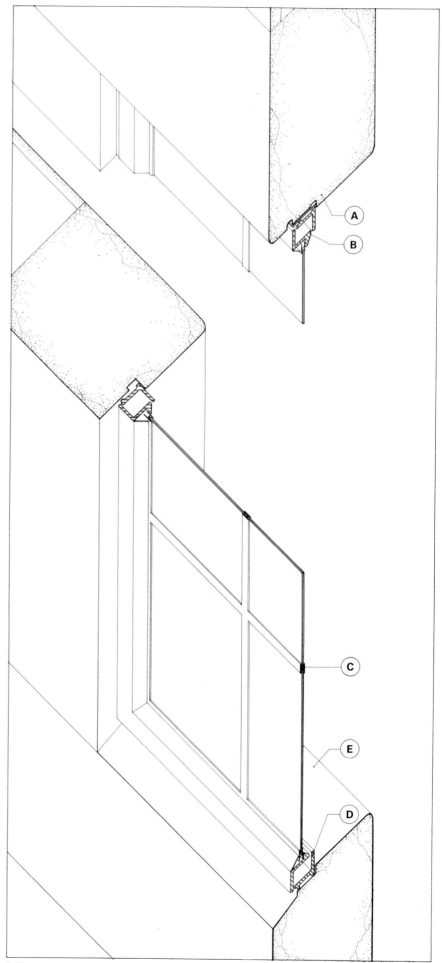

5.19

Stoneywell Cottage

Ernest Gimson

Leicestershire, 1899

5.17 **exterior**

(Lethaby, *The Life and Work of Ernest Gimson.*)

5.18 **floor details**

A 8 × 8 purlin supporting wood planks to which thatch is applied. (The thatch is not shown.)

B Wood sill to receive rafters.

C 6 × 6 beams, about 24″ on center.

D 9 × 9 rafters.

E Wood-plank floor with plaster ceiling.

F 16 × 16 girder supporting 6 × 6 floor beams.

G 6 × 6 edge beam and thatch roof (not shown).

H Load-bearing fieldstone wall, plastered on the interior.

(Lethaby, *The Life and Work of Ernest Gimson.*)

5.19 **C. A. F. Voysey, typical window detail**

(from a drawing for an unnamed house).

A Stone lintel. This supports the masonry over the opening.

B Out-swinging metal casement window. Although similar to medieval types, this is actually a prototype of the modern steel casement window.

C Preformed lead H bead. These were commonly used at the turn of the century to give the appearance of medieval leaded glass while simplifying the process of assembly.

D Sill of casement frame. All stone-to-metal joints are notched or lapped to ensure that they will not open as the metal expands and contracts.

E Stone sill. Voysey does not use the standard projecting sill and drip. This gives the building an appealing simplicity, but it is a poor detail to use with stucco.

(*RIBA Drawings Collection, drawing* [143].)

with plaster, but it is supported by a timber frame (figure 5.4), which provides its own timber lintels at the openings. The roof is an equally strange mixture of clay tile supported by rough timbers. In the interior, there is extensive use of exposed chestnut timbers. Few if any of these timbers are solid; most are built of rough 4 × 8 timbers wrapped in ¾-inch finish wood. The living room was too large for a single span of these beams, so a steel girder was added; this was also clad in ¾-inch chestnut.

Stickley's use of a wood-clad steel beam raised a number of questions regarding "deceits." The veneering of rough wood with finish wood was common practice and common sense. Ruskin had forbidden intentionally deceptive cladding, and he opposed the structural use of steel or iron. Gimson, judging from his work, considered veneering acceptable in furniture but not in buildings. Stickley, perhaps because of his background in cabinetry, thought the process of veneering was as applicable to architecture and made frequent use of clad beams. In response to a reader's inquiry as to the propriety of covering iron beams with wood or of using wood beams that were purely ornamental, Stickley replied:

As to the writer who spoke of "fake"—we imagine that . . . he was not familiar with the practical side of woodwork. . . . As every carpenter is aware, the use of solid beams for ceilings is becoming more and more impracticable, for several reasons.

In the first place, it is difficult to season [i.e. dry] wood of more than three inches in thickness, and a solid beam would need to be seasoned for at least three to five years. Even if this were feasible, it would be too expensive, for the price of lumber is increasing and people can no longer afford to use fine hardwood for such purposes. Therefore where carrying beams are needed, some inexpensive kind of wood is used and encased in boards of a better quality to match the rest of the trim. . . .

Where the floor overhead is carried by iron beams, . . . it is as natural to encase the iron in wood as in plaster, plaster being preferable in some rooms and wood in others, according to the decorative scheme of the interior.[12]

Stickley does not explain why he went to so much trouble to use solid structural timbers on the outside of his house while using clad steel and wood beams on the inside. Interestingly enough, he felt that there was nothing wrong with ornamental beams, which he thought were completely compatible with the goals of the Arts and Crafts movement:

It seems to us perfectly legitimate to use built-up beams and posts and other forms of woodwork simply for their decorative value, and it seems only natural to place them as they would be placed if they were necessary parts of the construction. This is done not for the purpose of deceiving anyone into thinking they are performing some definite structural service, but merely to satisfy the eye. For almost everyone possesses, in some degree, an instinctive knowledge of structural fitness, of mechanical balance and proportion, of the relative strength of materials, and will consciously or unconsciously resent any actual or seeming infringement of these physical laws. On the other hand, compliance with such laws, whether for the sake of strength or beauty, will satisfy the observer's sense of mechanical and artistic propriety.[13]

Although the Greenes were undoubtedly familiar with the work of their British contemporaries, their primary exposure to Arts and Crafts ideals came through Stickley and *The Craftsman*, and their treatment of exposed and concealed structures and of joinery generally conforms to Stickley's ideas.

Like Gimson and Stickley, Charles Greene had learned carpentry and woodcarving. And, like them, he seldom executed his own designs, working by closely supervising craftsmen. Virtually all of the Greenes' mature buildings were executed by the workshop of Peter and John Hall, who served as general contractors and who did both the rough carpentry and the finish millwork. C. R. Ashbee visited the Hall's shop in 1908 and found it to be a model of Arts and Crafts practice: ". . . the men who were doing the work were old men—some quite old . . . men who

"SEACROFT," near Seabright, New Jersey.

West Elevation

5.20

5.21

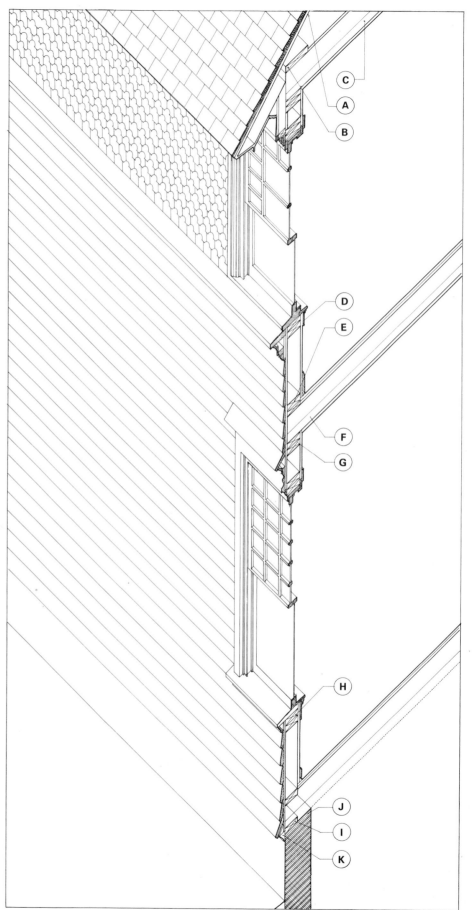

5.22

Seacroft

Bruce Price

Seabright, New Jersey, 1882

5.20   west elevation

(American Architect and Building News, 1883.)

5.21   south front

(American Architect and Building News, 1883.)

5.22   wall section

(typical of a balloon-frame house of the nineteenth century).

A   2 × 6 rafters, 16″ on center. 16″ is the effective span of both 1″ sheathing and plaster; this establishes the basic spacing.

B   Plate to receive load of rafters.

C   2 × 8 ceiling joists, 16″ on center.

D   Window trim. This is made of higher-quality wood than the studs and joists.

E   Sole plate. Since this is a balloon and not a platform frame, this acts only as brace and nailer.

F   2 × 8 floor joists, 16″ on center. The 1″ wood subfloor is a structural element that braces the structure and distributes loads on one joist to adjacent ones. The finish floor was installed much later in the construction sequence.

G   2 × 4 top plate and 2 × 4 splice plate. The 2 × 4 wall is sheathed with 1″ boards laid diagonally, which laterally brace the structure and tie the studs together.

H   Two 2 × 4's, framing window. Since the openings must be framed before the window is installed, the window has two types of wood: the rough 2 × 4's of the opening and the window frame itself.

I   2 × 4 mudsill. Mudsills are often made of redwood, to resist decay. They are always set in a bed of grout to ensure that they will be level.

J   8″ brick foundation wall. Wood-frame buildings are typically placed several feet above grade to discourage rot and termites.

K   Water table. This sheds water away from the joint at the foundation, and also serves to visually terminate the wall.

(American Architect and Building News, 1883.)

have still a traditional feeling for craftsmanship in wood, and who had learned their tradition before the days of machine development—before American Wood-craft had been 'Grand-Rapidized'"[14] Though the Halls' workmen were undoubtedly extraordinary men, it is doubtful that they had anything to say about the designs. Charles Greene made almost daily visits to their shop, and he provided full-size drawings of many of the details. Given the similarity of many of these details, the workmen probably learned over time what was expected.

In his scant writings, Charles Greene seemed to advocate the Arts and Crafts ideals of truth to materials and honesty of expression. In 1908 he wrote: "We have got to have bricks and stone and wood and plaster; common, homely, cheap materials, every one of them. Leave them as they are—stone for stone, brick for brick, wood for wood, plaster for plaster. Why are they not better so? Why disguise them? . . . The noblest work of art is to make these common things beautiful for man."[15] To the contemporary mind this idea is impossible to reconcile with beams that are not really beams and fasteners that are not really fasteners. The physical evidence indicates that Greene might have been in agreement with Stickley—at different times, he used false half-timbering, false interior beams, and veneered steel beams. But there is also considerable evidence that he and his brother tried to reconcile their decorative and structural ideas.

The Greenes, like Gimson and Stickley, were alienated from the mainstream of Western architecture and sought their formal models outside the existing classified styles such as Classic and Gothic. Like their English contemporaries, they looked for inspiration in vernacular examples. Those houses that come close to fulfilling the ideal of a monolithic exposed wood frame, including the Bandini house (1903), follow local vernacular traditions. The single-story building is U-shaped, with a veranda surrounding the resulting courtyard. The walls are faced with board and batten siding inside and out, and the wooden roof structure is exposed. There is no plastering and no highly finished wood paneling. These houses have a sort of controlled rusticity. Though they are considerably more polished than Stickley's log cabins and brush arbors, they are crude in comparison with the Greenes' later Gamble house. As Makinson has shown, this was the Greenes' preferred type of construction.

The one-story courtyard house, executed in a rustic, monolithic style, presented certain problems of construction, and the plan was not acceptable to many of the Greenes' clients. A more typical construction type is represented by the Cole house, completed in 1906, in which the Greenes combined features of the Japanese, the Swiss, and the platform frame. With minor modifications, the Greenes employed this style in almost all of their later executed commissions. It is not one of the Greene brothers' outstanding achievements, but its construction is well documented by a series of detailed construction photographs taken by Charles Greene (figures 5.25 and 5.26). The basis of this type is a large hipped roof volume, to which are attached a number of open pavilions containing sleeping porches, large bay windows, and porte-cochères. The main volume is platform-framed and clad in shingles. While a number of pieces of the frame are exposed, the shingled surface encloses the structure of the house, wrapping the corners and dominating the frame. In the pavilions, the frame elements dominate. These frames resemble more traditional prototypes, particularly Japanese ones. In the case of porches the structure is completely exposed, and the enclosed porches are framed with exposed corner posts and sills; the shingles are infill material, somewhat as in English half-timber construction, and the frame dominates the skin.

The Cole house does not have the uniform level of craftsmanship found in Japanese work. There are two distinct types of structural members, made of different materials, joined in different ways, and finished with different techniques. Most of the exposed timbers are made from large redwood sections, cut in standard sizes with circular saws. Where these pieces are exposed, as at the gable ends, the mill marks were sanded off by hand and the ends rounded. The 2 × 4 studs and 2 × 8 joists of the platform frame, and all the other concealed wood, is Oregon pine, which is less attractive but also less expensive than redwood. These members are

5.23

5.24

5.25

5.26

left as they came from the mill, and are fastened with nails. This is an entirely logical method of wood construction. If one studies the proportion of exposed to concealed lumber in the building, one can see the absurdity of the idea that the concealed pieces should be larger redwood timbers, sanded by hand and fastened with pegs.

The Cole house, a platform-framed block surrounded by traditionally framed pavilions, is typical of the Greenes' mature work. The most innovative aspect of this type is not the traditionally framed pavilions but the transformations of the platform-frame block. Before we examine the unique aspects of the Gamble house, it is useful to examine those characteristics of the house that typify the Greenes' mature work.

The details of the central block of the Gamble house show the way in which the Greenes transformed a standard platform frame into a structure resembling a vernacular wood frame. The details have also been transformed to comply with Arts and Crafts ideals of revealed joinery and to emphasize the constructivist impulse—the maximum articulation of the elements without destroying the perception of the whole. A comparison of a typical section of the wall of the Gamble house with a more standard contemporary structure will clarify this.

Seacroft, designed by Bruce Price in 1882, uses the same basic systems and materials as the Gamble house: platform frame structure, shingles, clapboards, and plaster. It resembles some of the Greenes' earlier buildings, and it is technically similar. However, the Greenes achieved different visual results by exposing certain structural members, articulating certain joints, and extending and separating pieces that are commonly joined to emphasize their individual identity.

The foundation wall of Seacroft is brick, and the house is raised several feet above grade to protect the wood from water and termites. The foundation walls of the Gamble house are also brick, covered with stucco. The key piece of lumber in any platform frame is the mudsill, which transfers the entire load of the wood frame to the foundation. It is often made of redwood to discourage rot. Because of its structural importance, the mudsill must be absolutely level and in continuous contact with the foundation wall below. Since the top of the foundation wall is often irregular, the mudsill is placed in a bed of grout (a mixture of cement, sand, and water) to ensure this. At Seacroft, the mudsill and the grout are concealed behind the sheathing and the shingles. In the Gamble house, both are pushed forward to the face of the wall and exposed. Exposing elements is not simply a question of peeling back the shingles; exposed members require higher standards of finish than concealed members. Thus, the mudsill had to be planed and sanded to remove mill marks and round the corners. The Greenes provided special templates to ensure that the lip of the grout bed would have a uniform profile.

Typically, two mudsills are joined at an exterior corner by means of a lap joint (figure 5.6). In the Gamble house the Greenes use a similar detail, the cross lap, in which the timbers project beyond the corner of the building so that they appear to interpenetrate (figure 5.28). This detail, adapted from typical Japanese building, adds considerably to the constructivist feel of the finished building. In long walls it is sometimes necessary to splice two mudsills. In the typical condition as it occurs at Seacroft, a lap joint is used to ensure an even foundation. The Greenes use a similar joint, but exposed and connected with an oak wedge. Unlike many other wedges in the firm's work, this one is real.

An element missing from the Gamble house but present at Seacroft is the water table. A board is placed under the shingles so that the wood wall flares out at the base. This throws the water away from the wall, but it also acts to make the building visually bottom-heavy. The Greenes used the traditional water table detail in some of their earlier work, but they abandoned it in favor of one in which the exposed timber and its shadow created the opposite visual effect, that of floating the building above its foundation (figure 5.28). (This recalls the pole foundations of many Japanese buildings.)

5.27

5.28

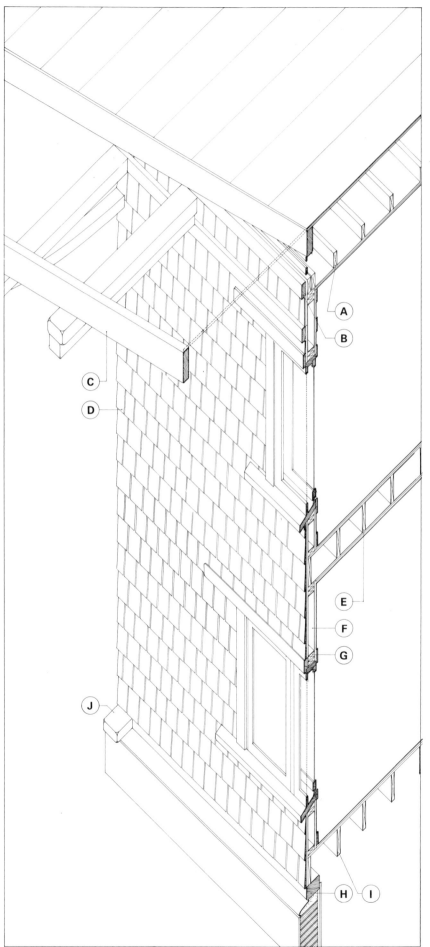

5.29

David B. Gamble house

Charles and Henry Greene

Pasadena, California, 1908

5.27   **exterior**

5.28   **detail at mudsill**
        Notice that the marks left by the
        rotary saw blade have not been
        completely sanded and planed off.

5.29   **wall section at front bedroom**
  A   2 × 6 pine ceiling joists. The
        standard 16″ spacing of the
        platform frame is reduced to half of
        the spacing of the heavy timber
        rafters, which are 24″ on center.
  B   3 × 6 exterior trim.
  C   4 × 12 verge board with rafters
        beyond.
  D   Split wood shingles, 11″ to weather.
        Shingles are usually set 6″ or 8″ to
        weather. The Greenes double the
        exposed portion, put a ½″ gap
        between shingles, and cut the ends
        irregularly to destroy the long
        horizontal lines of conventional
        shingle walls.
  E   2 × 12 floor joists, 12″ on center.
  F   2 × 4-wood-stud wall sheathed
        with 1× 6 boards set diagonally.
        Except for the sill and the top, the
        internal wood frame is a standard
        platform frame.
  G   Double 2 × 4′s over opening, with
        1 × 6 pine trim on exterior and
        1 × 6 cedar trim on interior. The
        2 × 4′s support the studs over the
        window opening.
  H   8 × 6 redwood sill. The portions of
        the exterior most subject to rot,
        such as the window sill and the
        mudsill, are made of redwood. The
        mudsill is set on a bed of grout so
        that the framing will start perfectly
        level. The Greenes took a typical
        segment of the platform frame—the
        mudsill—and exposed and enlarged
        it.
  I   2 × 10 floor joists, 12″ on center.
  J   Lap joint of mudsill at corner.
        Mudsills were typically lapped in
        standard construction, but they are
        extended here in a Japanese
        fashion.
        (Greene and Greene Library.)

The wall treatment of the Gamble house continues the tendency to articulate the individual element. Whereas the shingles and clapboards of Seacroft are in even neat 6-inch rows, the shingles of the Gamble house are spaced ½ inch apart, and their ends are not cut evenly but are at slightly varying angles to the horizontal, giving the wall the "rudeness" that Ruskin desired. At the same time the wood structure seldom interrupts completely the continuity of the surface. In the main block of the Gamble house, the second-floor framing and corner posts are completely concealed behind the shingles and sheathing. The walls here are never allowed to become frame and infill, as they are in the surrounding pavilions.

The windows continue the theme of articulating the individual parts through discontinuity. The exterior trim of Seacroft is classical in inspiration, forming the juxtaposition of classical and vernacular that was so important to the shingle style. Here the trim forms a complete frame around the window opening. In the Gamble house, however, the sill and head trim are continued past the edge of the opening, so that we perceive the trim as four separate pieces forming a rectangle and not as a frame. The interior trim, executed in finish woods to match the interior paneling, echoes this treatment, and the Classical base formed by the apron and sill of the Seacroft window is here replaced by flat trim echoing that above. The Greenes might be accused of a Ruskinian deceit: making an ornamental piece appear to be structural. On the exterior the window trim appears identical to the timbers above and below, and one has no way of knowing that it is only a ¾-inch piece nailed over the sheathing rather than a 6 × 6 timber. In some of their houses, notably the Irwin house, the Greenes differentiated the trim from the structure by leaving the trim square-edged and flat while rounding all the corners of the structural timbers. But in the Gamble house the trim is planed and sanded to match the structural beams. But from another point of view this is not really a deceit, since there is a beam here made up of the two Oregon pine 2 × 4′s and the trim piece is simply their finish wood or veneer cladding.

At Seacroft the shingles and clapboards continue uninterrupted past the second floor to the roof above, forming a continuous membrane emphasizing its volume. In the Gamble house the volumetric treatment ends abruptly at the top of the second floor; the wall above consists practically of lattice and structure.

It is in the roof structure that the platform frame undergoes its greatest transformation and comes close to becoming a traditional frame. At Seacroft joists and rafters are spaced 16 inches on center and made from 2 × 8′s and 2 × 10′s. The Greenes increased the spacing of the exposed pieces to 24 inches, to increase the scale, while reducing the spacing of the concealed joists to 12 inches. Virtually all of the rafters and girders are exposed, and here the cost of completely dressed and shaped redwood used in the Cole house was prohibitive. Thus the exposed framing of the Gamble house is of Oregon pine, with the ends and the corners gently rounded.

The themes of discontinuity and separate articulation of the parts continue. Note in figure 5.38 the means of ending the roof rafters and their relationship to the building's exterior finish. The barge board is raised above the rafters to form a gutter and the rafter ends are extended beyond, maximizing the discontinuity and separateness of the parts. Extension of the rafters has the unfortunate effect of exposing their ends to the weather. The end grain of wood, being the most porous, is the most susceptible to water. (Strangely, the Greenes made only minimal use of metal caps to protect these ends—a common feature in Japanese architecture. Cost may have been a factor here.) The roof itself, with its tapered profile, recalls Japanese thatched roofs such as those at Ise. It is covered with malthold, an asbestos-based material resembling the modern asphalt shingle.

The various pavilions which are added to the main volume are detailed in subtly different ways, so that here the frame dominates the skin in a way that it does not in the main volume. In the porch, structural members serve as corner posts and window supports are exposed. Here again it is not a question of exposing what would normally be concealed. The corner post, which is typically three concealed

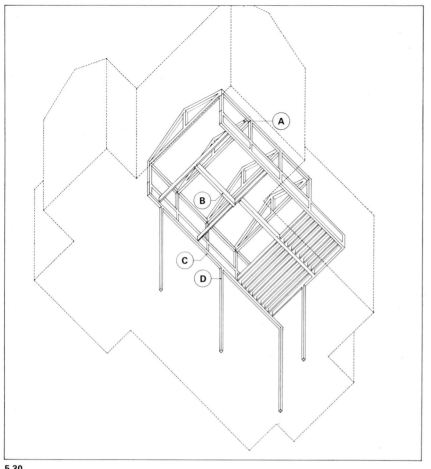

5.30

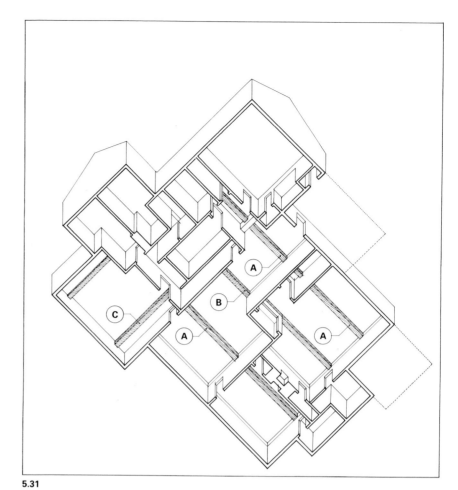

5.31

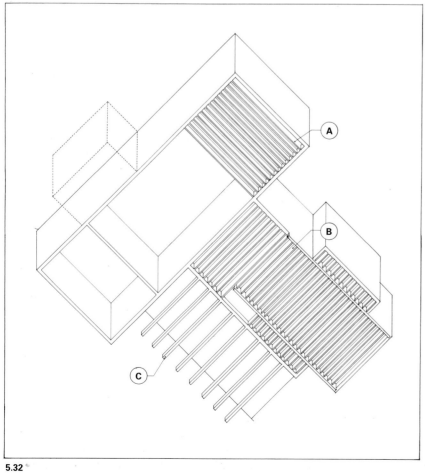

5.32

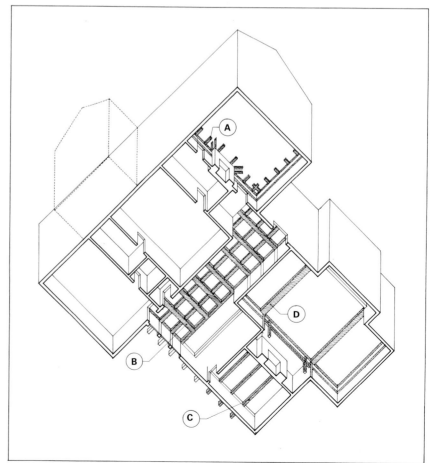

5.33

David B. Gamble house

Charles and Henry Greene

Pasadena, California, 1908

5.30 framing plan for billiard room

A Exposed rafters of billiard room above. This is one of only two rooms in the house where the structural wood timbers are exposed.

B Girder of two 2 × 16's. This supports the floor joists of the billiard room at midspan and is in turn supported by heavy timber beams spanning between columns.

C Truss supporting billiard room walls. This is exposed in the billiard room but concealed in the rooms below.

D 4 × 4 and 4 × 8 wood columns. These are concealed within the walls of the house. Although their structural arrangement is not illogical, it shows that structural regularity is subordinate to picturesque effect in the Greenes' work.

(Greene and Greene Library.)

5.31 reflected ceiling plan, second floor

A ¾" white cedar cover on wood trusses above.

B White cedar cover on two 2 × 14's above. These covers are not necessary; the beams and the truss could have been concealed in the ceiling above.

C White cedar cover of beams in front bedroom. See figure 5.35.

(Greene and Greene Library.)

5.32 second-floor framing

A 2 × 12 joists spaced at 16" on center with ¾"-thick subfloor above supported by 2 × 4 wood stud walls.

B 2 × 12 joists spaced at 12" on center, supported by 2 × 4-stud walls and girders made from three 2 × 14's.

C 6 × 12 Oregon pine beams. The larger, more widely spaced timbers are used for those beams that are wholly or partially exposed.

(Greene and Greene Library.)

5.33 reflected ceiling plan, first floor

A Dining room, finished in San Domingo mahogany. The ornamentation of the ceiling, although it appears structural, is not, nor does it have any relation to the real structure above (a simple wood-joist floor).

B Entry hall. The wood ceiling trim clads the pine beams above in the long direction; but the shorter, deeper beams are hollow and have no corresponding element in the structure.

C Study. Here the structural pine beams are exposed.

D Ornamental beam in living room.

(Greene and Greene Library.)

timbers, becomes an exposed dressed post. At the second-floor extensions, such as the balcony, the normally concealed structure of two 2 × 12's becomes an 8 × 12 dressed beam, tapered at its cantilevered ends to express the location of maximum stress. But it would be wrong to interpret the Greenes' work as rigorous structural rationalism. Many details are arbitrary, illogical, or purely aesthetic when analyzed structurally.

Certain details of the Gamble house are unique, but most of those discussed here occur repeatedly in the Greenes' work between 1904 and 1914. There are many variations and some refinements, but seldom are there radical differences. When they occur, it is often due to economic constraints. The Garfield house (figure 5.24), for example, was a much less ambitious building than the Gamble house, and it can be seen as a sort of economy version of the typical Greene and Greene house. None of the timbers of the Garfield house have rounded ends or edges, nor does any of the trim; all are left square, greatly reducing the amount of hand labor required to finish them. Many timbers that were exposed in the Gamble house are here concealed, and while the foundation retains its boulder finish and grout molding, the mudsill is a concealed piece of rough pine instead of a dressed piece of redwood. The integral gutter of the Gamble house is gone, and with it the tapered form it produced; thus, the roof is a simple plane. In its place is a standard metal gutter, which hides most of the exposed rafter ends. The Garfield house is not one of the Greenes' more interesting houses; it demonstrates by elimination precisely those elements that made the Greenes' larger houses so difficult to execute.

The Gamble house is the best known and most accessible of the Greenes' houses, and has received the most criticism. Most contemporary critics have agreed with Banham that the Greenes were not truly dedicated to the ideals of the Arts and Crafts movement but were interested only in its imagery. True Arts and Crafts works are presumably those, such as Gimson's Stoneywell Cottage, with monolithic exposed structure, traditional construction methods, no ornamental structural elements, and a uniform level of craftsmanship. The Gamble house, with its frequent use of veneers and its numerous trusses, fasteners, and beams installed long after the building was structurally complete, is seen, in comparison with Gimson's work, as "dishonest."

Ruskin would not have liked the Gamble house, and the Greenes were certainly guilty of using elements and joints that appear to be structural but are not. On the other hand, their houses are not pastiches of technical images without a rational order. Many of the exposed structural elements are exactly what they appear to be and are joined and fastened in the way that they appear to be joined and fastened. Some of the interior beams, brackets, and joints bear not even a faint resemblance to the true construction that they conceal, but the most common system, particularly in the interior, employs we might call analogous structures—structures which in themselves are ornamental, but which closely parallel the true structural elements they conceal. This system may lack the conceptual purity of Gimson's cottage, but it is infinitely better suited to the realities of wood construction. Regardless of the degree of industrialization, a theory of construction (particularly wood construction) that does not allow for the veneering of high-quality materials onto poorer ones, varying levels of perfection in workmanship, and the correct sequencing of these types of work in the construction of the building is a severely deficient theory.

Although most of the exterior wood members of the Gamble house are structural, most of the wood in the interior is not. Figures 5.35–5.37 show three typical conditions that occur in the Gamble house. In the first, an Oregon pine beam is exposed on an interior ceiling. In the second (which occurs at the second-floor hall), an ornamental beam made up of thin boards is suspended below the real beam, which is made of rough Oregon pine. Notice that this differs from a veneered beam, and that there is enough room in the ceiling so that this beam could have been concealed completely. Figure 5.38 shows a condition that occurs in the hall: the real ceiling beams of Oregon pine are clad in Burmese teak, but they are also

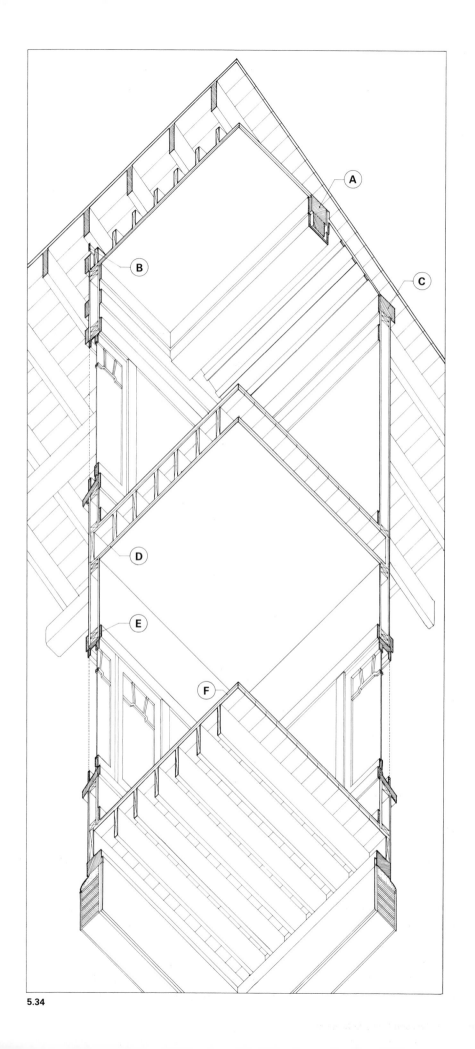

5.34

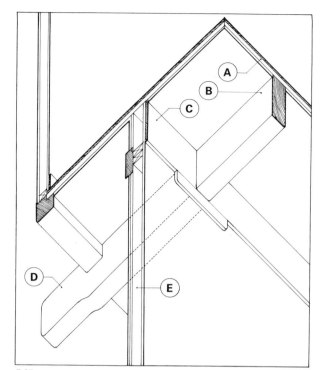

5.35

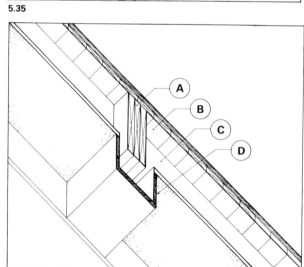

5.36

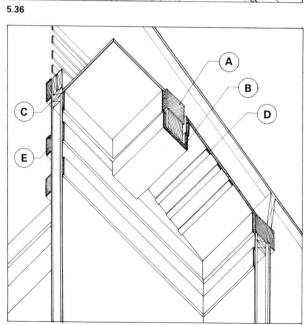

5.37

David B. Gamble house

Charles and Henry Greene

Pasadena, California, 1908

5.34 wall section,
interior of front bedroom

A 8 × 6 and 6 × 6 Oregon pine beams clad with 1″ white cedar boards.

B Lattice. This provides ventilation to the attic and also increases the openness and the frame quality of the structure.

C Some of the cedar interior trim corresponds to pine structural pieces (as at the crown mold); some does not (as in the molding just below).

D Plaster-on-wood-lath ceiling. Most of the interiors were completely plastered before any of the wood trim was installed.

E Cedar casing at window head. Although this trim is used for conventional purposes—to cover joints between plaster and wood— it does not have conventional shapes. Interior and exterior window trim are almost identical and are indistinguishable from the solid structural elements.

F Floor construction: 1 × 6 pine subfloor with finish-wood floor above. The floor is oak in the major living areas, maple in the kitchen and pantry, and red birch in the upstairs hall and bedrooms. Oak is the most durable and attractive of these woods, maple the most resilient, birch the most economical.
(Greene and Greene Library.)

5.35 beam details,
study

A Floor construction: 1 × 6 pine subfloor with birch finish floor above.

B 6 × 12 solid Oregon pine beam. This is one of two locations where actual structural members are exposed on the interior.

C Wood trim. This covers the rough edge of the plaster where it meets the ceiling.

D 6 × 12 beam.

E 2 × 4 Oregon pine stud wall supporting beams.
(Greene and Greene Library.)

5.36 beam detail,
second-floor hall

A Girder made from three 2 × 14's.

B $\frac{13}{16}$″ × $2\frac{1}{4}$″ red birch finish floor on subfloor of 1 × 6 Oregon pine boards.

C 2 × 12 joists at 12″ on center.

D 1″ white cedar boards. Although this hollow beam is not structural, it does locate and describe the real girder above.
(Greene and Greene Library.)

5.37 beam details,
front bedroom

A 8 × 6 and 6 × 6 Oregon pine beams.

B 1″ white cedar cladding on structural beams.

C 3 × 6 Oregon pine facing on two 2 × 6 joists. The outer 3 × 6 is rounded at the corners, while the rafters retain the square shape given by the mill.

D $\frac{3}{4}$″ white cedar ceiling boards with $\frac{3}{4}$″ battens at joints.

E 3 × 6 Oregon pine facing board. This piece serves no structural purpose.
(Greene and Greene Library.)

connected by short false beams, which have no parallel in the real structure. For convenience we may refer to these three types as *real beams, analogous beams,* and *ornamental beams.* The most common type in the interior is the analogous beam. Instances of the ornamental type are rare, and the Greenes often insisted on applying the analogous beam in situations in which it was detrimental to the visual effect.

Why is the Greenes' mature work so different from Gimson's? If they were in agreement as to the principles involved, why are the results so different? Why is the complex system of structure and ornament in the Gamble house better than the simple solid timbers of Stoneywell Cottage? The reason has to do with materials—specifically, with the species of wood and their characteristics.

The wood of Gimson's house is all of one type (solid English oak), and most Arts and Crafts buildings are similar in using one type of interior finish throughout. It was common in the more elaborate houses in the nineteenth century to use a different finish in each major room, and often a different type of wood paneling, to give "character" to the individual rooms.

Some of the Greenes' more rustic works, such as the Bandini house, have a uniform quality of finish and workmanship, but their larger commissions—particularly those for wealthy clients, such as the Gambles—have a hierarchy of finishes, with the finest and most expensive in the major public rooms and the less expensive in the more private areas. Thus, in the Gamble house the hall and the living room are finished in Burmese teak, the dining room in mahogany, the study in oak, the kitchen in maple, and the upstairs bedrooms in white cedar. There is little real structural timber that is exposed in the interior; most of the remaining areas are finished in plaster, the notable exception being the billiard room.

If one wishes to build a wood building in the monolithic, exposed style of Gimson and of the Bandini house, there are limits on the type of wood and the type of finish that can be used. Only certain types of wood can be obtained in the large sizes that are necessary. For the Greenes, the choices were Oregon pine and sometimes redwood. Neither of these woods is particularly good for interior finish. They are fairly soft and are not as durable as oak, nor can they be polished to the same degree. Redwood timbers are seldom given the sort of precise finish that is seen in the teak of the Gamble house. Even if the redwood were finished it would not produce the beauty of color and grain that the teak would have. The timbers, being structural, have to be installed early in the construction process and are much more susceptible to damage than work done at a later time; thus, even if the redwood had been given a high polish, the contractor would have had the additional problem of protecting this finish from damage.

If one wishes to have the type of interior finish seen in the Gamble house—quality interior woods with a high degree of finish—one has little choice but to build in the veneered style. Burmese teak and mahogany are more durable, more beautifully grained, and more easily finished than redwood or pine, but they are difficult to obtain in the large sizes required for the structural members. Even if they were available in these large sizes, the results might not have been acceptable. The larger a timber, the more susceptible it is to cracking as it dries out; thus, the longer it must be seasoned. A crack might be visually acceptable on an exposed redwood rafter on the exterior, but not in a living-room ceiling. The cladding of rough pine beams with thin pieces of these finish woods solves all of the problems as well as making the construction much easier. Since the finish woods are not structural, they may be finished in the shop and installed at the end of the construction process, when the likelihood of damage is much less. In fact, the Greenes did not allow any finish wood to be installed before the completion of plastering, so that the wood would not be affected by the presence of water.

The exterior wall has two types of wood structure and two levels of craftsmanship. The concealed elements of the platform frame are rough Oregon pine, nailed together, and the exposed timbers are dressed (planed and sanded) Oregon pine. The fact that much of this work is not complete (notice the mill marks of the

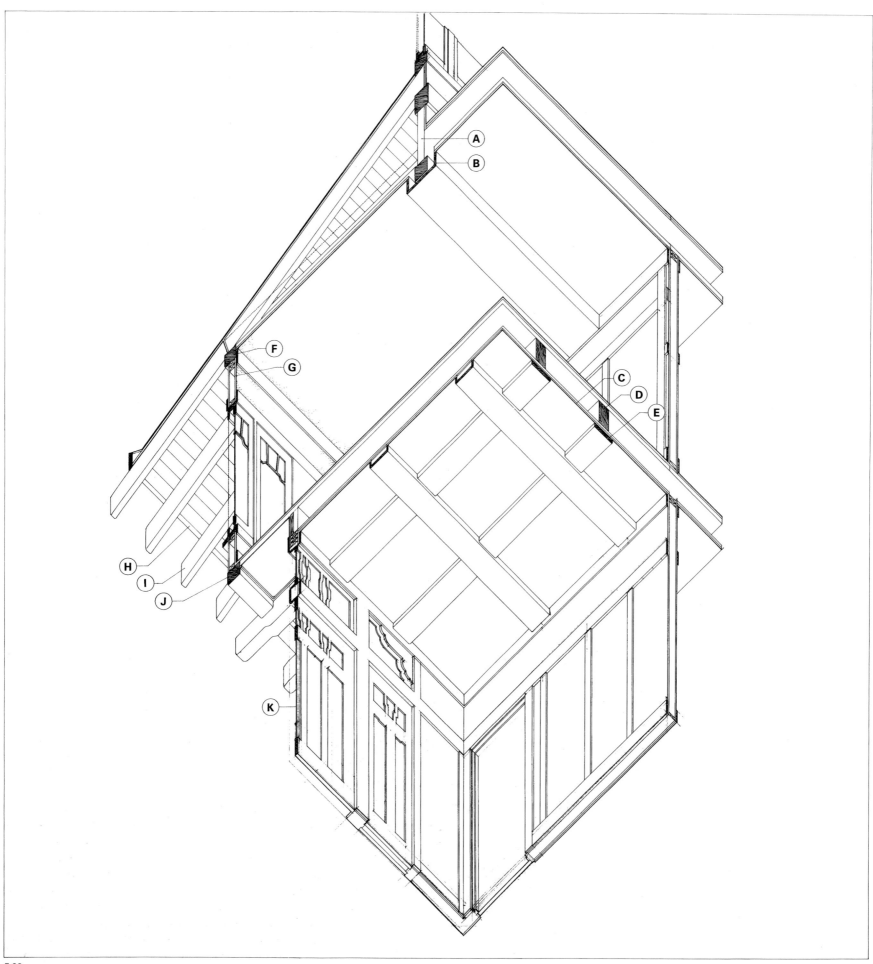

David B. Gamble house

Charles and Henry Greene

Pasadena, California, 1908

5.38 **wall section,**
interior of entry hall

A Wood truss supporting walls of
billiard room above.

B 1" white cedar boards covering
bottom chord of truss.

C Ceiling: plaster on wood lath.

D 6 × 12 Oregon pine beam,
concealed on the interior but
exposed on the exterior.

E Burmese teak ceiling trim. This trim
corresponds to the real beams
above. The trim that is
perpendicular to it has no relation
to the structure, real or symbolic.

F 8 × 6 pine beam on exterior, faced
with 1⅞ × 6½ white cedar trim on
the interior.

G 2 × 4-wood-stud wall

H Roof construction: 1 × 6 Oregon
pine boards covered with sheets of
Malthoid.

I 3 × 8 rafters spaced at 24" on
center.

J 8 × 6 edge beam.

K 2 × 4-wood-stud wall.
(Greene and Greene Library.)

circular saw in figure 5.28) may be an indication of the increasing cost of this intensive handwork. Some of these timbers are real structure (such as the mudsill); some of them are analogous (such as the board over the window head, which simulates the concealed headers). Wherever portions of the structure are exposed, the size and spacing of the timbers is increased to make the structure resemble a traditional wood frame. Thus, while most of the first-floor framing is concealed standard framing spaced at 12 inches on center, the exposed portions (such as the cantilever over the front door) are made from 6 × 12 timbers spaced at 4 feet on center. The roof rafters are enlarged and are spaced at 24 inches. Certain economies were made here; for example, the ridge pole, which is a dressed 4 × 10 on the exterior, changes to two rough 2 × 10's as soon as it penetrates the wall.

Including the interior, there are three general types of wood used in the Gamble house, and there are three different levels of craftsmanship in finish and joinery that correspond to them. The Oregon pine platform frame is completely concealed. Its boards are left unfinished as they came from the mill, and its joints are made with nails. Most of the exposed exterior structure is also of Oregon pine timbers, planed to produce round ends and edges and sanded to remove most of the mill marks. The pieces are joined with oak wedges and pegs, although they often cover screws and nails. The finish wood of the interior (teak, mahogany, white cedar, etc.) is shaped and joined with a high degree of finish, and it is polished much more than the exposed exterior timbers. It is joined with wood screws covered with wood pegs. Like the beams themselves, the joint materials—wedges, pegs, or screws—are usually used to cover the real fasteners and sometimes are purely ornamental. The first two systems are usually structural; the third is not, but it is less an ornamental system than an analogous system that parallels the real structure which it conceals.

If one accepts this analogous system of construction as a reasonable way to construct wood buildings, an immediate problem arises: Must the analogous system replicate what is covered, or can it be altered to emphasize or clarify architectural readings? The Greenes' works give no clear answer; in some of them the analogous system follows the underlying system fairly closely, but in others it comes very close to being "deceitful" in Ruskin's terms.

A comparison of the real structure of each room of the Gamble house with its analogous structure reveals a variety of answers to the above question. The most literal representation of structural reality is found in the upstairs front bedroom (figure 5.34). The structure of this wing is self-contained; a series of rafters are tied with collar beams to form trusses, and then supported both by the exterior walls of the platform frame and by two intermediate beams. This use of four rather than two supports may seem somewhat redundant, but the span is somewhat long for a simple joist, and the Greenes were fond of doubling the means of structural support. The framing is all of Oregon pine, rough finished where it is exposed on the exterior. None of the structural wood is exposed on the interior, which is finished entirely in white cedar. However, the interior trim is designed to appear exactly as it would had the exterior timbers been exposed inside. The two pairs of Oregon pine beams are covered with ¾-inch white cedar in a form that implies two beams. The two 3 × 6 timbers at the gable end are echoed by two ¾ × 6 pieces of wood trim on the interior. But not all of the structure is expressed in this way; the rafters, for example, are simply covered with a plaster ceiling.

A less literal representation is found in the living room (figures 5.40 and 5.46). The room is cruciform and structurally self-contained. The floor above is standard platform framing, with 2 × 12 joists at 12 inches on center. The long span exceeds the maximum span for these joists; additional support is provided by two built-up beams, each made of three 2 × 16's. The 2 × 16's are deeper than the 2 × 12's, and thus the beam projects below the ceiling. This portion is covered with ¾-inch teak boards. The analogy does not end here. Below the real beam is a truss of Burmese teak, with dog-leg diagonals resembling Japanese construction. This truss is strong enough to support the joists, and it adds additional support to the structure; however, since the truss is installed much later than the joists, with

5.39

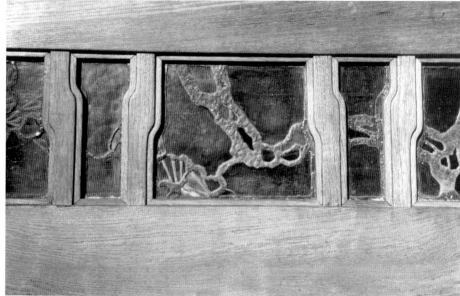

5.41

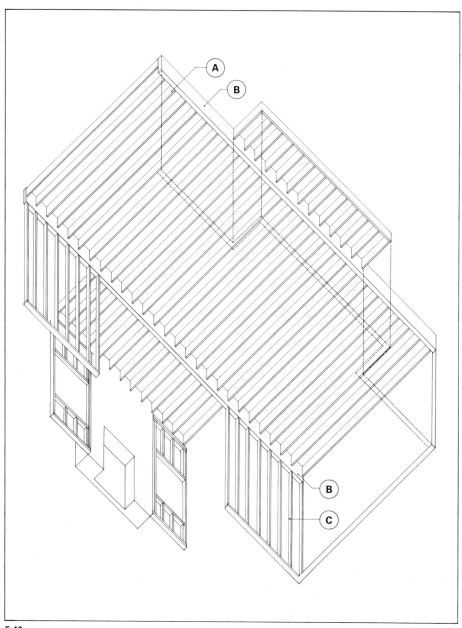

5.40

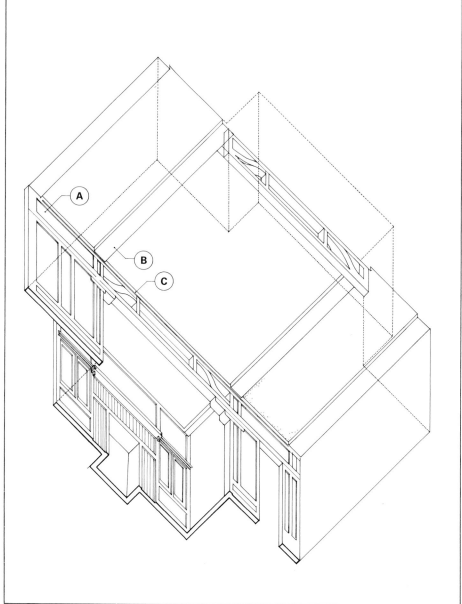

5.42

David B. Gamble house

Charles and Henry Greene

Pasadena, California, 1908

5.39 **porch detail**

5.40 **framing of living room**

A Floor construction: subfloor of
1 × 6 boards on 2 × 12 joists 12″
on center.

B Girder made from three 2 × 16
boards.

C 2 × 4-wood-stud wall supporting
girder.

(Greene and Greene Library.)

5.41 **detail of window in front door**

5.42 **ceiling plan of living room**

A Burmese teak paneling.

B Ornamental teak beams. Unlike the
truss, these elements have no
relation to the real structure.

C Burmese teak truss. This has no
structural purpose, but it is
analogous to the real structure and
parallels the three 2 × 16's above.

(Greene and Greene Library.)

the finish carpentry, the three 2 × 16's must be capable of carrying the entire load. Thus, although this truss could be described as an analogous rather than a purely ornamental structure, it is considerably overdesigned, being heavier and more elaborate than is structurally necessary. Some of the pieces, such as the two strips on the ceiling that connect the trusses, have no counterparts in the real structure. In this sense it is less accurate in describing the concealed structure, but at the same time it makes possible other analogies between itself and other real structures in the building.

The analogous structural systems of the interior can also be interpreted as symbolic recapitulations of the real structures of the exterior porches and pavilions. Thus, in the main elevation, the analogous wood structure of the front bedroom parallels the real wood structure of the sleeping porch at the opposite end of the facade. The living room, in a similar way, can be seen as analogous to the real structure of the rear sleeping porch, for (unlike the front porch, which is constructed with brackets) the rear porch is constructed with a truss, which is closely paralleled in the adjacent living-room truss. The differences between the two trusses can be seen as distinguishing between one that is structural and one that is not. The diagonals of the real truss are straight, and align exactly with the forces that they carry. The distortion of this form into a dog-leg brace in the interior truss acts to signal its lack of structural importance. The purely ornamental crosspiece is also detailed to make clear its nonstructural nature. The bracket, which would normally support this if it were a real beam, is dropped several inches, so that the bracket and the beam never make contact.

It can be argued that these analogous structures are due to a combination of coincidence and the necessary cladding of exposed beams, but the treatment of the second-floor hall and bedrooms shows the use of analogous structure where it is functionally unnecessary and detrimental to the visual unity of the whole. These rooms are not structurally self-contained but are traversed by a complex structure carrying the roof and the third floor. The most important elements are the two large trusses supporting the billiard room. Although completely contained by the attic, so that they do not protrude below the ceiling level, they are expressed by two analogous beams of white cedar (figures 5.32 and 5.33). Three beams run across the master bedroom and hallway ceiling in a way that awkwardly divides the space. Surely if these beams were purely ornamental they would have been used in a way more complimentary to the rooms they occupy. The central beam covers three 2 × 14's, which act as additional joist supports; perhaps to show that this beam is secondary in importance to the trusses, it is "broken" between the hall and the bedroom.

There are rooms in the Gamble house that fall outside this system of analogous construction—some because they are ornamental, but others because they expose the real structure. The den on the ground floor exposes the Oregon pine timbers, here suitably finished for interior use, and the billiard room on the third floor is built in the monolithic style of the Bandini house. There are several possible reasons for this. The architects and the client may have felt that the more rustic finish of exposed pine or redwood was more suitable to those two male-dominated areas of the house. In the den the Greenes had been forced to use Mr. Gamble's existing furniture and oak paneling. The Greenes rarely used oak, which they disliked, probably because of its strong grain. The billiard room can be interpreted as another traditional frame pavilion, similar to the sleeping porch, and this reading may explain why a man who did not play billiards should have a room that would accommodate several tables.

The entry hall is less easily understood as analogous; its wood ceiling only faintly resembles the structures above. What appear to be the minor beams are in fact teak covers on the Oregon pine timbers above (figures 5.30, 5.31), but the short teak beams running across the hall have no basis in structural reality, unless they conceal bridging or cross-bracing not shown on the drawings.

5.43

5.45

5.44

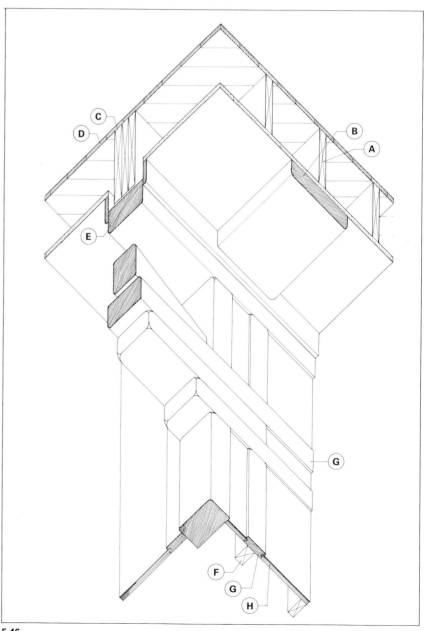

5.46

David B. Gamble house

Charles and Henry Greene

Pasadena, California, 1908

5.43 **entry hall and living room**
(Marvin Rand.)

5.44 **detail**

5.45 **dining room**
(Marvin Rand.)

5.46 **details of truss in living room**

A   2 × 10 pine joists spaced at 12″ on center.

B   Burmese teak ornamental beam.

C   Girder made from three 2 × 14 pine boards.

D   Subfloor of 1 × 6 Oregon pine boards laid diagonally.

E   Burmese teak truss.

F   2 × 4 pine studs, 16″ on center.

G   Teak trim, $\frac{7}{8}$″ thick.

H   Teak veneer on plywood.
(Greene and Greene Library.)

The dining room also appears to be primarily ornamental rather than analogous. The true framing is a simple platform-frame box. The posts and cross-rails of the paneling can be seen as analogous to the framing around the numerous door and window openings, but the boards and brackets that form a cornice around the room have no basis in the real structure of the dining room, although they resemble and occupy the same position as the real brackets on the south sleeping porch. In its defense, one can say that the wood is detailed in a way that makes its ornamental function clear. The boards of the cornice are joined in a way that shows that they are less than an inch thick and incapable of taking loads. Likewise, the brackets are quite thin and could not easily be perceived as a real structure.

The Gamble house is a fairly systematic mixture of real and analogous structural systems, with its combination of solid exposed real structure on the exterior and an analogous veneered system on the interior, but it is isolated in the Greenes' work in this regard. While accepting the fact that analogous systems were often preferable to monolithic ones, and feeling (like Stickley) that purely ornamental gestures were sometimes desirable, they always felt (like Stickley) that the best solution occurred when structural and ornamental concerns coincided in monolithic structures. The reasons why they chose not to use this system in the interior of the Gamble house can be explained by examining a case where they did: the hall of the Blacker house.

The Blacker house was under construction while the documents for the Gamble house were being prepared. Like the Gamble house, it has three primary levels of craftsmanship and uses real, analogous, and ornamental structural systems. Still, the Greenes were careful to distinguish among these types, partially through detailing, but primarily through the use of different species of wood. This explains, in part, why the hall of the Blacker house has four different finish woods (figure 5.38). The first-floor ceiling of the hall is a monolithic structure of oak and Oregon pine. All the beams are dressed, and some are carved at their ends. The only exception to the monolithic nature on this structure is the sandwich construction of the floor, in which Oregon pine decking is sandwiched in between finish flooring above and white cedar paneling below. On the side walls this structure converts to an analogous one, such as at the stair, where the real beam end is enclosed by a $\frac{3}{4}$-inch board of Oregon pine veneered against the wall beyond. Like those in the Gamble house, this interior bracket mimics an exterior one but is detailed in such a way (with a round end) as to deny its support. The second-floor ceiling and vestibule are faced with hollow oak beams, which are mostly ornamental. The main truss is echoed by the main oak beam below, but the smaller cross-beams have no counterpoint except the joists above, which are much more tightly spaced. Those around the entry vestibule are perhaps the most deceitful, since the beams whose ends are visible are solid, while those whose ends are not are hollow box beams. The wood paneling is in two parts. The panels themselves extend from the ground floor to the tops of the doors at the second floor, and are made of monolithic slabs of teak or mahogany. Separated from the paneling by a band of plaster is a frieze of redwood panels with oak trim. It recalls the living-room frieze of the Gamble house, and it may have been intended that these panels be carved.

Each of the structural types used in the Blacker house—solid, clad, and paneled—is delineated in a different type of wood, which adds clarity to the distinction between real and ornamental pieces. Clearly, there was a decision to use a monolithic structure wherever possible, while using a veneered analogous system where conditions (or funds) did not permit monolithic construction. The price of this decision is the collision of these systems and species in one space. While the Blacker hall is in its general outlines more impressive than the Gamble hall, it lacks the unity of detail achieved in the latter, and as we have seen, only the den and billiard room in the Gamble house are detailed in a method comparable to the Blacker hall.

A comparison of the wood paneling systems of the Blacker and Gamble houses also reveals an initial preference for monolithic systems followed by an acceptance of the need to use veneers. Almost all the panels in the Blacker hall are monolithic;

5.47

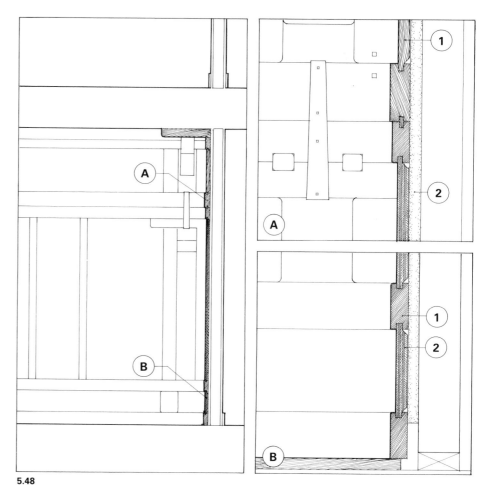

5.48

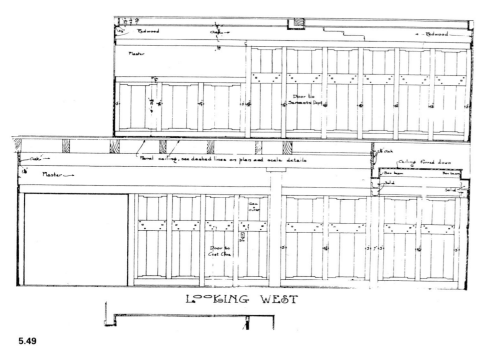

LOOKING WEST

5.49

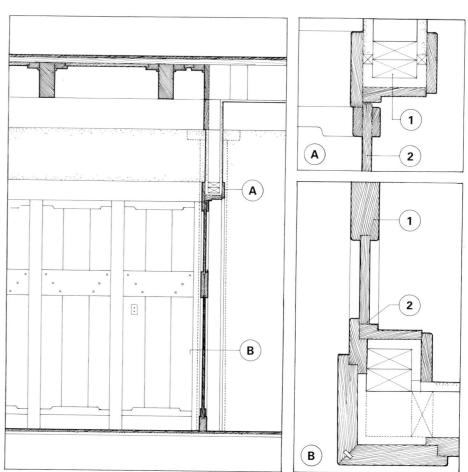

5.50

David B. Gamble house

Charles and Henry Greene

Pasadena, California, 1908

5.47   **detail of living room**

(Marvin Rand.)

5.48   **details of paneling**

A   Intermediate railing.

  1 Solid wood panel with carving.

  2 Plaster on wood studs.

B   Base.

  1 Solid teak rail.

  2 Most of the larger pieces are five-ply plywood veneer with only the outer ply of teak.

(Greene and Greene Library.)

R. R. Blacker house

Charles and Henry Greene

Pasadena, California, 1907

5.49   **section at hall**

(Greene and Greene Library.)

5.50   **details of paneling**

A   Head at closet door. This detail forms an "invisible" door in the hall paneling.

  1 Two 2 × 4 wood headers. These support the studs over the door openings.

  2 Door, made mostly of solid lumber.

B   Corner, closet door jamb.

  1 Solid rail of door.

  2 Door jamb, designed to make the door indistinguishable from the paneling.

(Greene and Greene Library.)

the only exception is the doors, some of which face onto rooms finished in a different type of wood. These are built of pine cores and veneers with different woods on each side to match the rooms that they face.

The architect who wished to use solid paneling in 1900 faced a number of problems. Architects who favored monolithic construction often used a simple pattern of tongue-and-groove boards. This was too rustic for the tastes of the Greenes and their clients, as they obviously wanted a system with the repetitive elements of traditional stile-and-rail paneling. The Greenes' solution was the H-shaped system shown in figure 5.50, which had a number of functional and aesthetic advantages. It used relatively narrow boards (thus eliminating concealed joints in the panel itself). It did not have the visual completeness of traditional paneling, since the surrounding frame was discontinuous. In accordance with Arts and Crafts doctrine, it did not use molding to hide the joints or the workmanship; instead, the fasteners (or at least their ebony caps) were used as ornament.

Just as the monolithic interior of the Blacker house evolved into the veneered one of the Gamble house, so did the paneling. The Gamble house's dining room does have monolithic panels of mahogany that resemble those of the Blacker house, but the hall and the living room are paneled in a system that makes extensive use of veneers (figure 5.48). The panel itself is fine-grained, clear Burmese teak; the inner layers are of inferior woods. As in the Greenes' furniture, the grains of the veneers are book-matched on each panel. The panels are joined with solid pieces of teak, which project beyond. The veneer panels are set into the solid rail with a rabbet joint.

The veneering used in the Gamble house was undoubtedly the more inexpensive system. The only real advantage of the monolithic system was the smaller amount of labor involved in its fabrication, and the development of power tools in the nineteenth century eliminated this advantage, so that the cost of large, defect-free pieces of solid wood far outweighed the cost of producing veneers.

The Greenes' extensive use of analogous structures, clad beams, and veneered panels did not mark the beginning of a new style. The prejudice in favor of monolithic systems remained, and both systems—the monolithic and the analogous—were elaborated on in the Greenes' later work.

Perhaps because they sensed that the Gamble house represented something of an idea carried to its conclusion, the Greenes pursued a number of different directions in their subsequent work, both in planning and in construction. The Pratt house was their most extreme attempt to build a monolithic timber-frame building within the constraints of modern construction. The Bentz house represents an acceptance of the fact that modern construction favors concealed structural systems and layered and veneered assemblies, and an architectural exploration of the plastic possibilities of this system.

The exterior construction of the Pratt house is similar to that of the Gamble house, with minor changes that can be interpreted as refinements. The wall uses two systems—a concealed platform frame and a large-scale timber frame of Oregon pine—just as in the Gamble house. But the interior details, unlike the analogous and ornamental systems of the Gamble house, make extensive use of exposed structural members.

Figure 5.53 shows a detail of a structural beam in the ceiling of the dining room. In the bedrooms of the second floor, the real Oregon pine beam is exposed on the exterior and clad with pine on the interior to create an analogous beam. In the dining room, a larger Oregon pine beam is split into two beams, one exposed on the outside and one on the inside. Similarly, the ceiling beams are not rough lumber clad in finish wood, as in the Gamble house and other houses, but monolithic Oregon pine beams dressed where they are exposed. It should be noted, however, that nowhere is a structural beam exposed on the interior and the

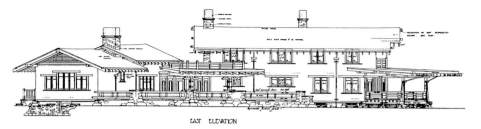

5.51

5.52

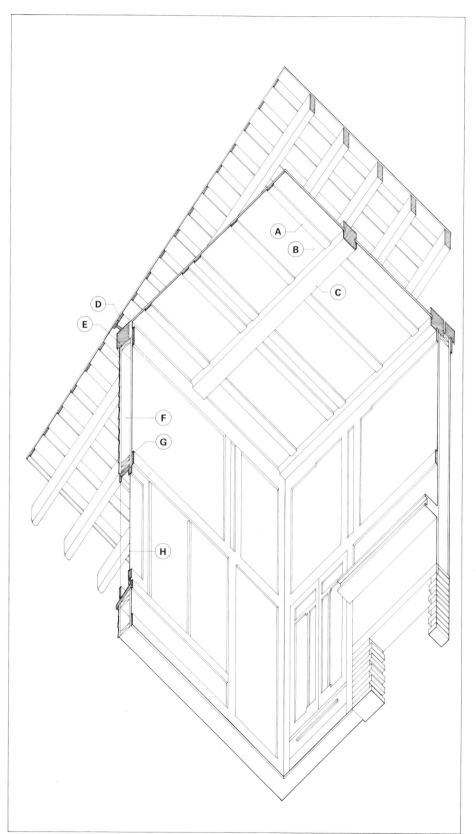

5.53

C. M. Pratt house

Charles and Henry Greene
Nordhoff, California, 1909

5.51 **east elevation**
(Greene and Greene Library.)

5.52 **dining room**
(Marvin Rand.)

5.53 **wall section at dining room**
A   White cedar battens.
B   24" redwood boards.
C   8 × 8 Oregon pine beam. Unlike the Gamble house, this house has many of its structural timbers exposed on the interior.
D   1 × 4 lath, supported by 3 × 6 Oregon pine rafters.
E   8 × 8 Oregon pine beam, exposed on the exterior but clad on the interior.
F   Wall construction: 2 × 6 Oregon pine studs spaced at 12" on center and sheathed with ⅞ × 6 Oregon pine boards.
G   Two 2 × 6's over window opening.
H   In swinging wood casement window. The sash is sugar pine, veneered to match the paneling.
(Greene and Greene Library.)

exterior. This would have made the finishing and the alignment much more difficult, since it would have been impossible to dimensionally adjust the framing to take up inaccuracies in construction. The dining room, in fact, is almost a separate frame set within the larger frame of the house.

Perhaps the most striking feature of the Pratt house is the distinction between the wood structure and the wood paneling and the difference in detail between them. Here, for the first time, the Greenes fully exploited the possibilities of veneered plywood, using much wider sheets than in the Gamble house. This is in sharp contrast to the Blacker hall, where the solid paneling and beams are closely integrated. Perhaps this is why the Pratt house is so appealing to modern sensibilities that demand a sharp distinction between that which supports and that which is supported. By emphasizing the monolithic quality of the structure and the layered and veneered quality of the paneling, the Greenes anticipated the construction philosophies of Modernists like Kahn. At the same time, it should be remembered that there are functional differences as well. The exposed Oregon pine structure of the Pratt house was put in place with the rest of the major framing, whereas the paneling was added much later (after the building was closed in). In the Gamble house, the paneling and the beam covers were installed simultaneously, making installation much easier.

The dining-room paneling of the Pratt house is itself something of an analogous structure. (It is one of the few two-story spaces in the Greenes' work. Many Arts and Crafts architects, including Voysey, disliked two-story spaces on the grounds that they were inappropriately monumental for domestic interiors.) The Greenes use a double-tiered system with white cedar panels below and redwood above, all covered with white cedar battens. The battens are single on the bottom tier and doubled on the top, recalling the doubling of columns in the Gamble house's porch.

Unfortunately, the Pratt house, like the Gamble house, marked an end and not a beginning for the Greenes. Makinson has detailed the decline in their fortunes after 1909 as tastes changed and the cost of their buildings and services increased. The problem was not, however, the cost of building in wood. Most of the single-family houses built in California then (and now) are platform-frame wood structures. Their frames, however, are seldom exposed. The expense of the Greene brothers' work was due to the way they built, not to the materials they used. The cost of large structural members, the cost of hand-finishing these members, the cost of woods good enough to merit exposure, and the cost of workmanship of a quality to be exposed were all factors in increasing the cost of the Greenes' type of wood-frame construction. The exposed beams of the Pratt house are in some places very crudely finished, perhaps reflecting this increase in costs. The correspondence between Charles Greene and Charles Pratt gives a clue to another problem: the cost of architectural supervision. The typical Greene and Greene house required extensive coordination between architect and contractor. Since most of the Greenes' houses were built in Pasadena, close to both the Halls' workshop and the Greenes' office, coordination was simplified, and Charles visited both workshop and sites almost daily. The Pratt house's location, in Ojai, made communication considerably more difficult and required considerably more of the architects' time. Charles Greene's letters to Pratt make it clear that the client was extremely unhappy with the cost of the extensive supervision required to finish the house.

By the time they designed the Bentz house, the Greenes clearly realized that the bungalow style had to be modified to survive. This house (not one of their best) shows that the Greenes were trying to minimize the problems of wood construction by making use of new techniques and materials.

Of all the Greenes' houses in the bungalow style, the Bentz house probably has the least amount of exposed timber. Certain of the standard details are here (the heavy timber base, the typical casement window and eave detail), but many others are gone. There are no sleeping porches, no open gable ends with lattice vents.

5.54

5.55

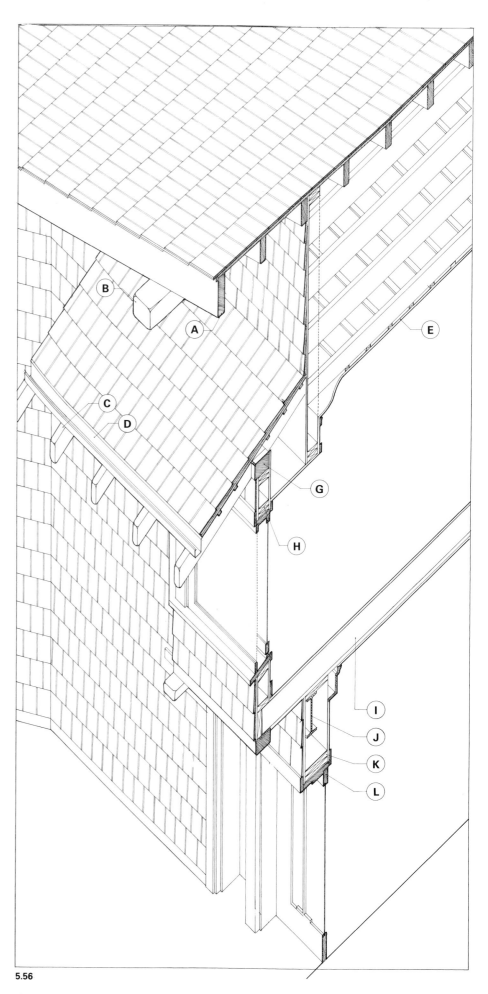

5.56

N. Bentz house

Charles and Henry Greene

Santa Barbara, California, 1911

5.54   **under construction**

(Greene and Greene Library.)

5.55   **exterior**

5.56   **wall section at entry**

A   Roof construction: 3 × 6½. Rafters spaced at 24″ on center, supporting wood deck and shingles.

B   8 × 10 beam, supporting rafters.

C   3 × 6½ rafters, 24″ on center.

D   Metal gutter.

E   Ceiling: plaster on 1 × 2 furring, 12″ on center.

G   8 × 6 beam, supporting rafters of small roof.

H   Wall construction: 2 × 4 studs with shakes 11″ to weather.

I   Floor construction: 2 × 12 wood joists with wood subfloor.

J   14″-deep steel beam.

K   2 × 10-wood-stud wall. The wall is considerably thicker than the normal 5″ here to accommodate the steel structure.

L   Wood door.

(Greene and Greene Library.)

There is a trellis, but it is supported by brick walls; and there is little interior paneling, only trim. The most surprising change is the extensive use of steel and concrete structural members. The brick base of the building is supported principally by concrete cross-beams holding wood joists. The radial beams of the hall, which were Oregon pine timbers in the Pratt house, are steel here (figure 5.57). The most drastic change is in the interior, where the constructivist aesthetic of wood is replaced by an expressionist aesthetic of plaster, which covers the steel and concrete beams.

In the Bentz house's interiors, the Greenes moved completely away from the idea of building represented by the Bandini house. Monolithic exposed wood was replaced by layered, veneered, and concealed construction of steel, wood, and plaster.

When last they had used steel extensively, in the Libby house (1905), the Greenes had constructed the beam covers of plaster, not wood, to avoid what Ruskin would have called a "deceit." This philosophy of cladding in plaster rather than wood was maintained in the Bentz house's living room, with its elaborate plaster covers (figure 5.57), but not in the hall, where the ceiling is plaster but the beam covers are wood.

The treatment of the plaster ceiling signals another change in Charles Greene's work, and an increased interest in the plastic, fluid, and sculptural qualities of materials at the expense of the constructivist and elemental qualities of construction. Exposed joinery and visually independent structural members are rare in his later work. In the James house, for example, the wood windows and the stone trim were carved, and the plaster was molded into curved shapes that extend uninterrupted across joints in material.

The use of a steel-and-concrete frame clad in plaster, and the use of a concealed wood frame, were also prophetic of the direction that modern construction was to take, but not of the direction Charles Greene was to follow. In the few works that he executed after 1917, the construction was monolithic exposed masonry and wood.

It is tragic that Charles Greene, born in the same year as Frank Lloyd Wright, built only two major buildings after 1918 (the James house and the Flavin Library). Yet it may be that Greene, like Gimson, found success on his own terms, building a few buildings the way he felt they should be built. His last works were built of monolithic wood and stone, without the extensive use of machinery. Greene molded the plaster and carved the woodwork himself, and (like Gimson) acted as his own contractor, supervising a few trained workmen. Perhaps he was thinking of his problems with the Pratt house when he wrote, describing the construction of the James house:

Ordinarily, when plans are made for a house, after careful study they are practically final, and the specifications minutely exact. These are turned over to a contractor who by contract produces the completed product. Whether he does the work by percentage or a stated sum doesn't matter, he directs the work. Now the James house was not built that way. The architect hired the men and directed the work personally; except for plumbing, electric work and tiling, there were no contracts.

Here is the difference; prevailing custom is a system of administration by recorded instruction; mine is not any system, but personal direction on the job. The first is fixed, the second is elastic, yielding to contingencies, open to inspiration.[16]

Charles Greene's last significant work was the Flavin Library in Carmel. It was finished in 1932, the year the International Style Exhibition opened at the Museum of Modern Art in New York.

If the Greenes' work was honest or dishonest or had lost the moral content of the Arts and Crafts movement, it was not in this respect different from the work of their contemporaries. If the Greenes' work is dishonest, then so is the work of Voysey and Webb. However, what is perhaps more important than the effect of

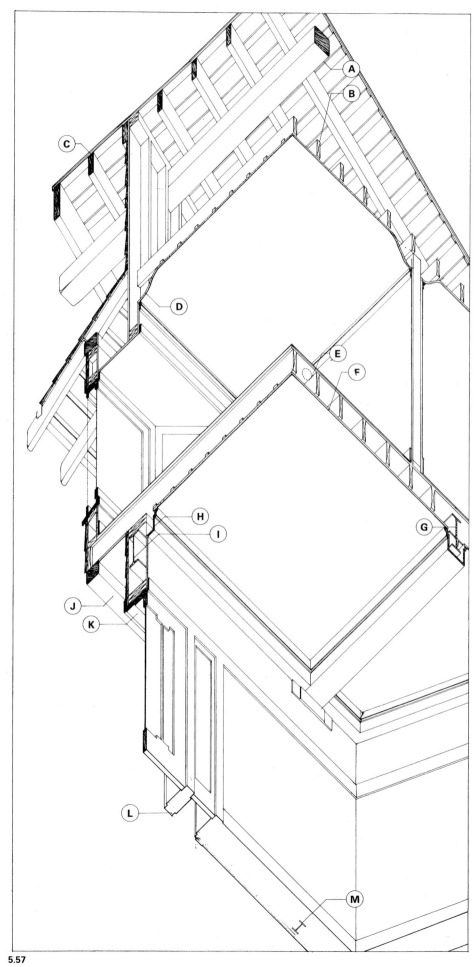

5.57

N. Bentz house

Charles and Henry Greene

Santa Barbara, California, 1911

5.57 interior wall section

A 8 × 10 beam.

B 2 × 6 ceiling joists.

C Roof construction: 3 × 6½ rafters supporting lath and shakes.

D Plaster cove. Contrast this detail to the corresponding detail in figure 5.38.

E 6″ round ventilation duct.

F Floor construction: 2 × 12 joists.

G Steel beam: 18″-deep, 56-lb. I section with 5″ × 3″ × ⅜″ steel angles to support wood joists.

H Plaster cove.

I 14″-deep steel beam, supporting floor joists over door opening.

J 6 × 8 beam.

K 2 × 10 plates.

L Wood door frame.

M Steel column: 5″ I section.

(Greene and Greene Library.)

Arts and Crafts theories on Arts and Crafts architecture is the effect of those theories on Modern architecture.

Historians have always been aware of the close link between the progressive ideals of Modernism and the conservative ideals of the Arts and Crafts movement, despite the stylistic differences. The outstanding example of this link is the effect of Morris's ideas on the founding and organization of the Bauhaus.

Three ideas of Arts and Crafts detailing became important ideas of Modernist detailing. The first of these ideas (an idea that is related to Ruskin's idea of rudeness, and to what might be called picturesque as opposed to Classical craftsmanship) is that the imperfections and marks left by the individual workman are desirable over perfection of joinery and finish. If the marks of the hand tool are virtuous, why not the marks of the machine tool? That later architects were to consider Wagner's exposed bolts, Le Corbusier's board-formed concrete, and Kahn's form-tie holes aesthetically desirable is, in part, due to the Arts and Crafts ideal. The second of these ideas is a result of the application of the first idea to the methods of joinery. Classical joinery concealed fasteners and covered difficult joints with moldings and trim. Arts and Crafts sought the opposite—exposed fasteners and joints—as an ideal, since it allowed the evidence of craft to show. The result, of course, was that a higher level of finish came to be demanded in these operations, as awareness of joinery was not to be equated with rudeness. Subsequent architects, both Modernist and traditional, were to make extensive use of the exposed fastener and the exposed butt joint, and to demand the level of craftsmanship from man or machine that would make them possible. The third idea was the postulation of an ideal building as one with exposed monolithic construction with a uniform level of craftsmanship. Exposed monolithic construction had already been advocated by Pugin and others, but the uniform level of craft required to produce it became for the British Arts and Crafts architects an end in itself. By 1900 it was clear that this was not a practical method of building for many jobs, but this was a problem of society, not of architecture; it was the society that needed to be changed, not the building. These architects were well aware that this was a utopian and not a practical ideal. Subsequent architects who were to advocate this type of construction were less utopian, but this ideal retained its power well into the next century and did not really begin to die until the social ideals of Modernism did so.

The Greenes were not utopians. To criticize them for the use of layered construction, analogous structural systems, and hierarchies of craftsmanship is to criticize them for accepting the world as they found it. Like Stickley and Wright, they often spoke of the uniquely American qualities of their work with an enthusiasm we associate with the turn of the century. They were not alienated from the world they lived in (at least not before 1914), and utopia seemed to them to be within reach (at least a utopia they could live with). It seemed to them unnecessary and foolish to postulate a method of building that ran counter to their world as it was. Their dedication to the Arts and Crafts ideal was as strong as Gimson's, but it was not the same ideal. To criticize the Greenes for not building according to the ideals of Gimson or Dresser is to criticize them for not sharing their alienation. When the Greenes were rediscovered in the 1950s, they were seen as the embodiment of these ideals—something they never claimed to be. Disillusionment with them came when they were discovered not to be what some had tried to make them into. As we shall see, the ideals to which they did conform proved quite relevant to the directions that architecture and building were to follow.

6   Frank Lloyd Wright in Oak Park

Whether or not Hemingway ever said that Oak Park was full of "wide lawns and narrow minds," the wisecrack defined his position.

For forty years he insisted that he hated the place and that he had more than once run away from it.

Kenneth S. Lynn

In 1912 Montgomery Schuyler reviewed the recently published Wasmuth's portfolio of Wright's work for the *Architectural Record.* Although generally favorable, Schuyler was quite specific about the deficiencies of Wright's details: "The defect of their [the designs] will be evident to every practiced inspector. Those functional modifications of surface or of line, commonly by means of moldings, to form a footing, to emphasize a division, to soften or sharpen a transition, to mark a projection or a recess, which have been employed in every artistic mode of building from the Egyptian downward, are here almost altogether absent. . . . The stark unmodeled transitions give an air of something rude, incomplete, unfinished. The buildings seem 'blocked out' and awaiting completion rather than completed."[1] Schuyler was not alone in this sentiment. C. R. Ashbee, in his introduction to the same book, wrote of "a certain barrenness and sterility of detail . . . a certain disregard of the intimate and personal things that make a building lovable in the sacrifice of tenderness for integrity,"[2] and Russell Sturges, reviewing the Larkin Building, wrote: "An extremely ugly building. It is in fact a monster of awkwardness if we look at its lines and masses alone. . . . We find in this building none of those familiar motives—those accepted details which are architecture for us."[3]

It is not surprising to find adverse criticism of Wright at this time, but Schuyler, Ashbee, and Sturgis were not reactionaries. They were, to varying degrees, progressive critics, and Schuyler and Ashbee were supporters of Wright. Ashbee was a key member of the English Arts and Crafts movement. In the same year, Wright wrote to him: "You will count me one of your warmest friends and admirers."[4] And in 1914, Wright said of Schuyler: "When . . . I took my stand, alone in my field, the cause was unprofitable . . . unhonored and ridiculed; Montgomery Schuyler was the one notable exception to the rule."[5] All three of these men admired the absence of literal historical references in Wright's work, but all three saw his harsh geometric trim detail as a flaw in work that was otherwise admirable.

The reservations of Wright's early critics have been forgotten, mainly because Modern critics saw in the geometric simplicity of his ornament and his trim the origins of the minimalism and abstraction of Modern architecture. Wright was after all "a pioneer of modern design," although even Nikolaus Pevsner, describing

6.1

6.2

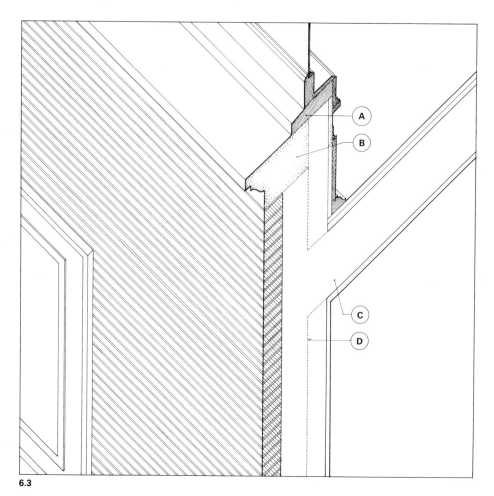

A

B

C

D

6.3

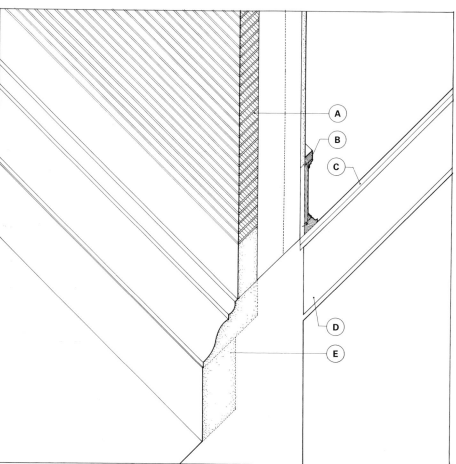

A

B

C

D

E

6.4

W. Winslow house

Frank Lloyd Wright

River Forest, Illinois, 1893

6.1 **exterior**

6.2 **detail**

6.3 **wall section at window**

A   Double-hung wood window with trim not unlike that used by McKim and White.

B   Stone sill. Note use of cyma recta curve to visually support the projected sill. In Wright's later work, he simplified and then eliminated this detail.

C   Floor construction: finish floor on subfloor of wood joists with plaster below.

D   Wood studs. The house is a platform-frame building with wood veneer.
(Frank Lloyd Wright Foundation, drawing 9305.11, HABS.)

6.4 **wall details at base**

A   Brick veneer. The "Roman" brick, being thinner than "common" brick, produces more horizontal lines.

B   Wood base. The shape of this wood base replicates at a smaller scale the shape of the exterior stone base.

C   Finish-wood floor and subfloor.

D   Wood-joist floor.

E   Stone base (a typical Classical molding, given a horizontal emphasis).
(Frank Lloyd Wright Foundation, drawing 9305.11, HABS.)

the Larkin Building's interior, wrote of "Wright's never abating desire for harsh angular decorative forms."[6] Wright's thinking at the time was quite different, for Wright and his critics saw the characteristic detail of his work as an application of the ideals of the Arts and Crafts movement to the ideals of classicism.

WRIGHT AND CLASSICISM

Sturgis, in his rather hostile review of the Larkin Building, also called attention to what he felt was inadequate in Wright's detailing: "... while everything has been carried out with a view to practical utility there has also been some attempt to adorn, to beautify. But we have already seen reason to think this attempt has failed. See for the attempt and for the failure that curious base arranged beneath brick piers on the right [figures 6.5, 6.6]; it is the attic base reduced to its simplest form, the familiar old attic base, with its round moldings turned back into the square edge bands which these moldings were in their origin."[7] History's assessment of the Larkin Building was different from Sturgis's, but on this point one has to agree he was right. The inspiration for the column base was undoubtedly Classical.

It is hard for us to look at Wright's work from before 1910 and not think about what came later, especially from Wright. Later in Wright's life it was equally difficult for him. The majority of his writings were done many years after he left Oak Park, and the descriptions of his early buildings in these writings were written with an eye to establishing precedents for his later work. All this obscures some of the finer qualities of his early buildings, particularly the details. Wright changed his detailing methods quite radically after 1910, and he ignored many of the qualities of his early work in his later writings.

WRIGHT AND THE ARTS AND CRAFTS MOVEMENT

After meeting with Wright in 1908, Ashbee's wife Janet wrote in her journal: "Lloyd Wright is a strange delightful soul, a radical original thinker working out his ideas consistently, as an artist, in his architecture not bothering about the 'sociology' of it ('it destroys' the art) putting up building after building in queer square blocks with squares and long straight lines for decoration. 'The mechanical must be utilized and beautiful,' he says 'we cannot reject it—we cannot go back to previous conditions or methods. We must use things as they are to create a new beauty from apparent ugliness.' Much of this building is too bizarre [and] away from all tradition to be beautiful [and] the decoration of squares [and] geometric lines I find fussy and restless."[8]

Despite his progressive ideas about the machine, Wright's credentials as a member of the Arts and Crafts movement were much better than those of the Greene brothers. He was a founder of the Chicago Arts and Crafts Society, and was the corresponding secretary of Ashbee's British National Trust.

When he delivered his lecture "The Art and Craft of the Machine" at Hull House, he invited several of his subcontractors to attend, in the hopes that they would "tell us what we might do to help them."[9] Later in his life Wright gave the impression that this lecture, with its emphasis on the possibilities rather than the limitations of industrialization, went against the grain of the Chicago Arts and Crafts Society in particular and the Arts and Crafts movement in general; however, many members of the movement shared his sympathies. Ashbee wrote in 1900: "He threw down the glove to me in characteristic Chicagoan manner, in the matter of Arts & Crafts & the creations of the machine. 'My God' said he, 'is machinery and the art of the future will be the expression of the individual artist through the thousand powers of the machine, the machine doing all those things that the individual workman cannot do.' ... He was surprised to find how much I concurred with him."[10] As H. Allen brooks has pointed out, "in terms of the British Arts and Crafts Movement, Wright's words were absolutely revolutionary, but in Chicago they were a succinct reaffirmation of the spirit of the times."[11]

Ashbee's introduction to the Wasmuth portfolio is, curiously, not particularly flattering. In addition to declaring that he prefers Charles Greene's work, he makes some fairly critical comments on Wright's buildings: "I have seen buildings of

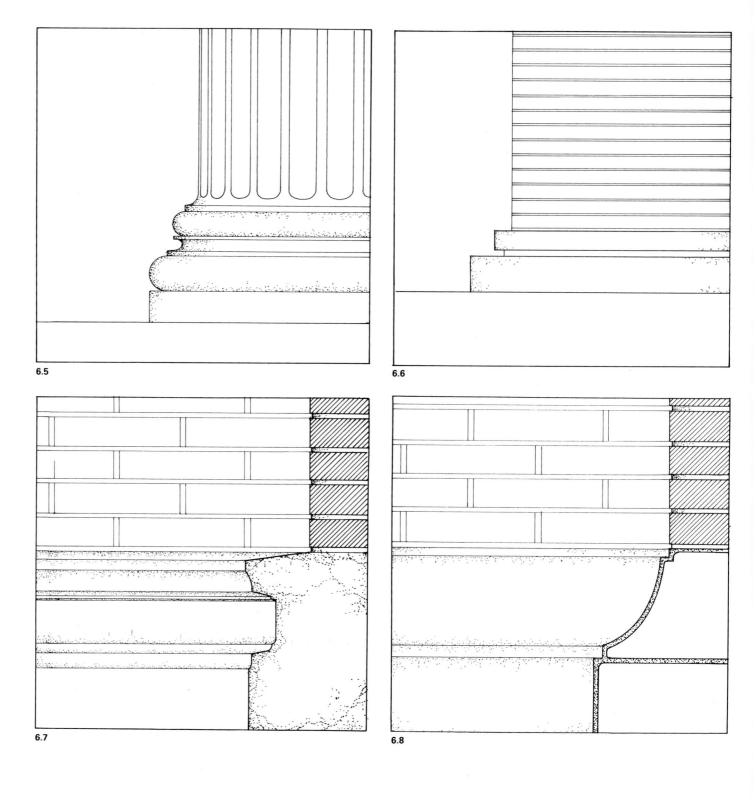

6.5

6.6

6.7

6.8

Frank Lloyd Wright's that I would like to touch with the enchanted wand; not to alter their structure in plan or form, or carcass, but to clothe them with a more living and tender detail."[12] But Ashbee did not really wish to see Wright's buildings altered. He considered them an accurate reflection of the state of craftsmanship in architecture. He goes on to say: "I do not know how, and the time is not yet—nor would I like to see Wright do it himself, because I do not believe he could; for thus to clothe them would mean a school of Craftsmanship that would tell of the intimate life of America, and would imply a little of that quietude and poetry and scholarship which our English churches and country houses have received from the caressing hands of generations of craftsmen."[13] This lack of tradition of craftsmanship is, Ashbee suggests, aggravated by the presence of machine tools: "Through the United States indeed the traditions of craftsmanship, upon which the arts professedly rest, have been broken down by mechanical power more than with us in Europe, and the American Architects . . . have not yet devised a way of reestablishing them, of finding their equivalent, or readjusting the balance. It is to the credit of Frank Lloyd Wright that he is the first American architect who has sought consciously to express this fact, to readjust the balance."[14]

Wright was in agreement with Ashbee and the Arts and Crafts architects that machine-made ornament had destroyed the handcrafted nature of true ornament. In his lecture to the Arts and Crafts Society in 1901, he said: "Machinery has been invented for no other purpose than to imitate, as closely as possible, the wood-carving of the early ideal—with the immediate result that no ninety-nine cent piece of furniture is salable without some horrible botchwork meaning nothing unless it means that art and craft have combined to fix in the mind of the masses the old hand-carved chair as the *ne plus ultra* of the ideal."[15] In the same talk, Wright's discussion of the use of stone provides an answer to those critics (including Schuyler and Ashbee) who would call for a softening of his detailing through moldings: "In the stone cutting trade the stone planer has made it possible to cut upon stone any given molded surface, or to ingrain on that surface any lovely texture the cunning brain may devise, and do it as it never was possible to do it by hand. What is it doing? Giving us as near an imitation of hand-tooled chiseling as possible, imitating moldings specifically adapted to wood, making possible the lavish use of miles of meaningless molded string courses, cornices, base courses—the giant power sneered at by the 'artist' because it fails to render the wavering delicacy of 'touch' resulting from the imperfections of 'handwork.'"[16]

Wright, like Ashbee, felt that sharp rectilinear trim, such as that of the Larkin Building, was inevitable in a country where a tradition of building craft did not exist and stone and wood trim was cut by machine. Unlike Ashbee, he was optimistic about the result. He felt this geometric simplicity, which the machine facilitated, brought out the nature of the materials, since carving and molding obscured the graining of wood and stone: "You may try to imitate the hand carving of the ancients in this matter, baffled by the craft and tenderness of the originals, or you may give the pneumatic chisel and power plane suitable work to do which would mean a changed style, a shift in the spiritual center of the ideal now controlling the use of stone in constructing modern stone buildings."[17]

Wright's description of rational building in 1901 was largely a sociological one. As his relation to society was to change, so was his defense of the abstract nature of his detail.

WRIGHT, STRUCTURAL RATIONALISM, AND ORNAMENTATION

Writing in 1911, Ashbee described his idea of rational building and what he believed were those of Wright and the other Arts and Crafts architects: "We guard in common the lamp of truth. We hold equally with Frank Lloyd Wright that structure should be self-explanatory, that iron is there for man's service, only he must learn to use it rightly, and not learn to lie or cheat about it."[18]

Wright certainly believed in the lamp of truth, but what was an honest building, particularly of wood? To the Gothic rationalists, honesty meant that structural members must be exposed monolithic pieces without veneers or cladding. To the

6.9

6.10

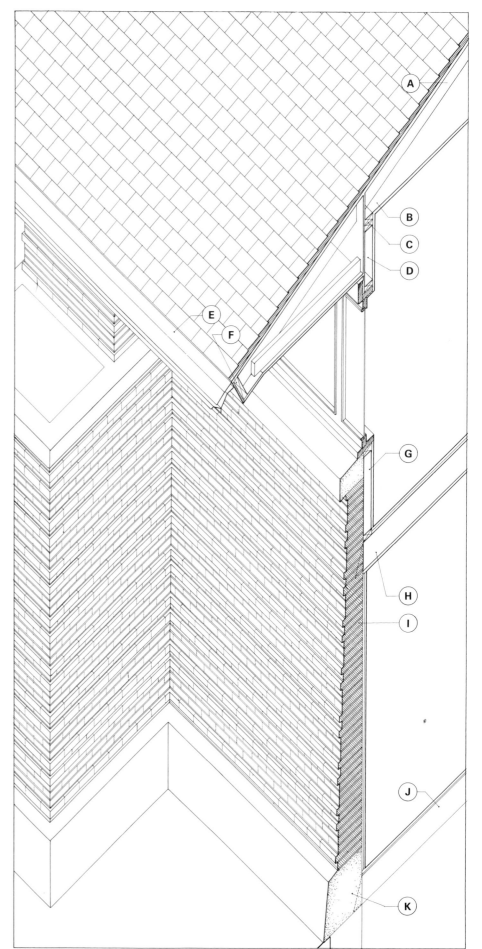

6.11

A. Heurtley house

Frank Lloyd Wright

Oak Park, Illinois, 1902

6.9   exterior

6.10   detail

6.11   wall section

A   Roof construction: tiles on 1″ wood sheathing on 2 × 6 wood rafters.

B   Wood ceiling joists.

C   Two 2 × 4 wood top plates.

D   Wood-stud wall. The upper part of this wall is standard 2 × 4 platform-frame construction. Wright avoided the use of either exposed or concealed lintels supporting brick in this house.

E   Gutter. Gutters should be curved or tapered rather than square to prevent damage from the expansion of freezing water. In the Prairie Houses, Wright exaggerates the curved or tapered shape into a triangle. The sharp edges reduce the apparent visual size of the gutter.

F   Wood fascia.

G   2 × 4-stud wall.

H   Floor construction: wood subfloor and joists supported by masonry wall.

I   Brick wall. The wall is tapered so that it is thickest toward the bottom, where the load is greatest. This is structural expression, not structural necessity; the increased wall thickness is unnecessary in this small building. The projecting bricks may be an expression of the header courses, in which bricks have their short side exposed.

J   Floor construction: finish-wood floor on 1″-wood-slat subfloor on 2 × 10 joists 16″ on center.

K   Stone base. Like the wall, the base is tapered to exaggerate the massiveness of the building.

(Frank Lloyd Wright Foundation, drawing 0204.011.)

Arts and Crafts architects, the monolithic system was preferable, but an analogous system in which the true structure was clad was acceptable if the ornamental system was not deceptive as to the true nature of the structure.

We think of Wright as a structural rationalist, and it is something of a surprise to discover that his work before 1910 is analogous rather than literal in its structural expression. Exposed structural members other than brick load-bearing walls are almost totally absent from his early work. It can be argued that the Martin house and the Larkin Building both have exposed concrete frames, but they might be more accurately described as composite—a mix of steel frames clad, and concealed, with concrete. Exposed framing members of wood or steel do not appear in Wright's work until the 1920s. If we consider the exposure of these elements as a criterion for either structural rationalism or Modernism, then we must consider Henri Labrouste far more "Modern" than Wright.

The equating of exposed structure with rational building was to be one of the great fallacies of Modernism. Perhaps it is a measure of Wright's genius that if he succumbed to this dogma, he did so at a very late date. Ironically his nearly exclusive use of analogous systems in this period is probably due to the influence of an architect who was less interested in structural rationalism than most of his contemporaries: Louis Sullivan.

Both Wright and Sullivan spoke of ornament as effervescent, as being *of* and not *on* the material. Sullivan dissociated ornament from many of its traditional uses. Traditional ornament consisted of moldings such as the ovolo, with or without enrichments such as egg-and-dart. These moldings were used to cover joints, to support projections, and to ease transitions. As Sullivan's style developed, he used ornament less and less for these purposes. In Sullivan's later work, ornament (particularly in terra cotta) occurs on flat surfaces, and either flows smoothly across joints and corners or avoids them altogether. Cornices, capitals, baseboards, and crown molds disappear or are brutally geometric.

The development of Wright's ornament parallels his relationship with Sullivan, from imitation to rejection to reacceptance. Much of his early (pre-1900) ornament is Sullivanesque in form and style, but as early as the Winslow house there is a reassertion of the Classical conceptions of moldings as transitions (although it is a highly personal reinterpretation of the Classical ornament). In the Martin house of 1904, ornaments and moldings begin to become "plastic" (in Wright's terminology), breaking away from joints, corners, and edges, which were left in pure if not brutal geometric simplicity. In style this ornament was the opposite of Sullivan's, being totally geometric in contrast to Sullivan's abstract but sinuous interpretations of plants. However, in concept and in the way in which it was used, it was identical. The other primary influence of Sullivan was, indirectly, on Wright's ideas of structural expression. Sullivan had little or no interest in structure, real or symbolic, and exposed structural elements are rare in his work, but he did impart to Wright the idea of structure clad in an expressive way.

Wright wrote in 1901: "The steel frame has been recognized as a legitimate basis for a simple, sincere clothing of plastic material that idealizes its purpose without structural pretense."[19] Clearly, he did not feel at this point in his career that the exposure of structure was necessary for the expression of structure.

In his autobiography, Wright admits to two other influences: Viollet-le-Duc's *Discourses on Architecture* and Owen Jones's *Grammar of Ornament*. (The latter book undoubtedly influenced Sullivan, too.) Since Wright was not one to readily acknowledge influences, his admission must be taken seriously. But the views of these two on ornament and its relation to structure are in many ways opposite and, not surprisingly, correspond to the two different trends in Wright's ornamentation. Despite his love of Gothic, Viollet-le-Duc's view of moldings was Classical. The purpose of moldings, he wrote, was to form a footing, mark a height, define an opening, or support a projection—in short, to make joints and transitions. Jones, in contrast, disliked this aspect of Classicism. He wrote of Greek ornaments:

6.12

6.13

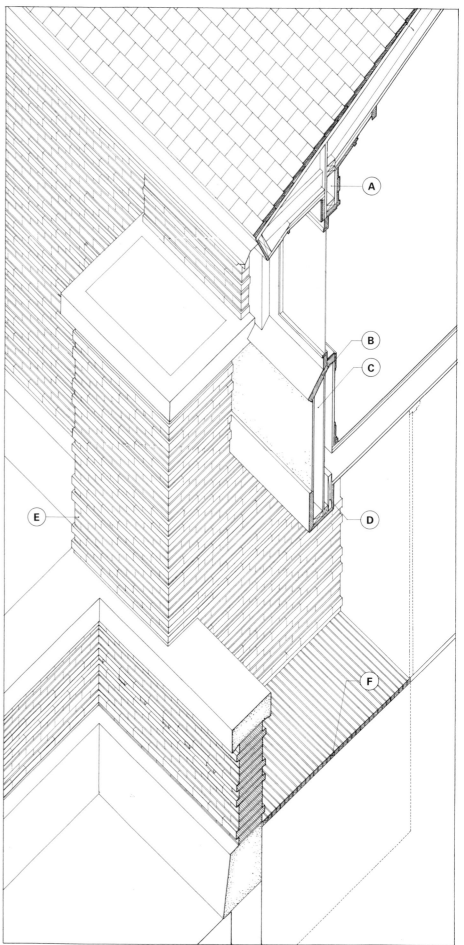

6.14

A. Heurtley house

Frank Lloyd Wright

Oak Park, Illinois, 1902

6.12 **interior of living room**

(Herbert Barnett.)

6.13 **detail**

6.14 **wall section at balcony**

A 2 × 4-wood-stud wall frame over opening. Faced with sheathing and stucco.

B Wood sill. The slope of this sill is much greater than that of the adjacent windows in masonry walls.

C Wall construction: two layers of 2 × 4 wood studs with wood sheathing between, faced with stucco on exterior. Wright avoids using masonry to span large openings; instead he uses a wood wall, doubled to make it appear more massive.

D 2 × 10 joists supporting plaster wall. The floor joists of the balcony are supported by the piers beyond.

E Brick pier.

F Wood deck with open joints.

(Frank Lloyd Wright Foundation, drawing 0204.011.)

Greek ornament was wanting, however, in one of the great charms which should always accompany ornament—viz. Symbolism. It was meaningless, purely decorative, never representative, and can hardly be said be constructive; for the various members of a Greek monument rather present surfaces exquisitely designed to receive ornament, which they did, at first, painted, and in later times both carved and painted. The ornament was no part of the construction, as with the Egyptian: it could be removed, and the structure remained unchanged. On the Corinthian capital the ornament is applied, not constructed: it is not so on the Egyptian capital; there we feel the whole capital is the ornament—to remove any portion of it would destroy it.[20]

By contrast, Jones saw certain types of Gothic ornament as integral with the structure. Wright spoke often of the idea of integral ornament, ornament that was "of" and not "on" the surface of the material, as did Sullivan, and in this they were repeating Jones's demand for ornament that was constructive and not applied.

To Wright, as to Ruskin, it was not necessary to expose (or even express) structure. It was mandatory that the structure not be clad in a deceitful way. At the same time, it was critical to Wright that his ornament be integral, meaningful, and not applied. Thus, when Wright condemned buildings such as the Art Institute in Chicago for having steel frames clad with traditional forms, he was objecting to the use of the forms rather than to the cladding, and in his early work his intention was to develop a system of ornament that described structure in a way that was analogous rather than literal.

THE WINSLOW AND HEURTLEY HOUSES

The Winslow house is one of Wright's finest buildings, but it is not typical of his work. Many elements and details used here—the symmetrical facade, the centered entrance door, double-hung windows, and wooden arches—do not appear in Wright's mature Prairie houses and are in many ways antithetical to them. The Winslow house has a wood platform frame with brick veneer, a construction system which Wright seldom used again, evidently feeling that a wood frame clad in brick was "dishonest." And, in contrast with the later buildings, there is no detail, inside or out, that expresses the true nature of the concealed structure. The details of the Winslow house are also atypical, with their literal use of Classical elements; however, they merit a close examination, since the abstract details of the Prairie houses evolved from them.

If Sturgis had examined the Winslow house in detail, he would have found much to admire. It has precisely those qualities that he found lacking in Wright's mature work, particularly the Larkin Building. Classically derived moldings are used liberally to "form a footing, to emphasize a division, to soften or sharpen a transition," and to create "delicate light and shade."[21] At the same time Wright had already begun to transform these classic details into something that is truly his own.

The Winslow house does have in common with the other Prairie houses the basic division of the wall—the "grammar," as Wright called it. The house sits on a projecting base, so that "all the structures stand upon their foundations to the eye as well as physically."[22] The brick wall then extends, relatively unbroken, to a horizontal band or string course at the sill of the second-floor windows, creating a sort of frieze between the window sill and the roof. The roof projects well beyond the wall line, so that the frieze and most of the windows are in shadow.

The typical wall of the Winslow house is of orange Roman brick. It is the same width as common brick, but much thinner; as a result, the building has a decidedly horizontal emphasis. This is a technique we commonly associated with Wright: to the smallest detail, the horizontal is expressed and the vertical is not. The Winslow house is a unique version of this, in that it has Classical elements distorted horizontally. Figure 6.4 shows the base of the Winslow house; figure 4.30 shows the similar Classical base of Lutyens's Cenotaph. Both moldings use a large

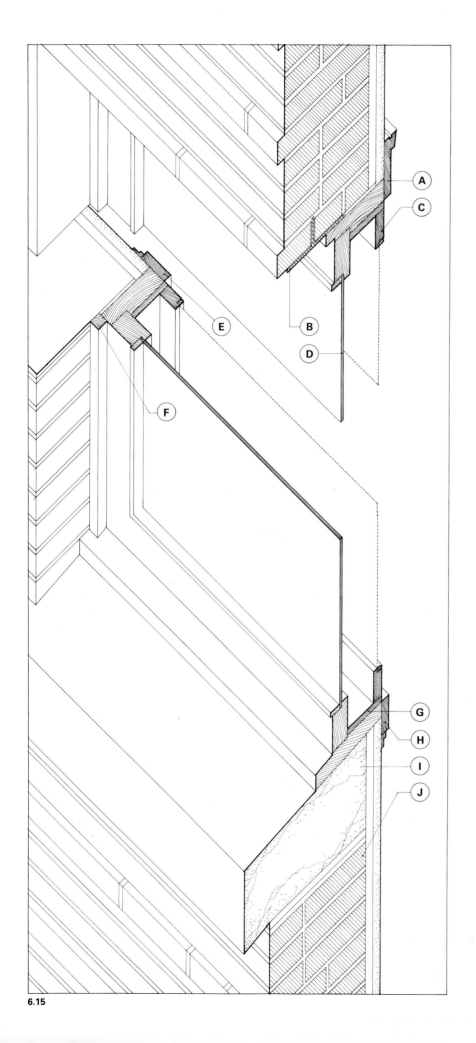

6.15

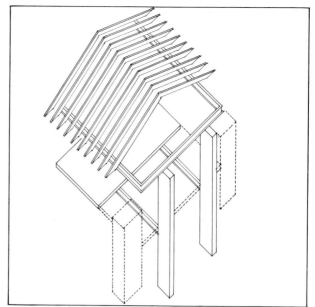

6.16

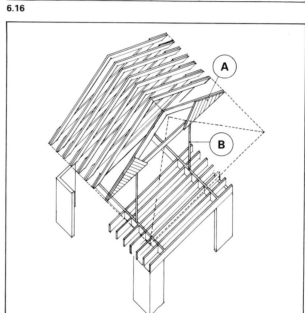

6.17

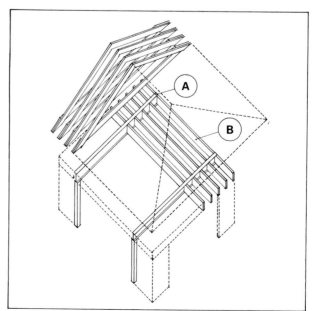

6.18

A. Heurtley house

Frank Lloyd Wright

Oak Park, Illinois, 1902

6.15   window details

A   Wood picture rail. This forms a continuous horizontal line around the room.

B   Steel lintel. In contrast with Wright's other contemporary work, the lintel is not expressed in any way on the exterior.

C   Insect screen in wood sash.

D   Out-swinging wood casement window.

E   Interior wood trim. This covers the joint between the plaster and the wood frame.

F   Brick molding. This covers the joint between brick and window.

G   Finish-wood cover on sill. Like many wood windows, this is of two types of wood: a paint-grade wood on the exterior and a finish-grade wood (to receive a semi-transparent stain) on the interior.

H   Interior wood trim. The profile of the panel molding is similar to that in the Willets house.

I   Stone sill.

J   Brick wall.

(Frank Lloyd Wright Foundation, drawing 0204.011.)

6.16   Brick-pier house type:

Martin house prototype

6.17   Wood-box house type:

prototype of Bradley and Willets houses.

A   Wood truss in attic above second floor.

B   Steel hangers supporting flush wood girders below.

(John Eiffler.)

6.18   Wood-box house type:

Willets house as built.

A   Steel beam and column flush with floor joists.

B   Wood floor joists.

(John Eiffler.)

---

concave molding, the cyma recta, in combination with a smaller concave quarter-round molding, but Wright's molding has been distorted parallel to the ground to give a greater projection to the base and a pronounced horizontal emphasis.

The molding at the top of the string course under the windows fulfills Viollet-le-Duc's first and third criteria—marking a height and supporting a projection—since not only the molding cap but the entire frieze projects slightly from the face of the brick wall (figure 6.3). The molding here is also a cyma, but it is smaller and occurs alone. Here we see, as in Classicism, moldings being used to give scale and emphasize mass. Where the weight is greater, at the base, the molding is larger. And as the convex molding becomes larger, it is "doubled" by the addition of the concave quarter-round to create what John Belcher called "proportionate comparison—creating apparent greater size by the addition of a smaller one."[23] This type of base detail is common in Classicism but rare in Wright's work. The base and windowsill–string course details of the Heurtley house (figure 6.32), although similar in size and material, are reduced to simpler rectangles, distorted only to create a wash and drip to protect the wall from water; this results in the geometric harshness that Ashbee and Sturgis found so disturbing. This elimination of the molding gives Wright's later buildings an ambiguous scale that makes them appear larger than they are.

The moldings of the Winslow house are equally dissimilar to Wright's earlier work and his work with Sullivan. Figure 6.8 shows the base detail of Sullivan's Adams Bank; figure 6.4 shows the base of the Winslow house. Sullivan's molding (executed in terra cotta rather than stone) is complex but does not employ the "doubling" effect used in the Winslow house; it consists of a simple concave quarter round, again making the scale of the building somewhat ambiguous. The Winslow house base is "doubled," but the effect of this on our perception of the mass of the building is considerable, since the convex bulge of the cyma recta describes the weight of the building being carried to earth. Sullivan's concave base does the opposite, making the Adams Bank appear less massive.

The interior trim of the Winslow house continues the theme of a horizontally distorted Classicism. Figure 6.30 shows a typical wood base in the interior. Figure 3.60 shows a similar detail in Stanford White's Gibson house. As on the exterior, Wright transforms a Classical molding by horizontal distortion. Notice also that the bottom portion of the molding repeats at a small scale the stone base outside, but is once again "doubled" by the base molding above, which is again an alternating convex and concave surface. This same type of horizontal distortion can be seen in other details throughout the Winslow house. Compare the glass stops (figure 6.30), for example, with those in McKim's University Club (figure 3.16).

In contrast with the exterior stone moldings, the interior trim of the Winslow house is extremely complex in relation to the small size of the pieces. This illustrates two more axioms of the traditional use of moldings: that interior trim should be finer and more delicate than exterior and that all ornamentation should be appropriate the the material.

The moldings of the Winslow house conform to the three basic uses described by Viollet-le-Duc: forming a footing (the base), marking a height (the picture rail at the door top), and softening a transition (the crown mold).[24] However, Viollet-le-Duc was writing about stone construction, and one of the primary purposes of trim in wood buildings is to conceal joints between materials—particularly those which are likely to be irregular or subject to movement. The real purpose of a base molding is to allow for movement of the wood floor relative to the wall, and the purpose of the molding at the top of the base is to hide the rough wood screed that ends the plaster.

Despite their elegance, the moldings of the Winslow house represents exactly those practices which Wright ridiculed in *The Art and Craft of the Machine*. Is not the stone base an example of the "miles of meaningless molded string courses, cornices, base courses" that the machine produces? Is the wood trim not an example of the use of "wood carving to imitate handicraft patterns"? This conflict

6.19

6.21

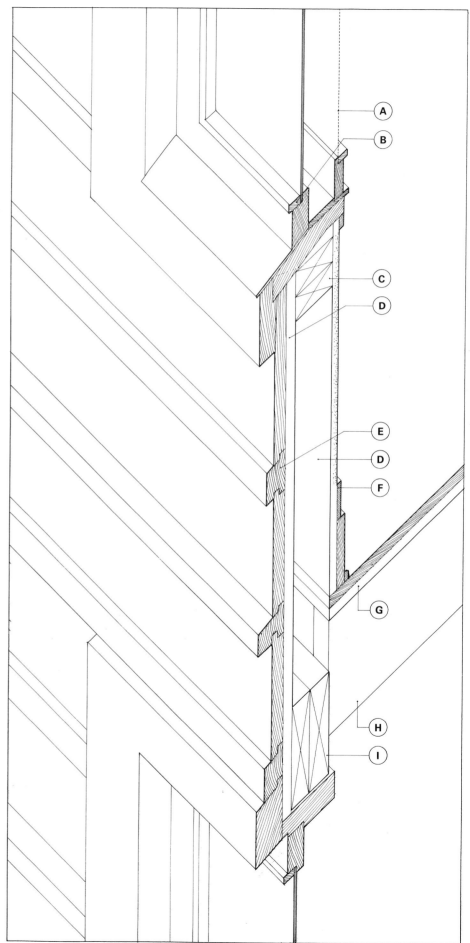

6.20

W. Glasner house

Frank Lloyd Wright

Glencoe, Illinois, 1905

6.19 **exterior**

(*Art Institute of Chicago.*)

6.20 **wall detail**

A   Insect screen.

B   Out-swinging wood casement window.

C   Two 2 × 4's. This is part of the platform framing that forms the window opening. It was installed during the erection of the frame; the wood window itself was installed much later.

D   2 × 4 studs, 16" on center, with sheathing. In this period, Wright used standard platform-frame and balloon-frame construction.

E   Siding. The batten profiles alternate between a wide/flat and a narrow/projecting profile. All are rabbeted into the siding boards to ensure that the joint remains closed as the wood moves with changes in temperature and humidity.

F   Wood base (simple version of Wright's typical abstracted Classical base).

G   Finish flooring and subfloor. The subfloor makes the finish floor level, and structurally unites the floor joists to prevent deflection. It also allows the finish floor to be installed at the end of the construction.

H   2 × 12 yellow pine joists at 16" on center.

I   Two 2 × 8's, supporting the wall studs over the window opening.

(*Frank Lloyd Wright Foundation, drawing 0505.011,HABS.*)

6.21 **B. Bradley house,** F. L. Wright, Kankakee, Illinois, 1900, dining room.

(*Art Institute of Chicago.*)

in the Winslow house between the nature of the details and Wright's conception of the relation of ornament to the machine explains in part the transformations that took place in Wright's details around 1900.

The ornament and the trim of the Winslow house tell us little or nothing about the nature of the structure. Many of the visible elements are misleading. The arched arcade in the entry vestibule is an excellent example of a structural form derived from stone construction executed in wood. It can hardly be said to be "in the nature of the material." But the real structure of the building is the wood frame, and on the interior the details are not so much misleading as to the nature of the structure as they are mute. The structure is nowhere exposed, but neither is it expressed. Unlike the Greenes' ceiling, which described the concealed structure above in an analogous way, the Winslow house ceilings are completely flat, having only the crown mold at the perimeter. Wright, even by his own standards, was under no obligation to express the structure. But in any case he seldom treated a ceiling in this manner in his later buildings, choosing instead to endeavor to describe the structure above without exposing it.

The Heurtley and Winslow houses both have compact plans based on a simple rectilinear prism under a single hip roof. This is rare in Wright's work; he generally preferred a cruciform plan, particularly when the exterior finish was brick. Despite the use of brick veneer in the Winslow house and load-bearing brick in the Heurtley house, their structural systems are similar, employing the standard platform-framing joist flooring. The exception is the living room of the Heurtley house, where two wood trusses were required to support the long span.

The Heurtley house employs the same grammar as the Winslow house, with a stylobate, an uninterrupted shaft of brick to the string course at the second-floor windows, then a frieze and an overhanging eave above. But in the Heurtley house the grammar is clarified by a major change in plan. The rooms that require the most light, the living and dining rooms, are located on the second floor, and the ground floor consists mainly of service areas and thus requires fewer openings. This increases the number of openings in the frieze while decreasing those in the base.

The stylobate and the water table of the Heurtley house (figure 6.11) are about the same size and proportions as those of the Winslow house, but the similarities end there. All of the Heurtley house's moldings are simple four-sided sections with unbroken plane surfaces. The combinations of curves, the play of light on curved surfaces, and the contrasts of scale of traditional moldings are all gone. Most of the departures from simple rectilinear shapes are for functional reasons. The top of the stylobate is sloped so that water will run off. The bottom of the string course slopes up to create a drip. The only exception is the sloping face of the stylobate. Here, in accordance with his doctrine of the craft of the machine, Wright exploits the geometric precision that the machine-powered masonry saw makes possible. These elements are "honest" in the terms of truth to materials and processes, but they cannot be called functional in the modern sense of that word, since neither piece of stone is technically mandatory. The string course protects the top of the masonry wall, but it could have been made of brick, as it was in Wright's later houses, and the stylobate is much wider than is really necessary to make the transition to the thicker wall below grade. This is not yet the grammar of Modernism; it is a grammar of abstracted Classicism.

A more subtle Classical influence can be seen in the construction of the wall of the Heurtley house. Like Lutyens, Wright "batters" the surface of the wall so that it becomes noticeably thicker near the ground, thus visually emphasizing the mass and weight of the wall. (Wright used the same technique in the Hickox and Bradley houses.) The notable difference here is that Wright allows the headers (the bricks turned sideways to bond the wall together) to project beyond the face of the wall, creating a series of horizontal shadows. (Wright also may have wished to articulate the bonding function of the headers.)

6.22

6.23

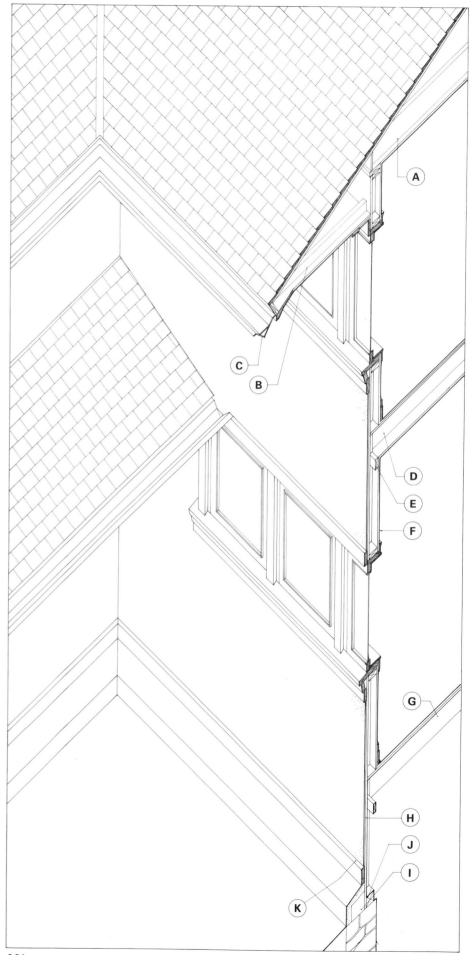

6.24

W. Willets house

Frank Lloyd Wright

Highland Park, Illinois, 1902

6.22 exterior
(Art Institute of Chicago.)

6.23 detail at windowsill string course
(John Eiffler.)

6.24 wall section at living room

A Roof construction: wood shingles on 1" wood sheathing on 2 × 6 rafters 16" on center.

B 2 × 4's spaced at 16" to support plaster soffit.

C Metal gutter.

D Floor construction: 2 × 12 wood joists 16" on center supported by steel beams.

E Ribbon strip of balloon frame. This ties the studs together and provides additional support for the joists. See figure 5.10.

F Interior finish: plaster on wood lath.

G Floor construction: finish-wood flooring on subfloor on 2 × 12 wood joists with plaster-on-wood-lath ceiling below.

H Exterior finish: stucco on metal lath, building paper on diagonal wood sheathing.

I Concrete sill and rubble foundation wall.

J 4 × 4 wood mudsill. This transfers the load of the individual studs to the foundation wall below. Placing the wood sill below rather than on top of the adjacent concrete sill caused major problems, since water trapped between the two rotted the sills over the years.

K Galvanized steel sheet-metal flashing.

(Frank Lloyd Wright Foundation, drawing 0208.007.)

The interior trim of the Heurtley house shows a similar transformation from Classicism to abstraction. The same basic pieces occur in the same location as in the Winslow house, and have similar relationships to the exterior, but again they are reduced to nearly rectilinear forms. As in the Winslow house, the base molding replicates in wood, at a smaller scale, the stone exterior base, complete with wash and batter. The typical plaster trim of the Winslow house recurs here in the same locations; it is no less complex, but it is composed of complete rectilinear forms (figure 5.32). Here again Wright exploits the potential of the modern milling machine to create a series of sharp, continuous squares. In the case of wood, these flat shapes served to "bring out the nature of the material" by allowing the grain of the wood to show.

The most marked difference between the interior trim of the Winslow and Heurtley houses is in the relationship of trim to structural expression. The trim of the Winslow house tells us little or nothing about the nature of the structure (and, in the case of the exterior, is actually misleading). In the mature Prairie Houses, Wright used the trim to create an analogous structural system—an ornamental system of trim that describes the structure it conceals.

The plans and the perspectives of Wright's *Ladies' Home Journal* house projects indicate the use of beamed ceilings. Whether the beams were to be solid or veneered is not clear, but few if any of the beams that appear in Wright's work before 1920 are real, monolithic, exposed beams. The Bradley house (figure 6.21) has dropped beams in the entry hall, but the ceilings of the living and dining rooms—formed of plaster and thin wood strips—parallel the ceiling joists above.

The ceiling ornamentation of the Heurtley house is more complex, since here there are no rooms above the living and dining rooms and the ceilings may project into the attic space. The living and dining rooms have ceilings that imitate in miniature the hip roof outside. The ceiling shapes follow the profile of the real roof structure in a very rough way, but since they have their own system of rafters to support the plaster, independent of the roof joists, it is difficult not to see them as what Pugin would call "constructed ornament." The trim of the living room follows the edges of the hip roof, but the dining-room ceiling has bands of trim that parallel the rafters above, although the trim spacing is much greater than the structural joist spacing.

It is interesting to note the similarities and the differences between the ceiling treatments of the Heurtley house and those of the Gamble house, built several years later by the Greene brothers. The Greenes' analogous beam clads the bottom of the joist and corresponds exactly to the real structure (figure 5.36). The teak boards that clad the joists are mitered and splined at the corners, and this detail, in combination with the fact that teak is not a strongly grained wood, makes it easy to mistake this beam for a monolithic one. Wright does not follow so precisely the structure above, but each beam is detailed so that it cannot be mistaken for a monolithic beam. Wright's analogous beams are more widely spaced than the real ceiling joists above, and Wright does not miter the corners of the cladding but allows the two vertical pieces to extend beyond the bottom of the beam, making it clear that it is composed of three pieces of wood.

A similar detail is used in the wall details. Figure 6.29 shows a typical jamb between two windows in the living room of the Willets house, which is similar to those in the Heurtley house. Here two 2 × 4's of rough lumber, which act to support the roof, are clad with finish lumber. Once again, Wright extends the side pieces to clarify that this is a clad and not a monolithic structural member.

There is little in the Winslow or the Heurtley house that is technically innovative. In essence, Wright restyled traditional systems of exterior moldings and interior trim, and he used these elements in the ways that Viollet-le-Duc and Schuyler thought they should be used: to cover joints and to mark the transitions between the major parts of the structure. This conventional treatment of the ornamentation

6.25

6.26

W. Willets house

Frank Lloyd Wright

Highland Park, Illinois, 1902

6.25 exterior
(John Eiffler.)

6.26 living room
The ceiling beam in the foreground is ornamental rather than structural, but it marks the location of the steel beam above.
(Art Institute of Chicago.)

6.27 exterior base details
(Frank Lloyd Wright Foundation, drawing 0208.007 and photographs.)

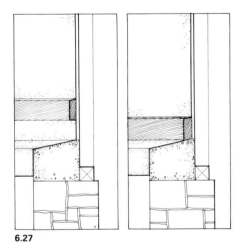

6.27

is in part a reflection of the conventional nature of the construction. Wright's most unique systems of ornamentation were to occur in his most structurally innovative buildings, particularly the larger Prairie Houses.

THE WILLETS HOUSE

Wright's only formal education in architecture was received at the engineering school of the University of Wisconsin, from which he never graduated. Later in life he was fond of saying that he had spent just enough time there to learn that the best place to support a slab or a beam was not at its corners, but at two points halfway between the end and the center. Under certain conditions, such as uniform loading, this construction will minimize the bending stresses at the center of the beam; however, it is not necessarily a universal formula for economy in construction (figure 6.34). The advantage of this system was that it allowed the corners to be open. Wright never executed this idea precisely (he came closest in the Bach house and Unity Temple), but in modified form this principle was important in the larger Prairie Houses.

Figure 5.6 shows the structure of a simple one-room platform-frame building; figures 6.16 and 6.17 show the structure of the central pavilions of the Willets and Martin houses as they were originally designed. In the typical platform frame the joists are supported by the two side walls. The structurally logical place to locate an opening is in the middle of the non-bearing wall parallel to the joists. Openings may be put in the side bearing walls; however, the more openings, the weaker the wall. The most difficult place to locate an opening is at the corner, and the corner, in a wood-frame building, is one means by which the structure withstands lateral loads.

The structure of the Willets house is of wood and steel; that of the Martin house is of steel, concrete, and wood. But these two houses support their roofs and floors in similar fashion. Rather than spanning between the cross walls, the joists and rafters are supported not at their ends but at two intermediate points. The means of support are different (wood trusses and girders in the Willets house, steel beams in the Martin house), but the results are similar: an uninterrupted strip of windows under the eaves with an open corner. But this occurs only at the second floor; the corners remain solid below the second-floor window sill line. Although they do not carry the roof, they still act to give lateral bracing to the structure.

This solidity of the corner is somewhat masked by the way in which it is inverted, in the Martin house, so that it appears to be two independent piers rather than a corner. To Wright this was another means of expressing the nature of the material: "Bricks naturally make corners and the corners are easily used for the play of light and shade. The Martin house is an organized brick-pier building. It is when assembling piers in a rhythmical relation to the whole that brick comes out best according to its nature."[25] Wright generally adhered to this rule of using more boxlike volumetric treatments for stucco and more pierlike forms for brick, but there are notable exceptions: the Gale house, which has a composition of planes with stucco finish, and the Barton house, with its boxlike composition in brick.

The increasing structural complexity of the larger houses was reflected in the ornamentation and expression as well. Without entirely breaking free of its Classical origins, Wright's ornamentation began to take on the quality that Wright later described as plasticity, which he saw as ornamentation expressing continuity of structure. Traditional ornament and trim in emphasizing joints and transitions emphasized this structural independence. Wright felt that, given the integrated nature of steel and concrete, the ornament should emphasize continuity. His writings on this concept were done many years after the Prairie Houses, and he wrote then that the idea was not clearly formed, at least verbally, before 1910.

Nevertheless, beginning with Unity Temple (1906), it becomes more and more characteristic of his work.

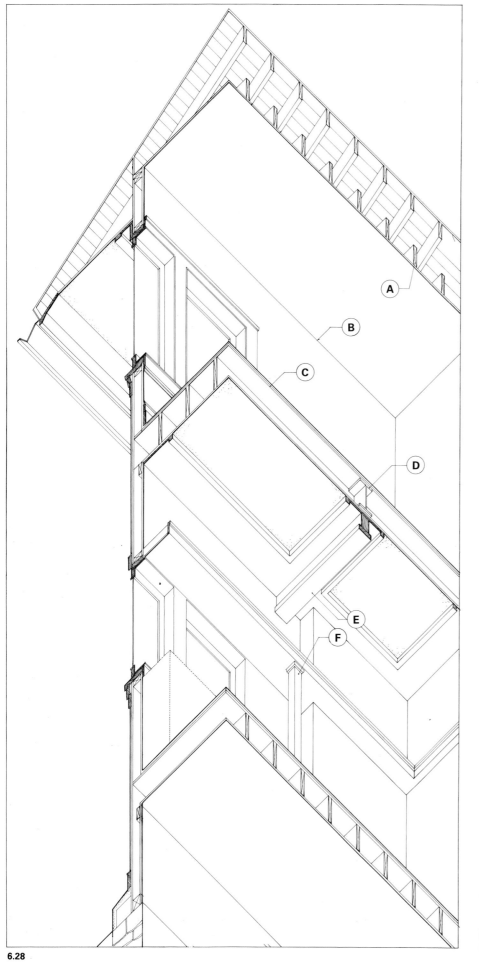

6.28

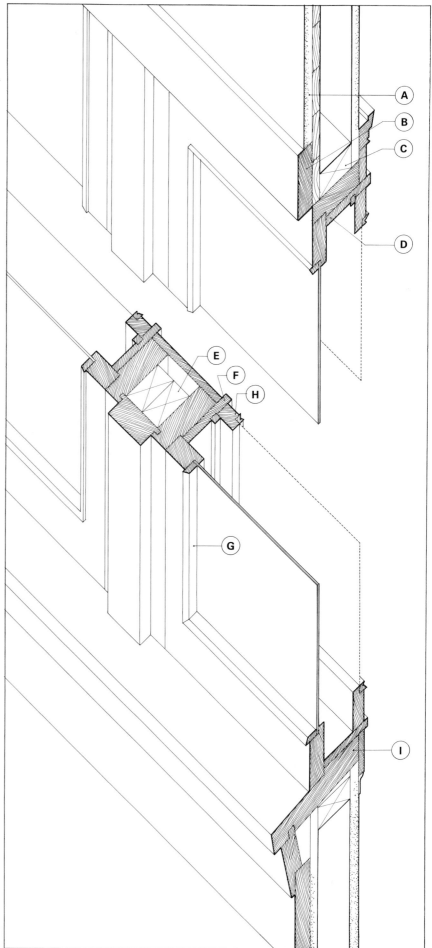

6.29

W. Willets house

Frank Lloyd Wright

Highland Park, Illinois, 1902

6.28 **interior wall section at living room**

A Typical roof and ceiling construction: 2 × 6 rafters spaced at 16″, with 2 × 10 ceiling joists.

B The crown mold is omitted in the upstairs bedrooms, in accordance with Wright's increasing tendency to place trim on surfaces rather than at corners.

C 2 × 12 wood joists, 16″ on center.

D 12″-deep steel beam. This supports the floor joists, allowing large window areas in the walls. It is supported by a steel post concealed in the wall beyond.

E Ornamental wood beam paralleling the steel beam above.

F Wood column at buffet. This marks the location of the steel column in the wall beyond. See figure 6.18
(Frank Lloyd Wright Foundation, drawing 0208.007.)

6.29 **window details**

A Typical wood-stud exterior wall.

B Exterior wood trim. This covers the joint between sheathing and window. It is capped with galvanized metal to protect the horizontal surface of the wood from water.

C 2 × 4 studs. These are part of the balloon frame of the house; they carry the load of the wall above, which cannot be supported by the window.

D Joint stop. The Z-shaped joint ensures that the joint of sash and frame remains closed as the wood expands and contracts.

E Two 2 × 4 wood studs. These act to support the wall and lintel above the window. The window jamb cannot be structural, as it is installed after the basic framing is complete.

F Interior trim.

G Out-swinging casement sash with projecting glass stop.

H In-swinging insect screen.

I Wood sill.
(Frank Lloyd Wright Foundation, drawing 0208.007.)

It never occurred to Wright to expose any of these structural systems, any more than it occurred to Sullivan. They are all expressions of his flesh-and-bones concept of structure and form—particularly the Martin house, with its steel and concrete beams. The ornament and trim were what Wright called the "efflorescence" which expressed the nature of that structure.

In its simplest form we see this in the front of the Willets house, where the analogous structure used in the Heurtley house's ceiling is applied to the stucco facade. The horizontal and vertical boards are simply applied to the sheathing, and are merely symbols of the real studs behind (which are spaced much more closely than the trim).

The exterior trim follows the pattern of simplified Classical elements seen in the Heurtley house, which was designed a year later. Wright tries a variation here by slanting much of the trim slightly in order to retain the quality of light and shade seen in Classical moldings without sacrificing geometric simplicity. The base detail is just as Wright described in it his 1908 article in the *Architectural Record*. The wood-frame walls are pulled into the inside face of the foundation wall to create a projecting plinth. Because of the thinness of the wood wall in relation to the foundation below, a flat band of wood is placed at the bottom of the stucco next to the concrete. It serves no purpose other than to create a visual transition. In some of his other Prairie Houses, Wright raised this piece slightly to create a recess between the concrete base and the trim (figure 6.27). It is hard not to see in this detail exactly what Sturgis saw: the base of an Ionic or Corinthian capital, with its concave scotia between two convex tori, the one on the bottom slightly larger. Wright did not change the conceptual or even the specific nature of Classical ornament; he simply restyled it into an abstract form.

For the molding of the string course below the second-floor windows, Wright selected a more literal Classic shape than he did for the Heurtley house, but his transformation was equally abstract. In previous designs he had used a simple rectilinear stone sill (as in the brick portions of the Heurtley house) or a sharply sloping wood sill (as in the Bradley house or the stucco portions of the Heurtley house). In the Willets house he introduced an intermediate piece of wood just below the window sill proper (figure 6.29), which slopes back to create a transition to the flat trim below. This piece too is unnecessary; it serves only to visually connect the sill and the trim below, just as a molding does. The transition here is considerably less harsh than that at the Heurtley house, although it lacks the subtleties of light and shade that traditional curved forms would have given. This detail also occurs in the identical shape and size at the sill of the ground-floor windows and on top of the low retaining walls. Classical rules of proportion would dictate that it be different, particularly at the low wall.

The interior detail continues the theme of simulating classical elements through the use of angular trim. If we compare the major details of interior trim of the Winslow and Willets houses, we can see the way the Willets trim approximates the same profile; it simply does not use curved lines. This is particularly true of the backband and picture-rail pieces. At the same time we can see indications of Wright's mature style. The glazing bead, for example, projects rather than recedes—a detail used in all the Usonian Houses of the 1930s.

Like the Heurtley house, the Willets house uses trim to create a structure analogous to the real structure which it clads. It is much more elaborate, including false columns as well as beams, and, like many analogous structural systems, it describes with varying degrees of accuracy the true structural system which it clads. But the differences in trim design can be interpreted as a reflection of the differences in structural design.

Originally the living room of the Willets house was to be framed in much the same way as that of the Bradley house (figure 6.17): wood joists spaced at 16 inches on center, supported by two flush girders which were to be suspended by means of steel tie rods from wood trusses in the attic. This system proved difficult to

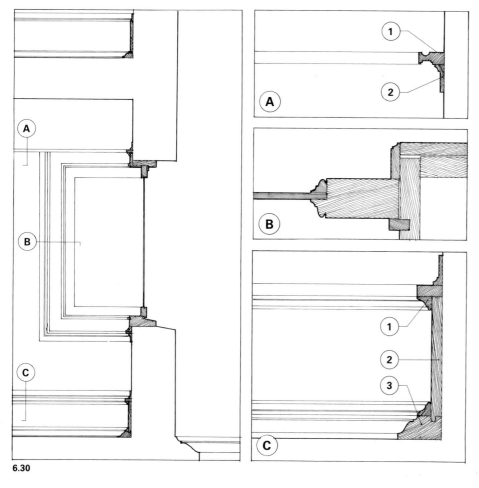

6.30

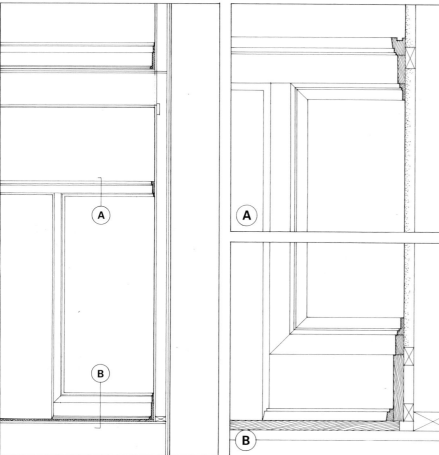

6.31

6.30 Winslow house, interior trim. The Winslow house's trim is in a traditionally Classical style, although slightly distorted horizontally. Like all Classical trim, it combines contrasting concave and convex curves separated by portions of rectangles.

A Picture rail.

　1 The picture rail is designed to receive hooks for hanging pictures, but its real purpose is to establish the scale of the room.

　2 Panel molding. This elongated piece, with its concave quarter round, is used as a cover on all joints of plaster and trim.

B Window-jamb details. Except for the addition of the small quarter-round, the shape of the glazing bead is identical to that used by McKim, Mead & White (see figure 3.16.)

C Base details.

　1 Trim. This piece is used typically to join a horizontal and a vertical piece of wood, visually softening the transition.

　2 $\frac{3}{4}''$ base piece. This is rabbeted into the base below to maintain a closed joint.

　3 Base mold. This covers the joint between the wood floor or the carpet and the wall, which is usually crude because of the joining of dissimilar materials.

(Frank Lloyd Wright Foundation, drawing 9305.011.)

6.31 Willets house, interior trim

A Detail at picture rail. Compare the panel molding here with that in the Winslow house. The rounded profiles have been changed to angles.

B Base detail. As in the panel molding, the quarter circle and cyma recta moldings of the Winslow house have been changed to angular shapes, which Wright felt were more appropriate to the material and to the power tools used to shape it.

(Frank Lloyd Wright Foundation, drawing 0208.007.)

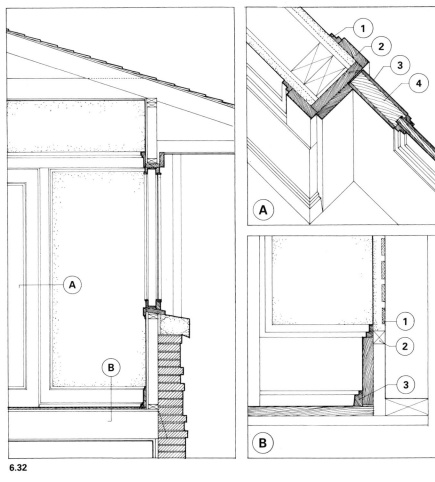

6.32

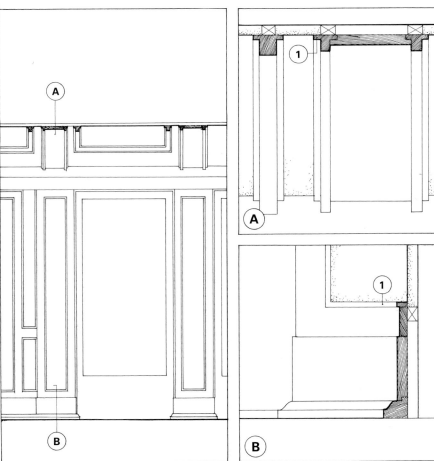

6.33

6.32 Heurtley house, interior trim.

A Door detail. Note the use of veneering on the central door panel.

   1 Typical wood panel molding.

   2 Jamb casing. This covers the joint between the door frame and the plaster.

   3 Finish-wood veneer.

   4 Wood core.

B Base detail. Wright uses a variant of the angular system used in the Willets house.

   1 Wood lath. Nailed to the studs, this forms the base for plastering.

   2 Wood screed. This provides an even edge for the plasterer to work to, as well as a nailer for the trim.

   3 Base molding. This matches in profile the stone base of the exterior.

(Frank Lloyd Wright Foundation, drawing 0204.011.)

6.33 Robie house, interior trim.

A Detail at ceiling trim. Unlike the base detail, the trim at this location is unrelated to joints in materials or junctures of wall and ceiling. Note that the rabbet which connects the two pieces of wood on one side is duplicated on the other.

B Detail at base. The panel molding here has been inverted from its position in the Winslow house, so that it projects rather than recedes.

(Survey.)

6.34 Structural diagram of beam support

A1 Beam simply supported at its ends.

A2 Deflection of this beam.

A3 Diagram of bending stresses, which are greatest at midspan.

B1 Beam supported at its quarter points.

B2 Deflection of beam B.

B3 Diagram of bending stresses in beam B, which are at a minimum at midspan.

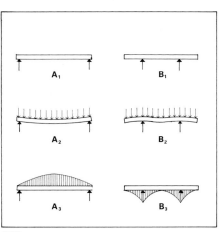

6.34

6.35

6.36

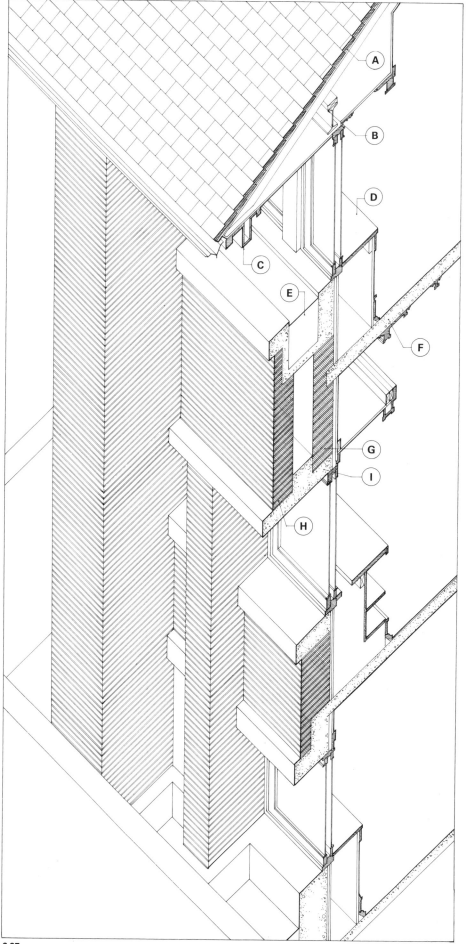

6.37

D. D. Martin house

Frank Lloyd Wright

Buffalo, New York, 1904

6.35   **exterior**

6.36   **detail**
The mortar is flush with the brick in
the vertical joints and recessed in
the horizontal joints.

6.37   **wall section at library**
A   Roof construction: 2 × 8 wood
    joists, 16″ on center, with wood
    sheathing.
B   Steel beam with wood blocking.
    The blocking is bolted to the beam
    to provide a nailer for the wood
    joists.
C   Plaster soffit with wood trim.
D   Wood cover for radiator.
E   Concrete sill and planter.
F   Concrete floor slab.
G   Interior brick wall.
H   Exterior brick wall. The outer wythe
    is of "Roman"-size brick.
I   Concrete lintel.
    (Frank Lloyd Wright Foundation,
    drawing 0405.009, HABS, Survey.)

execute, primarily because the second floor had to be built before the first so that the steel tie rods could be installed. The structure was then changed to that shown in figure 6.18, in which wood joists, running in the opposite direction to those of the original design, are supported by steel beams and columns.

The analogous system of wood trim that describes this steel-and-wood structure is shown in figures 6.26 and 6.28. The steel beams are concealed within the wood floor structure, but corresponding to each steel beam is a section of wood ceiling trim that is itself in the form of a wide flange beam, although it is purely ornamental. The steel columns are concealed within the wall construction, but their location is marked by an ornamental wood column which, although located directly under the wood trim and the steel beam, supports only the soffit above the window.

Wright differed from the Greenes in his method of detailing analogous beams in a way that makes clear that they are neither structural nor monolithic. The side pieces of the dining-room beams are extended vertically below the bottom of the beam (figure 6.28), and the bottom piece of the living-room beam is extended horizontally—in both cases demonstrating that this is a clad and not a monolithic beam.

This detail reveals another "Classical" characteristic of Wright's detailing, particularly if compared with a similar Greene and Greene detail (figure 5.38). The Greenes allow the plaster ceiling to butt against the side of the wood beam, with no transition and no molding. Wright extended the wood horizontally and added a typical backband, so that each plaster panel of the ceiling has a wooden opening almost forming a frame between ceiling and beam.

Why did Wright not merge these two structural systems? He obviously did not want to expose structural steel members, but he was also dealing with a problem similar to one faced by the Greene brothers: Finish woods, such as oak, were available only in small pieces. More important, the finish wood had to be installed at the end of the construction process to avoid damage by the elements and by workmen. Thus the real structure went up first, and the analogous structure went up last (after the completion of the roof, the plastering, etc.).

THE MARTIN HOUSE
The Martin house was designed and constructed almost simultaneously with the Larkin Building. This explains many of its atypical aspects, including the use of a concrete and steel composite structural system. Such a system is unusual in residential construction. Even Wright's houses were usually built of steel and wood, or wood alone. But it is also the system used in the Larkin Building. The Martin house is thus, among others things, an attempt to develop a universal building system, applicable to both large-scale and residential projects.

Given Wright's ideas about the relationship between expression and ornament, and given the structures clad, one would expect to see different systems of ornamentation to correspond to the different systems of construction in the Martin house. This is in fact the case. There are several systems of trim and ornament, and they delineate precisely which portions are concrete and which are wood. These ornamental systems express Wright's interpretations of the nature of the structural systems they clad.

Perhaps it is the close relationship with the Larkin Building that gives the Martin house its other unique quality: the use of structural subsystems to establish scale. By eliminating moldings, Wright had severely limited his ability to establish scale. Here he explored a number of alternatives, particularly the use of what Sir John Summerson calls *aedicules*—little buildings within a larger one.

Compare the main pavilion of the Martin house (figure 6.16) with the corresponding pavilion of the Willets house. Like the Willets house, the Martin house uses pairs of beams—in this case steel—to support the ceiling joists and the concrete slab at their third points, freeing the side walls for larger openings. But whereas

6.38

6.40

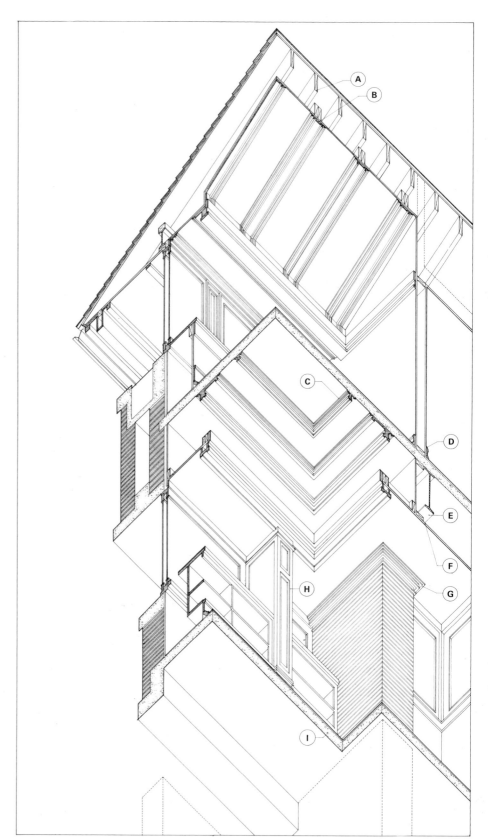

6.39

D. D. Martin house

Frank Lloyd Wright

Buffalo, New York, 1904

6.38 **detail**

6.39 **interior wall section at library**
(reverse view of figure 6.37).

A Roof construction: 2 × 8 wood
rafters, 16" on center, with
sheathing.

B Ceiling supports and wood trim.
Note the difference in character
between the wood trim of the
second-floor ceiling (which covers a
wood structure) and that of the
first-floor ceiling trim (which covers
a concrete structure).

C Wood trim on concrete slab. See
figure 6.49.

D Wood trim at second floor (base).

E 8"-deep steel beam. This supports
the concrete slab, and bears on the
brick pier beyond. See figure 6.42.

F Plaster ceiling. This covers the steel
beam as well as reducing the scale
of the room.

G Wood trim at top of brick pier.

H Interior wood-and-plaster pier. This
corresponds to the location of the
brick pier on the exterior.

I Concrete slab over basement.
*(Frank Lloyd Wright Foundation,
drawing 0405.009, HABS, Survey.)*

6.40 **Willets house,** detail
This photograph, taken during
restoration, shows the soffit of one
of the overhanging eaves. The two
V-shaped plaster ridges mark the
location of a concealed steel beam
in the roof above.
(John Eiffler.)

the Willets house maintains its volumetric character, the Martin house is developed into a series of piers and lintels. From the exterior, the main pavilion of the Martin house appears to be composed of three independent structural systems (figure 6.35), the largest being the roof (which is supported by the two large piers in front), the next largest being the second floor (which appears to be supported by the two corners piers), and the smallest being the two small brick piers that appear to support the lintels. In fact the three systems are connected, so that they do not really act independently. The two main corner piers, for example, are connected to provide lateral bracing, and to a certain degree all three pairs of brick piers act to support the second floor. Wright's intention here is to establish scale by means of multiple scales of "orders," just as Palladio might have used an interlocking giant and smaller order to establish the scale of a facade.

The exterior trim of the Martin house is stark and simple, even for Wright. The string courses are simple rectangles, as is the base (which lacks even the notch and batter typical of the other Prairie Houses). This is in part due to the exposed concrete trim, which Wright used here for the first time. Poured-in-place concrete does not easily lend itself to small, complex forms, although this did not deter Wright from experimenting with cast-in-place ornament beginning with Unity Temple in 1904.

In contrast with the Heurtley and Willets houses, where the interior trim replicated at small scale the exterior stone trim, the interior wood trim of the Martin house is much more varied, intricate, and complex than the stark concrete forms of the exterior. This may be due to the fact that much of the interior trim serves a different purpose, or in many cases serves no functional purpose at all, given the nature of the structural systems employed.

Most of Wright's pre-1910 buildings have concealed, or at least partially concealed, structural systems. The wood frame of the Willets house is plastered over inside and out, and the brick walls and rafters of the Heurtley house are concealed by plaster and trim on the interior. This is a layered, as opposed to monolithic, system of building. Much of Wright's later work, and much of Modern architecture in general, was monolithic in construction, and the Martin house, the Unity Temple, and the Larkin Building represent the beginning of this trend.

The concrete first and second floors of the Martin house are exposed, and the majority of the supporting walls and piers are of Roman brick, matching the exterior. Only at the roof is the structure clad primarily in plaster, since it is constructed of steel and wood and thus must be concealed. In accordance with the two systems of construction, Wright developed two types of trim.

The ground-floor interiors of the Martin house have a great deal of oak trim. Although it conforms to the traditional locations, forming a footing, marking a height, and supporting a projection, it serves no functional purpose. The primary use of trim in residential construction is to cover joints particularly those that are subject to irregularity of construction and thermal movement. The joints that occur in the Martin house (tile floor to brick pier, brick pier to concrete beams) do not require a cover, as is evidenced by the absence of such transitional moldings in the exterior.

Traditionally the material of a base is harder than the material of the wall above, to protect the latter from damage. To use an oak base on a brick pier is a reversal of functional logic, since the wood is more vulnerable than the brick above. But no one would argue that the Martin house would be a better building without this trim. It acts to give the interior the quality of scale, which many of Wright's later buildings lack. This assertion of scale is due not only to the combination of different moldings but also to the variation from one element to another.

Figures 6.49–6.52 show various base details that occur in the Martin house. These details vary in height and design depending on location. The second-floor moldings are shorter than those at the ground floor, although the cyma recta molding is about the same size. The bases for brick and plaster walls at the ground floor are

6.41

6.43

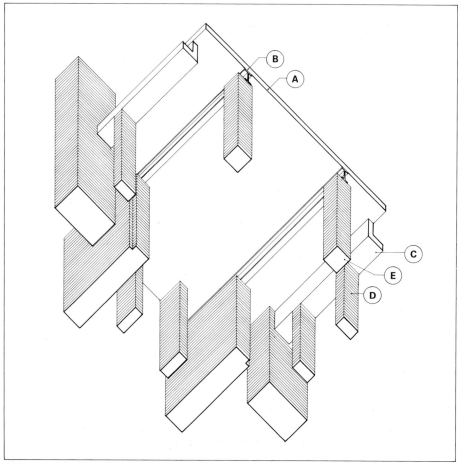

6.42

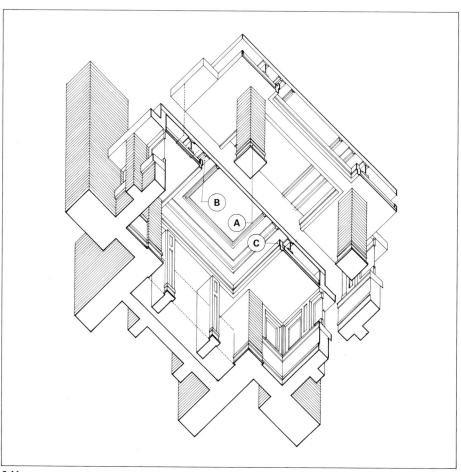

6.44

D. D. Martin house

Frank Lloyd Wright

Buffalo, New York, 1904

6.41 **living room**
(Canadian Center for Architecture.)

6.42 **first floor framing of library**
(showing only structural elements).

A 6″ concrete slab.

B 8″-deep steel beam.

C Concrete lintel. This supports the brick above and helps support the concrete floor slab.

D Small brick piers. These primarily support the lintel, but probably take part of the floor load as well.

E Large brick piers. These support the steel beams and thus the concrete floor slab.
(Frank Lloyd Wright Foundation, drawing 0405.009, HABS, Survey.)

6.43 **interior showing heat and light unit**
(Canadian Center for Architecture.)

6.44 **ceiling plan of library**

A Wood trim at base of brick pier. This trim, unlike that in a wood-and-plaster wall, serves no functional purpose.

B Wood trim on concrete slab. The trim here is unrelated to joints or transitions and takes a form completely different from that used under wood ceilings.

C Plaster soffit supported by 2 × 4 wood framing hung from steel beam.
(Frank Lloyd Wright Foundation, drawing 0405.009, HABS, Survey.)

identical except that the typical board and backband trim has been added to the base at the plaster wall. At the same time, the furniture at the ground floor has a base which is similar but noticeably smaller. This technique is again an abstraction from Classicism, which dictates not only that the height of the base should be proportionate to the height of the wall but also that, by its design, it should visually show the greater weight being carried. The furniture moldings of the Martin house are smaller than the wall moldings, and the cyma recta is enlarged to explain the greater weight it supports. The variation in detail has the additional advantage of explaining the scale of the building; just as the combination of large and small curves in moldings and large and small structures on the exterior act to establish scale, so does the combination of large and small base details.

The complex ceiling trim of the Martin house describes the structures which it clads. Since the structure is a combination of traditional and modern structural systems—post and lintel systems of masonry and wood and steel and concrete frame systems—there are two systems of ornament and trim: one that articulates joints and transitions of traditional construction and one that emphasizes the visual and structural continuity of modern construction.

The top of the piers is given a traditional crown molding, which works with the base detail to create a Classical composition of base, shaft, and capital. This molding marks a height, supports a weight, and articulates a transition. Running atop this piece is a continuous band that suggests an entablature, particularly in its use of a continuous band of dentils. Wright sometimes uses this piece traditionally (to form an entablature for the brick column) and sometimes plastically (to describe structural continuity).

This entablature detail is used as an edge on the dropped beams in the library and the dining room. It is free of the wall, and, although it spans between two piers, at no point does it touch the column capital. Wright's intention here was to create an analogous structure. The real structure of these rooms is steel beams supporting a concrete slab, and this wood entablature is generally used to define the location of the steel beams (figures 6.42, 6.44).

The ceiling lacks the traditional crown mold at the juncture with the wall, and since there is no wood structure above there are no analogous wood beams. Wright applied a molding to the surface of the concrete and allowed it to pass by some of the brick piers uninterrupted, defining larger areas than those described by the entablature below. Figure 6.47 shows a view of the living room and the vestibule. The ceiling molding unites these two spaces by means of a simple rectangular form. At the same time, the entablature below spans between the fireplace and the piers, dividing the rectangle into two rooms. This use of two overlapping figures (Robert Venturi would call it a "both-and" spatial ambiguity) would be impossible without the use of different moldings to define these spaces as figures, as complete shapes which overlap. And when Wright abandoned the use of trim, he abandoned with it this method of spatial composition, using instead the "continuous" and "flowing" compositions we associate with his later work.

In the wood-frame portions of the Martin house, Wright used ornamental systems similar to that of the Willets house. The ceiling of the master bedroom, unlike the unbroken surfaces of the library, has a series of flat wood strips to describe the wood joists and rafters above. The same type of detail is used throughout the second floor, which also has wood structure above. The detailing of these pieces is similar to the analogous beams of the Willets house, but with important differences. Rather than ending at the edge of the ceiling, they continue down the face of the wall to the entablature molding, and the crown molding is again omitted altogether (figure 6.41). This is an example of Wright's concept of "plasticity" in ornament.

The Martin house is, in some ways, one of Wright's most innovative buildings. The concrete and steel structural system, the monolithic wall structures, the integration of utilities, and the use of overlapping spatial figures are seen here more clearly and strongly than in many of the Prairie Houses, before or after.

6.45

6.47

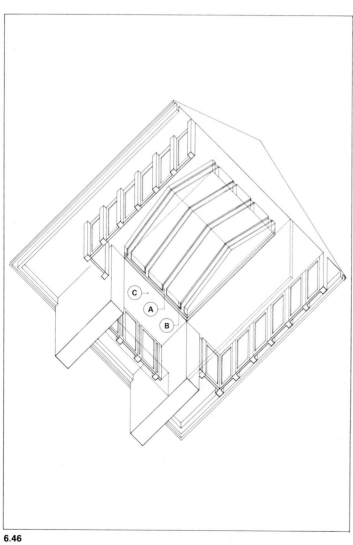

6.46

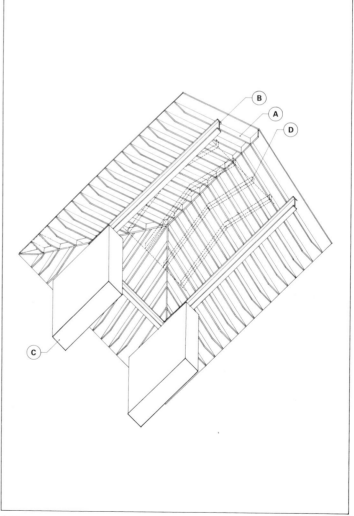

6.48

D. D. Martin house

Frank Lloyd Wright

Buffalo, New York, 1904

6.45 **dining room**
(Canadian Center for Architecture.)

6.46 **ceiling plan of master bedroom**

A Interior wood trim. The trim follows the line of the paired rafters above. This ceiling trim is more typical of Wright's earlier ceiling trim, since it clads a wood and not a concrete ceiling.

B The crown mold is omitted, so that the two plaster surfaces simply butt together. This is an example of the beginning of Wright's "plastic" ornament.

C Ceiling: plaster on wood lath.
(Frank Lloyd Wright Foundation, drawing 0405.009, HABS, Survey.)

6.47 **reception room**
(Canadian Center for Architecture.)

6.48 **roof framing at master bedroom**

A Roof construction: wood sheathing on 2 × 8 rafters spaced at 16″ (which is the effective span of the sheathing). Typically the rafters would be connected with a horizontal joist to form a triangle and thus a truss, but the interior ceiling configuration does not permit this.

B Steel beam (8″-deep I section). Because of the large horizontal openings in the wall, the load from the rafters must be picked up by the steel beam and carried to the brick piers.

C Brick piers. These carry most of the load, but pairs of studs within the window mullions may also help to support the roof.

D Two 2 × 6 rafters. These support only the plaster ceiling below, which slopes in a direction opposite to that of the roof rafters above.
(Frank Lloyd Wright Foundation, drawing 0405.009, HABS, Survey.)

The variations in detail in the Martin house—particularly in the base heights—are atypical in Wright's work. In the Willets house, the base, string course, and windowsill details are identical throughout the house, regardless of their proportional relationship to the walls on which they are placed. To some degree this is a product of Wright's endless experimentation. He frequently returned to old details after experimenting with new ones; for example, in the Coonley house (1908) he used details identical to those of the Bradley house, which he had designed eight years earlier. But the desire to establish scale, and the devices used to achieve it, are less and less evident after 1910. The multiplicity of types and sizes of trim detail and the use of substructures within a larger structure were never repeated as systematically again. This was due not to an increased interest in geometric abstraction, but to a redefinition of the rule of trim and ornament in architecture.

THE ROBIE HOUSE

Wright rarely used the composite steel and concrete system in a house; most of the subsequent Prairie Houses with extensive structural requirements were steel and wood. (The Coonley Playhouse, which Hitchcock describes as being concrete, is in fact built of structural clay tile and wood, covered with stucco.)

The structural and detailing systems of the Robie house are much less dogmatic than those of the Martin house. There is no attempt here to develop a universal building system of steel and concrete. Although dependent upon steel for its more dramatic effects, it is in essence a combination of load-bearing brick and platform frame, heavily modified by the introduction of steel members.

Although it appears much simpler than the Martin house, the Robie house is structurally much more complex. It lacks the close correspondence between structure and form that exists in works such as the Larkin Building, and many of the primary structural elements are obscure or concealed. As in the Willets house, the rafters are supported at their third points, just below the collar beam. Yet the piers that support these beams at the building ends are almost completely within the building, and the large corner piers visible on the exterior (figure 6.62) are really of secondary importance structurally.

The steel channels supporting the balcony cannot span the distance without additional support. This is provided by a second steel beam cantilevered from the fireplace to support the steel channel at mid-span, but there is not even a hint of this in the exterior expression of the building. Most disturbing is the structure of the third floor, which meets the structure below at such an awkward location that it is built of brick veneer on wood framing in order to reduce its weight, there being inadequate structure below to support masonry. As an architectural totality, the Robie house may be preferable to the Martin house; but in clarity of structural expression, the latter is far superior.

Yet it is what the steel frame makes possible that gives the Robie house its niche in architectural history. Critics have long considered it the best of the Prairie Houses, primarily because it anticipated some of the characteristics of Modernism. To critics such as Nikolaus Pevsner and Sigfried Giedion, buildings such as the Robie house were evaluated insofar as they did or did not establish precedents of the International Style. Whether or not one agrees with their assessment (Wright thought the Avery Coonley house the best house from this period), one must agree that it is the most proto-Modern of his early houses and that it does the most to exploit the potential of steel. The Heurtley and Martin houses, with their small spans and openings, do not appear to be beyond the limitations of brick and wood construction. If we did not know that they used steel, we might not easily guess. Not so with the Robie house; it is clear from the huge cantilevers that something other than brick and wood is present. This house seems to precisely fulfill Ruskin's prediction that, with the use of steel as a structural material, the old rules of composition (based on the limitations of masonry) would disappear.

Before discussing the details of the Robie house, we should look at the module system that plays such an important part in the ornamentation. Beginning around

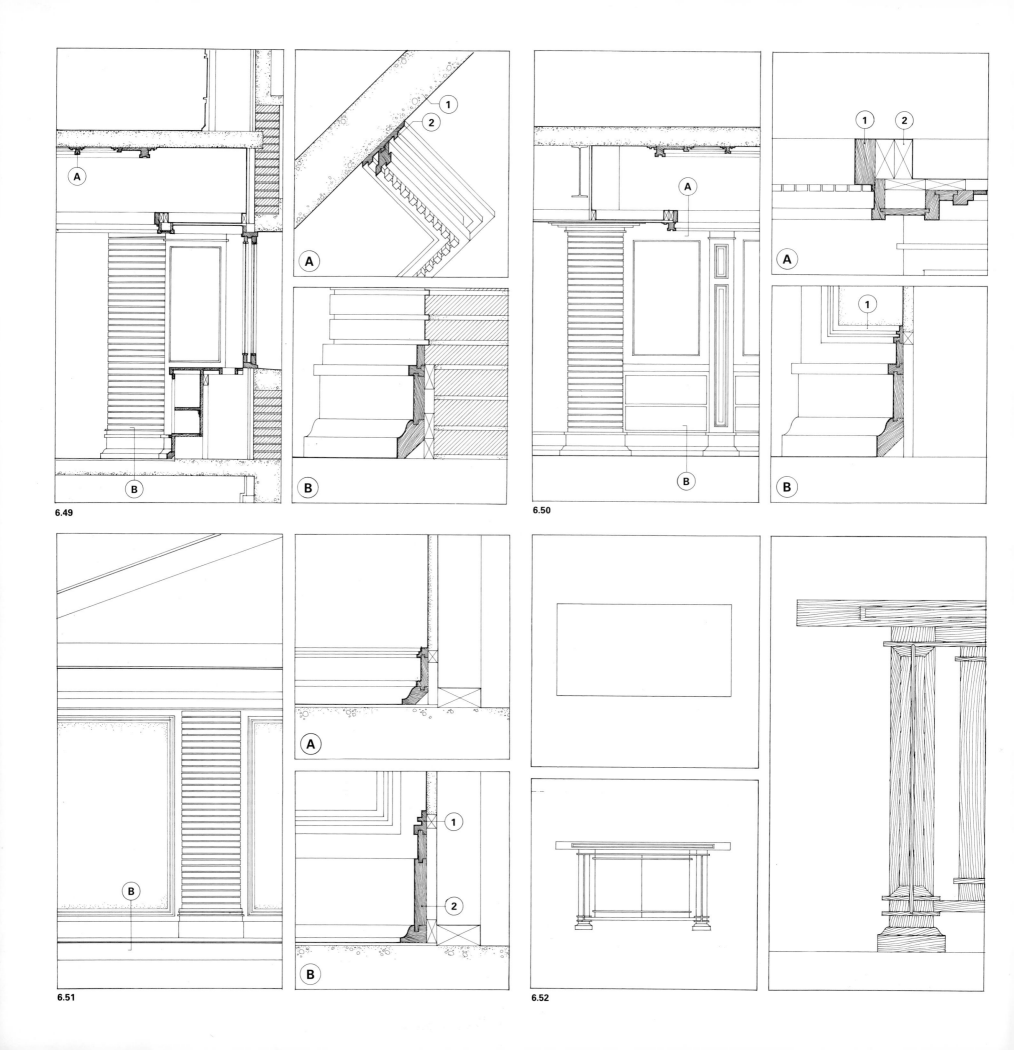

6.49

6.50

6.51

6.52

D. D. Martin house

Frank Lloyd Wright

Buffalo, New York, 1904

6.49 **interior trim of library**

A Trim detail at concrete slab.

   1 Concrete slab.

   2 The exposed projection of the horizontal piece matches exactly that which is concealed to make the connection with the vertical piece, and the projecting dentils below are also the same size as the concealed projection. This can be interpreted as an example of Wright's call for an ornament appropriate to the machine.

B Base detail. Connections in finish wood are typically made by means of rabbet joints in which the pieces interlock rather than butting together. This ensures that the joints will not open as the wood shrinks and swells with changes in humidity.

(Survey.)

6.50 **interior trim of library**

A Details of picture rail.

   1 Wood edge.

   2 2 × 4 wood support framework.

B Base detail.

   1 Panel molding. The exposed projections are identical to those that are concealed to make the rabbet joints.

(Survey.)

6.51 **interior trim on second floor**

A Base detail at plaster wall in bedroom. In rooms where no other wall trim occurs, the base is considerably smaller.

B Base detail at plaster wall in hall of second floor.

   1 Panel molding.

   2 Base. The lowest piece of the base here is smaller than that on the first floor (figure 6.50), where the ceiling is higher.

(Survey.)

6.52 **table**

Note that the base molding of the leg of the table is a small-scale version of the adjacent wall base.

(Survey.)

1905, Wright planned each of his buildings on a uniform, tightly spaced grid. Writing in 1928, Wright stated that the grids were based on "the nature of the material." Thus, the Martin house has a 3'9" module (brick), Unity Temple has a 2' module (concrete), and the Coonley house has a 4' module (stucco). The Willets house appears to have a module but does not; the livng-room windows, for example, are 1" farther apart than the dining-room windows. The choice of a 3'9" module for the Martin house is a strange one. A 4' module is logical for brick or wood, since it corresponds to three 16" spaces and to standard lumber lengths as well as equaling six 8" bricks or four 12" bricks. The 3'9" module that was used is not equally subdivided by any building material, and could only have been a purely aesthetic choice. (In fact, many portions of this house are off the module, and Wright may have been rationalizing after the fact.) The module of the Robie house is 4'0", and this quickly became the standard dimension for all rectilinear grids regardless of the material. It is seen most clearly in the Robie house in the spacing of the brick piers, but it controls all other aspects of the design as well, particularly the ornamentation.

The exterior trim of the Robie house is even simpler than that of the Martin house. In the Martin house, the horizontal trim varies in size, if not in shape, depending on location. In the Robie house, all the string courses are 8" high, excepting only the base, which is a simple rectangle. This reflects Wright's denial of scale in the Robie house, in contrast with his assertion of scale in the Martin house.

One of the most dramatic exterior details of the Robie house is the copper gutter of the main roof. Wright's gutters show the most variation of any of the Prairie House details, perhaps indicating Wright's dissatisfaction with each of the solutions. Whatever the reason, it is the gutter and eave details that give many of the Prairie Houses their character. In the Dana house Wright used a concealed gutter and barge board flush with the rafter ends to create a strong and heavy roof edge. This detail, along with the gable roof, gives the Dana house its unique character in Wright's work. In subsequent efforts; Wright tried to make the roof appear as light as possible by reducing its profile with a knife-like edge (figure 6.58). In the Heurtley and Willets houses, the eave is sloped back for a distance parallel to the rafter and the rafter end is cut at an angle, both devices to increase the visual lightness of the roof. The gutter, a sort of abstract geometric version of a conventional gutter, is also given sharp edges to minimize its profile. Downspouts presented a visual problem, since the gutter was so far out from the wall. This problem was solved easily, if not professionally, by eliminating the downspout and letting the water fall to the ground at a point as far removed from the wall as possible. In this regard the Greene brothers' details are superior to Wright's. Although they used equally large overhangs, they never did away with downspouts.

In his pier-plan buildings, Wright preferred to keep the soffit parallel to the ground, to give the different piers a uniform, flat surface to join. In the Martin house, Wright retained the triangular gutter and added an ornamental trim just behind the point of the eave, perhaps feeling that some transitional element was necessitated by the heaviness of the base. This solution is not wholly satisfactory, and the type developed for the Robie house is superior in every way. The Robie house's gutter is a flat gull wing of copper with ornament stamped on its underside. While still functioning as a gutter, it gives a paper-thin edge to the roof. Its slight "lift" gives the roof a visually weightless character so that it seems to have floated down onto the brick piers.

The interior trim of the Robie house is varied in a way similar to that seen in the Martin house. The base detail varies from the first floor to second floor to the furniture; however, its impact is considerably less, since the Robie house lacks the piers, the subpiers, and the structures within structures that characterize the Martin house. The cyma recta is again used at the base (although it is much reduced in size and the dentils are gone), but the trim is used in a significantly different way.

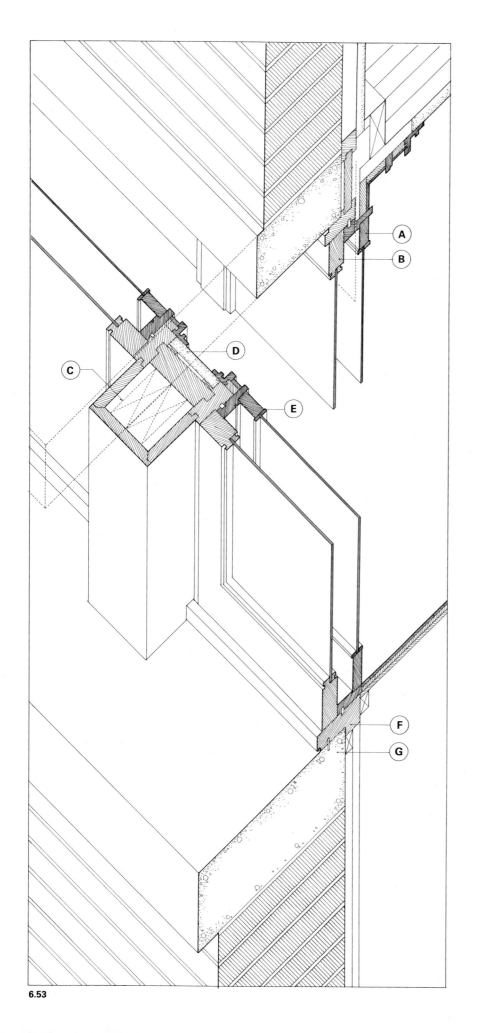

6.53

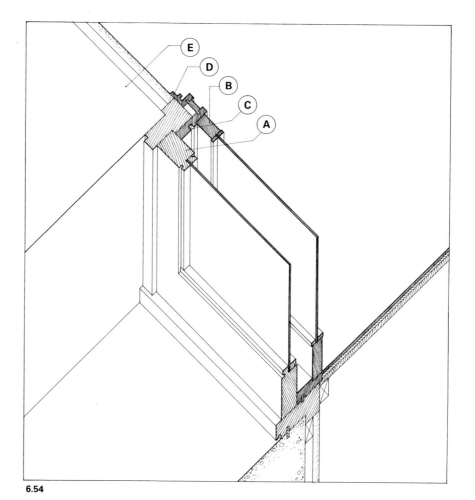

6.54

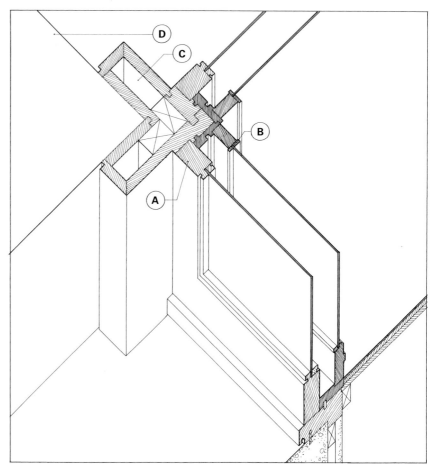

6.55

D. D. Martin house

Frank Lloyd Wright

Buffalo, New York, 1904

6.53 window details

A Oak interior window with concrete lintel above (not shown).

B Wood exterior window. The transparent interior varnish used on the oak will not stand up when exposed to the elements, so a cheaper wood, such as pine, is used here.

C 2 × 4 wood studs. These help support the roof above. The least expensive wood is used for the structure which is concealed from view.

D Plaster on wood lath.

E Glass stops. These hold the glass in place and allow for replacement. Wright uses the typical projecting stop for the interior window.

F Wood sill with drip.

G Concrete sill. This is sloped to allow water to run off, but no drip is provided at the bottom.

(*Frank Lloyd Wright Foundation, drawing 0405.009, Survey.*)

6.54 window-jamb details at brick pier and plaster wall

A Wood exterior window.

B Oak interior window.

C Groove. This acts as a guide for the roll-down windowshade.

D Panel molding. This covers the joint between the wood window frame and the plaster wall.

E Brick pier, plastered on interior.

(*Frank Lloyd Wright Foundation, drawing 0405.009, Survey.*)

6.55 window-jamb details at corner brick pier

A Wood exterior window.

B Oak interior window.

C Exterior wood trim.

D Brick pier.

(*Frank Lloyd Wright Foundation, drawing 0405.009, Survey.*)

In the early Prairie Houses, moldings are used to make transitions and cover joints. Thus, the junctions of wall and floor, of wall and ceiling, and of column and beam are all locations for elaborations. In the Robie house, trim is used for one dominant purpose: to delineate structure. Other uses for moldings are eliminated or minimized. There are no crown moldings at the ceiling-and-wall junctions, either above the windows or at the fascia. There is no molding where the brick fireplace meets the floor or the ceiling. In the Martin house, the trim ran along the inside and outside corners of the ceiling recess (figures 6.49, 6.50). The ceiling at the Robie house is similar in outline, but the corners are left exposed and the trim runs uninterrupted across the surfaces and around the corners of the ceiling.

In view of the structural basis of the ornamentation, it is not surprising to find the trim of the Martin and Robie houses so different. Whereas the Martin house is concrete, the Robie house is wood and steel, and the trim that crosses its ceiling is simply a more elaborate version of the analogous wood beams of the earlier houses. But Wright was also trying to develop a system of ornamentation that would be in accordance with the qualities of modern structural systems. He referred to both effects as *plasticity*. Structurally, this term referred to the continuity of steel-and-concrete construction. In his later writings Wright described plasticity as an expression of modern materials. In traditional wood and stone buildings, columns and beams when joined continue to act largely as independent structural members. This is not true of steel or concrete. Wright saw traditional moldings and trim, correctly, as the expression of these joints, and he saw their elimination as the expression of the character of steel and concrete joints. Before 1910 this idea took the form not of the elimination of ornament, but of the independence of ornament and joints. In Wright's words: "The ceilings [could be] thus expanded, by extending them downward as the wall band above the windows, gave a generous overhead to even small rooms. The sense of the whole was broadened and made plastic, too, by this expedient. The inclosing walls and ceilings were thus made to flow together. Here entered the important element of plasticity—indispensable to successful use of the machine, the true expression of modernity."[26] Wright's application of this idea in the Prairie Houses was, as he admitted, largely intuitive and hardly rigorous. In many examples, it was purely aesthetic.

Another innovative aspect of the Robie house's trim is what might be called inversion: the reversal of a detail from what one would expect. For example, the glazing beads of the casement windows, which are normally recessed behind the face of the sash, here project, creating a frame around the window. Wright did the same with the backband detail (figure 6.33). In the Winslow and Willets houses, it was recessed behind the trim. In the Robie house, it projects. Wright had done this before, but never so extensively as here. He was to repeat and expand upon this concept in his later work.

The construction of the Robie house seems to have gone fairly smoothly and to the satisfaction of everyone, even though while it was in progress Wright left his office and the country, and even though he is said to have been indifferent to the status of projects in construction and to have refused to answer letters asking for guidance. This success was due in part to the capability of the contractor and of Wright's staff and to the sympathy of the client, but one must also bear in mind that the Robie house was not as technically revolutionary as has been supposed. With his later houses in the Textile Block and Usonian series, Wright attempted to change not only the form of modern residential architecture but also the materials and processes. In time he would reject entirely the standard platform-frame and masonry systems, which were the typical methods of building houses in America, but he did not do so in the Robie house. Despite the quantity of steel and the many technical and architectural innovations, it was built by relatively conventional methods, with load-bearing brick walls, wood-frame floors, and standard balloon framing; it stretched these systems to their limits, but it did not go outside them.

6.56

6.57

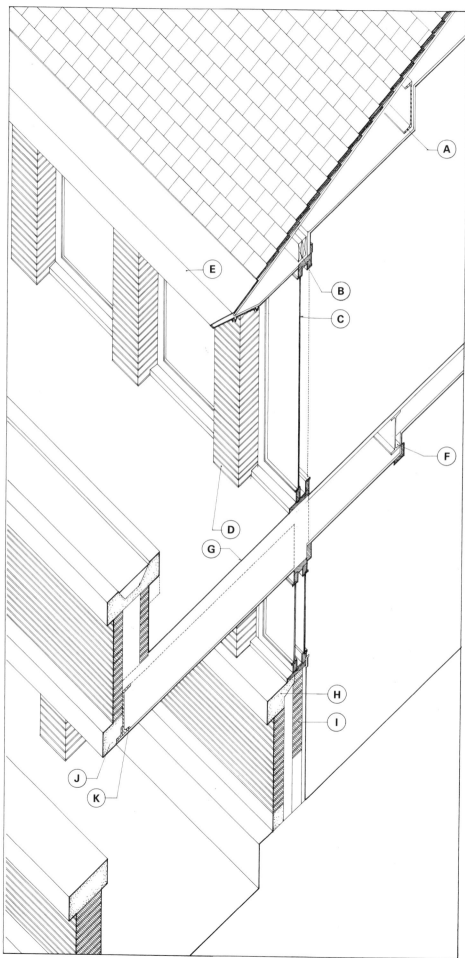

6.58

F. C. Robie house

Frank Lloyd Wright

Chicago, 1909

6.56 exterior

6.57 detail

6.58 wall section

This drawing is based on the original working drawings. Modifications were made during construction, particularly to the planter at the edge of the terrace and to the first-floor framing.

A 15" steel channel. This is primary support of the 2 × 8 wood rafters; it is supported by large brick piers and by the fireplace.

B Girder made from two 2 × 8's. This is the secondary support of the rafters at their ends.

C Wood window.

D Brick pier supporting wood girder.

E Copper gutter, supported by iron T stiffeners.

F 15" I-section steel beam. Most of the first-floor framing is steel.

G Balcony deck.

H Limestone sill.

I Brick wall. Unlike many of Wright's earlier masonry houses, this one has a cavity wall.

J Limestone trim. This appears to support the brick, but in fact the trim is supported by the steel beam. Its upper horizontal surface had little slope, and as a result much water penetrated the brick wall at this point.

K 15" steel channel with 3 × 3 steel angle supporting wood joists and limestone trim.

(Frank Lloyd Wright Foundation, drawing 0908.24, HABS, Survey.)

THE LARKIN BUILDING

Wright brought over a hundred projects to completion between 1893 and 1910, the vast majority of them residences. His experience in large-scale building had been acquired in the office of Alder and Sullivan. Paul Mueller, who was the contractor and perhaps the engineer for the Larkin Building, had also worked for Alder and Sullivan. Despite this, the building bears little resemblance to the mature office blocks of the Chicago School. Its closest relatives are the adjacent concrete-frame factories of the Larkin Company, but for the most part it is an original creation in its technical systems. Unlike the majority of the Prairie Houses, the Larkin Building was not "conformed to this world." The integrated structure and utilities that were to become the ideal of modern construction were seen here for the first time. But despite the brilliance of its achievement, it remains outside the course of development of modern construction (as opposed to Modern architecture). That kind of construction is more accurately represented by Chicago Style office buildings such as the Wainwright Building.

The well-known black-and-white pictures of the Larkin Building are somewhat misleading as to color. The major exterior materials were cinnamon-colored sandstone and dark red brick. In color, it was very similar to the Wainwright Building, which is also primarily red. The first major difference between the two buildings is in their structures. The Larkin Building has an integrated structure and skin; the Wainwright Building's skin is supported by a complete structurally self-sufficient steel frame. The extensive masonry of the exterior is only a cladding. Finish and structure are independent. The brick piers of the Larkin Building are structural, although they support pairs of steel beams encased in concrete. The Larkin Building is a load-bearing masonry structure, and its structure and its finish are one. This is a more efficient use of material; however, it was not to develop as a more efficient means of construction, because of the development of independent systems and subcontractors.

Reyner Banham has described extensively the integration of ductwork and structure in the Larkin Building.[27] Portions of the structure are hollowed out to contain the services while not concealing the structure. Vertical distribution is through hollow brick shafts; horizontal distribution is in the voids between pairs of steel beams. The concept has obvious suggestions (not surprisingly) of an organism. Subsequent architects emulated this example, but as with the structure the trend has been toward independent rather than integrated systems. The ductwork of the Modern office building is distributed vertically through shafts in a central core and horizontally in a plenum between the floor structure and the plaster ceiling. What this system loses in expression, it gains in efficiency by allowing services and structure to be designed and built independently. The principal advantages of Wright's concept was that it allowed the structure to remain monolithic. Structure was expressed through exposure.

Wright said of the Larkin Building: "It is the simple, dignified utterance of a plain, utilitarian type, with sheer brick walls and simple stone copings."[28] This is, of course, not true. There are a great many elements in the Larkin Building that have no functional purpose, particularly in the stonework. Russell Sturgis was correct in interpreting the stone trim as a highly abstracted Classical order. The two rectilinear bands at the base of the piers correspond to the torus and scotia of an Ionic base (figures 6.5, 6.6), and the terra cotta capitals at the tops of the piers form a highly abstracted equivalent of Corinthian columns.

In 1909 Wright wrote a reply to Sturgis's unfavorable review. In this reply, which was not published (out of deference to Sturgis, who had just died), Wright justified many of the formal characteristics—particularly the absence of moldings and enrichments—that he had argued for in his 1901 Hull House lecture. However, his reasoning in 1909 lacks the concerns with craft and industry that characterize his earlier lecture. There are references to the unique industrial conditions in America, and certain details are defended on the basis of expression of the material, but on the whole Wright's tone is more abstract, hermetic, and purely architectural. The central issue (as with Schuyler and Ashbee) is that, although the Larkin

6.59

F. C. Robie house
Frank Lloyd Wright
Chicago, 1909

6.59 dining room
(Art Institute of Chicago.)

6.60 ceiling plan of living room
A   Wood trim. This parallels the joists
    and rafters above, although its
    spacing is much wider.
B   The crown mold is omitted,
    allowing the plaster to form a
    simple corner. Wright has
    eliminated the traditional function
    of trim—to cover joints and make
    transitions—in favor of ornament
    that describes without duplicating
    the structure it clads.
C   Wood grill concealing lights above.
D   Surface-mounted globe lights (not
    shown.)
    *(Frank Lloyd Wright Foundation,
    drawing 0908.24, HABS, Survey.)*

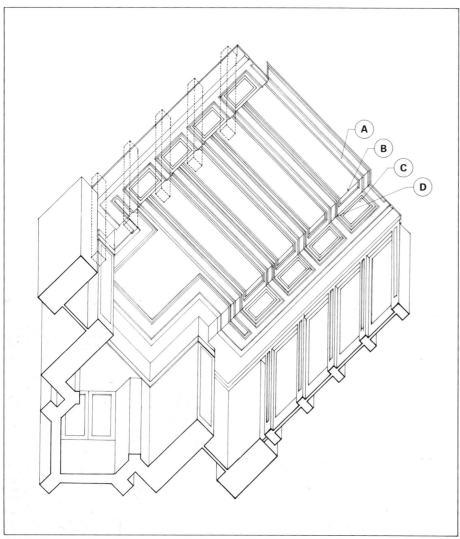

6.60

6.61

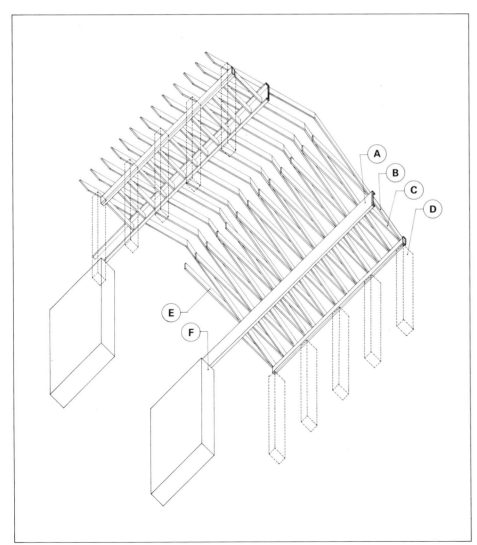

6.62

F. C. Robie house
Frank Lloyd Wright
Chicago, 1909

6.61   **under construction**
(Regenstein Library, University of Chicago.)

6.62   **framing plan**
- A   15″ steel channel supporting rafters.
- B   2 × 8 rafters, 16″ on center. These support 1″ boards forming a roof deck.
- C   Two 2 × 8's forming girder supporting rafters at their ends.
- D   Brick piers supporting girder.
- E   2 × 8 collar beam and ceiling joists, 16″ on center. The rafters have a tendency to spread apart when the roof is loaded. This acts as a tension member to hold them together, as well as supporting the plaster ceiling.
- F   Brick pier supporting steel beam.
  (Frank Lloyd Wright Foundation, drawing 0908.24, Survey.)

6.63   **under construction**
(Regenstein Library, University of Chicago.)

6.63

6.64

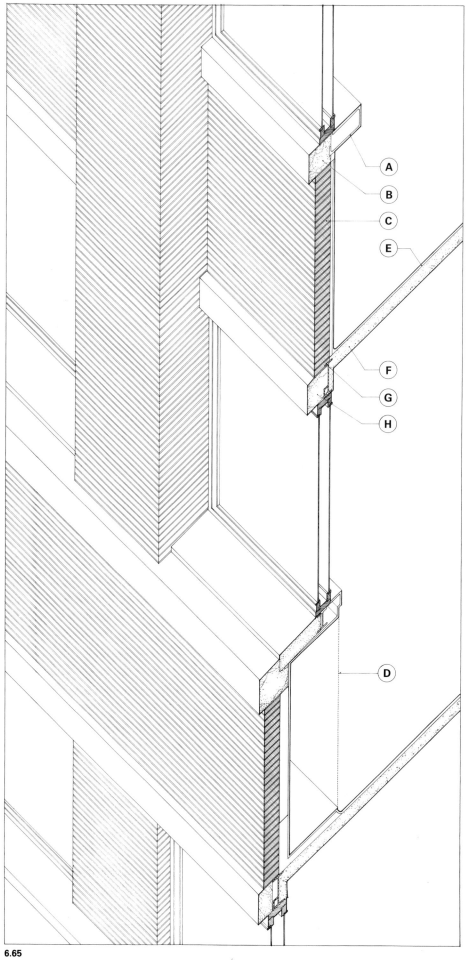

6.65

Larkin Building

Frank Lloyd Wright

Buffalo, New York, 1904

6.64 **exterior**

(Buffalo and Erie County Historical Society.)

6.65 **wall section**

A Terra cotta interior sill. Although the interior is similar in form to the exterior, the materials are subtly different, with terra cotta instead of stone trim and a different type of brick.

B Red sandstone exterior sill.

C Brick wall. The brick piers are load-bearing and do not contain steel columns.

D Space for file cabinets (not shown).

E Magnesite finish floor. Magnesite is a poured-in-place flooring material made from a cement containing magnesium carbonate.

F Concrete floor slab.

G Steel beam and angle. Although the brick wall appears to be supported by the sandstone lintel, both are supported by this steel beam spanning between the brick piers.

H Double wood window. Two windows are used here to reduce heat loss in a manner similar to today's double glazing.

(Frank Lloyd Wright Foundation, drawing 0403.083.)

Building has numerous bases, plinths, capitals, architraves, and entablatures, none are softened or eased by moldings. Wright first argues, echoing Owen Jones, that traditional moldings, such as those that Sturgis suggests, are applied rather than integral and thus are "constructed ornament" rather than ornamented construction: ". . . we are further away from a living style of architecture than ever, chiefly because of the conception rooted in the mind of architect and critic alike that architecture consists, or ever did consist, in manufacturing with ornamental moldings and chamfered edges a fabric flickering with light and shade, to be applied to a structure as a porous plaster might be applied to an aching back. . . ."[29]

Although the Larkin Building lacks the "plastic" qualities of ornamentation found in Unity Temple and the Robie house, where ornament and joinery are dissociated, Wright argues that moldings and ornamentation are unnecessary additions to structure: ". . . a molding is only a means of articulating the elements of structure. . . . Moldings could have said nothing in this structure that is not better said without them or by the plain stone courses which say all that is artistically necessary."[30] Wright also defends the absence of ornament (or enrichments). It is, of course, possible to have ornament without moldings; the Imperial Hotel is a prime example. Wright wrote of the Larkin building:

It is not the awkward groupings of masses that troubles Mr. Sturgis, but simply that they are not modified by the means of grace he must have if "Architecture" is a consideration. . . . When forms are modified the modification should mean something. Unless you know what the modification means let the form alone. . . .

The building is, frankly, "a group of bare, square edged, parallelopipedons, . . . but fitted to one another organically and with aesthetic intent, and with utter contempt for the fetish so long worshiped that architecture consists in whittling their edges or in loading their surfaces with irrelevant sensualities.[31]

Like many of his contemporaries, Wright was seeking an astylistic architecture, one devoid of specific historical associations. Webb and Voysey avoided stylistic association in moldings by a strategy of deliberate naiveté, copying vernacular examples and using simple and traditional moldings in an unsophisticated way. Wright did the same by avoiding moldings altogether.

But the dominant theme of Wright's defense of the Larkin Building is the virtue of geometry—not because it is the expression of the machine, or because it has no historical associations, but because it is in itself beautiful: "I confess to a love for a clean arris; the cube I find comforting; the sphere inspiring. . . . I can marry these forms in various ways without adulterating them but I love them pure, strong, and undefiled."[32]

The criticism of Ashbee, Schuyler, and Sturgis must have hurt Wright deeply, for in 1923, with Sturgis and Schuyler long dead and Ashbee more or less retired, he seemed to be responding to them in his description of the Imperial Hotel:

. . . Its structure asserts itself so boldly as to pain the sensitive beholder committed by use and wont to the modifying member. Having devoted my life to getting rid of that expedient in Architecture, or in Society or in Life—it is with difficulty that I realize the shock to sensitive Renaissance nerves, the utter neglect of this member causes.[33]

In his 1901 Hull House lecture, Wright defended the absence of moldings in his work on grounds that were largely sociological. In his 1909 reply to Sturgis he defended the same characteristics of his work for reasons that were almost totally aesthetic, and it is not an accident that the appearance of this attitude coincides with the end of his Oak Park period.

CONCLUSION

When Ashbee returned to Chicago in 1908 he perceived a change, both in the intellectual climate of the city and in Wright's attitude: "The great vainglorious one is not what she was. She is not so cocksure, not quite herself. . . . The soul of the city is sick. . . . Lloyd Wright, who eight years ago was so full of fire and belief, . . . has grown bitter. He has drawn in upon himself. It is the bitterness of

6.66

6.67

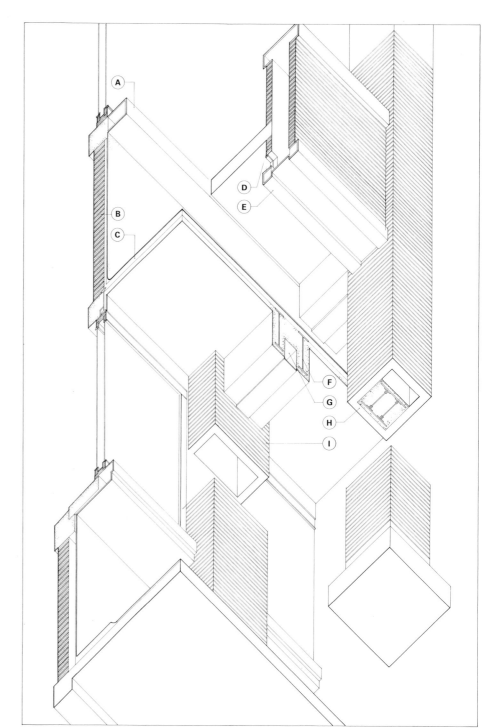

6.68

Larkin Building

Frank Lloyd Wright

Buffalo, New York, 1904

6.66 interior

(Buffalo and Erie County Historical Society.)

6.67 fragment of existing wall

6.68 interior wall section

(reverse view of figure 6.65).

A Interior terra cotta sill with exterior sandstone sill.

B Typical brick exterior wall.

C Concrete slab.

D Interior spandrel of brick with cavity for air distribution.

E Terra cotta trim.

F Two 18"-deep steel beams.

G Cavity in beam for ductwork carrying air to the register in the bottom of the beam.

H Typical interior pier. Exterior piers are load-bearing solid brick; interior columns are steel encased in brick and concrete. The cavity contains a void for a duct riser, which carries air from the basement to the cavities in the spandrels and beams.

I Typical exterior brick pier with air shaft. Air from all floors is exhausted from vents near the floor.

(Frank Lloyd Wright Foundation, drawing 0403.083.)

an archaic socialism.''[34] Ashbee was at least partly correct in his perception of Wright's mood. A year later, Wright abandoned his family and his office and left Oak Park.

The extent to which Wright's withdrawal was the result of his personal life and the extent to which it was the result of "the bitterness of an archaic socialism" will never be completely understood. Ashbee's phrase is a curious one; Wright would not have enjoyed being called a socialist, archaic or otherwise. Did Ashbee see mirrored in Wright his own disillusionment with the Arts and Crafts movement, or did Wright share this disillusionment? Like many other Modernists, Wright saw his abstractions as justified by social and industrial conditions, but he also saw abstraction as virtuous in a purely aesthetic sense.

Wright was indeed "drawn in on himself." Before 1910 he had been an eccentric; after 1910 he was an outcast. N. K. Smith has written that Wright left Oak Park because he had failed:

For seventeen years he had wrestled with the problem of resolving the polar tension between the personal and the institutional, between freedom and loyalty, between the individual and state, between music and architecture; and during that time he had invented many different forms, always in an effort at finding adequate expression of that resolution in the public art of building. But had he succeeded at any single point?[35] . . . It must have seemed to him that in the very act of defying law and custom, he was breaking his way out of the trap of conventionality in which he felt himself to be caught, and was clearing the way for a new life that would now have to be built, whatever form it might take, upon the idea of the supremacy of individual freedom over social conformity.[36]

Smith points out that many of the elements and ordering devices that denote connections to society, such as formal dining rooms, are rare in Wright's work after 1910.

This alienation affected Wright's patterns of building and detailing as well. In his work prior to 1910, Wright was more optimistic and reconciled to the world as it was. He was certainly a reformer, but he was not yet a social revolutionary. His buildings may have been revolutionary, but he did not yet reject the pattern of American cities or the pattern of American building. He wished to change it, to improve it, but he did not reject it. Not until the 1920s, after he had cut himself off (or been cut off) from society, did Wright attempt to reinvent American building.

Wright's post-1910 buildings are largely monolithic and largely without trim, although often heavily ornamented. Structural systems are largely exposed, and there is a minimum of distinction between structural and finished materials. None of this is true of his earlier work, in which trim is abundant and in which structures are concealed and are described by the systems in which they are clad. Wright's disassociation of trim from joints and transitions and his development of wood ornament appropriate to modern forming techniques—perhaps his most significant achievements—are absent from his later work.

Despite the brilliance of his work in the 1930s, it is somewhat unfortunate that Wright abandoned this attitude toward building, which was much closer to the direction in which construction was developing. Wright's building methods of the 1930s were as revolutionary as his forms. As utopian as the Broadacre City Plan, they were ill-suited to the society in which they were used—and they were meant to be. Although Wright carried many of his ideas regarding trim and ornament to what was perhaps their logical conclusion in the 1920s, he abandoned the idea of modifying standard building systems in favor of totally new ones. Nevertheless, there is much more to be discovered in Wright's early work besides precedents for later phrases of Modernism, including his own Modernism.

7 Otto Wagner and Adolf Loos: Viennese Rationalism

In 1898 Otto Wagner completed a project for the Akademie der Bildenden Künste (Acadamy of Fine Arts) in Vienna. It has been largely ignored by his Modernist admirers, since it is covered with symbols of the sort that make them so uncomfortable. Snakes swirl around columns, smoking urns on tripods decorate the windows, and statues of Victory hold out laurel wreaths for our inspection. These elements may be interpreted in several ways. Some of them are programmatic; that is, they describe the function of the building. Wagner wrote that the groups of figures on each corner represent the arts of Architecture, Sculpture, Painting, and Graphics, that the figures next to them are teachers and pupils, and that the floral ornament of the corners identifies the structural support of these piers. Unless one is cynical about art schools, this does not explain the snakes, and one can assume that on a second level the elements are mythic. The snakes, tripods, and laurel wreaths of the facade are all elements of the story of Apollo and the founding of the Temple at Delphi. Joseph Rykwert has explained the significance of this myth as it pertains to the mythic origins of architecture; however, on a third level we may see these elements as reflecting the influence of Gottfried Semper, for the tripod, the urn, and the wreath are three of the major elements of the decorative arts out of which Semper felt that the language of architecture grew.

Semper also wrote of the mystical significance of the Delphic tripod, but more important to him were the transformations which it underwent in the development of art. In his view the tripod and kettle represent, along with the stand of the ritual chalice, the origins of the characteristic ornament of the Corinthian order, and it is not by accident that in Wagner's building the tripods are located precisely where one would expect to see a column. To Semper the ornaments of Classicism came not from the nature of stone, or from a transformation of primitive wood construction, but from ornaments taken from the ritual implements of the ancient temple. The wreath was the "ultimate textile object" and "the archetypal work of art."

Semper felt that the language of architecture was born, not out of the branches of Laugier's primitive hut, but out of the artifacts—the textiles, ceramics, and metal—that were hung on the primitive wood frame. It is not by accident that

·MITTELBAV·DER·GESAMMTANLAGE·

PROJECT·FVR·DEN·NEVBAV·
DER·KAIS·KÖNIGL·AKADEMIE·
····DER·BILDENDEN·KVNSTE····

7.1

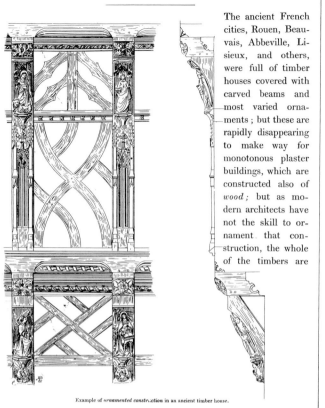

PRINCIPLES OF POINTED OR

The ancient French cities, Rouen, Beauvais, Abbeville, Lisieux, and others, were full of timber houses covered with carved beams and most varied ornaments; but these are rapidly disappearing to make way for monotonous plaster buildings, which are constructed also of *wood*; but as modern architects have not the skill to ornament that construction, the whole of the timbers are

Example of *ornamented construction* in an ancient timber house.

concealed by mock cornices and pilasters, so that the houses of modern

7.2

7.3

7.1 Akademie der Bildenden Künste
Otto Wagner
(Project), 1898.
(Wagner, *Einige Skizzen, Projekte und Ausgeführte Bauwerke.*)

7.2 Detail of ancient timber house, from Pugin's *Principles of Pointed or Christian Architecture.*

7.3 Details of a Swiss timber building, from Semper's *Der Stil.*

7.4 Wreath, from Semper's *Der Stil.*

7.5 Tripod on top of the monument of Lysicrates, from Semper's *Der Stil.*

7.4

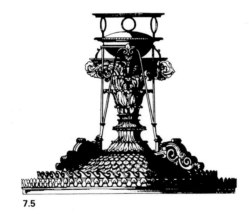

7.5

Wagner selected one artifact from each of Semper's four major categories of artifacts: textiles (the wreath), ceramics (the urn), metalwork (the tripod), and stereometry (the building itself). Although Wagner criticized Semper for stopping at a symbolism of construction, and although these symbolic elements occur much less frequently in Wagner's work after 1905, they never disappear completely, the wreath being the predominant ornament in both the Postsparkasse (Post Office Savings Bank) and St. Leopold's Church. But the relationship of Semper and Wagner involves much more than symbols. In Wagner's later work, two of Semper's ideas have considerable influence: the theory of cladding *(Bekleidung)* and the theory of change in materials or vestigial forms *(Stoffwechsel).* These two concepts represent a position opposite to that of many of Wagner's contemporaries, particularly the Gothic Revivalists.

GOTTFRIED SEMPER AND RATIONAL BUILDING

In 1855, two years after Pugin's death, Gottfried Semper completed the manuscript of the first volume of *Der Stil,* a projected three-volume study of all the decorative arts. His intention had been to write a book on architecture, but he found, unlike Pugin or Viollet-le-Duc, that he could not do so without first discussing what he called the technical arts—ceramics, textiles, and metalwork. He wrote to his publisher: "I wanted to have the technical arts precede architecture because stylistic laws and symbols that later were employed in architecture were first developed in works of the technical arts."[1]

From this unlikely source came the second major theory of building of the late nineteenth century, one that was in practice the opposite of the Gothic Rationalist school of monolithic exposed construction. Semper was to make explicit what was only implied in the teaching of the Beaux-Arts: that rational building could be achieved by means of analogous structural systems, by finish materials that describe the true structural systems they conceal (or, as Semper would put it, "cladding").

Semper was an architect, a Classicist, and a better designer in any style than Pugin or Viollet-le-Duc. Despite the fact that his major writings have never been translated into English, his ideas had some influence on subsequent architectural thought, through H.P. Berlage but also, strangely enough, through Louis Sullivan and John Root in Chicago. But Semper's thought ultimately ran counter to Modernist theories of building. With its dependence on symbols rather than facts, it could not easily have done otherwise. However, Semper was to have an enormous effect on the Modern movement in Vienna, where he did some of his own finest work.

The Gothic Rationalists had argued directly and indirectly that good building used monolithic components and exposed structures. Pugin wrote in praise of medieval English timber houses that "we do not find a single feature introduced beyond what is necessary for their substantial construction."[2] And by criticizing the use of plaster ceilings to conceal roof trusses and screen walls to cover buttresses, Pugin advocated an architecture in which finish materials would be eliminated, leaving only pure structural elements. Equally distasteful were forms that had originated in the structural limitations of one material and were then executed in materials of dissimilar character. The arch and the vault were forms that had originated in stone, and to execute them in wood or plaster was, to Pugin, a sham.

For Viollet-le-Duc, "all architecture proceeds from structure and the first condition at which it should aim is to make the outward form accord with that structure."[3] In order to do that this structure must be exposed, both inside and out, and thus the building must be essentially monolithic. He recognized that it was sometimes desirable to cover the structure and to limit the use of valuable materials by using veneers, but this must be done in a way so as not to hide or deceive. For Viollet-le-Duc, the medieval stone-walled and wood-roofed church represented the construction ideal, with its solid beams, its exposed wood deck inside and metal roof outside, and its monolithic stone walls. All was visible. All was clear. All was solid.

7.6

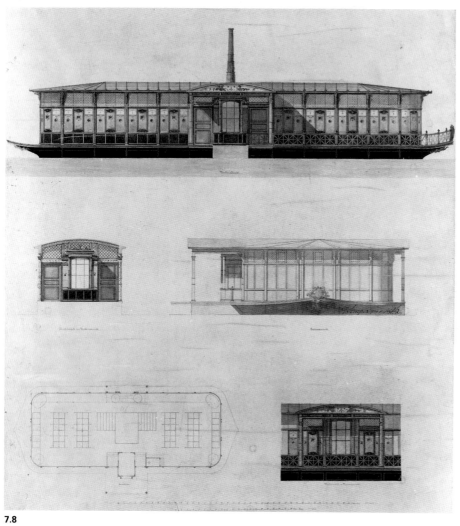

7.8

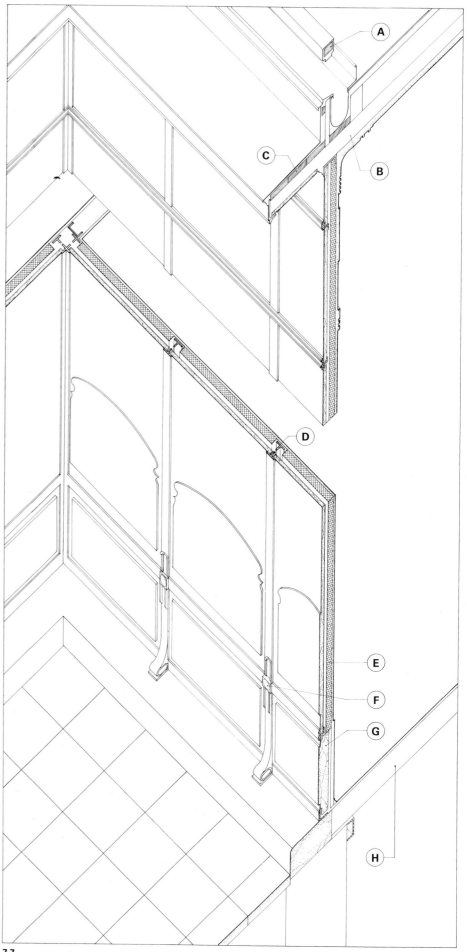

7.7

Karlsplatz Station

Otto Wagner

Vienna, 1896

7.6 **entrance**

7.7 **wall section**

A Baluster railing.

B Roof construction: wood beams supporting wood planks. In contrast to the wall, the roof structure is conventional wood framing.

C Cornice: metal brackets supporting wood decking cased in sheet metal.

D Typical column. See figure 7.13.

E Wall construction: 2-cm marble supported by 5-cm gypsum block wall plasterd on the interior.

F Cast-iron applied ornament.

G 5-cm rusticated granite base.

H Floor construction: iron beams supporting metal decking and concrete fill. The building sits on what is essentially a steel bridge spanning the railway tracks below.

(Kartographische Sammlung, Wiener Stadtarchiv.)

7.8 **Semper, project for a laundry barge,** Paris, 1862.

(Semper Archive, Eidgenossischen Technischen Hochschule, Zurich.)

To Semper, construction was by its very nature layered and not monolithic. Architecture was always structure plus cladding. In his discussion of a type of Swiss timber house similar to that described by Pugin, he points out that the real frame is always concealed behind a cladding of clapboards and carved wood panels. These are sometimes expressive of the real wood structure, but more often they are antique ornaments that originated in other materials, such as the braid molding (which originated in textiles) and the quoin (which originated in masonry). Semper writes of these buildings:

In the Gothic [wooden buildings] the tendency is to base the form on the needs of the support—these are carved with figures etc. In between the framework is either left as constructed . . . or the space is broken down with highly carved subordinate columns and panels. . . . later all the diagonal bracing is hidden behind wooden paneling. This tendency to cover up the diagonal bracing, partly with decoration, completely eliminates their anti-monumental quality. . . . As opposed to the framework, [these decorative panels are] the blank in-between space. Since this space has no dynamic use, it is developed as panels for the blooming of free, decorative art that has no connection with the structure. The Gothic building style uses decoration based on the ability of the craftsman, rather than on structural tendencies, or rather that make the structural dynamic clear.[4]

Semper's concept of ornament is a complex one that allows ornamentation to be simultaneously expressive of both the structure and the art of the craftsman, and allows the use of decorative art forms that were traditionally executed in entirely different materials.

Semper recognized that in architecture, forms that grew out of the characteristics of one material would inevitably be adapted to another, but he also recognized that these forms would be changed by the new processes and materials in which they were executed. Style was evolutionary, and although Semper allowed for the existence of vestigial forms (forms detached from their technical origins) he also recognized that these forms might eventually disappear.

Wolfgang Herrmann writes: "[Semper] was of the opinion that the decorative parts of Greek architecture were closely connected to the construction and that their purpose was to express symbolically the mechanical functions of the structural parts—giving support, carrying load, countering pressure. 'Greek ornaments,' he declared in an English lecture, 'are emanations of the constructive forms, and, [at] the same time, they are symbols of the dynamical functions of the parts to which they belong.' . . . Hellenic techtonics . . . envelop bare form with explanatory symbolism."[5] Greek architecture illustrates an elaboration of this concept that constructive forms and ornamentation are subject to independent development, which can result in vestigial forms and sometimes the fusion of two elements into one; the Greek temple contains not only vestiges of wood construction in stone, but structure and cladding which became fused.

An example of this influence of the decorative arts on architecture is the relationship of the Delphic tripod to the Corinthian column illustrated by Wagner in his project for the Akademie der Bildenden Künste. To Semper this relationship was proved by example in the building in which he thought the Corinthian order had first appeared, the monument of Lysicrates in Athens. Semper wrote of this monument:

In this period occurs the discovery, or at least the definition and spreading of the Corinthian order. . . . Among the still preserved early Corinthian works none is so important as the Choregic Monument of Lysicrates in Athens. . . . The actual key to this building gives it its crowning Corinthian composition. The whole monument is only a fantastic holder for the "Omphalos," the middle support of the horned tripod. This composition contains the Doric-Corinthian flower petal detail; as an expression of its spanning strength in many upwards and downwards stepping repetitions. Finally, the most luxurious Acanthus growth extends from the tripod to the location of the missing vessel. It is the essence of the perapatetic

7.9

7.10

7.9   **detail**

7.10 **detail**

column in its plastic-Corinthian form. In it are the base, the shaft, the capital, all in the original luxuriant Alexandrian forms. With this appropriate crowning of the work the individual columns stand in clear harmony.[6]

Note that Semper writes of the importance of three different aspects of Corinthian ornamentation. It is first derivative of a symbol, the "Omphalos," the navel or center of the world in Greek mythology. It is derivative of the decoration of an ancient piece of furniture of mystical importance, the Delphic tripod, but it is also an expression of the structural forces at work in the column. The fact that these symbols have been transposed from furniture to architecture, or from metal to stone, has not altered their symbolic structural importance.

Semper's ideas on the nature of structural ornament were based, like Laugier's, on theories of the primitive origins of architecture. Using a Caribbean hut as his paradigm, Semper conceived of the origin of building in a wood roof supported by posts and enclosed with wickerwork. This was then covered with carpets, mats, or weavings, which was thus the primordial origin of cladding. It is for this reason that Semper saw the origins of architectural ornament in the technical arts of textiles, ceramics, and metalwork. Since these made up the original cladding systems, their specific elements were particularly important.

According to Rykwert, Semper felt that "the wreath is the prime example of a textile object. The functions which first lead man to connect pieces of material . . . were first the desire to order and bind and, second, that to cover and shelter, to delimit. . . . The knot is 'perhaps the oldest technical symbol and the expression of the first cosmogonic ideals which arose among the people.'"[7] This concept implies a different type of ornamentation and joinery than the traditional Classical and Gothic systems, which were, in theory, based on primitive systems of wood and stone construction, since the techniques of joining textile fibers, and the resulting ornamentation, are fundamentally different from the means of joining pieces of wood or stone.

Metal was another of Semper's primordial cladding materials. With the gradual disappearance of the wood base, the use of metal cladding gave rise to a tubular, hollow system of metal construction, which Semper considered superior to monolithic construction. Semper felt that the proper use of metal in buildings was in sheet-metal ceilings and in cast columns with hollow centers. At the same time, he opposed the use of structural steel beams.

According to Semper, the origin of walls as carpets had resulted in languages of ornamentation based on textile art, such as the seam and the border. The seam was thus, as Rykwert says, "an analogue and symbol which has archaic roots, for the use of joining originally separated planes."[8]

Mosaics, Semper wrote, were derivative of carpets, and thus glazed tile and brick were a part of the primal system. Semper was careful to point out that primitive (in this case Assyrian) glazed walls were not glazed brick but an encrusted layer of tiles independent of the structure.[9]

WAGNER'S THEORY

Otto Wagner was heavily influenced by Semper's writings but had difficulty accepting some of his major premises. This ambivalence is clear in Wagner's major theoretical work, *Moderne Architektur*, written in 1896 and periodically revised in later years. In places it closely resembles Semper's *Der Stil*, such as in Wagner's description of the origins of building: "Man's earliest constructional form was the roof, the protecting ceiling. . . . It preceded pillars, walls, and even the hearth, being succeeded by supports artificially built of tree trunks or stones, later followed by wattled work, the wall, [and] the partition."[10] But Wagner uses these arguments to do something Semper never did—to call for a new style in architecture, based on modern materials:

7.11

7.12

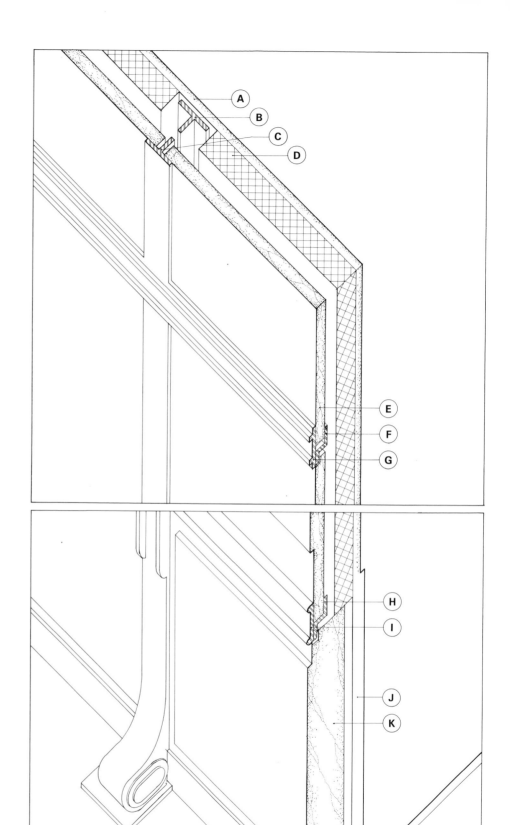

7.13

Karlsplatz Station

Otto Wagner

Vienna, 1896

7.11 **detail**

7.12 **detail**

7.13 **wall details**

A Plaster.

B 7 cm × 10 cm iron I section, made from two T sections.

C Outer T section. Since this section cannot be attached until the marble is in place, it is largely ornamental, forming part of the "cladding."

D 5-cm-thick gypsum block wall.

E 2-cm-thick marble facing.

F Z section to support marble supported by the columns beyond.

G Molded Iron band.

H Iron Z section.

I Molded iron band.

J Plaster interior base.

K 10-cm-thick rusticated granite base. In Classical architecture marble walls often sit on granite bases, since granite is less easily damaged by elements that may be present at grade.

L 7 cm × 7 cm iron angle. Although the granite base implies that this is a load-bearing wall, the metal angle shows that it is not.

(Kartographische Sammlung, Wiener Stadtarchiv.)

"Necessity is the sole mistress of art." Gottfried Semper himself was the first to direct our attention to this truth (even if he later deviated from it), thus clearly showing the path to be pursued. . . . *"Every architectural form originates from construction, and it has gradually become an art form."* . . . Hence a constructive basis influences forms, and it may therefore by deduced with certainty that new constructions must likewise yield new forms.[11]

Wagner agreed with Semper on many issues, such as the importance of symmetry, but at the time he wrote *Moderne Architektur* he could not accept completely the concept of cladding: "Unlike Darwin [Semper] did not have the courage to fully complete his theories upwards and downwards, and stopped at a symbolism of construction, instead of designating construction itself as the germ-cell of architecture. Construction always precedes, for no art form can originate without it, and the task of art, which is to idealize existing objects, becomes impossible without the existence of the object."[12]

Despite Wagner's criticism of the concept of cladding, his buildings clearly show its impact. What he disliked was not so much the concept of cladding itself but the idea that the structural language of the cladding could exist independently of its structural base. He did not, like Pugin, prefer that structure and finish (base and cladding) be one. In Wagner's work different types coexist: monolithic exposed structures, structures clad in accordance with their bases, and buildings clad with vestigial stylistic elements.

But what were the new forms to be? What were the effects of modern technology on building? In view of the fact that these effects were only beginning to be felt in Vienna in 1900, Wagner's analysis of the new technology is remarkable for its perception of the course modern building was to follow. In 1900, although concrete and steel framing were in use in Vienna, and although the stone industry was being transformed by the use of modern tools, construction methods were traditional in comparison with American practice. Wagner's Post Office Savings Bank, completed in 1910, makes use of modern techniques such as concrete framing and veneered marble, but has load-bearing exterior walls and contains few elevators. By contrast, the Chicago-style office building, with its self-supporting steel frame and its banks of elevators contained in a core, was fully developed by 1890. In the context of these conditions, Wagner's analysis is remarkable in its insight into modern construction. Wagner, working with only limited exposure to modern building systems, saw their consequences more clearly than Le Corbusier or Louis Kahn.

Wagner saw three major differences between modern construction and traditional construction (or Renaissance construction, as he called it):

Time of construction. Wagner wrote in *Moderne Architektur:* "In the methods of construction employed in all periods there is an evident tendency to impart buildings with the greatest possible stability and permanence in order to obtain eternal duration. . . . After modern construction produced a complete revolution in the time of erection required, though the principle of durability remained the same in art, construction was required to solve this problem, and it was compelled to adapt new means to satisfy this requirement. These methods were chiefly the use of new materials and the introduction of machines. Their influence on forms of art must certainly become apparent. . . . Forms of art where the time of erection neither corresponds to the effect nor to the material employed, always have something untruthful or irritating."[13] The idea that construction time must be expressed in form was unusual; it had few precedents and fewer subsequent adherents. His chief means of achieving this expression was to transform traditional Classical construction by means of veneers, exposed fasteners, and the replication of traditional masonry forms in exposed metal. But this was only part of an overall system of separation of components.

Independent systems. Wagner wrote: "It must be natural for modern men, who prize the value of time, to promote those systems of construction that can satisfy their wishes in this respect. This again occurs by the use of materials which are quickly obtained and of good quality, by division of labour, thus by commencing

7.14

7.15

7.16

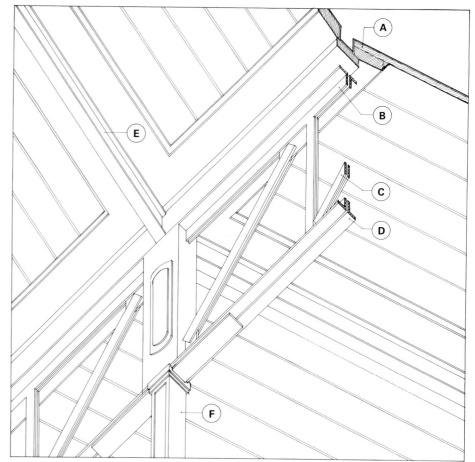

7.17

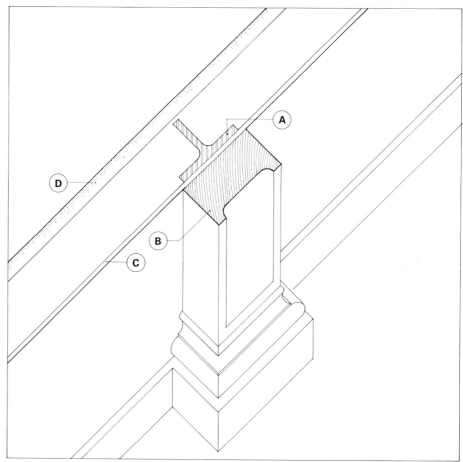

7.18

different portions of the structure at the same time, so that a quicker method of erecting the edifice results. If the structure be solidly constructed, it will supplant earlier methods in spite of increased cost. It is evident that new forms must result from this procedure."[14] Many of Wagner's contemporaries and successors perceived the importance of specialized labor; however, being concerned with industrialization, they saw its main effects in prefabricated components. Wagner again was one of the few to perceive that this would result in increased independence and in a specialization of operations at the job site. Eighty years later, it is easy to see that this has been a more important consequence of specialization than prefabrication.

Steel structures. Much of the construction section of *Moderne Architektur* is devoted to the praise of steel construction: "The properties of steel are indeed so extraordinary that it is able to satisfy almost any requirement. . . . The possibility and the facilitation of so many constructions, the unlimited choice of dimensions of rooms, the execution of any prescribed pier construction, the free selection of form of ceiling, with artificial lighting of the interior at pleasure, the great reduction of thickness of walls, security against fire, and the great reduction in time required for erection . . . are entirely due to the use of this material."[15] This is a curious passage, since Wagner built few steel buildings that used a complete steel frame. (He did use steel framing extensively in the bridges he built for the city of Vienna.) The majority of his larger buildings are framed with concrete, a material which is hardly mentioned in *Moderne Architektur*. When Wagner wrote the original version, he had completed only one building (the Landerbank) that made extensive use of steel, and even that building did not have a complete, independent steel frame. It is important not to take these remarks out of context. The complete and independent steel frame with a curtain wall, already well established in Chicago, was relatively rare in Wagner's Vienna. Two of Wagner's best-known buildings (the Karlsplatz Station and the main room of the Postsparkasse) have what appear to be exposed metal frames, but the remainder of his buildings have load-bearing exterior walls with concrete frames in the interior and thus are similar in structure to many pre-1880 American buildings.

Wagner's descriptions of the possibilities of steel—particularly his descriptions of the aesthetic changes that steel would make possible—appear to anticipate Modernist attitudes, but the aesthetic theme of *Moderne Architektur* is, in some ways, conservative. Ruskin and Semper had criticized the use of iron and steel as structural materials, arguing that perceptions of architectural form were based on a knowledge of the structural limitations of stone and that the long spans and large openings possible with steel would be visually disturbing and destructive of the qualities of mass and interplay of solid and void found in traditional stone architecture. Wagner welcomed the functional advantages of steel framing, which he felt would transform architectural form, but he insisted that the perceived permanence, solidity, stability, and monumentality of traditional architecture should be maintained. Wagner's architecture, despite its abstract overtones, has none of the weightlessness, the tautness, or the membrane-like quality of the International Style.

THE KARLSPLATZ STATION

In 1898, the year of the second edition of *Moderne Architektur* and the project for the Academy of Fine Arts, Wagner completed the Karlsplatz Station. The few symbols he used in that building, such as the sunflower, were not derived from Semper. The form, with its small-scale uprights and chamfered corners, resembles Semper's 1862 project for a laundry barge in Paris, but the greatest influence of Semper on this work is not in form but in conception, in the application of the theories of cladding, incrustation, and vestigial forms to metal-frame building.

It is something of a shock to realize that the Karlsplatz Station is Wagner's only building with a complete metal frame. Twenty years after the first steel-frame skyscrapers in Chicago, Wagner was building load-bearing masonry buildings with wood or concrete floors. It would seem that the use of an exposed frame is contradictory to the concept of cladding; however, what appears to be the frame

7.19

7.20

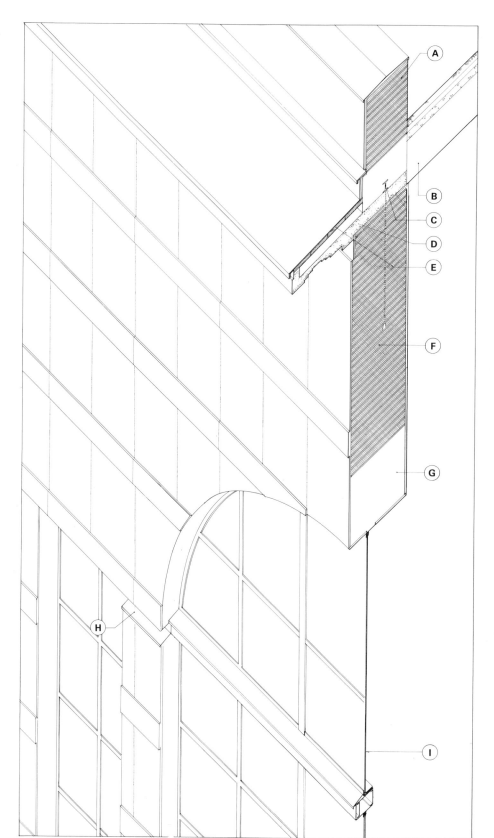

7.21

St. Leopold's

Otto Wagner

Vienna, 1907

7.19 **exterior**

7.20 **detail**

7.21 **wall section**

A   Parapet: typical marble-faced brick wall with metal copings.

B   Roof construction: asphalt cement on concrete deck.

C   8-cm-deep I section, 70 cm long. This is cast into the concrete cornice to anchor the steel rods extending into the brick. The long cantilever of the cornice requires that it be anchored into the wall.

D   Concrete cornice.

E   Wood-and-metal cornice cover. See figures 7.22 and 7.23.

F   Wall construction: 2-cm-thick marble facing on solid brick wall plastered on interior.

G   Brick or concrete arch supporting wall over window opening.

H   The channel passes across the top of the pier to form the lintel. A concrete lintel is located above the small window.

I   Iron, copper, and glass window. See figure 7.28.
    (Technische Betriebsleitung, Psychiatrisches Krankenhaus Baumgarten.)

is not the true frame at all but a network of iron that overlays the real steel structure. The iron columns that support the roof are concealed within the block-and-plaster wall, but corresponding to each column is a iron tee on the face of the building. This tee is not structural; although it holds the marble facing in place, it was added after the structural frame was erected. The true structure of the frame is clad with an analogous frame, which describes the frame behind without precisely duplicating it.

If Semper's concept of cladding encompasses a layer of vestigial elements that act as symbols, Wagner's concept of cladding encompasses a layer of structural elements that are largely symbolic; although the Karlsplatz Station has no urns, snakes, or wreaths, it does have numerous vestigial structural elements: a rusticated base, an attic story, a cornice, and (more faintly) column bases and capitals. Each of these elements has been transformed by the materials and processes of modern construction. The base is rusticated granite, in contrast to the smooth marble of the main wall. In the language of traditional Classicism, its dark color, rough surface, and greater thickness increase the mass of the building at the base. In a conventional load-bearing wall this acted to functionally and visually strengthen the building by increasing the bearing capacity of the wall at grade, and to make this solidity apparent. In the Karlspaltz Station, where an iron frame sits not on the ground but on girders spanning the tracks below, the base serves no structural function; thus it is encased on all four sides by an iron angle, showing that it is a supported and not a supporting element. It has become, in Semper's terms, a vestigial form, one that is evolving toward a new manifestation. The marble slabs are polished, book-matched, and stenciled, all of which act to emphasize their thinness and lightness. This deemphasis on weight is made even more dramatic by the cornice, where slabs of marble are hung from iron brackets.

Most of the structure, both real and analogous, is of rolled iron angles and tees, to which are attached ornaments (brackets, consoles, etc.), which, being of cast iron, are considerably more complex in design. Nineteenth-century steel and iron were greatly inferior to today's steel in strength and ductility, but the architects had the advantage of being able to freely mix rolled and cast sections. The profiles of rolled sections can be varied only in one plane and in limited ways. Cast sections, although greatly inferior structurally, can be made into much more complex configurations, the principal limitation being that the overall thickness cannot be greatly varied within the same section. This combination of cast and rolled sections enabled nineteenth-century architects to articulate junctions and termination, and to join pieces in a method reminiscent of Classicism.

Despite the formal similarities to Semper's work that are evident in the Karlsplatz Station, the influence of Semper on Wagner's mature work is more in the realm of ideas than in that of forms. Semper's theory of cladding was a description of a historical phenomenon; it had little to do with his architectural work. It was Wagner who made the theory of cladding into a theory of building—but his reasons for doing so, or at least his arguments for doing so, were not historical but pragmatic.

Wagner designed over forty stations for the Stadtbahn (Vienna's municipal railway), most of which were variations on a series of standard designs. These stations were much less opulent in their materials and much more conventional in their technology than the Karlsplatz. The walls were of brick clad in stucco, and the roofs were wood-framed. Exposed iron was used in the exterior porches and canopies, but for the most part Wagner used the technology of conventional load-bearing masonry.

A typical station of the Stadtbahn is Schönbrunn (figure 7.14). A square masonry block is covered with a pyramidal wood-framed roof. Carved out of the center is an entry portico supported by iron columns and brackets. The all-wood framing of the interior is completely concealed. The framing of the portico is of iron and wood, and is exposed. Each of these types, the exposed and the concealed, is given its own specific type of details. The masonry walls are in the spirit of much of

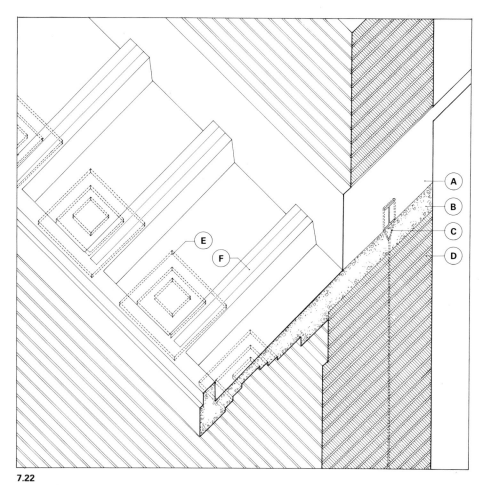

7.22

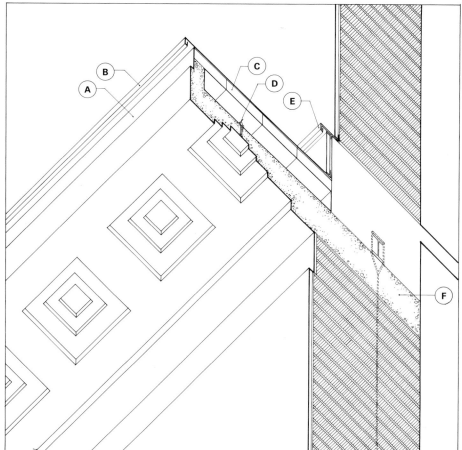

7.23

7.24

7.25

St. Leopold's

Otto Wagner

Vienna, 1907

7.22   structural support of cornice

A   Concrete roof deck. This is essentially a ribbed one-way slab with a slight pitch for drainage.

B   Concrete cornice.

C   Iron I section, 8 cm deep and 70 cm long, anchored to brick wall by metal straps 1.6 m long. This counteracts the overturning moment created by the cantilevered concrete cornice.

D   Brick wall.

E   Coffer below.

F   Concrete rib with cast-in wood nailer. These stiffen the slab and provide a surface to receive the wood deck.
(Technische Betriebsleitung, Psychiatrisches Krankenhaus Baumgarten.)

7.23   cornice with cladding

A   Concrete cornice. This is the only exposed structural element in the building.

B   Copper roof.

C   Wood-plank deck. This spans between the concrete ribs to support the metal roof.

D   Bolt to support rossette (not shown). This is the most literally Classical element of the cornice.

E   Copper flashing. Both the flashing and the roof extend behind the marble, where they are turned up to prevent water from seeping through the horizontal joint. The flashing and the roof are also extended beyond the wall and the cornice face and turned down to form a drip.

F   Brick wall clad with marble on exterior and plaster on interior.
(Technische Betriebsleitung, Psychiatrisches Krankenhaus Baumgarten.)

7.24   detail

7.25   interior

traditional Viennese Classicism; brick load-bearing walls are covered with stucco, which is then molded to resemble stone. None of the joints, the moldings, or the trim in this portion of the building can be seen, even remotely, as an interpretation of the clad structure; they can be seen only as vestiges of cut-stone construction. The corner pieces are rusticated and separated from the rest of the wall by a reveal, but the implication of this detail—that it is a detail of a frame-and-curtain wall—is not structurally correct, as both portions of the wall are structural (perhaps to emphasize this, the articulations between parts—column and entablature, for example—are minimal). The portico, by contrast, is ornamented construction. A truss fabricated from tees and angles is supported at its third points by two cast-iron columns. To this structure are attached wrought-iron and cast-iron ornaments. The columns are given wreaths closely resembling those shown by Semper, and the floral elements that cover the diagonals of the truss suggest Semper's description of the decorated primitive hut.

ST. LEOPOLD'S CHURCH

With St. Leopold's (also known as the Kirche am Steinhof) Wagner perhaps came closest to building an expression of Semper's thought. Not by coincidence, it is his least "rational" building, at least by the rules of International Style Modernism. The form of the building (completed in 1907) is not a new one, based on the needs of modern life and construction; it is an archaic form transformed by the conditions of modern life. This went directly against the dogma of the Gothic rationalists, to whom form and material were inseparable and to whom forms that had evolved from the characteristics of one material were not appropriate to materials that did not share those characteristics.

Semper, although interested in the relation of form and material, acknowledged that forms could be "vestigial" and could remain valid after their functional purpose no longer existed. St. Leopold's abounds in vestigial forms; however, these forms are detailed not only in accordance with Semper's conception of cladding, but also in accordance with Wagner's demand for an expression that acknowledged the process of modern construction.

The primary vestigial form of St. Leopold's is the dome. In section it resembles Wren's dome of St. Paul's; the inner and outer shapes are almost independent of each other; the internal supports form a cone. This is precisely the type of dome Pugin disliked. Pugin would have been even more appalled to discover that the dome is not stone but metal. In unreinforced masonry construction, a vault or a dome is necessary to cover a large space. Not so with steel, which could easily have spanned this distance without curvature. By the standards of Gothic rationalism this was inexcusable, but by Semper's reasoning it was logical. One of the primitive methods of cladding had been the covering of wood structure with metal plates; after this in the course of development, the internal structure disappeared, leaving the tubular structure. Conceptually, Wagner's dome is a tubular structure of this kind, with the wood replaced by metal and then clad with plates inside and out.

The primary framework of the dome is a network of metal tees and angles. On the outside this is covered with wood decking and then interlocking copper tiles. The inner dome (actually a cross-vault) is made of rabitz panels set in a grid of gilded iron tees. One can see in this exposed seam and fastener a reflection of Semper's feeling for the origin of ornament in textile art. It is clear from the grid details and from the way in which stained glass is substituted for the rabitz panels in some locations that this is not a real vault but what we would today call a suspended ceiling.

The walls were constructed by two contrasting methods, and this again is a reflection of Semper's ideas about the origins of building. The base is monolithic, composed of rough granite stones trimmed on their faces but not squared. The stone is set in the method Semper called "Polygonneck," which he felt was a reflection of the crystalline nature of stone. The wall above, on the other hand, is layered and clad, being composed of thin slabs of marble fastened to the brick load-bearing wall with bolts.

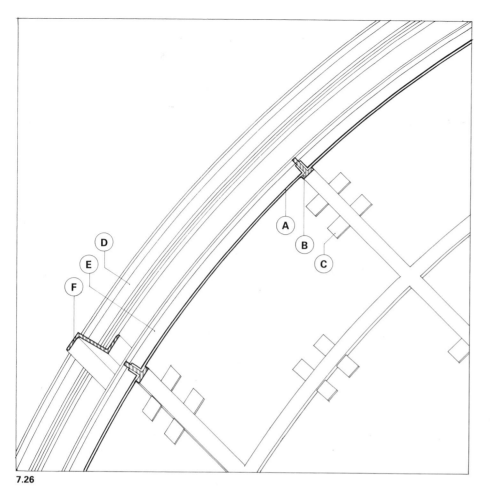

7.26

7.27

7.28

7.29

7.30

St. Leopold's
Otto Wagner
Vienna, 1907

7.26 ceiling construction

A   Rabitz plaster panel.

B   3 cm × 4 cm iron face T. These form a grid to support the rabitz panels. The exposed faces of the T's are gilded.

C   This appears to be a fastener holding the panel in place, but it is largely ornamental.

D   Upper chord of iron truss, fabricated from two iron angles, supporting Z section below.

E   Iron T connecting the grid of T's carrying the panels to the Z above.

F   5 cm × 8 cm iron Z. Located at every third face T, these form the principal support of the ceiling.
(*Technische Betriebsleitung, Psychiatrisches Krankenhaus Baumgarten.*)

7.27 section
(*Wagner, Einige Skizzen, Projekte und Ausgeführte Bauwerke.*)

7.28 "Majolikahaus," Otto Wagner, 1889, cornice.

7.29 Kaiserbad Dam Building,
Otto Wagner
1908, cornice detail. Here the traditional Classical cornice has been reduced to a series of metal brackets supporting stenciled tongue-and-groove boards.

7.30 Villa Wagner II, Otto Wagner
Vienna, 1912, cornice.

The upper wall is detailed so as to bring out its clad character and to emphasize the nonstructural nature of the cladding and the manner and time of its erection. The typical joint pattern, rather than forming voisseurs around the arched opening, is simply cut off at the edge of the curve, exposing the edge of the marble (figure 7.21). The true arch, formed of brick or concrete, is hidden beyond. The metal channel that forms the base line of the arch runs across the pier (figure 7.34), thus interrupting the stone at its most important bearing point. While the wall retains the form of the arch, it is detailed as cladding.

The top of the wall is adorned with bronze wreath ornaments (Semper's primordial technical symbol) and a cornice. This wall and its cornice is a transformed Classical element. It is in accordance with Semper's theory of cladding, but also with Wagner's theory of modern construction. In *Moderne Architektur* Wagner described the nature of what he called Renaissance construction, as opposed to modern construction:

For a prominent monumental edifice [in Renaissance construction] a colonnade with entablature is executed as the chief motif. . . . The building is constructed of horizontal courses of stone, and the material is procured with a great expenditure of time and money. Immense stone blocks, that recall the system of construction used by the ancient Romans, are employed for the lower members of the main cornice, being structurally necessary because the modillions of the entablature are wrought in them. The procuring and dressing of these blocks causes great sacrifices of time and money. This mode of execution should be termed "The Renaissance Mode of Construction," and a "Modern mode of construction" will be contrasted to it, for the same problem. Stone slabs are employed for the external cladding (for the plane surfaces) of the building (based on the same premise). The volumes of slabs being materially less, they may be of nobler materials, as in marble. The anchoring of these would occur by means of bronze knobs or rosettes. Anchored steel supports would be used to bear the strongly projecting cornice, divided into thin courses, and these supports would be covered with gilded bronze coverings in the form of consoles. The result of this comparison would be that the volume of stone work would be from one-fifth to one-sixth that of the first method, the number of ashlars would be less, the monumental effect would be enhanced by the nobler material, the amount of money required would be largely reduced, and the time of erection would be brought down to the normal and the desired limit. [16]

The construction of the wall of St. Leopold's differs in some details from the ideal system described in *Moderne Architektur*. The cornice is not stone, but a ribbed concrete slab with coffers on its underside and ribs on top to hold the wood nailers to receive the metal roof. In earlier buildings Wagner had used a cornice similar to that described in *Moderne Architektur*, such as the Kaiserbad Dam Building (1906), where he used cast metal to support a wood plank platform which was then stenciled. The concrete cornice at St. Leopold's is heavier in appearance and in fact more closely resembles the Classical prototype. Wagner's use of it here was probably due to financial limitations rather than to stylistic preference, as he returned to it in the extension of the Post Office Savings Bank in 1912.

Some elements of the interior of St. Leopold's are detailed in the monolithic rather than the clad style, although they are no less elegant for it. The confessional and the pews, for example, are monolithic wood frames resembling stile-and-rail paneling, except here the wood panels are tongue-and-groove boards that are rabbeted into the frame (figure 7.33). With their solid pieces and ornamented joints, the furnishings seem much closer to contemporary British Arts and Crafts detailing than to the other works of Wagner.

THE POST OFFICE SAVINGS BANK
For many present-day architects, the Postsparkasse (Post Office Savings Bank) represents an ideal structure in which good urban design and the qualities of Classical buildings were maintained without recourse to literal Classical forms and without the denial of modern building systems. There is some danger in

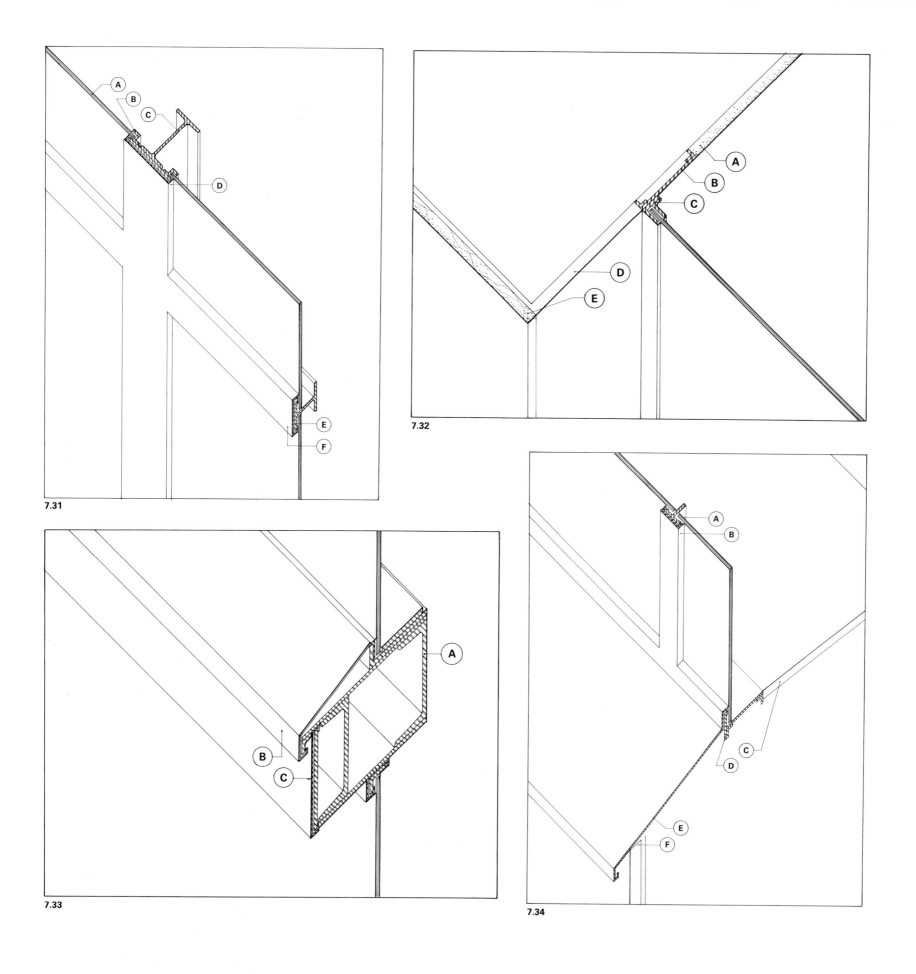

7.31

7.32

7.33

7.34

St. Leopold's
Otto Wagner
Vienna, 1907

7.31 window details at vertical mullion

A Leaded art glass (not shown).

B Iron Z forming stop to secure glazing.

C Main vertical mullion of rolled I section.

D Copper cladding on exterior of mullion. The copper protects the iron from corrosion on the exterior, but it also conforms to the Semper-Wagner conception of cladding in architecture.

E Small horizontal mullion.

F Copper cladding.

(Technische Betriebsleitung, Psychiatrisches Krankenhaus Baumgarten.)

7.32 window detail at jamb

A Interior plaster.

B Iron plate with angles.

C Mullion, made from two angles.

D 2.5-cm plaster.

E 2-cm-thick marble facing.

(Technische Betriebsleitung, Psychiatrisches Krankenhaus Baumgarten.)

7.33 window details at horizontal mullion

A Major horizontal mullion, made from two rolled channels connected with flat plates.

B Sloped copper sill with drip. This sheds water away from the window.

C Copper facing on iron plate.

(Technische Betriebsleitung, Psychiatrisches Krankenhaus Baumgarten.)

7.34 window details at sill

A Smaller vertical mullion.

B Copper facing.

C Interior sill.

D Sill mullion (similar to jamb).

E Metal exterior sill.

F Exterior wall: brick faced with 2-cm marble.

(Technische Betriebsleitung, Psychiatrisches Krankenhaus Baumgarten.)

treating the building this way, for although it is progressive in its attitudes it is somewhat archaic in its technology. In St. Leopold's Wagner used traditional forms, such as the dome that had lost their original structural purposes if not their symbolic meanings. The bank uses fewer of these forms, but it is also a "transformed" Classical building. The difference is that the use of traditional forms is in less conflict with the actual building systems.

Unlike modern concrete buildings in which the frame is self-supporting and the masonry is non-load-bearing infill, the Post Office Savings Bank is a hybrid building, with a concrete floor and beams supported internally by concrete columns and externally by load-bearing masonry walls. It is neither a true frame nor a true load-bearing building. This type of structure is almost unknown today, but it was popular in the late nineteenth century. Many American buildings, such as Richardson's Albany City Hall and McKim, Mead & White's State Savings Bank in Detroit, used exterior load-bearing walls with internal steel or concrete frames. Historians such as Carl Condit have described this type of structure as backward, since the first frame-and-curtain-wall buildings of Chicago were already over 20 years old. But these historians were tracing the development of the all-glass-and-steel systems of the 1950s. If for architectural purpose it is desirable to have the quantity of masonry wall used here, it seems only logical that it be used structurally. What has made this system obsolete is the way in which brick and concrete are tightly integrated. In 1905 this was a logical structure, since today's system of highly independent subcontractors and building systems was only beginning to develop (although Wagner was one of the few to perceive this trend). More important, unlike later Modernists, Wagner did not have to deal with the problem of reconciling the language of Classicism with the curtain wall. Auguste Perret, who also tried to transfer the rules of Classicism to concrete construction, had to reconcile rules that required columns to be 2 diameters apart with a structural system that could easily span ten times that distance. Wagner had no such contradictions to reconcile; the rules of Classicism were determined by load-bearing masonry, and he was designing a load-bearing masonry wall.

The front facade of the Post Office Savings Bank is composed of a vestigial element, just as that of St. Leopold's was. If we read the spaces between windows (figure 7.35) as columns, as Franco Borsi has shown, this facade becomes a columned portico between two towers resembling some of Schinkel's churches. The applied aluminum ornaments of the facade can also be seen as a column, a base, a capital, and a frieze applied to the marble. Wagner, like Semper, saw architecture as evolutionary rather than revolutionary, and was pressing Classicism into its next phase, a phase in which Classical elements would become more layered and more abstract. The idea of flattening three-dimensional objects into two-dimensional symbols brings us, surprisingly, to the work of Robert Venturi, conceptually if not formally.

The wall of the bank has the base, shaft, and cornice typical of Classicism, but the detailing follows the system described in *Moderne Architektur* and used at St. Leopold's—with refinements. The base here is not monolithic but veneered, and it is detailed in a way that maintains it as more massive than the wall proper, i.e., a rusticated base transformed by modern construction processes. The thin slabs of stone are curved heavily toward the bottom to create a shadow line and increase the visual weight, but at the same time the exposed edge at the corner (figure 7.39) and the recessed bolt hole make it clear that this is a veneered wall and not solid masonry.

The stone veneers of the typical floors are set in three patterns. In his previous work Wagner had set the stone in a bonded rather than a gridded configuration. The bond pattern emphasizes the load-bearing nature of the wall, whereas the grid emphasizes the veneer nature of the slabs. Here Wagner used both. There are three principal patterns: (1) The stones of the central portion are flat squares set in a grid. (2) The slabs of the two flanking towers are set in a bonded pattern, and each stone has a slight convex curvature. These are fastened with iron bolts, which are then covered with a sheet of lead and an aluminum cap. (3) The stone slabs of the

7.35

7.36

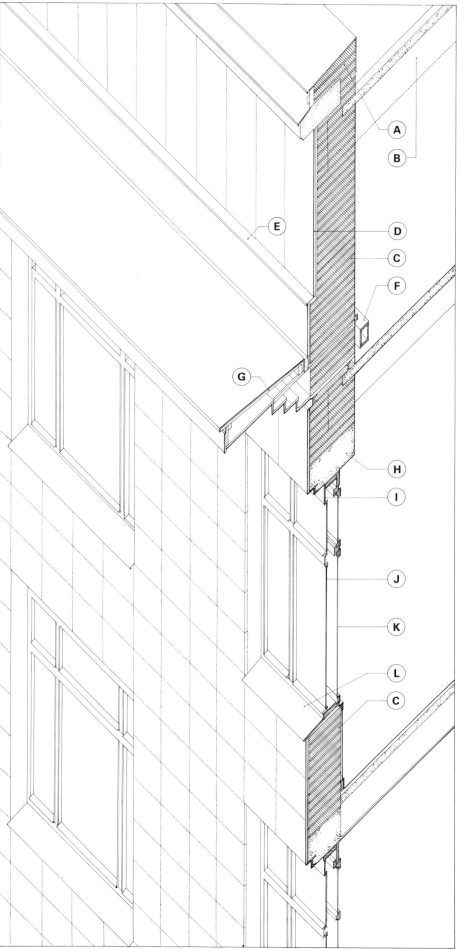

7.37

Postsparkasse

Otto Wagner

Vienna, 1906

7.35 **main facade**

7.36 **detail**

7.37 **wall section**
(This drawing is based on a
surviving wall section of the
building and shows a design earlier
than that built, although there
appear to be no major
discrepancies at this scale.)

A   Metal coping. This protects the top
of the brick-and-marble wall from
water.

B   Roof construction: Concrete slab
covered with asphalt, gravel, and
sand.

C   Brick wall.

D   2-cm marble facing, fastened wqith
4-cm-round by 12-cm-long iron
pins, which are then covered with
lead and given an aluminum cap.
Additional hidden fasteners may
have been used.

E   Metal flashing.

F   Gutter to collect water runoff from
cornice.

G   Cornice. Wagner argued that the
cornice is functional, since water
running down the facade will
deposit dirt on the marble.

H   Concrete lintel.

I   Ornamental lintel. Although it
appears to support the masonry,
this is only an enlarged portion of
the window frame.

J   Iron outer window, clad with
aluminum on the exterior and
glazed with plate glass. The double
window was a typical middle
European solution to the problem
of heat loss.

K   Iron inner window.

L   Metal sill.
(Postsparkasse)

side walls facing the streets are also set in a grid, but the aluminum fasteners have a simplified design.

Architects and historians have long admired the exposed bolts of this facade. It is a practice more admired than imitated, since in contemporary construction it is easier to conceal the stone fasteners in the edges of the panels, where they are protected from water and where their craftsmanship and finish may be more crude since they are concealed. But the bolts that we see are more symbol than tool. What we see are really aluminum covers concealing the actual bolts, and in many instances the panels are also held by fasteners set in their edges, making the exposed bolts, in a way, an extension of the concept of cladding.

There are, in Wagner's work, two contradictory means of expression. The first follows the tradition of exposed and expressed construction; the second is more concerned with expressing the qualities of the veneer than with expressing the structure it clads. These same two tendencies, and Wagner's vacillation between them, can be seen in the development of the window details. Wagner's initial competition drawings emphasize the structural qualities of the lintel. The outermost steel lintel is exposed and given its own structure by two free-standing metal columns (figure 7.40). The bearing of the lintel on the jamb is also exposed, expressed, and ornamented. Wagner has almost created an aedicule, or miniature building, to support the masonry above. Steel and iron lintels were relatively new but commonplace in 1900, and it was unthinkable to traditional architects to simply let the masonry run across the opening with no visible support as is often done today. The weight of the masonry and the inability of the masonry to span a large flat opening had to be expressed. The usual procedure was, in the manner of McKim, to place a stone lintel or arch in front of the metal lintel. Here Wagner followed a procedure that a Gothic Rationalist would have approved by exposing and ornamenting the metal lintel itself. In the executed version, the design has been greatly simplified, perhaps because of money, but the detail has been changed into a Semper-type clad expression. Although the form of a beam supported by two columns remains, it is a purely ornamental form, and it is clearly not supporting the wall above. The lintel is concealed, and its sheet-metal cover stops at the jamb. It has become, like St. Leopold's dome, a vestigial form. It has lost its structural function, but it is detailed to clarify that it is a veneer.

The cornice is, like that of St. Leopold's, a Classical stone cornice transformed into metal, and the attic story is decorated with Semper's wreaths in three places. A statue of Victory on either side of the main facade holds a wreath aloft in each hand, and the central portion of the attic story has a wreath on each pier.

ADOLF LOOS

The discussion of Loos's details must be brief, not because of a lack of importance, but because of a lack of evidence. Loos destroyed many of his drawings, and for many of his details drawings may have never existed, for Loos preferred when possible to solve detailing problems on the site. Richard Neutra recalls:

In the year 1900, Adolf Loos started a revolt against the practice of indicating dimensions in figures or measured drawings. He felt, as he often told me, that such a procedure dehumanizes design. "If I want a wood paneling or wainscot to be of a certain height, I stand there, hold my hand at that certain height, and the carpenter makes his pencil mark. Then I step back and look at it from one point and from another, visualizing the finished result with all my powers. This is the only human way to decide the height of a wainscot, or the width of a window." Loos was inclined to use a minimum of paper plans; he carried in his head all the details of even the most complex designs, and prided himself on being an architect without a pencil.[17]

Like many of his contemporaries, Loos was influenced by the English domestic architecture of the time. But, as the above passage indicates, he was also influenced by the Arts and Crafts movement and by its ideas regarding craftsmanship, materials, and "honesty" in construction. Despite his love for Anglo-Saxon culture

7.38

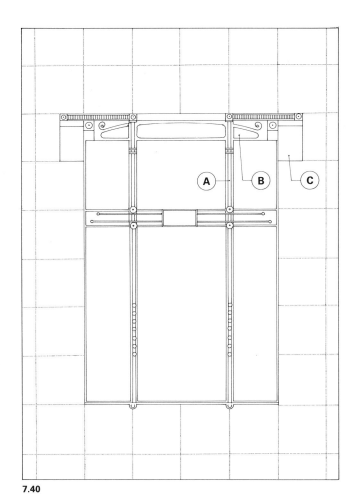

7.40

7.39

7.41

7.38 detail
While the lintel does not project into wall, as it does in figure 7.40, the metal ornamentation of the marble slab adjacent to the lintel does differ from the typical marble panel.

7.39 detail at granite base

7.40 lintel of competition design

A   Vertical mullion. Although it is probably nonstructural, its form implies that it helps to support the lintel above.

B   Metal lintel. Although not completely detailed, the implication is that this is the last in a series of parallel I sections supporting the masonry above. See figure 7.41.

C   Stone corbel. This element is perhaps not structurally necessary, since the lintel does not project, but it does demonstrate the wall support of the lintel.
(Historisches Museum, Vienna.)

7.41 project for Kaiser Franz Josef Stadtmuseum,
Otto Wagner, 1902,
detail of cornice and lintel. Note that the lintel over the window opening is formed by a series of I-shaped iron sections, the outermost of which is exposed.
(Historisches Museum, Vienna.)

and his dislike of much of German culture, the dominant source of his ideas about building was Gottfried Semper.

If it was Otto Wagner who saw the potential of the theory of cladding in the Modern era, it was Adolf Loos who saw its dangers. And if Wagner recognized that modern processes of building made possible a language of architecture that was largely analogous and symbolic in its expression of structure, Loos recognized that it made possible a language of Kitsch.

Loos and Semper had many common interests: the evolutionary nature of culture and architecture, the relationship between clothing design and architectural design, and (most important) the concept of cladding. Loos wrote his own essay on the subject with the same title as Semper's ("The Principle of Cladding"), and many of Loos's passages are almost direct quotes from Semper. But Loos's concept of cladding was also influenced by the ideas of John Ruskin, particularly the latter's idea of honesty in building.

Loos's ideas of the nature and origins of building closely parallel Semper's, particularly in emphasizing the importance of textiles (especially carpets hung over the timber frame) as the source of building:

The architect's general task is to provide a warm and livable space. Carpets are warm and livable. He decides for this reason to spread out one carpet on the floor and to hang up four to form the four walls. But you cannot build a house out of carpets. Both the carpet on the floor and the tapestry on the wall require a structural frame to hold them in the correct place. To invent this frame is the architect's second task.[18]

And, like Semper, Loos uses this idea to justify the principle of cladding as the basis of architecture:

In the beginning was cladding. Man sought shelter from inclement weather and protection and warmth while he slept. He sought to cover himself. The covering is the oldest architectural detail. Originally it was made out of animal skins or textile products. . . . Then the covering had to be put up somewhere if it was to afford enough shelter for a family! Thus the walls were added, which at the same time provided protection on the sides. In this way the idea of architecture developed in the minds of mankind and individual men.[19]

To Loos, as to Wagner, the idea of cladding coincided with one of the major effects of industrialization: the increased use of veneered construction. But to Loos, writing in 1898, the adverse effects of this type of construction were much clearer than they had been to Semper, writing in 1855. The practice of veneering and the development of synthetic materials had resulted in what many, including Loos, felt was "dishonest construction." Loos singled out the use of terra cotta and cement to simulate stone, citing contemporary Viennese examples: "Nowadays one nails the structure to the facade with aplomb and hangs the 'keystone' under the main molding with artistic authority."[20] Architects of the Gothic Revival, such as Street and Pugin, had demanded or at least requested the use of monolithic systems without veneers for this very reason. Perhaps taking his cue from Ruskin, who thought there was nothing wrong with veneers provided they were not "deceitful," Loos developed the "law of cladding":

The law goes like this: We must work in such a way that the confusion of the material clad with its cladding is impossible. That means, for example, that wood may be painted any color except one—the color of wood. . . . Applied to stucco-work, the principle of cladding would run like this: Stucco can take any ornament with just one exception—rough brickwork. . . . The cladding material can keep its natural color if the area to be covered happens to be of the same color. Thus I can smear tar on black iron or cover wood with another wood (veneer, marquetry, and so on) without having to color the covering wood; I can coat one metal with another by heating or galvanizing it, but the principle of cladding forbids the cladding material to imitate the coloration of the underlying material. Thus iron can be tarred, painted with oil colors, or galvanized, but it can never be camouflaged with a bronze color or any other metallic color.[21]

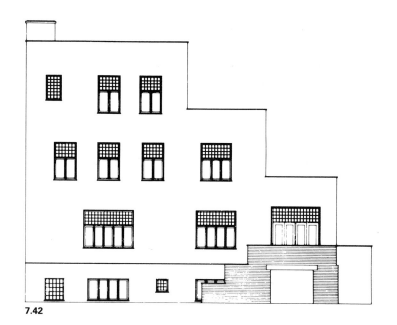

7.42

7.43

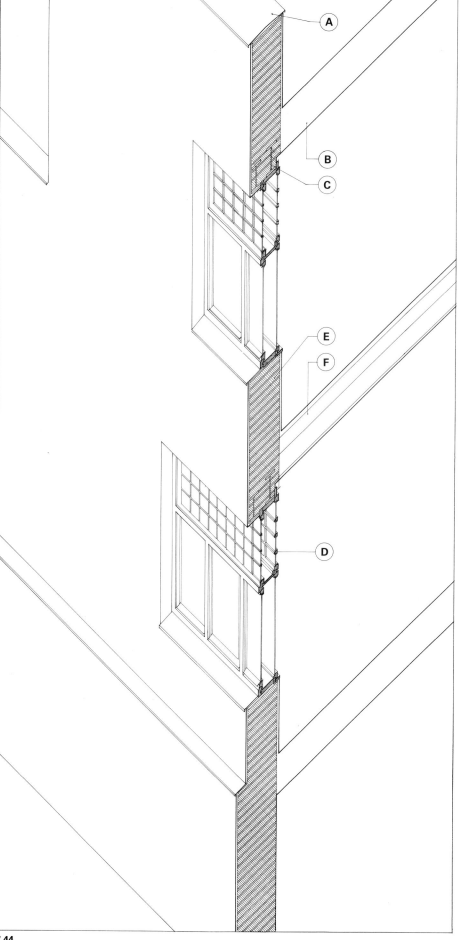

7.44

Scheu house

Adolf Loos

Vienna, 1912

7.42   elevation

(Gustav Pichelmann.)

7.43   study area

(Gustav Pichelmann, Michael Stoger.)

7.44   wall section

A   Metal coping. As is typical in stucco construction, the horizontal surfaces are capped with metal to prevent water from penetrating the wall.

B   Roof construction: wood beams supporting wood deck. Most of these beams are concealed by plaster ceilings.

C   Steel or iron beams supporting brick over the window openings. There is no exterior expression of the lintels, although in some interior locations they are marked by wood trim.

D   Double wood window. (See figure 7.47.)

E   Brick wall faced with stucco.

F   Floor construction: wood beams supporting wood deck.

(Floor drawings by Gustav Pichelmann.)

Loos also reiterated an idea shared by Semper and the Arts and Crafts writers, the importance of material to design:

Every material possesses its own language of forms, and none may lay claim for itself to the forms of another material. For forms have been constituted out of the applicability and the methods of productions of materials. They have come into being with and through materials. No material permits an encroachment into its own circle of forms. Whoever dares to make such an encroachment notwithstanding this is branded by the world a counterfeiter. Art, however, has nothing to do with counterfeiting or lying. Her paths are full of thorns, but they are pure.[22]

Loos's Scheu house is based on a cube with one quadrant displaced to form a stepped volume with roof terraces. Contrary to expectation, the building's steps are parallel, not perpendicular, to the street. The interior shows Loos's concept of the *Raumplan* at work, but it also shows the similarity of the *Raumplan* to English house plans such as those of Voysey and Baillie-Scott. The major living areas are connected but retain their distinct identities. Each of the major living spaces is given its own character through different ceilings, paneling, and trim. This is in sharp contrast to the exterior, which seems to conceal rather than articulate the function of the rooms beyond.

The Scheu house reveals Loos's attitude toward structure, form, and the transformations of modern technology. Despite its abstract qualities and its superficial resemblance to International Style buildings, it is completely traditional in structure. Three brick cross-walls running perpendicular to the terraces support wood beams and a wood deck. The load-bearing wall at the center severely limits the interior planning, and in the living room large steel lintels are required to frame the large opening. On the other hand, it can be said that traditional masonry-and-wood-beam construction, which tends toward cellular planning, is ideally suited to Loos's *Raumplan,* with its cellular arrangements of space.

The expression of this structure illustrates the differences between Loos's concept of cladding and Wagner's. The ceiling beams are concealed under flat plaster ceilings except in the dining room, the hall, and the inglenook, where the beams are cased in oak (figure 7.46). Unlike Greene or Wright, Loos does not "finish off" these beams with a board of equal depth where they meet the wall; he stops them abruptly against the plaster to show their continuity. To expose or express beams in one room while concealing them in another was common nineteenth-century practice, but Loos took this a step further. The two steel beams supporting the opening in the masonry wall between the living room and the library are also cased in oak to visually "explain" how the opening is supported. Where the steel beam ends, just beyond the inglenook, this trim stops also, so that it will not be interpreted as part of the paneling (the rails of which are much smaller—see figure 7.49).

As in much of Loos's other work, the exterior of the Scheu house seems almost the work of a different architect. Other than the projecting base, and the design of the windows, it has few architectural elements: no cornice, no trim, no rustication. The windows seem at first to have been designed to obscure rather than explain the rooms inside. They are modular, each window being a multiple of a unit consisting of a single-pane casement below and a casement divided into a grid with muntins above. A typical bedroom has two of these units, the dining room and hall four each, and the living room five, so that they do in fact articulate the relative importance of the spaces they serve. From the exterior, they appear to be aligned in accordance with the plan while ignoring the resulting pattern on the facade. In general this is true, but in many locations windows are located off center to a room in order to align with a window above or below on the facade.

The interior detail of the Villa Wagner and the Scheu house shows a contrast similar to that between the exterior and interior of the Scheu house. Both interiors can be seen as abstractions of classical moldings. Both use simple rectilinear pieces of wood for base and picture rails (figures 7.49 and 7.51). Both use stile-and-rail

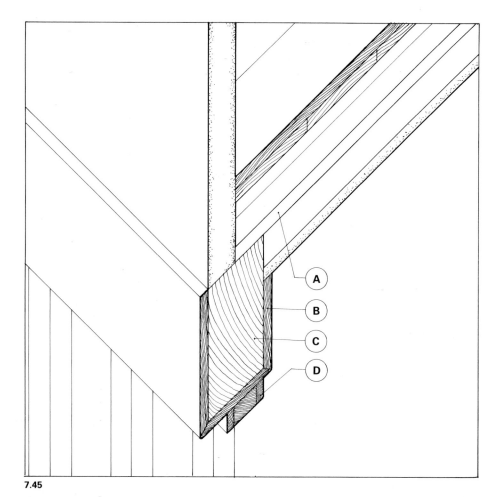

7.45

7.46

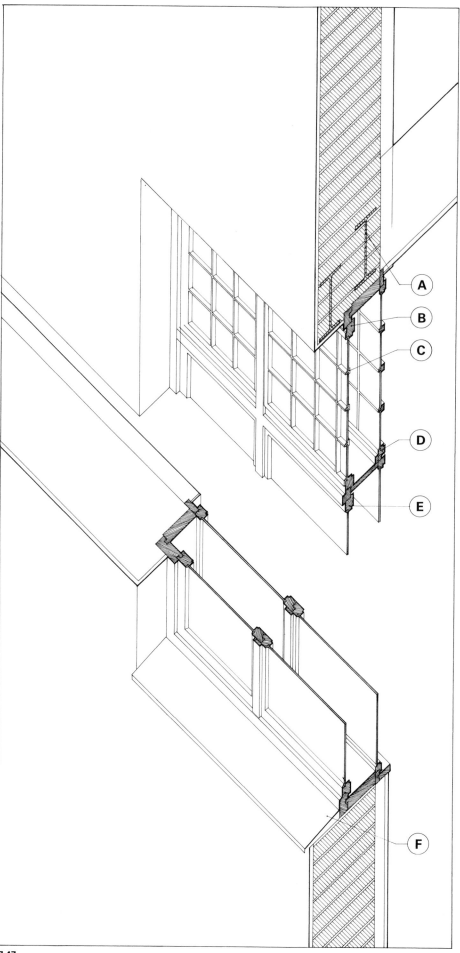

7.47

Scheu house

Adolf Loos

Vienna, 1912

7.45   beam detail at stair

A   Floor construction: 20-mm-thick wood boards on wood beams.

B   Finish-wood casing on solid beam. Here Loos disobeys his own law of cladding by cladding wood with wood.

C   14 cm × 24 cm solid wood beam.

D   Trim to secure stair railing.

(From drawings by Gustav Pichelmann.)

7.46   main staircase

(Gustav Pichelmann, Michael Stoger.)

7.47   window details

A   Steel or iron beams supporting masonry over window opening.

B   Wood outer window sash.

C   Metal T muntin. The inner muntins, unlike the outer ones, are wood. The metal here creates a smaller profile on the exterior.

D   Inner wood window sash.

E   Outer wood casement.

F   Metal sill. This prevents water from getting behind the stucco or running down the face of the wall, where it would stain.

(From drawings by Gustav Pichelmann.)

paneling abstracted into simple rectangles with no moldings to ease the transitions. Doors are made in similar fashion. The principal differences are Wagner's "inversions." In his paneling and doors, the positions of stile and rail are reversed so that the stile projects, making clear its veneered and layered nature. Loos retains the traditional configuration while stripping it of any moldings or ornaments that might create sytlistic associations. Although Loos's paneling is similar to English work, the intentions and the results are different. Whereas Voysey used simple paneling with minimal trim and crude joining techniques to suggest the vernacular, Loos eliminates trim to eliminate all stylistic associations.

The paneling in these two houses also illustrates another crucial difference between Wagner and Loos: their differing attitudes toward material. Loos's oak was lightly stained, to bring out its strong grain; Wagner's was always stained dark brown or black. Wagner was inclined to suppress the natural character of his materials; Loos would use materials so strongly marked as to often obscure their form. Wagner's marble was almost pure white; Loos's colored marbles were so strongly veined as to be unacceptable to many architects. This strength of surface acted to emphasize the veneered quality of Loos's stone (in some of his buildings it almost appears to be wallpaper). His intent was the same as Wagner's, but his means were different. Wagner articulated cladding by altering the configuration of traditional elements; Loos did so by his use of material.

The window details and the paneling details of the Scheu house show another important aspect of Loos's detailing, particularly in regard to his influence on International Style detailing: Loos eliminated ornament and moldings, but he did not eliminate trim. Window and door casings, baseboards, and other traditional trim elements are present in his work; they are simply reduced to rectilinear shapes. Loos never demanded the seamless perfection of many Modernists, or the waste of skilled labor he thought necessary to produce it.

Compare the Scheu house's windows with those of the second Villa Wagner (figures 7.47, 7.50). Both have the double wood casements that were commonly used at the time in Austria and Germany. In both cases, the inner window is flush with the inside wall and the outer window is set back in the opening to create a shadow on the exterior. All the windows have trim, and it is always square and never molded (although Loos cut a square notch in the corner to decrease the apparent width of the mullion). Voysey insisted that lintels be exposed or expressed, but neither Wagner nor Loos did so. Wagner placed a large piece of trim at the top of the window to visually, if not actually, support the wall. Loos was not concerned with this, and in the Scheu house there is no hint on the facade of the large steel lintels beyond. Wagner's windows, like Loos's, are repetitive units, but they are arranged, as in the Post Office Savings Bank, to suggest a Classical order. At the same time, they are aligned with the interior beam spacing. Wagner was working with a transformed Classicism, while Loos was deliberately avoiding any stylistic reference, however remote. Wagner was interested in structural expression via cladding; Loos avoided the use of any language, and in so doing he denied any expression of structure on the facade. This same opposition may be seen in other elements of the facades. Both houses have projecting bases. However, Wagner's base is grooved to suggest, without imitating, a rusticated base in stone; Loos's base simply projects, with no articulation other than its metal coping.

CONCLUSION

Both Wagner and Loos were Classicists, each in his own way. Wagner sought a transformed Classicism, while to Loos a Classicism transformed was no longer Classicism. Classical elements (particularly the Doric order) are common in Loos's work, but they are never transformed, even in a mannerist way. This is perhaps one reason why Loos's work, unlike Wagner's, is so devoid of structural expression. To achieve the degree of structural expression found in Wagner's work, Loos would have had to manipulate and transform the Classical language (the only architectural language he thought acceptable). This he was unwilling to do. Loos wrote in *Ornament and Crime:* "Since ornament is no longer organically linked with our culture, it is also no longer the expression of our culture."[23]

7.48

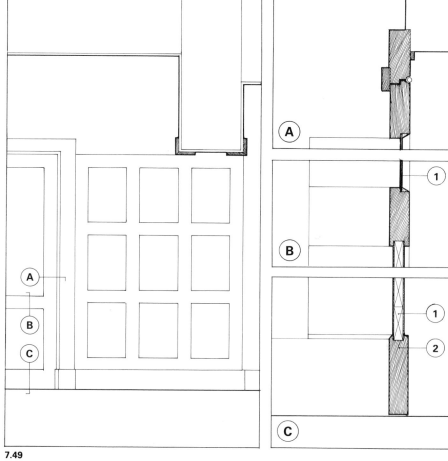

7.49

7.50

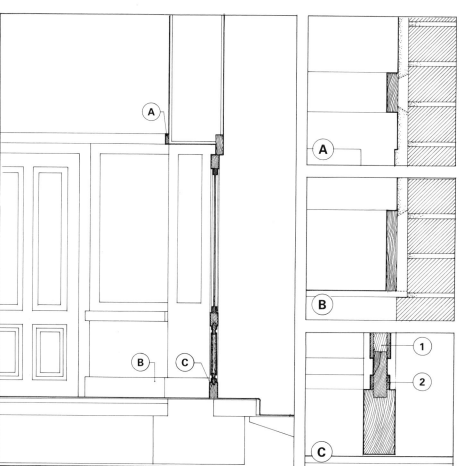

7.51

Scheu house

Adolf Loos

Vienna, 1912

7.48   library

(Gustav Pichelmann, Michael Stoger.)

7.49   paneling details

A   Door jamb.

B   Horizontal door rail.

  1   Glass.

C   Base rail of door.

  1   Wood-veneered panel.

  2   Solid wood rail.

(From drawings by Gustav Pichelmann.)

Villa Wagner II

Otto Wagner

Vienna, 1913

7.50   exterior

7.51   interior trim details

A   Horizontal trim. Like Loos, Wagner eliminates most moldings and transitions.

B   Base detail.

C   Base rail of door.

  1   Veneer plywood door molding.

  2   Panel molding.

(Historisches Museum, Vienna.)

One of Loos's better essays on detailing was *Ornament und Erziehung* [*Ornament and Education*], written in 1924. By that time, Loos was uneasy with the uses to which his ideas and forms were being put by architects such as Le Corbusier. "The teaching of drawing," wrote Loos, "must be based on Classical ornamentation. . . . Classical teaching created the unity of Western Civilization in spite of the divisions caused by languages and borders. . . . Therefore we must not only cultivate Classical ornaments but also study ornaments and moldings."[24]

In order to understand the differences in detailing between Wagner and Loos one must look at their attitudes toward the technical transformations of the nineteenth century, and in order to understand their attitudes toward technology one must understand their attitude toward society. Wagner, despite his numerous disappointments and the vituperative attacks to which he was subjected, was much more an establishment figure than Loos. He was a successful developer, and he executed a number of large commissions. He welcomed the transformations created in architecture by the use of steel and concrete and by the modern methods of fabricating old materials. Most of Loos's work was of residential scale. He was not financially successful. Though not a pariah, he was certainly more of a Bohemian than Wagner. He was 30 years younger than Wagner, and he had none of Wagner's faith in the future of technology or society. He made use of modern materials, such as concrete, but this had little effect on the forms of his buildings.

The great current interest in both Wagner and Loos is due to the very same things that produced so many reservations about them among the architects of the 1920s and the 1930s: the Classical elements in the works of both men, and the pessimistic tone of many of Loos's writings. Unfortunately, what should have been the most important aspect of their work and thought has been forgotten.

8   Le Corbusier: The Classic Villas

"Don't you think that she's the most wonderful woman in the world?" said Paul.

"No," said the Professor (Silenus, the new architect) after a few moments' consideration. "I can't say that I do. If you compare her with other women of her age you will see that the particulars in which she differs from them are infinitesimal compared with the points of similarity. A few millimeters here, a few millimeters there, such variations are inevitable in the human reproductive system; but in all her essential functions—her digestions, for example—she conforms to type."

Evelyn Waugh, *Decline and Fall*

Few major architects of the twentieth century have received as much criticism for the technical shortcomings of their buildings as Le Corbusier, and, in truth, much of it is deserved. Finding flaws in architects of his stature is a popular activity, but the seemingly endless series of stories of leaky roofs, crumbling walls, environmentally uninhabitable spaces, and constant restoration seem to indicate that Le Corbusier's ambitions exceeded his abilities, and that he lacked the patience to deal with the technical minutiae of making his ideas work and was unwilling to let others do it for him. It is perhaps not an accident that what is probably his best-detailed building, the Heidi Weber Pavilion in Zurich, was completed by others after his death.

Many of the systems used in Le Corbusier's buildings are now antiquated. Those architects working today who are stylistically indebted to Le Corbusier, such as Richard Meier and Werner Seligmann, are using completely different materials and systems. There would be little point in adding to the criticisms of Le Corbusier, but there is a great deal to be learned by examining his buildings on their own terms. How did their details succeed or fail in terms of Le Corbusier's own criteria? What technical choices were necessary? What options were available? Were the right choices made?

LE CORBUSIER AND HIS PREDECESSORS

Figure 8.4 shows Le Corbusier's house for his parents (Villa le Lac) of 1924, and figure 8.2 shows one of its antecedents: Tony Garnier's project for a house in the Cité Industrielle. All of the elements of the Corbusian wall section are present in Garnier's project: the roof terrace, the absence of a cornice and of exterior window moldings, and the rolling shutter recessed in a pocket above the window. The structural system of the floor slabs is almost identical to Le Corbusier's, but it is in the support of this slab that the difference lies. Despite its modernity, Garnier's house has traditional load-bearing walls (as the narrow window openings testify). The Villa le Lac, with its pipe-column supports, is a primitive version of a frame-and-curtain-wall building.

8.1

House in Cité Industrielle
Tony Garnier
1904

8.1 **exterior**

(A. Morancé, *L'Architecture Vivante*.)

8.2 **wall section of typical street facade**

A Roof terrace.

B Concrete floor slab, made by lost-tile process.

C Gutter and coping. The horizontal surface at the top of the wall and the joint between roof and parapet are particularly susceptible to water penetration. The metal covering protects both.

D Typical wall construction. Although the drawings imply that this wall is of concrete, it undoubtedly would have been made of masonry and stucco for economy had the project been realized.

E Roll-down shutter.

F Wood window.

(A. Morancé, *L'Architecture Vivante*.)

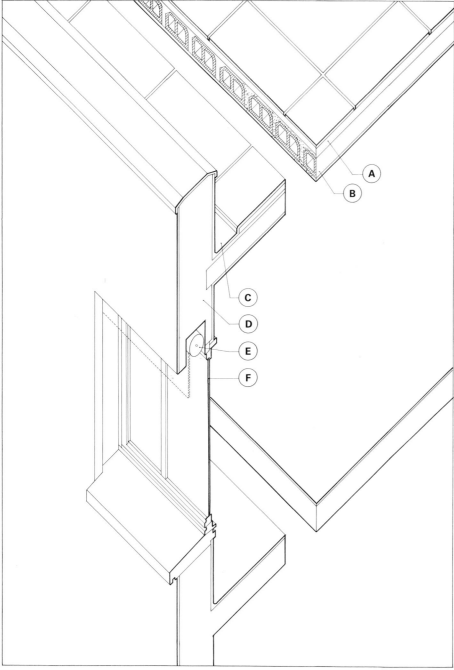

8.2

8.3

Villa le Lac
Le Corbusier
Lake Geneva, 1924

8.3 **exterior**
(Photo by Bruce Abbey, model by Brian Sawyer.)

8.4 **wall section of south facade**
A Concrete roof structure, made by lost-tile process.
B Tile.
C Coping. Le Corbusier's typical coping was made by carrying the plaster up and over the coping to avoid the trim that metal copings would require. This is probably one of the major causes of leakage in his buildings.
D Roll-down shutter.
E Wood-frame window with operable steel sash.
F Steel-pipe column.
G Typical wall construction: concrete masonry with plaster on both sides.
(Fondation Le Corbusier, drawing 415.)

8.5 **Francois Hennebique's lost-tile system of construction**
A Temporary steel beams supporting wood formwork.
B Tile.
C Steel reinforcing bars.
D Concrete.
(Fondation Le Corbusier, Gregh, "The Dom-Ino Idea.")

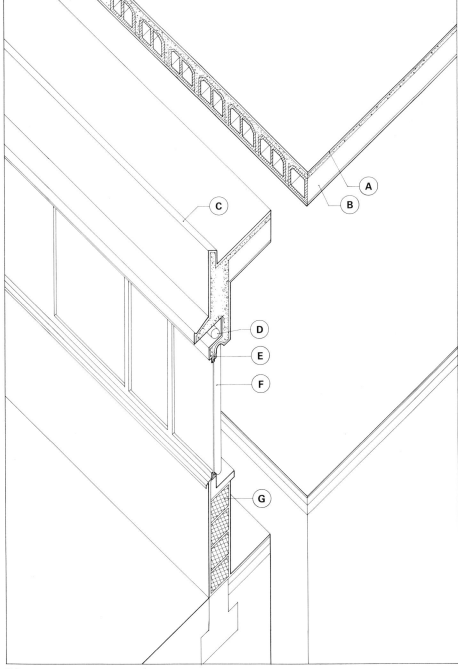

8.4

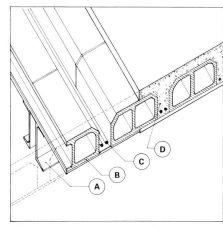

8.5

8.6

Cité Frugès
Le Corbusier
Pessac, Bordeaux, 1925

8.6   exterior from street
(A. Morancé, *L'Architecture Vivante.*)

8.7   window details, typical window
A   Sheet-metal cover.
B   Roll-down shutter.
C   Fixed steel frame. Le Corbusier's drawings show details of two other systems: an all-steel system and an all-wood one similar to that used at the Villa Cook. Presumably this one was chosen for cost reasons.
D   In-swinging wood casement.
E   Removable stop, to allow replacement of glass.
F   Metal sill.
(Fondation Le Corbusier, drawing 30.581.)

8.8   window types

8.9   Structural bays of Le Corbusier's villas
1   Cité Frugès, Pessac.
2   Weissenhoff I.
3   Weissenhoff II.
4   Villa Cook.
5   Villa de Monzie (Garches.)
6   Villa at Carthage.
7   Villa Savoie (Poissy.)

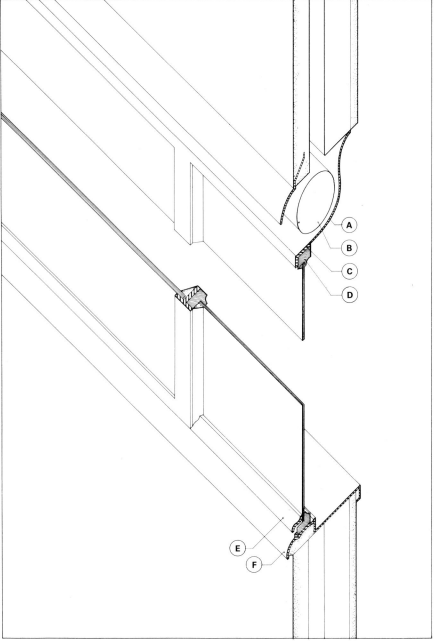

8.7

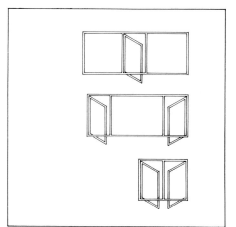

8.8

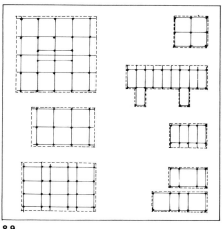

8.9

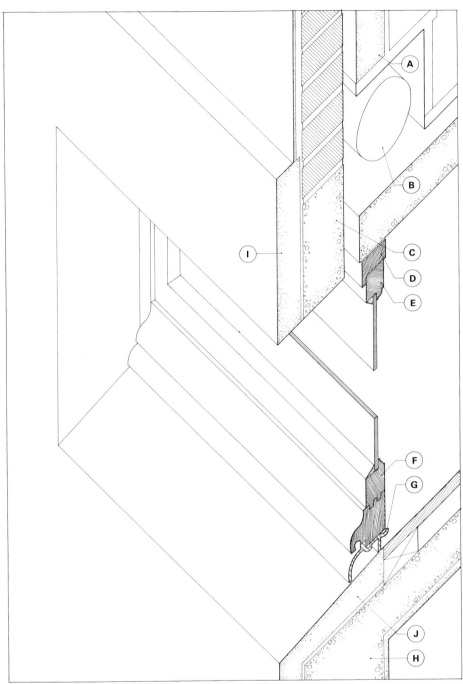

8.10

8.10 **window details of principal facade, second floor**

A Typical wall construction. The exterior layer of the wall is composed of brick covered with "Lithogne" plaster; the interior layer is plaster tile with a coating of "Lyonnaise" plaster.

B Roll-down shutter.

C Lintel. This is actually part of the concrete floor slab.

D Fixed wood frame.

E Head of in-swinging wood casement.

F Sill of casement. The curved drip mold protects the joint below from water running down the face of the wall.

G Metal sill. The interlocking joint prevents water from entering the building via wind or air pressure.

H Typical floor construction: flat concrete slab with edge beams, supported by a combination of load-bearing walls and concrete columns.

I Plaster window surround.

J Plaster sill.

(A. Morancé, *L'Architecture Vivante.*)

8.11 **exterior**

(A. Morancé, *L'Architecture Vivante.*)

8.11

8.12

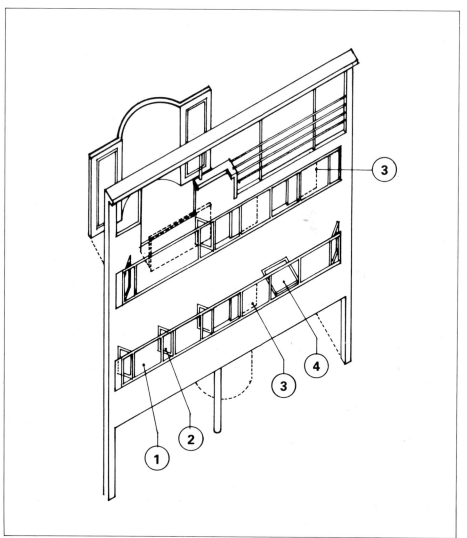

8.13

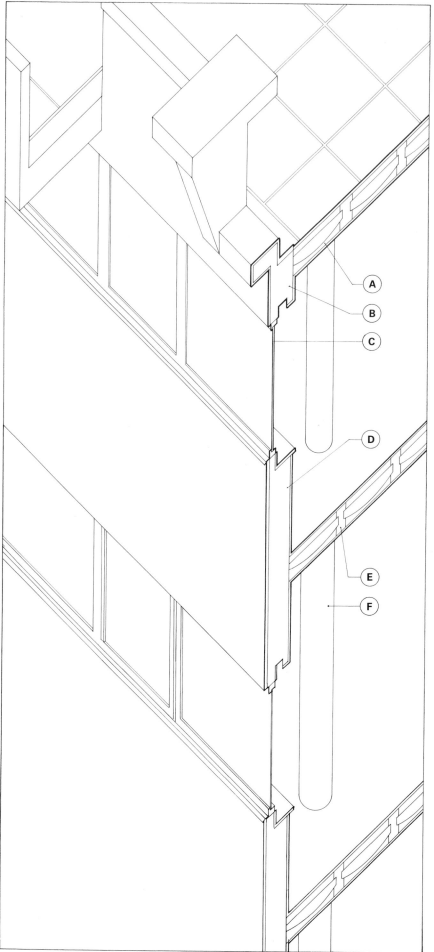

8.14

Villa Cook

Le Corbusier

Paris, 1926

8.12 exterior

(Fondation Le Corbusier.)

8.13 window types

1 Fixed wood window.

2 In-swinging metal casement window.

3 Sliding wood window.

4 In-swinging horizontal pivoting window.

(Fondation Le Corbusier, drawing 748.)

8.14 wall section, street facade

A Roof terrace. The typical Corbusian roof terrace consists of flagstone pavers set on a bed of sand and gravel, with a layer of pitcholine between it and the concrete deck. Slab construction is identical to E below.

B Concrete beam.

C Wood window system. (See figure 8.15.)

D Typical wall construction: masonry faced with stucco on exterior and plaster on interior.

E Typical floor construction. Of Le Corbusier's early concrete buildings, this is the only one not to use the Hennebique system.

F Concrete column. These columns decrease in diameter at each floor.

(Fondation Le Corbusier, drawings 698 and 8293.)

The majority of the buildings designed by Le Corbusier in the 1920s use the same structural system for the floor, a modification of the Hennibique system for reinforced concrete first used by Le Corbusier in the Dom-Ino House project of 1914. Unfortunately, the well-known illustration of this system has created the impression that it was a simple slab of concrete of uniform thickness. It was, in fact, a ribbed slab created by the ''lost tile'' process, which is much more efficient, uses less concrete, and weighs considerably less. In this system, hollow clay tile units are placed on flat wooden scaffolding with spaces between. When concrete is poured on top of the tile units, a ribbed slab is formed. Upon the removal of the scaffolding, the tiles remain embedded in the concrete, creating a flat surface on the underside of the slab. Colin Rowe has pointed out how dependent the idea of the free plan was on this system, since any structure in which beams or ribs fell below the plane of the slab implied a natural division of interior space.[1]

Given these two concepts of the nature of the wall, the load-bearing mass of Garnier, and the independent plane of Le Corbusier, one would expect to see a corresponding difference in detail.

The windows of the Villa le Lac could serve as ideal illustrations of Le Corbusier's concept of the free facade. Whereas the load-bearing wall of Garnier's house requires narrow, punched openings, Le Corbusier's frame and curtain wall makes possible the *fenêtre en longuer*. The details of the two window systems accept these characteristics, but also act to visually emphasize this difference. Garnier's windows are deeply recessed, revealing the full thickness of the wall and creating a deep shadow at the head, thus celebrating the mass of the wall although it is a single plane. Although one cannot say that Le Corbusier's wall is perceived as a membrane, as the walls of some later International Style buildings can be, it is visually ''lighter'' than Garnier's. While both buildings are notable historically for the relative absence of trim, each of them does have a little. The Villa le Lac has a thin metal projecting sill at the base of the window, and Garnier's house has the thick projecting sill of traditional architecture (albeit in concrete and in a simplified form). Le Corbusier does seem to have felt the necessity for articulation at the head of the window; he used a cover for the rolling shade opening as a means of achieving this. (Later designs, such as at Garches, conceal the shutter almost completely.)

Figure 8.10 shows the window of a house by Perret on the Rue Nansouty, also designed in 1924. Perret's fenestration system has more in common with Garnier's than with Le Corbusier's. His windows are deeply recessed within the wall, and although they are not as small as Garnier's, they extend from floor slab to floor slab rather than from wall to wall. To Perret a window was anthropomorphic. His windows are not simple incisions in a mass, as Garnier's were; each one is surrounded by a projecting frame. The typical Perret facade is a frame with infill, but whereas in such buildings as the Rue Franklin Apartments the frame is the true structural frame of the building, in this case the window surrounds are unrelated to the concrete columns beyond and are simply a thickening of the plaster wall. These window projections are not an expression of a concealed structure, but a stripped-down and simplified version of the Classical window surround. Perret's intention was to modernize Classicism, not to create a new architecture.

A comparison of the window details of Perret's Rue Nansouty house with the typical window details of Le Corbusier's housing at Pessac illustrates precisely the Classical and Modernist conceptions of the window. Both use the same materials (metal and wood), the same means of operation (in-swinging casements), and (in some cases) the same standardized parts (e.g., the metal threshold at the sill; see figure 8.10). The sash of Perret's window is fairly wide, to provide an appropriately thick transitional element between wall and void, and the profile is composed of simple and compound geometric curves. Le Corbusier's window has vestiges of all these characteristics, such as the inverted quarter-round on the interior of the wood casement, but it also shows the direction the typical modern

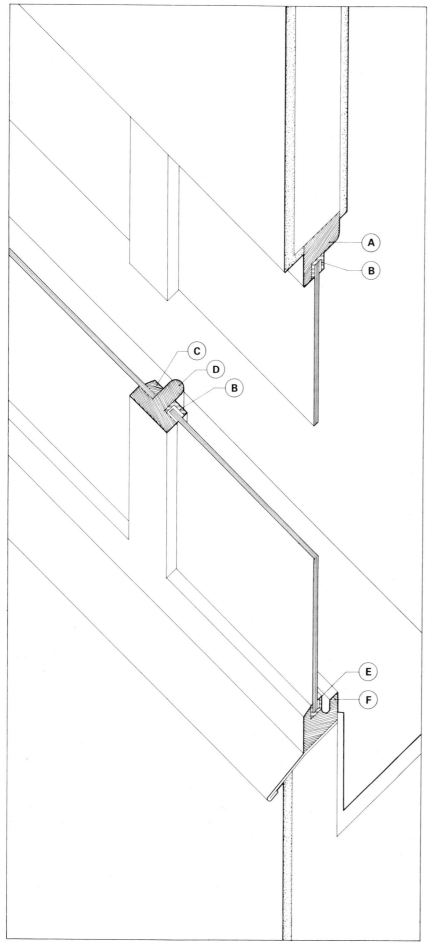

8.15

8.16

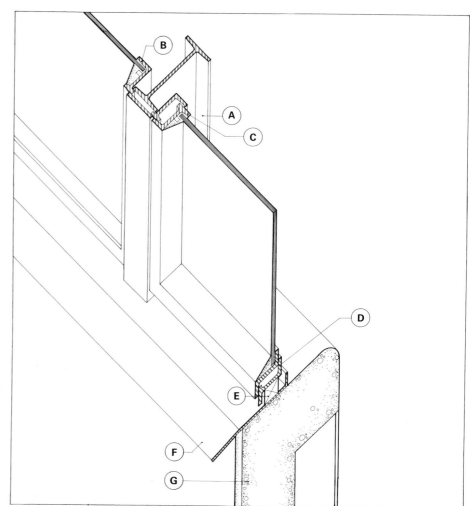

8.17

Villa Cook
Le Corbusier
Paris, 1926

8.15   window details

A   Fixed wood sash at head.

B   Operable metal sash. In order to minimize its profile, the metal section is quite small and probably very weak.

C   Wood glazing bead. This permits installation and removal of glass.

D   Vertical wood sash. Unlike most window units that combine fixed and operable units, this frame does not require a larger frame for the operable sash.

E   Condensation gutter. This collects water that condenses on the window. It is provided with weep holes to drain the water to the outside.

F   Fixed wood sash at sill. Although it has visual advantages, this is a poor detail for preventing infiltration of water.

(Fondation Le Corbusier, drawing 9.415.)

8.16   Open-Air School
Johannes Duiker
Amsterdam, 1930
(William Wischmeyer.)

8.17   Zonnestraal Sanitarium,
Johannes Duiker
Hilversum, 1928
window details.

A   Fixed mullion made from steel I section.

B   Fixed steel frame.

C   Steel casement window with operable sash. This window is composed of the Z-shaped pocket typical of all casements.

D   Fixed sash.

E   Wood blocking. This acts as a "shim" allowing for discrepancies between the size of the factory-made window and the field-made opening, while supporting the weight of the window.

F   Metal sill. This is made of sheet metal, probably zinc. It throws the rainwater that accumulates at the bottom of the window clear of the wall and prevents it from entering the wall through the joint at the base of the window.

G   Concrete wall.

(P. Bak et al., J. Duiker Bouwkundig Ingenieur.)

window was to follow. The frames and the sash are as thin as possible, given the nature of the materials involved, and one can see in these two illustrations the potential of steel-frame windows to produce much thinner profiles. The thickness and bulk of the traditional wood frame was essential to the Classical aesthetic because it could be used to ease transitions and to frame and highlight openings. The steel frame was to become equally essential to Modernism because its thinness and lightness made possible the simple geometric forms and openings we associate with the International Style. However, as will be shown, the mature detailing style of Le Corbusier was not a purely Modernist one.

Though there is nothing particularly inspiring about the window detailing of Pessac (it is not inconsistent with the building's intent, but it does little to add to it), it does demonstrate the one aspect of Le Corbusier's detailing that he usually executed well. The conceptual system of the fenestration is a small model of the conceptual system of the building as a whole. Le Corbusier was, at this time, extremely interested in compositions based on multiples of a fixed module. The unit plans at Pessac are based on a module of 2.5 × 5 meters, and its double (5 × 5 meters), composed and arranged in a variety of ways. The window openings are developed in similar fashion. The basic unit is a casement window, and its double is a fixed window twice its size. All the windows and openings in every unit are combinations of this basic module, so that the system of detailing is a direct outgrowth of the building's parti.

THE DETAILING OF THE CLASSIC VILLAS
Few would describe Le Corbusier as a great detailer. He lacked the patience, the eye for precision, and perhaps even the technical knowledge. Kahn, Mies, Aalto, and even Gropius developed details which are integral to the success or failure of their architectural intentions. However superior one may consider Le Corbusier in other fields, as a detailer he was clearly inferior to them. However, he was able to develop detailing systems that reproduced, on a small scale, the organizational ideas of the buildings themselves.

This correspondence of detail and parti is particularly true with regard to his ideas about standardization and object types. The mature buildings show a remarkable degree of standardization, even at the smallest level. All of the houses from Pessac (1924) through the Villa Savoie (1931) have certain elements and systems in common: (1) All have structural bays of 5 × 5 or 2.5 × 5 meters and are constructed of a one-way concrete slab system formed with structural clay tile. (2) The windows of all major spaces (living room, dining room, bedroom, etc.) are composed of combinations of a single unit—a sliding wood window, 1.0 × 2.5 meters—so that each structural bay is one or two windows wide. (3) Windows in minor spaces, ground-floor rooms, and circulation areas are non-operable and made of steel. The Villas at Garches and Carthage, the Weissenhof Exhibition, the Villa Savoie, and the League of Nations project all conform closely to this model, subject to certain distortions. There are notable exceptions, particularly the Villa Cook, but for the most part this system was relentlessly applied regardless of the building's use, size, and internal or external organization.

This system had its purest application at the Villa de Monzie (Garches) and perhaps its most interesting variations at the Villa Savoie (Poissy), so let us examine it at work in each of these cases. Both buildings use the "lost tile" system of poured-in-place concrete, which was so essential to the concept of the free plan, and both use standardized bay sizes of 2.5 × 5 and 5 × 5 meters. An examination of a typical bay at Garches reveals a strange inconsistency: the typical 5-meter bay is not a multiple of the typical tile width. Although the size of the structural bay is remarkably consistent, the size of the tiles of which it is composed varies from building to building. The choice of 5 meters was a formal or programmatic choice, not a structural one. At Garches, the need to locate columns on the grid is dominant, except where the cantilevers occur; at the Villa Savoie, they were displaced or split in two when in conflict with the plan (most noticeably at the ramp that splits the center column line). Garches is similarly dogmatic in that

8.18

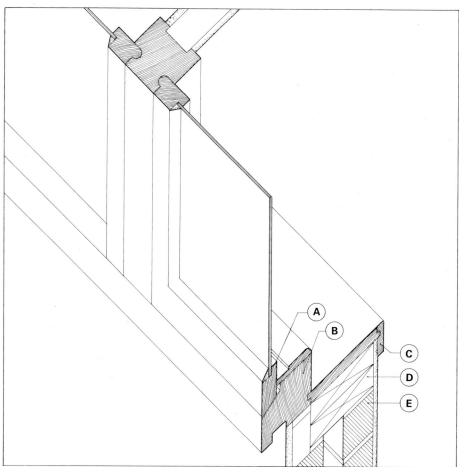

8.19

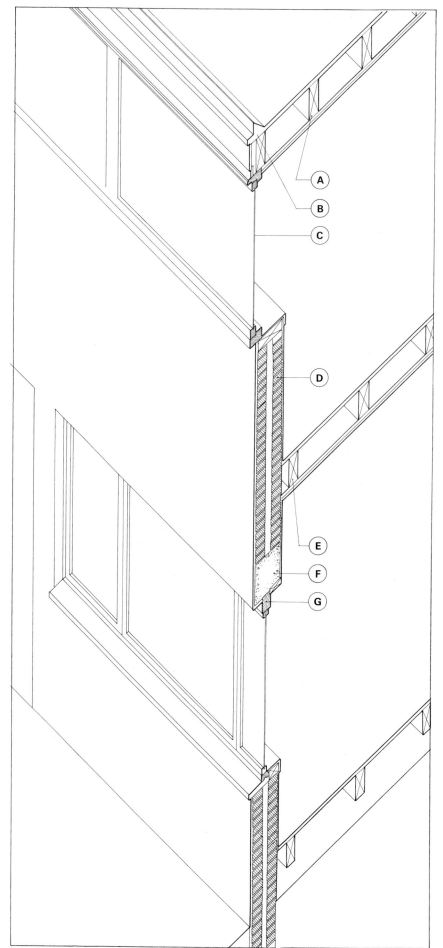

8.20

Kiefhoek Housing Estate
J. J. P. Oud
Rotterdam, 1930

8.18 exterior
(A. Morancé, *L'Architecture Vivante.*)

8.19 window details at second floor

A Wood casement with operable sash. This window is constructed to form the Z-shaped pocket common to all casement windows.

B Fixed wood sash.

C Wood sill and apron. In addition to the architectural advantages of projecting the window in front of the wall, it eliminates the need for a projecting sill and drip.

D Wood blocking. It is difficult to attach a piece of finish wood directly to masonry, since the openings are dimensionally inaccurate and the means of fastening are crude. The blocking allows for dimensional adjustments while providing a nailing surface for the wood window.

E Typical wall construction.
(A. Morancé, *L'Architecture Vivante.*)

8.20 wall section

A Typical roof construction. The basic structure of the house is that of a traditional row house: wood joists spaced about 20″ on center spanning between two masonry party walls. Each roof joist is set at a slightly different elevation to achieve a slope for drainage.

B Metal coping.

C Upper wood casement.

D Typical wall construction. The wall is composed of two wythes of brick, with plaster on their exposed faces. The cavity wall is superior to the solid one for water protection and insulation.

E Typical floor construction. The basic construction is described in A above.

F Concrete lintel. This supports the masonry over the window opening.

G Lower wood casement.
(A. Morancé, *L'Architecture Vivante.*)

8.21 League of Nations (left) and Villa de Monzie (right)
Wall sections
(*Une Maison—Une Palais;* Fondation Le Corbusier, drawing 10.578.)

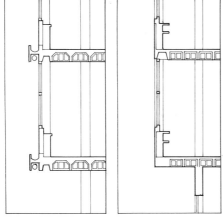

8.21

the underside of the slab is kept as a simple plane to facilitate the free plan. The Villa Savoie again presents a modification to the system: The major girders (those which pick up the loads of the minor beams created by the tiles) are dropped below the bottom of slab, creating a series of frames parallel to the major axis of circulation.

The fenestration of the two buildings shows a similar contrast between a system rigidly applied (at Garches) and a system distorted and displaced (at Poissy). At Garches the typical 2.5-meter sliding window is uniformly applied to the facades of the second and third floors in bands one window high on the front (north) facade and two windows high on the rear. The regular spacing and rhythms of the sash are unaffected by internal partitions or programmatic use. All the other windows—those on the ground floor and those on the north side of the terrace—are of varying sizes and shapes and are formed of a system of tightly spaced steel sections which are for the most part fixed. In the Villa Savoie, the 2.5-meter window is confined to an almost continuous band around the second floor. All ground-floor windows, including the curving glass wall at the entry and the triangular windows between the ramps, are made from the same rolled-steel frame, with tightly spaced mullions used at the ground floor of Garches. The large rolling window between the roof terrace and the living room constitutes a distinctly independent third system. Figure 8.33 shows the south facade as it was illustrated in the 1910–1929 volume of the *Oeuvre Complete* (at the completion of the design), and the facade as built. The original design, which conformed closely to the principles established at Garches, was distorted in the execution for a number of reasons. The typical bay was reduced from 5 meters to 4.75 meters, and, rather than change the size of his standard window, Le Corbusier shifted the spacing off the column center lines. Other changes, such as the use of windows of completely different dimensions, were caused by relocated partitions, but this was a problem the initial scheme did not recognize. The complexity of the plan of the Villa Savoie simply could not be accommodated by a fenestration system that required walls to be spaced on multiples of 2.5 meters.

One should not search too deeply for architectural significance in these modifications. Tim Benton has described the changes that were made between the initial and final designs. (The size of the building was greatly reduced.) The modifications were due less to architectural whim than to economic necessity. Standardization is all very well and good, but then, as now, the most significant way to reduce the cost of a building was to reduce its size. In terms of Le Corbusier's desire to use the "object type" in detailing, Poissy is a relative failure and Garches a relative success.

Le Corbusier's use of the sliding wood window is a curious one. Whereas in a fixed or casement window all the individual panes and frames are usually in the same vertical plane, in the case of the sliding window, since one sash must move behind the other, this relationship is not possible. The success or failure of a facade of this type is often dependent on the way in which the wall plane and the glass plane are related. Because there are two glass planes in a sliding window, this relationship is hard to establish. The other curious choice is the use of a wood rather than a steel frame, since a wood frame has to be much larger and thicker. The general tendency of Modernism has been toward a light membrane with simple, geometrically pure openings, an effect that is much more easily accomplished with a thin steel frame than with a thick wood one.

The view of the interior of the Villa Savoie shown in figure 8.35 may give a clue as to what Le Corbusier thought was so virtuous in the sliding wood window. The recessed notch at the head, the projecting sill, and the two planes of the sliding window make it possible to see the wall as a series of parallel planes, in contrast with the traditional solid mass of Perret or Garnier. The wall thus becomes an analogue or subsystem of the building itself. Colin Rowe has described this type of spatial organization in Le Corbusier's work; and many Corbusian buildings (particularly Garches) can be read in the same way, as a series of parallel planes receding in space.

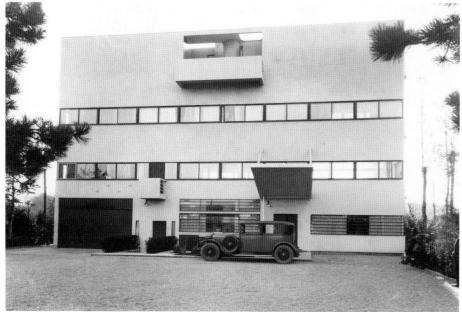

8.22

8.23

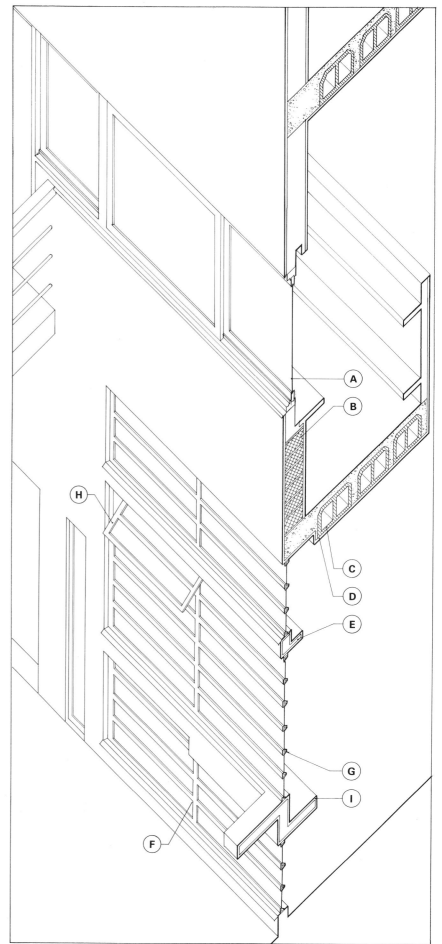

8.24

Villa de Monzie

Le Corbusier

Garches, 1927

8.22   **exterior**

(F. R. Yerbury, Architectural Association Library.)

8.23   **exterior**

(Fondation Le Corbusier.)

8.24   **wall section**

A   Sliding wood window, almost identical to the window shown in figure 8.36.

B   Typical wall construction: hollow pumice concrete masonry covered with "Kalk Cement" externally and plaster internally. No insulation or waterproofing.

C   Typical floor construction: concrete and lost tile.

D   Structural clay tile.

E   Concrete beam.

F   Steel-pipe column. Because the concrete sill and transom beams span such a long distance with such a shallow section, two intermediate supports are provided.

G   Fixed steel sash.

H   Operable steel sash. This is a hopper, or horizontally pivoting, window.

I   Concrete sill beam.

(Fondation Le Corbusier, drawing 30.235.)

8.25   **framing plan**

1   Concrete column.

2   Concrete girder. The bottom is flush with the ceiling.

3   Beams formed by lost-tile process.

(Fondation Le Corbusier, drawing 10.578.)

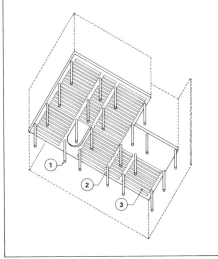

8.25

Not all of the departures from the standard system are as easily explained as those at Poissy, which brings us to the curious example of the Villa Cook. On the surface, Garches and Cook seem quite similar. Both embody the major tenets of the classic Corbusian villa: pilotis, roof terrace, *fenêtre en longeur*, and piano nobilé. These design principles are applied first to a cube (Cook) and then to a solid based on the Golden Section (Garches). A comparison of details reveals something quite different. Cook is the only villa of the 1920s that does not use the 2.5-meter or the 5-meter structural bay (its bay is 4.65 meters square). This could be a product of circumstance, as at Poissy, but in this case the structural system itself is entirely different. In place of the "lost tile" system of Garches is a deck composed of precast I sections with lightweight infill.

In his idealized projects of the 1920s Le Corbusier had proposed the use of a number of new products and assemblies for the basic wall. The Monol Houses (1919) were to have walls of two layers of ¼-inch asbestos sheeting with rubble from the site and cement poured between, leaving enough air pockets to provide insulation. This project was obviously meant to combine precision factory labor (the asbestos sheets) with unskilled on-site labor. Later projects were to use more sophisticated techniques. The Citrohan House (1922) and the Artisan's House (1922) were to have walls of two layers of gunite (cement sprayed on metal lath) with an air space between. The walls of the Artisan's Housing were to be rigid insulation (compressed straw sheets) with 1½ inches of gunite on the exterior and plaster on the interior. These walls were to be "industrialized" architectural products, analogous to cars or airplanes.

It is thus disappointing to discover the crude nature of the walls in Le Corbusier's executed buildings of the late 1920s. Garches has walls of a single layer of concrete block, stuccoed outside and plastered inside. At the Villa Savoie, two wythes (layers) of masonry were used with an air space between. This cavity was of little waterproofing value; it kept water that had penetrated the exterior from entering the interior, but did not allow it to escape. It was probably thought to have insulating qualities, but such air spaces are of limited value without insulation to keep the air still. Convection currents in this cavity would allow heat to easily escape from the building. In any case the design is hardly progressive; it is the same as that used by Perret in the building discussed above.

It is in the fenestration system that the greatest variations occur. It appears to be similar to Garches, with a tightly spaced steel sash at the ground floor and a *fenêtre en longuer* of wood sash above; however, the wood sash and its subdivisions are quite different in this case. In place of the regularly spaced sliding sashes of equal size, there are a variety of different glass sizes, mullion spacings, and window types. Fixed glass, sliding windows, casement windows, and horizontally piveting windows all occur on the same facade. A functionalist might hope to see in this a sensitive response to the precise ventilating requirements of each space, but it is not so simple. One room, the dining room, has all four types in a space of 15 feet. Comparing the plan to the facade, we may assume that this complexity was caused by an irregular spacing of mullions, which in turn was caused by a desire to express internal spatial organization.

Not surprisingly, the window frames of the Villa Cook themselves are quite different in design from the standard 2.5-meter windows of Garches and Poissy, and for a very logical reason: In any window system that mixes fixed and operable sashes, the architect must deal with the fact that the operable sash is visibly larger and thicker than the fixed, being composed of two pieces (one that moves and one that does not) whereas the fixed sash has only one frame and is therefore thinner. This is true of the typical 2.5-meter window; one can see very clearly in a close-up view of the Villa Savoie which pairs are fixed and which are operable. The particular frame used in the Villa Cook is somewhat unique in not having this feature. The operable glass panes are held in a thin U-shaped metal frame small enough to be contained within the standard wood T-shaped mullion.

8.26

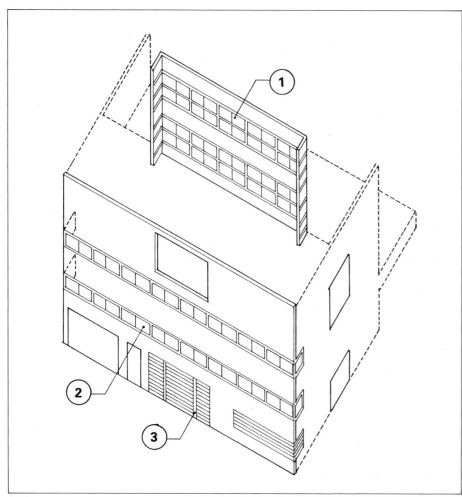

8.27

8.28

Villa de Monzie

Le Corbusier

Garches, 1927

8.26 rear facade

(F. R. Yerbury, Architectural Association Library.)

8.27 window types

1 Double row of Le Corbusier's standard 1 m × 2.5 m sliding wood windows.

2 Single row of 1 m × 2.5 m sliding wood windows.

3 Fixed steel window.

(Fondation Le Corbusier, drawing 10.420.)

8.28 window details at ground floor

A Anchor and head of frame. The anchor is case into the concrete slab and bolted to the frame.

B Steel frame, composed of rolled steel L and T sections glazed from the inside and held in place with putty. Many more horizontal mullions are provided than are structurally necessary.

C Typical intermediate steel rail.

D Sill with condensation gutter.

E Projecting metal sill, formed from a thin piece of zinc.

(Fondation Le Corbusier, drawing 30.235.)

Le Corbusier abandoned this system of rigid standards after 1930, perhaps in part because of the difficulties he experienced on the Villa Savoie. But before doing so, he produced a project that carried this system to its logical, or perhaps illogical, extreme. Figure 8.21 shows, at the same scale, a section of the south wall of Garches and a typical wall of Le Corbusier's project for the League of Nations. Except for the change in cladding from stucco to stone, and the relocation of the rolling shutter to a projecting fin, they are identical. Le Corbusier was clearly interested in a system of standards to apply not just to housing, but to all building types. He even wrote a book, *Une Maison—Une Palais,* arguing the virtues of this point and demonstrating how the facade of the League of Nations project was simply a multiple of that at Garches. This is an idea not only of profound architectural implications, but of social ones as well. If architectural components are the same for all types of buildings, then they will be the same for all types of occupants, rich or poor.

Le Corbusier was never to realize a large-scale building using this system, and it is probably just as well, for he could not have been more wrong in his evaluation of the development of an architecture of "object types." His errors were rooted in three misconceptions of the nature of Modern construction: (1) He failed to recognize the differences in economy and functional requirements between large-scale office-type buildings and small-scale residential buildings, although the lost-tile system is still in use for many building types in countries with unsophisticated building processes. (A poured-in-place concrete frame is seldom economical for an individual residence.) In the 1970s, when a number of American architects built houses using a formal vocabulary reminiscent of the white stucco buildings of the 1920s, they were invariably executed in wood framing with steel reinforcement, never in concrete. (2) He greatly overemphasized the importance of standardized sizes of building components. Although there was undoubtedly some economy in using a single window size within the same building, there was very little advantage in using custom-made windows of the same size in two buildings built over an interval of two years. In any case, this degree of standardization has become neither necessary nor desirable. Two of the major manufacturers of residential windows in the United States today, Pella and Anderson, manufacture, respectively, 46 and 42 different sizes of casement windows alone. (3) In addition to failing to recognize the differences in economy of structure between residential and large-scale buildings, he failed to recognize the difference in environmental requirements and its effect on the architecture. The increased floor-to-ceiling depth in an office building is mandated by the increased requirements for mechanical equipment. In fairness to Le Corbusier, this was not as clear in 1930 as it is to us today, but throughout his career he failed to deal conceptually with the integration of mechanical services into the floor-ceiling assembly.

It is as unfair to criticize Le Corbusier's detailing for falling short of its technologically utopian goals as it would be to criticize Russian Constructivism or German Expressionism for falling short of their socially utopian goals. It is perhaps more productive to evaluate his detailing system as to how it fails or succeeds on its own terms. For this purpose, let us take a closer look at his typical fenestration systems, particularly the standard sliding 2.5-meter-wide window. To understand the opportunities and limitations of his design, it is necessary to consider what options were open to him. This is best done by comparing his details with those of his contemporaries.

LE CORBUSIER AND HIS CONTEMPORARIES

The public perception of Le Corbusier as the father of a machine-age architecture is, of course, inaccurate. In comparison with other architects active in the 1920s, he was neither the most interested in nor the most indifferent to the possibilities of new methods and materials. There were many architects of this period, most of them associated with the De Stijl group, who were fully committed to the forms of modernism but were neutral or even hostile to the futurist preoccupation with the machine. The most prolific architect of this group was J. J. P. Oud. His Kiefhoek housing estate at Rotterdam illustrates this attitude. To Henry-Russell

8.29

8.30

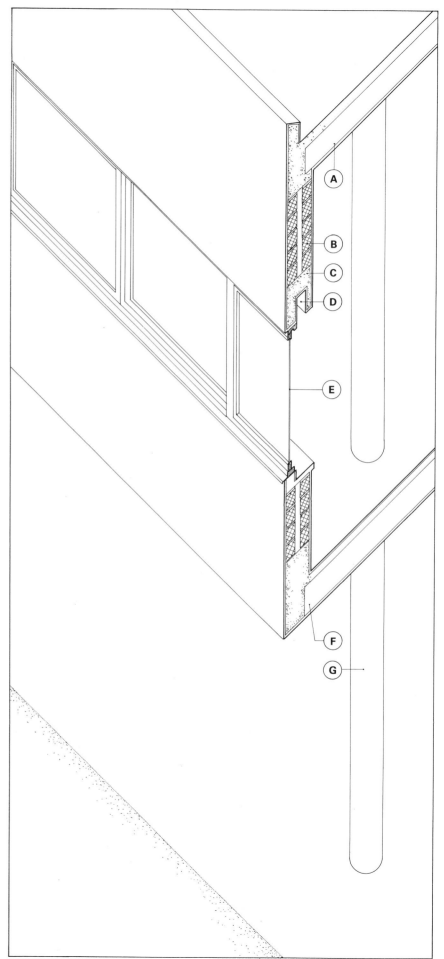

8.31

Villa Savoie

Le Corbusier

Poissy, 1932

8.29 **exterior**

8.30 **detail**

8.31 **wall section, south wall at second floor**

A Roof construction: layer of bituminous mastic (durumfix) on concrete slab covered with layer of sand and gravel. This roof was built with no apparent slope.

B Wall construction: cavity wall formed of two layers of concrete masonry.

C Concrete lintel. This acts to support the masonry above. It is not a true lintel; it is suspended from the floor above rather than bearing on the masonry walls.

D Pocket in lintel for rolling shades.

E Sliding wood window. This is the typical window of most of the villas of the 1920s. It was patented by Le Corbusier and Pierre Jeanneret.

F Typical floor construction: lost tile and concrete.

G Concrete column.
(Fondation Le Corbusier, drawing 19.651 and as-built drawings made in 1965.)

8.32 **framing plan**

A Cast-in-place concrete column.

B Lost-tile slab.

C Opening for ramp.

D Dropped girder.

E Cantilever.
(Construction photographs.)

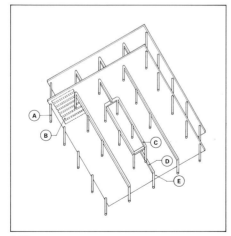

8.32

Hitchcock and Philip Johnson, writing in *The International Style* in 1932, Kiefhoek was stylistically similar, if not identical, to the buildings of Le Corbusier, although the technology was quite different.[2] Figure 8.20 shows the structure of a typical Kiefhoek dwelling, with wood joists spaced at about 20 inches spanning between masonry party walls. It is in fact the structure of a typical nineteenth-century row house.

In contrast to the rather mundane structural system, the fenestration system of Kiefhoek is adventurous enough to merit close analysis. All the windows are outswinging wood casements of a fairly thick and wide section, in violation of the general Modernist preference for the light, thin frames that steel made possible. The second floor has a continuous ribbon of casements, which extend all the way to the roof and project about 3 inches in front of the building face. The windows of the first floor, although the frames are of the same general profile, are set in narrow punched openings and recessed from the face of the wall. This system of openings is quite consistent with the structure of a load-bearing masonry row house, and although it differs from Le Corbusier's system it is (not by accident) very similar to certain Frank Lloyd Wright houses, such as the Coonley house. The technique of varying the location of the glass plane in relation to the wall, a recurrent one in Modern architecture, is probably derived from Gropius. Oud realized that, just as the way to make a wall appear massive was to recess the glass plane behind the wall plane, the way to make a wall appear light and taut was to project the window frame to bring the plane of the glass forward of the wall plane. Oud used both of these techniques to make the wall appear heavier at its base and lighter at the top, reinforcing the overall facade composition. While the use of the heavy wood frame is unfortunate, Oud's facade is in this respect much more successful than the typical Corbusian facade. The manipulation of the glass plane in relation to the wall plane, which is often so critical in this type of building, was never a tool that Le Corbusier used effectively in his Purist phase. In fact he could not do so and use the sliding wood window as a primary element, since by its very nature it has two different glass planes. It is in this sense that Oud's facade is superior to that of Villa Cook, where in a single strip of window the glass is in at least three different planes.

By Le Corbusier's own criteria, his fenestration systems are unsuccessful. A more common window detail of the period is shown in figure 8.17. This particular detail is from Johannes Duiker's Sanatorium at Zonnestraal, but similar details can be found in similar buildings by Gropius, Meyer, and even Oud. The steel window was the preferred type of the modernists of the 1920s. Not only did it make possible the light thin glass membranes of the International Style, but it carried with it the association of the factory, in which it had found its principal use up to that time. Curiously, this is a trend Le Corbusier pursued and later abandoned in favor of the one described above. The Ozenfant house has all-steel windows, and a steel system was investigated for Pessac. He did not use the steel frame again as a primary element until he began to develop the all-glass curtain walls of the 1930s.

A simple explanation for Le Corbusier's attitude is that he did not see the factory and its imagery as a model for the modern house. Saying that a house should be factory-made and saying that it should look like a factory are two different things. Le Corbusier had a fundamentally different conception of the nature of the facade and the nature of the wall than his contemporaries, particularly the members of the Neue Sachlichkeit. He conceived the wall as the surface of a solid. Architecture was "forms brought together in light." The problem of the window was the problem of "how to model the plain surface of a primary and simple form," and the solution was to "borrow the generating and accusing lines of these simple forms."[3] Duiker and Gropius, on the other hand, saw the wall as a membrane, stretched over and infilling the structural frame. The steel frame, with its thin sash and narrow profile, is obviously much more essential to the "glass wall as membrane" concept, and Duiker used it in this way, wrapping windows around corners and extending them unbroken from floor slab and spandrel to ceiling.

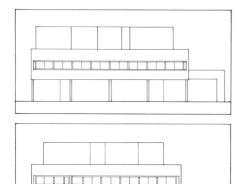

8.33

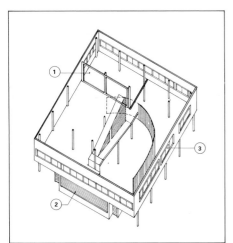

8.34

8.35

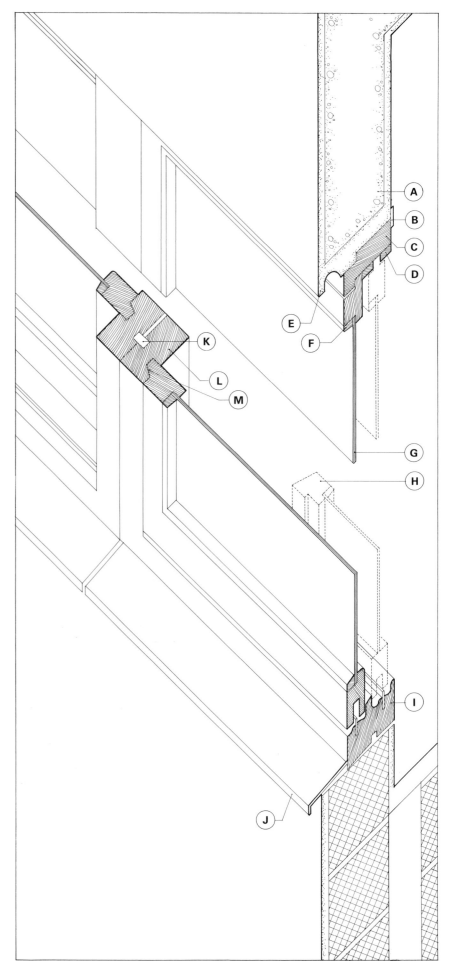

8.36

Villa Savoie

Le Corbusier

Poissy, 1932

8.33 preliminary and final elevations

8.34 window types

1 Sliding glass wall connecting living room and terrace.
2 Fixed steel windows at circulation and service areas.
3 Band of Le Corbusier's standard 1 m × 2.5 m sliding wood windows.

8.35 window

8.36 window details

A Typical wall. (See figure 8.32.)

B Batten. This covers the joint between the wall and the wood frame, which is likely to be uneven and subject to movement. It replaces traditional wood trim in a simple-minded way, and is an example of Le Corbusier's detailing as its crudest.

C Fixed wood frame.

D Removable stops. These permit installation and removal of the sliding portions of the window.

E Drip. This prevents water running down the face of the wall from reaching the joint between the frame and the wall, where it might enter the building. Often this is accomplished with an applied molding. Hiding it under the lintel maintains the clean lines of the opening.

F Removable glass stop, permitting installation and replacement of glass.

G Outer leaf of sliding wood sash. The notch in the bottom of the sash holds small wheels which run along the metal rail below.

H Inner leaf of sliding wood window. The leaves of the sash must be in different planes so that one may pass behind the other.

I Base of fixed wood frame. The wood upright at the center separates the two leaves of the sash. The depressions in the frame act as condensation gutters and are provided with weep holes to the outside. In the undulating profile of this frame can be seen a characteristic form used in Le Corbusier's later buildings.

J Projecting metal sill.

K Mullion reinforcement. This metal piece gives the frame additional stiffness at its main structural member.

L Fixed intermediate wood frame. The notch in the frame which receives the protecting tongue of the wood sash forms a "rabbet" joint ensuring that the joint will remain closed despite changes in the shape and size of the wood sash due to moisture, heat, etc. The joint between the two fixed pieces allows for on-site joining of larger units made in the factory.

M Rabbet. This notch ensures that the joint will remain closed despite movements in the wood sash.
(Fondation Le Corbusier, drawing 19.455 and as-built drawings made in 1965.)

THE DEVELOPMENT OF THE CURTAIN WALL

Beginning with his designs for the Salvation Army Hostel, Le Corbusier began to pursue a direction opposite to that he had proposed in *Une Maison—Une Palais*. Rather than develop a system of standard dimensions and "object types" which would be applied equally and uniformly to buildings of all scales and uses, he chose to explore the multi-story frame building and the frame-and-bearing-wall residence as distinct and independent types. Many factors, some of them far from technological, were behind this change—among them the decline of Purist and Cubist aesthetics in favor of Surrealist ones, the decline of the Futurist-inspired fascination with the machine, and the influence of contemporary Modern architects. It is ironic that, concurrent with the decline in the fervor with which industrialization was discussed, there was a marked increased in the technological sophistication of building systems. This period saw the completion of Le Corbusier's three major steel curtain-wall buildings: Centrosoyus (1935), the Salvation Army Hostel (1933), and the Swiss Pavilion at the Cité Universitaire (1932).

The Swiss Pavilion, despite its well-documented technical shortcomings,[4] is Le Corbusier's best-detailed building up to this time. Though his earlier work should be lauded for the development of detailing that was conceptually analogous to the building's parti, he was not using the full range of techniques and materials at his disposal, particularly in his manipulation of the surface of the wall and the glass plane (as the comparison with Oud and Duiker has shown). The Swiss Pavilion shows an altered set of technical priorities, a wider vocabulary of materials, a different attitude toward the relation of structure and space, and a greater sensitivity to the relation of the wall plane to the glass plane. Undoubtedly, Le Corbusier had been influenced by the work of his contemporaries—Gropius, the architects who built at the Weissenhofsiedlung, and even Neutra's Lovell house (which was published in *L'Architecture Vivante* in the 1920s). But for purposes of discussion and comparison, the Workshop Block of the Bauhaus Building is most informative.

The Bauhaus wall is very much like Duiker's Zonnestraal—a glass membrane stretched over the structure—while the Swiss Pavilion wall is very much a plane punctured in accordance with *traces reguler*. The structural systems disclose certain differences. The structure of the Bauhaus and Zonnestraal are the same: a flat concrete plate with dropped beams at major spans, tapered in accordance with decreasing loads. This system, because of its dropped beams, does not permit the same freedom in locating partitions as that used at Garches, with its completely flat slab, and the plans of the two buildings reflect this. The framing of the Swiss Pavilion, however, employs a system entirely different from the lost-tile system used in the houses. Le Corbusier used the tile system in at least one large-scale building, the Cité de Refuge (Salvation Army Hostel); subsequently, he experimented with a dropped-beam system similar to that of the Bauhaus (at the Centrosoyus), and then with the hybrid system used at the Swiss Pavilion.

The Swiss Pavilion consists of three separate systems: (1) a concrete slab supported by concrete columns and load-bearing masonry walls, which form the small sub-buildings on the ground floor, (2) a concrete platform supported by pilotis, which forms the second floor, on which sits the third system, and (3) a steel cage, which supports composite floor slabs of concrete, tile, and steel and which makes up the dormitory rooms. The structural bay is identical to one room, 2.7 × 4.0 meters, and the steel columns are entirely concealed within the partitions (although they are exposed on the south facade). This system is the opposite of the free plan—since the spatial divisions of the building are defined by the structural divisions, one cannot move a wall without moving a column. In the building as a whole, different parts of the program are defined by separate volumes with their own structural systems, in contrast to Garches and Poissy, where all programmatic parts are made to fit into a regular structural grid. Le Corbusier did not use this precise structural system again, but he did continue to experiment with hybrid structures of load-bearing and frame elements. Other architects pursued the concept of separate volumes and structures for separate parts of the program with more interest than Le Corbusier, especially after 1945.

8.37

8.38

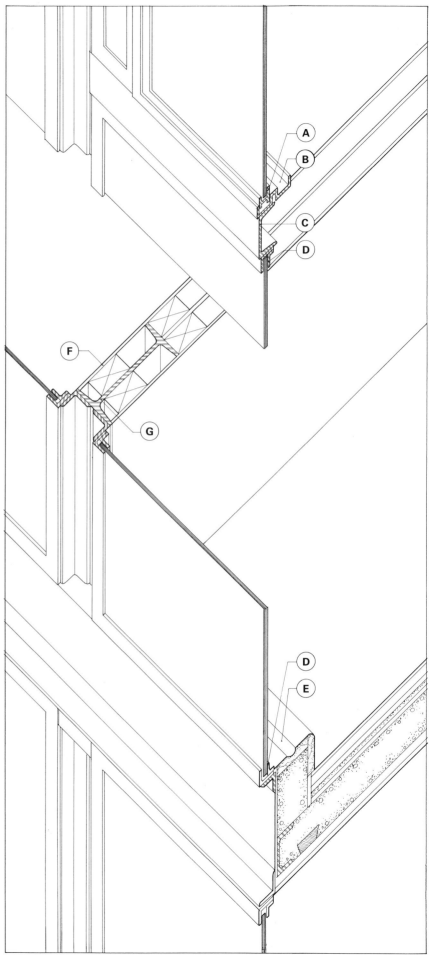

8.39

Pavillion Suisse

Le Corbusier

Paris, 1932

8.37 exterior

(Fondation Le Corbusier.)

8.38 window detail

8.39 window details

A Sliding steel window. The operable window consists of two horizontally sliding sashes made from rolled steel sections. The track in which they slide is formed from steel sheet braked (bent) into roughly a W shape to form grooves.

B Track for sliding window.

C Steel channel support. In addition to forming the traditional rail 3 feet from the floor, this supports the considerable weight of the glass and the frame above.

D Typical steel frame and stop, made from two rolled-steel angles (L-shaped pieces): a larger one on the exterior, forming the frame proper, and a smaller one on the inside, forming a removable stop for reglazing.

E Sill with condensation gutter.

F Typical partition.

G Steel column, concealed within partition.

(Fondation Le Corbusier, drawings 15.400 and 15.401 and construction photographs.)

It is in the curtain wall of the dormitory that Le Corbusier's detailing shows its greatest improvement over that used in the early villas, and the curtain wall of the Swiss Pavilion is in many ways superior to its possible inspiration at the Bauhaus. The concept of the plane in contrast to the glass membrane has not changed, but the means of execution has.

The first change is in the relationship of structure to exterior wall. At the Bauhaus, since the slab edge is cantilevered, the columns are several feet behind the wall face, but are articulated on the outside by means of a U-shaped metal piece that engages the projecting beam at each column line (figure 8.42). The structural frame of the Swiss Pavilion is in the same plane as the outside wall and is necessarily expressed where the wall is mostly glass; it conveniently divides the facades into a series of squares corresponding to the room divisions.

But what of the element that was such a shortcoming in the early houses, the lack of a consistent relationship between glass and wall and the failure to manipulate the surface to enhance the parti? The Bauhaus wall achieves its tautness by setting the glass plane several inches in front of the base wall, which in turn is cantilevered several feet in front of the wall of the ground floor. At the top, however, the wall projects in front of the glass plane. The coping, in turn, projects beyond the wall, forming a sort of simplified Classical cornice. To have set the wall back here in the same plane as the wall below would have been difficult and dangerous, since it would have exposed the top of the window frame to the weather at a location where it would have been likely to leak. While the solution as it exists is undoubtedly better technically, it gives the building a Classical top-heaviness not totally appropriate to its elementarist aesthetic.

The most noticeably similar feature of the Swiss Pavilion and the Bauhaus is that they are both inside-glazed (the glass is installed and replaced from inside the building). The Corbusian mullion is a flat rectangle whose face is close to the plane of the glass, resulting in a taut surface to the wall. The glass plane here is not set forward of the solid wall but is virtually in the same plane. The two planes never touch, since they are always separated by a recessed notch formed of two steel angles and a plate. This same notch also is used to divide each floor and each room. Rather than decrease the visual tension in this facade, it actually increases it. Additional evidence of Le Corbusier's awareness of the potential for manipulating the wall plane and the glass plane is provided by the detailing of the small punched windows on the north side of the building, where the glass is set deep into the wall, creating the same type of contrast and ambiguity that Oud created at Kiefhook.

A problem for both Le Corbusier and Gropius was how to include operable windows without destroying the visual integrity of the basic system. Le Corbusier had already tried to get along without them in a similar curtain wall, at the Salvation Army Hostel, with disastrous results[5] (the building was initially uninhabitable). Gropius used a series of horizontally pivoting windows in a series of vertical bands from the top to the bottom of the wall. The additional thickness of the mullion caused by the addition of the operable sash is clearly visible on the building's exterior and gives it a definite vertical emphasis. In some respects, the facade of the Bauhaus has a Classical feel, with its series of verticals running from the top of the building to the bottom, capped by a cornice and entablature. Le Corbusier stubbornly refused to abandon the sliding window; however, he did substitute steel for wood in order to make the sash compatible with the rest of the curtain wall, and thus he was again faced with the problem of dealing with two different glass planes. His solution here was to add a narrow fixed piece of glass to the end of each sliding window (figure 8.41). Though this did not eliminate the problem, it reduced the recessed portion of the glass to simply a punched opening. (Not surprisingly, it also made the width of this window 2.5 meters.)

To most contemporary observers, the Swiss Pavilion comes off better in this comparison, not only as an architectural composition but also in the way in which it is detailed. Just as he had done in the past, Le Corbusier adopted the detailing

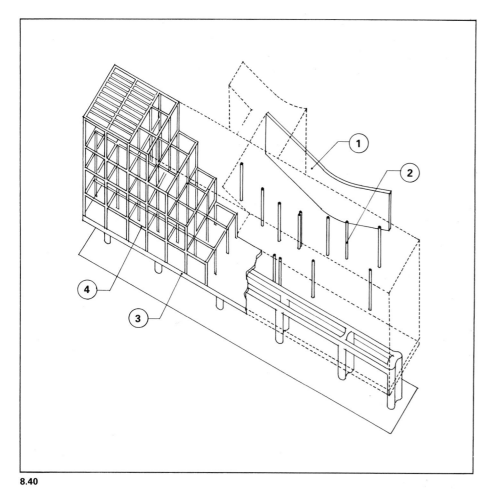

8.40

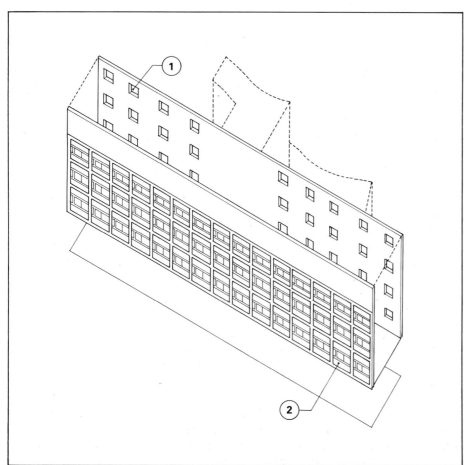

8.41

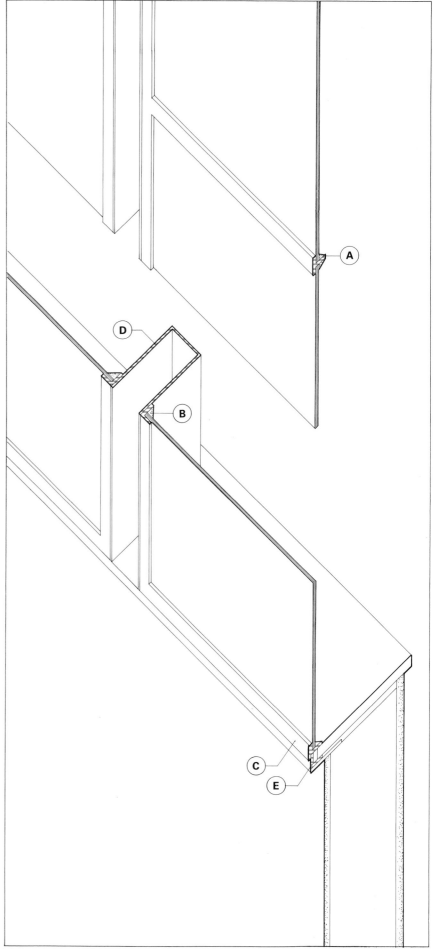

8.42

Pavillion Suisse

Le Corbusier

Paris, 1932

8.40 framing diagram

1 Load-bearing fieldstone wall.

2 Cast-in-place concrete columns framing common room.

3 Cast-in-place concrete platform (open below).

4 Steel frame at dormitory room.

(Fondation Le Corbusier, drawing 15.518 and construction photographs.)

8.41 window types

1 Recessed window windows.

2 Steel curtain wall with sliding steel window in center portion.

Bauhaus building

Walter Gropius

Dessau, 1926

8.42 window details of workshop block

A Typical horizontal sash: steel, glazed from the inside.

B Vertical sash at column.

C Sash at sill.

D Typical mullion at column. This is made from braked steel sheet and attached to the beams projecting from the columns at each floor, strengthening the wall and giving a subtle articulation to the column bays.

E Support angle at sill. Projecting the glass plane in front of the wall creates a considerable structural problem, since the weight of the glass wall does not rest on the masonry wall.

(Architectural Record.)

ideas of his contemporaries and made them his own. But it is probably unfair to compare him with Oud, Gropius, and Duiker, since their architectural intentions were so fundamentally different. In contrast with those men, he comes across as something of a Classicist, and as an architect who exploited the possibilities of modern technology but did not celebrate them to the same extent. A more accurate analysis will arise from a comparison with contemporary architects of a more conservative intent.

Within the detailing systems of Le Corbusier, and within the detailing systems of International Style Modernism, there are two strains, one of which is based on the simplification and abstraction of traditional details and one of which is based on the inversion and reversal of traditional detailing practice. The works of Oud and Gropius are examples of the latter. For an example of the former, it is necessary to look at the work of architects such as Guiseppe Terragni.

Terragni's Casa del Fascio was originally designed as a traditional building with a hip roof, a heavy rusticated base, and traditional window openings. It evolved over the course of its design into a Modernist building, while retaining some of the compositional character of its original form. It is visually bottom-heavy, and it shows a Classical distribution of mass, becoming lighter toward the top. This is a characteristic it does not share with Le Corbusier's buildings—particularly the Swiss Pavilion, in which the distribution of mass is just the reverse (i.e., the weight of the building appears to be suspended above the ground). Otherwise the two buildings have much in common: the same building systems were used, the openings and proportions were determined by regulating lines, and there was a tendency to treat the building envelope as the surface of a primary form rather than a frame covered or infilled with a membrane of glass. On a more superficial level, the Casa del Fascio resembles the Swiss Pavilion in that its primary facade is composed of closely spaced squares or rectangles. Let us examine this facade as another option open to Le Corbusier. First, however, an examination of the structural systems of both buildings will be useful.

Terragni's building, like Le Corbusier's, uses a lost-tile system to form a one-way ribbed slab, although with a different tile in a square bay. Rather than keep the underside of the slab flat, as Le Corbusier had done, Terragni dropped the major beams below the slab a distance equal to the thickness of the column. Thus, instead of the flat slabs of Le Corbusier's Dom-Ino System, we have a cage of cubes made of square members that bring to mind the later works of O. M. Ungers and Arata Isozaki. This is obviously not a condition that facilitates a free plan, and Terragni made no effort to achieve one. All partitions in the building extend between columns, and thus meet a beam at the underside of the slab. This places extreme restrictions on planning, since sizes can only be multiples of the structural bay, or the bay size must be changed to accommodate the offices. Despite the limitations of this concept (which would be unacceptable in any present-day office building), it is perhaps a more accurate expression of the nature of the concrete frame, but it is also the antithesis of the free plan. In traditional masonry buildings there is a fairly exact correspondence between the structural organization and the spatial and plan organization. The concept of the free plan is that this relationship is no longer either necessary or desirable. The Casa del Fascio is in no sense a free-plan building. The structural bays and the room divisions correspond exactly, and in this conceptual way Terragni's building is traditional in its attitudes toward the relationship of structure and space.

It is in the wall system of the Casa del Fascio that we find its chief virtue. Although this building has an elegant and elaborate series of sliding and pivoting wood windows, their design is, at least from the outside, almost irrelevant. The solid portions of the wall and the window portions exist at two independent planes. The building is a box within a box. And the window frames are so far behind the outside wall face that one sees only the clear, simple lines of the stone wall. Although this is an extreme solution, it is easy to see the advantages of this technique: Differences in glass planes and in sash profiles cease to matter. On the other hand, Terragni is attempting to conceive the building envelope in a way that

8.43

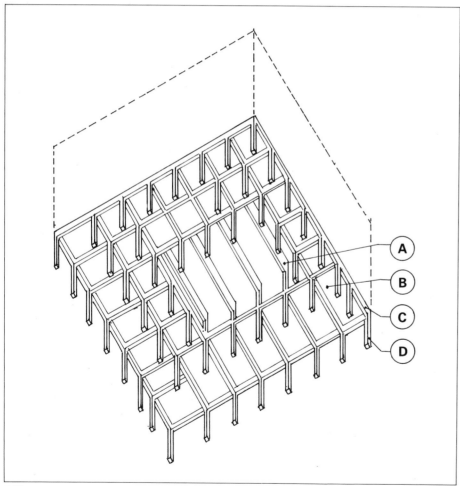

8.44

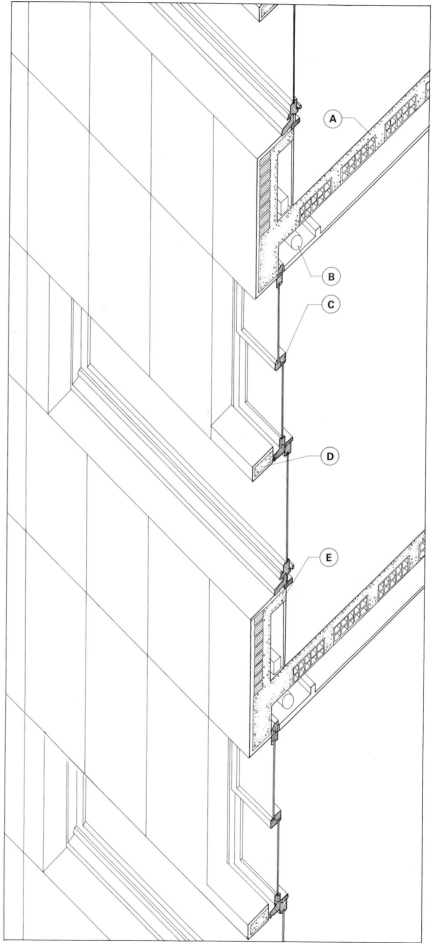

8.45

Casa del Fascio

Guiseppi Terragni

Como, 1936

8.43 **exterior**

(Quadrante.)

8.44 **framing plan**

A Large concrete girder over courtyard.

B Concrete floor slab.

C Concrete beam. These coincide exactly with the location of the walls.

D Concrete column.

(Quadrante.)

8.45 **wall section, south facade**

A Concrete structure of lost tiles with dropped beams.

B Rolling shutter.

C Wood sliding and pivoting windows.

D Concrete and marble fin.

E Typical wall construction: single layer of brick faced with 5-cm-thick marble slabs, sometimes with a concrete backup.

(Quadrante.)

is neither the membrane of Gropius nor the articulated pure form of Le Corbusier. First, Terragni treats the glass almost as if it were invisible—of all the buildings in this chapter, the Casa del Fascio is the one that would gain rather than lose in appearance if its glass were to be taken out. Despite the abstract Modernism of Terragni's facade, the fenestration is traditional in the sense that it is based on a relationship of solids and voids rather than an exploitation of the qualities of glass as a membrane. A second advantage of this technique is that by moving the exterior wall slightly forward of the columns, Terragni frees himself of the necessity of expressing them on the outside and enables himself to treat the wall sometimes as an unbroken plane and sometimes as a frame.

It is important to note that this facade, despite its elegance, in no way represents a model for emulation in present-day buildings. The shortest spans of the bays are 2.75 and 4.75 meters, both of which are well below economical spans for steel and are close to the minimum for concrete. However, the desire to make the structural module and the spatial module coincide, in opposition to the spatial independence of the free plan, remained a strong Classical ideal in Modernism and resurfaced in the 1950s and the 1960s.

CONCLUSION

The influence of Le Corbusier transcended purely formal ideas. Just as his concepts of city planning enjoyed a life independent of architectural taste, his ideas of construction influenced architects who were not necessarily his stylistic progeny. The difficulty was (and is) that his ideas were based on two concepts that were far from universal in their applicability.

First, most of Le Corbusier's projects for industrialized building systems (none of which were executed) were to use thin walls made up of a number of layers of specialized and preferably synthetic components. This was true of the Monol Houses of 1919 and of the Loucher Houses of 1929, but the white villas of the 1920s used simple monolithic walls, without insulation or waterproofing. In his more rustic work of the 1930s, Le Corbusier resigned himself to simple monolithic walls of stone, presumably because the available budgets and technology did not permit the more complex wall. Perret pursued the monolithic wall in another way, through the use of precast concrete. In buildings such as his Bley house, precast elements (although complex ones) constitute the entire building's structure and interior and exterior finish. This was the fulfillment of nineteenth-century ideas in twentieth-century terms: one universal, monolithic building material. This conception of modern building is very much alive today. The precast buildings of Ricardo Bofill, despite differences in style, are a continuation of this trend.

The second of Le Corbusier's difficult concepts was his idealization of automobile and aircraft manufacturing as models for the building industry. His analysis was not an in-depth one; it consisted generally in standardization, maximum off-site work, and minimum on-site work. This was to be achieved by fabricating large components off site and by making a minimum number of joints and connections at the site. Economy in building was to be achieved by simplification—a minimum number of materials fabricated into a minimum number of components assembled with a minimum number of joints. The best materials, and the best components, would therefore be those that performed the most functions. Rather than have separate components, materials, and laborers for structure, insulation, waterproofing, and finish, it seemed infinitely better to have one material and component to do all four. It would require fewer joints, fewer workers, and fewer materials. Precast concrete seemed the ideal building component. The fact that this theory does not resemble the ways cars and planes are actually built was unknown or ignored.

Both of these conceptions led to the conclusion that modern buildings would be simple, monolithic structures. The monolithic style exists today in the form of precast concrete architecture, but except in the mass housing projects of Europe and in certain types of American buildings (such as parking garages) it is not the

8.46

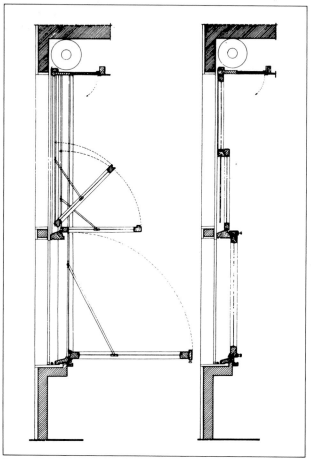

8.47

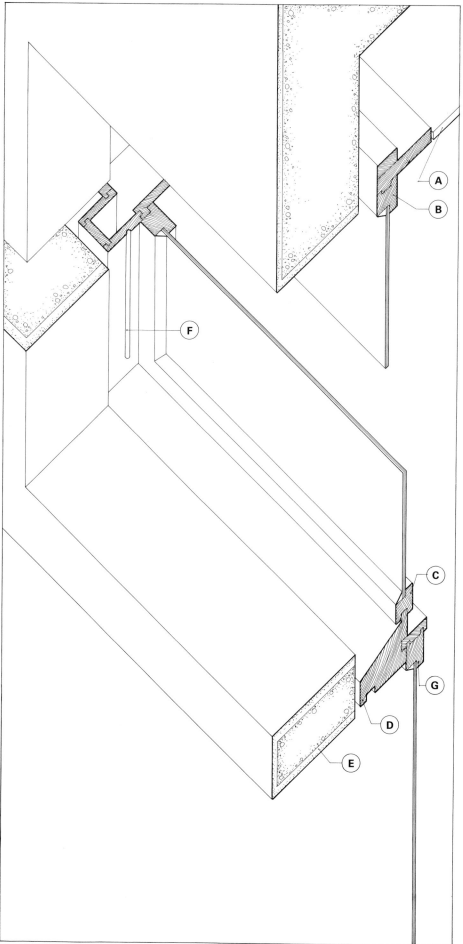

8.48

Casa del Fascio

Guiseppi Terragni

Como, 1936

___

8.46 **interior**

(Quadrante.)

8.47 **window operation**

(Quadrante.)

8.48 **window details**

A   Hinged wood panel. This permits access to the rolling shutter above for repairs and adjustments.

B   Vertical sliding wood upper sash. The typical joint, consisting of a tongue and a groove, acts like the Z-shaped joint to keep the joint closed despite dimensional changes in the wood sash.

C   Vertical sliding wood lower sash. The typical sash is glazed from the outside.

D   Fixed horizontal rail.

E   5-cm marble on concrete screen wall.

F   Typical jamb. The groove is for the sliding sash above.

G   Pivoting wood sash. See figure 8.47 for operation.

(Quadrante.)

dominant system of building. This is particularly true in America, where a majority of residential buildings are wood-frame and a majority of larger buildings are steel. Wood and steel frames almost demand a layered system of building with specialized components, and efforts to bring them into the monolithic systems have led to much frustration.

The chief virtue of the study of Le Corbusier's details is not what it tells us about the qualities of fine details, but what it tells us about Le Corbusier's architecture. His major accomplishment was that he was sometimes able to produce detailing systems that were exact parallels of his formal systems. In terms of his ability to select materials and assemblies and to configure them in a way that would strengthen his formal intentions, he was less successful, and it has remained to his followers to develop details appropriate to his vision. There is an irony, and it is one that Le Corbusier would not appreciate: Although his formal ideas are still very much alive, the technological ideals that were so integral to them—the concrete-frame house, the standardized wood and steel windows, the universal structural bay size—are very much dead.

Le Corbusier's legacy is not, however, a purely formal one. His ideas about the building industry, although formulated sixty years ago, also have had a life of their own. Despite his overemphasis on standardization, despite his failure to recognize the differences between small-scale and large-scale construction, and despite his general misinterpretation of the nature of industrialization, they still dominate our conception of the building industry. The idea that building must become like the automobile industry, that economy is to be obtained by off-site manufacture of large-scale standardized components by repetitive "Taylorized" processes, has refused to go away, despite any number of failed attempts to put it into practice—perhaps because no comprehensive vision of comparable scope has come along to take its place.

The Swiss Pavilion and the Cité de Refuge do represent detailing achievements in their own right, and show considerable improvement over their predecessors, but they are an end, not a beginning. The order of standardized equal parts was to give way to the order of progressive series, based on modules. Stucco walls and steel frames gave way to stone and concrete walls and wood frames, and with them came a new language of detailing.

9 Ludwig Mies van der Rohe and the Steel Frame

One thing will be decisive. The way we assert ourselves in the face of circumstance.

Mies van der Rohe, 1930

There have always been two Mies van der Rohes. There was the European Mies, who did many projects and built little, and there was the American Mies, who built one major building a year from 1950 till his death in 1969. There was the Mies who belonged to De Stijl and the Novembergruppe, edited the Magazine *G*, and designed a monument to the Communist martyrs Karl Liebknecht and Rosa Luxemburg, and there was the Mies who, after the Seagram Building, gave corporate America its architectural language. The buildings were different as well. There was the Mies of the expressionistic glass skyscraper projects, the brick country house, and the Barcelona pavilion, and there was the Mies of the Farnsworth house, Crown Hall, and the Berlin Museum. The European buildings were irregular, asymmetrical, fragmented, and touched by Expressionism and De Stijl; the American buildings were regular, symmetrical, and complete and recalled the work of Schinkel. The European buildings were known only by a few sketchy drawings and old photographs; the American buildings were documented down to the last bolt. The European buildings were mysterious, inaccessible, enigmatic, and often unrealized; the American buildings were close at hand, held no mysteries or secrets, and were almost too well known, sometimes almost boring.

The changes of form and detail across Mies's career were not caused by changes in technology, but changes in technology made them possible and gave them direction and shape. There are considerable technological differences between a house built in Germany in 1930 and an office building built in New York in 1960, but there are also differences in attitude, differences in detailing style, and differences in concepts of construction. Although we associate Mies with the steel frame, exposed rolled steel sections did not appear in his work until 1943, sixteen years after Neutra's Lovell house and ten years after the Swiss Pavilion. We associate him with the International Style, but he designed only two major buildings faced in stucco.

Before 1940, Mies (unlike most Modernists) favored the layered rather than the monolithic system. His work after he came to America favors the latter. Ironically, in many of his later commissions he could not expose the frame because of the building type, so both systems occur throughout his work. Mies's great virtue was his ability to accept conditions adverse to his ideas and deal with the problem at hand.

9.1

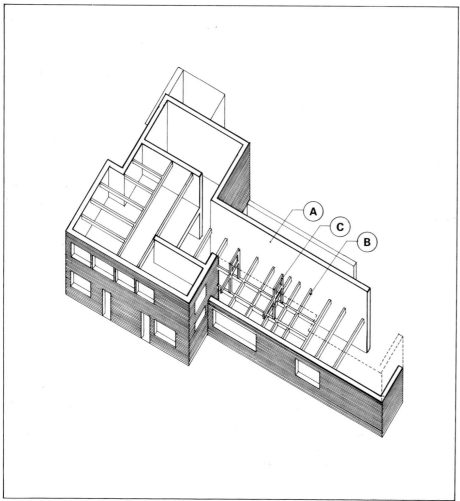

9.2

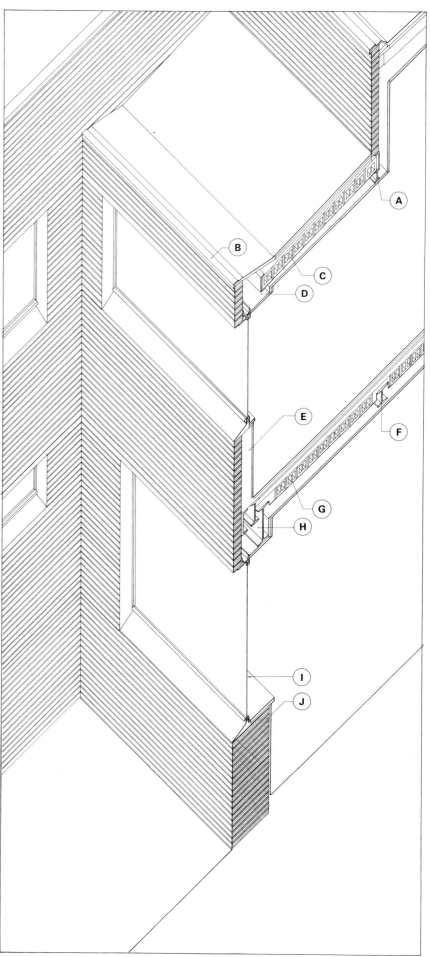

9.3

H. Lange house

Mies van der Rohe

Krefeld, 1928

9.1 exterior

(Museum of Modern Art.)

9.2 framing plan

A   Load-bearing brick walls.

B   Steel beams. These support a floor deck of tiles and concrete, which is supported by masonry load-bearing walls.

C   Steel bracket. The set-back wall of the second floor has no wall below to support it, unlike the other load-bearing walls. Thus it must be supported by a steel bracket, spanning between two bearing walls. The X bracing is concealed within the walls of the second floor.

(Museum of Modern Art, drawing 6.30.)

9.3 wall section

A   Steel I section and channel, supporting brick wall above. This is part of the steel brace shown in figures 9.2 and 9.4.

B   Parapet and roof. The edge of the built-up roof is held down with a section of a rolled steel T, rather than the standard sheet-metal gravel stop, to lessen the possibility of warping.

C   Roof construction: deck of prefabricated sections, probably structural clay tile, covered with concrete and supported by steel beams.

D   Pocket for roll-down shutter.

E   Upper wall construction. The upper wall is veneered rather than monolithic, probably to accommodate the steel bracket.

F   Steel beam supporting concrete-and-tile floor.

G   Floor construction. This is similar to the roof construction, and except for the steel beams it is not unlike the Hennebique system used by Le Corbusier (figure 8.5).

H   Pocket for roll-down shutter.

I   Steel window. The use of a thin steel sash, rather than the larger traditional wood sash, creates a simpler and more abstract opening.

J   Lower brick wall. Most of the walls are monolithic brick, rather than the cavity type associated with modern construction.

(Museum of Modern Art, drawings 6.115 and 6.174.)

9.4 steel brace at second floor

(Museum of Modern Art, drawing 6.174.)

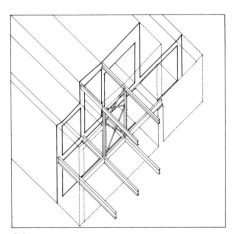

9.4

Mies preferred steel structure, but he would accept concrete if necessary; he preferred, in later life, to expose the steel, but he would accept concealment if required. Proportions were important, but could be altered slightly to suit conditions. But one idea—the concealment of joints—was inviolate, and that idea is a constant thread running through all Mies's work.

Mies said that the work of H. P. Berlage—particularly the Amsterdam Stock Exchange—had formed his ideas of rational building. "I used to try to get him to talk about Schinkel," said Philip Johnson, "but . . . he would never really discuss [him]. . . . The only man he mentioned was Berlage. He never mentioned Behrens."[1]

The Amsterdam Stock Exchange is perhaps the finest and most original example of the monolithic style of building. The walls are monolithic brick, unplastered inside and out, and the roof trusses of the major spaces are completely exposed. It is a building very much in accordance with the Puginesque theory of construction, in that there is no distinction between what is structure and what is finish, or between what is structure and what is architecture. Ironically, although Berlage was influenced by Semper's ideas in a variety of ways, the Stock Exchange is devoid of cladding. It is strange that Mies should have admired this building in 1910. It has little to do with the work he did between 1910 and 1930—a period in which exposed structures are rare in his work—although it has great similarities with the work he was doing in the 1940s. Mies made considerable use of monolithic brick walls in his early work in the United States, although the development of the modern cavity wall and the use of insulation made this increasingly difficult. Mies's greatest problems, however, occurred in his attempts to use exposed steel frames.

Exposed iron and steel frames were common in the nineteenth century but became considerably less so as the twentieth century progressed. Modern fire codes require steel frames to be covered with fireproofing when buildings are more than two or three stories in height, are above a certain moderate size, or are located in dense urban areas. Steel exposed to the weather must be repainted often. Exposed frames require greater craftsmanship and hence are more expensive. Mies developed a number of clever ways of evading the codes to expose the steel frames of lower buildings, but in his high-rise buildings he had no choice. For these buildings he developed wall systems which gave an indication as to what the real structure was. There are many exposed steel sections in his work, but seldom are they part of the real structural frame. Although functional, they form an analogous structure to that which they clad. Mies clearly preferred exposed frames, and in many of his buildings he could have exposed the structure by substituting concrete for steel; however, he chose instead to retain steel framing clad in an ornamental frame.

If he really was fascinated with Berlage in 1910, then Mies must have had a bias toward monolithic building systems and the beginnings of an obsession with precision craftsmanship. The crystallization of his ideals, however, occurred in the early 1920s. Like most of his contemporaries, he was influenced by the revolutionary atmosphere of postwar Berlin and by German Expressionism. During this period, when many German architects (among them Gropius, the Taut brothers, and the Luckhardt brothers) designed buildings and wrote manifestos that they would find somewhat embarrassing in later years, Mies produced his glass skyscraper and brick and concrete country house projects, which he seems to have always been proud of; however, his writings of this period—which are some of his best-known—are as unlike his later work as are those of Gropius.

In 1923 Mies wrote in the revolutionary journal *G:*

We reject all esthetic speculation, all doctrine, all formalism.
Architecture is the will of an epoch translated into space; living, changing, new.
Not yesterday, not tomorrow, only today can be given form.
Only this kind of building will be creative.
Create form out of the nature of our tasks with the methods of our time.
This is our task.[2]

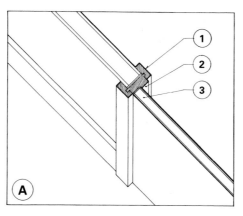

A

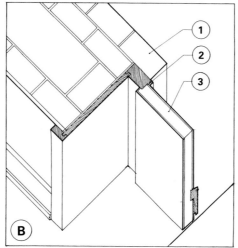

B

9.5

9.6

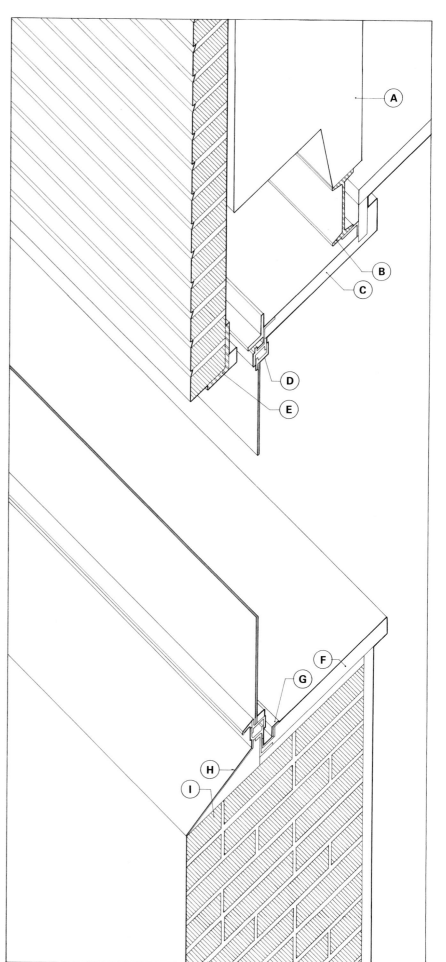

9.7

H. Lange house

Mies van der Rohe

Krefeld, 1928

9.5 interior trim

A Interior door jamb.

  1 Wood trim, rabbeted into door jamb. Although "Modern" in its geometric simplicity, it is traditional in that the trim is applied rather than recessed.

  2 Door frame.

  3 Veneered wood door.

B Exterior door jamb.

  1 Brick load-bearing wall. The door jamb is recessed behind the brick wall to minimize the visual profile of the frame on the exterior.

  2 Rabbet joint. This Z-shaped joint acts as a stop to keep the door stationary, and keeps the joint closed when the wood expands and contracts.

  3 Wood door.

  (Museum of Modern Art, drawings 6.70 and 6.86.)

9.6 interior

  (Volker Döhne.)

9.7 window details

A Cast-in-place concrete beam.

B Steel beam to support floor over window opening.

C Access panel to pocket for roll-down shutter above.

D In-swinging steel casement window.

E Steel angle supporting brick above. Whereas in traditional construction the lintel is exposed and becomes part of the architectural expression, this lintel is concealed.

F Interior sill.

G Metal condensation gutter.

H Sheet-metal sill. Metal, rather than stone, is used so that it will not be visible from the exterior.

I Brick wall faced with plaster on interior.

  (Museum of Modern Art, drawing 6.174.)

We refuse to recognize problems of form, but only problems of building.
Form is not the aim of our work, but only the result.
Form, by itself, does not exist.
Form as an aim is formalism; and that we reject.[3]

Essentially our task is to free the practice of building from the control of aesthetic speculators and restore it to what it should exclusively be: building.[4]

These statements have been reprinted many times and presented as a description of the ideas behind Mies's mature work. Nothing could be further from the truth. In practice Mies never denied that design involved an aesthetic choice. All of his buildings contain structural elements which are expressed and structural elements which are repressed to give certain readings to the building. Exposed structural elements are uncommon in his work except in that of the 1940s; analogous structural systems, designed to represent the structures they clad, are more common.

An important aspect of the revolutionary fervor of the postwar period was the concern with industrialization. In the early 1920s there was an obsession with traditional handicraft methods of building, and Gropius and Meyer (who had produced the glass-and-steel Werkbund Pavilion at Cologne in 1914) designed the Sommerfeld house, which can only be described as a log cabin. This attitude was soon replaced with an equally revolutionary zeal for industrialization, which was so popular that even some of the German Dadists joined in. Although Mies was always interested in modern materials, his attitude toward industrialization was lukewarm. He was far more cognizant than Gropius or Le Corbusier of the degree to which Modern forms were dependent on traditional craftsmanship, and he did not consider this necessarily undesirable:

There have been many attempts to find new building methods which have succeeded only in those branches of the industry in which industrialization was possible. The potentialities of assembly methods in building have also been exaggerated; they are in use only in factory and barn construction. The steel industry pioneered the manufacture of fabricated parts ready for assembly, and today the lumber industry is trying the same thing. In all other building, however, the rough work and most of the interior fittings are carried out in the traditional way—by hand work. Hand work cannot be eliminated by changes in organization of the building industry, nor by improving work methods, for it is just this hand work that keeps small contractors going. It has been demonstrated that the use of larger masonry blocks can lower material and labor costs, but this in no way eliminates hand labor. Besides, the old brick masonry has many advantages over these newer methods. The problem before us is not the rationalization of the present methods, but rather a revolution in the whole nature of the building industry. The nature of the building process will not change as long as we employ essentially the same building materials, for they require hand labor.[5]

In 1930 Mies wrote:

Let us not give undue importance to mechanization and standardization.
Let us accept changed economic and social conditions as a fact.
All these take their blind and fateful course.
One thing will be decisive: the way we assert ourselves in the face of circumstance.[6]

Mies desired order—not the "mechanistic principle of order," not the "idealistic principle of order," but the "organic principle of order . . . the successful relationship of parts to each other and to the whole . . . allocating to each thing its proper place and giving to each thing its due according to its nature."[7] But if Mies was indifferent to mass production, he was obsessed with workmanship and craft.

When one thinks of good detailing in Modern architecture, the names that most often come up are Greene and Greene and Mies van der Rohe. This is understandable, but it is curious in that their approaches to joinery and craftsmanship were diametrically opposed. The Greene brothers felt, as did Kahn, that the joint was the source of ornament. Their work is a celebration of the act of joining materials.

9.8

9.9

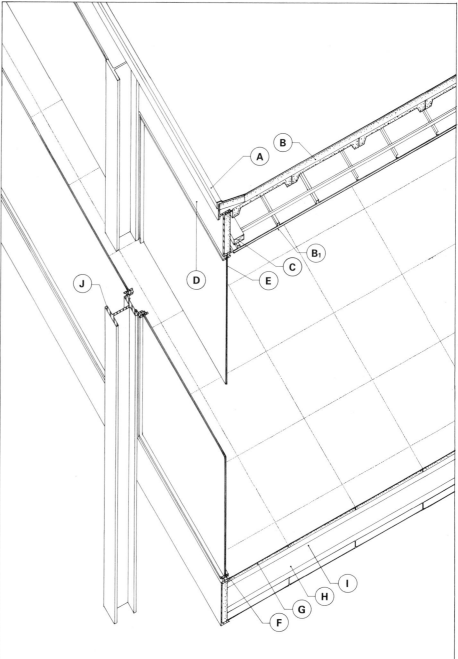

9.10

E. Farnsworth house

Mies van der Rohe

Plano, Illinois, 1950

9.8 exterior
(Hedrich-Blessing.)

9.9 construction photograph
Note the transverse beams of the roof (concealed in the finish construction), and the difference in craftsmanship between this frame and that in figure 9.13.
(Museum of Modern Art.)

9.10 wall section

A Steel coping with lead flashing. As in the Lange house, this piece is made from a rolled steel section.

B Roof construction: built-up roof on foam glass insulation on precast planks supported by steel beams (not shown).

B1 Suspended plaster ceiling. This conceals the complex steel-and-concrete structure above, reducing it visually to a simple plane.

C Wood 2 × 4. This provides an attachment for the plaster ceiling at its edge.

D 15″-deep steel channel backed with insulation. This is an unusually deep section for a channel; a wide flange section would have been much easier to obtain, but Mies wanted a flat surface on the exterior.

E ¼″ plate glass.

F Window frame fabricated from simple $1\frac{1}{4}″ \times \frac{5}{8}″$ and $1″ \times 2″$ steel rectangles.

G Travertine floor set in bed of grout.

H Floor construction. The bottom layer is precast concrete planks. A layer of insulation is placed on top; and then covered with poured-in-place concrete.

I Radiant heating coils. There is little or no space for ductwork in the floor or the ceiling. Radiant heating provided a convenient solution, since it requires only pipes.

J Steel column. Unlike the Barcelona column, the structural column here is monolithic and exposed. It is joined to the steel channel by plug welds on the concealed side, so no means of fastening are visible.
(Museum of Modern Art.)

Exposed fasteners abound, and each piece of wood retains its identity as a part of a whole. Often the exposed fasteners are ornamental, concealing the real ones below, but the Greenes' work explains the process of its becoming. Mies celebrated the joining of materials, but not the means by which it was accomplished. Exposed fasteners are almost unknown in his work. Important connections, such as column to slab and column to beam, are concealed deep within construction. It is often easier to conceal a connection than to expose one, but it is also often easier to expose than to conceal, and Mies went to extraordinary lengths to erase the marks of joining in his work, particularly in the steel frame. Of course, Mies is well known for his use of the reveal (the notch at the joining of dissimilar materials); however, this occurs only at such locations as the joining of brick to steel; the joining of steel to steel is seamless and invisible. Mies was no follower of William Morris; no one asked greater perfection of workmen than he. He demanded precision workmanship, and he avoided the use of materials that were not suited to precision; exposed concrete, for example, is absent from his mature work. It is perhaps for this reason that in his first buildings to make extensive use of steel, such as the Lange house, the framing is completely concealed.

THE LANGE HOUSE

It is difficult to believe that the Lange house was designed almost simultaneously with the Barcelona Pavilion. Both in form and in technology, it straddles the fence between tradition and Modernism. Its materials are modern (steel beams, concrete planks, and steel windows), but their configuration is not; it is essentially a load-bearing masonry building. The walls are configured in the loose, open relationships associated with Constructivism and De Stijl, but they do not attain the independence of structure and wall, or of wall and wall, that characterizes the Barcelona Pavilion. But this house does illustrate the beginnings of Mies's ideas on modern materials and structure, and of his obsession with precision craftsmanship.

Despite its large wall openings and the planar extensions of walls from its main volume, the Lange house is essentially a load-bearing brick box. The floors are constructed of hollow tiles (probably of structural clay tile or precast concrete). The voids between tiles are filled with concrete and steel reinforcing to create a ribbed slab similar to Le Corbusier's typical floor system. This ribbed slab is supported by steel beams, which are then supported by the wall. The exception to this is the set-back wall of the main facade, which is supported by a complex bracing system (figure 9.4). This is not the clarity of structure of which Mies spoke. It is an excellent example of form determining structure rather than structure determining form. But despite its complex nature and the modernity of its systems, the steel-and-concrete floor structure is neither exposed nor expressed; it is covered with a flat plaster ceiling.

This is not to say that there is not a connection between technology and form in Mies's early work. His pre-World War I work was traditional in form and technology. In the period of 1920–1925, when many of his ideas were crystallized, he built little, and when he returned to real commissions in the late 1920s he used building systems based primarily on steel and concrete. He was not alone in this, or even necessarily an innovator. The constructional systems of the Lange house closely resemble those of Gropius's 1926 houses for the Bauhaus masters, and many others (including the Luckhardt brothers) used concrete and steel for single-family houses. There were many Modern architects who continued to use load-bearing masonry with wood framing in single-family houses, among them Peter Behrens and Erich Mendelsohn, and architects such as Heinrich Tessenow continued to use traditional forms and technology. In October 1928 Walter Esters, the client for the house built simultaneously with and adjacent to the Lange house, complained: "The amount of steel has turned out to be quite large. This is mainly a result of the liberal use of Peiner beams and your foolish estimates of carrying capacities."[8] The extensive use of concrete and steel in single-family houses may have been due more to architectural dogma than to economic analysis.

9.11

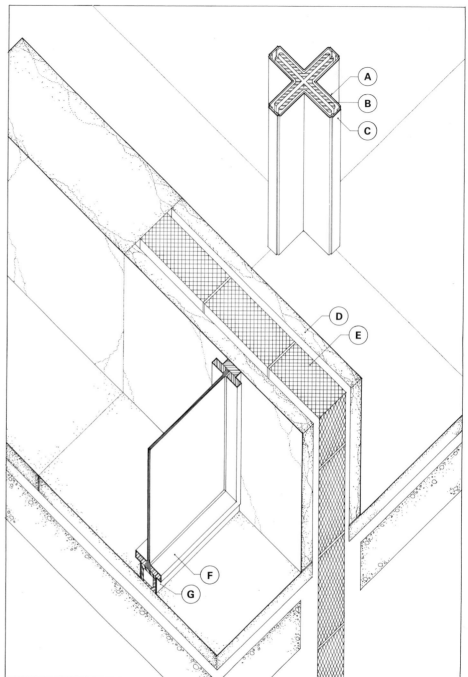

9.12

Barcelona Pavilion

Mies van der Rohe

1929

9.12 **wall details**

A Chrome-plated sheet-metal column cover.

B Structural column: four rolled steel angles bolted together.

C Chrome-plated sheet-metal cover, attached with machine screws (a rare example of exposed fasteners in Mies's work).

D Marble facing. The marble is made as thin as possible to reduce expense. Only the end pieces are solid, so the entire wall appears monolithic.

E Brick or concrete masonry-core wall.

F Bronze glass stop, attached to base with machine screws.

G Window-frame base, fabricated from two structural steel angles which are then clad with bronze sheets.

(Museum of Modern Art, drawings 14.9, 14.11, 14.14, 14.20, and 14.24.)

The most Modern details in the house are those of the walls, particularly the windows. Just as the traditional window is designed to emphasize the mass of the building and the support of the weight above the opening, the Modern window is designed to emphasize the membrane quality of the wall. The steel beams that support the brick above are concealed, and nothing in the brick pattern acknowledges their presence. The windows are pushed forward in the opening toward the face of the wall. The windows themselves are steel—"Modern" windows, as opposed to the traditional double wood windows used in traditional German domestic architecture. The industrial imagery of these windows is their only advantage, the traditional window generally being thermally superior and requiring less maintenance. The principal advantage to the steel window is its narrow profile, which by making the frame almost invisible enables Mies to compose with windows which are abstract rectangles. This is equally true of the small steel tee that forms the coping, which (unlike one of stone or sheet metal) is almost invisible.

In his 1947 book, Philip Johnson tells the story of Mies personally sorting the facing bricks, placing the overburned and thus shorter bricks on the side walls and the longer underburned bricks on the front and the back. The working drawings locate precisely each vertical joint, whereas contemporary practice locates only horizontal joints and allows vertical joints to be random, since they are staggered. One must admire Mies for his devotion to precision, but one must also ask if it was worth the trouble. Ruskin had said that the demand for perfection is always a misunderstanding of the ends of art. Mies was no disciple of Ruskin or of the picturesque architecture he advocated, but there is a question of the appropriateness of this aesthetic to the material at hand. In requiring the precise placement of the brickwork, with faces and joints precisely aligned, Mies was attempting to give the building envelope a more abstract, perhaps more industrial appearance (the abstract and the industrial were closely associated in the 1920s); however, the appearance of the finished building suggests that he may have been demanding a precision from the material that was inappropriate to its nature.

The interior details of the Lange house are unlike Mies's later work, but they are a point of departure for understanding the interiors of works such as the Tugendhat house. The interior trim, the door and window casings, and the baseboards are all simple rectangles without moldings, curves, or transitions of any kind. They are abstracted to a degree to which even Wright would not have gone, and in this way they recall the interiors of Adolf Loos. But they are simply that: abstractions of traditional trim. They are used to cover joints between dissimilar materials (at doors) and surfaces (baseboards), and they always project beyond the surfaces they cover. This is much more in keeping with traditional attitudes toward craftsmanship. Instead of demanding that wood and plaster or wood and wood meet in a precise geometric butt joint, Mies covers and conceals the joint. Mies's subsequent work was to depart from this attitude and from this solution.

THE BARCELONA PAVILION

Figure 9.13 shows the steel frame of the Barcelona Pavilion under construction. Figure 9.10 shows the steel frame of the Farnsworth house. The frame of the Farnsworth house was and is exposed; the frame of the Barcelona Pavilion was not visible in the completed building. If one looks at these pictures and if one understands Mies, one can see why. Each column of the Barcelona Pavilion is a cross made from four angles bolted together, and on top of each column is an octagonal plate. This plate has sixteen holes to receive the bolts of the girder above. Four pairs of these columns carry four wide flange beams, which form the main girders. Smaller wide flanges are connected to these beams to form the cantilever. Between the main girders are wide flange beams, which are bolted to the main girder by clip angles. Below the stone floor in the photograph is a concrete slab; the steel columns extend below the stone, where they are bolted to the slab, probably with a base plate. The deepest steel member in the Barcelona Pavilion is about 16 inches deep; the deepest steel member in the Farnsworth house is 15 inches deep. All of the joints in the Barcelona Pavilion are bolted. All the exposed

9.13

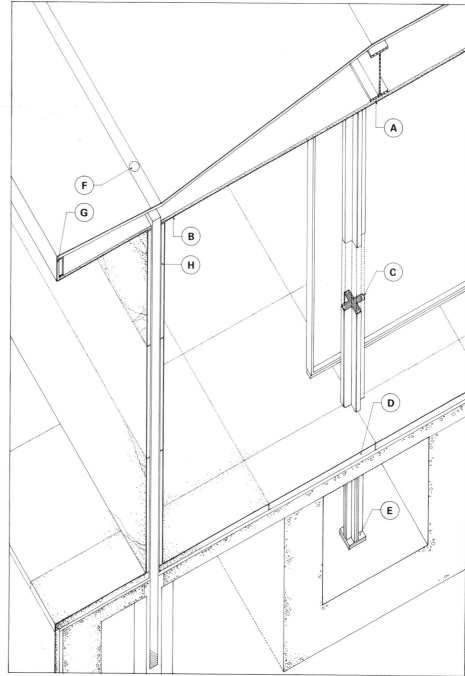

9.14

Barcelona Pavilion

Mies van der Rohe

1929

9.13 **under construction**

Note the crudeness and complexity of the column-to-girder connection, which is concealed by the plaster ceiling in the finished building. *(Museum of Modern Art.)*

9.14 **wall section**

A Steel beam. None of the steel structure is exposed.

B Plaster ceiling. The ceiling is completely flat, with no recognition of the steel beams above.

C Structural steel column, faced with chrome-plated sheet metal.

D Travertine on concrete slab.

E Detail of steel column base. This is set in a hollow cavity to allow for dismantling of the frame. In a permanent building, it would have been encased in concrete.

F Roof drain. The pipes for these are concealed within the masonry walls, as are some of the columns.

G Steel channel and fascia. The roof is tapered toward its edges so that it appears as a thin plane from ground level. The steel beams in fact require it to be much deeper.

H Brick or masonry wall, faced with one of three kinds of marble. *(Building Center Trust.)*

connections in the Farnsworth house are welded. The tolerance (degree of inaccuracy) of the steel in the Barcelona Pavilion is probably about ⅜ inch; the tolerance of the exposed steel in the Farnsworth house is probably less than 1/16 inch. The frame of the Barcelona Pavilion is crude, rough, and inaccurate, and it bristles with bolts, plates, joints, and connectors; the frame of the Farnsworth house is precise, monolithic, and seamless. Between 1927 and 1951 the technology of steel had changed. Mies's knowledge of the technology of steel had also changed, and his methods of buildings had changed accordingly.

Composite or built-up sections, such as the cruciform columns, were common in the 1920s. A column of about 14 inches, which today would be one piece, would in those days have been made up of angles and plates. Some architects appreciated and exploited the patterns of bolts thus created. McKim's Pennsylvania Station and Wagner's Postsparkasse would have lost a great deal if their columns had been monolithic rather than built-up. To Mies, however, if bolts were necessary they should be hidden. Hence the steel-angle columns at Barcelona are clad with chromium-plated sheet metal. The column base plates are hidden under the stone paving. The girders, beams, bolts, plates, and angles of the roof structure are all hidden from view by the flat plaster ceiling.

A great deal can be understood about the Barcelona Pavilion from this principle. Mies wished to conceal the means of connecting the steel frame and the inaccuracy, or tolerance, of this steelwork.

Certain joints of the Barcelona Pavilion are expressed, and some fasteners are exposed. The window frames are formed with projecting glass stops fastened with visible machine screws, forming a precise reveal between the panes of glass and between the metal frames and the floor and ceiling above. This detail was obviously derived from the projecting stops and trim of Wright's work, which Mies knew and respected, but Mies used this detail in his own way, to make the planes of metal and glass appear to float. This detail, the reveal, occurred more and more frequently in his work, most commonly as a joint between different materials. Like many modern details, this is an inversion of a traditional detail; the glass stop, instead of being recessed, projects beyond the frame. In subsequent works Mies applied this type of inversion to many other details.

Other aspects of the structure can only be described as *ad hoc*, and illustrate how different is the structural reality from the structural image. The plane of the roof is too thin to contain the deep girders required for the cantilevers. These girders are tapered at their ends to create the thin edge that Mies desired. In addition to the eight free-standing columns, there are others concealed within the stone walls. These crude compromises may be attributed to the speed with which the pavilion was designed and built; in subsequent buildings, Mies was more systematic in his acknowledgment or denial of the column. Other aspects of the Barcelona Pavilion in which structural reality differs from structural imagery are more important, as they continue to occur in Mies's later work.

There is no exposed structure in the Barcelona Pavilion; it is a layered and analogous building system, not a monolithic and literal one. As mentioned, rough cruciform columns are clad with chromium-plated sheet metal. The concrete base is clad with Travertine. The irregular frame of the roof structure is clad with boards and a smooth unbroken plane of plaster. Much of what appears to be monolithic stonework is actually thin slabs mounted on masonry. In addition to allowing for the concealing of the steel connections, this allowed Mies to use only thin layers of the expensive materials, and to veneer these materials with a layer of precision craftsmanship atop the rough work of steel and concrete below. But the greatest advantage of this system was that it allowed Mies to express certain aspects of the structure while concealing others. If we look at the Barcelona Pavilion in its completed state, we see what historians have always seen: eight free-standing columns supporting a flat slab, and free-standing screens that carry no loads. It is a conception identical to Le Corbusier's free plan, and, like Le Corbusier, Mies conceals those aspects of the structure that confuse this reading

9.15

9.16

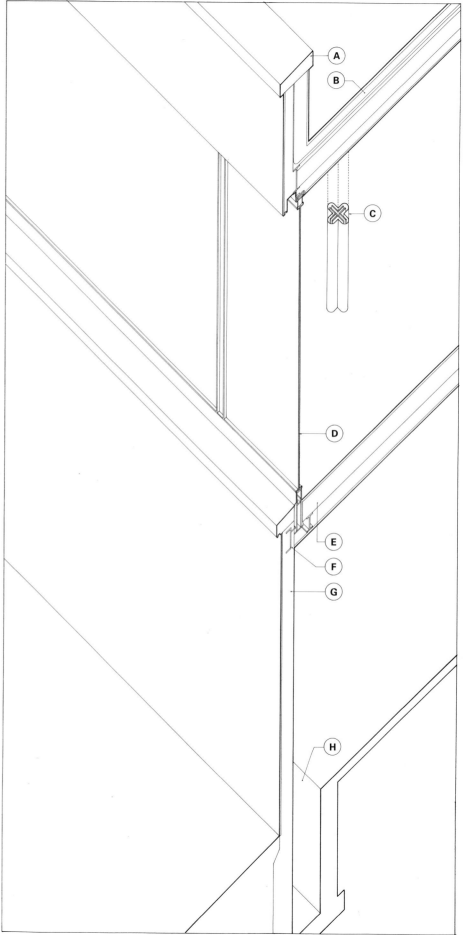

9.17

Tugendhat house

Mies van der Rohe

Brno, Czechoslovakia, 1930

9.15 **exterior**
(Museum of Modern Art.)

9.16 **under construction**
(Museum of Modern Art.)

9.17 **wall section at living room**
(Interior rail and drapery track not shown.)

A Parapet of masonry faced with stucco.

B Floor and deck construction: hollow tiles (probably structural clay tiles), covered with cinder concrete and torfoleum insulation and supported by steel beams. Deck is covered with asphalt and paving slabs of yellow travertine.

C Steel column: four steel angles bolted together, with chrome-plated bronze cover.

D Retractable window. The large windows are bronze, the smaller ones steel.

E Floor construction: similar to floor above, with linoleum finish.

F Steel channel.

G Wall construction: brick walls, with cement plaster on exterior and a layer of torfoleum insulation (compressed peat) covered with plaster on interior.

H Foundation, with pocket to receive retractable window.
(Museum of Modern Art, drawings 2.108, 2.249, and 2.265.)

---

of the building. Thus, we do not see expressed the concrete frame of the podium, the light steel framing supported the stone slabs, or (more important) the beams and girders of the roof. Had these been exposed or expressed, it would have detracted considerably from the concept of the free plan. If a ceiling is flat, partitions may be placed in any location, independent of the structure; if a ceiling consists of a grid of beams connecting to columns, the space tends to be divided into cells defined by the structural bay. And partitions of full height must inevitably follow the grid of the beams above if one wants to avoid visual and constructional chaos. What we see at Barcelona is an analogous, not a literal structure system, and it is the inevitable result of the layered system of building.

Another explanation for the predominance of layered systems in the Barcelona Pavilion is based on the materials themselves. Mies loved expensive materials, such as onyx, marble, ebony, and bronze, and given their cost it is somewhat inevitable that he used them as veneers. To have made the walls of solid marble, or to chromium-plate the actual steel angles of the columns, would have been ridiculously expensive if not impossible. Mies was careful, however, to preserve the appearance of a monolithic building. The last piece of each marble wall (and the short screen of onyx) is solid, so that the veins flow unbroken around corners and edges. Wagner, in contrast, exposed the edges of his veneers.

In that he favored clad construction. Mies's detailing follows the principles of Wagner and Loos. In that he reduced the cage of the skeletal frame to a diagram of flat slabs supported by columns, Mies recalls Le Corbusier. His systems of cladding are less sophisticated than Wagner's, and his methods of achieving the flat slab are less integral than Le Corbusier's monolithic concrete. The principal virtues of the Barcelona system are related to craftsmanship. By minimizing the number of exposed connections, Mies minimized the number of exposed joints and fasteners by cladding the crude structural framework in precise layers of plaster, stone, and sheet metal. He allowed hierarchies of craftsmanship in the construction of the building, from the very crude to the very precise, allowing each structural component and each material to be executed with a precision appropriate to its nature. In this regard the Barcelona Pavilion is much more in line with the development of modern building than Mies's later works (such as the Farnsworth house, which has a monolithic exposed steel frame and which required a uniformly high level of craft throughout).

THE TUGENDHAT HOUSE

Mies said that the Barcelona Pavilion was the first building in which he achieved independence of column and wall. He might have added that it was also the last, for he was seldom able in subsequent buildings to achieve an equally strong separation. Most of his subsequent houses employ complete and regular steel frames, unlike the distorted load-bearing volume represented by the Lange house, but the frame is usually partly concealed.

Figure 9.20 shows the framing plans of various types of Miesian pavilions and houses of the late 1920s and the 1930s. The first type, represented by the pavilions at the Barcelona and Berlin building expositions, consists of a regular frame of free-standing columns with walls arranged as (apparently) non-load-bearing planes. In the second type, represented by the Tugendhat house, only some of the columns are exposed, the others being contained in walls. The third type, represented by the Hubbe house project and other courthouse projects of 1931–1935, consists of two intersecting but independent volumes, one of which is a regular frame and the other of which is load-bearing with columns sometimes displaced by walls. That the first type was an ideal form is evidenced by its use only for exhibition pavilions. The development of the second type suggests that it was a compromise. Mies had intended that all the columns of the Tugendhat house be free-standing, but at the client's request columns in the smaller rooms were moved back into the walls. (The drawings of the Nolde house suggest a similar history.) The third type, in which wall and frame structures are treated in a more systematic way, is evidently another ideal prototype, but one that Mies developed to accommodate

9.18

Tugendhat house

Mies van der Rohe

Brno, Czechoslovakia, 1930

9.18 **interior**
(Art Institute of Chicago.)

9.19 **framing plan**
A Steel beams. As in the Barcelona Pavilion, all beams are concealed above the flat plane of the plaster ceilings.
B Steel columns. They follow a regular grid, but most are concealed within interior walls.
C Onyx wall in living room.
D Ebony wall in dining room.
(Museum of Modern Art, drawings 2.238 and 2.239.)

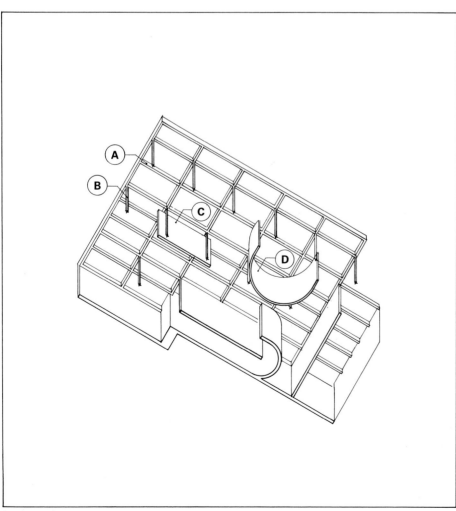

9.19

9.20 **structural diagrams of Miesian houses**
A Barcelona Pavilion. Except for the small room in the upper left there are no load-bearing walls, and all columns appear to be exposed.
B Tugendhat house. This is also almost entirely a frame-and-curtain-wall structure, but most of the columns are concealed within walls. They are exposed (although clad with sheet metal) only in major spaces, such as the living room.
C Hubbe house. This house (never built) was to be a systematic combination of a load-bearing masonry structure and a frame structure with exposed columns.
(Museum of Modern Art.)

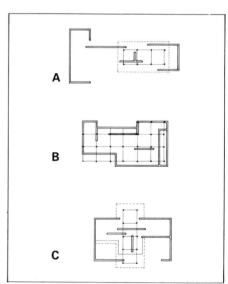

9.20

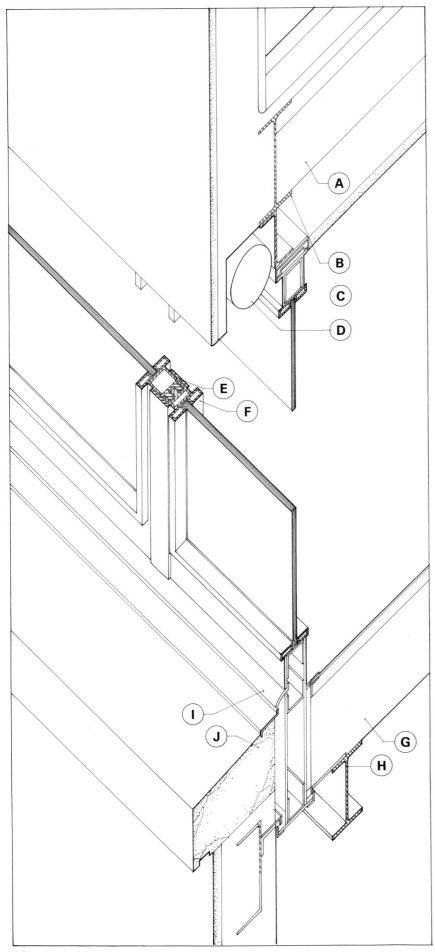

9.21

Tugendhat house

Mies van der Rohe

Brno, Czechoslovakia, 1930

9.21 window details at living room

A   Floor construction. (See figure 9.17.)

B   Steel beam. This is part of the structural support of the floor.

C   Plaster ceiling suspended from the structure.

D   Roll-down shutter.

E   Jamb of movable window. The interlocking shape holds the sash in place horizontally while allowing it to move vertically.

F   Removable glass stop. This projects in the manner typical of Mies and Wright.

G   Floor construction: linoleum on concrete-and-tile slab.

H   Steel beam. Since the floor is slotted to allow the window to retract into the basement, it cannot bear on the exterior wall. Therefore, there is a structural channel in the wall and a steel beam on the other side of the slot.

I   The sill joint of the movable window is the point at which it is most vulnerable to water penetration; therefore, it is provided with a metal drip cap above and a flexible seal below.

J   Stone sill. Compare this with the typical Corbusian sill, a thin piece of sheet metal. Mies's is much more substantial and thus more visible, forming a base for the glass portion of the house.

(A. Morancé, *L'Architecture Vivante.*)

9.22

9.22 ebony screen wall

(Art Institute of Chicago.)

9.23 details of ebony wall

A Details at ceiling.
  1 Steel beam. This is part of the floor framing.
  2 Steel bracket. This braces the top of the wall against the beam.
  3 Wood rail. This is cut in a circle to form a template for the curve.
  4 Ebony-veneered plywood.

B Detail at glass wall.
  1 Bronze mullion.

C Detail at vertical joint.
  1 Wood stud. The larger, structural pieces are made of a less expensive wood.
  2 Solid ebony connector. Rather than cover the joint with a projecting molding in the traditional manner, Mies recesses it into the joint.

D Base detail.
  1 Solid ebony base.
  2 Wood plate. Besides acting as a brace, this serves as a "template" for the curve.

(Museum of Modern Art, drawings 2.140 and 2.141.)

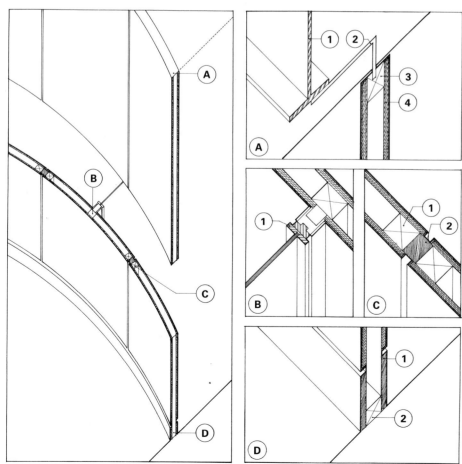

9.23

9.24

Tugendhat house

Mies van der Rohe

Brno, Czechoslovakia, 1930

9.24 **onyx screen wall**

(Art Institute of Chicago.)

9.25 **details of onyx wall**

A   Detail at ceiling.

1 Plaster ceiling.

2 Metal clip angle. All connections are made at edges of the stone panels so connectors can be concealed.

B   Detail at vertical joint.

1 Onyx panel, finished on both sides. (Compare figure 9.12.)

2 Mortar pocket to connect panels. This cements the panels together while keeping a hairline joint on the panel face.

C   Base detail.

1 Metal spline bracing bottom of stone panel.

2 Clip angle tying clip to steel beam below.

(Museum of Modern Art, drawings 2.207, 2.87, and 2.208.)

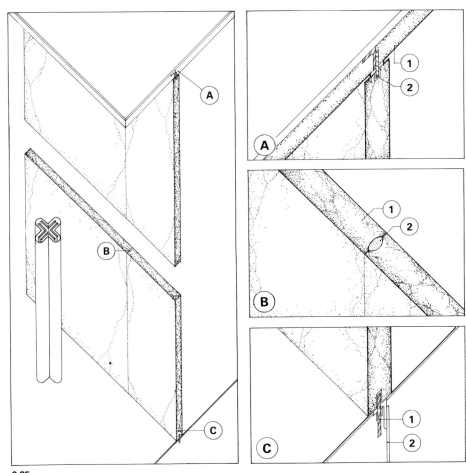

9.25

9.26

9.27

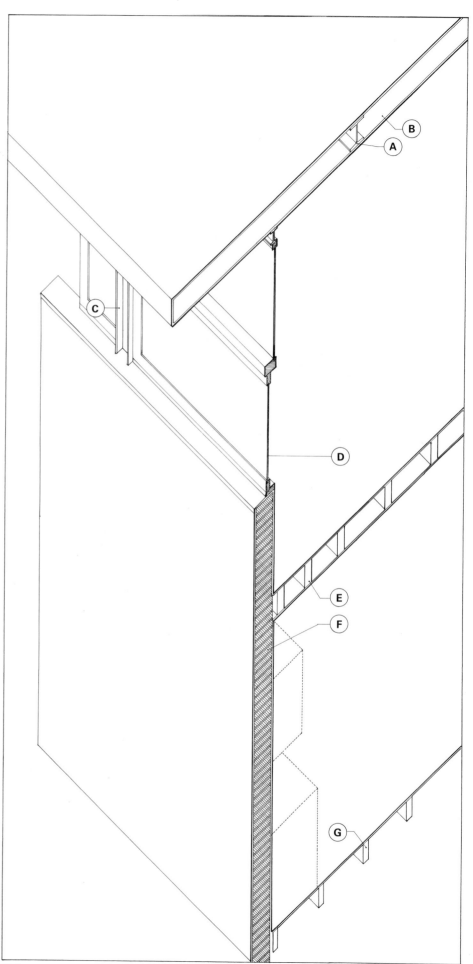

9.28

Schröder house
Gerrit Rietveld
Utrecht, 1924

9.26 exterior
(Central Museum der Gemeente Utrecht.)

9.27 contemporary photograph of interior
(Central Museum der Gemeente Utrecht.)

9.28 wall section at dining area

A Steel beam. Four of these beams support the wood roof joists, taking their loads to the columns at the windows. (See figure 9.32.)

B Roof construction: wood beams spanning between steel beams. Although it appears flat, the roof has a slight pitch for drainage. It is covered with a "ruberoid" mastic cement and has galvanized steel flashing.

C Steel column. There is no regular column grid, and some columns do not extend to grade.

D Wood window. The windows are of pine except for those on the east side of the second floor, which are fir.

E Floor construction: 20 mm × 15 cm floor boards on wood beams. The ceiling below is of cement plaster rather than gypsum plaster, which is usually used on interiors.

F Wall construction: solid clinker brick, faced with Portland cement plaster on both sides. Three different colors of cement were used to achieve the gray tones of the facade.

G Floor construction: 20-mm boards on wood beams.
(Central Museum der Gemeente Utrecht.)

9.29 Red, Blue, and Yellow Chair
Gerrit Rietveld

9.30 Berlin Chair
Gerrit Rietveld

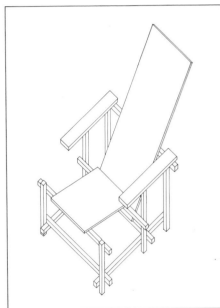

9.29

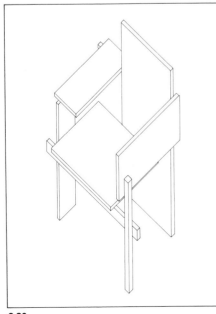

9.30

his clients' dislike of free-standing columns in small rooms. Mies was perhaps also interested in the purely formal possibilities of combining load-bearing and frame structures; around the same time, Alvar Aalto and Le Corbusier were experimenting with similar structural concepts at the Villa Mairea and the Swiss Pavilion.

Thus, the Tugendhat house is something of a transitional work in its wall-and-column relationships. It is a complete two-story steel frame, portions of which are eroded to form the upper terrace. Free-standing columns occur only in the major living and circulation areas. On the other hand, the expression of some columns and the concealment of others is quite consistent with Mies's method of abstracting a real structure into an ideal one. Note that the typical square bay is not structurally equal in both directions (as in a true two-way system), but consists of two major girders running in one direction and three minor beams in the other. As in the Barcelona Pavilion, this is all covered by a flat plaster ceiling. Again Mies has clad the structural system to create an abstract image of that structural system, one that resembles but does not precisely follow the real structure.

An important result of this process of abstraction is, again, the exposure of a minimum number of joints and fasteners. Figure 9.16 shows the steel frame of the Tugendhat house during construction. As at Barcelona, the connections are made with bolts or rivets. Most of these connections are hidden by the plaster ceiling. The steel column base is recessed below the slab, and the free-standing columns are given (as at Barcelona) chrome-plated sheet-metal covers. The actual steel columns, both engaged and free-standing, are a cross made from four steel angles. The cover is similar to that at Barcelona, but it is detailed so as to hide the joints and the screws that were required there.

The stucco walls of the Tugendhat house show an increased interest in layered as opposed to monolithic construction. The walls of the Lange house were solid brick, although they consisted of both facing and common brick. The walls of the Barcelona Pavilion had no environmental requirements other than waterproofing; they were brick walls on which the marble and travertine were hung. The walls of the Tugendhat house were deliberately layered, with each of the layers performing a specialized function. The wall proper is two layers or wythes of brick and a cavity between. Applied to the inner face of the outer brick wythe is a layer of rigid insulation (torfoleum, made from compressed peat). The exterior finish is stucco; the inner finish is plaster.

This wall system reflects the influence of Mies's contemporaries who were investigating industrial building systems. Mies first used this wall in his apartment block at the Weissenhof in 1927, where, as the director of the exhibition, he became familiar in detail with the work of other architects who were using this system. It is a much more sophisticated and proto-Modern wall than that of the Lange house.

The only monolithic wall in the Tugendhat house is the onyx wall in the living room, and its details show the difficulty of achieving Mies's precise and seamless style of detailing. Since both faces are exposed, each piece must be precisely the same thickness, and since there is no "back" to the panel, all fasteners must occur at the edges. This is not a great problem at the base and the top, where the fasteners may be concealed by the concrete floor and the plaster ceiling (figure 9.25), but at the vertical edges grout pockets and splines had to be fitted into the panels' narrow edges. This detail achieves a much thinner wall than that at Barcelona while maintaining continuity of the veining.

There are two window types: standard rolled steel casements are used for the small openings, while the larger windows are bronze, with profiles closely resembling those at the Barcelona Pavilion. The added complexity is a result of the fact that every other window here may be lowered into the basement. Mies again uses the "inverted" window stops here, which project rather than recede. He also applies the concept of inversion to other joints in the house; this was to become, perhaps, the most influential detail of the Tugendhat house.

9.31

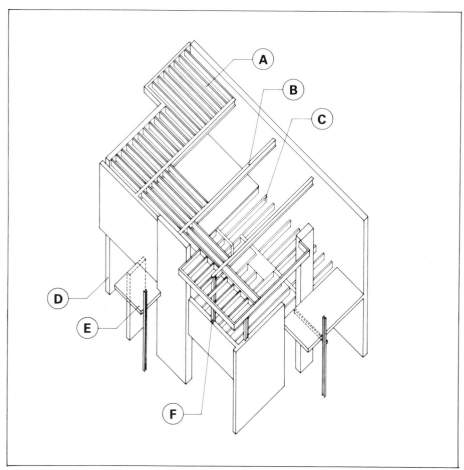

9.32

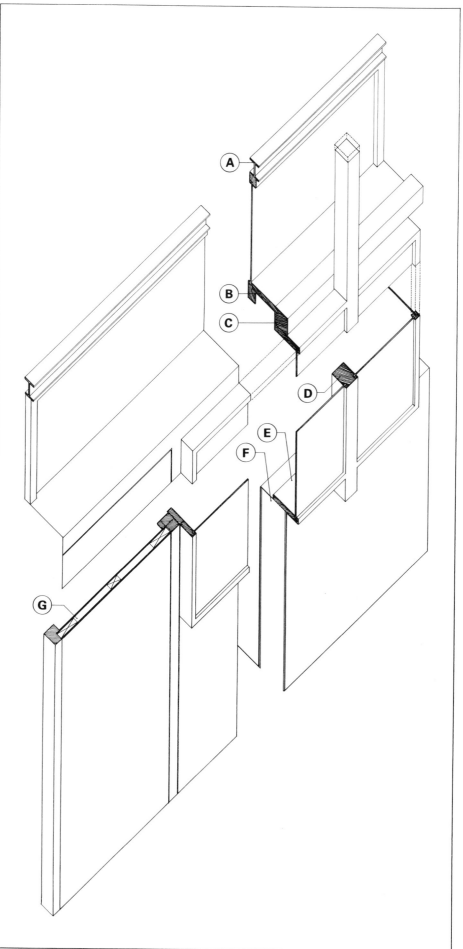

9.33

Schröder house

Gerrit Rietveld

Utrecht, 1924

9.31 exterior

(Elroy van Groll.)

9.32 framing plan

A Wood joists, about 2′ on center.

B Steel beams, about 10″ deep. These beams are concealed within the flat ceiling.

C Wood floor joists.

D Masonry load-bearing wall.

E Concrete balcony supported by steel I section.

F Steel column.

(Central Museum der Gemeente Utrecht.)

9.33 window details at studio

A Steel section. This may assist in supporting the masonry wall above, but is probably more ornamental than structural.

B Triplex (three-ply plywood) panel.

C Pine mullion.

D Pine mullion with square glazing bead holding double thick ($\frac{1}{8}$″) French glass.

E Interior sill.

F Base wall of clinker brick with Portland cement on both sides.

G Door: 1-cm triplex screwed to wood rails.

(Central Museum der Gemeente Utrecht.)

Figure 9.23 shows a typical joint in the Macassar ebony screen that forms the dining alcove. Like most paneling in fine woods, whether traditional or modern, it is made by veneering thin sheets of the ebony over a lower-grade wood. In this respect, it is not different from McKim, Mead & White's paneling in the Gibson house (figure 3.60). What is different is the methods of joining the veneered pieces. White's paneling is formed by applying solid strips of the veneered material over the joint. This forms a projection, which is softened with suitable moldings. Mies's panels are also joined by a solid piece of ebony, but here it is recessed rather than projecting, and it is square-edged. What was a molding in White's work had become a reveal in Mies's. As in his window details, Mies had arrived at the modern by an inversion of the traditional.

Although he did not leave Germany until 1938, Mies completed few significant buildings after the Tugendhat house before his departure, except for the pavilion at the Berlin Building Exhibition of 1931. He designed many houses, but almost none were built. He began to receive numerous commissions of considerable scope almost immediately after his arrival in the United States. There, many of his attitudes changed, including his attitude toward construction. He abandoned his layered and structural ideal in favor of one that was monolithic and literal.

MIES'S CONTEMPORARIES

The dedicated Modernist or the diehard Miesian might interpret the Barcelona Pavilion as the inevitable result of the state of steel framing in 1928, or, as Mies would say, "the will of the epoch translated into space." Given the state of technology and the course of its development, what options did he have? How else could one put steel, plaster, and stone together in an honest way? A comparison with two contemporary buildings—one steel and one wood—will give the answer.

Despite Mies's claims that he was not influenced by De Stijl, the Barcelona Pavilion would seem to be an answer to Theo van Doesburg's call for a new architecture in 1922:

The creative painter has to organize contrasting, dissonant or complementary energies in two or three spatial dimensions to produce an unambiguous harmony, and the creative architect has to do the same with his material. Not decoratively, to produce an effect which makes an easy appeal to the senses, but creatively, exploiting the contrasts of energy inherent in the materials. In creative painting, yellow and blue, for example, express two contrasting energies; in architecture this is done by two contrasting materials, e.g.:

Wood—compression.

Concrete—tension.

On the other hand dissonant materials are, for example:

Concrete—rigid tension.

Iron—elastic tension (a pulling quality).

Only those works in which the creative forethought of the builder has allowed the force of energy a maximum of expression are created works.

An iron bridge is good, i.e., it has been created, when the various materials are so organized and unified that a maximum of energetic force is obtained.[9]

The way in which Mies uses contrasting planes of materials contributes to the idea that he was influenced by De Stijl. Thus, it may be useful to compare Mies's steel buildings of the 1920s with a steel residence by the De Stijl architect Gerrit Rietveld.

It may seem strange to call the Schröder house a steel-frame building, as it has been described as almost everything but. Gropius described it as built of concrete. (This was Rietveld's original intention, but cost limitations forced him to use a hybrid of modern and traditional systems.) Brown, in his monograph on Rietveld, describes it as having conventional masonry and wood framing. In fact, the house

9.34

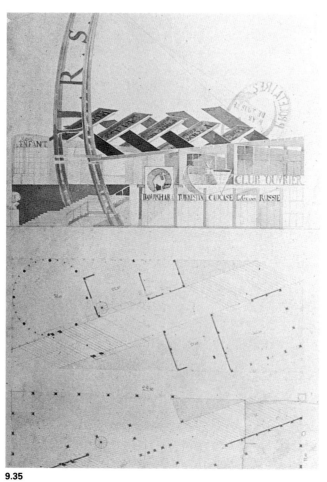

9.35

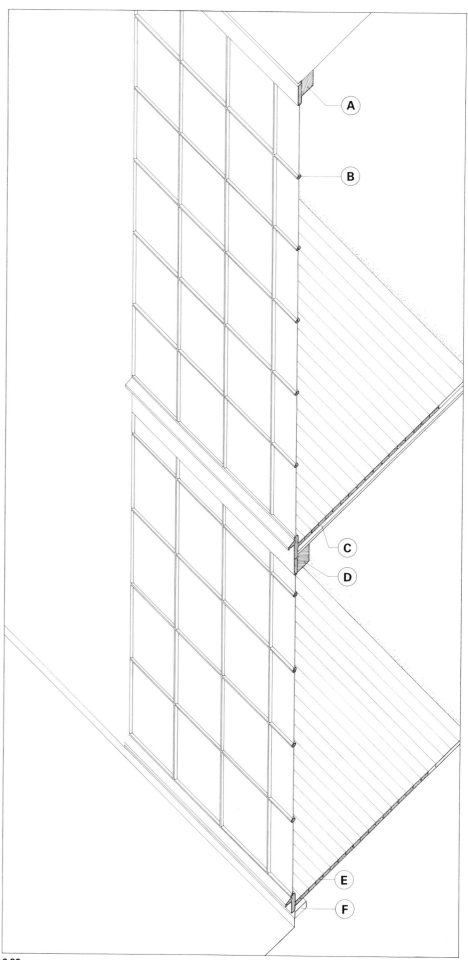

9.36

USSR Pavilion

Exposition des Arts Décoratifs

Konstantin Melnikov

Paris, 1925

9.34 **exterior**
(Eva Aver, Princeton University Press.)

9.35 **schematic design drawing**
Melnikov Archive, Princeton University Press.)

9.36 **wall section**

A   8 × 8 wood beam.

B   Wood window system. The mullions are small by today's structural standards for such a large wall.

C   Floor construction: floor and ceiling of tongue-and-groove boards supported by exposed wood beams.

D   8 × 8 wood beam.

E   Floor construction: similar to C above.

F   Mudsill.
(Charpentiers de Paris.)

contains steel, concrete, brick, and wood framing, and although its floors are predominantly of wood and its walls of brick, its particular form would be impossible without steel. An accurate description would be to say that it is, like the Robie house, a conventional brick and wood building that has been considerably modified by the introduction of steel framing.

Figure 8.20 illustrates the framing of a unit in Oud's Kiefhoek housing in Rotterdam. Figure 9.32 illustrates the framing of the Schröder house. Both houses occupy similar sites, as the units in a series of row houses. Despite its external appearance, the framing of Oud's project is quite conventional, with wood joists spanning between two party walls. The framing of the Schröder house can be seen as a distortion of this system. The end party wall has been eroded to the point that it is necessary to introduce steel beams and columns to support the roof. The columns do not stand free of the walls, as at Barcelona, but emerge from them. Grouped around the main volume of the house as a series of balconies, which are supported by additional steel columns and the walls of the house. This is not a pure frame-and-skin building, but a hybrid. At Barcelona, all roofs are supported by frames and all masonry walls are non-load-bearing. In the Schröder house, masonry walls carry loads when they can, but in other locations the roof and the floors are supported by the frame. Nor is the steel frame used only as structure; it serves as handrail supports, window mullions, and balcony supports as well.

Traditional modern historians, such as Gideon and Condit, saw such hybrid structures as transitional and impure, since they saw the ideal modern building as a complete, pure frame carrying a complete, pure curtain wall. But the hybrid building, although now outdated, had a certain logic in its day (as we have seen in the works of Richardson, McKim, and White), and modern architects were not so quick as modern historians to condemn it. Rietveld, Mies, Le Corbusier, and Breuer all experimented with hybrid frame and wall structures in the 1920s and the 1930s. In Mies's Lange house of 1935, two of the steel columns are replaced by load-bearing walls (figure 9.20). Aalto's Villa Mairea and Le Corbusier's Maison Loucher have similar mixtures of frame and wall. Given the complexity of these relationships in the Schröder house (columns that don't reach the ground, etc.), one might be tempted to say that Rietveld was indifferent to structural expression and that the ambiguity is unintentional; however, the evidence does not bear this out. Rietveld's later works distinguish clearly between frame elements and supporting walls. The design of his furniture follows the opposite trend. Whereas the Red-Blue Chair of 1917 consists of frame elements and supported planes, the Berlin Chair of 1923 is ambiguous; its frame elements are incomplete, and its planar elements are sometimes supporting and sometimes not.

Certain elements of the Schröder house resemble Meis's early work. Like Mies, Rietveld keeps the ceiling a flat plane of plaster, with no exposure or expression of the steel frames above, and he does so for a similar reason: to allow for uninterrupted movement of the sliding screens. Like Mies, Rietveld "floats" certain planes and walls, but in a much more obvious way. Unlike Mies, and unlike most Modernists, he does not use the thin window frames made possible by steel but chooses instead heavier wood frames. Painted in primary colors, they form an integral, if subordinate, part of the facade composition.

Another interesting comparison involves Konstantin Melnikov's USSR Pavilion for the Paris Exhibition of 1925. Although its forms originate in the same Cubist-Constructivist sensibility that produced the Schröder house and ultimately the Barcelona Pavilion, its attitudes toward structure and industrialization are opposite to those of Mies.

While unquestionably Modern in its forms, Melnikov's pavilion is unquestionably primitive in its technology. The only materials in the building are wood, glass, and plaster. There is no steel, no concrete. The structure is completely of wood. The windows, despite their apparent thinness, are wood, and not steel as one might suspect. Although there are large areas of glazing, the individual panes are

9.37

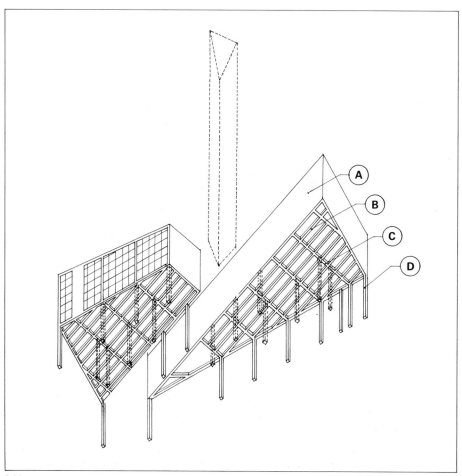

A
B
C
D

9.38

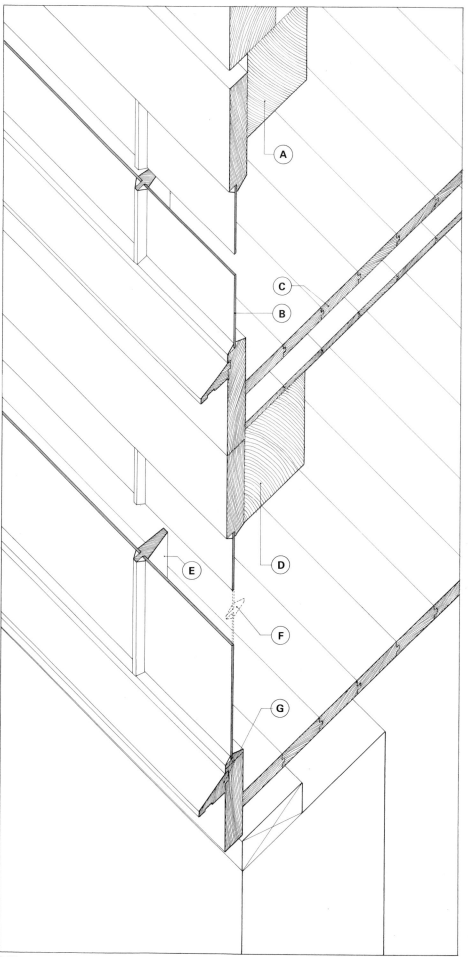

A
C
B
D
E
F
G

9.39

USSR Pavilion

Exposition des Arts Décoratifs

Konstantin Melnikov

Paris, 1925

9.37 **construction photograph**

(Eva Aver, Princeton University Press.)

9.38 **framing plan**

A Floor opening for ramp.

B 8 × 8 wood beams, spaced at about 24″ on center.

C 8 × 8 wood girders.

D Wood columns. Although generally located at the ends of girders, their placement is irregular.

(Charpentiers de Paris.)

9.39 **window details**

The building's temporary nature accounts for much of the simplicity and crudeness of its interior finish, and for its lack of technical sophistication.

A 8 × 8 wood beam.

B Glass.

C Floor construction: floor of 1″ tongue-and-groove boards and ceiling of ½″ tongue-and-groove boards, separated by two 12″ boards running perpendicular to them.

D 8 × 8 wood beam.

E Vertical mullion.

F Horizontal mullion. Note that the vertical mullion is much deeper than the horizontal.

G Projecting wood sill.

(Charpentiers de Paris.)

fairly small. There is little in the technology of this building that was not available to Palladio or Wren.

The modernity of Melnikov's building is a result of the structural arrangement, not the materials. It is an arrangement that has little in common with the contemporary work of Mies. Mies's pavilions were clad steel frames in which the structure was analogous and literal. Melnikov's structure is a monolithic exposed wood frame. Mies's floor and roof beams are covered with a flat plaster ceiling to make possible the free plan. Melnikov's beams and girders are exposed to form an irregular gridded ceiling, which largely determines the partition layout. Miesian walls are layered in construction and columns either stand free or are concealed within the wall; Melnikov's wall is a frame-and-infill system in which beams and columns lying within the plane of the wall are exposed inside and out, with glass and plaster as infill.

Melnikov's window-framing system has some of the traditional character of a Miesian building and some of the Constructivist character of Rietveld's Schröder house windows. Miesian mullions have a constant profile so that the projecting stops form a complete and continuous frame around the opening. Rietveld used different sizes, types, and colors of mullions to create discontinuities between the different parts of the frame and to give the identity of each element that is associated with De Stijl and Constructivism. Melnikov's glazing, viewed from the outside, forms a uniform square grid in which the mullions appear to be of the same size and form complete continuous frames around the openings. Viewed from the inside, the mullions vary in depth and are discontinuous, recalling the disjointed frames of Rietveld. The variations are not arbitrary but systematic. All the mullions are tapered to make them appear as small as possible. The depths of the mullions vary according to the loads they must carry. The vertical mullions, which must carry the wind loads from the glass to the floor and the roof, are the most stressed and thus the largest. The horizontal mullions, less structurally important, are shallower. Stiffness is required of the vertical mullions at midspan (halfway up the wall), not at its ends, and thus these mullions stop short of meeting the floor and roof. This, of course, adds to the general perception of discontinuity. These details also illustrate that the life of details and the life of forms in architecture are not parallel. Whether through tradition, influence, or coincidence, these same window details occur in Wright's Storer house (1923) and Aalto's Town Hall at Saynatsalo (1952).

The most important difference between the pavilions of Melnikov and Mies lies in their attitude toward craftsmanship and joinery. Mies's clad structural systems, continuous window frames, and revealed wood joints were all designed to minimize and conceal the act of joining and to emphasize the abstract continuity of elements. By concealing the structure, Mies conceals most of the joints—particularly the crudest ones, which occur in the steel structure. Those joints that are exposed are executed with a precision that must have been, at times, unreasonable. Melnikov, in using an exposed monolithic structure, exposed most of the joints at the cost of precision. It was a price he was willing to pay, since he would not have desired a Miesian continuity even if he had been able to achieve it.

Melnikov deliberately designed the windows with a Constructivist sensibility, allowing each piece to seek its own identity and celebrating the resulting discontinuity. His attitude toward the structural elements was the same.

CONCLUSION

Many things separate the American Mies of the 1950s from the European Mies of the 1920s: different compositional techniques (Classical symmetry rather than Expressionist or Constructivist asymmetry), different political associations (conservative rather than radical), and different building techniques (monolithic and literal rather than layered and abstract). Some things remained constant, however: Mies's love of materials, his respect for traditional building, and (more important) his attitude toward workmanship. Mies demanded seamless perfection. He hated visible joints and exposed fasteners. He systematically avoided the very same

9.40

9.41

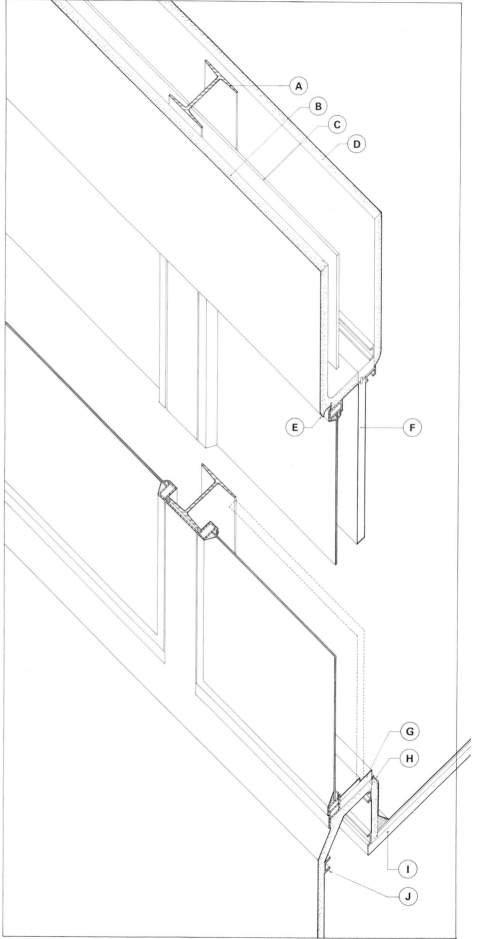

9.42

Lovell house

Richard Neutra

Los Angeles, 1929

9.40   **exterior**

(UCLA Special Collections, courtesy of Dion Neutra.)

9.41   **detail**

(UCLA Special Collections, courtesy of Dion Neutra.)

9.42   **column and wall details**

A   4″ H column, faced with steel plate.

B   Exterior wall: cement plaster sprayed on metal lath.

C   Insulation.

D   Interior finish: 1″ plaster on metal lath.

E   Drip and steel casement window.

F   Interior shutter.

G   Wood sill.

H   Casing bead. This provides a hard, even edge to the plaster surface. In traditional construction this joint would be covered with wood trim.

I   Floor construction.

J   Furring channel. These span between the steel columns to support the interior finish.

(UCLA Special Collections, courtesy of Dion Neutra.)

elements that the Greene brothers systematically pursued. Ruskin's ideal of rudeness and of perfection as a misunderstanding of the ends of arts is totally foreign to Mies's work and thought. The Constructivist desire for maintaining the visual identity of the individual member, although common in his formal vocabulary, is absent from his detailing. To find this one must look to Rietveld or Melnikov. It could be argued that the reveal is a celebration of the act of joinery, but as Mies used it—as an inversion of the traditional molding—it became a minimalization of a necessary joint.

But Miesian ideas of craftsmanship cannot be separated from Miesian ideas of building. Mies used layered and clad systems of building not because he was a follower of Semper (who he probably never read) or because he saw it as the nature of twentieth-century construction (although it has become that). He used layered systems because they enabled him to achieve the level of precision in joinery he desired. By cladding the structure in simple seamless envelopes, he was able to hide the crude structural joints, minimize the number of joints exposed, and execute these exposed joints with the required precision. Mies was probably quite sincere in his praise for Berlage's Stock Exchange, with its monolithic exposed brick walls and trusses. He did not follow its example because he could not execute it in steel and concrete with the necessary precision. When he began working in America, where he felt this degree of precision was possible, he pursued the monolithic ideal; the exposed seamless frames of the Farnsworth house and the Illinois Institute of Technology, where joints were endlessly welded and ground smooth, were the result.

Just as the European Mies must be separated from the American Mies, so must Mies the architect be separated from Mies the polemicist. In the discussion of Mies's buildings, little attention was given to his brief but well-known writings. Simply put, this is because there is little if any correspondence between the writings and the buildings. Mies had argued in 1923 for an architecture free from aesthetic speculation—an architecture of pure building, in which form was a result, not an end. It could be argued that this is impossible under any circumstances. The simplest steel frame can probably not be erected without some decision in which aesthetics plays a part. When this frame is clad, however, aesthetic decisions become mandatory. The cladding must emphasize certain aspects of the structure it clads while concealing others. Mies expressed the columns in the strongest way possible while hiding the girders and beams above a flat plaster ceiling. Why not express both columns and beams? Why express some columns and not others? If this is not aesthetic speculation, what then is?

10 Residential Construction in America: Rudolf Schindler, Walter Gropius, and Marcel Breuer

My house never pleased my eye so much after it was plastered, though I was obliged to confess it was more comfortable.

Henry David Thoreau, *Walden*

In 1782, in describing the conditions in the state of Virginia, Thomas Jefferson wrote: "Private buildings are very rarely constructed of stone or brick, much the greater portion being of scantling and boards, plastered with lime. . . . It is impossible to devise things more ugly, uncomfortable, and—happily—more perishable."[1] Jefferson, in his own buildings, used primarily brick, and although the American architects' preference for masonry was to continue to the present day, the economic advantages of wood framing were also to continue. Despite long-standing prejudices, the primary residential building system in the United States has always been wood. A typical present-day suburban house with brick exterior finish will almost invariably, on examination, prove to be a wood platform frame with brick veneer.

Sigfried Giedion was one of the first to recognize the platform frame as one of the great American inventions.[2] (He refers to it as the "balloon frame," its original manifestation. It has been largely replaced by the platform frame, a variation on it, in this century.) Had Giedion lived to see the domestic architecture of the Postmodern era, he might have had cause to regret his assessment. The platform frame met many of the criteria set down by modern advocates of industrialization, but it has also proved to be remarkably adaptable stylistically, accommodating the work of architects as diverse as Stanford White and Richard Meier. At the same time, while undergoing countless improvements and modifications and the addition of many components and materials since its invention in 1833, it has changed very little. The technology of a McKim, Mead & White residence of the 1880s is not substantially different from the technology of a Venturi residence.

Perhaps it is because of this flexibility that architects' feelings toward the platform frame have been so equivocal. Succeeding generations of American architects have seen it either as a national treasure to be cherished or as an archaic, "inorganic" system unsuitable to a true "modern" architecture. Frank Lloyd Wright carried on his own private war with the platform frame in the latter part of his career, beginning with the Textile Block houses of the 1920s, but the first great assault came from the Viennese immigrants Rudolf Schindler and Richard Neutra. Despite the similarities in their backgrounds (both trained under Wagner and Loos) and the similarity of their initial experiences in America (both worked with Wright),

10.1

10.3

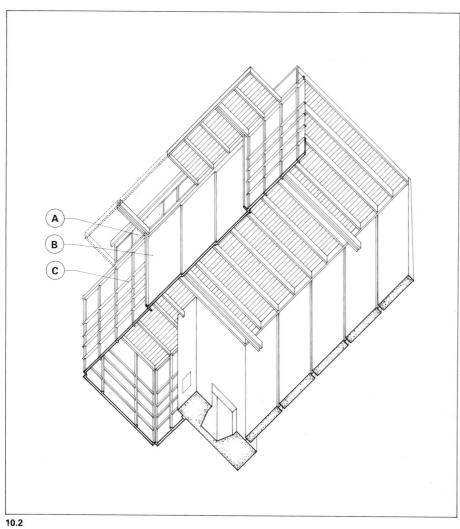

10.2

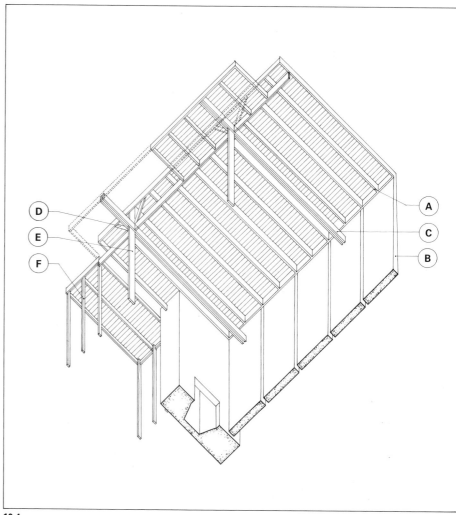

10.4

Schindler-Chase house

Rudolf Schindler

Los Angeles, 1922

10.1 Photograph taken during restoration. Note the diagonal bracing in the clerestory, which was concealed behind Insulite panels. *(Architectural Drawings Collection, University Art Museum, Santa Barbara.)*

10.2 **ceiling plan of Schindler's studio** (This view shows the finished building; figure 10.4 shows the structural components only.)

A Insulite panels concealing diagonal bracing. This is the only portion of the structure that is concealed.

B Sliding redwood-and-canvas doors.

c Window mullions. *(Architectural Drawings Collection, University Art Museum, Santa Barbara.)*

10.3 **interior** *(Architectural Drawings Collection, University Art Museum, Santa Barbara.)*

10.4 **framing plan of Schindler's studio** Note that few elements of the design are not part of the essential structure of the building.

A Roof construction: 3 × 8 redwood joists at 24" on center, supporting a deck of 1 × 4 redwood roof boards.

B Tilt-up-concrete slabs. These taper toward the top as the load decreases. They are connected to the slab with reinforcing bars in a grout pocket at the base. The spaces between floor panels are filled with glass set in grout with no frame.

c Double beam made from two 2 × 6's. The double beam simplifies the connection to the column.

D 1 × 4 redwood diagonal bracing.

E 3 × 8 redwood column.

F $1\frac{1}{2}" \times 2\frac{1}{2}"$ redwood columns supporting lower roof. These are also window mullions. Structural purists of the International Style would never use a multifunctional and visually ambiguous element of this sort. *(Architectural Drawings Collection, University Art Museum, Santa Barbara.)*

---

their responses to the American building industry had only one thing in common: rejection of the platform frame. Both these architects sought to reform and transform the materials and methods of the American housing industry, Schindler primarily with concrete and Neutra primarily with steel.

There was much in American building that Schindler admired, and much that he detested. He described the typical stuccoed wood-frame residence as "an inorganic, unelastic, plaster slab supported by means of an organic swelling and shrinking skeleton."[3] As an alternative he proposed, taking his cue from Wright and Gill, a system of concrete walls with wood floor and roofs. Unlike those two, however, he exposed the wood ceiling joists and deck rather than plastering over them. Between 1920 and 1928 he designed a series of variations on this theme, each using a different type of concrete structural system. His own house (1922), had tilt-up concrete walls; the Pueblo Ribera apartments (1923) had "slab-cast" concrete walls; the Howe house (1925) had slab-cast and platform-frame walls; the Packard house (1924) had gunite walls; and the Lovell house (1926) had cast-in-place load-bearing walls with gunite non-bearing partitions.

The house Schindler designed for himself and Clyde Chase is built of tilt-up concrete slabs and a roof structure of exposed redwood. It is an almost totally monolithic system, with few finish materials. One of the major problems with any building system in which structural materials and finish materials are identical is the need for a uniformly high level of craftsmanship and finish. Both the walls and the roof structure of the Schindler-Chase house presented difficulties in this regard.

The walls of Schindler's house were undoubtedly inspired by Irving Gill's work with the tilt-up system, in which the concrete walls are cast on the floor slab and then tilted into an upright position. In the Schindler-Chase house, the small voids between the concrete slabs were filled with thin strips of glass. The problems of uniform craftsmanship in the wall construction relate to the issue of tolerance. Cast-in-place concrete is often an inexact material, and the voids between panels in the Schindler house vary as much as $\frac{1}{2}$ inch in width, so that each piece of glass had to be measured and cut individually. Since the glass was set with no frame, there was no means of accommodating either inaccuracy of construction or thermal movement.

The redwood roof structure is a variation on typical platform-frame construction, with the joists more widely spaced. The craftsmanship problems here relate to the level of finish given to the wood. When wood members are exposed, the quality of the wood and the degree of finish must be higher than if the wood were concealed. Schindler solved this problem by lowering the acceptable level of finish. Few if any interiors by the Greene brothers have the rough timbers and crude joinery of the interior of the Schindler house, although roughness is common on the exteriors of their houses.

Pueblo Ribera was one of Schindler's finest compositions, but it was a technological disaster. It deserves close analysis for both reasons. The monolithic walls, formed by what Schindler called the "slab cast" system (figure 10.15), are 8 inches thick and are made from concrete mixed at the site and formed with reusable horizontal wood forms. Wood strips within the forms create a series of recessed horizontal joints, establishing the vertical module of the building and also hiding the cold joints between separate concrete pours. (Cold joints are the visually disturbing joints that are created when wet concrete is poured on top of older concrete that has begun to set.) The floor construction is similar to a typical platform frame, but it has larger joists (3×8 instead of 2×8) with wider spacing (24 inches instead of 16). Celotex insulation is placed between the joists and a roofing membrane and concrete topping are placed on the wood floor deck, but no other provision is made for insulation or waterproofing.

Schindler's conception of construction was the opposite of Semper's and Loos's. Those two men saw building as the cladding of structure with successive layers

10.5

10.6

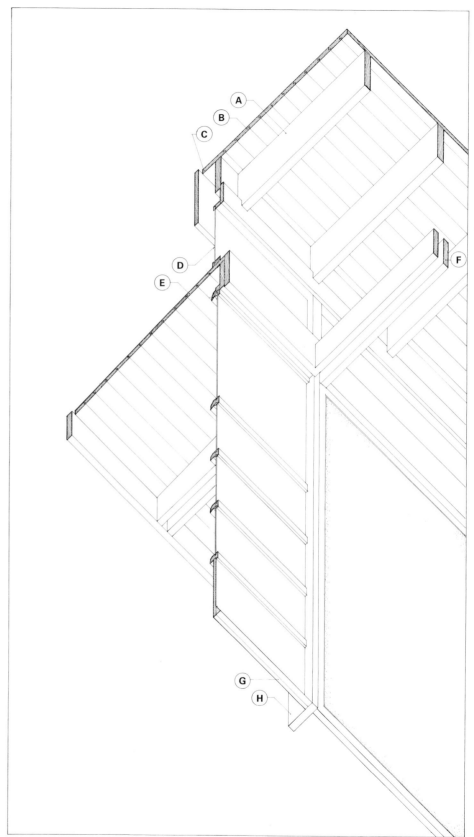

10.7

Schindler-Chase house

Rudolf Schindler

Los Angeles, 1922

10.5   **detail**

10.6   Detail of joint between two tilt-up concrete panels, photographed during restoration. The small reinforcing bars extend into the panels; the larger bars extend into the floor slab.

10.7   **wall section**

A   3 × 8 redwood joists, spaced at 24" on center.

B   Roof: 1 × 4 redwood boards, covered with composition roofing.

C   The composition roofing is turned down over the edge of the deck into a 1" slot between the deck and the fascia board. A better detail would extend the roof membrane upward to keep water away from the edge of the roof.

D   Clerestory window.

E   Low roof (similar in construction to main roof).

F   Two 2 × 6 redwood beams.

G   Window. (See figure 10.9.)

H   3 × 8 redwood column.
    (Architectural Drawings Collection, University Art Museum, Santa Barbara.)

of materials. Schindler wrote, in describing his own house of 1922, that "the traditional method, by which structural members are covered onion-like, with layers of finishing materials . . . is abandoned."[4] If these two attitudes are compared with contemporary practice, Loos is much nearer the mark; Schindler's monolithic wall has no insulation, no waterproofing, none of the successive layers of specialized components that characterize the modern wall. Schindler, despite his Viennese background, conceived the wall in the monolithic terms of traditional architecture.

The floor construction of Pueblo Ribera is superior to the wall, since it does contain insulation and building paper. But a comparison with the roof structure of Loos's Scheu house shows another important difference. While Schindler's exposed wood beams recall the houses of Loos and Wagner, his method of execution is quite different. The beams of the Scheu house, where exposed, are rough lumber clad in finish wood—"onion-skin like," as Schindler described them. In Schindler's own work, the rough carpentry is simply exposed. This idea was to become one of the great fallacies of Modernism—that construction could be made more simple, more economical, and more expressive by peeling back and eliminating these layers. The layers of traditional construction permit a corresponding hierarchy of the levels of craftsmanship required to execute them; the outermost layers can be composed of higher-quality materials executed with closer tolerances and superior finishes. In Schindler's system, since everything is exposed, everything must be of the same quality of workmanship, and although it may be rougher than traditional finish-level craftsmanship, it will not be as crude, and hence as economical, as traditional concealed construction.

Before the construction of Pueblo Ribera began, Schindler wrote to Lloyd, his skeptical client, to reassure him about the monolithic concrete walls: "Your banker's apprehension lest concrete walls not be waterproof is utterly unfounded. A well-mixed concrete of proper proportions is in itself waterproof. It is only to guard against possible carelessness in the mixing that it is advisable to add any of the well-known waterproofing ingredients."[5] Schindler's statement is not false. A properly mixed concrete wall can be waterproof. However, the client's general apprehension was well founded.

David Gebhard has described the unfortunate history of Pueblo Ribera. In summary, it began leaking upon completion and continued to do so for some time. The balconies were enclosed in the 1920s, but this did not stop the leaks entirely. In recent years portions of the concrete walls have begun to disintegrate. It is impossible to accurately assess blame after sixty years (the contractor may have been at fault), but Schindler did make some fundamental errors in detailing, particularly in regard to windows and doors. These were inserted into the form work, along with plumbing and other items, prior to the pouring of the concrete, resulting in a finished detail in which the wood is tightly butted against the concrete, with no trim or moldings (figure 10.16). This is the reverse of present-day practice, in which the frame is installed in an oversized opening after the concrete is set and the space between frame and concrete opening is covered with trim. The latter procedure allows for differential thermal movement between frame and walls and for dimensional inaccuracies in construction, and it permits installation of the frames at a much later stage, lessening the chance of damage during construction. Schindler, like Wright, allowed that sand from the building site could be used in the concrete mix to give a contextual color to the finish. This would not be allowed under current practice, since the sand might contain organic compounds that would interfere with the setting of the cement.

There is in these details something of a correlation to Schindler's ideas about indoor-outdoor living. In his early buildings, responding to the benign climate of California, he was inclined to minimize or even ignore the differences between inside and outside, making extensive use of sleeping porches, sliding glass doors, and outdoor rooms. He was at the same time inclined to ignore the environmental differences between interior and exterior; he often neglected the effects of heat transfer, thermal expansion, and water migration.

10.8

Schindler-Chase house
Rudolf Schindler
Los Angeles, 1922

10.8 exterior
*(Architectural Drawings Collection,
University Art Museum, Santa Barbara.)*

10.9 window details
A Redwood mullion. These project beyond the vertical mullions to give a horizontal emphasis to the windows. They are tapered to a point to make them appear light.
B Glass.
C Putty holding glass in place.
D $\frac{3}{4}''$ redwood panel.
E Grout base. This seals the joint between wood and slab.
F "Insulite" panel.
G $1\frac{3}{8}'' \times 2\frac{5}{8}''$ redwood stud with $\frac{3}{4}'' \times 1\frac{3}{8}''$ redwood cap. The stud supports part of the low roof. The cap acts as a glazing bead.
(Architectural Drawings Collection, University Art Museum, Santa Barbara.)

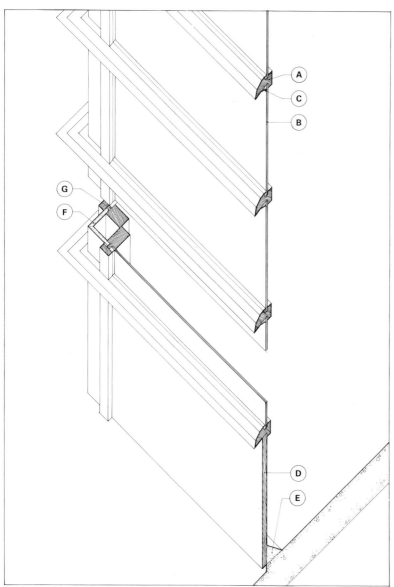

10.9

10.10

J. Howe house

Rudolf Schindler

Los Angeles, 1925

10.10 exterior

(Architectural Drawings Collection, University Art Museum, Santa Barbara.)

10.11 window details

A Redwood horizontal mullion.

B Removable redwood glass stop.

C $\frac{1}{8}''$ fixed plate glass, with $\frac{1}{4}''$ sliding glass pane beyond. The glass is set at a slight angle. The sliding glass is set in a small metal U but is otherwise frameless.

D Wall construction: 2 × 4 wood studs spaced at 16″ on center, faced on the exterior with 1 × 16 redwood boards and on the inside with plaster or redwood boards. Although this is a conventional wood-stud wall, sheathing and building paper are omitted (not shown).

E Typical redwood batten.

F 1 × 3 vertical redwood mullion, with slot to allow glass to slide. There is no weatherstripping or mechanical seal at the joint between the operable glass and the wood frame. Schindler considered the California climate so hospitable that he abandoned the idea of walls and windows as environmental membranes that keep heat in or out; he abandoned the traditional details for doing so as well.

(Architectural Drawings Collection, University Art Museum, Santa Barbara.)

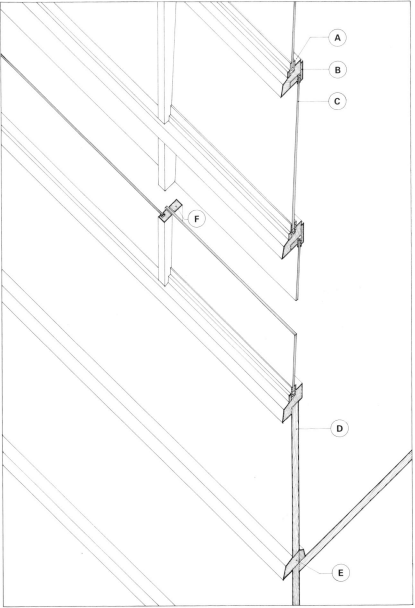

10.11

10.12

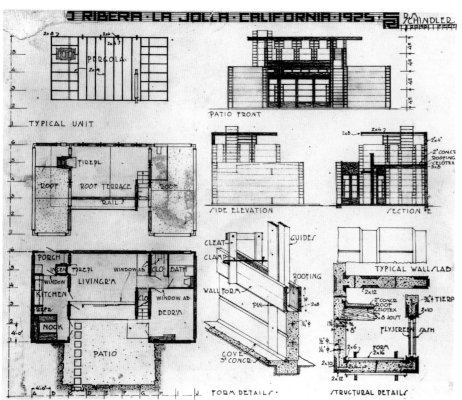

10.13

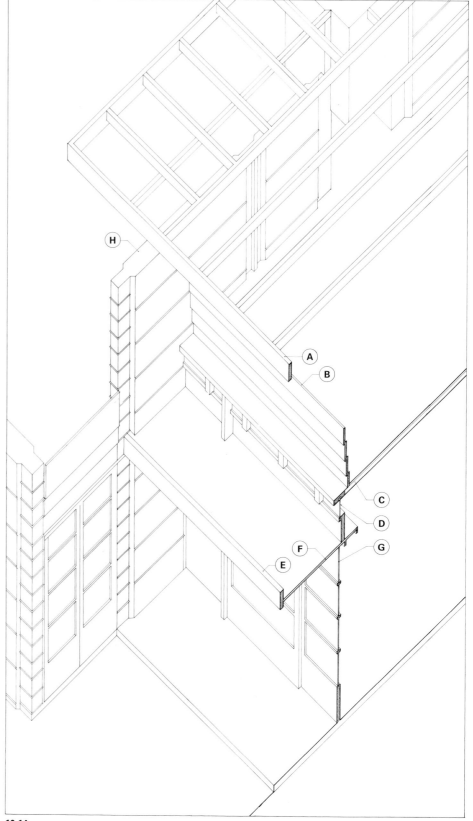

10.14

Pueblo Ribera
Rudolf Schindler
La Jolla, California, 1925

10.12 exterior
(Architectural Drawings Collection,
University Art Museum, Santa Barbara.)

10.13 plans and sections
The details of the slab-cast system
are shown at lower right.
(Architectural Drawings Collection,
University Art Museum, Santa Barbara.)

10.14 wall section

A Trellis. The major beams are 2 × 8
redwood; the smaller ones are 2 ×
4 redwood.

B Railing of 1″ redwood boards.

C Floor construction: 2″ concrete slab
on wire-mesh composition roof and
Celotex, resting on 3 × 8 redwood
joists spaced at 24″ on center. The
absence of adequate waterproofing
in this floor was a major omission.

D Glass set between 2 × 14 redwood
beams. This supports the joists
above and spans between concrete
walls.

E 3 × 8 redwood fascia.

F Construction of low roof:
composition roof on 1″ boards
supported by 2 × 4 redwood
beams 24″ on center.

G Sliding wood-and-glass door.

H Cast-in-place concrete wall. This
was built using the slab-cast
system illustrated in figure 10.15.
(Architectural Drawings Collection,
University Art Museum, Santa Barbara.)

Equally innovative in building techniques, but far more successful in performance, was the Howe house of 1925. Like all Schindler's buildings of this period, it is planned on a 16-inch vertical module and a 4×4-foot planning module. The walls and windows show his detailing at its best, although they are still riddled with technical problems (at least by the standards of the 1980s). The quality of this work results from the evolution of the abstract idea of the 16-inch vertical module into the actual details of the building and the transformations that took place during this process. Others had employed similar modules and detailing (notably Wright), but none so successfully as Schindler, who used the notches and battens of the materials to weave the planes and volumes of the house together. In the concrete walls the module is established by the notches left by the formwork; in the wood walls it is established by a projecting wood batten. The batten retains its profile, despite all the different ways in which it is used: fixed window mullion, sliding window mullion, and molding between wood boards (see figure 10.11). This is probably the primary reason for the sloping of the glass—to avoid weakening the batten by cutting notches opposite each other, top and bottom, although it also creates a crisp shadow line below each mullion. Not accidentally, it is similar to Wright's Usonian House wall of the 1930s, and it shares with this wall the same fundamental technical problem: in order to emphasize the horizontal joints, the verticals must be deemphasized by means of butted and mitered joints, which tend to open up during the constant movement to which wood structures are subjected.

The Lovell house, Schindler's best-known work, is also transitional in its detailing. Like his earlier buildings, it is organized on a 4×4-foot plan module and a 16-inch vertical module, but the plan module is visible only in the joist spacing and the vertical module is expressed only in the windows and the built-in furnishings. The three primary systems of the house are the five parallel concrete frames, the exposed wood floors of tongue-and-groove decking on 3×8 joists, and the non-bearing partitions of 2-inch gunite. Although the concrete frames are left exposed, the rustication strips of the slab-cast system are eliminated, leaving the cold joints exposed at varying intervals. The floor joists are exposed construction-grade wood spaced at 24 inches (rather than the usual 16) to conform to the 4-foot module. Gebhard has attributed this stylistic change toward a more volumetric abstract architecture to the influence of De Stijl and the International Style. This is undoubtedly correct, but the structural origins of the idea are in Vienna. Schindler's concept of a series of parallel foundations linked by wood floor and roof systems, as opposed to the more standard box foundation, was probably inspired by Adolph Loos's patented system for low-cost row housing of 1921. But in any case it is the interplay between the taut, white, paper-thin gunite skin and the dark articulated skeleton of concrete and wood that makes the building so memorable in that we perceive the building either as pure volume or as skin and bones depending on one's point of view. The crude but careful joining of gunite to wood to concrete adds to this, and the upside-down nature of the composition makes these details all the more visible.

The windows of the Lovell house, which to the modern eye are so essential to its character, were fairly controversial at the time of its completion and were the primary reason for the house's non-inclusion in the International Style Exhibition of 1932. Dr. Lovell himself asked Schindler to change to the more conventionally modern steel frames. It is somewhat surprising to discover that the window frames are not steel, given the length of span and delicacy of profile of some of the mullions. It is difficult to understand how some of the larger glass areas, such as those on the west facade, can withstand heavy wind loads. (According to Lovell, they could not, and they began to sag upon completion.) Here Schindler departed from the flat-bottomed wedge-shaped profile he had used in the King's Road and Howe houses. In its place is a mullion tapered to a $\frac{1}{4}$-inch face on both sides so that the mullions appear as only thin lines, and outside-glazed to a minimum depth to make the glass wall into a thin membrane (figure 10.35). Whereas the International Style used such membranes flush with opaque surfaces, Schindler's are always recessed and not used to create volume. Occasionally the openings are

10.15

10.17

10.16

Pueblo Ribera

Rudolf Schindler

La Jolla, California, 1925

10.15 detail of concrete wall

Note deterioration of concrete.

10.16 interior wall section

A Trellis. Major beams are 2 × 8 redwood; smaller beams are 2 × 4 redwood.

B Floor construction: 2″ concrete slab on wire mesh, composition roof, and Celotex, supported by 3 × 8 redwood joists, 24″ on center.

C Cast-in-place concrete wall.

D Glass in voids between beams.

E 2 × 14 redwood beam supporting 3 × 8 joists

F Construction of low roof: composition roof on 1″ boards supported by 2 × 4 redwood beams 24″ on center.

G Sliding redwood-and-glass door.

H 2 × 8 redwood column. The redwood beam spans between concrete walls, and this column serves only to shorten the span.

I Redwood-and-glass door.
(Architectural Drawings Collection, University Art Museum, Santa Barbara.)

10.17 J. Howe house

detail of concrete wall

glazed with ⅜-inch plywood in lieu of glass to create a De Stijl-like composition of solid and void. There is nothing innovative about this system; it is in fact only a modification of the traditional stile-and-rail system of building doors. Given the thinness of profile he desired, it is difficult to understand why he did not use steel, but it is one of Schindler's great virtues that his attitude toward industrialization was undogmatic. While eager to experiment with gunite walls and spray-on paint, he was perfectly satisfied to use traditional wood floors and windows.

The furniture of the Lovell house shows Schindler's attitudes toward structure and craftsmanship in miniature. Compare the bedroom table with a similar table by Frank Lloyd Wright in the Martin house. They are both small-scale conceptual models of the buildings they occupy, using the same compositional and structural systems, particularly the cantilever. Schindler's table is constructed almost entirely of 8-inch-wide boards and is based on an 8-inch module, as is all the furniture in the house (in addition to the fence, the stair rails, and the window mullions). Wright's piece has more Classical overtones, but it is in the joinery that the major differences occur. Wright's table top is a sort of over-scaled plywood. This construction allows a lower grade of wood to be used for the core, since most of the defects (knots, etc.) will be concealed. Schindler's piece is much more Constructivist. There is no joinery to speak of; each 8-inch board is articulated as an independent object. Save for the mitered and turned-down ridges of the top pieces (a means of avoiding exposure of the end grain), no concessions are made to the inhomogeneous nature of wood, since all surfaces of each board and somewhere exposed. Modern practice is, of course, much more similar to Wright's, relying heavily on the veneering of thin sheets of higher-quality wood onto substrates of poorer quality—once again, a process very close to the "cladding" principle described by Semper and Loos.

Gebhard and McCoy both describe Schindler's loss of interest in technological innovation after 1930 in favor of an increased interest in abstract form. But the two changes did not take place simultaneously, nor was the change toward a more conventional technology necessarily the result of stylistic evolution. In the late 1920s, as Schindler began to develop an aesthetic similar to the white volumes and planes of the International Style, he also developed building systems to construct them which were as revolutionary as those of the period 1922–1930. His shift to the use of conventional wood platform framing did not occur till later, and then for primarily economic reasons.

The Wolfe house was Schindler's first major executed project after the completion of the Lovell house, and his approach to construction here may be in part a reflection of the difficulties experienced in the construction of the latter. The skin-and-bones aesthetic implied in the Lovell house becomes dominant. A wood frame is partially covered with a taut skin of stucco and arranged in such a way that it can be sometimes perceived as a volume and sometimes as a series of planes. While obviously influenced by International Style buildings, it is different in its intentions. Le Corbusier and Gropius would not, in 1928, have exposed the beams of the roof and ceiling as Schindler did. They desired a much more unified volumetric effect, which Schindler opted to abandon in favor of expression of structure in contrast with skin. But more significant than the changes in aesthetic attitudes are the changes in technical attitude.

Like the Lovell house, the Wolfe house is a combination of new materials (concrete and steel) and a traditional one (wood) configured in a new way. The floors are formed of metal deck with concrete topping supported by double beams of two 2×6's with spacers. The double joists allow an easy junction with the columns (single 2×6's). On the open side they occur as individual columns; on the closed side they become studs in a wall. It could be argued that this is only a sort of overscaled platform frame with the spacing of members increased from 16 to 48 inches, but this dimensional change is a significant one. The essence of the platform frame is that its individual members act together as a unit, much as the

10.18

10.19

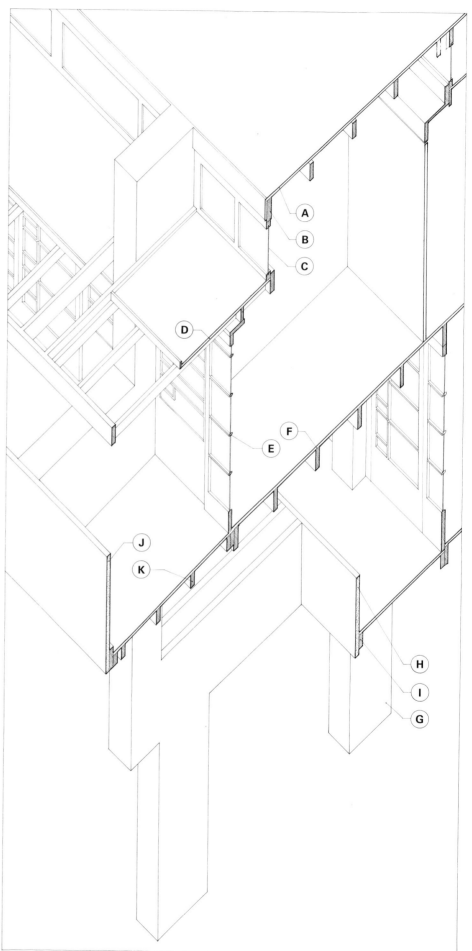

10.20

P. Lovell house

Rudolf Schindler

Newport Beach, California, 1926

10.18 exterior
(Architectural Drawings Collection, University Art Museum, Santa Barbara.)

10.19 construction photograph
(Architectural Drawings Collection, University Art Museum, Santa Barbara.)

10.20 wall section

A Roof construction: composition roof on 1"-thick shiplap boards supported by 2 × 6 redwood joists at 24" on center. Blocking of various sizes is placed between the shiplap and the joists to achieve the slope necessary for drainage.

B 2 × 8 wood beam faced with 1" stucco.

C Glass in wood frame.

D Construction of low roof: 2 × 8 redwood beams spanning between the concrete frames support 2 × 4 redwood beams (24" on center), sloped for drainage. A partial roof of 1" shiplap is covered with composition roofing, with edging of 1 × 3 wood.

E Wood-and-glass door. The balcony was later closed in, and these doors were modified into windows.

F Floor construction: 1" wood boards spanning between 2 × 8 redwood beams 24" on center.

G Concrete frame. The 2 × 8 floor joists are supported by five cast-in-place concrete frames.

H 2" stucco railing.

I Floor construction. In some locations, beams are suspended from the concrete frame above by steel rods.

J 2" stucco railing. The use of solid stucco permits these railings to be much thinner than wood-stud construction would have permitted.

K Deck construction: 1" boards on 2 × 6 redwood beams, 24" on center, sloped to drain.

(Architectural Drawings Collection, University Art Museum, Santa Barbara.)

bricks in a bearing wall do. The widening of columns and joists and the elimination of much of the sheathing cause the members of the Wolfe house to act structurally as independent members and to be perceived as individual members.

The fenestration of the Wolfe house is not extensive; most of the terraced openings have doors. It does show a careful sensitivity to the differing perceptions of the wall. One type of window occurs as an opening in the stucco membrane and is thus contained in the platform-frame wall. A simple wood frame is used here of the same width as the stud, so that the window is perceived as an opening created by peeling back the stucco and the window frame as part of the platform frame. The windows and doors on the terraces are of a different type. The doors are located between the 4-foot grid of 2×6 columns, and the window is an infill in a frame rather than a punched opening. The doors are set completely behind the column, while the window is set completely in front. This minimizes the visual disturbance of the different planes of the sliding door, while increasing the tautness of the window since it is uninterrupted by the column.

In 1933 Schindler developed a system of industrialized building, the "Schindler Shelter," which used both the 4-foot grid and semi-industrialized techniques. There were actually two systems, one of steel and concrete and one of wood panels, but the steel-and-concrete one was the preferred type. Referred to as the "garret system," it consisted of light steel bar joists, spaced 24 inches on center, sandwiched between two layers of cement plaster (presumably gunite) on metal lath. The cement layers were to act as structural skins forming a sandwich panel with a hollow center. Other components were to be industrial as well, such as the sheet-metal windows. The Schindler Shelters were not an economic or a popular success, and only a few were built, but they formed a sort of ideal building system for the projects of the 1930s.

In the same year, Schindler attempted to use this system in a single-family house for W. E. Oliver. His experiences here may have had a major effect on his subsequent attitude towards structural innovation. There are three separate versions of this house. The first radical redesign occurred when the site was changed. The second design is an outstanding example of Schindler's De Stijl style, but it is not one of his more systematic designs (although it does conform to the 4-foot grid). The site was narrow, and the building's corners were chamfered to fit. A deed restriction required a sloped roof; Schindler used this restriction playfully to his advantage so that the house appears to be a flat-roofed Corbusian volume on the entry side but is in reality a hip roof, visible at the rear. The result is a very complex volume that does not lend itself easily to the use of standardized components.

But the constraints and opportunities of the site only partially account for its complexity, for there are second and third versions of the design on the new site. The second version, designed in 1933, applies the system of the Schindler Shelters (figures 10.28, 10.29). The framing is of steel bar joists, irregular in shape, covered with a layer of gunite on each side. This structure is supported by a concrete frame. The frame is not of the typical Modernist "skin and bones" or "column and curtain wall" type, as the columns are contained and concealed within the walls. It resembles closely the system proposed by Le Corbusier for the construction of the "Citrohan" houses of 1921—a system that Le Corbusier was never able to execute.

Obviously this system was too expensive, and in 1934 Schindler produced a third version of the house, using primarily a wood platform frame. The large strip windows and cantilevers of the original design were impossible in wood framing, and steel beams and columns were substituted for the concrete beams of the second design—but only where wood would not do the job. The primary system is thus a platform frame modified by steel framing. The visual differences between the second and third designs are small, but the structural differences are considerable. In the earlier design the skin of the building is an integral part of the structure. In the latter, the concealed wood sheathing does the work of the gunite.

10.21

10.22

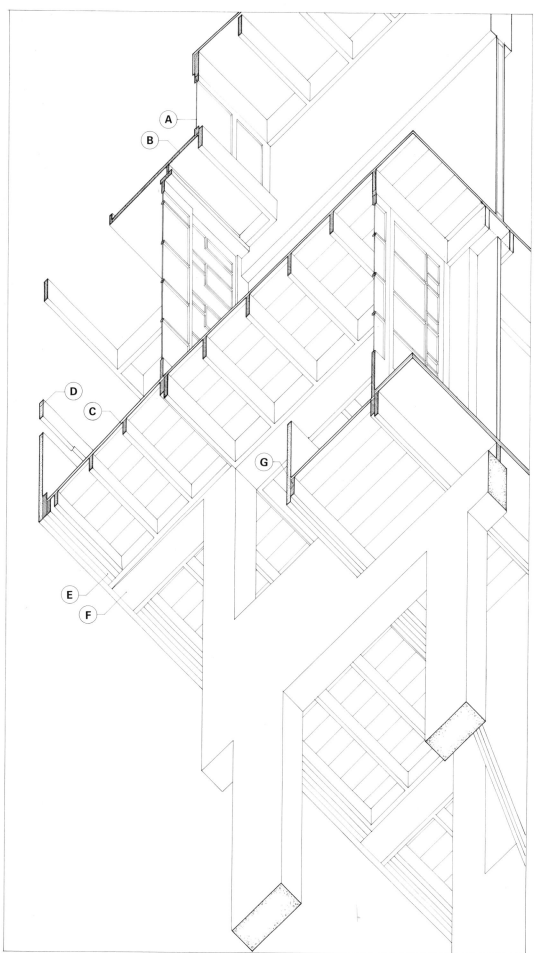

10.23

P. Lovell house

Rudolf Schindler

Newport Beach, California, 1926

10.21 interior

(Architectural Drawings Collection,
University Art Museum, Santa Barbara.)

10.22 interior

(Architectural Drawings Collection,
University Art Museum, Santa Barbara.)

10.23 interior wall section

A Clerestory window.

B Balcony roof: 1″ shiplap covered
   with composition roof on 2 × 8
   redwood beams.

c Floor construction: 1″ wood boards
   spanning between 2 × 8 redwood
   beams, 24″ on center.

D 2″ solid stucco balcony rail.

E Deck construction: 1″ boards on 2
   × 6 redwood beams, 24″ on center.

F Concrete frame. There are no
   concrete elements tying the frames
   together, but there are diagonal
   steel rods hidden in the walls.

G Second-floor construction (same as
   C above, except that some beams
   are supported by tie rods
   suspended from the floor above).

(Architectural Drawings Collection,
University Art Museum, Santa Barbara.)

The stucco has become only another onion skin of cladding. After ten years of experimentation, Schindler had arrived at a system of building that did not differ substantially from that used by Wright in the Robie house twenty years earlier or from that used by Meier in the Douglass house fifty years later.

Mention should be made of the windows of the Oliver house, which were the one holdover from the Schindler Shelter concept. They are steel, but unlike the typical rolled steel sections used by Gropius and Duiker they are made from bent sheets of metal. Normally this had been done by forming the metal into a tube, a shape that is structurally efficient but is thick and bulky and resembles wood after painting. Schindler used the metal primarily in the form of angles, so that the mullions are smaller, the glass is tauter, and the window is more of a glass membrane. It is a detail of elegance in comparison with Schindler's other work. The system has not seen general application and was never mass-produced, but Kahn was to use it effectively in many of his later buildings.

Schindler never really lost interest in technological innovation. There are many experiments in his later work, but they are most often attempts to modify or improve, rather than replace, existing systems. Although most of his residential buildings after 1930 are platform-frame wood houses, they do contain such items as precast concrete floor systems and custom-designed steel windows. With the lifting of the constraints caused by the Depression and World War II, he proposed a panelized system of wood construction similar to that used in the Case Study houses, and in the 1940s he made use of the Schindler Frame, a modification of the platform frame.

None of Schindler's many innovations were picked up by other architects. Despite the fact that we now can see Schindler as an architect equal if not superior to Gropius and Neutra, his evaluation of modern construction, in comparison to theirs, was far off the mark. Single-family houses of poured-in-place concrete are a rarity in the United States. For both economic and aesthetic reasons, the Schindler Shelter and the Schindler Frame were never utilized on a large or even a modest scale, and although mass-produced wood-panel houses have become a reality, they are "modular" only in the broadest sense of the term. Schindler's most idiosyncratic idea was his concept of eliminating the distinction between finish-grade and construction-grade work, a concept that gives some of his work what Charles Moore calls a "nail it up yourself shack" quality. But it is more than an idiosyncrasy; it is an idea that recurs throughout the history of modernism.

Richard Neutra arrived in California in 1926 and immediately began a campaign to reform American, if not international, systems of construction. Despite the similarity of his background and Schindler's (both men were influenced by Loos, Wagner, and Wright), Neutra's analysis of the problems of American building was quite different from Schindler's and much more in line with the mainstream of Modernism in Europe. The problem for Neutra was industrialization, and the solution was steel: steel framing, steel windows, and (when possible) cladding with steel panels. He was not so much hostile to traditional wood platform-frame construction as he was indifferent to it. Like other Modernists of the 1920s, he felt industrialization would mean that small-scale residences would be built with the same materials and techniques as large-scale commercial and institutional buildings.

The best-known and most spectacular of Neutra's buildings is the Lovell town house (figure 9.40). It has some similiarities to Wright's and Schindler's work—particularly in its use of the planning module, which is ubiquitous in Modern architecture in California—but it has much more in common with contemporary European work. Steel window units are "standardized" in double casement units, in contrast to the complex rhythms of Schindler. The structural columns are exposed, but the floor and roof structures (steel joists, also on a module) are concealed by flat plaster ceilings.

10.24

10.25

10.26

C. H. Wolfe house

Rudolf Schindler

Catalina, California, 1934

10.24 exterior

*(Architectural Drawings Collection,
University Art Museum, Santa Barbara.)*

10.25 interior

*(Architectural Drawings Collection,
University Art Museum, Santa Barbara.)*

10.26 interior wall section

A Roof deck: 2" of concrete on corrugated metal deck. The standard deck of 1" boards is insufficient to span the 4' between double beams.

B Beam made of two 2 × 10 redwood beams. Doubling the beam simplifies the connection to the 2 × 6 column.

C 2 × 6 wood columns.

D Balcony construction. The deck is sloped but is otherwise identical in construction to the interior floor.

E Planter made from 1" solid plaster and wire mesh.

F Wood-and-glass windows and doors.

*(Architectural Drawings Collection,
University Art Museum, Santa Barbara.)*

Neutra's structural system is less ambitious then those of his European contemporaries, such as the typical Corbusian 5-meter grid of concrete and the typical Miesian 20-foot steel grid. Neutra's system is a tightly spaced series of H columns forming rectilinear bays, mostly located on the exterior walls. This is not an efficient system by modern standards, owing to the large number of footings and columns, but it does acknowledge that steel structures, being "one way," are much better suited to rectilinear bays than to square bays. This system seems original, at least to domestic architecture, and seems to have been developed with the Bethlehem Steel Corporation, which helped finance the house (although its tightly spaced grid of columns resembles that of Wagner's Karlsplatz Station).

While obviously a skeletal frame building, the Lovell house does not have the skin-and-bones structure that we associate with European Modernists. The typical Corbusian villa has free-standing columns a foot or so inside the exterior wall. Neutra's H-shaped steel columns are placed within the wall and are exposed by peeling away the layers of stucco and plaster. This layering effect is reinforced by the detailing of the windows, panels, and steel columns. All are located in such a way the the wall is made up of two planes of each face. On the exterior a plane of white stucco stands several inches in front of the steel plane made up of the outside faces of the steel windows, columns, and panels. On the inside is a comparable system in which a plane of plaster stands in front of the plane made by the interior shutters. The outside layer is progressively peeled away toward the bottom of the building until only the columns remain.

Neutra's concept of the wall was much closer to Semper's idea of cladding than Schindler's, and in many ways it was the opposite of Schindler's concept of the monolithic building, in which all levels of workmanship would be the same. Neutra recognized the complexity of modern building systems. He wrote in the 1950s:

Once upon a time, the material specifications had been short and simple. For the Parthenon they were marble, quarried in the neighborhood. This was the only material employed, from flooring to roofing. Now, the material specifications, not only of a huge monument but even of a little roadside service station, could easily fill a heavy tome if they were to be pounded out on a typewriter. There are fire-enameled sheet metal and glazing and structural steel, conduits, wires, pipes, plumbing installations, sash, roofing, plated hardware, and what-have-you. Countless finished products of complex industries which are located in many sections of the country—of the globe—make up the "raw materials" of even the smallest building.[6]

Neutra applied the system of steel framing used in the Lovell house, to several other houses in the 1930s, making additions and improvements. Metal panels were used for exterior finish in the Beard house (1935) and the Von Sternberg house (1936). The Beckstrand house employed radiant heating and shop-welded steel strip windows. But by 1936, when he designed the Brown house, Neutra had adopted the use of standard wood joists supported by steel columns (similar to those of the Gropius house), and by 1937, in the McIntosh house, he was using standard wood construction. Neutra cites as his reason for this the desires of his clients, but the high cost of small-scale steel frames must have been a factor. The Lovell house, for example, cost $50,000 more than projected, despite a substantial subsidy from Bethlehem Steel.

Neutra saw the future more clearly than Schindler in his recognition that modern construction would involve multiple components and layered construction, but he erred badly in applying the methods and standards of large-scale steel structures to residential buildings. The very characteristics of the steel frame that Neutra found so virtuous (exactness, standardization, and organized methods of design and production) made it unsuitable for residential construction, and the very qualities of the platform frame that he most disliked (imprecision, lack of sophistication, and the crude and simple method of fabrication and assembly) were those that made it suitable. It is one of the great merits of the platform frame, in

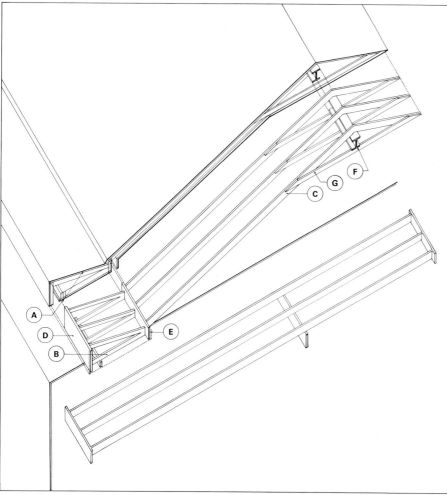

10.27

W. E. Oliver house

Rudolf Schindler

Los Angeles, 1934

10.27 framing as built
A Roof deck of 1 × 8 boards.
B 2 × 4 wood joists, 16″ on center.
C 2 × 6 wood joists, 16″ on center.
D 2 × 14 wood fascia beam.
E 2 × 12 wood beam.
F 8″-deep steel I beam supporting rafters.
G 2 × 4 wood collar beam.
(Architectural Drawings Collection, University Art Museum, Santa Barbara.)

10.28 proposed steel-and-gunite framing
A 1″ cement plaster on wire mesh, top and bottom.
B Trusses at 16″ on center, made from galvanized iron sheet metal braked into U shape.
C Cast-in-place concrete beam.
D Concrete beam.
(Architectural Drawings Collection, University Art Museum, Santa Barbara.)

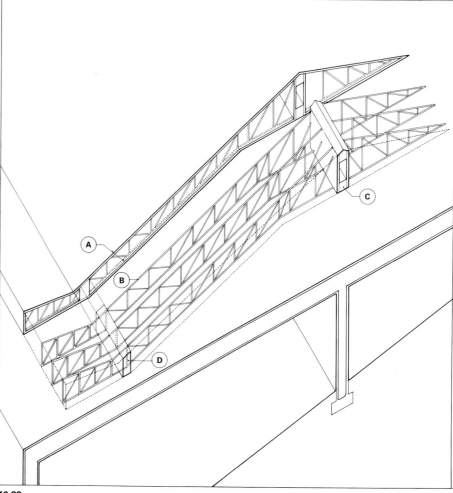

10.28

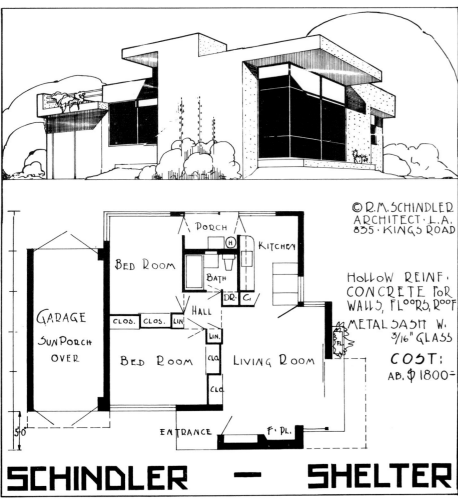

10.29

10.29 **Schindler Shelter**
Rudolf Schindler

10.30 **structural system of Schindler Shelter**
- A Galvanized iron U-shaped channel.
- B Gunite (2″ cement plaster).
- C Wire mesh.
- D 2″ cement plaster floor.
- E Galvanized iron U channel.
- F Horizontal reinforcing bars forming bottom chord of truss.
- G Wire mesh.

(Architectural Drawings Collection, University Art Museum, Santa Barbara.)

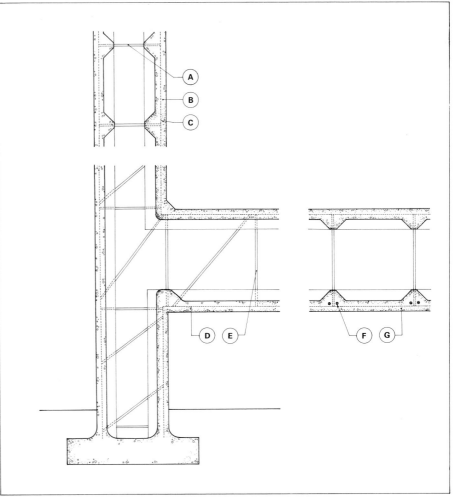

10.30

10.31

W. E. Oliver house
Rudolf Schindler
Los Angeles, 1934

10.31 exterior
*(Architectural Drawings Collection,
University Art Museum, Santa Barbara.)*

10.32 window details

A Exterior wall: stucco on 2 × 4 wood studs.

B Plaster ceiling.

C 1 × 3 wood ground. The frames are screwed to these pieces, which are in turn nailed to the studs.

D Cadmium-plated sheet-metal frame. This section holds the insect screen. The sections were custom-made to Schindler's design. The frames were partially bolted and partially spot-welded together.

E $\frac{3}{16}''$ demiplate glass.

F Floor of linoleum on 1″ wood flooring.

G This upturned metal leg provides a rail for the roller of the sliding window above.

H Sloped metal sill.

I Sliding casement sash.

J Stationary sash with L-shaped stop.
*(Architectural Drawings Collection,
University Art Museum, Santa Barbara.)*

10.33 J. J. Buck house
Rudolf Schindler, Los Angeles, 1934
window detail.

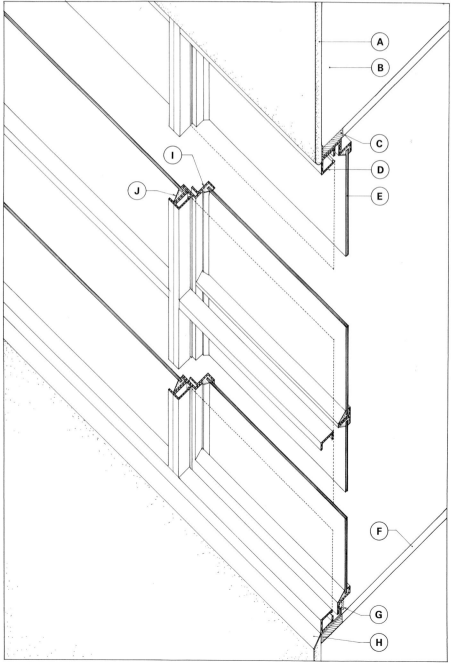

10.32

10.33

10.34

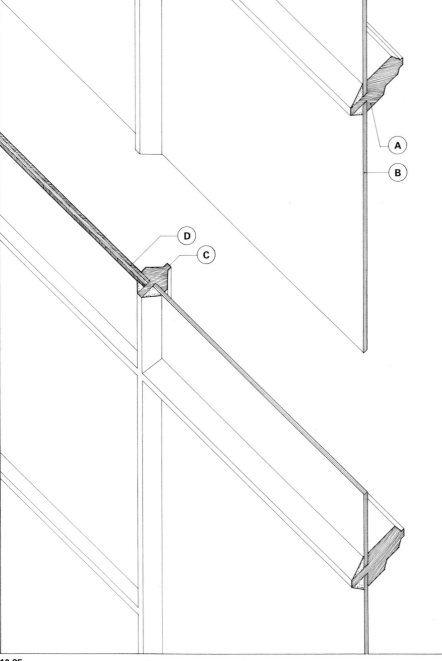

10.35

P. Lovell house

Rudolf Schindler

Newport Beach, California, 1926

10.34 detail

10.35 window details

(as shown in construction
drawings)

A Horizontal mullion, $2\frac{1}{2}''$ deep. This
carries the main load of the
windows back to the jambs. It adds
greatly to the transparency of the
wall. It should be much deeper in
such a large window.

B Glass.

C Vertical mullion, $1\frac{3}{8}''$ deep. The
corners are chamfered to minimize
the visual profile of the mullion.

D Three-ply veneer plywood panel.
*(Architectural Drawings Collection,
University Art Museum, Santa Barbara.)*

10.36

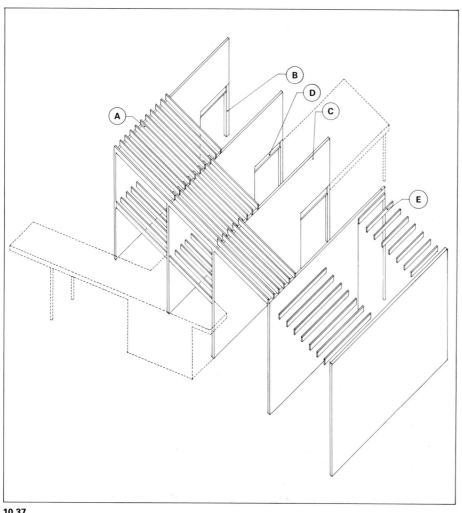

10.37

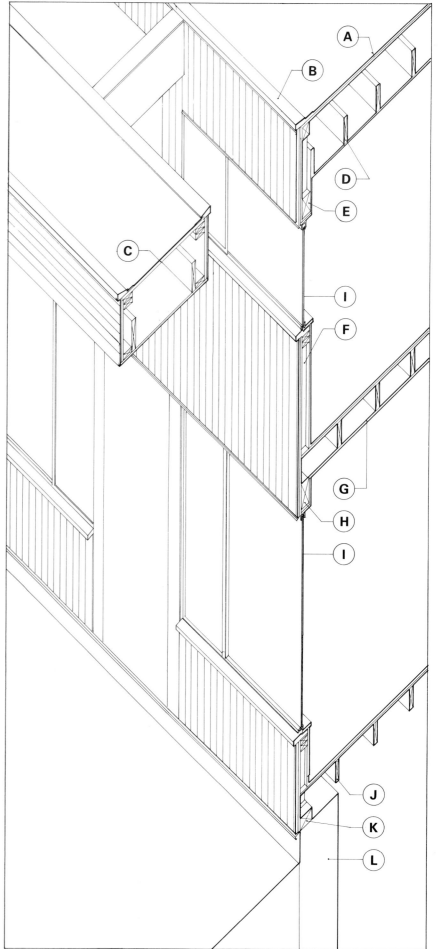

10.38

W. Gropius house
Walter Gropius and Marcel Breuer
Lincoln, Massachusetts, 1939

10.36 rear view
(Busch-Reisinger Museum, Harvard University, Paul Davis photograph.)

10.37 framing plan
A 2 × 10 fir or spruce joists, 16″ on center, supporting the roof.
B 4 × 4 wood post. These are concealed within the stud walls.
C Interior load-bearing partition of 2 × 4 studs, 16″ on center.
D Steel beam (wide-flange 6 × 12), supporting studs of the load-bearing wall over door opening.
E Exposed rafters at roof terrace. These run perpendicular to the real joists, which span between the cross walls.
(Busch-Reisinger Museum, Harvard University, drawing 6A 82.1-20.)

10.38 wall section at rear facade
A Roof construction: five-ply built-up roof with gravel on ⅞″ boarding, sloped ¼″ per foot.
B Gravel stop: 16-ounce lead-coated copper with 2 × 4 wood nailer. This covers the joint between the built-up roof and the wood siding while holding down the edge of the roofing.
C Vermiculite plaster soffit (later replaced with cement plaster).
D 2 × 10 fir or spruce roof joists, 16″ on center.
E 4 × 8 fir or spruce beam supporting wood studs over window opening. (This is not a load-bearing wall, as the joists span between the perpendicular cross-walls.)
F Wall construction: vertical tongue-and-groove redwood siding with V joints; building paper; sheathing; 2 × 4 wood studs; plaster on metal lath for interior finish; 3″ fiberglass insulation in voids.

G Floor construction: 2 × 10 joists, 16″ on center; ⅞″ wood subfloor, carpet floors and plaster ceilings.
H 4 × 8 fir or spruce beam.
I Steel casement window.
J Floor construction: 2 × 10 fir or spruce joists, 16″ on center.
K 4 × 6 mudsill and termite shield.
L Fieldstone foundation wall.
(Busch-Reisinger Museum, Harvard University, drawing 6A 82.1-20.)

comparison to steel, that it requires little advance planning and drawing and can easily be modified in the course of construction, giving the builders and carpenters considerable flexibility. It is the great difficulty of the steel frame that it requires shop (fabrication) drawings and cannot easily be altered at the site.

At about the same time that Schindler and Neutra were reluctantly abandoning their fight to replace the platform frame, a second wave of Modernist immigrants arrived who saw the issue in a different light. To Gropius and Breuer, the platform frame was an inspired vernacular creation, entirely in sympathy with the ideals of Modernism and ripe for expropriation into the new architecture. This was the time of what Giedion called "the New Regionalism," and it would have been unthinkable that these two, faced with the context of New England, would not respond by studying local vernacular forms, materials, and building methods.[7]

Shortly after their arrival in the United States, Gropius and Breuer produced a series of houses illustrating the merging of the new architecture with American tradition, beginning with their own houses in Lincoln, Massachusetts (1938 and 1939) and continuing with the Ford (1939), Hagerty (1939), and Chamberlain (1941) houses. The basic system was born more out of necessity than out of dogma. Gropius wished to produce a model of the modern house. A benefactor offered to finance the construction of two houses which would be leased to Gropius and Breuer. They were thus working not only under the economic constraints of the Depression but also under the economic constraints of not really being their own clients. Accordingly, at an early stage in the design process Gropius and Breuer consulted a local contractor to ensure that the designs would not stray beyond the bounds of standard practice.

Giedion called of the Gropius house a primary example of the "new regionalism" because of "its use of traditional methods and materials." This is only partly true. In fact, the house contains so much steel that it is almost a skeletal frame building. Yet—unlike the doctrinaire buildings of the 1920s, which clearly distinguished both conceptually and visually between the structural skeleton and the skin of the curtain wall—this building is a hybrid. A structural element may be wood or steel, wall or frame, or plane or column, depending on its location and its role in the building. Gropius and Breuer thus began, in effect, where Schindler left off with the Oliver house.

Whereas each of Schindler's houses was a unique formal and structural experiment, the Gropius and Breuer houses belong to a more rigorous typology. The first type, represented by the Breuer house in Lincoln and the Chamberlain cottage in Wayland, consists of two volumes forming a T shape, one being a load-bearing, platform-frame box and the other being a frame-and-curtain-wall structure (both are constructed of wood). This type of parti—a load-bearing wall structure intersected by a frame—is structurally analogous to contemporary work in Europe, particularly Mies's Hubbe house and Aalto's Villa Mairea, both of which are masonry load-bearing volumes intersected by steel-frame skeletal volumes. The second type is less interesting spatially, but it deals more directly with the problem of accommodating the aesthetic goals of Modern architecture to the platform frame. It is represented by the Ford and Hagerty houses, and it takes as its starting point a simple elongated platform frame box, 16–20 feet wide and two stories tall. The elements that project from this volume, such as stairs, are those that would interfere with this standard framing. In the Modernist ideal of building, this is the most functional solution, since structural limitations rather than programmatic ones determine the massing. The various spaces simply fill up the volume rather than determining it. In addition, the integrity of the structure—or at least that of the floor and the roof structure—is maintained, since the joists are all cut to the same length (standardization again) and are uninterrupted by openings.

The walls of this second house type are more complex, being composed in the manner of a free facade with long strip windows. This feature causes much structural difficulty, since these long slits cut the load-bearing stud wall in half and decrease the lateral rigidity. It is for this reason that steel columns and beams are

10.39

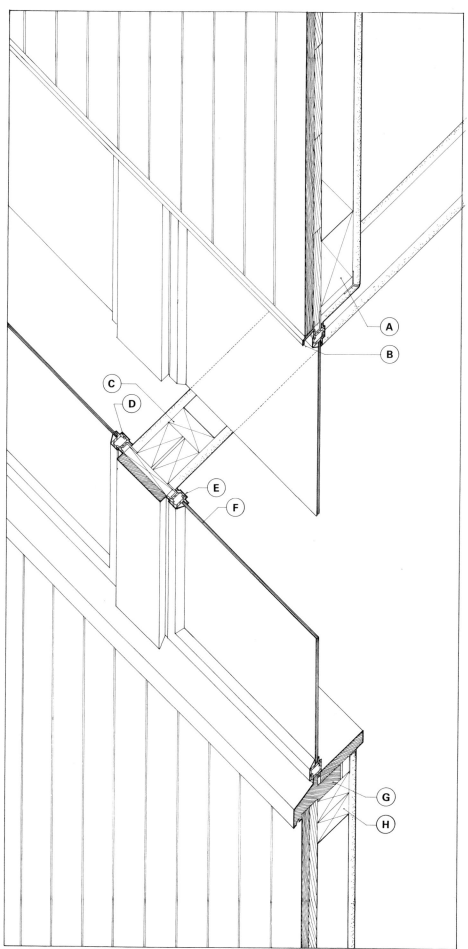

10.40

W. Gropius house

Walter Gropius and Marcel Breuer

Lincoln, Massachusetts, 1939

10.39 exterior

(Busch-Reisinger Museum, Harvard University, Paul Davis photograph.)

10.40 window details

A 4 × 6 or 4 × 8 wood beam, supporting wall over long horizontal window opening.

B Metal drip.

C 2 × 4 wood stud framing. The roof and floor joists are actually carried by these interior partitions.

D Finish-wood facing.

E Steel casement windows.

F $\frac{1}{4}$″ glass. Polished plate glass is used for the large living room windows, pull glass for the smaller bedroom windows.

G Sloped wood sill.

H 2 × 4 wood stud framing. This forms the rough opening in the framing to receive the finished window.

(Busch-Reisinger Museum, Harvard University, drawing 6A 82.1-20.)

required in this type of house. Although the long windows recall the International Style facades of the 1920s, they do not follow a regular module; they vary in size and type, depending on the rooms which they serve. The long banks of operable windows of identical size that were so important to Wright, Le Corbusier, and Neutra are replaced here by fixed wood windows of varying size. Where operable windows are required, steel casements are set into the wood frames. The pattern of openings (both vertical and horizontal) is determined by the types and sizes of the spaces behind, not by modules or standardization. The basic envelope is cut out to capture exterior space on the interior of the volume, and in some locations the sheathing and siding are peeled away to expose the structure of joists or studs below, such as in the trellis of the second-floor balcony of the Gropius house.

The interest of Gropius and Breuer in the platform frame, and the extent to which they allowed it to influence the form of their designs, was not due entirely to economic constraints. They saw it as a vernacular building type, just as Le Corbusier saw Catalonian vaults as a vernacular building type. At the same time, it is clear that this idea was of greater interest to Breuer than to Gropius. This makes a comparison of their postwar work all the more revealing.

Gropius and Breuer dissolved their partnership in 1941, and after the war they followed opposite paths in their domestic work. Gropius, in collaboration with Konrad Wachsmann, returned to his first love—industrialized housing—and developed a system of panel houses based on a type of industrialized platform frame. Breuer remained preoccupied with variations on the standard platform frame. His use of vernacular elements (such as fieldstone walls and natural siding) increased, and he began to experiment with the structural capabilities of the platform-frame box: its ability to cantilever, or to act as a diaphragm and/or a frame.

Like Loos (and unlike Schindler), Breuer saw modern construction as inherently layered. Breuer wrote: ". . . the building is an organism of many parts: there is the structure, and then there are different layers or specialized skins wrapped around that frame. There are layers to insulate against heat or cold, against dampness, against too much sky glare. These are the skins of the building—just as 'true' as the structural frame."[8]

Breuer's concept of the layered wall is illustrated by the house he built for himself in New Canaan after ending his partnership with Gropius (figure 10.48). The face of the wood mullions is placed in the plane of the structural studs and stained dark to express the "cut-out" nature of the window opening. Likewise, the jamb and head of the window are detailed to express the thinness of the wall layers, either by recessing the sheathing to form a notch between the siding and the frame or by recessing the frame halfway under the siding. In Breuer's later buildings, such as the Geller house, the frames are painted white while the wood siding is stained. At the base, the foundation wall is recessed to the plane of the structural studs, articulating the thinness of the sheathing and the siding.

The concept of layering, which was so successful on the exterior, ran into more difficulty inside. Whereas the exteriors were primarily wood volumes, the interiors tended to be De Stijl-like compositions of planes of different materials. In one corner of the first Breuer house, for example, a plaster ceiling intersects one wall of fieldstone and one of wood siding. These junctions were to be made without transitions and without trim, as were any openings in these planes. Even exposed lintels over openings in stone walls were eliminated in favor of concealed steel ones, as in the fireplace of the Hagerty house. To many Modernists this detail would be "dishonest."

To Breuer, the Modern ideal was a detail-free architecture:

The architectures of past periods tended to lend melodies of their own to the details: the head of a column was a piece of sculpture in itself, . . . even without the building. Our details tend to be completely for the service of the whole structure. . . . Often our details completely fuse with the greater "architectural"

10.41

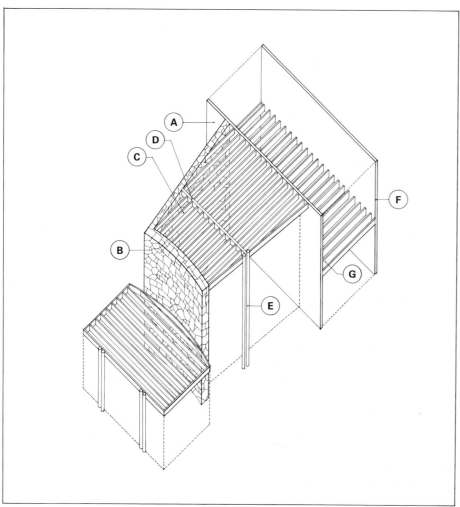

10.42

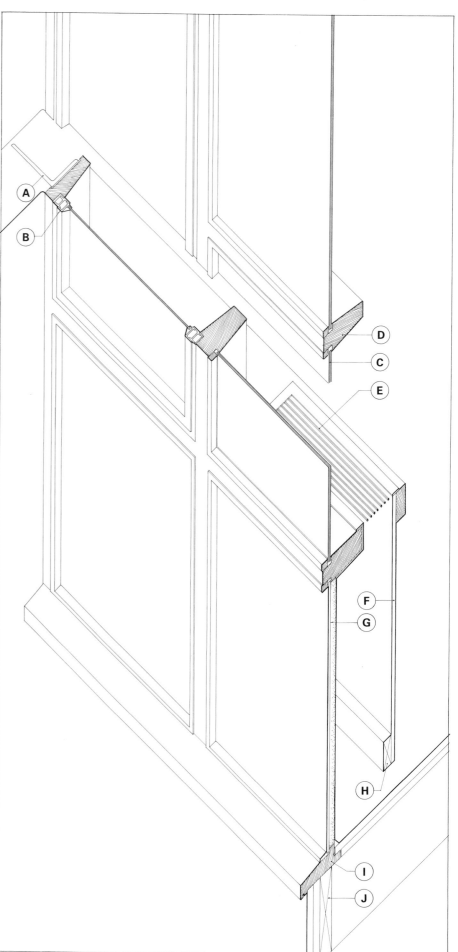

10.43

M. Breuer house

Walter Gropius and Marcel Breuer

Lincoln, Massachusetts, 1939

10.41 exterior

(Busch-Reisinger Museum, Harvard University.)

10.42 framing plan

A Wood-stud load-bearing wall.

B Fieldstone load-bearing wall. Like Mies and Le Corbusier, Breuer often combined frame structures using industrial components with load-bearing masonry structure using vernacular components.

c 2×8 wood joists, 16" on center.

D $8\frac{1}{2} \times 5\frac{1}{2}$ WF 21. The wood joists are set into the web of the beam rather than on top of it so that the ceiling below remains flat.

E Two round steel-pipe columns, exposed on the exterior.

F 2×4 wood stud load-bearing wall. This portion of the house is a conventional platform frame.

G 2×8 wood joists, 16" on center.

(Busch-Reisinger Museum, Harvard University, drawing 6A 84 1/2.)

10.43 window details

A $4" \times 6" \times \frac{3}{8}"$ steel angle to support wood frame.

B Out-swinging steel casement window. The small thin steel sash is used to make the profile of the operable window as close as possible to that of the fixed one.

c $\frac{1}{4}"$ plate glass

D $5\frac{1}{2}"$ hard pine mullions, joined with visible lag-bolted steel angles.

E Metal grille. This allows warm air from the radiator to rise up the face of the glass, preventing condensation and reducing drafts.

F $\frac{3}{8}"$ plywood radiator cover.

G Opaque panel of $\frac{1}{4}"$ Masonite backed with $\frac{3}{4}"$ Celotex insulation.

H Slot for air circulation around radiator.

I Wood sill.

J Floor construction: 2×10 fir joists.

(Architectural Record.)

form: it is indeed difficult to draw a demarcation line between an overall design and a definition of the details. It seems more and more nonsensical to say: ". . . he might have been a great architect, if only someone had done the details for him. . . ."[9]

A comparison of a typical Breuer wall (that of Breuer House I in New Canaan) with a typical traditional wall (such as that of Seacroft, built by Bruce Price in 1882) shows both the radicalness of a "detail-free" architecture and the difficulties of achieving it. The structural components of the Price and Breuer houses are the same, and the exterior finish materials are essentially the same, but their configurations are different. Most of the technology of the Breuer house was available to Price. Breuer's aim was to eliminate and minimize all trim and modulations associated with ornament. On the exterior he was successful: the task performed by the drip cap and the window flashing of the Price house is achieved in the Breuer house by cutting the edge of the siding at an acute angle to form a minimal drip without the use of trim, and the use of vertical siding eliminates the need for exterior jamb trim. Breuer's use of a projecting sill is an exception; it was necessitated by the increased danger of leakage at this point. Price's window is an object applied to the surface of the wall. Breuer's is a cutout. The softness of the plaster on the interior makes this elimination of trim less easy. Elimination of the baseboard would result in the destruction of the bottom of the wall, so it is simply detailed as if the base were invisible. In the Price house the termination of the plaster at the window is covered with trim; in Breuer's case it is left exposed. This latter operation is a much more difficult one for the plasterer in this exposed location, since he must create a perfect joint of plaster and wood. Even if he succeeds, the two materials will shortly separate because of differential movements due to temperature and moisture. Again the wood trim in the window would hide this crack when it occurs. The substitution of plywood for plaster in some of Breuer's later houses does not solve the problem, since the two pieces of wood will also undergo differential movements and eventually separate.

This is another case in which the Modernist notion equating geometric simplicity with efficiency in construction does not agree with the facts. The trim used in traditional architectural detailing allows for the expansion and contraction of materials, permits the joining of materials of radically different character, and does not make unreasonable demands of the craftsman. In many modern buildings the desire to eliminate trim has resulted only in a lack of attention to the design of trim.

The irony of Breuer's New Canaan house is that it shows the degree to which Modern architecture is aesthetically independent of modern materials. Although the house has many elements of the typical Corbusian facade of the 1920s, such as the strip window and the cantilevered second floor, they are executed in traditional materials. There is no steel or structural concrete in the house; all cantilevers and openings are accomplished by means of large timbers or by the use of the diaphragm action of the platform-frame walls themselves (in which the entire wall acts as a large beam). Another irony is the expression of this cantilever. The wood siding of the projecting portion is set on a diagonal, in accordance with the stresses created by the cantilever. However this siding is not structural, but is applied to the true structure of the studs and sheathing. What appears on the exterior of the building is, in effect, ornament.

Gropius and Breuer accepted the technology of American housing as they found it, made only minor modifications, and established a system of detailing that remained influential through the 1950s and is still in use today. Richard Meier's Douglass house (1973), for example, is a wood platform-frame building, supported in some key locations by steel beams and columns. It has vertical wood siding, and operable steel sashes set in fixed wood frames. However much this house may recall the forms of Le Corbusier, its structural systems and details are those of the Gropius and Breuer houses.

10.44

J. Ford house

Walter Gropius and Marcel Breuer

Lincoln, Massachusetts, 1939

10.44 exterior

(Busch-Reisinger Museum, Harvard University.)

10.45 framing plan

A 2 × 10 roof joists, 16″ on center, supporting flat roof.

B Wood-stud load-bearing wall. The framing here is much simpler than that of the Gropius house, since the width of the building is kept within the standard limits of platform framing and the joists span between the exterior walls.

C 2 × 10 floor joists, 16″ on center, and wood sheathing. The subfloor of sheathing also acts as a diaphragm to laterally brace the structure.

D 4 × 6 wood post supporting 6 × 10 wood beam

E Exposed wood joists forming trellis. Like many Modernists of the 1930s, Gropius and Breuer exposed a small portion of the structure.

(Busch-Reisinger Museum, Harvard University, drawing 6A 91.1-37.)

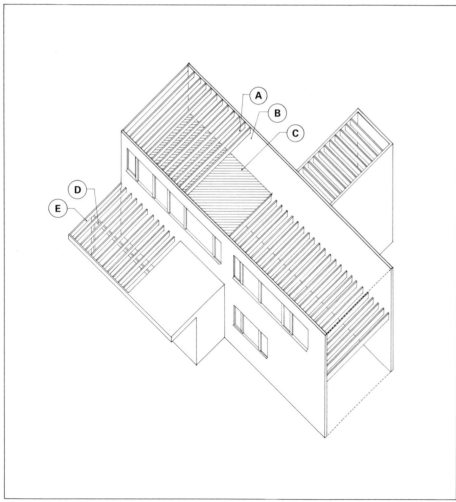

10.45

10.46

J. Hagerty house

Walter Gropius and Marcel Breuer

Cohasset, Massachusetts, 1939

10.46 exterior

(Busch-Reisinger Museum, Harvard University.)

10.47 framing plan

A   2 × 10 roof joists, 16″ on center.

B   7″ I 15.3 steel beam supporting roof joists. The roof and the floors are supported by steel beams rather than by the walls (which are, in effect, curtain walls.)

C   Two 2 × 10 wood joists. Since this joist connects the columns, it is doubled to provide additional lateral stability.

D   6″ I 12.5 steel beam supporting floor joists.

E   4″ round steel-pipe column. The Hagerty house comes close to being a steel-frame-and-curtain-wall structure.

F   Stair. A bedroom added during construction (shown in dotted lines) compromised the structural clarity of the original scheme.
In 1949 John Hagerty, the son of the original client, published in *Interior Design and Decoration* an article highly critical of many technical aspects of the design.
(Busch-Reisinger Museum, Harvard University, drawing 6A 85.1-15.)

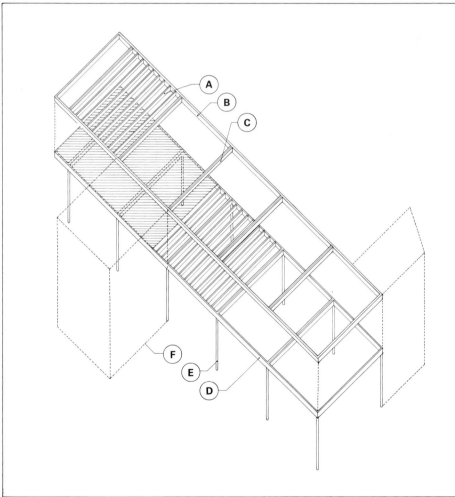

10.47

10.48

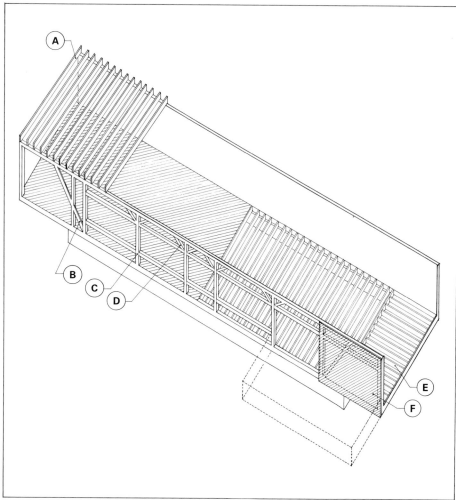

10.49

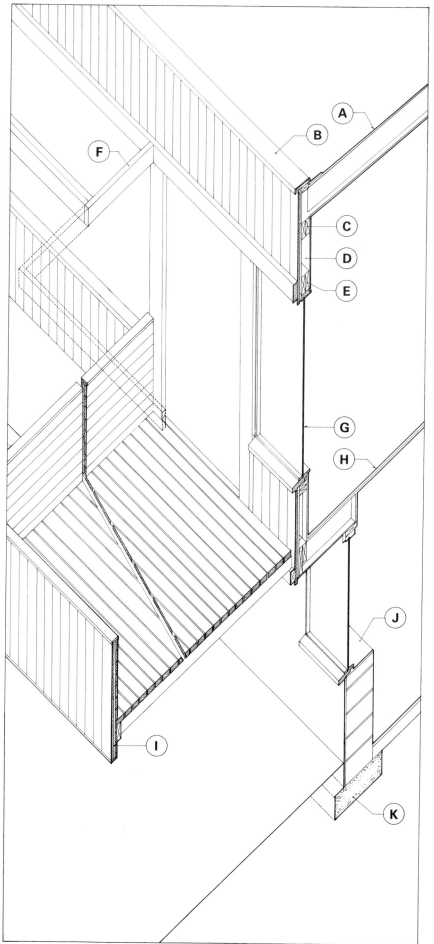

10.50

Breuer House I

Marcel Breuer

New Canaan, Connecticut, 1948

10.48 exterior

(Architectural Record,
Damora photograph.)

10.49 framing plan

A 2 × 6 wood roof joists, 16″ on center.

B 1 × 6 diagonal bracing cut into columns and studs. This also assists in bringing the roof load of the cantilevered portion to the foundation wall.

C 4 × 4 wood columns.

D 1 × 6 diagonal bracing.

E 2 × 8 floor joists, 16″ on center. The joists must run parallel to the cantilever and thus must change directions.

F Wood sheathing boards, placed diagonally.

(Architectural Record.)

10.50 wall section

A Roof construction: 2 × 10 wood joists, 16″ on center, supporting $\frac{3}{4}$″ wood deck. Voids between joists are filled with insulation.

B Copper gravel stop. This waterproofs the horizontal surface at the top of the wood wall and seals the edge of the built-up roof.

C Two 2 × 6 wood joists supporting roof joists.

D Wall construction: 2 × 4 wood studs, $\frac{3}{4}$″ wood sheathing faced with building paper, $\frac{3}{4}$″ tongue-and-groove wood siding.

E Lintel: Two 2 × 6's supporting studs over the long horizontal window opening.

F Trellis made from 2 × 6 wood boards.

G Fixed wood window, with steel operable windows set in frame.

H Floor construction: 2 × 8 wood joists, 16″ on center, supporting $\frac{3}{4}$″ subfloor and $\frac{1}{2}$″ finish floor.

I Balcony rail. Sandwich panel construction, similar to that of Wright's Usonian wall, results in a much thinner wall than wood studs would have produced.

J 12″ concrete masonry foundation wall, faced with $\frac{3}{4}$″ stucco.

K Concrete footing and 4″ concrete slab on grade.

(Architectural Record.)

Despite the failure of the specific systems developed by Neutra and Schindler to gain popular acceptance, the ideals that produced them were far from having run their course. The dreams of the mass-produced steel-frame house, the exposed wood frame, and monolithic concrete construction, and the detailing ideals of a wall with pure minimal junctions and openings, were still very much alive, and were to reappear in a variety of manifestations after the Second World War.

Yet in the late 1930s, Schindler, Neutra, Gropius, and Breuer all accepted, with varying degrees of enthusiasm, the platform frame as the logical system of residential construction in America. This was due in part to a fascination with vernacular building systems, in part to the trends in construction, and in part to the economic constraints of the Depression. But not all architects accepted the platform frame as inevitable, and if the conditions of the 1930s drove these architects to accept (at least temporarily) the platform frame, they drove another to reject it altogether: Frank Lloyd Wright.

11　Frank Lloyd Wright: The Usonian Period

The year 1932 was a triumphant one for Modern architecture in America. The International Style Exhibition opened at the Museum of Modern Art, and the first Modern skyscrapers, the RCA and Philadelphia Savings Fund Society buildings, were under construction. It was not, however, a triumphant year for Frank Lloyd Wright. He had no work, he was near bankruptcy, and his name had appeared more often in the yellow press than in architectural journals in recent years. Whether by his own choice or by the choice of society, he was something of a pariah.

Wright was neither idle nor alone, and in the same year he founded the Taliesin Fellowship. But both he and the fellowship were detached from the society around them, physically and economically. Living on Wright's family farm in Wisconsin, the fellowship grew much of its own food and was in many ways self-sufficient. Timber and wood lath for the renovations and additions were cut on site, stone was quarried nearby, and limestone was burned to make lime mortar. The work was done mostly by young and untrained apprentices, and Wright altered his details to suit the available level of craftsmanship. Later, when Taliesin West was built as a winter camp, its details reflected its temporary nature, its construction by apprentices, and the self-sufficient nature of the entire process.

The year 1932 also saw the publication of *The Disappearing City* and the beginning of the Broadacre City Plan, which included Wright designs for everything from houses to helicopters to automobiles. Its implementation would have required massive political and social changes, and it is not surprising that, in addition to utopian schemes for architecture, transportation, and planning, Wright should have adopted utopian systems of building. What is surprising is the rigor with which he applied them. Unlike Le Corbusier, Gropius, or Schindler, he would not bend to accommodate individual circumstances.

The year 1936 was a triumphant one for Wright. It saw the completion of the Jacobs, Hanna, and Kaufmann houses and the Johnson Wax Building, four of his best works. It was inevitable that the attitudes and techniques developed at Taliesin should find their way into the details of these buildings. This is the only explanation of Wright's cavalier attitude toward certain traditional standards of

11.1

11.2

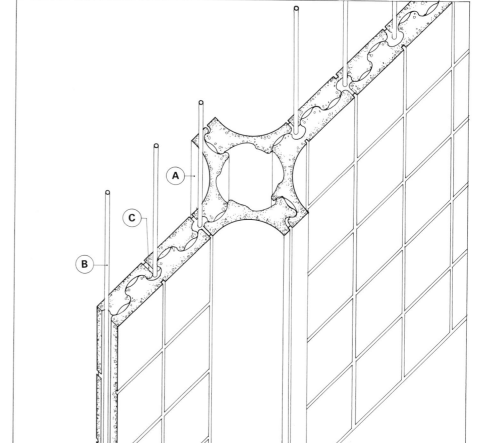

11.3

11.4

Gage Building

Louis Sullivan

Chicago, 1899

11.1 **exterior**

11.2 **detail**

11.3 **F. L. Wright, textile-block system**
A Reinforcing bars.
B 16″ × 16″ × 4″ concrete blocks, cast on site in wood molds.
C Pocket to receive reinforcing bars.
   (*Historic American Buildings Survey.*)

11.4 **W. B. Griffin, Knit-Lock system**
A Cast concrete block. In contrast with Wright's system, Griffin's blocks interlock and have staggered joints so that none go straight through the wall. This makes Griffin's wall stronger but more difficult to assemble.
B Reinforcing bars. Griffin's bars typically run only vertically.
C Pocket to receive reinforcing bars.
   (D. L. Johnson, *The Architecture of Walter Burley Griffin.*)

11.5 **Willets house, framing diagram**
Because of the moderately wide window openings, the studs must be cut to varying lengths to frame around the openings.
(From construction photographs, *F. L. Wright Newsletter.*)

11.6 **Ready-cut Homes, framing diagram**
By narrowing the windows and widening the stud spacing to 24″, the openings were made to match the stud spacing; thus, no cutting was necessary, and all studs were the same length.

the building industry—standards to which he had adhered in his earlier work. The technical faults of these buildings, which were many, cannot be blamed on the apprentices, who saved Wright from embarrassment on more than one occasion by ignoring his instructions.

In his Oak Park years, Wright had worked, on the whole, with the standard materials and methods of the building industry. The construction system of the Robie house might appear somewhat unusual, but it is essentially the same as that of the Greenes' Bentz house. Both use what is essentially wood platform or balloon framing reinforced with steel and concrete at critical locations. Architectural innovation, even in Modernism, does not require technical innovation.

Wright's work after 1920 has none of this character of working within conventional systems. In the Textile Block Houses of the 1920s and the Usonian Houses of the 1930s and the 1940s he sought to alter not only the forms of American architecture but also the forms of construction and the processes of contracting, challenging the most fundamental assumptions about the use of materials and the accommodation of environmental requirements. As the distance increased between himself and society, Wright's theories of building became more and more radical.

Wright experimented with modifications and alternatives to the basic systems of American building, the platform frame and the masonry load-bearing wall with joists. He identified three of these alternatives as systems for general application, and he proclaimed that the buildings designed to use them were prototypes. These were the Ready-cut Home System of 1915, the Textile Block Houses of the 1920s, and the Usonian Houses of the 1930s and the 1940s. All three of these systems were characterized by the use of exposed construction and of structural systems that resembled those in nature.

The structural frames of Wright's early buildings seldom were exposed. The wood and steel framing was covered in layers of interior and exterior finish materials. They were in Loos's terms "clad"; in Schindler's terms, this was an "onion skin" system. Even the concrete buildings had concealed steel sections. After 1920 Wright made increasing use of exposed, unclad wood structural members and of unclad concrete, so that there was no longer a distinction between structure and finish materials. As a result, the ornamental system of analogous structure was eliminated, and the architectural expression was confined to the structure itself. But while favoring exposed construction, he did not necessarily favor the monolithic. He made use of assemblies, such as the sandwich panel, in which the structure was external.

Throughout his career Wright was fond of organic metaphors, particularly the comparison of the building and the tree or plant. In his early work this metaphor was primarily in the ornamentation, as in the sumac-tree decorations in the Dana house or the recurring hollyhock motif in the Barnsdall house. Along with the change from clad to monolithic construction came an increased level of abstraction and an elimination of ornament. Thus, in Wright's later work the natural metaphor occurs in the structure rather than in the ornamentation. For example, the columns of the Johnson Wax Building imitate the form of the tree. Whenever possible, Wright made his structural systems analogous to natural systems.

THE AMERICAN READY-CUT HOME SYSTEM
Wright's first effort at mass-produced housing, unlike the later ones, was intended for mass production from the outset. In 1911 Wright was commissioned by the Richards brothers of Milwaukee to produce a series of what we might today call model homes. A client could select from a number of alternative plans, each of which would be built for a guaranteed price. A few of the houses were built in Milwaukee without Wright's supervision; they are among the least interesting of his executed buildings, being watered-down versions of the late Prairie Houses. The system was, on the whole, a failure, but Wright's effort in the project was considerable. The Ready-cut system occupies one of the largest of the drawing files at Taliesin, and its failure, after so extensive an effort, may have affected

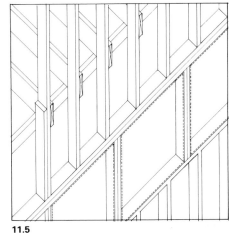

11.5

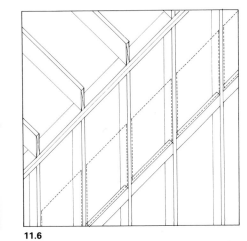

11.6

11.7

11.8

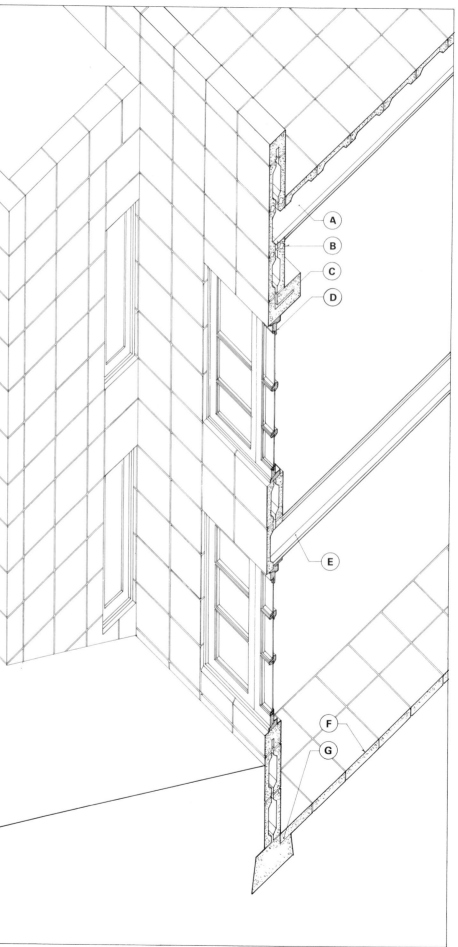

11.9

J. Storer house

Frank Lloyd Wright

Los Angeles, 1923

11.7 **exterior**
  (Marvin Rand.)

11.8 **living-room ceiling**

11.9 **wall section at bedroom**
  A Roof-deck construction: cement tiles on subfloor on 2 × 10 wood joists, 16″ on center.
  B Textile-block wall.
  C Lintel block.
  D Wood window.
  E Floor construction: 2 × 12 wood joists, 16″ on center, with subfloor and ⅞″ finish floor above and plaster ceiling below.
  F Ground-floor construction: concrete tiles set on grade.
  G Concrete footing.
  (Frank Lloyd Wright Foundation, drawing 2304.015.)

Wright's attitude toward later projects, since the system was not based on radically different materials or methods of building but on modifications of the common balloon-frame system.

The basis of the Ready-cut system was, as with most prefabrication systems, that a limited number of standardized elements could be assembled in a variety of ways. Economy was to be achieved as a result of mass-producing the wood members, and thus the architectural designs had to use the minimum number of types of studs and joists. Wright's method of doing this can be seen by comparing the framing of a typical window band in the Willets house with the window band in the Ready-cut system. In the Willets house the windows, although narrowly spaced at 3′2″, are wider than the 16-inch spacing of the studs (figure 11.5). In the Ready-cut system the windows are narrowed and the stud spacing is increased to 24 inches so that the studs continue uninterrupted from foundation to roof (figure 11.6). A carpenter cutting studs for the Willets house would have to plan his work carefully, cutting many studs of varying lengths to accommodate the unique openings in the walls. The studs of a Ready-cut house were nearly identical and were to be cut beforehand to uniform length, since they had no relationship to the pattern of openings.

Thus Wright for the first time brought his grid system of planning into conformity with a system of construction. In his early buildings the grid had been used mainly for visual effect. The module of the Martin house seems to be an arbitrary choice having little to do with units of construction. The Coonley house uses a 4-foot visual module, which is a threefold enlargement of the 16-inch structural module. Only in the Ready-cut system do the planning module and the structural module coincide exactly.

The American Ready-cut System was a financial failure. Wright and the Richards brothers had a falling out at some point, and Wright was not involved in the completion of the concept. It is unlikely that the system of construction was a factor in this failure. Changes in taste and in the economy, and the disruption caused by the First World War, probably affected the marketing of the units. Whatever the reason, this was Wright's last attempt to work within the rules and standards of the construction industry. His subsequent attempts were to be far more radical in their scope.

THE TEXTILE BLOCK HOUSES

During the first two decades of the twentieth century there was a gradual increase in the price of lumber, particularly the large timbers favored by the Arts and Crafts architects. At the same time, portland cement and reinforced concrete were becoming popular in all areas of construction. This led many to believe that concrete would replace or at least compete with wood as a structural material for houses. Although concrete masonry is common, wood framing was and is the dominant structural system in American single-family housing. However, in the 1920s many architects experimented with concrete houses.

Thus, Wright was neither the only nor the first architect to experiment with concrete in housing. Henry Mercer built several cast-in-place buildings in Doylestown, Pennsylvania, in the early 1900s. Gustav Stickley published many designs for concrete houses in *The Craftsman*. More closely connected with Wright was Irving Gill, who built many concrete tilt-slab buildings in Southern California. Wright had known Gill in Sullivan's office, and his son Lloyd worked for Gill. Walter Burley Griffin developed a concrete-block system called the "knit-lock system," which was similar to Wright's; it is a matter of dispute as to who originated the idea. Griffin had worked for Wright in the early 1900s, but they were not on speaking terms after 1910.

The basis of Wright's system is a concrete block cast in a wood mold with an ornamental design. Today it would be called cast stone, since it requires a finer mix of water, cement, and aggregates than standard concrete to produce the fine detail on the surface. Wright's first use of these blocks was purely ornamental. The Midway Gardens (1914) and the German Warehouse (1915) both make exten-

11.10

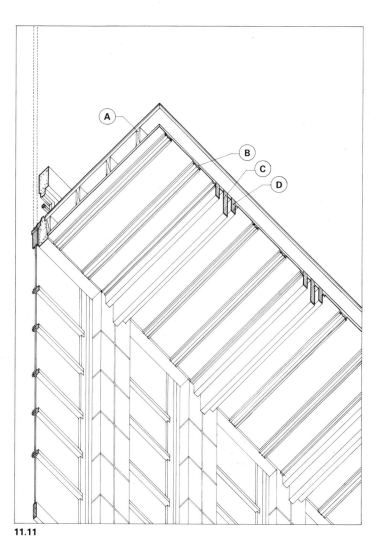

11.11

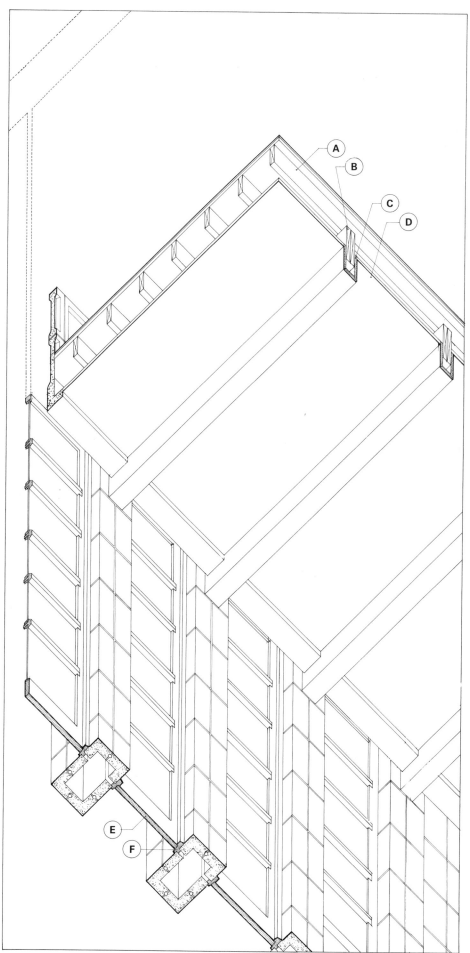

11.12

11.10 detail

11.11 interior wall section as built

A Floor construction.

B Wood paneling with battens.

C Solid 3 × 6 wood beam. In the final design the beams are solid rather than clad.

D Solid 4 × 10 wood beam. There is no particular structural advantage to using beams of two different sizes, but the spacing of the small beams corresponds to the width of the concrete-block column.
(Frank Lloyd Wright Foundation, HABS, drawing 2304.015 and survey)

11.12 interior wall section as originally designed

A Floor construction: ⅞″ oak finish floor and wood subfloor on 2 × 4's.

B Girder of two 2 × 12's.

C Redwood cladding on girder.

D Redwood plywood ceiling.

E Wood door.

F Textile-block column supporting 2 × 12 girder.
(Frank Lloyd Wright Foundation, drawing 2304.015)

sive use of these ornamental blocks in combination with brick. They are not used in any structurally unique way; they are laid up the wall in the same way as brick. The first houses to use textile blocks exclusively in a reinforced load-bearing wall were the Storer and Millard houses of 1923.

The Usonian and Ready-cut systems were both meant to minimize labor and materials, within aesthetic limits. The textile-block technique was also meant to be a universal system, but economy was not its primary objective. It was more an exploration of the possibilities of concrete construction. Wright felt that in terms of character, concrete was an inferior material, lacking the qualities of veining, grain, and texture of stone and wood. He felt the way to bring out the character of wood and stone was to use flat plane surfaces so that these qualities would become apparent. By contrast, he felt the way to bring out the character of concrete was to texture the surface and thus hide the absence of these qualities. In the Unity Temple (1904) and to a lesser extent in the Barnsdall house (1920) Wright had experimented with exposed flat cast-in-place concrete surfaces and with cast-in-place concrete ornament. Evidently he was not happy with the result, for he seldom used either technique again. In his work of the 1920s, concrete surfaces were always textured to some degree—and although the ornaments and blocks were usually cast at the site, they were not cast in place; they were cast on the ground in wooden molds. Many of Wright's buildings of this period which are often described as monolithic concrete, such as the Coonley Playhouse and the Hollyhock house, are in fact stucco on wood or masonry.

Equally important to these houses is Wright's grid planning system. Wright used it in all his buildings after 1904, but never so literally as in the Textile Block Houses, where he actually built the grid. All the houses are on a 16-inch grid in both plan and section. The standard blocks are 16 × 16 inches, and a double-layered wall is 8 inches thick (i.e., half a module). The structural modules of the houses are usually 4 feet (three 16-inch modules). This planning grid was for Wright, as it was for Sullivan, an important part of the organic metaphor. Sullivan wrote, regarding the use of grids and axes in the construction of ornament:

[They are] . . . *rigid in their quality, are to be considered in our philosophy as containers of radical energy, extensive and intensive; that is to say: extension of form along lines or axes radiating from the center and (or) intention of form along the same or other radials from the periphery toward the center. . . . Note also that we assume energy to be resident in the periphery and that all lines are energy lines. This may be called plastic geometry.*[1]

Wright perceived the development of an architectural plan in the same way.

The only sure way to hold all to scale is to adopt a unit-system. . . .

. . . sticks will not space the same as stones nor allow the same proportions as steel. . . .

A wood plan is slender: light in texture, narrower spacing.

A stone or brick plan is heavy: black in masses, wider in spacing.[2]

The Storer house, one of the first of the Textile Block series to be completed, shows the changes in Wright's attitudes toward the nature of construction. It uses primarily monolithic systems of buildings, and it shows the trend away from clad structures and analogous systems of ornament in his work. Plaster, stucco, and paint are uncommon in the Usonian Houses, and often the exterior finishes are identical to the interior. Ceiling and roof framing are sometimes exposed, and when they are not there is seldom an attempt to mimic in ornament the structure above.

11.13

11.15

11.14

11.16

The roof and floor structures of the Storer house are not concrete but wood, used here in a way not seen before in Wright's work. The major structure is a series of beams on 4-foot centers, resting on concrete block piers. Spanning across these beams are joists spaced at 16 inches, which is, of course, the effective span of the wood floor deck. Both dimensions fit the building module exactly.

Wright's first design (figure 11.12) clad the bottoms of the major beams in a way reminiscent of some of the Greenes' work. Subsequently these were changed to smaller monolithic beams. This system is generally more expensive, of course; it is cheaper to clad rough construction lumber with finish woods than to use large monolithic pieces of the more valuable wood (which are also much more likely to crack), but the latter creates a much more monolithic design. At this point Wright was still using moldings to cover joints between panels (they also are on the module), but they become increasingly rare in his work. Ten years later he would announce "interior trim is no longer necessary"[3] without explanation. The framing of the exterior soffits is identical to the interior, in keeping with Wright's tendency to blur this distinction, although the wood here is stenciled. The stenciling is quite beautiful, but it is difficult to see how it is "integral" ornament.

The exterior wall design also is identical inside and out, and it continues the tendency toward monolithic construction. Figure 11.9 shows a typical section of this wall. The typical block is nominally 16×16×4 inches. The blocks are tied together with reinforcing bars running through each joint and running across the cavity at each intersection to tie the two layers (or wythes, as they are called) together. The edge of each block has a round groove to receive the bars, which are set in a bed of grout about 1½ inches in diameter. When the walls became wider, an air space was created between the wythes and the reinforcing bars running across the space were exposed. Wright said that he built the walls hollow for insulation, but the two wythes were equally important to the ease and accuracy of the construction. To have cast a block with two ornamental sides rather than one would have been extremely difficult, since the blocks are never of uniform width. Concrete block is not a precision material, and it is much easier to make a wall of two layers smooth on both sides than a wall of one layer. The result is the appearance, if not the reality, of a monolithic masonry wall.

The basic wall system as shown in figure 11.3 matches closely that of Wright's generic drawing of the textile-block system in *The Natural House* (1954), but the real system is not so simple. There are two texture patterns, a flat block, a coping block, and numerous types of L-shaped blocks to form door jambs, corners, and fascias. In certain areas additional reinforcing was required, such as over the door openings, and here a solid block was cast with additional reinforcing. In the later block houses the voids between the blocks were filled with concrete and additional reinforcing where greater strength was required. In other locations, soffits and ceilings were covered with standard blocks tied with wires to the wood joists above, giving the impression of a concrete slab.

The window details also show new departures for Wright. They generally follow an angular design that recalls the Willets house. This acts to ease the transitions, as a molding would do, and to make the individual members appear lighter than they really are by tapering their edges. But Wright does not make the sash a visually continuous frame, as in the Prairie Houses. The glass stops do not project, but the muntins project beyond the line of the sash (figure 11.12), giving the joints of the frame a kind of discontinuity we do not associate with Wright. Most striking, and most unlike Wright, is the monumentality of these doors. In the Prairie Houses Wright had deliberately lowered the height of doors and soffits to uncomfortably low levels, emphasizing the scale of a person, and he adhered to this idea in the Usonian Houses. The doors of the Storer house are almost 12 feet high, and there is no clear distinction between these and the windows above (which makes them appear to be almost continuous). Nowhere in the house is the "horizontal earth line" to be seen. Although Wright later returned to the human-scale door, he retained the tapered, discontinuous sash design in later buildings.

11.17

11.18

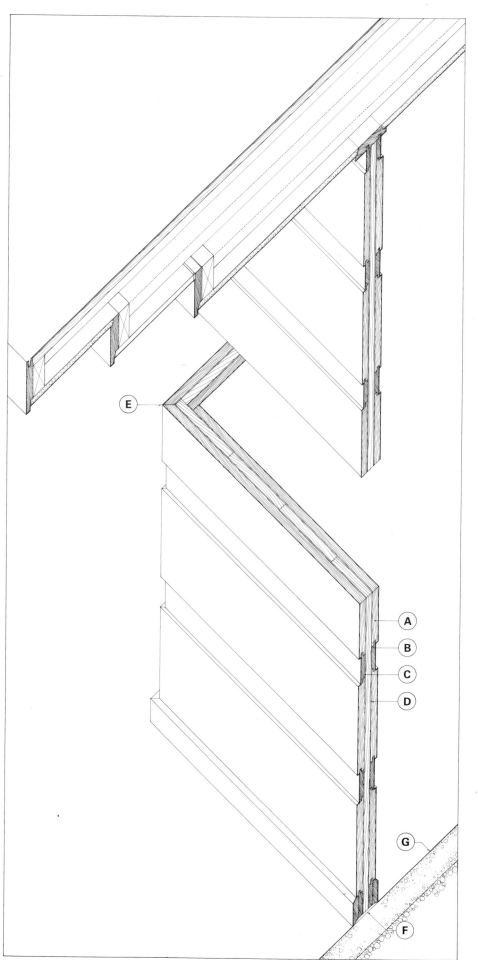

11.19

H. Jacobs house

Frank Lloyd Wright

Madison, Wisconsin, 1936

11.17 exterior
(Wayne Cable.)

11.18 detail
(Wayne Cable.)

11.19 wall section

A Pine board. A low-grade wood was used.

B Redwood batten. The darker redwood sets off the batten on the exterior.

C Building paper.

D Building paper.

E Corner joint. In order to maintain continuous horizontal bands, Wright used a miter joint here, rather than a batten as in the horizontal joint. This joint has a tendency to open up as the wood moves.

F Base trim. Wright used the traditional projecting base to cover the wall-to-floor joint.

G Concrete slab. Wright omitted the traditional footing in favor of a gravel trench.

(Frank Lloyd Wright Foundation, drawing 3702.18.)

The textile-block system was not as successful as Wright hoped it would be. Few architects other than his close associates used the system, but Wright himself used it in a number of buildings throughout his career and updated it in the 1950s to what he called the "Usonian automatic." The reasons for its lack of success have less to do with its shortcomings than with the steady resistance of the building industry to anything other than the platform frame, but there was and is considerable debate as to its shortcomings. (Spalling and cracking have occurred in some of the houses, particularly the Ennis and Freeman houses.) Some architects maintain that it is a good building system, and that the problems are caused by improper construction or poor maintenance. To determine the cause of these problems is beyond the scope of this work, but it is instructive to note the ways in which Wright's system departs from conventional practice in the building industry.

Current practice, of course, discourages monolithic masonry walls in many building types, since modern walls require a cavity to intercept water that penetrates the wall and insulation to meet current standards of energy performance. The air cavity in the textile-block wall does not really provide insulation as Wright claimed. Air is a good insulator only if it remains still; if convection currents develop inside the cavity, the air will only accelerate heat loss. The cavity in Wright's wall will intercept water, but there is nothing to get the water out of the cavity, such as flashing or weep holes. More important, there is nothing to protect the reinforcing bars in the joints or the cavity from rust if water does penetrate the wall surface. (It is not entirely fair to judge the Storer house by present-day standards, as the insulated cavity wall is a relatively recent development and monolithic masonry walls were common in the 1920s.)

The cracking and spalling of the concrete block are undoubtedly caused by water rusting the steel, which breaks the bond between the concrete and the steel. Were this structure duplicated today, certain procedures would probably be altered to conform to present-day industry practice:

· The reinforcing bars would not be exposed inside the cavity, where they are subject to damage from leaks or from condensation (admittedly, less of a problem in California than in some places).

· Wright was fond of mixing earth and sand found at the site with the concrete for the blocks to give them a natural color. This would be forbidden today, since these materials may contain organic compounds that can interfere with the setting process of concrete. Modern ingredients in concrete are required to be sterile.

· Reinforcing bars in monolithic concrete walls are now normally encased in at least 2 inches of concrete to prevent water from the outside from coming into contact with the steel. In walls that combine masonry and concrete, they may be encased in as little as $\frac{1}{2}$" of concrete, depending on the diameter of the bars, but this type of wall is heavily dependent on the use of precisely the correct mortar mix in order for the wall to be waterproof and for the reinforcing bars to remain protected.

These rules, of course, are the work of engineers, of whom Wright said "They are no more capable of making architecture than a professor of mathematics can make music,"[4] but the reasoning behind these rules is much sounder than the reasoning behind Wright's rejection of them.

THE USONIAN SYSTEM

The houses Wright built during the early 1930s employ an interesting variety of construction types. The Willey house (1933) was Wright's last house to use simple platform framing. The Kaufmann house, Fallingwater (1935), had a generous budget and used cast-in-place concrete slabs and steel windows, which were more commonly used in larger commercial buildings. But it was the Jacobs house (1936), one of Wright's most inexpensive buildings, that became the prototype for the Usonian System. It is the first of his houses to use the wood sandwich wall system of construction, which bears little resemblance to the platform frame but which is totally residential in scale.

11.20

11.21

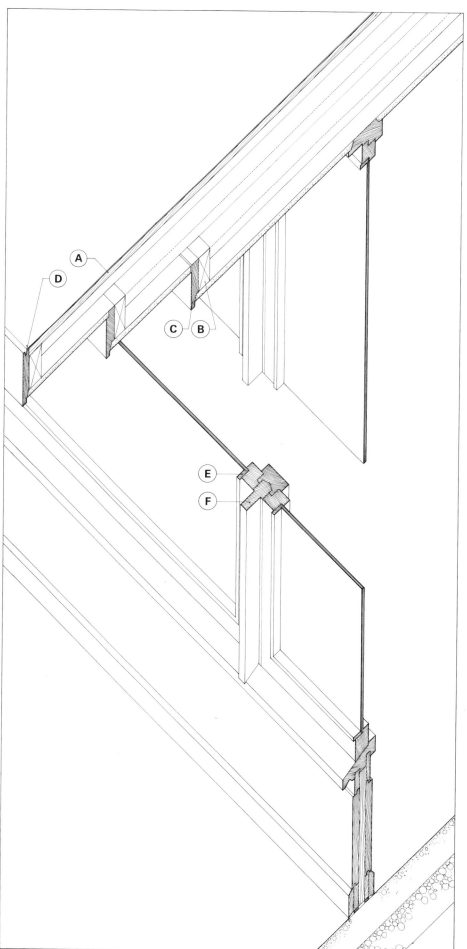

11.22

H. Jacobs house

Frank Lloyd Wright

Madison, Wisconsin, 1936

11.20 **exterior**

(Wayne Cable.)

11.21 **exterior**

(Wayne Cable.)

11.22 **window details**

 A Roof construction.
 B Roof joists. Instead of one 2 × 12 joist, Wright used three 2 × 4's. They are connected with a 2 × 4 header. This structurally ties the joists together.
 C Redwood fascia.
 D Flashing.
 E Projecting glass stop.
 F Mullion.

(Frank Lloyd Wright Foundation, drawing 3702.18.)

When Wright was approached by the Jacobs family, whose financial resources were quite limited, he clearly saw public-relations value in their commission. European ideas of urbanism and low-cost housing were becoming well known in America just at the time when the Depression was at its worst. Wright was horrified by many of these proposals and ideals, and he saw a need to develop a radical alternative that would be "American" in nature. Wright, without exaggeration, rethought the procedure for building wood residences from top to bottom, eliminating and simplifying to an extreme degree. In evaluating this system, one should remember that cost was initially a major concern.

The nature of the transformation can be seen in a comparison of the Jacobs house wall with the stylistically similar wall of the Glasner house (1905). Both are based on a similar composition of horizontal wood bands, but the means of execution are totally different, the Glasner house being of conventional balloon-frame construction.

The foundations of the Glasner house are conventional spread footings. The wall is carried below grade and rests on a concrete pad, which distributes the weight of the building over a larger area of earth than the wall alone would have. The distance below grade is determined by the frost line, the line below which the soil does not freeze. If the footing were placed above this line, water in the ground might freeze, expand, and push up on the footing, cracking or even toppling the wall. (This is known as a frost heave.) For this reason, spread footings are used almost universally for single-family houses.

Wright's first method of cost-cutting was to eliminate not only the basement but the entire spread footing foundation system, thus saving the costs of excavation, materials, and construction. In its place he substituted the "dry wall footing" he had used in farm buildings in Wisconsin. The wall rests on a shallow pad set in a sloped trench filled with gravel to enable water to flow away from the wall. According to Wright, no frost heaves would occur because no water would be present. Thus the Jacobs house has only a thickened slab on a gravel bed at the building perimeter. The action of frost is further discouraged by the heating system, which in the process of warming the building also warms the earth beneath the wall.

The exterior wall structure of the Glasner house is traditional balloon-frame construction: 2×4 studs, 16 inches on center, with a ¾-inch layer of wood sheathing on the outside for lateral bracing. This is covered on the inside with plaster, and on the outside with a layer of waterproof building paper and then the horizontal boards and battens of the exterior finish. The building paper acts to intercept any air or water that might penetrate the siding. This construction, if built today, would not be substantially different. The voids between studs would be filled with insulation, and the sheathing would be plywood or insulation board. The Glasner house wall is not only a layered system but also a specialized system. It uses two different trades—carpentry and plastering—and several different operations. The structural materials (studs and sheathing) and the finish materials (plaster and siding) are independent of each other.

Wright's concept of the Usonian wall was to use one trade and to unify structural and finish materials into one system. Thus his wall is finished inside and out with horizontal siding, which acts to structurally support the wall. If the siding were removed from the Glasner house, it would not be affected structurally. If this were done to the Jacobs house, it would collapse.

Wright described this wall as the principle of plywood applied on a large scale. A simple piece of wood, because of its grain, is stronger in one direction than in another. Plywood derives its strength by overlaying alternating sheets of wood with their grains running perpendicular to one another. The center core of the Jacobs house wall is composed of vertical boards, the outer layers of horizontal boards. The inner layer, being concealed, is made of much cheaper wood. This construction is what we would today call a sandwich panel. Being thinner than a

11.23

11.24

P. Hanna house

Frank Lloyd Wright

Palo Alto, California, 1936

11.23 exterior

(Ezra Stoller, ESTO.)

11.24 wall section

A Composition roofing on two-ply foil-covered paper on ⅞" sheathing.

B Joists made of 2 × 9 on top of 2 × 6.

C ½" "Nu Wood" soffit.

D Redwood corner piece. In contrast with the Jacobs house, the corners were not mitered.

E Wall cavity.

F ⅞" × 8" stud.

G Redwood batten.

H ⅞" redwood board. The Hanna house uses the more expensive but more visually appealing redwood for both boards and battens.

I Two-ply oil-coated paper.

J Whereas the base trim of the Jacobs house projects in the traditional manner, the base trim of the Hanna house is recessed in the more typically Wrightian manner.

K Concrete slab with metal spline.

L ½" plywood ceiling. This ceiling, in which joints are made with applied rather than recessed battens (as in the wall), is one of the house's least successful details.

(Frank Lloyd Wright Foundation, drawing 3701.23.)

11.25 Flitch beam similar to that used in the Hanna house. The flitch beam is a method of increasing the strength of a beam without increasing its depth; a steel plate is bolted between two wood joists.

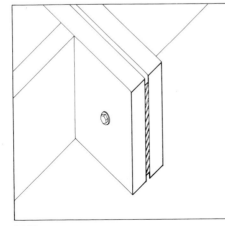

11.25

conventional stud wall, it is considerably less rigid. Wright compensated for this weakness by limiting it to one story, and by using it in short lengths with frequent turns to stiffen it against lateral loads. The longest wood wall is the front side of the living room, and according to Wright the long rows of wood bookcases here act to stiffen the wall.

The differences between the board and batten details are a good indication of the change in style between 1905 and 1936. The boards of the Glasner house are simple elongated rectangles; the battens are simple parallelograms, given a wash and a drip to protect the wall from water. The battens vary in width to create alternating wide and narrow horizontal bands. This detail, along with the accompanying window and door details, shows the conventional use of trim; the molding is used to cover the joint. The Jacobs house wall is a typical Wrightian inversion of the normal. Here the battens are recessed, rather than projecting, and they interlock with the boards in a complex way that discourages penetration of water and allows for movement of the wood. All of the Glasner siding was put in place with finish nails. In the Jacobs wall the batten holds the board in place and is attached with screws, the slots of which are turned horizontally. This same inverted detail is used at the door and window jambs, which—like the battens—recede rather than project, giving an impression of layering to an already thin wall. This is the typical modern attitude toward joinery: Rather than rely on moldings to cover joints, Wright relies on the precision of the machine to create an exposed joint. This was one of the economic drawbacks of the Usonian wall: It required considerably more skill and sophisticated machinery to build than walls such as those of the Glasner house, and the siding for the Usonian Houses was sometimes made in the millwork shop rather than at the site.

The roof structure of the Jacobs house is more conventional. It is composed of joists 16 inches on center, but instead of using a 2×12 Wright uses three 2×4's. Because larger defect-free boards are harder to obtain than small ones, three small boards are often cheaper than a large board of equivalent depth. Wright's intentions were not purely technical; this construction also enabled him to use the three-layered roof detail, which made the roof appear considerably thinner.

The innovation of which Wright was most proud was the radiant heating system (or Gravity Heat, as he called it). In his previous houses he had used forced air or steam radiators, or a combination of the two. The radiant system uses a loop of tightly spaced pipes cast into or under the slab. Heated water circulates throughout these pipes, is transferred to the slab, and is radiated into the room. This was not a cost-saving device, but it did have the tremendous advantage of being invisible, so to speak. There were no duct shafts, dropped ceilings, registers, or radiators to be integrated into the architecture. In this regard the savings were considerable, in comparison with the many radiator pockets and grilles of the Robie house.

Wright went to great lengths to hold down costs in the Jacobs house, not only out of genuine concern for the budget but also because he wished to publicize the house as a prototype for low-cost housing. Bricks rejected for use in the Johnson Wax Building were sold at a reduced price for use in this house, and a low grade of pine was used for the siding (although the narrow battens were made of redwood). Wright was successful from the point of view of economy. The final cost was $5,500, according to Wright—inexpensive for a custom-designed house in the 1930s. The economizing had its effect on the design, however; the Jacobs house is architecturally inferior to many of the subsequent Usonian Houses, particularly because of the low-quality wood used in much of the siding.

The Hanna house, finished later the same year, was much larger, used finer materials, and was much more expensive. Having made his polemical statement about low-cost housing, Wright then felt comfortable applying the Usonian system to larger and less economical commissions. Partially as a result of this, and partially because of lessons learned in the Jacobs house, the Hanna house incorporates many improvements in the basic Usonian system.

11.26

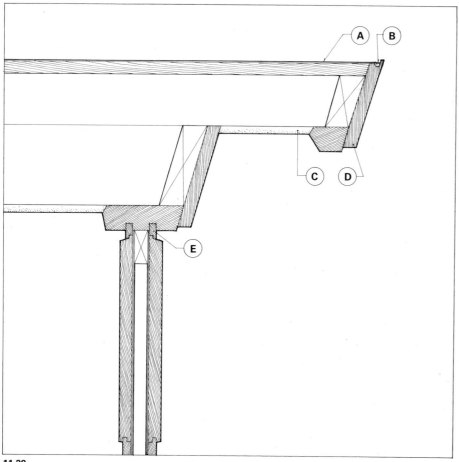

11.28

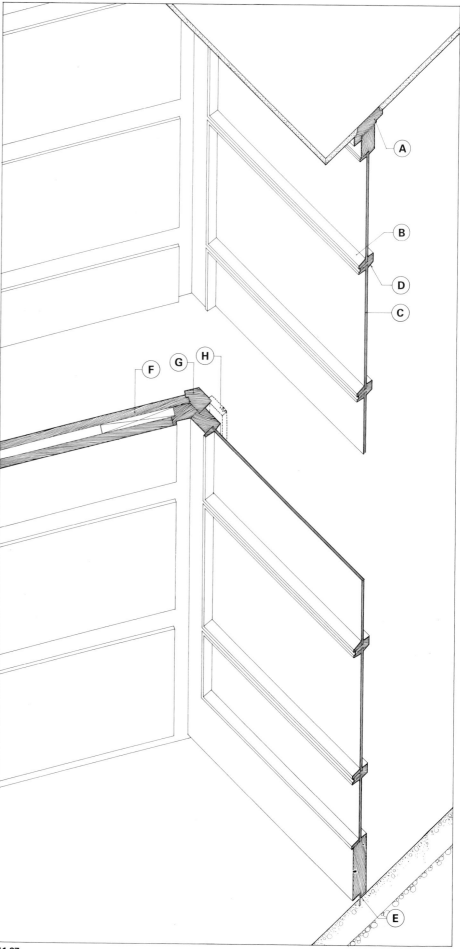

11.27

P. Hanna house

Frank Lloyd Wright

Palo Alto, California, 1936

11.26 exterior

(Ezra Stoller, ESTO.)

11.27 window detail

A Head of door frame.

B Projecting, tapered glass stop.

C $\frac{1}{4}$" glass.

D Redwood muntin. Like the glass stop, this is tapered to minimize its profile and to bring it into character with the angular detailing of the house. Wright used more muntins than were functionally necessary in order to maintain the horizontal module.

E Weatherstriping.

F Typical sandwich panel wall.

G Redwood corner piece.

H Redwood frame holding insect screen.

(Frank Lloyd Wright Foundation, drawing 3701.23.)

11.28 coping detail

A Composition roofing on wood sheathing.

B In conventional detailing, metal flashing would cover the end of the composition roofing and lap over the wood fascia to ensure that no water would penetrate the joint. Here the flashing is turned down into a notch so that it is not visible on the exterior.

C $\frac{1}{2}$" "Nu-wood" soffit.

D Redwood fascia. The fascia and trim is angled here, in keeping with the geometry of the house in plan.

E Redwood batten. One of the problems of Wright's modular grid is that the last piece of trim is half the width of the others.

(Frank Lloyd Wright Foundation, drawing 3701.23.)

The Hanna house winds around the crest of a hill and has numerous retaining walls. The foundations are much more elaborate than those of the Jacobs house, but they adhere in principle to the "dry wall" system. The use of a hexagonal rather than a rectilinear unit grid system does not alter the details in any fundamental way. The special milled pieces made for the corners were vastly superior to the mitered corners of the Jacobs house (which were much more likely to come apart as a result of movement in the wood).

The fundamental technical difference is in the structure and its effect on the wall details. In the Jacobs house, the wood walls were load-bearing and carried the roof joists. The structure of the Hanna house is complex, but can generally be described as a series of flitch beams (a steel plate bolted between two wood joists; see figure 11.25) and trusses spanning between hollow brick piers. Thus, the wood walls of the Hanna house are for the most part non-load-bearing. Accordingly, their cores are not solid wood but a series of very flat studs. In place of the rough pine siding of the Jacobs house, the Hanna house uses fine-grained redwood for both board and battens.

There is no gravity heating system in the Hanna house. It has forced-air heating, because the client feared (correctly) that radiant heating would be slow to respond to temperature changes. Although the house has no basement, it does have an extensive system of utility trenches. In fact, most of the cost-saving devices of the Jacobs house are either missing or deprived of their economic justification here. This does not stop the Hanna house from being a superior building. The Usonian system has many virtues other than economy, and it is best to look at the Hanna house as a statement of the purely architectural qualities of the Usonian system.

Like the textile-block system, the Usonian system was used only by Wright and his close followers; it had little impact on the residential construction industry. Wright was very pleased with it, and virtually all of his wood buildings built after 1936 use it in some way. Given the undoubted architectural quality of the houses built with this system, it deserves a full analysis as to its merits and shortcomings, both in relation to the standards of its own day and with the hindsight we now have as to the technical issues.

By the current standards of performance, the Usonian system has some obvious shortcomings:

Insulation. Wright felt that the only place insulation was really required was the roof, and that it was unnecessary in the walls and floor. Insulation is normally provided only at the edge of the building at grade, since little heat is lost to the earth directly under the building. Energy was cheap in 1936, and, as Wright said, "the insulation of the walls and the air space within becomes less important, with modern systems of air conditioning and heating you can manage almost any condition."[5] By eliminating the traditional cavity between studs in the Jacobs house, Wright eliminated the possibility of insulation. In the Hanna house the cavity exists, although it is thin, but no insulation is provided. An even more serious problem is at the slab perimeter, where the absence of insulation allows much of the heat provided by the radiant heating system to escape into the ground.

The radiant heating system. This has not proved to be popular, perhaps because it is not always cost effective and because it presents serious maintenance problems. Other heating systems make more efficient use of fuel. Part of the problem is that the slab cannot be too hot to touch. Maintenance of the heating coils in a radiant system is not a common problem, but when it occurs it is a major one since the coils are imbedded in the slab. These problems have kept radiant heating out of general use. But it is still used today, for the same reasons for which Wright used it. It is easily integrated into monolithic construction, and it is extremely comfortable for the building's occupants.

Foundations. Wright's elimination of the traditional footing is a highly questionable decision. The "dry wall" system may be adequate, but it is hardly superior to the conventional system. The elimination of conventional footings in the low-

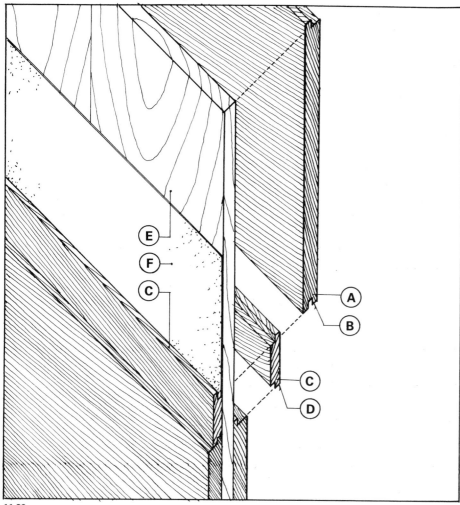

11.29

11.30

11.29 H. Jacobs house
wall detail

A Pine board.

B Groove to receive tongue of batten.

c Redwood batten.

D The tongue-and-groove is altered
here so that the joint is running up,
not down, to discourage water
from penetrating the wall.

E Core boards.

F Building paper.
*(Frank Lloyd Wright Foundation,
drawing 3702.18.)*

11.30 L. Pope house
wall detail

cost Jacobs house is understandable, but their omission from the Hanna house, with its larger budget, seems absurd. There is evidence on both sides of this argument. The "dry wall" system is not used today, and no engineer would recommend it for permanent construction in an area subject to subzero temperatures. On the other hand, it seems to have worked well on the whole as Wright used it. In a survey of Wright house owners in the 1970s, few indicated that they had foundation problems.

These considerations, other than the code restrictions, probably had little to do with the Usonian system's lack of acceptance with the building industry. Style certainly was a factor (not everyone wants a Frank Lloyd Wright house), but other things were involved:

·There was not much wrong with the old system. Builders and architects were happy with the platform-frame system for home building. It was easy to execute, was understood by all, and was stylistically versatile. Gropius, Breuer, and Schindler (as well as the Colonial Revivalists) all built within this system, as did Wright himself in the Glasner house. There was no compelling reason to change.

·The system was tailor-made to Wright's type of house and was limited in its applications. It was essentially a one story system, owing to its thinness, and it could accommodate multiple stories only with a secondary frame, as in the Hanna house. There was much skepticism at the time as to whether the Usonian wall could support even one story. Building officials, quite justifiably, demanded that sample walls be built for structural testing.

·Wright's concept of integrating and unifying trades to save money ran counter to the ultimate direction that American building was to take. It saved material by getting as many uses as possible out of each wood member, but it could require more time, more labor, and more coordination between separate trades (such as millwork and rough carpentry). The sandwich wall system provides an example. Whereas the balloon-frame Glasner house was structurally complete without the finish materials, the builder of a Usonian House had to wait for the boards and battens to be milled (sometimes off site) and put in place before the house would be structurally sound. The development of modern construction has encouraged the development of independent systems and trades. Wright got around these problems at the time by becoming his own contractor. For the construction of each house, one of his apprentices would live at the site and would subcontract and coordinate the work.

Wright failed to produce a system for building houses that was adopted by a major segment of the industry, but Schindler, Gropius, Neutra, Mies, and Eames also failed in the same way. The only viable low-cost alternatives to standard housing today are mobile and modular housing, the architectural results of which have not been inspirational. But although Wright's system does not easily provide, either in its design or in its procedures, a model for today, we should recognize that by the criteria of 1936, when labor and energy were cheap, it was a remarkable achievement.

THE KAUFMANN HOUSE AND THE JOHNSON WAX BUILDING
Both the idea of a building as a metaphor of an organism and the idea of form being inherent in the nature of the materials had been present in Wright's work since 1900. Both ideas were present in Sullivan's work, but mainly in the ornament. Thus the columns of the Gage Building, rather than being separated from their entablature by a molding, run across the joint and burst into flower in what Wright and Sullivan called a plastic treatment. Sullivan, like the Arts and Crafts architects, felt that ornament should be appropriate to the material that received it. Wright expanded this metaphor into the structure of the building—the columns of the Johnson Wax Building are almost literally concrete trees. This is the most obvious example, but the idea has more subtle effects on the structure.

The primary rule of truth to materials required that they be used as they occur in nature. Thus, after 1930 Wright used stone set in its natural bed, with few arches or lintels. Wood, although never used in a rustic way, is cantilevered, just as the

11.31

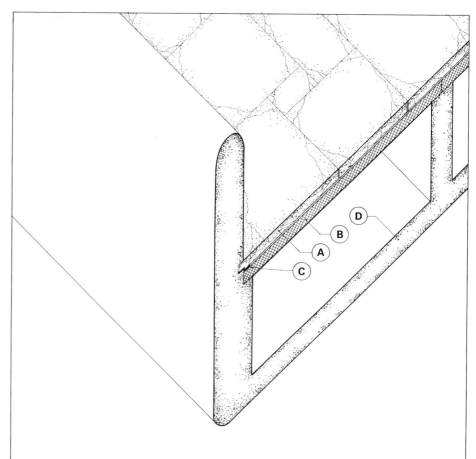

11.32

11.33

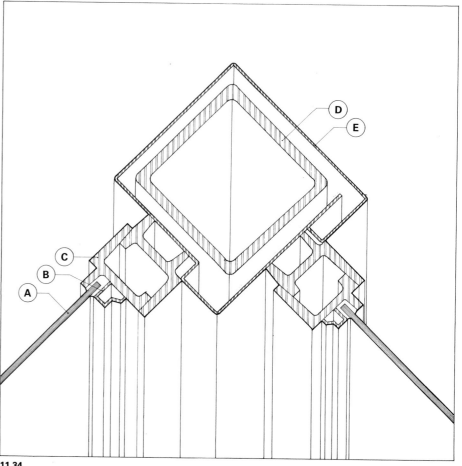

11.34

"Fallingwater"

(E. Kaufmann house)

Frank Lloyd Wright

Ohiopyle, Pennsylvania, 1936

11.31 exterior

(Hedrich-Blessing.)

11.32 balcony detail

A Flagstone paving.

B Two layers of asphalt-saturated felt on gypsum block. The block supports only the stone and is itself supported by the concrete beams.

C Lead flashing set into notch in concrete.

D Concrete slab with upturned concrete beams. Like Le Corbusier and Mies, Wright hides the beams within the depth of the floor to maintain a continuous flat ceiling below.

(Frank Lloyd Wright Foundation, drawing 3602.12 and construction photographs.)

11.33 detail

11.34 window profile

A Glass.

B Glazing bead.

C In-swinging steel casement sash (standard steel sash manufactured by Hope Company). The joint formed by two L-shaped frames allows the metal to move without opening the joint, and creates a pocket of air to ensure that a negative pressure does not force water through the joint.

D $3'' \times 3'' \times \frac{3}{4}''$ steel tube.

E Sheet-steel cover.

(Hope's shop drawings, Avery Library, Columbia University.)

branches of a tree are cantilevered. Artificial materials were to be used as the natural materials they most resembled. Thus brick, which resembles stone in its inability to take tensile stress, is also used with only occasional lintels or arches. Reinforced concrete, like wood, can sustain tensile stress, so its appropriate form is also the cantilever.

Figure 11.38 shows the typical structure of the Johnson Wax Building; figure 11.36 shows the structure of the Kaufmann house. The structure of the Johnson Building is clear and regular, both structurally and metaphorically. The structure of the Kaufmann house is complex by comparison. In the Kaufmann house Wright sacrificed structural clarity to achieve certain visual effects.

The framework of the Kaufmann house consists of four piers—three of concrete and one of stone—which are set on the rock and which support the main floor. The main structure of the second floor is supported by four stone piers forming a square; they rest on the first and the third of the four piers and define the living room. A balcony cantilevers from the main floor parallel to the stream, and a second balcony cantilevers from the second floor perpendicular to the stream, forming the familiar image of the two slabs floating over the waterfall. The upper cantilevered terrace is supported at the edge of the living room by four small steel tees that appear to be part of the window system. An irregular line of rectangles on the uphill side holds the kitchen and bedroom wings.

The column and pier supports are all of monolithic fieldstone except for the four piers and the four steel tees. The concrete floors are of three types, all of which occur in a 2-foot-deep layer reserved for structure. The simplest type is a flat slab at the top of the layer, varying in thickness from 4 to 7 inches. This is used primarily in the kitchen-bedroom wing, which has small spans and load-bearing walls of stone around most of its perimeter. The second type is the stepped structure between the square piers that define the living room (the most geometrically regular portion of the house). Architecturally and structurally, the third type is the most complex; it forms an inverted ribbed slab in which the flat concrete portion forms the ceiling rather than the floor. This structure occupies the full 2 feet of the structural layer, this depth being necessary to achieve enough stiffness in the cantilevers. The floors are formed by gypsum planks spanning between the tops of the concrete ribs, which are then covered with stone paving.

The window details of the Kaufmann house, although some of Wright's most elegant, are uncharacteristic of his work. Wright used wood in all the Usonian Houses to blend with the wood siding, and had also used wood in the California Textile Block Houses. The Kaufmann house's windows are steel, which he had seldom used (e.g., in the Richard Lloyd Jones house of 1929 and the Imperial Hotel of 1915). Steel was popular with the European Modernists of the 1920s, and this may be a case of their influence on Wright. Interestingly enough, they are the only articulation of the unit grid system in the building (in section it is 17 inches); in plan it is impossible to detect if the module is used. (The module was reduced in places by $1\frac{1}{2}$ inches because of changes during construction.)

The window details resemble in concept the detailing of the Usonian wall in that Wright treats horizontal joints differently than vertical joints. Horizontal joints are emphasized and articulate the separateness of the pieces; they are executed in accordance with good practice. The vertical joints are detailed to emphasize continuity and to deemphasize the joint, often at the expense of good practice. Here Wright was working with standard Hopes steel sections; he could not custom-design them as he did with wood, but he did modify them to meet his ends. Thus, a typical horizontal joint of operable window and fixed frame (figure 11.34) is the standard Hopes detail of interlocking sections forming an intermediate air pocket between interior and exterior. At the joining of the two operable pieces at the corner, the fixed vertical rail is omitted. Thus, when both windows are open the room has no corner, and Wright achieves the sort of ambiguity between inside and outside that he was so fond of. Likewise, where the window meets the stone wall the vertical rail is set directly into the stone with only a space to hold the glazing

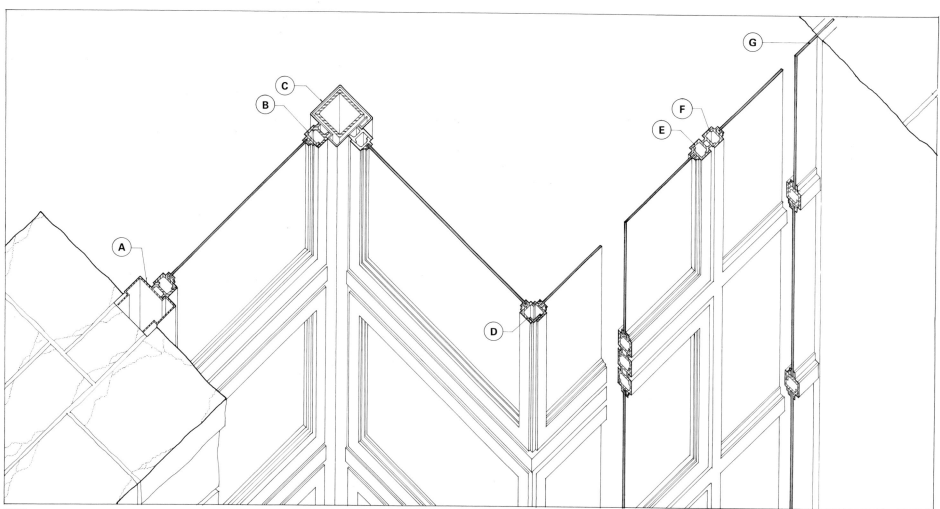

11.35

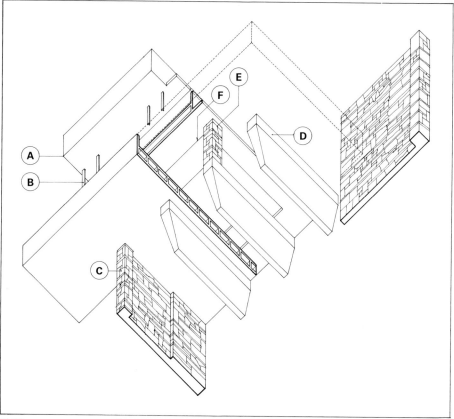

11.36

"Fallingwater"

(E. Kaufmann house)

Frank Lloyd Wright

Ohiopyle, Pennsylvania, 1936

11.35 window details

A Jamb of operable sash at stone wall.

B In-swinging steel casement window.

C 3″ × 3″ × ⅜″ steel tube clad with sheet steel.

D Corner of out-swinging steel casement windows.

E Operable sash.

F Fixed sash.

G Jamb of fixed glass at stone wall. The frame is omitted; the glass is set into a notch in the stone with glazing compound.

(Hope's shop drawings, Avery Library, Columbia University.)

11.36 framing plan

A Cantilevered balcony. This is actually an upside-down ribbed slab, with the ribs concealed within the 2′ depth of the structural cavity.

B 2″ × 2½″ steel T's. Although they appear to be part of the window system, these four posts are major supports of the balcony above.

C Masonry pier. The outermost pier is of stone rather than concrete, since it is the most visually prominent.

D Concrete piers supporting first floor and resting on rock.

E Stone columns. The main living area is framed by four stone columns resting on concrete piers.

F The concrete slab above the living room steps up to become a simple flat slab at the center.

(Frank Lloyd Wright Foundation, drawing 3602.12.)

compound. This, again, emphasizes continuity between interior and exterior, and—by giving the windows a visual discontinuity—merges them with the rest of the composition. Neither of these details is technically desirable. The omitted corner rail would act to keep the joint closed should the steel frames twist or warp, and reglazing of the glass set into the wall is extremely difficult. But these are not major flaws, and no one would want to see them detailed otherwise.

To many the Kaufmann house is Wright's masterpiece and one of the greatest American buildings. The role that detailing plays in this assessment is not easy to judge. One might say of this house, as Philip Johnson said of the Guggenheim Museum, that it has no details. Its dominant elements are stone and concrete, and our major response is to the spaces and forms they create. At the same time, the bands of bright red steel windows are just as integral a part of the house. There are also a few sour notes. The streamlined metal shelves in the living room, with their Art Deco styling, introduce the style of the moment into what is otherwise a timeless piece. On the other hand, the wood trim and cove lighting in the concrete coffer of the living room, with its rows of dentils, is a leftover from Wright's Prairie House years, and seems out of character here. Not accidentally, it recalls the trim in a similar location in the D. D. Martin house of 1904.

The Kaufmann house has a sort of spiritual relationship with the Martin house. In 1904, having just finished the steel-and-concrete Larkin Building, Wright used those same materials in the next house he designed, the Martin house. Afterwards he returned to more conventional housing construction systems. The Johnson Wax Building and the Kaufmann house share a similar relationship, having been designed almost simultaneously, and show a similar relationship of systems and materials.

The Johnson Wax Building is at the same time one of Wright's best and most problematic buildings. Jonathan Lipman and Edgar Tafel have detailed the numerous problems that arose during design and construction and continued after the building's completion. These problems are not all circumstantial; many were the direct outgrowth of a conflict between Wright's vision and the conventions of the American building industry.

A greatly simplified description of the Johnson Wax Building is that it consists of a grid of 60 tree-like columns forming a large single hall with balconies, surrounded by an almost windowless wall of brick. The metaphor of the forest is completed by the skylights that fill the spaces between the round column capitals.

The columns of the Johnson Wax Building are probably Wright's most literal expressions of the organic metaphor. In the working drawings he refers to the top as the petal and the throat as the calyx. The metaphor extends further. Rather than the standard round reinforcing bars, Wright used a membrane of expanded metal mesh (figure 11.47). While in Arizona he had become fascinated with the structure of the Saguaro and the Cholla cactus. Both have wood lattice skeletons of a diamond-like pattern, which are concealed in the green pulpy outside of the Saguaro and the fine crust of needles that cover the Cholla. Both plants recalled to Wright not only the skeleton-and-flesh nature of the human body, but also the structure of reinforced concrete. Wright proudly announced that "this marks the end of rod-reinforced concrete."[6]

The columns are not exactly what they appear to be. They are not solid, but are composed of two cross-beams and three concentric rings. They are not free-standing; they are tied at points of tangency to provide lateral bracing, and the cross-beams are continuous. The structure is in fact a continuous grid of columns and beams. Wright was fond of telling and retelling the story of how the sample column withstood many times the load it was required to sustain, but the Johnson Wax Building was hardly an engineering triumph. The columns are on a 20-foot grid—rather small for a contemporary office—and they support only the roof. However, the structure is undeniably beautiful.

11.37

11.38

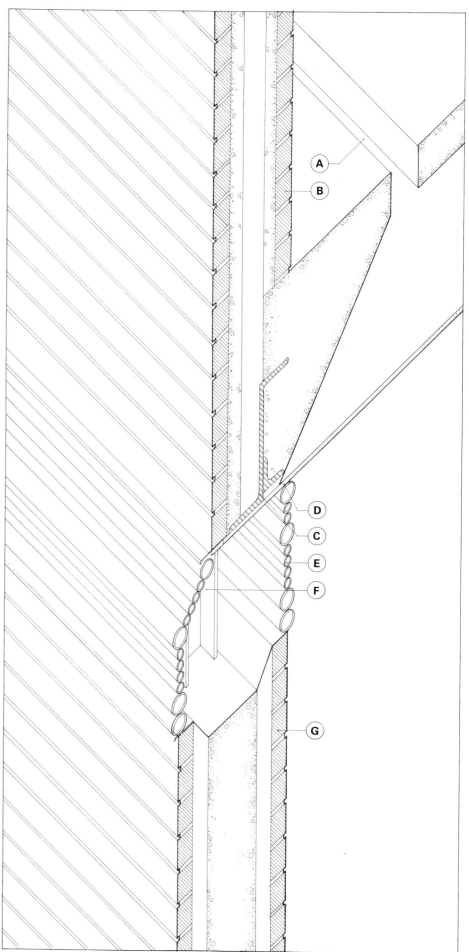

11.39

S. C. Johnson and Son Office Building

Frank Lloyd Wright

Racine, Wisconsin, 1939

11.37 aerial view
(Johnson Wax Company.)

11.38 interior
(Johnson Wax Company.)

11.39 wall section

A Concrete floor slab with slot for air distribution.

B Upper wall construction. A layer of brick on each face forms a cavity, which is then filled with cork boards and then concrete with reinforcing on either side.

C Structural steel Z and angle. This is supported by a steel column (not shown in the drawing).

D Plaster ceiling. The space between the concrete slab and the plaster ceiling is used for air distribution.

E Pyrex glass tubing.

F Cast-aluminum rack to hold glass tubes.

G Lower wall construction. The cork layer here is separated by a concrete wall.

(Frank Lloyd Wright Foundation, drawing 3601.10.)

The walls of the Johnson Building are brick inside and out, showing again Wright's desire to use monolithic construction and to blur differences between interior and exterior. The design of this wall is in many ways superior to the textile-block and Usonian walls, but it has the potential for some of the same problems. Two walls are used in the building, both of the sandwich type. The first type occurs in the lower portion of the wall below the window; it is structural in that it supports one end of the balcony. It has an inner core of concrete faced on both sides first with layers of cork insulation and then with bricks (figure 11.39). The second type extends from the balcony floor to the clerestory. It is not structural, but must support itself since it is unbraced at the top. It is formed by laying up two wythes of brick, placing a layer of cork in the center of the cavity, and then placing concrete with a reinforcing grid in the spaces left on either side.

The strong point of this design is the insulation. Wright was extremely thorough in this regard throughout the building, insulating the footings and providing an insulating slab on top of the columns. Its weak point is again a lack of concern with water. As a rule concrete, provided it is not cracked, is impervious to water. Brick and mortar as a rule are not. It is possible in theory to build a waterproof wall of brick and mortar, but the chances of failure are so great that the practice has been to use the cavity wall—that is, to assume that the wall would leak and make allowances for it. The concrete core of the Johnson design could have conceivably made the wall impervious, but only by the use of a carefully designed and controlled concrete mix.

Wright's wall shows a sensitivity to the nature of construction not shared by many Modernists. Many, like Wright, desired to build monolithic masonry walls with identical interior and exterior finishes, despite the tendency toward the insulated layered cavity wall. Louis Kahn struggled with this problem. Wright, at an early date, realized this contradiction and brought it into his conceptual thinking with the sandwich wall concept.

The windows and skylights of the Johnson Wax Building leaked badly for many years. They are the building's architectural glory and its technical nightmare. Wright's attitude is somewhat baffling, since he neglected some fundamental practices of construction that, to judge from his earlier work, he understood very well. His method was, to say the least, experimental. Construction was underway before the basic glazing system was even decided upon, and a number of products that had just become available (such as Pyrex tubing and silicone glazing) were used. Perhaps Wright placed too much faith in the ability of these new materials to change the nature of architectural detailing.

The skylights and the windows are similar in design. Both use various sizes of round Pyrex tubing, held in place by cast aluminum racks. The windows have two layers of tubes, the skylights one. All joints between tubes and between frames are butt joints caulked with a silicone glazing compound. The designs of both systems violate a number of industry practices of the 1930s:

· Butt joints in glass were unacceptable. Glass is subject to large thermal movements, and the traditional U-shaped window frame joint when filled with putty or glazing compound allows for these.

· Skylights were never flat. All exterior horizontal surfaces were sloped to avoid standing water, which will eventually soak through most materials. It would not soak through glass, of course, but it would soak through the joints.

· Skylights were usually fitted with condensation gutters to draw off water from condensation before it could fall to the floor.

Wright had followed all the standard practices in the past. The Larkin Building's skylight is an excellent example; it has a flat ornamental glass light and a sloped glass skylight (with condensation gutters). His previous window designs had not drastically altered the fundamental technology of the window.

11.40

11.41

11.42

11.43

S. C. Johnson and Son Office Building

Frank Lloyd Wright

Racine, Wisconsin, 1939

11.40 interior

(Johnson Wax Company.)

11.41 skylight detail

showing installation of caulking at
glass skylight. These skylights
became a major source of leaks, in
part because rainwater could not
adequately drain off the flat top
and in part because of the
numerous crevices between the
glass tubes.

(Johnson Wax Company.)

11.42 view

(Johnson Wax Company.)

11.43 masonry wall under construction

The cork insulation and the steel
reinforcing are visible. The
remaining cavity was filled with
concrete.

(Johnson Wax Company.)

Wright obviously felt that the standard practices were no longer necessary, but he was correct in only one of his assumptions—butt glazing of windows has become commonplace, largely because of silicone. The design of skylights still follows the general practice used in the Larkin Building and in standard commercial systems. A distinction is always made between a window system and a skylight system.

Through the course of construction, the contractor and even Wright's apprentice Edgar Tafel argued with Wright to change the skylight design. Wright apparently saw no reason why a good window system would not be a good skylight system. He could not have been more wrong. After 20 years during which the skylights were almost constantly being recaulked, the Johnson Company finally covered the leaky skylights with conventional sloped and framed skylights in 1957.

Wright's attitude toward detailing in the Johnson Wax Building was what might be called perfectionist. Every element had to be executed as specified, put in exactly the right place, made to exactly the right size, and made of precisely the components and the materials that Wright called for. If the contractor or the workman erred, there was nothing in the construction to accommodate the results. Most common detailing practice, in 1935 or in 1989, is the opposite. It assumes errors and inaccuracies will occur during construction and takes steps to accommodate them. The cavity wall, which makes allowances for leaks, and the typical molding, which makes allowances for inaccuracies in size, are examples. The majority of architects detail in this way, assuming that mistakes will occur and must be accommodated. Others, such as Wright in his later years, have taken the opposite view: that the architect should demand and ensure that the building be executed correctly, and that the architect should detail accordingly.

When Wright presented the schematic design to Herbert Johnson in August of 1936, he informed him that the office building would cost $250,000. The building was completed in April of 1939, behind schedule and $600,000 over the budget. The research tower, finished in 1950, had similar problems. When construction began the estimated cost was $1.2 million. It was completed for three times that amount. What caused this? Many of the problems resulted from Wright's indecision and delay in providing drawings to the contractor as they were needed. Some factors make Wright seem somewhat unprofessional; for example, even when construction was well underway, Wright had no idea how he would enclose the windows. But most revealing as to the separate courses being taken by modern architecture and modern construction are the problems caused by the building's tightly integrated systems, and the problems caused by the degree of tolerance, or accuracy, that was required.

Wright, like many modern architects, thought that a functional building would be a tightly integrated one, and a cheaper one as well. In an integrated building—one in which the separate systems tightly interlocked—fewer elements would be used, and more functions would be performed by each element. Simplicity would yield not only order but economy. Concrete, for example, can serve as both structural and finish material, and is therefore preferable in this system to steel, which can only be structural and must be plastered over for finish. Another example is one we have already seen in the Usonian House wall: Rather than use the traditional system, in which exterior siding, wood structure, and interior plaster are three different systems performing three different roles and installed by three different workmen, Wright combined them all into one system in which exterior and interior finish were not only the same material but also part of the structure. This attitude is very much like that of the traditional architect. The stone walls of Chartres Cathedral are structure, interior finish, and exterior finish. Ironically, the tendency of modern construction is to do the opposite of what Wright intended and to have independent and specialized elements rather than integrated and multifunctional ones. The primary reasons for this are organizational and have to do with specialization of labor and materials within the building industry, particularly in the case of large-scale buildings.

11.44

11.45

11.46

11.47

S. C. Johnson and Son Office Building
Frank Lloyd Wright
Racine, Wisconsin, 1939

11.44 Johnson Wax tower
(Johnson Wax Company.)

11.45 interior
(Johnson Wax Company.)

11.46 installation of glass tubing
In the original building, the Pyrex glass tubes were joined with a simple caulk joint. In later additions the joint was made with a gasket that fit into grooves in the tubing, as shown. This lessened the possibility of joint failure as the glass expanded and contracted.
(Johnson Wax Company.)

11.47 installation of steel reinforcing
Note the use of both conventional bar reinforcing and expanded metal (the diamond-shape material). Wright felt the latter was more organic because of its resemblance to natural structures.
(Johnson Wax Company.)

11.48 diagram of Johnson Building-type skylight

11.49 diagram of Larkin Building-type skylight

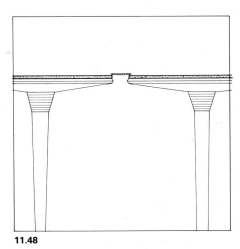

11.48

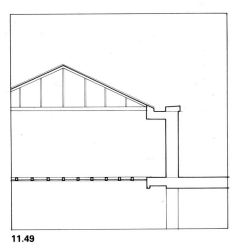

11.49

A building like the Johnson Wax Building is not built by one company but by a general contractor. He may have a large number of employees himself (he did not in this case), but he basically hires a number of other companies—subcontractors—who specialize in certain trades, such as concrete, brick, heating, and plumbing. A bricklayer working on the Johnson Building would only lay bricks, being an employee of the brick subcontractor. He would not work on concrete or insulation or other related aspects of the wall, and when he was done he would lay bricks on another building. Chartres Cathedral might be said to have had four subcontractors: one for stone, one for wood, one for metal, and one for glass. The Johnson Wax Building had over a hundred.

The more obvious implications of this type of organization can be seen in the debate between the various unions as to which union should install the glass tubing. Under union regulations, masons could not install windows and glazers could not lay bricks. Wright confused the issue by using glass tubing instead of windows. This did not fit into the neat system of division of labor. Who should install it: glaziers? masons? concrete workers? In the tower, the solution was a compromise: Glaziers and masons did alternating floors.

In a more subtle way, the implications can be seen in the problems of constructing a typical wall. Wright's design called for the laying of two layers of brick, which were then to be filled with insulation and concrete. If the finished construction is considered, this appears logical; the brick and the concrete bind together as a unit. If the realities of the procedure are considered, it was a nightmare. The concrete workers had to stand and wait (while being paid) until the masons had completed the outer walls. In the construction of the main block, which was only two stories tall, this did not cause severe problems. In the construction of the 15-story tower the problem was aggravated. The client, the contractor, and Wright's apprentices determined that it would be cheaper to build the concrete separately and apply the brick layer as a veneer. Wright refused to permit this. The result is a testament to the degree of Wright's alienation from the society in which he lived: The contractor, the client, and the apprentices agreed to build the systems independently and not to tell Wright. Cram, the Greenes, and Gimson were all alienated in similar ways. Their concepts of logical building did not coincide with those of the men with whom they worked. But Wright was comfortable in his defiance. Whether he was foolishly defying the realities of modern life or heroically defying the absurdities of modern society is impossible to say.

12   Conclusion

What does architecture amount to in the experience of the mass of men? I never in all my walks came across a man engaged in so simple and natural an occupation as building his house. . . . It is not the tailor alone who is the ninth part of a man; it is as much the preacher, and the merchant, and the farmer. Where is this division of labor to end?

Henry David Thoreau, *Walden*

An architect cannot construct a building without a theory of construction, however simple-minded that theory might be. Construction is not mathematics; architectural construction is just as subjective a process as is architectural design. Construction involves a more complex set of concerns, the application of scientific laws, and a tradition (or perhaps a conventional wisdom) as to how things ought to be built, but that tradition and that wisdom are no more or less valid than the tradition or conventional wisdom as to how buildings should appear.

Each of the architects considered in this study had a theory of construction and a theory of detail. Some of these theories, like those of Wagner, were sophisticated in thought and in execution. Some, like those of McKim and White, were crude in conception but sophisticated in execution. Some, like those of Lutyens, were sophisticated in detail but crude in construction. And some, like those of Le Corbusier, were sophisticated in conception and crude in execution. All these men had in common the fact that, in order to build, they had to compromise; the degree of the success or failure of each depended on how their perceptions of the reality of building, or their conception of an ideal form of building, differed from the construction industries' conception of good building. It is no accident that the most successful of these architects in numbers of commissions were those who were the least systematic and the most inconsistent in the application of their ideas.

It is surprising how great, in almost every case, is the difference between conception and reality. But this is less surprising if we examine the origins of these architects' ideas about building. Some came from nineteenth-century theoreticians such as Pugin and Viollet-de-Duc, whose ideas in turn came from the analysis of archaic masonry buildings that had little in common with modern structures. Other ideas were drawn from the architects' perceptions of the process of industrialization—the way they believed cars or airplanes were built. These perceptions were often based more on images than on realities. Few ideas were drawn from an analysis of the building industry as it existed.

As architects' ideas about modern construction developed, modern construction developed as well—often in the opposite direction. Architects were aware of the major changes in architectural technology after 1875, such as the development of the skeletal frame and the enormous increase in the quantity and sophistication of mechanical equipment. Architects responded to these changes, and architectural historians (Giedion, Frampton, and Banham in particular) have described their responses in detail.

Some subtler but equally important changes have also occurred:

The development of layered construction. The idea that walls in ancient or medieval architecture were monolithic was largely an illusion. Marbles have always been veneered, interiors have always been plastered, and even in a simple stone wall the quality stone was always placed on the faces. In the 1930s and the 1940s, developments occurred which created a trend toward layered construction: the development of machinery to veneer expensive woods, stones, and metals; the widespread use of the brick cavity wall; and the development of frame buildings, which freed the wall of its load-bearing function and enabled it to be designed specifically to accommodate insulation and waterproofing. There are and always will be building systems and building types with monolithic structures and finishes, but the trends of the construction industry of the present and the recent past have gone in the opposite direction.

The development of specialized components. In the traditional monolithic wall, all functions—structure, insulation, waterproofing, and finish—are performed by one or two materials. In the modern layered wall, there is a separate component for each function—structural frame, insulation, waterproofing (cavity or membrane), vapor barrier, interior finish, and exterior finish. This is only scratching the surface of this phenomenon. The medieval parish church might have five or six different materials in addition to wood and stone; its modern equivalent, regardless of exterior appearance, would require over a hundred.

The specialization of labor. Accompanying the specialization of components was the specialization of labor. Each of the specialized components was installed by a specialized craftsman. The English parish church might have involved specialized masons and carpenters; its modern equivalent would require a hundred different types of workmen, corresponding to the hundred different specialized materials. Within this multiplicity of materials and skills is an exact hierarchy of craftsmanship. Exterior stonework is precise in its finish and tolerances; concealed steelwork and concrete are not. Unit masonry and rough carpentry lie somewhere in between. In contemporary construction, this tolerance or allowable degree of inaccuracy is almost legislated by a multiplicity of standard specifications, manufacturers' organizations, and building codes.

The development of independent building systems. Many of the buildings discussed in the beginning of this book are hybrids of load-bearing wall and frame. Many of the larger buildings of Richardson, McKim, Lutyens, and Wright are made from modern structural components, but these components are arranged in a tightly integrated way, so that masonry, ironwork, and carpentry had to be erected almost simultaneously. The development of independent subcontractors, specialized workmen, and specialized materials made this degree of integration undesirable. The modern steel subcontractor wishes to erect his frame and leave the site as quickly as possible, with a minimum of interaction with other subcontractors.

The development of building typologies. This is not so much a development that occurred as one that did not. The artisan who worked on Chartres Cathedral did not live in a house with stone vaults. Different materials and different assemblies of those materials have always been used for different building types, and the greatest difference has always been between the single-family house and the large-scale institution. Many expected that industrialization would erase this difference, that all buildings would be built of standardized, factory-made components. Modern building techniques, if they have affected this distinction at all, have probably increased it. This is less true in Europe, where single-family houses are not as common and lumber not so plentiful as in America. In America there exist two separate and independent building industries, which use different materials and procedures and which do not operate by the same rules. Much of the specialization of labor that has occurred in the construction of larger buildings has not occurred in residential construction, where workmen often work at a variety of tasks.

This, then, was and is the reality of modern construction. There is no reason to assume that these characteristics are irreversible or inevitable. They represent only the tradition of building as it exists. Large-scale changes may reverse this tradition; for example, the long-awaited factory-produced house may become the standard. Or more subtle changes might have major effects; if steel were to become vastly more expensive than concrete, we might see a return to monolithic construction. Or the conventional wisdom, the modern traditions of building, may be wrong. Specialized components, specialized labor, and independent systems may not be the most inexpensive way to build. There is no reason to assume that the opinions of the American building industry are any more infallible than the opinions of the American automobile industry.

But the above-mentioned trends are the tradition of the modern building industry, and not of modern architects. While these modern building systems were developing, modern architects were pursuing their own theoretical agenda. Trends in the theory of modern building can be identified which are independent of, and often opposite to, trends in the development of modern construction. If these latter trends are striking in their independence from the former, it is because they are the result of responses to ideology and not of analysis:

The trend toward monolithic construction. In 1953, Mies van der Rohe, who had built the layered and veneered Barcelona Pavilion, built the monolithic exposed-frame Commons Building at the Illinois Institute of Technology. In 1935 Le Corbusier, who had proposed the multilayer, aircraft-like wall of the Loucher Houses in 1929, built the house at St. Cloud with monolithic stone walls; and in 1936 Frank Lloyd Wright, who had so carefully ornamented his early plaster-and-wood houses to describe their concealed structures, built the Kaufmann house with solid stone walls. How is it that these three "masters of modern architecture" were following a direction opposite to that of the construction industry? In fact it was due to circumstances: Cheap fuel, cheap labor, small buildings, and small budgets made monolithic construction seem viable during the Depression. But this does not explain the monolithic construction of the Farnsworth house or Fallingwater. Layered building systems conceal their structural frames—frames which these architects felt bound to express. To do so required either an analogous structural system or a partial exposure or expression. All of this implied the use of symbols and the making of purely aesthetic choices, which these architects found unacceptably subjective. Modern architecture was to be objective, inevitable, and free from style. It could not be so if the apparent structural system of its buildings was largely symbolic. The ideas of those who saw modern building as layered in nature, such as Wagner and Loos, were rejected by those, like Schindler, who might best have pursued them.

The desire for a uniform level of craft. This idea originated in the Arts and Crafts movement when writers such as Dresser and Cram called attention to Japanese and medieval building, in which the level of craftsmanship was uniformly high. It was also somewhat inevitable; in a building where everything is exposed, everything must achieve a minimum level of accuracy in execution. Writers have always admired architects (such as Mies) who demanded this level of perfection at considerable expense to his clients, without much explanation as to why it is so admirable. Ruskin's idea that a certain degree of inaccuracy and imperfection was desirable had a great deal of influence, and still does today, but controlling the degree of acceptable inaccuracy has proved as difficult as controlling the degree of acceptable precision. This is the most illogical of the constructional ideas of Modernism. It is certainly the most expensive, and (not by coincidence) the least adhered to in practice. The sins of the Greenes, who used milled and nailed lumber in the Gamble house attic, are no greater or lesser than those of any of their contemporaries or followers. Architects such as Cram solved the problem by demanding uniform craftsmanship of their disciples but not of their clients.

The desire for perfect joinery. In traditional joinery, ornament, trim, and craft were closely integrated. Moldings were used to cover joints and make transitions, both visually and technically. Modernists demanded the simplification and then the elimination of trim, and the seamless, perfect joint became the Modern ideal. The Arts and Crafts architects eliminated trim to display the craft of joining. Wright, feeling that the machine had eliminated the functional need for trim, dissociated it from joinery and then eliminated it altogether. Other Modernists, such as Mies and Le Corbusier, felt that industrialization was closely connected with abstraction and minimalism. In fact, most of the operations in question (plastering, for example) were little affected by mechanization, and these architects really were only finding ways to disguise trim. Where it could not be disguised, it was transformed to eliminate or at least contradict traditional associations. These details were certainly abstract, but there was nothing industrial about them; they often required more hand labor than traditional details. Trim has never disappeared from architecture; only the quality of its design has disappeared. But again architects abandoned a reasonable system not because it was outmoded, or irrational, but because it required them to make aesthetic choices—choices which they did not wish to make or appear to be making.

The industrialization of building. This is a dream that has and yet has not come true. No architect-designed prototypes were mass-produced on a large scale. Few architect-designed alternatives found their way into general use. The reasons for this failure have been described in depth by Gilbert Herbert[1] and others. On the other hand, mass-produced factory buildings exist. Modular housing, pre-engineered metal buildings, and precast concrete structural systems make up a substantial portion of buildings built in the United States, but architects as we think of them are not much involved in that industry. Standardization has occurred, but it is not of the scale and type envisioned, and in most instances it is a standardization so varied as to impose few limitations.

The desire for integrated building systems. It seems logical now, as it did fifty years ago, that a good building would use a minimum number of components, each of which would perform a maximum number of functions. It seems logical that the various systems in a building's structure, mechanical and architectural, should interact and determine each other's configurations, that there should be a "tight fit" between systems, that they should be integrated. It seems illogical to most architects, who are trained to value order for its own sake, that this is not true. The hybrid load-bearing and frame structures of the 1890s and the 1920s are logical in their conservation of material, but the amount of coordination that would be required to execute them today is often difficult. Wright's Johnson Wax Building, with its organic analogy of tightly interlocking concrete, brick, and ductwork, directly contradicts the organization of the American building industry, which has chosen to pursue specialized and independent components.

It seems hard to believe that so many leaders of the architectural profession in this century could be unaware of the developments of modern construction, or that they should be reluctant to make aesthetic choices. The answer is that they were not. But before we explore this dilemma, we must look at those aesthetic decisions that were made.

Of course Modernist detailing was not devoid of aesthetic decisions, any more than Modern architecture was. Nor was it as devoid of precedent as Modernists would like us to believe. One of the surprising characteristics of Modernism is how traditional it is. Sir John Summerson noted this in discussing buildings by Behrens and Perret:

In those buildings by two masters of the Modern Movement we have two statements regarding the possible interpretation of the classical language in terms of steel (Behrens) and reinforced concrete (Perret). Buildings such as these claimed in their day a new freedom, unrelated to specific orders and yet still closely related to the rhythms and general disposition of classical architecture. There was no reason at all why this kind of diagrammatic classicism should not prevail indefinitely as the medium for new constructions—indeed, plenty of buildings are still being built very close in expression to Perret's work of the 'twenties.[2]

A great deal of Modern architecture, and a great number of its details, are best understood as inversions of tradition. The composition of the detail reverses our expectations of what it should do. The base, which ought to project, recedes. The window stop, which ought to be recessed and curved, is projecting and square. The panel trim, which ought to project to cover a joint, recedes to reveal it. These details occur again and again in the works of Wright, Loos, Mies, and even Lutyens. These architects were aware, perhaps unconsciously, that an understanding of Classical detailing was somehow essential to the perception of Modern detailing.

Many of the typical facade details of Modernism are best understood as reversals, if not quite inversions, of the language of Classicism or perhaps of the language of load-bearing masonry. Classical facade details were designed to make the strength of the building not just adequate but apparent—to demonstrate literally how the weight of the building finds its way to the ground. The use of battered walls, rusticated joints, and larger stones in the lower courses, projecting plinths with moldings, and reductions in joint spacings toward the top of walls all acted to increase the apparent weight of these buildings at their bases and to increase the perceived stability of the building. Deeply recessed windows and the use of solid stones at corners and jambs acted to demonstrate the thickness of the wall with the same result.

Alan Colquhoun has shown how Modern facade composition is also often a reverse of the Classical.[3] The projecting ground floor is recessed so that the building floats, and the projecting massive cornice becomes the hollowed-out or recessed roof terrace. The details of these facades are also reversals of the Classical. The recessed window comes flush with the surface or even projects. The deeply recessed and staggered stone joints become minimal and gridded. Each element is manipulated to emphasize the thinness and lightness of the wall and to emphasize for the first time the continuity of wall and window.

The purpose of much of traditional detail was to provide scale. The essence of many Modern facades was abstraction, which requires a certain amount of scale-lessness. Many details were not reversed but eliminated or minimized. Thick wood window frames were abandoned for thinner and less visible steel windows. Eliminating trim and moldings eliminated the possibility of establishing scale through multiplication. But other details were transformed; for example, the balustrade, often used gratuitously in Classical buildings to define size, was replaced by a pipe rail fulfilling the same function.

While recognizing that Modern detailing was considerably affected by precedents in traditional architecture, it is equally important to acknowledge the impact of Modernism and the Modernist vision on traditional architecture in the twentieth century.

Critics who have focused on the extent to which McKim and White were copyists have obscured the extent to which they altered what they were copying. Their use of the orders was based not on ideal models from treatises and exact ratios, but on specific examples from antiquity, whose ratios and even configurations were often changed to suit conditions. Unlike those of Lutyens, these alterations were systematic and were made only when necessary, but it was a system based on perception rather than on ideal proportions. In this respect it was a "Modern system," one that Alberti or Palladio would find strange.

We usually judge architects to be Modernists by the extent of abstraction, and we have never really stopped using the definitions given by Hitchcock and Johnson in 1932. In this regard Lutyens is in the camp of the traditionalists. In other ways, the ways in which T. S. Eliot and James Joyce are Modernists, Lutyens is very much one. It is more than the rather loose way in which he uses traditional forms (his orders are almost never correctly proportioned); it is the inconsistencies and juxtapositions of the Classical and the vernacular, of Georgian and Tudor, and of varying levels of perfection and craft that occur in his work. Modern art and literature deal with more than just abstraction. They deal with shifting and simultaneous points of view, with the juxtaposition of disparate and even contradictory elements, with the displacement of object from context, with fragmentation, and with reconstruction. In this way Lutyens suggests avenues of Modernist detailing that we have not completely explored, although this same type of contradiction and inconsistency is present in the work of Wright and Rietveld.

To return to an earlier question: How is it that so many of the major architects of this century were so much at variance with modern building? Surely they must have realized that the building industry was evolving in ways often the opposite of those they were themselves pursuing. They, of course, did realize this. To varying degrees they understood what was happening, but they did not agree with it. Few based their ideas on an analysis of contemporary trends. More often they sought models of construction where they sought models of form and adapted them to current conditions. Cram looked to medieval England, McKim to ancient Rome, Le Corbusier to industry, and Wright to nature, not just for formal inspiration, but for the processes of building as well. In most cases they considered these formal models to be vastly superior to contemporary methods. These architects differed primarily in how they adapted these model techniques to suit contemporary conditions and in the degree to which they compromised their ideals when presented with difficulties.

Without intending to do so, I have shown much that was rational about the construction of traditional buildings in the twentieth century and much that was irrational in the construction of Modern architecture. But the architects of this century who challenged the status quo in form or technology should not be criticized for doing so. Lutyens, Richardson, and the early Wright dealt with the world as it is, to a point. Le Corbusier, Cram, and the later Wright dealt with the world as it might be, to a point. However admirable Schindler or Wagner and their work might be to us today, it is better to view them as role models than to study their methodologies. If we wish to use their forms, we must reconcile them with our technology, just as they reconciled their forms with the technology of their day. There are, perhaps, some lessons that can be learned:

· Traditional forms are not necessarily incompatible with modern technology. New techniques may require only the transformation of old forms, not the creation of new ones.

· There cannot be a value-free architecture based on objective decisions. The techniques of contemporary building are such that, for better or worse, aesthetic decisions must be made.

· Detailing is only appropriate or inappropriate, not good or bad; or it is good or bad only in the way a building is. Detailing is no more deterministic than design. It is simply a design process informed by technology.

Having established, I hope, that there is little objective basis for detailing and building in Modern architecture, I have also established that there is little objective basis for the technological criticism of Modern architecture. Design and criticism in form or in technology requires us to take a position in relation to building traditions, to the social order, and to our professional obligations. Whether we are, in the words of Saint Paul, "conformed to this world" or "transformed by the renewal of our minds to that which is good and acceptable and perfect" is a decision we must each make ourselves.

Notes

CHAPTER 1

1. G. E. Street, *Brick and Marble in the Middle Ages* (London: J. Murray, 1874), p. 400.

2. H. S. Goodhart-Rendel, *English Architecture Since the Regency* (London: Constable, 1953), p. 18.

3. John Ruskin, "The Seven Lamps of Architecture," in *Selected Prose of John Ruskin*, ed. M. Hodgart (New York: Signet, 1972), p. 66.

4. Julien Guadet, *Eléments et Théorie de L'Architecture*, fourth edition, volume 1 (Paris: Librarie de la Construction Moderne, 1901–1904), p. 214.

5. Ibid., p. 116.

6. Ibid., p. 117.

7. Kazimir Malevich, "God Is Not Cast Down," in *Essays on Art* (London: Rapp & Whiting, 1968), p. 201.

8. Goodhart-Rendel, *English Architecture Since the Regency*, p. 192.

9. John Ruskin, "The Stones of Venice," in *Selected Prose of John Ruskin*, ed. M. Hodgart, p. 123.

10. Montgomery Schuyler, "The Peoples Savings Bank of Cedar Rapids, Iowa—Louis H. Sullivan, Architect," *Architectural Record* 31 (January 1912), pp. 44–56.

11. Eugène-Emanuel Viollet-le-Duc, *Discourses on Architecture*, volume 1, tr. B. Bucknall (New York: Grove Press, 1959), p. 435.

12. *The Works of John Ruskin*, ed. E. T. Cook and Al. Wedderburn (London: Library Edition, 1903–1912), volume 20, lecture 1, paragraph 24.

13. Leopold Eidlitz, *The Nature and Function of Art* (New York: A. C. Armstrong, 1881; New York: Da Capo, 1977), p. 320.

CHAPTER 2

1. A. W. Pugin, *Principles of Pointed or Christian Architecture* (London: John Weale, 1841; New York: Academy Editions, 1973), p. 1.

2. Ibid., p. 25.

3. E. E. Viollet-le-Duc, *Discourses on Architecture*, volume 2, tr. B. Bucknall (Boston Ticknor, 1889; New York: Grove, 1959), p. 3.

4. Peter B. Wight, obituary of H. H. Richardson, *Inland Architect* 7 (May 1886), p. 59, reprinted in M. Friedlander, "Henry Hobson Richardson, Henry Adams, and John Hay," *Journal of the Society of Architectural Historians* 29, no. X (1970), p. 231.

5. H. H. Richardson to Henry Adams, June 7, 1885, quoted in J. F. O'Gorman, *Selected Drawings H. H. Richardson and His Office* (Boston: Harvard College Library, 1974), p. 78.

6. Henry Van Brunt, "The New Dispensation in Monumental Art," *Atlantic Monthly* May 1879; quoted in M. G. Van Rensselaer, *Henry Hobson Richardson and His Works* (New York: Houghton Mifflin, 1888), p. 61.

7. H. H. Richardson, "Description of Trinity Church," in *Van Rensselaer*, p. 143.

8. Van Rensselaer, p. 82.

9. Ralph Adams Cram, *Church Building*, second edition, revised (Boston: Small, Maynard, 1914), p. 264.

10. Ralph Adams Cram, *The Gothic Quest* (New York: Baker and Taylor, 1907), p. 191.

11. Cram, *Church Building*, p. 61.

12. Ibid., p. 84.

13. Cram, *Gothic Quest*, p. 171.

14. Ralph Adams Cram, *Impressions of Japanese Architecture and the Allied Arts*, second edition, revised (Boston: Marshall Jones and Co., 1930), p. 140.

15. Ralph Adams Cram, *My Life in Architecture* (Boston: Little, Brown, 1936), p. 122.

CHAPTER 3

1. Frank Lloyd Wright, "The Art and Craft of the Machine," in *The Future of Architecture* (New York: Horizon, 1953), p. 86.

2. Charles Moore, *The Life and Times of Charles Follen McKim* (Boston: Houghton Mifflin, 1929; New York: Da Capo, 1970), p. 281.

3. Marc-Antoine Laugier, *An Essay on Architecture* (Paris, 1753; New York: York, Hennessey & Ingalls, 1977), p. 17.

4. Captain John Sewall to McKim, Mead & White, July 15, 1905 (New York Historical Society).

5. *Frank Lloyd Wright on Architecture*, ed. F. Gutheim (New York: *Architectural Record*), p. 265.

6. Henri Labrouste, letter to the editor, *Revue générale de l'architecture et des travaus publics* 1 (1848), p. 543.

7. Julien Guadet, *Eléments et Théorie de l'Architecture*, fourth edition, volume 1 (Paris: Librarie de la Construction Moderne, 1901–1904), p. 518.

8. Ibid., p. 517.

9. Ibid., p. 518.

10. Ibid., p. 518.

11. Ibid., p. 518.

12. Ibid., p. 518.

13. P. J. Schneider, *The Works and Doctrine of J. I. Hittorf* (New York: Garland, 1977), p. 50.

14. H. Van Buren Magonigle, "A Half-Century of Architecture," *Pencil Points* 14 (March 1934), p. 116.

15. Memo, McKim, Mead & White to Columbia University, November 3, 1894 (New York Historical Society).

16. Ibid.

17. Henry MacCracken to Stanford White, August 2, 1898 (New York Historical Society).

18. William Ware to W. R. Mead, March 6, 1896; William Ware to Seth Low, March 6, 1896 (New York Historical Society).

19. Ibid.

20. Seth Low to Charles F. McKim, July 17, 1896; Norcross Brothers to McKim, Mead & White, November 17, 1896 (New York Historical Society).

21. Montgomery Schuyler, "A Modern Classic," *Architectural Record* 15 (May 5, 1904), p. 431.

22. Louis Sullivan, "The Tall Office Building Artistically Considered," *Lippincott's Magazine* 57 (March 1896), pp. 403–409.

23. Leland Roth, *McKim, Mead & White, Architects* (New York: Harper and Row, 1983).

24. Guadet, *Eléments* (see note 7), p. 17.

CHAPTER 4

1. Hannes Meyer, "ABC Demands the Dictatorship of the Machine," *Bauhaus* 2, no. 4; reprinted in *Programs and Manifestoes of Twentieth-Century Architecture*, ed. U. Conrads (Cambridge, Mass: MIT Press, 1964), p. 115.

2. Edwin Lutyens, "What I Think of Modern Architecture," *Country Life* 69 (June 20, 1931), p. 776.

3. Roderick Gradidge, *Edwin Lutyens, Architect Laureate* (London: Allen and Unwin, 1981), p. 74.

4. Christopher Hussey, *The Life of Sir Edwin Lutyens*, (London: Country Life, 1950), p. 493.

5. Gradidge, *Edwin Lutyens, Architect Laureate*, p. 3.

6. Lutyens, "What I Think of Modern Architecture," p. 776.

7. Hussey, *Life of Sir Edwin Lutyens*, p. 133.

8. Edwin Lutyens, "The Work of the Late Philip Webb," *Country Life* 37 (May 8, 1915), p. 619.

9. H. S. Goodhart-Rendel, *English Architecture Since the Regency* (London: Constable, 1953), p. 191.

10. Hussey, *Life of Lutyens*, p. 181.

11. Ibid., p. 133.

12. Ibid., p. 491.

13. Clayre Percy and Jane Ridley, *The Letters of Edwin Lutyens to his wife Lady Emily* (London: Collins, 1985), p. 75.

14. Ibid., p. 334.

15. Herbert Baker, *Architecture and Personalities* (London: Country Life, 1944), p. 16.

16. Edwin Lutyens, "Tradition Speaks," *Architectural Review* 72 (November 1932), p. 163.

17. Ibid.

18. Lutyens, "What I Think of Modern Architecture," p. 776.

CHAPTER 5

1. John Ruskin, "Seven Lamps of Architecture," in *Selected Prose of John Ruskin*, ed. M. Hodgart (New York: Signet, 1972), p. 65.

2. Ibid., p. 66.

3. John Ruskin, "The Stones of Venice," in *Selected Prose of John Ruskin*, ed. M. Hodgart (New York: Signet, 1972)., p. 125.

4. Ibid., p. 120.

5. William Lethaby, *Philip Webb and His Work* (London: Raven Oak, 1935), p. 122.

6. Ibid., p. 120.

7. Ibid.

8. Ibid., p. 127.

9. Ibid.

10. Reyner Banham, *Los Angeles* (New York: Harper and Row, 1971), p. 71.

11. Christopher Dresser, *Japan: Its Architecture, Art, and Art Manufactures* (London: Longmans, 1882), p. 230.

12. Gustav Stickley, "Practical Points about Craftsman Woodwork," *The Craftsman* 24 (April 1913), p. 125.

13. Ibid.

14. C. R. Ashbee journals, King's College Library, catalog no. 90/1908.

15. Charles Greene, "Bungalows," *Western Architect* 16 (July 1908), p. 3.

16. Elmer Grey "Some Country House Architecture in the Far West," *Architectural Record*, 52 (October 1922), pp. 308–315.

CHAPTER 6

1. Montgomery Schuyler, "An Architectural Pioneer: Review of the Portfolios Containing the Work of Frank Lloyd Wright," *Architectural Record* 31 (April 1912), p. 435.

2. C. R. Ashbee, "Frank Lloyd Wright, A Study and Appreciation," in *Frank Lloyd Wright: The Early Work* (New York: Horizon, 1968), p. 5.

3. Russell Sturgis, "The Larkin Building in Buffalo," *Architectural Record* 23 (April 1908), pp. 311–321.

4. Wright to Ashbee, 1908, Ashbee Collection, King's College Library, catalog no. 220/1908.

5. Frank Lloyd Wright, "In the Cause of Architecture," *Architectural Record* 35 (May 1914); collected by Frederick Gutheim in *In the Cause of Architecture* (New York: Architectural Record, 1975), p. 121.

6. Nikolaus Pevsner, *Pioneers of Modern Design*, (London: Penguin, 1940; reprinted 1964), p. 191.

7. Sturgis, "The Larkin Building in Buffalo," p. 320.

8. Ashbee Journals, King's College Library, catalog no. 325/1908. Although this entry is in Janet Ashbee's handwriting, it may have been dictated to her by C. R. Ashbee.

9. Frank Lloyd Wright, "In the Cause of Architecture VIII," *Architectural Record* 64 (October 1928); reprinted in Gutheim, *In the Cause of Architecture* (see note 5), p. 217.

10. J. Alan Crawford, "Ten Letters from Frank Lloyd Wright to Charles Robert Ashbee," *Architectural History* 13 (1970), p. 64.

11. H. Allen Brooks, "Chicago Architecture: Its Debt to the Arts and Crafts," *Journal of the Society of Architectural Historians* 30 (December 1971), p. 316.

12. Ashbee, "Study and Appreciation," p. 8.

13. Ibid.

14. Ibid., p. 5.

15. Frank Lloyd Wright, "The Art and Craft of the Machine" in *The Future of Architecture* (New York: Horizon, 1963), p. 96. This version of the lecture was read at Princeton in 1936 as a part of the Kahn lectures, and differs slightly from the older published versions (particularly in syntax). However, the 1936 version also contains previously unpublished sections of the original lecture, particularly those relating to stone construction. A careful reading of the 1901 version makes clear that this portion was included in the original talk but omitted from the original published version.

16. Ibid.

17. Ibid.

18. Ashbee, "Study and Appreciation," p. 7.

19. Wright, *Art and Craft of the Machine.*

20. Owen Jones, *The Grammar of Ornament* (1856; New York: Portland House, 1986), p. 33.

21. Eugène-Emanuel Viollet-le-Duc, *Lectures on Architecture*, volume I, tr. B. Bucknall (New York: Grove, 1959), p. 435.

22. Frank Lloyd Wright, "In the Cause of Architecture," *Architectural Record* 23 (March 1908); reprinted in Gutheim, p. 57.

23. John Belcher, *Essentials in Architecture* (London: B. J. Blatsford, 1908), p. 79.

24. Viollet-le-Duc. *Lectures*, volume 1 (Grove, 1959), p. 435.

25. Wright, "In the Cause of Architecture," *Architectural Record* 64 (January 1928); reprinted in Gutheim, p. 155.

26. Wright, *The Future of Architecture*, p. 153.

27. Reyner Banham, "The Services of the Larkin 'A' Building," *Journal of the Society of Architectural Historians* 37, no. 3 (1978), p. 195.

28. Wright, "In the Cause of Architecture," *Architectural Record* 23 (March 1908); reprinted in Gutheim, p. 57.

29. Wright, "Reply to Mr. Sturgis' Criticism," reprinted in J. Quinan, *Frank Lloyd Wright's Larkin Building: The Myths and the Facts* (Cambridge, Mass.: MIT Press, 1987), p. 165.

30. Ibid., p. 167.

31. Ibid., p. 168.

32. Ibid., p. 167.

33. Wright, "In the Cause of Architecture," *Western Architect* 32 (April 1923), p. 42.

34. C. R. Ashbee Journals, King's College Library, catalog no. 306/1908.

35. Norris K. Smith, *Frank Lloyd Wright: A Study in Architectural Content* (Englewood Cliffs, N.J.: Prentice-Hall, 1966), p. 83.

36. Ibid., p. 100.

CHAPTER 7

1. Quoted in Wolfgang Herrmann, *Gottfried Semper: In Search of Architecture* (Cambridge, Mass.: MIT Press, 1984), p. 91.

2. A. W. Pugin, *Principles of Pointed or Christian Architecture*, (London: John Weale, 1841; New York: Academy Editions, 1973), p. 73.

3. Eugène Emanuel Viollet-le-Duc, *Discourses on Architecture*, volume 2, tr. B. Bucknall (New York: Grove, 1959), p. 3.

4. Gottfried Semper, *Der Stil*, volume 2 (Munich 1863; Mittenwald: Maander Kunstverlag, 1977), p. 304.

5. Wolfgang Herrmann, *Gottfried Semper: In Search of Architecture* (Cambridge, Mass.: MIT Press, 1984), p. 144.

6. Semper, *Der Stil*, volume 2, p. 468.

7. Joseph Rykwert, "Semper and the Conception of Style," in *Gottfried Semper und die Mitte des 19. Jahrhunderts* (Basel and Stuttgart: Birkhauser, 1976), p. 69.

8. Ibid., p. 72.

9. Herrman, *Gottfried Semper*, p. 209.

10. Otto Wagner, *Modern Architecture* (English translation), in *9H*, no. 6 (1983), p. 76.

11. Ibid.

12. Ibid., p. 77.

13. Ibid., p. 78.

14. Ibid.

15. Ibid., p. 79.

16. Ibid., p. 78.

17. Richard Neutra, *Survival Through Design* (Oxford University Press, 1964), p. 300.

18. Adolf Loos, "The Principle of Cladding," in *Spoken into the Void: Collected Essays by Adolf Loos* (Cambridge, Mass.: MIT Press, 1982), p. 36.

19. Ibid., p. 66.

20. Ibid., p. 67.

21. Ibid., p. 68.

22. Ibid., p. 66.

23. Adolf Loos, "Ornament and Crime," reprinted in *Programs and Manifestoes of Twentieth-Century Architecture*, ed. U. Conrads (Cambridge, Mass.: MIT Press, 1970), p. 22.

24. Adolf Loos, "Ornament und Erziehung," quoted in Franco Borsi and Ezio Godoli, *Vienna 1900: Architecture and Design* (New York: Rizzoli, 1986), p. 150.

CHAPTER 8

1. Colin Rowe, *The Mathematics of the Ideal Villa and Other Essays* (Cambridge, Mass.: MIT Press, 1976).

2. Henry-Russell Hitchcock and Philip Johnson, *The International Style* (New York: Museum of Modern Art, 1932).

3. Le Corbusier, *Toward a New Architecture* (Paris: Editions Crès, 1923; New York: Praeger, 1960), p. 41.

4. Reyner Banham, *The Architecture of the Well-Tempered Environment* (University of Chicago Press, 1969), pp. 153–155.

5. Ibid., pp. 156–158.

CHAPTER 9

1. Philip Johnson, *Mies van der Rohe* (New York: Museum of Modern Art, 1947; reprinted 1978), p. 208.

2. Ludwig Mies van der Rohe, "Aphorisms of Architecture and Form," reprinted in Johnson, *Mies*, p. 183.

3. Ibid., p. 184.

4. Ibid.

5. Ibid., p. 124.

6. Ibid., p. 190.

7. Ibid., p. 194.

8. Walter Esters, Sr., to Walter Esters, Jr., quoted in Wolf Tegethoff, *Mies van der Rohe: The Villas and Country Houses* (Cambridge, Mass.: MIT Press, 1985), p. 61.

9. Theo van Doesburg, "From the New Aesthetic to its Material Realization," in *De Stijl*, ed. H. A. C. Jaffe (New York: Abrams, no date), p. 182.

CHAPTER 10

1. Thomas Jefferson, *Notes on the State of Virginia* (1782), quoted in James M. Fitch, *American Building*, (Boston: Houghton Mifflin, 1966), p. 55.

2. Sigfried Giedion, *Space, Time, and Architecture* (Cambridge, Mass.: Harvard University Press, 1967), p. 346.

3. Rudolf Schindler, unpublished notes on the Schindler-Chase House (1921), in archive of University of California, Santa Barbara.

4. Ibid.

5. Rudolf Schindler to W. L. Lloyd, May 14, 1923.

6. Richard Neutra, *Survival Through Design* (Oxford University Press, 1954), p. 51.

7. Sigfried Giedion, *Built in U.S.A.* (New York: Simon and Schuster, 1945), p. 14.

8. Peter Blake, ed., *Marcel Breuer: Sun and Shadow* (New York: Dodd, Mead, 1955), p. 70.

9. Tician Papachristou, *Marcel Breuer: New Buildings and Projects* (New York: Praeger, 1970), p. 21.

CHAPTER 11

1. Louis Sullivan, *A System of Architectural Ornament* (New York: Eakins, 1967), p. 3.

2. Frank Lloyd Wright, "In the Cause of Architecture" *Architectural Record* 64 (January 1928); in *In the Cause of Architecture*, ed. F. Gutheim (New York: Architectural Record, 1975), p. 154.

3. Frank Lloyd Wright, *The Natural House* (New York: Horizon, 1954), p. 73.

4. Frederick Gutheim, ed., *Frank Lloyd Wright on Architecture* (New York: Grosset & Dunlap, 1941), p. 140.

5. Ibid., p. 155.

6. Jonathan Lipman, *Frank Lloyd Wright and the Johnson Wax Building* (New York: Rizzoli, 1986), p. 62.

CHAPTER 12

1. Gilbert Herbert, *The Dream of the Factory-Made House: Walter Gropius and Konrad Wachsmann* (Cambridge, Mass.: MIT Press, 1984).

2. John Summerson, *The Classical Language of Architecture* (Cambridge, Mass.: MIT Press 1963), p. 44.

3. Alan Colquhoun, *Essays in Architectural Criticism: Modern Architecture and Historical Change* (Cambridge, Mass.: MIT Press, 1981), p. 51.

CHAPTER 2

Charles Maginnis, *The Work of Cram, Goodhue and Ferguson, Architects*. New York: Pencil Points Press, 1929.
An extensive monograph on the firm's ecclesiastical and academic work.

Henry-Russell Hitchcock, *The Architecture of H. H. Richardson and His Times*. New York: Museum of Modern Art, 1936.
The first monograph on Richardson.

Jeffrey Karl Ochsner, *H. H. Richardson: Complete Architectural Works*. Cambridge, Mass.: MIT Press, 1982.
Contains an individual listing and a description of each of Richardson's completed buildings.

James F. O'Gorman, *H. H. Richardson and His Office: Selected Drawings*. Cambridge, Mass.: MIT Press, 1974.
Contains a partial catalogue of Richardson drawings and extensive descriptions of the design of Austin Hall.

Frank Snyder, *Building Details*. New York: F. M. Snyder, 1908–1913.
Contains excellent technical and graphic information on details by Cram, McKim, Mead & White, and many others.

CHAPTER 3

A Monograph of the Work of McKim, Mead & White, 1879–1915. New York: 1914–1920.
Assembled by the firm itself, this contains a number of large drawings showing details of the construction of many of the major buildings.

Leland Roth, *McKim, Mead & White, Architects*. New York: Harper and Row, 1983.
Contains extensive information on the development and construction of the New York University and Columbia University Libraries, the banks, and the Cullum Memorial.

Richard Guy Wilson, *McKim, Mead & White, Architects*. New York: Rizzoli, 1983.
Contains extensive information on the major buildings and some information on materials and construction.

David Van Zanten, *Designing Paris*. Cambridge, Mass.: MIT Press, 1987.
Describes the work and thought of the rationalists of the Ecole des Beaux-Arts: Duban, Labrouste, Duc, and Vaudoyer.

CHAPTER 4

Colin Amory et al., *Lutyens: The Work of the English Architect Sir Edwin Lutyens (1869–1944)*. London: Arts Council of Great Britain, 1981.
Contains an essay by Sir John Summerson on Liverpool Cathedral and one by Gavin Stamp on New Delhi.

A. S. G. Butler, *The Architecture of Sir Edwin Lutyens*. Three volumes. London: Country Life, Ltd., 1950.
Most of Lutyens' construction drawings have been lost, and those that remain often differ radically from the completed buildings. These volumes, which contain numerous original drawings, are the primary source of information on Lutyens's detailing.

Roderick Gradidge, *Edwin Lutyens: Architect Laureate*. London: Allen & Unwin, 1981.
Gradidge is the chief proponent of the idea that Lutyens was interested in the expression of construction in his early work.

Christopher Hussey, *The Life of Sir Edwin Lutyens*. London: Country Life, Ltd., 1950.
A biography written to accompany the Butler volumes. Contains much information on certain buildings, particularly the Viceroy's House.

Robert Grant Irving, *Indian Summer: The Making of New Delhi*. New Haven: Yale University Press, 1981.
Contains a chapter detailing the construction of the Viceroy's House.

Jane Fawcett, *Seven Victorian Architects*. London: Thames and Hudson, 1976.
Contains a chapter by Gradidge describing the intricacies of the Thiepval Memorial.

CHAPTER 5

R. Makinson, *Greene and Greene*. Salt Lake City: Peregrine Smith, 1977.
A complete and comprehensive study of the Greenes' buildings and furniture.

W. R. Current and Karen Current, *Greene and Greene: Architects in the Residential Style*. Fort Worth: Amon Carter Museum of Western Art, 1974.
Contains many working drawings and much detailed information on the major houses.

Mary Comino, *Gimson and the Barnsleys*. New York: Van Nostrand Reinhold, 1980.
Primarily concerned with furniture, but details Gimson's life and architecture.

James Marston Fitch, *American Building: The Forces That Shaped It*. Boston: Houghton Mifflin, 1948.
Discusses the development of wood framing in America.

William Lethaby, Alfred Powell, and Frederick Griggs, *Ernest Gimson, His Life and Work*. Stratford on Avon: Shakespeare Head Press, 1924.
Contains a few technical drawings of Gimson's buildings.

CHAPTER 6

H. Allen Brooks, *The Prairie School*. University of Toronto, 1972.
Contains a description of Wright's early contacts with Ashbee and the Arts and Crafts movement.

Frederick Gutheim, ed., *In the Cause of Architecture*. New York: *Architectural Record*, 1975.
A collection of Wright's articles in the *Architectural Record*. Many of the articles are devoted to materials and industrialization, but are somewhat frustrating owing to the absence of specific information.

Donald Hoffman, *Frank Lloyd Wright's Robie House*. New York: Dover, 1984.
Contains most of the somewhat scanty information on the detailing and construction of the Robie house, including construction photographs.

Bruce Brooks Pfeiffer and Yukio Futagawa, *Frank Lloyd Wright: The Complete Works* Tokyo: A. D. A. Edita, 1984.
The archives of Wright's design development and construction drawings are the most extensive and complete of any modern master, and many of the important drawings are included in this set.

Jack Quinlin, *Frank Lloyd Wright's Larkin Building.* Cambridge, Mass.: MIT Press, 1987.
This is concerned primarily with the design of the building, but it describes the construction process, and it contains photographs taken during the demolition that show details of the brick-and-steel frame.

Reyner Banham, "The Services of the Larkin 'A' Building." *Journal of the Society of Architectural Historians* 37, No. 3, October 1978, p. 195.

CHAPTER 7

Frank Borsi and Ezio Godoli, *Vienna 1900.* New York: Rizzoli, 1986.
Contains excellent and extensive chapters on Wagner, on Loos, on their relationship to Semper, and on Wagner's students and their subsequent work.

Heinz Geretseggar and Max Peinter, *Otto Wagner.* Vienna: Residenz Verlag, 1964.
This is the most extensive Wagner monograph. It contains many construction photographs.

Otto Antonia Graf, *Otto Wagner: Das Werk des Architekten.* Two volumes. Vienna: Hermann Bohlaus, 1985.
Contains a complete catalog of the drawings of Wagner and his office, the text of *Modern Architecture*, and numerous project descriptions written by Wagner.

Wolfgang Herrmann, *Gottfried Semper: In Search of Architecture.* Cambridge, Mass.: MIT Press, 1984.
Herrman describes the development and the nature of Semper's key ideas and presents several of Semper's articles in English translation.

Gottfried Semper, *Der Stil.* Two volumes. Munich, 1863. Mittenwald: Maander Kunstverlag, 1977.

Otto Wagner, *Moderne Architekur.* Vienna, Verlag von Anton Schroll & Co., 1896 and 1898. Revised and reissued as *Die Baukunst unserer Zeit* in 1902 and 1914.

During the production of the present work, an excellent new translation of the 1902 edition of *Die Baukunst unserer Zeit* by H. F. Malgrave was published by the Getty Center. The introduction details Wagner's relationships with Semper and Karl Bötticher.

CHAPTER 8

P. Bak et al., *J. Duiker Bouwkundig Ingenieur.* Delft: Duikergroep, 1982.
Contains extensive technical information on all of Duiker's buildings.

Tim Benton, *The Villas of Le Corbusier, 1920–30.* New Haven: Yale, 987.
Deals primarily with the design history of the buildings of this period, but contains some technical information.

Peter Collins, *Concrete: The Vision of a New Architecture.* New York: Horizon, 1959.
Describes the development of the Hennibique system and the career of Auguste Perret.

Peter Eisenman, "From Object to Relationship II: Casa del Fascio." *Perspecta*, No. 13, 1971, p. 62.
Describes the evolution of the design of the Casa del Fascio.

Colin Rowe, *The Mathematics of the Ideal Villa and Other Essays.* Cambridge, Mass.: MIT Press, 1976.

Elenor Gregh, "The Dom-Ino Idea." *Oppositions*, No. 15/16, winter/spring, 1979.
Describes in detail the lost-tile system of concrete construction as used by Le Corbusier.

Brian Bruce Taylor, *Le Corbusier: The City of Refuge, Paris, 1929–33.* University of Chicago Press, 1987.

Quadrante, No. 35/36, October 1936.
The entire issue is devoted to the Casa del Fascio.

F. R. S. Yorke, *The Modern House.* London: Architectural Press, 1934.
Contains technical information on buildings by Le Corbusier, Gropius, Mies van der Rohe, and other modern architects of the 1920s and the 1930s.

CHAPTER 9

Arthur Drexler, ed., *An Illustrated Catalogue of the Mies van der Rohe Drawings in the Museum of Modern Art.* New York: Garland, 1986.
A complete catalog of the Mies van der Rohe Archive. (Only the European projects are included as of this date.)

Dirk Lohan, *Global Architecture Detail: The Farnsworth House.* Tokyo: A. D. A. Edita, 1976.
Contains the complete details of the house and a short commentary.

Paul Overy et al., *The Rietveld Schröder House.* Cambridge, Mass.: MIT Press, 1988.
Contains little technical information, but details the history of the design of the house and its restoration.

Franz Schulze, *Mies van der Rohe: A Critical Biography.* University of Chicago Press, 1985.
The most complete biography of Mies.

Wolf Tegethoff, *Mies van der Rohe: The Villas and Country Houses.* Cambridge, Mass.: MIT Press, 1985.
Contains extensive information on the design and construction of the Lange and Tugendhat houses and the Barcelona Pavilion.

CHAPTER 10

David Gebhard, *Schindler.* New York: Viking, 1972.

Ise Gropius, *History of the Gropius House.* 1977. Available from Gropius House, Lincoln, Mass.
Contains an outline specification of the building systems and a description of the design and construction.

Ester McCoy, *Five California Architects.* New York: Reinhold, 1960.
Includes chapters on the Greene Brothers and Schindler, and extensive information on the latter's ideas about American building.

Ester McCoy, *Vienna to Los Angeles: Two Journeys.* Santa Monica: Arts & Architecture Press, 1979.
Contains descriptions of the design and construction of Schindler's and Neutra's houses for Lovell and an interview with the client.

Winfried Nerdiner, *Walter Gropius*. Cambridge, Mass.: Busch-Reisinger Museum, 1986.
Complete catalog of Gropius's works and drawings.

Rudolf Schindler, "Schindler Shelters." *American Architect* 146, May 1935, pp. 70–72.

August Sarnitz, *R. M. Schindler, Architect*. Vienna: Christian Brandstater, 1986.
A complete catalog of Schindler's work.

CHAPTER 11

Paul F. and Jean S. Hanna, *Frank Lloyd Wright's Hanna House*. Cambridge, Mass.: MIT Press, 1981.
Describes the design and construction of the house. Contains excellent detail drawings of the wall and window systems.

Donald Hoffmann, *Frank Lloyd Wright's Fallingwater*. New York: Dover, 1978.
A detailed description of the problems encountered in design development and construction. Numerous construction photographs.

Herbert Jacobs, *Building with Frank Lloyd Wright*. San Francisco: Chronicle Books, 1978.
Jacobs built two houses with Wright, including the house in which the Usonian sandwich wall was first used.

Edgar Kaufmann, *Fallingwater: a Frank Lloyd Wright Country House*. New York: Abbeville, 1986.
Sone information on the construction of the house; extensive drawings of the house as built.

Jonathan Lipman, *Frank Lloyd Wright and the Johnson's Wax Building*. New York: Rizzoli, 1986.
Describes the construction sequences and problems of both the Administration Building and the Research Tower. Extensive information on the detailing and installation of the skylights and glass tubing, and on the problems created by the tightly integrated structure of brick and concrete.

Edgar Tafel, *Apprentice to Genius*. New York: McGraw-Hill, 1979.
Wright's on-site representative for both the Johnson Building and part of the Kaufmann house describes many of the problems that arose in the construction of those buildings.

Frank Lloyd Wright, *The Natural House*. New York: Horizon, 1954.
Describes in detail the theory and construction of the wood sandwich wall of the Jacobs house.